D1750119

Max Planck Yearbook of United Nations Law

Volume 16
2012

Max Planck Yearbook of United Nations Law

Founding Editors
Jochen A. Frowein
Rüdiger Wolfrum

Max Planck Yearbook of United Nations Law

Volume 16
2012

Editors
Armin von Bogdandy
Rüdiger Wolfrum

Managing Editor
Christiane E. Philipp

Max-Planck-Institut für ausländisches
öffentliches Recht und Völkerrecht

MARTINUS NIJHOFF PUBLISHERS
LEIDEN · BOSTON
2012

This book should be cited as follows: **Max Planck UNYB**

Printed on acid-free paper.

Articles from previously published Volumes are electronically available under www.mpil.de/red/yearbook

ISSN 1389-4633
E-ISSN 1875-7413
ISBN 978 90 04 22792-7

Copyright 2012 by Koninklijke Brill NV, Leiden, The Netherlands.
Koninklijke Brill NV incorporates the imprints Brill, Global Oriental, Hotei Publishing, IDC Publishers and Martinus Nijhoff Publishers.

All rights reserved. No part of this publication may be reproduced, translated, stored in a retrieval system, or transmitted in any form or by any means, electronic, mechanical, photocopying, recording or otherwise, without prior written permission from the publisher.

Authorization to photocopy items for internal or personal use is granted by Koninklijke Brill NV provided that the appropriate fees are paid directly to The Copyright Clearance Center, 222 Rosewood Drive, Suite 910, Danvers MA 01923, USA.
Fees are subject to change.

Contents

List of Contributors VII
Abbreviations IX

Krajewski, Markus/ *Singer*, Christopher,
   Should Judges be Front–Runners?
   The ICJ, State Immunity and the Protection of Fundamental
   Human Rights 1

Wood, Michael,
   The Immunity of Official Visitors 35

Roeben, Volker,
   Responsibility in International Law 99

Dingfelder Stone, John H.,
   Assessing the Existence of the Right to Translation under the
   International Covenant on Civil and Political Rights 159

Hertig Randall, Maya,
   Human Rights Within a Multilayered Constitution: The
   Example of Freedom of Expression and the WTO 183

Möldner, Mirka,
  Responsibility of International Organizations-
  Introducing the ILC's DARIO 281

Kirschner, Adele J./ ***Tiroch***, Katrin,
  The Waters of Euphrates and Tigris: An International Law
  Perspective 329

LL.M. Thesis:

Wehlend, Daniela,
  Improving Compliance Mechanisms of the International
  Waste Trade Regime by Introducing Economic Compliance
  Incentives 397

Book Reviews 467

List of Contributors

Dingfelder Stone, John H.
LL.M. (University of Nottingham School of Law); J.D. (University of Texas School of Law); Research Fellow at the Max Planck Institute for Comparative Public Law and International Law, Heidelberg, Germany

Hertig Randall, Maya
LL.M. (Cambridge); Professor of Constitutional Law at Geneva University, Switzerland

Kirschner, Adele J.
Senior Research Fellow at the Max Planck Institute for Comparative Public Law and International Law, Heidelberg, Germany; Ph.D. candidate at the Faculty of Law, University of Heidelberg, Germany

Krajewski, Markus
Professor of Public Law and Public International Law, School of Law, University of Erlangen-Nürnberg, Germany

Möldner, Mirka
Ass. Jur.; Senior Research Fellow at the Max Planck Institute for Comparative Public Law and International Law, Heidelberg, Germany; Ph.D. candidate at the Faculty of Law, University of Heidelberg, Germany

Roeben, Volker
Professor, Swansea University School of Law, United Kingdom

Singer, Christopher

Ass. Jur.; Maître en Droit; Research Fellow, School of Law, University of Erlangen-Nürnberg, Germany

Tiroch, Katrin

Senior Research Fellow at the Max Planck Institute for Comparative Public Law and International Law, Heidelberg, Germany

Wood, Michael

Senior Fellow, Lauterpacht Centre for International Law, Cambridge; Member of the International Law Commission

Abbreviations

ACABQ	Advisory Committee on Administrative and Budgetary Questions
AD	*Annual Digest of Public International Law Cases*
A.F.D.I.	*Annuaire Français de Droit International*
AJDA	*Actualité Juridique – Droit Administratif*
AJIL	*American Journal of International Law*
Am. U. Int'l L. Rev.	*American University International Law Review*
Am. U. J. Int'l L. & Pol'y	*American University Journal of International Law and Policy*
Anu. Der. Internac.	*Anuario de Derecho Internacional*
Arch. de Philos. du Droit	*Archives de Philosophie du Droit*
ASIL	American Society of International Law
Aus Pol. & Zeitgesch.	*Aus Politik und Zeitgeschichte*
Austr. Yb. Int'l L.	*Australian Yearbook of International Law*
Austrian J. Publ. Int'l Law	*Austrian Journal of Public International Law*
AVR	*Archiv des Völkerrechts*
Brook. J. Int'l L.	*Brooklyn Journal of International Law*
B. U. Int'l L. J.	*Boston University International Law Journal*
BVerfGE	Entscheidungen des Bundesverfassungsgerichts (Decisions of the German Federal Constitutional Court)

BYIL	*British Yearbook of International Law*
Cal. L. Rev.	*California Law Review*
Cal. W. Int'l L. J.	*California Western International Law Journal*
Cal. W. L. Rev.	*California Western Law Review*
Case W. Res. J. Int'l L.	*Case Western Reserve Journal of International Law*
Chi. J. Int'l L.	*Chicago Journal of International Law*
CLJ	*Cambridge Law Journal*
CML Rev.	*Common Market Law Review*
Colo. J. Int'l Envtl L. & Pol'y	*Colorado Journal of International Environmental Law and Policy*
Colum. Hum. Rts L. Rev.	*Columbia Human Rights Law Review*
Colum. J. Transnat'l L.	*Columbia Journal of Transnational Law*
Colum. L. Rev.	*Columbia Law Review*
Comunità Internaz.	*La Comunità Internazionale*
Conn. J. Int'l L.	*Connecticut Journal of International Law*
Cornell Int'l L. J.	*Cornell International Law Journal*
CTS	Consolidated Treaty Series
CYIL	*Canadian Yearbook of International Law*
Den. J. Int'l L. & Pol'y	*Denver Journal of International Law and Policy*
Dick. J. Int'l L.	*Dickinson Journal of International Law*
Duke J. Comp. & Int'l L.	*Duke Journal of Comparative and International Law*
Duq. L. Rev.	*Duquesne Law Review*
EA	*Europa-Archiv*
ECOSOC	Economic and Social Council
ed.	editor
eds	editors
e.g.	exempli gratia
EJIL	*European Journal of International Law*

ELJ	*European Law Journal*
Env. Policy & Law	*Environmental Policy and Law*
Envtl L. Rep.	*Environmental Law Reports*
et al.	et alii
et seq.	et sequentes
etc.	et cetera
EuGRZ	*Europäische Grundrechte-Zeitschrift*
FAO	Food and Agriculture Organization
Fla. J. Int'l L.	*Florida Journal of International Law*
Fordham Int'l L. J.	*Fordham International Law Journal*
Fordham L. Rev.	*Fordham Law Review*
Foreign Aff.	*Foreign Affairs*
Foreign Pol'y	*Foreign Policy*
Ga. J. Int'l & Comp. L.	*Georgia Journal of International and Comparative Law*
Geo. Int'l Envt'l L. Rev.	*Georgetown International Environmental Law Review*
Geo. L. J.	*Georgetown Law Journal*
Geo. Wash. J. Int'l L. & Econ.	*George Washington Journal of International Law and Economics*
Geo. Wash. L. Rev.	*George Washington Law Review*
GYIL	*German Yearbook of International Law*
Harv. Int'l L. J.	*Harvard International Law Journal*
Harv. L. Rev.	*Harvard Law Review*
Hastings Int'l & Comp. L. Rev.	*Hastings International and Comparative Law Review*
HRLJ	*Human Rights Law Journal*
HRQ	*Human Rights Quarterly*
HuV-I	*Humanitäres Völkerrecht – Informationsschriften*
IAEA	International Atomic Energy Agency
ibid.	ibidem; in the same place
IBRD	International Bank for Reconstruction and Development

ICAO	International Civil Aviation Organization
ICC	International Criminal Court
ICJ	International Court of Justice
ICLQ	*International and Comparative Law Quarterly*
ICSID	International Centre for Settlement of Investment Disputes
id.	idem; the same
IDA	International Development Association
i.e.	id est; that is to say
IFAD	International Fund for Agricultural Development
IJIL	*Indian Journal of International Law*
ILA	International Law Association
ILC	International Law Commission
ILCYB	Yearbook of the International Law Commission
ILM	*International Legal Materials*
ILO	International Labour Organization
ILR	*International Law Reports*
ILSA J. Int'l L.	*ILSA Journal of International Law (International Law Students Association)*
IMF	International Monetary Fund
IMO	International Maritime Organization
Ind. Int'l & Comp. L. Rev.	*Indiana International and Comparative Law Review*
Ind. J. Global Legal Stud.	*Indiana Journal of Global Legal Studies*
Int'l Aff.	*International Affairs*
Int'l Law.	*The International Lawyer*
Int'l Rev. of the Red Cross	*International Review of the Red Cross*
Iowa L. Rev.	*Iowa Law Review*
IP	*Die internationale Politik*
Isr. L. R.	*Israel Law Review*
Isr. Y. B. Hum. Rts	*Israel Yearbook on Human Rights*

J. History Int'l L.	*Journal of the History of International Law*
J. Int'l Aff.	*Journal of International Affairs*
JA	*Juristische Arbeitsblätter*
JIEL	*Journal of International Economic Law*
JIR	*Jahrbuch für internationales Recht*
JPR	*Journal of Peace Research*
JWT	*Journal of World Trade*
Law & Contemp. Probs	*Law and Contemporary Problems*
LJIL	*Leiden Journal of International Law*
LNTS	League of Nations Treaty Series
Loy. L. A. Int'l Comp. L. Rev.	*Loyola of Los Angeles International and Comparative Law Review*
McGill L. J.	*McGill Law Journal*
Miami U. Int'l & Comp. L. Rev.	*University of Miami International and Comparative Law Review*
Mich. J. Int'l L.	*Michigan Journal of International Law*
Mich. L. Rev.	*Michigan Law Review*
Mil. L. Rev.	*Military Law Review*
Minn. J. Global Trade	*Minnesota Journal of Global Trade*
N. Y. U. J. Int'l L. & Pol.	*New York University Journal of International Law and Politics*
N. Y. U. L. Rev.	*New York University Law Review*
NAFTA	North American Free Trade Agreement
NATO	North Atlantic Treaty Organization
NILR	*Netherlands International Law Review*
NJCL	*National Journal of Constitutional Law*
NJW	*Neue Juristische Wochenschrift*
Nord. J. Int'l L.	*Nordic Journal of International Law*
NQHR	*Netherlands Quarterly of Human Rights*
NYIL	*Netherlands Yearbook of International Law*
Ocean & Coastal L. J.	*Ocean and Coastal Law Journal*

Ocean Dev. Int. Law	*Ocean Development and International Law*
OJEC	*Official Journal of the European Communities*
Pace Int'l Law Rev.	*Pace International Law Review*
PCIJ	Permanent Court of International Justice
Pol. Sci.	*Political Science*
RADIC	*Revue Africaine de Droit International et Comparé*
RBDI	*Revue Belge de Droit International*
RdC	*Recueil des Cours de l'Académie de Droit International*
RDI	*Revue de Droit International, de Sciences Diplomatiques et Politiques*
RECIEL	*Review of European Community and International Environmental Law*
REDI	*Revista Española de Derecho Internacional*
Rev. Dr. Mil. Dr. Guerre	*Revue de Droit Militaire et de Droit de la Guerre*
RGDIP	*Revue Générale de Droit International Public*
RIAA	Reports of International Arbitral Awards
Riv. Dir. Int.	*Rivista di Diritto Internazionale*
RTDE	*Revue Trimestrielle de Droit Européen*
RUDH	*Revue Universelle des Droits de L'homme*
San Diego L. Rev.	*San Diego Law Review*
Santa Clara L. Rev.	*Santa Clara Law Review*
Stanford J. Int'l L.	*Stanford Journal of International Law*
Stanford L. Rev.	*Stanford Law Review*
SZIER/RSDIE	*Schweizerische Zeitschrift für internationales und europäisches Recht/ Revue*

	Suisse de Droit International et de Droit Européen
Temp. Int'l & Comp. L. J.	*Temple International and Comparative Law Journal*
Tex. Int'l L. J.	*Texas International Law Journal*
Tex. L. Rev.	*Texas Law Review*
Transnat'l L. & Contemp. Probs	*Transnational Law and Contemporary Problems*
Tul. Envtl L. J.	*Tulane Environmental Law Journal*
Tul. J. Int'l & Comp. L.	*Tulane Journal of International and Comparative Law*
U. Chi. L. R.	*University of Chicago Law Review*
UCDL Rev.	*University of California Davis Law Review*
UCLA J. Envtl L. & Pol'y	*University of California Los Angeles Journal of Environmental Law and Policy*
UCLA J. Int'l L. & Foreign Aff.	*University of California Los Angeles Journal of International Law and Foreign Affairs*
UCLA Pac. Basin L. J.	*University of California Los Angeles Pacific Basin Law Journal*
UNCIO	United Nations Conference on International Organization
UNCITRAL	United Nations Commission on International Trade Law
UNCTAD	United Nations Conference on Trade and Development
UNDP	United Nations Development Programme
UNEP	United Nations Environment Programme
UNESCO	United Nations Educational, Scientific and Cultural Organization
UNFPA	United Nations Population Fund
UNHCR	United Nations High Commissioner for Refugees

UNICEF	United Nations Children's Fund
UNIDO	United Nations Industrial Development Organization
UNITAR	United Nations Institute for Training and Research
UNJYB	United Nations Juridical Yearbook
UNRWA	United Nations Relief and Works Agency for Palestine Refugees in the Near East
UNTS	United Nations Treaty Series
UNU	United Nations University
UNYB	Yearbook of the United Nations
UPU	Universal Postal Union
Va. J. Int'l L.	*Virginia Journal of International Law*
Va. L. Rev.	*Virginia Law Review*
Vand. J. Transnat'l L.	*Vanderbilt Journal of Transnational Law*
Vol.	Volume
VRÜ	*Verfassung und Recht in Übersee*
VVDStRL	*Veröffentlichungen der Vereinigung der Deutschen Staatsrechtslehrer*
Wash. L. Rev.	*Washington Law Review*
WFP	World Food Programme
WIPO	World Intellectual Property Organization
WMO	World Meteorological Organization
WTO	World Trade Organization
Yale J. Int'l L.	*Yale Journal of International Law*
Yale L. J.	*Yale Law Journal*
ZaöRV/ HJIL	*Zeitschrift für ausländisches öffentliches Recht und Völkerrecht/ Heidelberg Journal of International Law*
ZEuS	*Zeitschrift für europarechtliche Studien*
ZRP	*Zeitschrift für Rechtspolitik*

Should Judges be Front-Runners?
The ICJ, State Immunity and the Protection of Fundamental Human Rights

Markus Krajewski and Christopher Singer

I. Introduction
II. Establishing and Revisiting State Immunity
   1. State Immunity, Sovereign Equality and the Law of Coexistence
   2. Modifications and Contestations
III. History and Factual Background of the ICJ's Judgment *Jurisdictional Immunities of the State*
   1. German War Crimes during World War II
   2. Peace Agreements and Compensation Schemes after the End of World War II
   3. Proceedings and Measures of Constraint taken by the Italian Judiciary
IV. The ICJ's Analysis of the German Claims
   1. Basic Principles of the Law of State Immunity
   2. Potential Limitations of State Immunity
      a. The Territorial Tort Exemption
      b. Grave War Crimes as a Limitation to State Immunity
      c. *Jus cogens* and the Hierarchy of Norms
      d. The Last Resort Argument
   3. Decision of the ICJ on Germany's Claims
V. The ICJ's Judgment: "No surprise, but wise?"
   1. The Dilemma of Detecting Customary International Law without Affecting its Development
   2. Choosing between the Preservation of the Law as it Stands and the Progressive Development of International Law
   3. The Missing Voices: Representing the Victims by the Home State or through other Means
VI. Beyond State Immunity
VII. Conclusion

Abstract

The present essay critically analyses the ICJ's ruling in *Jurisdictional Immunities of the State (Germany v. Italy)*. To contextualise the Court's judgment the essay begins with a brief reflection on the law of state immunity and recalls the historical and factual background of the case. The essay then discusses the ICJ's analysis of the claims of the parties. The main focus is not a challenge of the conclusions of the Court based on a positivist approach to customary international law. Instead, it is argued that faced with a methodological challenge and an institutional dilemma concerning the determination of customary international law, the Court opted for an approach which did not serve the progressive development of international law well.

Keywords

ICJ; State Immunity; Human Rights; Customary International Law

I. Introduction

The law of state immunity has been subject to numerous proceedings before domestic and international courts in recent years. Academic writings on the subject are abundant. In particular, the question whether the protection of fundamental human rights or the prosecution of serious violations of international law justify limitations of state immunity has been debated with passion and intellectual rigour.

The judgment of the ICJ in the matter of *Jurisdictional Immunities of the State (Germany v. Italy)* rendered on 3 February 2012[1] was therefore eagerly awaited by commentators and political actors alike. Not surprisingly the court's ruling in favour of Germany was welcomed by some and criticized by others. Unusually though, both par-

---

[1] ICJ, *Jurisdictional Immunities of the State (Germany v. Italy: Greece intervening)*, Judgment of 3 February 2012, <www.icj-cij.org>.

ties seemed to be satisfied with the outcome[2] even though Italy lost on all counts – an issue to which we will return. In any event, supporters and critics of the ICJ's decision will probably agree that the judgment is among the more important ones in recent years as it addresses fundamental issues of public international law which are of interest to the entire international community. It is quite likely that the decision will become one of the leading cases of the ICJ.

In a nutshell, the ICJ decided that Italy violated Germany's sovereign immunity by allowing Italian courts to adjudicate on claims against Germany even though Germany invoked its state immunity. The Italian courts were seized by victims of German war crimes during World War II in Italy who sought compensation. Furthermore, Italian courts allowed the enforcement of Greek judgments against Germany for compensation of victims of similar atrocities in Greece and placed constraint measures against German property in Italy in order to enforce those judgments. The ICJ rejected the argument of Italy (and its courts) that state immunity cannot be invoked where serious violations of international humanitarian and human rights law are at stake. The ICJ relied on a positivist analysis of customary international law and concluded that there was simply not enough state practice to support the Italian view.

Apart from deciding on Germany's claims and answering the question which had been debated so intensely in the past, the judgment of the ICJ raises important questions concerning its own role in the process of a progressive development of international law protecting individual rights. The case also highlights the methodological dilemma of determining customary international law. It showed that this is an exercise which cannot be disassociated from fundamental value choices. Furthermore, the ICJ's judgment affects the potential of cooperation between domestic and international courts in the development of international law in a multi-layered and decentralised system.

---

[2] See Auswärtiges Amt, Pressemitteilung: Außenminister Westerwelle zum IGH-Urteil in Sachen Deutschland/Italien, 3 February 2012, <www.auswaertiges-amt.de>. The Italian Foreign Minister welcomed the judgment's encouragement of dialogue and is quoted saying that "the sentence provides a useful clarification, especially considering the court's reference to the importance of negotiators to work with both sides to find a solution", *The Daily Telegraph*, "UN court rules against Italy in Nazi war claims row", 3 February 2012, <www.telegraph.co.uk>.

The present article aims to address these issues while critically analysing and commenting on the ICJ's ruling. It goes without saying that not all issues can be explored fully, but it is hoped that the contribution will stimulate debate, because the judgment of the ICJ should not be the last word concerning these issues.

In order to contextualise the Court's judgment we begin by briefly recalling the main contours of the law of state immunity (II.). In this section we show that state immunity is not a static concept, but subject to changes and reformulation reacting to changes in the international system. Furthermore we argue that state immunity is best understood and justified as a functional concept aimed at serving basic principles and values of the international community. Both aspects will be used in our analysis of the judgment to which we then turn.

We begin by recalling the historical and factual background of the case which is important to explain the sensitivity of the issues and the political importance of the case (III.) We then turn to a discussion of the ICJ's analysis of the claims of the parties, discussing the Court's arguments in the order of the judgment (IV.). Based on this we develop our critique of the judgment (V.). Like some of the distinguished authors of Dissenting and Separate Opinions our main focus is not a challenge to the conclusions of the Court based on a positivist approach to customary international law. Instead, we argue that faced with a methodological challenge and an institutional dilemma concerning the determination of customary international law, the Court opted – unnecessarily and regrettably in our view – for an approach which did not serve the progressive development of international law well. The penultimate section (VI.) of this contribution will then turn to related, but distinct developments in international law, namely the relationship between immunity of state officials and diplomatic immunity on the one hand and the protection of fundamental human rights on the other. We conclude with a brief outlook (VII.).

II. Establishing and Revisiting State Immunity

1. State Immunity, Sovereign Equality and the Law of Coexistence

The development of the contemporary understanding of state immunity is intrinsically linked to the development of the concept of state sovereignty and of sovereign equality of states.[3] State sovereignty implies two principles which would be affected if a foreign sovereign became the defendant in a domestic court of another nation: the principle of territorial jurisdiction of the forum state and the principle of sovereign equality of states.[4] The former demands unlimited exercise of jurisdiction, the latter implies that two equals cannot rule over each other (*par in parem non habet jurisdictionem*).[5] The resulting dilemma can only be avoided if state immunity is accepted as a deviation from the principle of unlimited territorial jurisdiction. This basic idea was already recognised by the United States Supreme Court in its famous 1812 judgment of *The Schooner Exchange* v. *McFaddon and Others*[6] which is generally seen as the first articulation of the principle of state immunity.[7]

Chief Justice *Marshall* delivering the judgment for the court wrote:

> "[The] full and absolute territorial jurisdiction being alike the attribute of every sovereign, and being incapable of conferring extraterritorial power, would not seem to contemplate foreign sovereigns nor their sovereign rights as its objects. One sovereign being in no respect amenable to another; and being bound by obligations of the highest character not to degrade the dignity of his nation, by placing himself or its sovereign rights within the jurisdiction of another, can be supposed to enter a foreign territory only under an express license, or in the confidence that the immunities belonging to his independent sovereign station, though not expressly stipulated, are reserved by implication, and will be extended to him. This perfect

---

[3] P.T. Stoll, "State Immunity", in: R. Wolfrum (ed.), *Max Planck Encyclopedia of Public International Law*, 2012, Vol. IX, 498 et seq., para. 4.

[4] L.M. Caplan, "State Immunity, Human Rights, and Jus Cogens: A Critique of the Normative Hierarchy Theory", *AJIL* 97 (2003), 741 et seq. (745).

[5] I. Brownlie, *Principles of Public International Law*, 7th edition, 2008, 325.

[6] *The Schooner Exchange* v. *McFaddon and Others*, 11 U.S. 116 (1812).

[7] R. van Alebeek, *The Immunity of States and Their Officials in International Criminal Law and International Human Rights Law*, 2008, 12.

equality and absolute independence of sovereigns, and this common interest impelling them to mutual intercourse, and an interchange of good offices with each other, have given rise to a class of cases in which every sovereign is understood to waive the exercise of a part of that complete exclusive territorial jurisdiction, which has been stated to be the attribute of every nation."[8]

Throughout the 19th century, the idea of absolute state immunity was generally accepted by domestic courts even though justifications of this principle differed. In particular, two issues seem to have been (and continue to be) controversial: first, whether state immunity was granted as a matter of law or on the basis of judicial discretion (comity) and second, whether state immunity was rooted in international or domestic law.[9] For the purposes of the present analysis both issues need not to be discussed because the ICJ and the disputing parties in *Jurisdictional Immunities of the State* agreed that state immunity was an issue of international law.[10]

The ICJ also recalled that state immunity derives from the principle of sovereign equality of states and therefore underlined the close connection between state immunity and sovereignty.[11] This aspect of the law of state immunity gives rise to a first important question in our context: if state immunity is a corollary of state sovereignty it has to be asked whether limitations of state sovereignty would also lead to limitations of state immunity. In fact, it is noteworthy that the basic principle of state immunity was developed at a time when the idea of absolute state sovereignty of the nation state was developed. However, the concept of state sovereignty underwent significant changes and limitations in the course of the second half of the 20th century, in particular through the adoption of the United Nations Charter and the recognition of inalienable human rights. Furthermore, most contemporary constitutional systems build the idea of sovereignty on the will of the

---

[8] *The Schooner Exchange* v. *McFaddon*, see note 6, 137. This quote – though undeniably the starting point of the modern doctrine – has been and continues to be interpreted in different ways in order to support different theories of state immunity, see J. Finke, "Sovereign Immunity: Rule, Comity, or Something Else?", *EJIL* 21 (2010), 853 et seq. (871).
[9] H. Fox, *The Law of State Immunity*, 2nd edition, 2008, 13 et seq.
[10] ICJ, see note 1, para. 53.
[11] ICJ, ibid., para. 57.

people and not on the existence of the state.[12] Yet, the law of state immunity as applied in practice does not seem to have reflected these changes.[13] Instead, the basic ideas of state immunity are closer to 19th century ideas of absolute state sovereignty than to an understanding of the early 21st century which sees a reformulation of the idea of sovereignty as a principle aimed at protecting human security and human rights.[14] One may even go as far as stating that the idea of state immunity remains a left-over of the traditional international law of co-existence, which was firmly rooted in the concept of sovereignty and sovereign equality.[15] As state immunity construes a boundary between two sovereign equals regardless of the underlying conflict or purpose of a claim it does not accommodate an understanding of sovereignty as responsibility to protect human rights and values of humanity.

2. Modifications and Contestations

Despite the observation that the idea of state immunity does not mirror modern reinterpretations of the concept of sovereignty, the law of state immunity is not static. Rather, the rules on state immunity have been subject to constant change.[16] In particular, the early 20th century saw the emergence of a significant modification of the doctrine relating to commercial or private law activities of the state. It is now widely accepted that these activities (*acta jure gestionis*) are exempt from state immunity and therefore subject to foreign jurisdiction.[17] It is usually argued that this shift in the doctrine of state immunity was a result of

---

[12] G.M. Badr, *State Immunity: An Analytical and Prognostic View*, 1984, 73 et seq.

[13] L. McGregor, "Torture and State Immunity: Deflecting Impunity, Distorting Sovereignty", *EJIL* 18 (2007), 903 et seq. (913).

[14] A. Peters, "Humanity as the A and Ω of Sovereignty", *EJIL* 20 (2009), 513 et seq. (524 et seq.).

[15] J. Kokott, "States, Sovereign Equality", in: Max Planck Encyclopedia, see note 3, Vol. IX, 571 et seq., para. 71. On the development from the law of coexistence to the law of co-operation see W. Friedman, *The Changing Structure of International Law*, 1964. See also van Alebeek, see note 7, 301.

[16] R.F. Lengelsen, *Aktuelle Probleme der Staatenimmunität im Verfahren vor den Zivil- und Verwaltungsgerichten*, 2011, 19.

[17] A. Aust, *Handbook of International Law*, 2nd edition 2006, 145, 152; M. Shaw, *International Law*, 6th edition, 2008, 707.

increased commercial activities in the late 19th and early 20th century.[18] The dynamic nature and its relativity was summarised by *Lady Fox*, one of the most eminent commentators on the matter, in 2008 as follows: "The last hundred years have seen enormous changes in the doctrine and the practice, and indeed in the last decade the changes have accelerated in response to the changing priorities of society."[19] It is possible that this sentence will be rephrased in the next edition of the book reflecting the ICJ's ruling. However, the quote highlights two aspects which are important for our analysis of *Jurisdictional Immunities of the State*.

First, the quote underlines that the changes of the law of state immunity were generated by changes in doctrine and practice, in particular changing approaches of the respective domestic courts seized with claims involving state immunity and through changes in domestic legislation.[20] In this context it needs to be recalled that the *acta jure gestionis*-exception was developed by domestic courts as a deviation from the doctrine of absolute state immunity which existed until then. Belgian and Italian courts were among the first to refuse to grant immunity to foreign states unless they acted in official capacity.[21] This approach gained rapid support in other countries in the early 20th century. It is important to note that the courts which dealt with this issue at the time were clearly aware that such a rule would be a deviation from earlier practice. In fact, the courts which adhered to the new approach based their decisions on the understanding that the law of state immunity was subject to changes developed and expanded through the practice of national courts.[22]

Second, and potentially even more important, the quote cited above, establishes a connection between state immunity and the priorities of the international society. When more and more states (and state-owned

---

[18] A. Cassese, *International Law*, 2nd edition 2005, 100.
[19] Fox, see note 9, 2.
[20] L.F. Damrosch, "Changing International Law of Sovereign Immunity Through National Decisions", *Vand. J. Transnat'l L.* 44 (2011), 1185 et seq. (1196 et seq.).
[21] van Alebeek, see note 7, 14.
[22] German courts were relatively late in accepting the restrictive approach, but when the German Federal Constitutional Court accepted the doctrine in the Iranian Embassy case, it did so fully aware of the historical context of the issue, see Bundesverfassungsgericht, Decision of 30 April 1963, 2 BvM 1/62, BVerfGE 16, 27 et seq. (33 et seq.).

enterprises) became actively engaged in commercial activities, the absolute understanding of state immunity no longer served the needs of the community of states. The courts therefore approached state immunity on a functional basis[23] trying to justify the refusal to exclude sovereign states from the jurisdiction of another state on the basis of practicability and a general understanding of fairness. It is precisely this aspect of state immunity which is closely connected to recent attempts of domestic courts limiting state immunity in order to protect fundamental human rights.[24]

Regardless of the respective legal approach of the courts (*jus cogens*, territorial tort exemption or special status of human rights[25]) they are (or were) united in the quest for a just and fair balance between the needs of inter-state relations warranting state immunity and the needs to protect fundamental values of the international community calling for an exception from state immunity. Indeed, it seems difficult to accept that states acting commercially would be subject to foreign jurisdiction while states violating fundamental human rights and humanitarian law would benefit from immunity.[26] This process of trial and error was nothing unusual regarding the development of the doctrine of state immunity which was always oriented towards the needs of the international community. The process may, however, have come to an end, or at least be put on hold by the ICJ's judgment of 3 February 2012 to which we turn now.

III. History and Factual Background of the ICJ's Judgment *Jurisdictional Immunities of the State*

On 23 December 2008, Germany initiated proceedings against Italy before the ICJ claiming a violation of international law by judicial actions brought against the Federal Republic of Germany before Italian courts.

---

[23] Brownlie, see note 5, 327.
[24] Fox herself, however, argues against a limitation of state immunity on those grounds, see note 9, 141.
[25] For a comprehensive treatment of these approaches before the ICJ's judgment see C. Appelbaum, *Einschränkungen der Staatenimmunität in Fällen schwerer Menschenrechtsverletzungen*, 2007. The ICJ also addressed these arguments, see under IV. 2.
[26] N. Paech, "Staatenimmunität und Kriegsverbrechen", *AVR* 47 (2009), 36 et seq. (89).

The judicial proceedings in question had been engaged by Greek and Italian nationals who sought redress for purportedly uncompensated war crimes perpetrated by German forces in Greece and Italy in the later stages of World War II.[27]

1. German War Crimes during World War II

After post-Mussolini Italy had broken away from the Axis powers to surrender to the Allies and declare war on Germany in September 1943, German forces began to inflict numerous atrocities on the population of the Italian territories it still occupied. It is uncontested and openly acknowledged by Germany that those perpetrations between October 1943 and the end of the War amounted to serious violations of international law.[28] In its present decision the ICJ classified those perpetrations into three different categories.[29]

The first category comprises murders and massacres of the civilian population in an occupied territory as part of political reprisals for resistance fighters' ambushes against the occupying forces. One of those massacres with relevance to the present judgment took place on 29 June 1944 in *Civitella in Val di Chiana* and its neighbouring villages when 203 civilians were taken hostage and killed by German soldiers in what was understood to serve as retaliation for the killing of four German servicemen. This large-scale killing was only adjudicated much later in the *Max Josef Milde* case in October 2006[30] – one of several proceedings that prompted Germany to sue Italy before the ICJ. Another war crime of similarly ferocious scale within this category which also underlies the present decision is the massacre of *Distomo*, a small Greek village where German occupying forces killed more than two hundred civilians on 10 June 1944.[31]

---

[27] See also C. Tomuschat, "The International Law of State Immunity and Its Development by National Institutions", *Vand. J. Transnat'l L.* 44 (2011), 1105 et seq. (1107 et seq.). For a summary of the main facts in German see J. Schaarschmidt, "Die Reichweite des völkerrechtlichen Immunitätsschutzes – Deutschland v. Italien vor dem IGH", in: C. Tietje (ed.), *Beiträge zum Europa - und Völkerrecht*, Heft 5, 2010, 6 et seq.

[28] Joint Declaration of Germany and Italy, Trieste, 18 November 2006.

[29] ICJ, see note 1, para. 52.

[30] ICJ, ibid., para. 29.

[31] ICJ, ibid., para. 30.

The second category relates to the deportation of members of the civilian population from Italy to Germany where they were subsequently subjected to forced labour. One of those victims, Mr. *Luigi Ferrini*, whose claims for compensation in Italian courts also formed grounds for Germany's application at the ICJ, was arrested in August 1944 and deported to Germany where he was held in custody and used as forced labourer in a munitions factory until the end of the war.[32]

The third category involves deportation of Italian servicemen to Germany and German-occupied territories where their status as prisoners of war was negated in order to exploit them also as forced labourers.

2. Peace Agreements and Compensation Schemes after the End of World War II

From the aftermath of the war to as late as the year 2000, unilateral and bilateral avenues were explored by the Allies, Germany and Italy to provide indemnification to Italy and Italian nationals for the atrocities and agonies suffered during the war. While the Peace Treaty of 1947, concluded between the Allied Powers and Italy, addressed the restitution of identifiable property of Italy and Italian nationals, the two bilateral Agreements concluded between Germany and Italy in 1961 aimed at solving outstanding economic questions as well as settling redress for Nazi war crimes. The 1961 Agreements *inter alia* stipulated that Germany would be exempt from future legal actions by Italian nationals related to war crimes against Italian nationals as it in turn entered into an obligation to pay a two-tier compensation to Italy settling both property-related economic issues and redress for Italian nationals who were "subjected to National-Socialist measures of persecution." Both the 1947 Peace Treaty and the 1961 Agreements contained waivers of claims against Germany by Italy or its nationals which became a major bone of contention in the parties' exchange of arguments as their validity and binding character was challenged by Italy. It remained, however, a moot point for the ICJ as its ruling did not attribute any relevance of a possibly persisting responsibility of Germany in respect of war crimes against humanity to the question of Germany's entitlement to immunity.[33]

---

[32] ICJ, ibid., para. 27.
[33] ICJ, ibid., para. 48.

Unilaterally, Germany enacted two laws seeking to compensate victims of wartime persecution. The Federal Compensation Law of 1953 amended in 1965, however, only applied to a small number of claims by Italian nationals. In fact, many claimants were either not considered victims within the definition of the law or were lacking permanent residence in Germany or refugee status. Consequently, the majority of claims by Italian nationals were dismissed by German courts.

The second law of 2 August 2000 establishing a "Remembrance, Responsibility and Future" Foundation allowed funds to partner organisations which allocated payments to victims of forced labour and other means of National-Socialist persecution. A significant number of former military captives, though, did not qualify for compensation as the law excluded those applicants from compensation who had held the status of prisoner of war at the time of the war. The Court observed this stance with "surprise-and regret-"[34] as Italian military internees were *de facto* deprived of their status as prisoners of war. Yet, German authorities argued that the German Reich had never been legally capable of altering the captives' status. According to the German view Italian military internees had never lost their prisoner of war status, effectively barring them from any benefits of the Foundation. This led to a strange consequence: the rights of the Italian military internees were first violated by the German Reich denying them the effects of the status of prisoners of war. The successor of the German Reich, the Federal Republic of Germany, does not maintain this position, which, however, effectively excludes them from compensation.

3. Proceedings and Measures of Constraint taken by the Italian Judiciary

The denial of Germany's jurisdictional immunity by the Italian judiciary can be summarised as an alleged three-pronged violation which saw lawsuits initiated before Italian courts against Germany not dismissed *a limine*, Greek judgments granting relief to war crime claims declared enforceable in Italy and eventually measures of constraint issued against German state property.

On 23 September 1998 Mr. *Luigi Ferrini* initiated proceedings which led to the present case by filing a lawsuit in the Court of Arezzo against Germany seeking relief for forced labour. After both the court of first

---

[34] ICJ, ibid., para. 99.

instance and the Court of Appeal in Florence had dismissed Mr. *Ferrini's* claims on the grounds of jurisdictional immunity, the Italian Court of Cassation ruled on 11 March 2004[35] that jurisdictional immunity does not apply where the act that the claim is based on amounts to an international crime. The case was then referred back to the Court of first instance in Arezzo which dismissed it again as time-barred, before the Court of Appeal in Florence rendered the final judgments on 17 February 2011, condemning Germany to pay damages to Mr. *Ferrini*.

The landmark ruling of the Italian Court of Cassation on 11 March 2004 most likely enticed twelve other victims to follow suit as *Giovanni Mantelli and others* started legal action against Germany in the Court of Turin only two days later. On 28 April 2004, another claim against Germany was brought before the Court of Sciacca by *Liberato Maietta*. In both cases, which were also founded on acts of deportation and forced labour, Germany lodged an interlocutory appeal requesting the Court of Cassation to suspend the proceedings due to a lack of jurisdiction. The Court of Cassation, however, dismissed the appeals by two orders of 29 May 2008 confirming that the Italian courts had jurisdiction to hear the cases.[36]

The Court of Cassation further cemented its view that immunity has to give way where international law is violated by war crimes on the occasion of deciding over Germany's appeal in the *Max Josef Milde* case on 21 October 2008,[37] after the Military Court of La Spezia and the Military Court of Appeals in Rome had sentenced Mr. *Milde* to life imprisonment and ordered him and Germany to pay damages to the relatives of the war crime victims. The jurisprudence of the Court of Cassation on allowing claims for compensation against Germany constituted the first alleged violation of Germany's state immunity.

The second aspect of Germany's claim concerned decisions declaring Greek judgments enforceable in Italy. In 1995, Germany was brought to court over the *Distomo* massacre with the Greek Court of first Instance of *Livadia* granting relief to claims for damages of the vic-

---

[35] *Ferrini* v. *Federal Republic of Germany*, Decision No. 5044/2004, *Riv. Dir. Int.* 87 (2004), 539 et seq., *ILR* 128 (2006), 658 et seq. On this case see also P. De Sena/ F. De Vittor, "State Immunity and Human Rights: The Italian Supreme Court Decision on the *Ferrini* Case", *EJIL* 16 (2005), 89 et seq.

[36] Italian Court of Cassation, Order No. 14201 (Mantelli), *Foro italiano* 134 (2009), I, 1568; Order No. 14209 (Maietta), *Riv. Dir. Int.* 91 (2008), 896 et seq.

[37] ICJ, see note 1, para. 29.

tims' successors in title on 25 September 1997. After Germany's appeal claiming the violation of state immunity was rejected by the Hellenic Supreme Court (*Areios Pagos*) on 4 May 2000,[38] the Greek claimants' success was effectively voided as they were denied the necessary authorisation from the Greek Minister of Justice to render the judgment enforceable.

An attempt to challenge this denial of authorisation before the European Court of Human Rights (ECtHR) was of no avail as the ECtHR held that the application of the Greek claimants was inadmissible.[39] Subsequently, the German Federal Court of Justice (*Bundesgerichtshof*) was seized to declare the Greek title enforceable in Germany. The German Court, however, ruled that the Livadia judgment was issued in breach of Germany's immunity and that therefore such decision could not be recognised in Germany.[40] After the landmark decision of the Italian Court of Cassation, the Greek claimants eventually turned their sights to Italy where their applications to declare the Greek awards enforceable in Italy, both in relation to the incurred legal costs as well as the awarded damages, were accepted by the Court of Appeal in Florence on 2 May 2005 and 13 June 2006 respectively. Germany's appeals against both decisions were each rejected by the Court of Cassation on 6 May 2008 and 12 January 2011.

In this context it appears also worth noting and of certain relevance for the ICJ's ruling that the Special Supreme Court (*Anotato Eidiko Dikastirio*) held in the *Margellos* case on 17 September 2002 – contrary to the Hellenic Supreme Court (*Areios Pagos*) which was initially seized with the case – that according to international law Germany's jurisdictional immunity barred claims for compensation of war crimes.[41]

Measures of constraint issued against German state property in Italy constituted the third alleged violation of state immunity. After the Greek judgment of the Court of Livadia in the *Distomo* case had been accorded *exequatur* by the Court of Appeal of Florence, the Greek

---

[38] *Prefecture of Voiotia* v. *Federal Republic of Germany*, case No. 11/2000, *ILR* 129, 513 et seq.

[39] *Kalogeropoulou and others* v. *Greece and Germany*, Application No. 59021/00, Decision of 12 December 2002, ECHR Reports 2002-X, 417; *ILR* 129, 537 et seq.

[40] *Greek Citizens* v. *Federal Republic of Germany*, case No. III ZR 245/98, *NJW* 2003, 3488, *ILR* 129 (2007), 556 et seq.

[41] *Margellos* v. *Federal Republic of Germany*, case No. 6/2002, *ILR* 129 (2007), 525 et seq.

claimants registered a legal charge over *Villa Vigoni*, a property of Germany, with the pertinent Land Registry Office in the Province of Como.[42] Located near Lake Como, *Villa Vigoni* serves as cultural centre of excellence founded to promote cultural exchanges between Germany and Italy and is used exclusively for such governmental purposes. By virtue of a decree-law the Italian authorities suspended, albeit not cancelled, the legal charge pending the decision of the ICJ.

IV. The ICJ's Analysis of the German Claims

The ICJ enters into its legal analysis by outlining the subject-matter – the alleged violation of Germany's jurisdictional immunity by the actions summarized above – of the decision before ascertaining its own jurisdiction by drawing reference to the European Convention for the Peaceful Settlement of Disputes which both Germany and Italy are parties to.[43]

The establishment of the Court's jurisdiction remained unchallenged by the parties, but the parties disagreed on *ratione temporis* limitations thereof. Their disagreement centred on determining the applicable temporal version of the law of state immunity.

Whereas Germany pleaded for the version valid during the underlying war crimes of 1943-1945, Italy advocated the application in its contemporary form due to its link with the pertinent Italian courts' decisions between 2004 and 2011. The Court followed Italy in that point by emphasising that Germany's application is based on the judicial proceedings before Italian courts and not on the war crimes of the German Reich which gave rise to the victims' lawsuits. In fact, the Court found that the law of immunity is procedural in nature and distinct from the substantive law that governs the acts of the German armed forces, which let the ICJ come to the conclusion that the law of immunity existing at the time of the proceedings in Italy has to be applied in the present case.[44]

The structure of the Court's substantive arguments follows the three claims of Germany outlined above, starting with the examination of the proceedings against Germany in Italian courts before turning to the de-

---

[42] ICJ, see note 1, para. 35.
[43] ICJ, ibid., para. 41.
[44] ICJ, ibid., para. 58.

cisions granting *exequatur* of Greek titles in Italy and the legal charge against *Villa Vigoni* as a measure of constraint.

We will broadly follow this approach but focus more on the legal points and less on their application to the facts which were relatively straightforward and undisputed between the parties. Consequently we begin by briefly commenting on the Court's general view on the basic principles of the law of state immunity (1.) and then turn to the four main sets of arguments concerning exceptions from that law (2.): the territorial tort exemption, the gravity of war crimes, the *jus cogens* argument and finally, the *ultima ratio* claim. Based on this, we briefly recall the Court's final decisions on Germany's claims (3.).

1. Basic Principles of the Law of State Immunity

The Court began its analysis by clarifying that the source of law for state immunity can only be derived from international customary law in relation to Germany and Italy as neither state is signatory to the United Nations Convention on Jurisdictional Immunities of States and their Property (UN Convention on Jurisdictional Immunities), while Italy has not acceded to the European Convention on State Immunity (European Convention). Following Article 38 (1) (b) of its Statute the Court notes that it has to identify the existence, scope and extent of international customary law documented in settled practice coupled with *opinio juris*.[45] It does so by referring to the ILC which showed that state immunity had become a general rule of law[46] deriving from the principle of sovereign equality set forth as one of the fundamental principles of international law in Article 2 (1) of the Charter of the United Nations.[47]

The Court then addressed the distinction between *acta jure gestionis* which entails limited immunity while *acta jure imperii* accorded impervious immunity to date. The Court concluded that the illegality of the underlying acts – not even the horrendous crimes of World War II – changes nothing in qualifying the deeds in question as *acta jure imperii*

---

[45] ICJ, ibid., para. 55.
[46] *ILCYB* 1980, Vol. II (2), 147, para. 26.
[47] ICJ, see note 1, para. 57.

as they genuinely signify sovereign power without any traces of private or commercial activities that *acta jure gestionis* require.[48]

While there is no question about the characterisation of the war crimes and violations of human rights as non-commercial, the Court did not address the question whether there is a third category of state acts apart from *acta jure gestionis* and *acta jure imperii*. This question was raised by Judge *Cançado Trindade* in the oral hearings. He asked the German delegation: "Can war crimes be considered as acts *jure* – I repeat, *jure* – *imperii*?"[49]

Indeed, it might have been worth contemplating whether certain crimes committed in the name of a state are so outrageous that no civilised nation could meaningfully claim that they are a legitimate exercise of its sovereign power. Developing the doctrine of state immunity on the basis of a modern concept of sovereignty as the responsibility to protect fundamental rights and principles of humanity could have led the Court to the conclusion that a third category would in fact be necessary to adequately evaluate such crimes: *Tertium datur!* Yet, the question of Judge *Cançado Trindade* remained unanswered by the Court as it did not address the idea of a third category.

In his Dissenting Opinion, Judge *Cançado Trindade* stated his own views claiming that international crimes labelled *delicta imperii* are neither acts of the state nor private acts and should not be covered by state immunity.[50] Unfortunately, the Dissenting Opinion does not reach this conclusion on the basis of an analysis of the changing ideas of sovereignty, but bases its view on a moral philosophical understanding of public international law which places individuals at the centre of a *jus gentium*.[51] As desirable as this perspective of international law might be, it can only be achieved if one closely analyses the function of state immunity in an era which sees a radically different notion of sovereignty compared to the 19th century.

---

[48] ICJ, ibid., paras 59-60.
[49] ICJ, Public sitting held on Friday 16 September 2011, 2:30 p.m., Verbatim Record, 54, <www.icj-cij.org>.
[50] ICJ, *Jurisdictional Immunities of the State (Germany v. Italy: Greece intervening)*, Dissenting Opinion of Judge *Cançado Trindade*, paras 181 and 184, <www.icj-cij.org>.
[51] *Cançado Trindade*, see note 50, paras 179 et seq.

2. Potential Limitations of State Immunity

a. The Territorial Tort Exemption

As a first line of defence, Italy argued that customary international law has nurtured an exception to the strict rule of impermeable immunity for acts qualified as *acta jure imperii* that were conducted in the forum state and caused personal injury and death. Italy based its argument on article 11 of the European Convention[52] and article 12 of the UN Convention on Jurisdictional Immunities[53] as both contain territorial tort exceptions, albeit not legally binding for the non-signatory parties, as well as on legislation on immunity enacted by a number of states which incorporated similar provisions.

The Court assessed Italy's argument by briefly pointing towards the development of the idea of the territorial tort exception stemming from road traffic accidents and other insurable risks before observing that, although originally designed for *acta jure gestionis*, contemporary legislation reveals that it in principle also applies to *acta jure imperii*.[54] The Court, however, dismissed Italy's assertion that the widely despised[55] European Convention and the UN Convention on Jurisdictional Immunities alone would suffice to constitute customary international law limiting state immunity.

---

[52] "A Contracting State cannot claim immunity from the jurisdiction of a court of another Contracting State in proceedings which relate to redress for injury to the person or damage to tangible property, if the facts which occasioned the injury or damage occurred in the territory of the State of the forum, and if the author of the injury or damage was present in that territory at the time when those facts occurred."

[53] "Unless otherwise agreed between the States concerned, a State cannot invoke immunity from jurisdiction before a court of another State which is otherwise competent in a proceeding which relates to pecuniary compensation for death or injury to the person, or damage to or loss of tangible property, caused by an act or omission which is alleged to be attributable to the State, if the act or omission occurred in whole or in part in the territory of that other State and if the author of the act or omission was present in that territory at the time of the act or omission."

[54] ICJ, see note 1, para. 64.

[55] As of August 2012 the United Nations Convention on Jurisdictional Immunities has 28 Signatories and 13 Parties; the European Convention a total number of ratifications/accessions of 8 – including Germany.

With regard to article 11 of the European Convention this follows from article 31 of the European Convention which provides a saving clause for the actions of armed forces of one contracting state on the territory of another contracting state. Contrary to Italy's view that article 31 was merely intended to avoid conflicts with the instruments governing the status of visiting forces, the Court holds that article 31 effectively excludes armed forces from the scope of the European Convention as clearly stipulated by the language of article 31[56] and in particular by the Explanatory Report,[57] a detailed commentary drafted during the negotiating process. This reasoning can also be found in a number of earlier European state court decisions – *inter alia* the Greek Special Supreme Court *(Anotato Eidiko Dikastirio)* in the *Margellos* case.[58]

Notwithstanding that a similar saving clause does not exist within the legal framework of the UN Convention on Jurisdictional Immunities, the Court ruled that article 12 of this Convention equally does not amount to customary international law in relation to jurisdictional immunity for acts of armed forces. The Court held that the ILC's commentary[59] on the text as well as statements of the Chairman of the Drafting *Ad Hoc* Committee[60] unequivocally suggest that article 12 of the UN Convention on Jurisdictional Immunities is not applicable to military actions.[61] This was not contested by the signatory states. Quite the contrary, two states officially declared their interpretation that the UN Convention on Jurisdictional Immunities does not affect the immunity of armed forces' actions.

Italy's attempt to construe an exception in customary international law by pointing to the fact that nine out of ten states which enacted legislation on jurisdictional immunity included territorial tort exceptions in the respective laws was also rejected by the Court on the grounds that at least two of those states explicitly excluded military acts, while

---

[56] "Nothing in this Convention shall affect any immunities or privileges enjoyed by a Contracting State in respect of anything done or omitted to be done by, or in relation to, its armed forces when on the territory of another Contracting State."

[57] "The Convention is not intended to govern situations which may arise in the event of armed conflict;…".

[58] ICJ, see note 1, para. 68.

[59] *ILCYB* 1991, Vol. II (2), 46, para. 10.

[60] Official Records of the General Assembly, 59th Sess., Sixth Committee, 13th Mtg, Doc. A/C.6/59/SR.13, 6, para. 36.

[61] ICJ, see note 1, para. 69.

there was no case-law in the other seven states that would support Italy's interpretation of the national legislation. In contrast, there are multiple judgments of national courts from a broad range of jurisdictions which granted immunity to acts of military forces both when visiting a foreign state by consent and during armed conflicts.[62] The only judgment outside Italy which did not explicitly exempt acts of armed forces from the territorial tort principle was the Hellenic Supreme Court's (*Areios Pagos*) ruling in the *Distomo* case. This reasoning, however, was subsequently disapproved with binding effect for all courts in Greece by the Greek Special Supreme Court (*Anotato Eidiko Dikastirio*) in the *Margellos* case. Given the fact that Greek courts, including the Supreme Court, adhered to that decision, the Court overall concluded that there is neither any state practice nor *opinio juris* upholding Italy's argument.

The analysis and discussion of the territorial tort exemption by the ICJ indicate that this exemption was not created to address war crimes and atrocities of the scale which were at stake in the present case. However, this observation does not exclude the possibility of applying it to such crimes. Even if one accepts that the territorial tort exemption did not apply to activities of military forces during armed conflicts, it is possible to argue that this would only apply to general war damages, but not to specific war crimes.[63] It should also be noted that the ICJ's approach to the question whether the territorial tort exemption could be applied to war crimes is based on a positivist understanding of customary international law: as long as there is not sufficient state practice following this approach, it is not part of the law.

Yet, state practice and *opinio juris* can be interpreted in various ways. For example, the fact that two states officially declared that the UN Convention on Jurisdictional Immunities does not affect the immunity of armed forces' actions can be interpreted as evidence that this is the view of the majority of the states – as the ICJ did – or as evidence of the contrary because two states felt that it was necessary to state their opposing view. As often, the analysis of state practice in order to detect a (new rule) of customary international law depends on the value choice

---

[62] ICJ, ibid., paras 72-75.
[63] For this line of arguments see Paech, see note 26, 74 et seq. A similar approach is developed by J. Bröhmer, *State Immunity and the Violation of Human Rights*, 1997, 204 et seq., who distinguishes between general violations of international law and individualised violations.

or on the normative *Vorverständnis* (pre-determination) with which one approaches the analysis.

b. Grave War Crimes as a Limitation to State Immunity

Despite discovering a "logical problem"[64] with the argument that serious violations of international humanitarian law would justify limitations of jurisdictional immunity as courts would always violate jurisdictional immunity by entering into the merits to examine whether an alleged serious violation of international law really exists, the Court scrutinised state practice to inquire whether international customary law has evolved in the way Italy alleges.

Apart from the *Distomo* decision of the Hellenic Supreme Court *(Areios Pagos)* which was repudiated, though, by the Special Supreme Court *(Anotato Eidiko Dikastirio)* in the *Margellos* case, the Court did not find any state practice that would support Italy's view.[65] It particularly deemed the United Kingdom's High Court decision in the *Pinochet* case as not pertinent for it concerned the immunity of a former head of state from criminal prosecution in a foreign country which High Court judges expressly distinguished from the immunity of the state itself.[66] The Court also noted that the ECtHR rejected the idea of limited immunity in the *Al-Adsani v. The United Kingdom* case in 2001.[67]

The ICJ also draws particular significance from the silence of the European Convention and the UN Convention on Jurisdictional Immunities on the issue of limitation of immunity in case of serious violations of international law as this question was raised and discussed at length within the Working Group and the United Nations Committee, but was eventually discarded as the members and states understood that customary international law did not limit state immunity in such cases.[68] In sum, the Court rejected Italy's argument that customary international law had developed to the point that it allowed exemptions from state immunity for claims based on serious war crimes.

---

[64] ICJ, see note 1, para. 82.
[65] ICJ, ibid., paras 83-85.
[66] ICJ, ibid., para. 87.
[67] *Al-Adsani v. United Kingdom* [GC], Application No. 35763/97, Judgment of 21 November 2001, ECHR Reports 2001-XI, 101, para. 61, *ILR* 123 (2003), 24.
[68] ICJ, see note 1, para. 89.

This part of the judgment is of great importance as it highlights – again – the dilemma in which the ICJ was forced by Germany's application: on the basis of a positivist approach towards Italy's argument any finding but an outright rejection would have been a surprise. Even to the most favourable commentators it was clear that the evidence Italy could rely on would hardly amount to sufficient state practice. The Court's answer to Italy's argument was therefore entirely correct if seen from a strict legalistic perspective. If the answer is correct, but the outcome is nevertheless unsatisfying, it is worth asking whether the problem lies not within the answer but within the question. As will be elaborated further in our critique of the judgment, Germany pushed the Court to search for the status of the law at a time when it would have been better to observe the development of a potentially new rule, rather than being forced to give a definite statement on something that could have been only an intermediate step in the process of the emergence of a new rule.

c. *Jus cogens* and the Hierarchy of Norms

The idea of a hierarchy of international norms claiming that human rights and humanitarian law is above the law of state immunity and therefore derogates from the latter has been discussed by some scholars and in a number of court cases.[69] Italy also followed this line of argument in its defence. It maintained that where peremptory rules of law, such as international humanitarian law, conflict with rules of a lower rank, as is the case for the rules of state immunity, the former renders the latter inapplicable.

However, the ICJ held that there is no such conflict in the present case as the two sets of rules govern entirely different matters as the law of state immunity by virtue of its preliminary and procedural nature does not address the questions of the substantive international humanitarian law.[70] The Court further reasoned that this stance remains unchallenged, even in the light of lacking compensation towards individual victims as there is no international rule of law which requires full reparation for each individual in the background of peace treaties that

---

[69] A. Orakhelashvili, "State Immunity and Hierarchy of Norms: Why the House of Lords Got it Wrong", *EJIL* 18 (2007), 955 et seq. (963 et seq.). For critical views see Caplan, see note 4, 771 et seq. and Schaarschmidt, see note 27, 21 et seq.
[70] ICJ, see note 1, para. 93.

either operate waiver clauses or lump sum settlements. The Court found this rationale affirmed by a series of decisions by national courts[71] which equally denied that *jus cogens* would set aside the rules of jurisdictional immunity and therefore also repudiated this strand.

This section of the ICJ's judgment is probably the most convincing one. Apart from the fact that it is still open to debate which international norms can be deemed to be *jus cogens*, the relationship between these norms is also not entirely clear. According to the law of treaties as stipulated in the Vienna Convention on the Law of Treaties, a treaty provision which violates *jus cogens* is void. This may establish a hierarchy between the two norms if there is a formal conflict, yet it is difficult to see how such a hierarchy could lead to a limitation of state immunity.[72] It would need to be shown that state immunity prevents a state from fulfilling its obligation not to violate norms of *jus cogens*. However, state immunity does not have this effect as can easily be seen in the present case: Germany was not prevented from compensating the Italian and Greek victims of war crimes through the notion of state immunity. Instead, it deliberately chose to invoke state immunity and therefore extend its violations of public international law.

d. The Last Resort Argument

Italy finally argued that the denial of jurisdictional immunity was justified by the fact that a significant number of Italian victims did not experience any form of redress despite all agreements and efforts emphasised by Germany during the proceedings before the Court. Similarly to the Court's reasoning on the *jus cogens* argument it rejected Italy's proposition by stating that the rules of state immunity are entirely distinct from the set of rules governing the state's responsibility and obligation to pay reparation. The Court further held that no customary international law has been developed to the point that would allow limiting jurisdictional immunity in favour of claims for alleged lack of compensation as no state practice in national courts or legislation can be found.[73] The Court therefore rejected this strand and additionally argued from a practical viewpoint that it would overstretch the national courts' tasks and abilities should they be seized with the questions to

---

[71] ICJ, ibid., para. 96.
[72] On this point see also O. Dörr, "Staatliche Immunität auf dem Rückzug?", *AVR* 41 (2003), 201 et seq. (215).
[73] ICJ, see note 1, paras 100-101.

determine if a state has failed in its obligation of compensation and if so to what extent.[74]

Two aspects are worth noting: first, Italy's argument was rather weak from the beginning, because Italy itself was apparently reluctant to exercise diplomatic protection to Italian victims of war crimes *vis-à-vis* Germany. In fact, Judge *Simma* specifically asked Italy to:

"describe in detail the attempts undertaken by the Italian Government at the diplomatic level to induce Germany to make reparation to Italian victims of German war crimes that is precisely the category of Italian victims allegedly excluded from German reparation measures during the period following the 1947 Peace Treaty up until the *Ferrini* case."[75]

Italy's answers to this question are not publicly documented, but the question shows that these activities of Italy – if any – were not widely known.

This leads to a second comment: the Court could have used the lack of significant Italian efforts as an argument to distinguish this case from other situations in which suits by individual war crime victims constitute the last resort to receive compensation. If a state which is responsible for international crimes seriously and continuously refuses to recognize its international obligations, in particular for reparation, the last resort argument could become more convincing. In his Separate Opinion Judge *Bennouna* supports this view arguing that a state could lose the benefits of its immunity if "the state presumed to be the author of unlawful acts rejects any engagement of its responsibility, in whatever form."[76] The Court's majority did not refer to this perspective. Yet, by developing a number of criteria for accepting the last resort argument and then showing that they are not met in the present case, the Court might have been able to escape the dilemma created by Germany's claim. Adopting such a line of argument would have at least saved the

---

[74] ICJ, ibid., para. 102.
[75] ICJ, *Jurisdictional Immunities of the State (Germany v. Italy: Greece intervening)*, Public sitting held on Friday 16 September 2011, 2:30 p.m., Verbatim Record, 53, <www.icj-cij.org>.
[76] ICJ, *Jurisdictional Immunities of the State (Germany v. Italy: Greece intervening)*, Separate Opinion of Judge *Bennouna*, paras 15 et seq. <www.icj-cij.org>.

Court from coming down so forcefully on a potentially emerging new international rule.[77]

3. Decision of the ICJ on Germany's Claims

Having concluded that none of Italy's arguments were convincing, the Court found by a majority of twelve to three[78] that the denial of jurisdictional immunity in proceedings before Italian courts amounts to a breach of Italy's international legal obligations towards Germany.

As for the second German claim, the Court turned to the decision to declare the Greek decision enforceable in Italy.

It held that the legality of the Italian *exequatur* with regard to state immunity is not linked to the question whether the Greek judgment violated Germany's immunity as the two proceedings have to be regarded as entirely separate.[79] The Court drew this conclusion from the consideration that the foreign court's decision on immunity must not necessarily run synchronously with the decision on immunity of the court granting *exequatur*.[80] This might happen for instance when the state waived its right to immunity in the country where proceedings were brought against it while its immunity still bars enforcement in the forum country where *exequatur* is sought.[81] The ICJ observed that although the Court of *exequatur* did not examine the merits, it exercises jurisdictional power by deciding whether to grant or deny *exequatur*.[82] Consequently, a Court which declares foreign judgments enforceable must adhere to the rules of immunity in the same fashion as it would if it had been seized to rule on the merits, for such decision affects the state party in a very similar way.[83] Therefore, the Court held with fourteen to one[84] that the decision on granting *exequatur* violated Germany's jurisdictional immunity on the same grounds as established above.

---

[77] See under V. 2.
[78] Judges *Cançado Trindade* and *Yusuf* and Judge *ad hoc Gaja* voted against this finding, see note 1, para. 139.
[79] ICJ, see note 1, paras 124-127.
[80] ICJ, ibid., para. 127.
[81] ICJ, ibid., para. 132.
[82] ICJ, ibid., para. 128.
[83] ICJ, ibid., para. 130.
[84] Judge *ad hoc Gaja* voted against this finding, see note 1, para. 139.

Lastly, the measures of constraint taken against German State Property in Italy were also addressed. Similar to its reasoning with regard to the decision of *exequatur,* the Court held that immunity from contentious proceedings in court is distinct from the immunity with regard to enforcement of the award and that therefore the alleged breach of immunity must be considered separately from the Greek proceedings and the declaration of enforcement in Italy. Germany proposed that article 19 of the UN Convention on Jurisdictional Immunities, which provides a detailed catalogue of conditions for the violation of immunity by measures of enforcements, constitutes in its entirety international customary law, whereas the Court was satisfied if at least one condition that – in view of extensive state practice[85] – could be effortlessly deemed as customary international law is met. With that condition being the exclusive use of the property which is subject to measures of enforcement for governmental non-commercial purposes, the Court held with fourteen to one[86] that the registration of the mortgage on *Villa Vigoni* constituted a breach of Germany's immunity.[87]

V. The ICJ's Judgment: "No surprise, but wise?"[88]

For most observers – even those in favour of limiting state immunity for international crimes – the ICJ's judgment should not have been a surprise. The Court could have only ruled otherwise if it had have adopted a different normative approach. However, any analysis of the existing state practice, in particular as evidenced by the judgments of a number of national and international courts, revealed that the doctrine Italy was relying on did not (yet) exist as a rule of customary international law. This was also the understanding shared by most commentators in the literature. In fact, those who argued that war crimes and gross violations of human rights should be exempted from state immunity did not base their arguments predominantly on a new rule of customary international law, but on a different understanding of the function and purpose of state immunity and the ultimate goal of public in-

---

[85] ICJ, see note 1, para. 118.
[86] Judge *ad hoc Gaja* voted against this finding, see note 1, para. 139.
[87] ICJ, see note 1, paras 118-119.
[88] This expression is borrowed from M. Hilf, "The ECJ's Opinion 1/94 on the WTO – No Surprise, but Wise?", *EJIL* 6 (1995), 245 et seq.

ternational law.[89] It was therefore not even particularly surprising that the outcome of the judgment proved to be relatively uncontroversial even among the Court's members.

If the principal judicial organ of the United Nations decides a case in a way expected – and hoped for? – by most states and anticipated by most scholars, one should assume a general satisfaction with the judgment. Yet, the judgment in *Jurisdictional Immunities of the State* cannot satisfy observers with an earnest interest in developing international law further in the interests of the protection of human rights. Three aspects which seem worth discussing further will be elaborated subsequently.

1. The Dilemma of Detecting Customary International Law without Affecting its Development

The judgment of the ICJ and its analysis of customary law on the day of the judgment show an effect which might be compared to an aspect of *Heisenberg's* uncertainty principle. One of the statements usually associated with this principle concerns the impossibility to measure the position of an object without disturbing its momentum.[90] In other words: the observation of an object will have influence on its location. For example, observing an object with the human eye requires that the object is illuminated which means it is subject to light waves affecting its exact position. Applying this idea to the analysis of customary international law by the ICJ in the present case, one could argue that the ICJ's attempt to measure the status of customary international law in relation to state immunity was not and could not have been without influence on the very development of the law at the moment of the ICJ's decision, i.e. the moment of observation.

In order to decide on Germany's claims, the ICJ analysed state practice and *opinio juris* regarding limitations on the principle of state immunity. It found a limited amount of practice supporting the claim that state immunity must be reduced if major international crimes are at hand. On the other hand, the Court found ample evidence of practice supporting the traditional view.

---

[89] Ample evidence for this can be found in the Dissenting Opinion of Judge *Cançado Trindade*, see note 50.
[90] P. Busch/ T. Heinonen/ P. Lahti, "Heisenberg's Uncertainty Principle", *Physics Reports* 452 (2007), 155 et seq. (155).

So far, the ICJ simply attempted to "measure" customary law at a given time. However, by concluding that there is not sufficient evidence for a new customary international law rule limiting the immunity of the state, the Court also influenced the development of such a new rule, by giving additional weight to the old rule. It is not very likely that in the aftermath of the ICJ's judgment many national courts will follow the example of the Italian courts and limit the immunity of the state in order to grant compensation to victims of gross violations of human rights and of humanitarian law.[91] Instead, it can be assumed that most – if not all – courts will take the judgment as an authoritative statement of the law and refrain from contributing to the development of a new rule.

This also reveals a structural methodological dilemma of the development of customary international law.[92] New rules of customary international law often emerge at first as a deviation, if not outright violation, of an old rule. The deviation only becomes the new rule if it finds a significant number of followers, as aptly recalled by Judge *Yusuf* in his Dissenting Opinion.[93] The establishment of a new rule therefore vindicates itself with hindsight: international law-breakers only become international law-makers when they attract a sufficient following to establish international practice.[94] Even if it was not its main intention, the ICJ ensured that the practice of the Italian courts will remain a transgression of international law for the foreseeable future.

The following thought experiment may highlight the problem associated with the Court's ruling in the present case: suppose the Permanent Court of International Justice had been confronted with the question about the extent of state immunity for *acta jure gestionis* in the early 1920s. At that time, a number of domestic courts already adopted the doctrine of limited state immunity while others maintained the idea of absolute state immunity. It was only in the second half of the 20th

---

[91] R. O'Keefe, "State Immunity and Human Rights: Heads and Walls, Hearts and Minds", *Vand. J. Transnat'l L.* 44 (2011), 999 et seq. (1033).

[92] On this dilemma see also W. Cremer, "Entschädigungsklagen wegen schwerer Menschenrechtsverletzungen und Staatenimmunität vor nationaler Zivilgerichtsbarkeit", *AVR* 41 (2003), 137 et seq. (151 et seq.).

[93] ICJ, *Jurisdictional Immunities of the State (Germany v. Italy: Greece intervening)*, Dissenting Opinion of Judge *Yusuf*, paras 46 et seq. <www.icj-cij.org>.

[94] C.I. Keitner, "Germany v. Italy: The International Court of Justice Affirms Principles of State Immunity", *ASIL Insights* 16, Issue 5 (2012), <www.asil.org>.

century that the idea that a state would not enjoy immunity for *acta jure gestionis* became widely accepted.[95] This development would have been seriously influenced, if not halted, by a judgment of the Permanent Court of International Justice ruling that an immunity exception for *acta jure gestionis* did not (yet) exist as a rule of customary international law. It can only be speculated how national courts would have reacted to such a decision of the Permanent Court, but one can be certain that the development of the law of state immunity would have been a different one.

2. Choosing between the Preservation of the Law as it Stands and the Progressive Development of International Law

The dilemma described above and the ICJ's decision to intervene in the development of a potential new rule of customary international law also blocked the progressive development of international law and preserved the traditional understanding of state immunity. In fact, the Court closed a door that stood open for a few years. In this respect, the Court may have followed *Christian Tomuschat*, Germany's representative who declared during the oral hearings: "Judges cannot be front-runners."[96]

Yet, domestic and international courts have been front-runners at various times in history and have shaped international law. The development of the law of state immunity is clear evidence of this. In fact, domestic courts may even serve as additional layer of implementing and developing international law in a progressive way.[97] Prominent commentators have therefore called upon the ICJ before the adoption of its judgment not to block national courts from further developing the law of state immunity in a way amendable to demands of remedies for serious violations of international law.[98] Unfortunately, the ICJ did not welcome the contribution of domestic courts to a new development. In

---

[95] Brownlie, see note 5, 704 et seq.; Cassese, see note 18, 327 et seq.
[96] ICJ, *Jurisdictional Immunities of the State (Germany v. Italy: Greece intervening)*, Public sitting held on Monday 12 September 2011, 10 a.m., Verbatim Record, 22, <www.icj-cij.org>.
[97] A. Fischer-Lescano/ C. Gericke, *Der IGH und das transnationale Recht. Das Verfahren BRD./. Italien als Wegweiser der zukünftigen Völkerrechtsordnung*, ZERP - Arbeitspapier 2/2010, 13 et seq.
[98] Damrosch, see note 20, 1197, 1200.

the words of *Nikos Lavranos,* the ICJ has put itself in a "position of slowing down rather than shaping as a front runner the developments in international law."[99]

But is the ICJ to blame? Could the Court have come to a different conclusion or should one criticize Germany for bringing its claims prematurely to the Court? As mentioned above, the Court could not have reached a different verdict on the basis of a positivist analysis of customary international law. Yet, the Court could have used language which would have indicated that the development is still in a state of flux or that its findings are restricted to the particularities of the case.[100] This could have left the door a bit open and would have allowed domestic courts to continue their quest for an adequate balance between the necessities of state immunity and the protection of fundamental human rights and principles of humanitarian law.

3. The Missing Voices: Representing the Victims by the Home State or through other Means

In its judgment the ICJ stated – although without any relevance to its analysis – that the war crimes at issue "can only be described as displaying a complete disregard for the 'elementary considerations of humanity'".[101] Furthermore, the Court considered it as "a matter of surprise- and regret-" that Germany denied compensation to forced labourers on the grounds that they were prisoners of war even though Germany refused to recognize that status at the time.[102] Yet, surprise and regret were the only condolences the Court was prepared to offer to the Italian and Greek victims of German war crimes.

At the end of the day, the ICJ referred these victims to the traditional means of diplomatic protection which requires the victims of a violation of human rights to pursue their claims through their home state. Yet, this avenue can be inadequate as shown in the present case: first, diplomatic protection does not provide for a proper alternative to judicial proceedings because diplomatic protection is exercised at the

---

[99] N. Lavranos, "National Courts, Domestic Democracy, and the Evolution of International Law", *EJIL* 20 (2009), 1005 et seq. (1011).
[100] See under IV. 2. d.
[101] ICJ, see note 1, para. 52.
[102] ICJ, ibid., para. 99. For a sharp, but convincing reaction to this expression see the Dissenting Opinion of Judge *Yusuf,* note 93, para. 10.

discretion of the state.[103] Victims will have to resort to political pressure which may or may not be successful.[104] Secondly, the home state may not be the best guardian of the interests of its citizens if it fears repercussions regarding its own potential violations of human rights and fundamental norms of international law. Italy, or rather the Italian government was, in fact, not very keen on defending the decisions of its courts denying Germany immunity,[105] because it might have feared similar cases against Italy for atrocities committed by its own military forces abroad. Even the Greek government did not appear with "clean hands" before the ICJ, because the Greek Minister of Justice refused to allow the execution of the judgment of the Hellenic Supreme Court *(Areios Pagos)* in the *Distomo* case.[106]

It could therefore be argued that the interests of the real victims were not present during the ICJ proceedings as their home states did not and could not argue forcefully in favour of the position of the victims. This leads to the question whether the procedural law of the ICJ needs to be amended to allow individual interests which are not adequately represented by the states to be heard through alternative means. In this context, it might be worth considering procedural instruments used in other international judicial bodies to compensate for the lack of representation of individual or collective interests not represented by the state.

WTO law and the law of international investment protection have developed the possibility of allowing so-called *amicus curiae* briefs submitted by non-state actors representing significant interests in the case at hand.[107] To date, the ICJ has never accepted any such briefs even though the possibility and desirability has been discussed repeatedly in the literature.[108] It might not even be necessary to change the ICJ Stat-

---

[103] McGregor, see note 13, 908.
[104] But see O'Keefe, see note 91, 1041, who actually advocates this approach as potentially more successful than litigation against the predatory state.
[105] O'Keefe, see note 91, 1033.
[106] See under III. 3.
[107] F. Ortino, "The Impact of Amicus Curiae Briefs in the Settlement of Trade and Investment Disputes", in: K.M. Meessen (ed.), *Economic Law as Economic Good*, 2009, 301 et seq.
[108] P. Palchetti, "Opening the International Court of Justice to Third States: Intervention and Beyond", in: J.A. Frowein/ R. Wolfrum (eds), *Max Planck UNYB* 6 (2002), 139 et seq. (165 et seq.) with further references.

ute in order to accept such interventions.¹⁰⁹ *Jurisdictional Immunities of the State* could be a good starting point to reconsider *amicus curiae* briefs in proceedings before the ICJ, in particular if individual claims for compensation are at the heart of the matter.

VI. Beyond State Immunity

Immunity issues in international law are not limited to state immunity.¹¹⁰ Diplomatic immunity and immunity of state representatives are the two other areas of the law of immunity which are also of relevance *vis-à-vis* the protection of human rights and the prosecution of international crimes.¹¹¹ Even though the different types of immunity serve different functions and the ICJ refused to draw parallels between state immunity and the immunity of the heads of state in the present case,¹¹² it is worth noting that the development of international criminal law has significantly reduced the personal immunity of state officials.

Article 27 of the Rome Statute of the International Criminal Court (ICC) specifically states that the statute applies equally to all persons. In particular, official capacity does not exempt a person from criminal responsibility under the Statute. Furthermore, immunities shall not bar the ICC from exercising its jurisdiction over such a person. However, in the 2002 *Arrest Warrant* case the ICJ did not deduce from this and other developments in international criminal law a new rule of customary international law limiting the immunities of state officials in general.¹¹³ Yet, in its recent judgment *Questions relating to the Obligation to Prosecute or Extradite* the Court did not pay any attention to the potential immunity of the former President of Chad *Hissène Habré*.¹¹⁴ Arguably, the issue at hand in that case did not involve the question of immunity directly, because the obligation to prosecute or extradite according to article 7 of the Convention against Torture and Other Cruel,

---

[109] Palchetti, see note 108, 170.
[110] Fox, see note 9, 665 et seq.; van Alebeek, see note 7, 103 et seq.
[111] D. Akande/ S. Sah, "Immunities of State Officials, International Crimes, and Foreign Domestic Courts", *EJIL* 21 (2010), 815 et seq.
[112] ICJ, see note 1, para. 87.
[113] ICJ, *Arrest Warrant of 11 April 2000 (Democratic Republic of the Congo v. Belgium)*, Judgment, ICJ Reports 2002, 3 et seq. (24).
[114] ICJ, *Questions relating to the Obligation to Prosecute or Extradite (Belgium v. Senegal)*, Judgment of 20 July 2012, <www.icj-cij.org>.

Inhuman or Degrading Treatment or Punishment does not have a direct effect on state immunity. However, from a broader perspective, the ICJ accepted in this judgment that even the position of a former President of a sovereign state would not prevent judicial proceedings *per se*.

The route towards limiting the immunity of state officials if international crimes are at stake has been long and not without detours. Yet, the direction of the general trend of the law is clear. It is noteworthy that the judgment of the ICJ in the *Arrest Warrant* case did not slow down the momentum. Instead, more and more laws and statutes restrict the immunity of state officials for international crimes, despite the verdict of the ICJ that no such rule existed in customary international law. This could be a glimpse of hope for the issue of state immunity as well. States may create new rules – either domestically or internationally – restricting state immunity even if such rules would not be grounded in customary international law.

VII. Conclusion

The judgment of the ICJ in the matter relating to *Jurisdictional Immunities of the State* supports the Court's position as a guardian of the *status quo* of international law. The Court made it clear that it does not see its role as promoter of a specific progressive judicial policy, but as an institution adjudicating disputes between states on the basis of a positivist analysis of public international law. This may be a relief to many, but a disappointment to some. Yet, this disappointment should not lead to frustration or unfair criticism of the ICJ. Instead, the judgment should be used as a stimulus to continue the quest for a modern law of state immunity. Such a law should be built on a reformulated understanding of state sovereignty allowing for proper balance between the protection of individual human and humanitarian rights and the functional necessity of allowing orderly processes of compensation for war crimes and violations of international law. Whether and how state immunity can play a useful role in these processes remains an open question.

The Immunity of Official Visitors

*Michael Wood**

---

*   I thank Penelope Nevill and Eran Sthoeger for their valuable assistance.

I. Introduction
II. Immunity *ratione personae* of serving Heads of State and other High-Ranking Officials; and "Official Act" Immunity
   1. Immunity *ratione personae* of serving Heads of State, Heads of Government, Ministers for Foreign Affairs and other High-Ranking Office Holders
   2. "Official Act" Immunity
III. The Convention on Special Missions
IV. Evidence of the Customary International Law on Official Visitors
   1. The Special Missions Convention and Customary International Law
   2. State Practice
   3. ICJ Case-Law
   4. Writings
V. The Customary International Law on the Immunity of Official Visitors
   1. Minimum Requirements for an Official Visit Attracting Immunity
      a. The Need for the Visitor to Represent the Sending State
      b. The Need for the Receiving State to Consent to the Visit as one Attracting Immunity
      c. Whether Consent is given is a Matter of Policy
      d. The Status of Persons on High-Level Official Visits
VI. Conclusion

Annex
State Practice

Abstract

This article reviews the customary international law concerning official visitors, in particular the inviolability of the person and immunity from criminal jurisdiction that they enjoy. It looks at State practice, including the case-law. It also considers the work of the ILC and the literature.

Three separate heads of immunity may come into play in the case of any particular official visit: the immunity *ratione personae* of holders of high-ranking office; "official act" immunity; and the immunity of official visitors, including those on special missions. As regards the third head, the rules of customary international law are both wider and narrower than the provisions of the *Convention on Special Missions*. They are wider in that the class of official visitors who may be entitled to immunity is broader than that foreseen in the Convention. They are narrower in that the range of privileges and immunities is more limited, being essentially confined to immunity from criminal jurisdiction and inviolability of the person.

Keywords

Official Visitors; Special Missions; Immunity; Inviolability; Convention on Special Missions

I. Introduction

The heir to the Throne of State A visits State B to receive an honorary degree. State A's former President visits State B for a reception in his honour, and also pays a courtesy call on the Prime Minister. The head of the national security office of State A visits State B intent on meeting officials of State B, but no meetings are arranged. The former Foreign Minister of State A, now leader of the opposition, visits State B to discuss with its Foreign Minister important questions of international relations. State A's Solicitor General visits State B to give a lecture at a university. Are these visitors, and persons accompanying them, entitled under customary international law to immunity from the jurisdiction of State B?

The aim of this article is to consider the customary international law concerning official visitors, in particular the inviolability of the person and immunity from criminal jurisdiction that they enjoy. In doing so, it looks at State practice, including the case-law, as well as the work of the ILC[1] and the literature.[2]

---

[1] In addition to the ILC's work on special missions, discussed in Section III below, its former Special Rapporteur on Immunity of State officials from foreign criminal jurisdiction (Kolodkin) produced three reports: *Preliminary report on immunity of State officials from foreign criminal jurisdiction* (Doc. A/CN.4/601, 29 May 2008); *Second report on immunity of State officials from foreign criminal jurisdiction* (Doc. A/CN.4/631, 10 June 2010); *Third report on immunity of State officials from foreign criminal jurisdiction* (Doc. A/CN.4/646, 24 May 2011) ("Kolodkin, Preliminary Report", "Kolodkin, Second Report" and "Kolodkin, Third Report"). The current Special Rapporteur (Escobar Hernández) submitted her first report in May 2012: *Preliminary report on immunity of State officials from foreign criminal jurisdiction* (Doc. A/CN.4/654 of 31 May 2012) ("Escobar Hernandez, Preliminary Report"). In addition, the UN Codification Division produced a Memorandum on *Immunity of State officials from foreign criminal jurisdiction* (Doc. A/CN.4/594, 31 March 2008) ("Secretariat Memorandum").

[2] C. Hyde, *International Law Chiefly as Interpreted and Applied by the United States*, Vol. 2, 2nd edition 1947, 1232-1234; C. Eagleton, "The Responsibility of the State for the Protection of Foreign Officials", *AJIL* 19 (1925), 293-314; H. Wriston, *Executive Agents in American Foreign Relations*, 1929; G.H. Hackworth, *Digest of International Law*, Vol. IV, 1940, 412-414; H. Wriston, "The Special Envoy", *Foreign Aff.* 38 (1959/1960), 219-237; M. Waters, "The Ad Hoc Diplomat: A Legal and Historical Analysis", *Wayne Law Review* 6 (1959/1960), 380-393; Ph. Cahier, *Le Droit diplomatique contemporain*, 1962, 361 372; M. Waters, *The Ad Hoc Diplomat: A Study in Municipal and International Law*, 1963; M. Bartoš, "Le statut des missions spéciales de la diplomatie ad hoc", *RdC* 108 (1963), 425-560; A. Watts, "Jurisdictional Immunities of Special Missions: The French Property Commission in Egypt", *ICLQ* 12 (1963), 1383-1399 (1383); J.V. Louis, "Le procès des diplomates français au Caire", *A.F.D.I.* 9 (1963), 231-251; J. Nisot, "Diplomatie ad hoc – les missions spéciales", *RBDI* 4 (1968), 416-422; M.R. Donnarumma, *La Diplomazia 'Ad Hoc'*, 1968; M. Whiteman, *Digest of International Law*, Vol. 7, 1970, 33-47; M. Bothe, "Die strafrechtliche Immunität fremder Staatsorgane", *ZaöRV* 31 (1971), 246-270; F. Przetacznik, "Jurisdictional Immunity of the Members of a Special Mission", *IJIL* 11 (1971), 593-609; M.R. Donnarumma, "La Convention sur les missions speciales (8 décembre 1969)", *RBDI* 8 (1972), 34-79; M. Paszkowski, "The Law on Special Missions", *Annuaire Polonais de Droit International* 6 (1974), 267-288; A. Maresca, *Le missioni speciali*,

Some 50 years ago, in 1963, Watts could write,

> "There is not yet any settled answer to the question whether, and if so to what extent, any jurisdictional immunity is enjoyed by government officials who are not members of an embassy or a consulate but who are sent on an official mission to a foreign State."[3]

That this is no longer the case is due in no small measure to the influence of the *Convention on Special Missions of 1969* and domestic

---

1975; M. Ryan, "The Status of Agents on Special Missions in Customary International Law", *CYIL* 16 (1978), 157-196; F. Przetacznik, "Diplomacy by Special Missions", *RDI* 59 (1981), 109-176; A. Verdross/ B. Simma, *Universelles Völkerrecht*, 3rd edition, 1984; J. Wolf, "Die völkerrechtliche Immunität des ad hoc-Diplomaten: untersucht anläßlich des Urteils des Landgerichts Düsseldorf in der Strafsache gegen Dr. Sadegh Tabatabai", *EuGRZ*, 10 (1983), 401-406; I. Sinclair, *The International Law Commission*, 1987, 59-61; L. Dembinski, *The Modern Law of Diplomacy*, 1988, 55-61; B. Murty, *The International Law of Diplomacy*, 1989, 262-266, 454-461; G. Dahm/ J. Delbrück/ R. Wolfrum, *Völkerrecht*, Vol. I/1, 1989, 296-298; M. Herdegen, "Special Missions", *EPIL* 4 (2000), 574-577; R. Jennings/ A. Watts (eds), *Oppenheim's International Law*, 9th edition, 1991, paras. 531, 533; J. Salmon, *Manuel de droit diplomatique*, 1994, 535-546; "Special Missions", in: A. Watts (ed.), *The International Law Commission 1949-1998*, 1999, Vol. I, 344-345; K. Ipsen, *Völkerrecht*, 5th edition, 2004, 591-596; P. Daillier/ M. Forteau/ A. Pellet, *Droit International Public*, 8th edition, 2008, para. 458; M. Shaw, *International Law*, 6th edition, 2008, 774-775; R. Van Alebeek, *The Immunity of States and Their Officials in International Criminal Law and International Human Rights Law*, 2008, 167-168; G. Buzzini, "Lights and Shadows of Immunities and Inviolability of State Officials in International Law: Some Comments on the *Djibouti v. France* Case", *LJIL* 22 (2009), 455-483; I. Roberts (ed.), *Satow's Diplomatic Practice*, 6th edition, 2009, 187-193; C. Wickremasinghe, "Immunities Enjoyed by Officials of States and International Organizations", in: M.D. Evans, *International Law*, 3rd edition, 2010, 390-392; D. Akande/ S. Shah, "Immunities of State Officials, International Crimes and Foreign Domestic Courts", *EJIL* 21 (2010), 815-852 (821-823); E. Franey, *Immunity, Individuals and International Law*, 2011, 135-149; J. Foakes, "Immunity for International Crimes? Developments in the Law on Prosecuting Heads of State in Foreign Courts", *Chatham House Briefing Paper*, November 2011 (IL BP 2011/2); N. Kalb, "Immunities, Special Missions", in: R. Wolfrum (ed.), *Max Planck Encyclopedia of Public International Law*, 2012; J. Crawford, *Brownlie's Principles of Public International Law*, 8th edition, 2012, 413-414; M. Wood, "Convention on Special Missions: Introductory Note", UN Audiovisual Library of International Law.

3 Watts (1963), see note 2, 1383.

case-law. The question of the immunity of official visitors under customary international law, including those on "special missions",[4] arises with increasing frequency. The law in this field may seem uncertain, given the variety of situations that arise. Yet, from the practice of States, the main outlines of the law are clear. The focus is on immunity from criminal jurisdiction since it is this that gives rise to most incidents in practice. But official visitors may enjoy a range of privileges and immunities, including in respect of civil and administrative jurisdiction. At least, they do so when the *Convention on Special Missions of 1969* applies.

With the introduction of permanent diplomatic missions in the fifteenth and sixteenth centuries, the institution of special missions declined, to reappear in full force by the time of World War II. As a working paper prepared in 1963 by the UN Secretariat explained,

"The custom of sending a special envoy on mission from one State to another, in order to mark the dignity or importance of a particular occasion, is probably the oldest of all means by which diplomatic relations may be conducted. It was only with the emergence of national States on a modern pattern that permanently accredited diplomatic missions, entrusted with a full range of powers, came to take the place of temporary ambassadors sent specially from one sovereign to another. However, although the legal rules which were evolved to determine diplomatic relations between States were therefore based largely on the conduct of permanent missions, so that special missions came to seem merely a particular variant of the other, the sending of special missions was never discontinued. During the eighteenth and nineteenth centuries such missions were frequently dispatched in order to provide suitable State representation at major ceremonial occasions, such as coronations or royal wed-

---

[4] The term "special mission" is in common use among international lawyers following the adoption of the 1969 Convention on Special Missions. But other terms are found in State practice and case-law. The term "official visit" may be preferable to "special mission". "Special mission" is not widely understood by those unfamiliar with diplomacy, and may conjure up unrelated images – of espionage, or the operations of special forces. In any event, the term is closely associated with the Convention on Special Missions of 1969, from which, as will be seen, customary rules differ significantly.

dings, or for the purposes of important political negotiations, particularly those held at international congresses."⁵

According to Milan Bartoš, also writing in 1963, it was widely assumed that *ad hoc* diplomacy was confined to ceremonial and protocol visits, visits by Heads of State, Heads of Government and Foreign Ministers (to which special rules already applied), and delegates attending international organizations and conferences. But, as Bartoš explains, this was not in fact the case. Especially from about 1941 onwards,⁶ *ad hoc* diplomacy to handle particular issues has become more and more common, both in bilateral relations and in the form of "special representatives" or "special envoys" designated by States (or international organizations) to handle particular issues.

The inviolability of the person and immunity from criminal jurisdiction of official visitors is distinct from other heads of immunity, such as those of (i) diplomatic agents;⁷ (ii) consular officers;⁸ (iii) representatives to international organizations and to international conferences;⁹ (iv) officials of international organizations;¹⁰ (v) persons associated with in-

---

5   "Special Missions. Working paper prepared by the Secretariat" (Doc. A/CN.4/155, in: *ILCYB* 1963, Vol. II, 151-158, paras. 3-11).
6   Bartoš, see note 2, 431-432.
7   E. Denza, *Diplomatic Law*, 3rd edition, 2008; R. van Alebeek, "Immunity, Diplomatic", in: Max Planck Encyclopedia, see note 2; H. Hestermeyer, "Vienna Convention on Diplomatic Relations (1961)", in: Max Planck Encyclopedia, see note 2.
8   L. Lee/ J. Quigley, *Consular Law and Practice*, 3rd edition, 2008; A. Paulus/ A. Dierselt, "Vienna Convention on Consular Relations", in: Max Planck Encyclopedia, see note 2.
9   The matter is governed by multilateral agreements on the privileges and immunities of particular international organizations, and by their respective headquarters agreements. The Vienna Convention on the Representation of States in their Relations with International Organizations of a Universal Character, 1975, has not (as of April 2012), entered into force. M. Hertig Randall, "The Vienna Convention on the Representation of States in their Relations with International Organizations of a Universal Character (1975)", in: Max Planck Encyclopedia, see note 2.
10 Wickremasinghe, see note 2, 398-400; H.G. Schermers/ N.M. Blokker, *International Institutional Law*, 5th revised edition, 2011, paras. 534-537; M. Möldner, "International Organizations or Institutions, Privileges and Immunities", in: Max Planck Encyclopedia, see note 2.

ternational courts and tribunals;[11] (vi) Heads of State, Heads of Government, Ministers for Foreign Affairs and certain other holders of high office in the State;[12] (vii) persons enjoying "official act" immunity;[13] and (viii) visiting forces.[14]

In each case, where appropriate, immunities may extend to members of the "entourage" or "retinue" of the persons concerned when they are visiting a foreign State. While these heads of immunity may overlap, in the sense that a person may enjoy (or claim) immunity under more than one head at the same time,[15] they are quite distinct.

In its Judgment of 3 February 2012 in the case of *Germany* v. *Italy*,[16] the ICJ indicated its approach to identifying the rules of customary international law in the field of State immunity. The Court made the important preliminary point, upon which both Parties agreed, "that immunity is governed by international law and is not a matter of mere comity."[17] The Court continued,

" ... the Court must determine, in accordance with Article 38 (1) *(b)* of its Statute, the existence of 'international custom, as evidence of a general practice accepted as law' conferring immunity on States and, if so, what is the scope and extent of that immunity. To do so, it must apply the criteria which it has repeatedly laid down for identifying a rule of customary international law. In particular, as the Court made clear in the *North Sea Continental Shelf* cases, the existence of a rule of customary international law requires that there be 'a settled practice' together with *opinio juris*. (*North Sea Continental Shelf (Federal Republic of Germany/Denmark; Federal Republic of*

---

[11] The matter is governed by particular treaties for each international court or tribunal.
[12] Section II 1 below.
[13] Section II 2 below.
[14] T. Desch, "Military Forces Abroad", in: Max Planck Encyclopedia, see note 2; P.J. Conderman, "Status of Armed Forces on Foreign Territory Agreements (SOFA)", in: Max Planck Encyclopedia, see note 2.
[15] As in *Khurts Bat* v. *The Investigating Judge of the German Federal Court* [2011] EWHC 2029 (Admin); [2011] All ER (D) 293 (Jul); *ILR* 147 (2012), 633, paras. 55-62 (Moses LJ); see R. O'Keefe, "Case-note", *BYIL* 82 (2011).
[16] ICJ, *Jurisdictional Immunities of the State (Germany* v. *Italy: Greece intervening)*, Judgment of 3 February 2012, <http://www.icj-cij.org>.
[17] Ibid., paras. 53, 55.

Germany/Netherlands), Judgment, I.C.J. Reports, 1969, p. 44, para. 77).''

Moreover, as the Court also observed,

"'It is of course axiomatic that the material of customary international law is to be looked for primarily in the actual practice and *opinio juris* of States, even though multilateral conventions may have an important role to play in recording and defining rules deriving from custom, or indeed in developing them. (*Continental Shelf (Libyan Arab Jamahiriya/Malta), Judgment, I.C.J. Reports 1985*, pp. 29-30, para. 27.)'

In the present context, State practice of particular significance is to be found in the judgments of national Courts faced with the question whether a foreign State is immune, the legislation of those States which have enacted statutes dealing with immunity, the claims to immunity advanced by States before foreign Courts and the statements made by States, first in the course of the extensive study of the subject by the International Law Commission and then in the context of the adoption of the United Nations Convention. *Opinio juris* in this context is reflected in particular in the assertion by States claiming immunity that international law accords them a right to such immunity from the jurisdiction of other States; in the acknowledgment, by States granting immunity, that international law imposes upon them an obligation to do so; and, conversely, in the assertion by States in other cases of a right to exercise jurisdiction over foreign States."[18]

Section II below recalls two additional heads of immunity that may apply to official visitors: that of serving Heads of State, Heads of Government, Ministers for Foreign Affairs and certain other holders of high office; and "official act" immunity. Section III then looks at the *Convention on Special Missions*. Section IV considers the evidence for the

---

[18] Ibid., para. 55. While the court was not concerned with the immunities of individual officials, its approach is relevant to the identification of the rules of customary international law in other cases where international immunities are governed by customary international law, including in the case of official visitors. See also Judge Keith, Separate Opinion, para. 4: "As appears from the Judgment in this case, the Court, for good reason, does give [decisions of national courts] a major role. In this area of the law it is such decisions, along with the reaction, or not, of the foreign State involved, which provide many instances of State practice. Further, the reasoning of the Judges by reference to principle is of real value."

rules of the customary international law on the immunities of official visitors. The emphasis is on State practice, including case-law. Reference is also made to such case-law of the ICJ as exists, and the literature. Section V seeks to restate the modern rules of customary international law in the field.

II. Immunity *ratione personae* of serving Heads of State and other High-Ranking Officials; and "Official Act" Immunity

The section briefly recalls two heads of immunity that sometimes apply in parallel with special mission/official visitor immunity.

1. Immunity *ratione personae* of serving Heads of State, Heads of Government, Ministers for Foreign Affairs and other High-Ranking Office Holders

The ICJ has held that, under customary international law, certain holders of high-ranking office, such as Heads of State,[19] Heads of Government[20] and Ministers for Foreign Affairs,[21] enjoy immunity *ratione per-*

---

[19] Kolodkin, Preliminary Report, see note 1, paras. 33-34. See also Doc. A/CN.4/650, para. 6 (summarising the 2011 Sixth Committee debate). Among recent cases where the immunity *ratione personae* of a serving Head of State has been recognized are *Affaire Ghaddafi*, Decision No. 1414, 13 March 2001, Cass. Crim.1; *President Yudhoyeno of Indonesia*, Rechtbanks Gravenhage, Sector civiel recht, 377038/KG ZA 10-1220, 6 October 2010. In English law, the immunity of Heads of State is now on a statutory basis: section 20 of the State Immunity Act 1978, which has been considered in a number of cases (*Halsbury's Laws of England*, 5th edition, Vol. 61, 178-179, para. 363). The leading case is *Pinochet (No. 3)* (2000) AC 147.

[20] Belgian *Cour de Cassation*, *H.S.A et al.* v. *S.A et al.*, 12 February 2003, *ILM* 42 (2003), 596.

[21] The ICJ's finding in respect of Ministers for Foreign Affairs has been criticized, but it reflects an emerging consensus in State practice, writings and case-law: Escobar Hernández, Preliminary Report, see note 1, paras. 33 and 63.

sonae while in office.[22] This includes inviolability of the person, and complete immunity from criminal jurisdiction.[23] After leaving office, such persons enjoy only immunity *ratione materiae*.[24]

In the *Arrest Warrant* case, the ICJ observed,

"that in international law it is firmly established that, as also diplomatic and consular agents, certain holders of high-ranking office in a State, such as the Head of State, Head of Government and Minister for Foreign Affairs, enjoy immunities from jurisdiction in other States, both civil and criminal."[25]

The three office holders listed by the Court – Heads of State, Heads of Government and Ministers for Foreign Affairs – are those who represent the State in its international relations by virtue of their office. They may, for example, sign treaties without having to produce Full Powers.[26] It is clear from the language used ("certain holders of high-ranking office in a State, such as ... .") that the list is not exhaustive, though it is confined to "a narrow circle of high-ranking State offi-

---

[22] Kolodkin, Preliminary Report, see note 1, paras. 109-121; Kolodkin, Second Report, see note 1, paras. 35-37; Kolodkin, Third Report, see note 1, paras. 23, 31; A. Watts, "The Legal Position in International Law of Heads of State, Heads of Government and Foreign Ministers", *RdC* 247 (1994), 9-130; Wickremasinghe, see note 2, 392-395; A. Borghi, *L'immunité des dirigeants politiques en droit international*, 2003; A. Watts/ J. Foakes, "Heads of State" and "Heads of Governments and Other Senior Officials", in: Max Planck Encyclopedia, see note 2.

[23] While there is little practice, it would seem that Heads of State-elect should also benefit from such immunity: Kolodkin, Third Report, see note 1; the same would also apply to the Heir to the Throne in a Monarchy. For a reference by the ICJ to a Head of State-elect, in which it seems to have treated his statements more or less on a par with those of a serving Head of State, see ICJ, *Application of the International Convention on the Elimination of All Forms of Racial Discrimination (Georgia v. Russian Federation), Preliminary Measures*, Judgment of 1 April 2011, <http://www.icj-cij.org/>, para. 77.

[24] On the distinction between immunity *ratione personae* and immunity *ratione materiae*, see Kolodkin, Preliminary Report, see note 1, paras. 78-83.

[25] *Arrest Warrant of 11 April 2000 (Democratic Republic of the Congo v. Belgium)*, ICJ Reports 2002, 3, 20-21, para. 51. See also *Certain Questions of Mutual Judicial Assistance in Criminal Matters (Djibouti v. France)*, ICJ Reports 2008, 177, 236-237, para. 170.

[26] Article 7, Vienna Convention on the Law of Treaties.

cials."²⁷ The same immunity *ratione personae* applies to certain other holders of high-ranking office to whom similar considerations apply,²⁸ such as others of Cabinet rank who similarly need to travel to represent their State at the highest levels.

In *Djibouti v. France*, the ICJ did not suggest that either the Djiboutian *Procureur de la République* or Head of National Security enjoyed immunity as persons occupying high-ranking offices in the State. Indeed, France considered that they "did not, given the essentially internal nature of their functions, enjoy absolute immunity from criminal jurisdiction or inviolability *ratione personae*."²⁹ And France pointed out that in the *Arrest Warrant* case, the ICJ had not suggested that the Minister of State charged with national education (which is what former Foreign Minister Yerodia had become since the proceedings commenced) fell within the class of high office holders enjoying immunity *ratione personae*.³⁰

The immunity of this "narrow circle" of high office holders applies whether or not they are on a special mission, and in addition to any immunity they may enjoy when they are official visitors.³¹ When they are on a visit, the immunity of members of their entourage or retinue may be that of persons on a special mission, but it may also be derivative of the status of the high official in question.³² This could be rele-

---

[27] Kolodkin, Second Report, see note 1, para. 94(i). English courts have recognized that immunity *ratione personae* extends to a Defence Minister (*Re Mofaz*, Bow Street Magistrates' Court, 12 February 2004, *ILR* 128 (2006), 709; *ILDC* 97 (UK 2004); *Ehud Barak*, Westminster Magistrates' Court, 29 September 2009 (unreported, described in Franey, see note 2, 146-147); and to a Minister of Commerce (*Re Bo Xilai*, Bow Street Magistrates' Court, 8 November 2005, *ILR* 129 (2007), 713).

[28] In modern times, other persons may exercise powers in the area of foreign relations: see *Armed Activities in the Territory of the Congo (New Application: 2002) (Democratic Republic of the Congo v. Rwanda), Jurisdiction and Admissibility*, ICJ Reports 2006, 6, 27, para. 47.

[29] *Certain Questions of Mutual Judicial Assistance in Criminal Matters (Djibouti v. France)*, see note 25, 241-242, para. 186.

[30] Ibid., French Counter-Memorial, paras. 4.31-4.35.

[31] Article 21, Convention on Special Missions 1969; article 50, Convention on the Representation of States in Their Relations with International Organizations of a Universal Character 1975.

[32] The ILC 1991 commentary on the draft articles on Jurisdictional Immunities of States and Their Property states that the draft articles "do not prejudice the extent of immunities granted by States to foreign sovereigns or

vant, for example, when they are travelling privately[33] and possibly in the case of certain close family members.[34]

The English High Court considered the immunity of high-ranking office holders in *Khurts Bat*.[35] The Court found that "there is no dispute but that in customary international law certain holders of high-ranking office are entitled to immunity *ratione personae* during their term of office. They enjoy complete immunity from criminal jurisdiction."[36] The Court concluded that *Bat*, a mid-ranking official, was not entitled to immunity *ratione personae* as a holder of high-ranking office.[37]

2. "Official Act" Immunity

State officials and former officials have "official act" immunity (immunity *ratione materiae*) from the criminal jurisdiction of foreign States.[38] This includes immunity from criminal jurisdiction in respect of acts

---

other heads of State, their families and household staff which may also, in practice, cover other members of their entourage", *ILCYB* 1991, Vol. II, Pt 2, 22 (draft article 3, commentary (7)). For a summary of discussions within the ILC, see Kolodkin, Preliminary Report, see note 1, paras. 13-44. There is little State practice or case-law on "entourage" or "retinue" immunity, though it is hinted at in the literature, and the considerations underlying the *Arrest Warrant* Judgment point would justify it: see M. Sørensen, *Manual of Public International* Law, 1968, 387; Watts, see note 22, 75-76; Jennings/ Watts, see note 2, para. 452.

[33] Even when travelling privately, a Head of State or Head of Government may well be accompanied by staff. In today's circumstances, they are never really "off-duty".

[34] See Kolodkin, Preliminary Report, see note 1, paras. 125-129.

[35] *Khurts Bat*, see note 15, paras. 55-62 (Moses LJ).

[36] Ibid., para. 55.

[37] In reaching this conclusion, the Court rejected the District Judge's view that *Bat* was not entitled to immunity since he was not engaged on foreign affairs, the stated purpose of his visit being to discuss matters of mutual security concern, ibid., paras. 62 (*Moses* LJ) and 107 (*Foskett* J). The Court accepted that security matters could be the subject of a special mission, but found that there was no such special mission in this case.

[38] C.A. Whomersley, "Some Reflections on the Immunity of Individuals for Official Acts", *ICLQ* 41 (1992), 848-858.

done in an official capacity, but not acts committed in a private capacity.[39] There may be exceptions:[40]

In *Pinochet (No.3)*,[41] the House of Lords held that there was an implied waiver of immunity from criminal jurisdiction by the parties to the UN Convention against Torture, since acts of torture within the meaning of the Convention could only be committed by persons acting in an official capacity. It is unclear how far this exception would apply to other "international crimes", such as war crimes.[42]

There is also authority to the effect that there is no immunity "where criminal jurisdiction is exercised by a State in whose territory an alleged crime has taken place, and this State has not given its consent to the performance in its territory of the activity which led to the crime and to the presence in its territory of the foreign official who committed this alleged crime."[43] This exception was applied by the High Court in *Khurts Bat*.[44] The issue only became clear during the High Court hearing,[45] and the Court was not called upon to consider the need to

---

[39] *Arrest Warrant of 11 April 2000 (Democratic Republic of the Congo v. Belgium)*, see note 25, 25-26, para. 61; Secretariat Memorandum, see note 1, paras. 154-212; Kolodkin, Second Report, see note 1, paras. 21-34.

[40] Kolodkin, Second Report, see note 1, paras. 54-93.

[41] *R. v. Bow Street Metropolitan Stipendiary Magistrate and others, ex p. Pinochet Ugarte (Amnesty International and others intervening)* (2000) 1 AC 147.

[42] Kolodkin, Second Report, see note 1, paras. 180-212; Van Alebeek, see note 2; A. Bellal, *Immunités et violations graves des droits humains*, 2011.

[43] Kolodkin, Second Report, see note 1, para. 94(p); see also paras. 81-86 and 90. The possible exception was evidently considered in *Pinochet (No. 3)*, see note 41, but the majority view does not deal with it explicitly. See, on the other hand, Lord Millett: "The plea of immunity *ratione materiae* is not available in respect of an offence committed in the forum state, whether this be England or Spain" (277C-D) and Lord Phillips, saying that he was "not aware of any custom which would have protected from criminal process a visiting official of a foreign state who was not a member of a special mission had he the temerity to commit a criminal offence in the pursuance of some official function ..." (283A-B). For practice, see Franey, see note 2, 244-281.

[44] *Khurts Bat*, see note 15.

[45] The claim to "official act" immunity had not been raised at first instance, and arguably should not therefore have been available on appeal. In the case of such a claim, "[t]he State which seeks to claim immunity for one of its State organs is expected to notify the authorities of the other State concerned": *Certain Questions of Mutual Judicial Assistance in Criminal Mat-*

exclude crimes committed during armed conflict from any territorial exception to immunity.[46] Moreover, it might have been more appropriate for the German Court, to consider the question of official act immunity for acts committed in the forum State in the light of all the facts before it.

III. The Convention on Special Missions

"Early codifications of the law of diplomatic immunity commonly included both permanent and temporary diplomatic agents."[47] The first official attempt to codify the law on *ad hoc* diplomacy was the *Havana Convention on Diplomatic Officers of 20 February 1928* (in force since 1929), which assimilates the status of "extra-ordinary diplomatic offi-

---

ters *(Djibouti v. France)*, see note 25, 243-244, paras. 194-197, especially para. 196; Kolodkin, Third Report, see note 1, para. 61(f), which reads: "When an official who enjoys functional immunity is concerned, the burden of invoking immunity lies with the official's State. If the State of such an official wishes to protect him from foreign criminal prosecution by invoking immunity, it must inform the State exercising jurisdiction that the person in question is its official and enjoys immunity since he performed the acts with which he is charged in an official capacity. If it does not do so, the State exercising jurisdiction is not obliged to consider the question of immunity *proprio motu* and, therefore, may continue criminal prosecution." The Special Rapporteur's explanation of this conclusion is at paras. 14-31 of the Report. But see also his somewhat inconclusive consideration of the question whether the official's State can also declare the individual's immunity at a later stage of the criminal process. (ibid., paras. 17 and 57) – this raises the question as to when immunity must be deemed to have been waived, if criminal proceedings are not to be frustrated at a late stage. On the possibility of implied waiver of immunity from foreign criminal jurisdiction, see Kolodkin, Third Report, see note 1, paras. 53-55 and 61 (l) to (o).

[46] Kolodkin, Second Report, see note 1, para. 86, makes an important qualification: "the issue of the criminal prosecution and immunity of military personnel for crimes committed during military conflict in the territory of a State exercising jurisdiction would seem to be governed primarily by humanitarian law *[that is, the law of armed conflict]*, and be a special case and should not be considered within the framework of this topic."

[47] Van Alebeek, see note 2, 168.

cers" to that of regular, permanent diplomatic agents.[48] The commentary to the definition of "mission" in the *Harvard Research Draft Convention on Diplomatic Privileges and Immunities of 1932* states that the term,

> "is broad enough to include special missions of a political or ceremonial character which are accredited to the government of the receiving state. Members of special missions probably enjoy the same privileges and immunities as do those of permanent missions."[49]

On 8 December 1969, the United Nations General Assembly adopted the *Convention on Special Missions*,[50] together with an *Optional Protocol on the Compulsory Settlement of Disputes*[51] and a reso-

---

[48] LNTS Vol. 155 No. 3581. See also the Vienna Règlement of 1815; the *Institut de Droit International*'s resolution of 1895; and the ILA's 1926 Vienna resolution.

[49] *Harvard Draft Convention on Diplomatic Privileges and Immunities, Commentary, Harvard Research in International Law* (*AJIL* Supplement 26 (1932), 15 (42)).

[50] UNTS Vol. 1400 No. 23431. The resolution adopting the Convention was adopted by a non-recorded vote of 98-0-1 (Malawi abstaining), A/RES/2530 (XXIV) of 8 December 1969. The Convention entered into force on 21 June 1985. As of August 2012, there were 38 States Parties: Argentina, Austria, Belarus, Bosnia and Herzegovina, Bulgaria, Chile, Colombia, Croatia, Cuba, Cyprus, Czech Republic, Estonia, Fiji, Georgia, Guatemala, Indonesia, Iran, Liberia, Liechtenstein, Lithuania, Macedonia, Mexico, Montenegro, Paraguay, People's Democratic Republic of Korea, Philippines, Poland, Rwanda, Serbia, Seychelles, Slovakia, Slovenia, Spain, Switzerland, Tonga, Tunisia, Ukraine and Uruguay. The Convention was open for signature until 31 December 1970. The States which signed the Convention but have not ratified are: El Salvador, Finland, Israel, Jamaica, Nicaragua and the United Kingdom. For the latest information about participation in the Convention, see the United Nations Treaty Collection website.

[51] UNTS Vol. 1400 No. 23431. The Optional Protocol is modelled on the corresponding Optional Protocols to the Vienna Conventions on Diplomatic and Consular Relations of 1961 and 1963 respectively. It entered into force on 21 June 1985. As of August 2012, there were 17 States Parties: Austria, Bosnia and Herzegovina, Cyprus, Estonia, Guatemala, Iran, Liberia, Liechtenstein, Montenegro, Paraguay, Philippines, Serbia, Seychelles, Slovakia, Spain, Switzerland and Uruguay. The Optional Protocol was open for signature until 31 December 1970. El Salvador, Finland, Jamaica and the United Kingdom signed but have not ratified it. For the latest information about participation in the Optional Protocol, see the United Nations Treaty Collection website.

lution concerning civil claims.[52] The Convention is the applicable international law as between the parties thereto. But it has attracted limited participation, and there are few other treaties on the subject.[53] So, as between most States, and in most circumstances, the governing rules are those of customary international law.

While the Convention has influenced the customary rules, it should not be assumed that all or even most of its provisions are now reflected in customary law, given the circumstances of its adoption and the lack of support among States. In summary, as we shall see, while the range of official visitors who enjoy privileges and immunities under customary law is wider than under the Convention, the privileges and immunities accorded under customary law are less extensive.

The key provisions of the *Convention on Special Missions* are articles 1 (a), 2, 3, 29 and 31 (1).

Article 1. Use of terms

For the purposes of the present Convention:

(a) a "special mission" is a temporary mission, representing the State, which is sent by one State to another State with the consent of the latter for the purpose of dealing with it on specific questions or of performing in relation to it a specific task;

---

[52] A/RES/2531(XXIV) of 8 December 1969 recommended "that the sending State should waive the immunity of members of its special mission in respect of civil claims of persons in the receiving State when it can do so without impeding the performance of the functions of the special mission, and that, when immunity is not waived, the sending State should use its best endeavours to bring about a just settlement of the claims."

[53] Ipsen, see note 2, 592 says that the legal basis for special missions is set out in individual bilateral treaties, but does not give references. For a possible example, see the Exchange of Notes between Switzerland and the United States, signed at Bern on 23 February and 5 March 1973 (TIAS 7582; 24 UST 772), which provides that certain US delegations were "considered to be special missions convened by the Governments of the USA and of the USSR on the territory of the Swiss Confederation. The two delegations and the persons of which they are composed enjoy on the territory of the Swiss Confederation the status, privileges and immunities which are accorded to a special mission, to the representatives of the sending State in a special mission ...": Washington, D.C. International Law Institute (ed.), *Digest of United States Practice in International Law*, 1973, 166-167.

Article 2. Sending of a special mission

A State may send a special mission to another State with the consent of the latter, previously obtained through the diplomatic or another agreed or mutually acceptable channel.

Article 3. Functions of a special mission

The functions of a special mission shall be determined by the mutual consent of the sending and the receiving State.

Article 29. Personal inviolability

The persons of the representatives of the sending State in the special mission and of the members of its diplomatic staff shall be inviolable. They shall not be liable to any form of arrest or detention. The receiving State shall treat them with due respect and shall take all appropriate steps to prevent any attack on their persons, freedom or dignity.

Article 31. Immunity from jurisdiction

1. The representatives of the sending State in the special mission and the members of its diplomatic staff shall enjoy immunity from the criminal jurisdiction of the receiving State.

The negotiating history of the Special Missions Convention[54] sheds light on a number of points important not only for the interpretation of the Convention but also as evidence of the customary law on the immunity of official visitors. These include the extent to which, already in the 1950s and 1960s, States and the ILC considered there were rules of customary international law in the field.

Three related issues were prominent in the negotiations:

1. Was it possible to define a "special mission" by reference to its level and functions? On the assumption that not all official visitors would enjoy immunity under the future Convention, how was the line to be drawn?

---

[54] Paszkowski, see note 2; Whiteman, see note 2. The two main stages were the preparation of draft articles by the ILC and the negotiation of the Convention within the Sixth Committee. M. Bartoš was Special Rapporteur for the Commission and Expert Consultant for the Sixth Committee. M.K. Yasseen was Chairman of the Drafting Committee.

2. While it seemed clear that the consent of the receiving State to the sending of the special mission was essential, what was the nature of that consent? Consent to what? Was prior consent needed, and if so prior to what? Entry into the territory, or at least to the commencement to the mission? Did consent need to be express or given through certain channels?
3. What scale of privileges and immunities should apply to special missions and their members? Should they enjoy the same level of privileges and immunities as permanent diplomatic missions?

The ILC had first considered the question of "*ad hoc* diplomacy" in the course of its work in the 1950s on the topic of "Diplomatic intercourse and immunities." Already in 1957 the Commission considered that other forms of diplomacy, under the heading "*ad hoc* diplomacy", "should also be studied, in order to bring out the rules of law governing them."[55] When presenting its final draft articles to the General Assembly in 1958, the Commission noted that diplomatic relations also assumed other forms, such as itinerant envoys, diplomatic conferences and special missions sent to a State for limited purposes.

The Commission appointed A.E.F. Sandström, Special Rapporteur for Diplomatic Intercourse and Immunities, as Special Rapporteur for Special Missions. In 1960, Sandström presented a report in which he explained that "a special mission can be characterized as performing temporarily an act which ordinarily is taken care of by the permanent mission. The head of a special mission is also generally, but not always, a diplomatic officer by profession." Sandström went on to refer to "the similarity between a special mission's activities and aims and those of a permanent mission."[56] On the basis of this report, and without the usual in-depth study, the Commission adopted three draft articles,[57] which were then referred by the General Assembly to the UN Conference on Diplomatic Intercourse and Immunities of 1961, in Vienna.[58]

Draft article 1 (1) contained the following definition:

---

[55] *ILCYB* 1957, Vol. II, 132-133.
[56] "Ad Hoc Diplomacy, Report by A.E.F. Sandström" (Doc. A/CN.4/129), paras. 5 and 6, in: *ILCYB* 1960, Vol. II, 108.
[57] *ILCYB* 1960, Vol. II, 179-180.
[58] For a summary of the Commission's consideration of special missions during its 1960 session, see "Special Missions: Working paper by the Secretariat", (Doc. A/CN.4/155), in: *ILCYB* 1963, Vol. II, 151-158, paras. 14-41.

"The expression 'special mission' means an official mission of State representatives sent by one State to another in order to carry out a special task. It also applies to an itinerant envoy who carries out special tasks in the States to which he proceeds."[59]

The draft articles would have applied the rules developed for the privileges and immunities of permanent diplomatic missions to special missions.

At the 1961 Vienna Conference, the question of special missions was considered by a Sub-Committee of the Committee of the Whole.[60] Upon the unanimous recommendation of the Sub-Committee, the Conference adopted a resolution, recommending that the General Assembly refer the subject back to the Commission.[61] And by Resolution 1687 (XVI) of 18 December 1961, the Assembly requested the Commission to study further the subject of special missions and report thereon to the General Assembly.[62] In 1962 the Commission placed the topic "Special missions" on its agenda once again, and requested its Secretariat to prepare a working paper, which served as a basis for the discussions in 1963.[63] In 1963 the Commission appointed Bartoš as Special Rapporteur. It instructed him to prepare draft articles based on the *Vienna Convention on Diplomatic Relations*, but to keep in mind,

" ... that special missions are, both by virtue of their functions and by their nature, an institution distinct from permanent missions."[64]

It further decided that the topic should include itinerant envoys, but not delegates to conferences and congresses, because the latter were re-

---

[59] Ibid., 179, para. 38. The term "itinerant envoy" refers to an envoy who visits several States successively.
[60] *United Nations Conference on Diplomatic Intercourse and Immunities, Official Records*, Vol. II (Doc. A/CONF.20/10), 45-46 and 89-90.
[61] Ibid., Vol. II (Doc. A/CONF.20/10/Add.1), Resolution I.
[62] For a summary of the work on special missions up to this point, see "Working paper prepared by the Secretariat", Doc. A/CN.4/147, in: *ILCYB* 1962, Vol. II, 155-156. For an account of developments in the Commission and at the Conference by an active participant see Bartoš, see note 2, 448-459.
[63] "Special Missions: Working paper by the Secretariat", see note 58, 151-158. The paper dealt with (I) preliminary survey of the topic and of previous attempts to determine the law relating to special missions; (II) prior consideration by the ILC etc.; and (III) the scope of the topic, and the form of the draft.
[64] *ILCYB* 1963, Vol. II, 225, para. 64.

lated to the topic of relations between States and inter-governmental organizations.⁶⁵

In 1964 the Commission presented 16 draft articles with commentaries to the General Assembly.⁶⁶ These contained rules concerning the sending, functioning and duration of special missions, but not their immunities and privileges. They made it clear that the consent of the receiving State was essential to the sending of a special mission.

Draft article 1 (1) provided:

"For the performance of specific tasks, States may send temporary special missions with the consent of the State to which they are to be sent."

The commentary emphasised the importance of consent: a special mission "must possess" certain characteristics, one of which is that "a State is not obliged to receive a special mission from another State unless it has undertaken in advance to do so" and "consent for it must have been given in advance for a specific purpose."⁶⁷

In presenting its final set of 50 draft articles to the General Assembly in 1967, the Commission stated that,

"In preparing the draft articles, the Commission has sought to codify the modern rules of international law concerning special missions, and the articles formulated by the Commission contain elements of progressive development as well as of codification of the law."⁶⁸

Under the heading "General considerations" at the beginning of Part II (which became articles 21 to 46 of the Convention), before discussing the scale of facilities, privileges and immunities to be accorded (on which there were differing views), the Commission said,

"Before the Second World War, the question whether the facilities, privileges and immunities of special missions have a basis in law or whether they are accorded merely as a matter of courtesy was discussed in the literature and raised in practice. Since the War, the view that there is a legal basis has prevailed. It is now generally recognized that States are under an obligation to accord the facilities,

---

⁶⁵ Ibid., para. 63.
⁶⁶ *ILCYB* 1964, Vol. II, 210-226.
⁶⁷ Ibid., 210 (para. (2)(c) of the commentary on draft article 1. Draft article 2 further required that "[t]he task of a special mission shall be specified by mutual consent of the sending State and of the receiving State" (ibid., 211).
⁶⁸ *ILCYB* 1967, Vol. II, 346, para. 12.

privileges and immunities in question to special missions and their members. Such is also the opinion expressed by the Commission on several occasions between 1958 and 1965 and confirmed by it in 1967."[69]

Draft article 2 read,

"A State may, for the performance of a specific task, send a special mission to another State with the consent of the latter."[70]

The Commission's commentary read,

"(1) Article 2 makes it clear that a State is under no obligation to receive a special mission from another State unless it has undertaken in advance to do so. Here the draft follows the principle stated in article 2 of the Vienna Convention on Diplomatic Relations.

(2) In practice, there are differences in the form given to the consent required for the sending of a mission, according to whether it is a permanent diplomatic mission or a special mission. For a permanent diplomatic mission the consent is formal, whereas for special missions it takes extremely diverse forms, ranging from a formal treaty to tacit consent."[71]

The draft articles were generally welcomed by States. However, some considered that they were too generous to special missions if the Convention was to cover all kinds of missions sent by one State to another, whatever their level and the nature of their functions. The overwhelming majority, however, rejected attempts in the Sixth Committee of the General Assembly in 1968 to lower the scale of privileges and immunities. When work resumed in 1969, certain States, led by France and the United Kingdom, pursued an alternative approach, seeking to establish a scope of application for the Convention which was appropriate to the extensive privileges and immunities granted. They were thus concerned to ensure that the Convention applied only to certain high-level missions conducting specific diplomatic tasks.[72]

There was much debate in the Sixth Committee on three related matters concerning the scope and definition of "special missions". First,

---

[69] Ibid., 358, para. (1) (footnote omitted).
[70] Ibid., 348.
[71] Ibid., 349.
[72] The negotiation of the Convention in the UN General Assembly is well described in Paszkowski, see note 2, 273-284.

the expression used by the Commission "of a representative character" proved controversial, and was replaced by the more neutral "representing the State."[73] Second, efforts expressly to limit the missions concerned to "high-level" missions were not successful.[74] On one point, and this was crucial, there was general agreement: the essential requirement of consent, both to the sending of the mission and to its functions. In the Sixth Committee, States were not fully satisfied with the Commission's approach to consent; hence the amendment requiring that consent be previously obtained through appropriate channels. In voting for the adoption of article 1 (a) of the Convention by the Sixth Committee on 20 October 1969, the United Kingdom said, in explanation of the vote (also on behalf of France),

> "[a] Special Mission is a temporary, *ad hoc* Mission. The existence of a particular Special Mission derives from an *ad hoc* expression of mutual consent by the sending and receiving States. A special Mission represents the sending State in the same sense of the word 'represents' as a permanent diplomatic mission represents the sending State. It represents the sending State in the external, international sense, in an aspect or aspects of its international relations. The normal task which a Special Mission will perform is a task which would ordinarily be performed by a permanent diplomatic mission of the sending State if one exists in the receiving State or if it had not been decided on the particular occasion that an ad hoc mission was called for."[75]

In fact, even if it were possible to interpret the Convention as adopted as applying only to those special missions that performed diplomatic tasks, there remained grave misgivings about the transposition to special missions, which by definition are temporary and limited in their functions, of virtually all of the rules in the *Vienna Convention on Diplomatic Relations*. This was controversial both within the Commission and the Assembly. A number of the provisions, such as the inviolability of the premises of the special mission (which may be a hotel

---

[73] Paszkowski, see note 2, 276-278. In the French text of the Convention the term is *"ayant caractère représentatif de l'État"*. See also the seventh preambular paragraph ("as missions representing the State").

[74] Paszkowski, see note 2, 278-279.

[75] Extract from the verbatim text of the statement made by Philip Allott, United Kingdom representative, in the Sixth Committee on 20 October 1969, cited in Roberts, see note 2, 190. For the summary record, see Doc. A/C.6/SR.1129, paras. 25-26.

room), were scarcely appropriate for a temporary mission.[76] It was probably for this reason that relatively few States became party to the Convention. Writing in 1987, Sinclair said,

> "[t]his effort at progressive development and codification has accordingly been only partially successful, no doubt because of the reluctance of Governments to accord a wide range of privileges and immunities to special missions and their members when, in the view of the Governments concerned, the grant of such privileges and immunities was not justified by functional reasons."[77]

Another concern may have been that "the definition of a special mission is not entirely clear."[78] While the United Kingdom and some others sought to clarify the essence of a special mission, their views may not have been widely shared by others.

IV. Evidence of the Customary International Law on Official Visitors

State practice is sufficient to establish rules of customary international law governing official visitors, in particular as regards their inviolability and immunity from criminal jurisdiction. Such inviolability and immunity are required by the nature of official visits, which often perform

---

[76] For extensive citation of the views of States during the negotiation, see Donnarumma (1972), see note 2, 47-49, who mentions an attempt to coordinate an approach within Council of Europe Member States.

[77] I. Sinclair, *The International Law Commission*, 1987, 61. Ten years later Watts wrote: "Reasons for this relatively modest appraisal by States of the Convention's worth are varied, but may include the view that special missions are so varied in their nature, scope and importance that any attempt to provide a single scale of treatment for all possible kinds of missions is bound to produce unacceptable results in relation to some kinds of missions. There are also serious political problems about the provision of extensive privileges and immunities to missions whose presence in a State is by definition temporary, and perhaps little more than transient. It cannot be denied that special missions need, and are entitled to, a degree of special protection and treatment when in the territory of another State on the official business of their sending State, but States have been reluctant to accept that missions always *need* the full range of privileged treatment which the Convention would require", Watts (1999), see note 2, 344-345. See also Salmon, see note 2, 546, and Daillier/ Forteau/ Pellet, see note 2, para. 458.

[78] Wickremasinghe, see note 2, 391.

similar functions and have similar needs to those of permanent diplomatic missions. The considerations underlying the immunity of permanent diplomatic missions are no less relevant to *ad hoc* diplomacy.

The issues that dominated the preparation of the Convention in the ILC and the General Assembly continued to be important after 1969. These included (i) whether it was possible to define which official visitors enjoyed immunity *ratione personae* by reference to their level and functions; (ii) the nature of the consent required from the receiving State; and (iii) the scale of immunities that should apply.

On many issues there is now widespread agreement. First, most States and courts that have opined on the matter are clear that there are rules of customary international law governing official visits.[79] Second, it is agreed that the consent of the receiving State is essential; such consent needs to be clear, and is normally given in advance of the visit. Finally, Heads of State, Heads of Government, Ministers for Foreign Affairs and certain other high office holders, when on official visits, continue to enjoy the facilities, privileges and immunities accorded by international law, including inviolability and immunity from criminal jurisdiction.

In considering the materials that evidence the rules of customary international law concerning the immunity of official visitors, it is convenient to consider (1) how far the provisions of the *Convention on Special Missions* now reflect rules of customary international law; (2) State practice, including in connection with cases before the domestic courts; and (3) the case-law of the ICJ, and (4) the writings of jurists.

1. The Special Missions Convention and Customary International Law

The elaboration of the Convention had a major impact on the development of rules of customary international law; it was a focus for State practice. As already noted, the Commission was of the opinion that its

---

[79] During its 2011 session, attention was drawn within the ILC to "the relevance of the law of special missions, both conventional and customary international law" for the consideration of the topic "Immunity of State officials from foreign criminal jurisdiction", *ILC Report*, 2011, 220, para. 119 *in fine*. The concluding preambular paragraph of the 1969 Convention affirms that "the rules of customary international law continue to govern questions not regulated by the provisions of the present Convention".

draft reflected, at least in some measure, the rules of customary international law, and this does not seem to have been contested by States. While it cannot be said that all – or even most – of the provisions of the Convention reflected customary international law at the time of its adoption, it is widely accepted that certain basic principles, including in particular the requirement of consent, and the inviolability and immunity from criminal jurisdiction of persons on special missions, do now reflect customary law.

At the time of its adoption, the United Kingdom's view was that the Convention was not declaratory of international law in the same way as the *Vienna Convention on Diplomatic Relations,* since there was not enough evidence of State practice for it to be said that existing international law was clear and settled in the matter. But the Convention was thought to be generally declaratory of what an international tribunal would probably have held international law to be, or what international law would have come to be in practice had the Convention not been concluded.[80]

The privileges and immunities enjoyed by special missions and their members have been afforded recognition in agreements adopted subsequent to the *Convention on Special Missions.* For example, article 3 (1) of the 2004 United Nations Convention on the Jurisdictional Immunities of States and Their Property[81] provides that that Convention "is without prejudice to the privileges and immunities enjoyed by a State under international law in relation to the exercise of the functions of (*a*) its ... special missions ...; and (*b*) persons connected with them."[82] Commentary (1) to the final draft article 3 of 1991 (which on this point was identical to article 3 of the Convention as adopted) says of article 3 (1) and (2), that "[b]oth paragraphs are intended to preserve the privileges and immunities already accorded to specific entities and persons by virtue of existing general international law and more fully by relevant international conventions in force, which remain unaffected by the

---

[80] Many official UK documents relating to the negotiation of the Convention, and the consideration given to signing and ratifying it, are available in the National Archives at Kew.

[81] See also Commentary (8) to article 1 of the Draft Articles on the Prevention and Punishment of Crimes against Diplomatic Agents and other Internationally Protected Persons, *ILCYB* 1972, Vol. II, 314.

[82] The Convention was adopted by the General Assembly, without a vote, on 2 December 2004, A/RES/59/38.

present articles."[83] Commentary (3) says that "[t]he extent of privileges and immunities enjoyed by a State in relation to the exercise of the functions of the entities referred to in subparagraph 1(*a*) is determined by the provisions of the international conventions ..., where applicable, or by general international law."[84]

2. State Practice

State practice is clear and consistent as to the main lines of the customary international law concerning official visitors. In this field, as with other heads of immunity (such as State and diplomatic immunity), much of the relevant State practice is to be found in or in connection with cases before the domestic courts of the various States.[85]

Domestic cases may contribute to the development of customary international law in this field in a number of ways. *First*, they may be the occasion for the sending or receiving State, or both, to indicate their position on the rules of customary international law. In other words, they may be the occasion for State practice in the form of expressions of the position of the executive branch. *Second*, the decisions of domestic courts may themselves amount to State practice and thus contribute to the development of rules of international law, since they indicate the

---

[83] *ILCYB* 1991, Vol. II, Part Two, 21.
[84] A Swiss speech in the Sixth Committee as circulated on 1 November 2011 stated "[f]or our part, we are of the view that certain principles of the [Convention on Special Missions] constitute a codification of international customary law, ..." "La pratique suisse en matière de droit international public 2011", No. 7.3, *SZIER/RSDIE* 22 (2012). At the same meeting, Austria referred to cases where "... immunity based on a special treaty regime, such as the Convention on Special Missions, or on a comparable rule of customary law, as in the case of an explicit invitation for an official visit ...", Doc. A/C.6/66/SR.26, 16, para. 80. See also Hungary, Doc. A/C.6/66/SR.19, 10, para. 56.
[85] As Rosalyn Higgins has written, "[i]n the related fields of jurisdiction and immunity – as in almost no other field of international law – the role of national courts and legislation has a very particular significance.": R. Higgins, "After Pinochet: Developments on Head of State and Ministerial Immunities", in: R. Higgins, *Themes and Theories. Selected Essays, Speeches, and Writings in International Law*, 2009, 409-423 (410). See also the passage from the ICJ's Judgment in *Germany* v. *Italy*, see notes 16, 18.

position of the judicial branch on the matter.[86] And *third*, depending on the care with which the court has approached the matter, domestic case-law may itself be valuable authority on the state of customary international law, insofar as it reflects the conclusion of the court on the matter, reached after thorough argument. Materials on State practice, in particular those connected with domestic cases in various jurisdictions, are summarized in the Annex below.

3. ICJ Case-Law

The ICJ has not had occasion to consider the law on official visits in any depth. In the *Arrest Warrant* case, the Court mentioned the *Convention on Special Missions* as providing "useful guidance on certain aspects of the question of immunities,"[87] but the point concerned holders of high-ranking offices, not special missions. The Court also mentioned the 1969 Convention in *Djibouti* v. *France*:

> "The Court notes first that there are no grounds in international law upon which it could be said that the officials concerned were entitled to personal immunities, not being diplomats within the meaning of the Vienna Convention on Diplomatic Relations of 1961, and the Convention on Special Missions of 1969 not being applicable in this case."[88]

The concluding words "not being applicable in this case" are not entirely clear. But there is no suggestion that the Court considered (and rejected) the customary international law on special missions; it seems that the question of the officials concerned being on an official visit simply did not arise on the facts.[89]

---

[86] M. Wood, "State Practice", in: Max Planck Encyclopedia, see note 2.
[87] *Arrest Warrant of 11 April 2000 (Democratic Republic of the Congo v. Belgium)*, see note 25, 21, para. 52.
[88] *Certain Questions of Mutual Assistance in Criminal Matters (Djibouti v. France)*, see note 25, 243-244, para. 194.
[89] For an analysis of *Djibouti v. France*, see Buzzini, see note 2. At an early stage in the proceedings, Djibouti had claimed special mission immunity for two of its officials, the *Procureur de la République* and the Head of National Security (Memorial of the Republic of Djibouti, at paras. 137-138), but it later amended its claim so as not to claim immunity *ratione personae* for officials other than the Head of State.

4. Writings

Some of the limited writings that touch on the customary international law regarding official visitors are dated and tentative. To a large extent they were written by those directly involved in developing the 1969 Convention, and focus on the Convention rather than on customary law. The writers are divided as to their conclusions (if any). But most recent contributions support the existence of some customary international law on official visitors, though usually not as detailed and precise as the rules set forth in the *Convention on Special Missions*.

Writing in 2011, in the *Max Planck Encyclopedia of Public International Law*, Kalb concludes that,

> "[t]he better view seems to be that under customary international law persons on special missions accepted as such by the receiving State are at least entitled to immunity from suit and freedom from arrest for the duration of the mission."[90]

The earlier *Encyclopedia of Public International Law* had an entry by Herdegen (writing in 1986, some 25 years before Kalb), concluding that,

> "[a] survey of State practice seems to support the conclusion that special agents, with the possible exception of members of government and other envoys on a high political level, are not (yet) entitled to privileges and immunities similar to those accorded to permanent diplomatic agents under customary international law (as opposed to mere comity)."

But Herdegen immediately added the caveat, "[t]his controversial inference calls for some caution, because it relies essentially on material prior to the adoption of the UN Convention on Special Missions of 1969". He goes on to say that "[w]ith respect to missions charged with negotiations on a high political level, the Convention may be regarded as an expression of the prevailing *opinio juris*."[91]

Oppenheim's International Law, published in 1991, is somewhat tentative: "The general recognition of the public and official character of these missions has not been accompanied by the development of

---

[90] Kalb, see note 2.
[91] Herdegen, see note 2.

clear and comprehensive rules of customary international law concerning their privileges and immunities."⁹²

Wickremasinghe, writing in 2010, says that "there is authority for the proposition that some special missions, and in particular high-level missions, enjoy immunities as a matter of customary international law."⁹³

Shaw (2008) cites *Tabatabai* to the effect that,

"it was clear that there was a customary rule of international law which provided that an ad hoc envoy, charged with a special political mission by the sending state, may be granted immunity by individual agreement with the host state and its associated status and that therefore such envoys could be placed on a par with members of the permanent missions of states."⁹⁴

An extended and recent treatment of the English case-law is given by Franey,⁹⁵ who is of the view that the *Convention on Special Missions*,

"is now considered to be declaratory of customary international law having been quoted with approval both in the *Pinochet* case, and in the *Arrest Warrant* case as providing, '*useful guidance on certain aspects of the question of immunities.*'"⁹⁶

As we have seen, this is true for only some central principles in the Convention.

The latest edition of *Brownlie* (2012) states that,

"[t]he [Special Missions] Convention has influenced the customary rules concerning persons on official visits (special missions), which have developed largely through domestic case-law. The Convention

---

⁹² Jennings/ Watts, *Oppenheim's International Law*, see note 2, para. 533.
⁹³ See note 2, 390, citing *Tabatabai*, and United States and United Kingdom decisions. It is no longer really the case that there are "relatively few decisions from national courts on the point". For *Tabatabai* see text at note 137 below.
⁹⁴ Shaw, see note 2, 775. *Satow's Diplomatic Practice*, see note 2, describes the uncertainty of the law before the Convention on Special Missions, and goes on to state that "the [Special Missions] Convention, unlike the Vienna Convention on Diplomatic Relations, has not acquired the status of customary international law" (para. 13.12). That, of course, is true up to a point; *Satow* does not seem to take a position on what the rules of customary international law actually are.
⁹⁵ Franey, see note 2, 135-149.
⁹⁶ Ibid., 136.

confers a higher scale of privileges and immunities upon a narrower range of missions than the extant customary law, which focus on the immunities necessary for the proper conduct of the mission, principally inviolability and immunity from criminal jurisdiction."[97]

V. The Customary International Law on the Immunity of Official Visitors

As with other areas of immunity, much of the most interesting State practice on official visitors consists of domestic case-law and the actions of Governments in the face of domestic cases and incidents. The rules of customary international law in the field of official visitors are supported by analogy with permanent diplomatic missions. It would be strange if members of permanent diplomatic missions enjoyed immunity while similar persons on official visits/special missions did not, since both are essential in today's world and the functional needs are similar.

It is inherent in the nature of a special mission that its duration is temporary. The mission ends when the specific questions have been dealt with or the specific task performed. This distinguishes a special mission from what is in principle a permanent but specialized mission, separate from the permanent diplomatic mission, such as the trade mission at issue in the *Krassin* case.[98] The status of such missions will usually be governed by specific agreements.[99]

At the time of the adoption of the *Convention on Special Mission*s in 1969, it was uncertain how far the new Convention reflected existing customary international law. Since 1969, the rules of customary international law have crystallized around certain central principles to be found in the Convention. On other respects, the provisions of the Convention are not apt for transformation into customary law. The text of the Convention is both very detailed and regarded by many as confer-

---

[97] *Brownlie's Principles*, see note 2, 414 (footnotes omitted).
[98] See note 160 below.
[99] See Bartoš, see note 2, on the distinction between special missions of limited duration and "permanent" missions established for a specific task of indefinite duration (for which special agreements are usually reached), such as those dealing with border issues. In addition to special agreements, obligations may flow from unilateral promises: see the Dutch Minister of Defence's 1994 Declaration, *ILCYB* 2000, Vol. II, Part 1, 267.

ring excessive privileges, and immunities, beyond those required by functional necessity. In addition, some of the bureaucratic requirements of the Convention hardly reflect State practice. The rules of customary international law are inevitably less technical than those in the Convention.

In light of Sections III and IV above, and the State practice described in the Annex (much of it comparatively recent), the broad outlines of the rules of customary international law concerning the inviolability and immunity of official visitors now seem well established. There are two key requirements: that the official visitor represents the sending State; and that the receiving State has consented to the visit as a visit attracting immunity.

1. Minimum Requirements for an Official Visit Attracting Immunity

Official visits form an important part of exchanges between States, the importance of which cannot be overestimated. Yet given the immunity *ratione personae* that may be enjoyed by persons on such visits, including inviolability of the person and complete immunity from criminal jurisdiction for the duration of the visit, not every official visitor (of whom there must be large numbers) will be accepted by the receiving State as entitled to immunity, even assuming (as will usually be the case) that the visit has been agreed and meetings arranged. Only certain visitors, principally those on high-level missions, are likely to be accepted as entitled to immunity *ratione personae*.

a. The Need for the Visitor to Represent the Sending State

The first key requirement is that the visitor, whoever he or she may be, "represents" the State. This is a matter of fact, and depends primarily on the attitude of the sending and receiving States. As is reflected in the terms of article 1 (a) of the 1969 Convention ("for the purpose of dealing with it on specific questions or of performing in relation to it a specific task"), the visitor may represent the State in a wide variety of capacities, not only to conduct Government-to-Government business.[100]

---

[100] The Convention on Special Missions contains no equivalent of article 3 of the Vienna Convention on Diplomatic Relations or article 5 of the Vienna

He or she may be present in a purely representational capacity, such as on "major ceremonial occasions, such as coronations or royal weddings."[101] Such seem to have been the primary occasions for special missions in the past. The same would apply to the representatives of a State present in the receiving State in order to attend a Presidential inauguration or a State funeral, or in any other capacity "as the representative of the Government of [the State] in the performance of official functions."[102] And nowadays, this might, for example, include high officials representing the Government at major international trade expositions, cultural festivals and sports events.

The range of official visitors enjoying immunity under customary international law is nowhere defined. For example, the precise meaning of the term "special mission", for the purposes of customary international law, is not defined. This is not a problem in practice, given the requirement described under b. below of mutual consent of the sending and receiving States to the visit as such and its functions. In practice, special missions are usually confined to high-level missions that represent the State in the same way as permanent diplomatic missions. This is perhaps why another term, commonly used in the United States, is "special diplomatic missions".

Official visitors enjoying personal immunity need not be members of the Government or Government officials or employees.[103] It is not

---

Convention on Consular Relations setting out the functions of diplomatic missions and consular posts respectively, see Paszkowski, see note 2, 270.

[101] "Special Missions. Working paper prepared by the Secretariat", see note 5; see also Bartoš, quoted at note 6; and the FCO statement at note 151 below.

[102] *Philippines* v. *Marcos*, see note 185 below.

[103] "Under the Convention on Special Missions participation in official missions is not limited to state officials. This broad interpretation makes it possible under the Convention to include, for example, family members who accompany state officials on special missions (such as state visits) or persons (such as a family member of a high-ranking dignitary or a former state official) who admittedly do not have or no longer have an official position, but who perform on behalf of their state a task in another state that meets the condition for full immunity, namely the smooth conduct of interstate relations, and should therefore enjoy full immunity during their visit", Advisory Committee on Issues of Public International Law (*Commissie van advies inzake volkenrechtelijke vraagstukken*, CAVV), *Advisory Report on the Immunity of Foreign State Officials, Advisory Report No. 20*, The Hague, May 2011, 34. The Dutch Government agreed with the main conclusions and recommendations in the report, see note 146 below.

uncommon for others to be received as such visitors, for example, personal or special envoys or representatives.[104] In the modern world, relations between States are not confined to those between members of the executive branch. Parliamentarians and members of the judiciary may on appropriate occasions represent their State. A State may be represented in its bilateral or multilateral relations by politicians or individuals who are not members of the Government or of the governing party/parties. These may include, for example, the leader of an opposition party (who, particularly in a democracy, may hold a special position recognized by law). Cross-party or *ad hoc* representation may, for example, occur in times of national or international crisis. In such circumstances, the function of the visitor may be to ensure that the receiving State is informed of the various currents of political or public opinion on matters of important bilateral or multilateral interest.

It has also been suggested that a mission representing an opposition faction in an internal conflict visiting the territory of another State to conduct peace negotiations could be a special mission.[105] The *Convention on Special Missions* also covers meetings of the representatives of two or more States in a third State.[106] There is no reason why such meetings should not equally be within the rules of customary international law.

---

[104] Special mission immunity was accorded, for example, to W., who was of Indonesian nationality and, as a former minister of foreign affairs, enjoyed only functional immunity, but who, as an adviser to the Indonesian president, paid an official visit to the Netherlands. See Judgment of The Hague District Court (*Rechtbank*) of 24 November 2010, LJN: 380820/ KG ZA 10-1453; <www.rechtspraak.nl>.

[105] "The Convention on Special Missions also allows scope for immunity to be granted to a mission that does not belong to the government of the sending state. An example would be where a mission representing an opposition faction in an internal conflict visits the territory of another state to conduct peace negotiations. However, the sending state must then notify the receiving state that members of the opposition belong to the special mission": Advisory Committee on Issues of Public International Law, see note 103, 34-35.

[106] Article 18, Donnarumma (1972), see note 2, 45-46.

b. The Need for the Receiving State to Consent to the Visit as one Attracting Immunity

The potentially broad scope of official visitors benefitting from immunity *ratione personae* is in practice limited by the second key requirement, that of the consent of the receiving State to the visit as one attracting such immunity. This requirement does not seem to have been clearly spelt out during the negotiation of the Convention, or in the text itself. But the better view is that, even under the Convention, the consent that has to be given is consent to the mission as a special mission.

The High Court in *Khurts Bat* considered the nature of the consent that was required before an official visitor would be entitled to immunity *ratione personae*. According to Moses LJ, "[t]he essential requirement for recognition of a Special Mission is that the receiving State consents to the mission, as a Special Mission."[107] And, he went on to say,

> "It is vital to bear in mind that the consent which must be previously obtained is consent to a Special Mission. A State which gives such consent recognises the special nature of the mission and the status of inviolability and immunity which participation in that Special Mission confers on the visitors. Not every official visit is a Special Mission. Not everyone representing their State on a visit of mutual interest is entitled to the inviolability and immunity afforded to participants in a Special Mission."[108]

As we have seen, the importance of such consent was clear during the negotiation of the *Convention on Special Missions* in the Sixth Committee of the General Assembly in 1968 and 1969, in the course of which the role of consent was enhanced. In the definition in article 1 the words "with the consent of the latter" [the receiving State] were added during the negotiations in the UN General Assembly. The ILC had added a commentary to its draft which contemplated tacit consent. That was clearly of concern to States, so in article 2 the words "with the consent of the latter" were expanded to read "with the consent of the latter, previously obtained through the diplomatic or another agreed or mutually acceptable channel."[109]

---

[107] *Khurts Bat*, see note 15, para. 27 (Moses LJ).
[108] Ibid., para. 29.
[109] In doing so, States were following the rules for the establishment of permanent diplomatic missions – article 2 of the Vienna Convention on Diplomatic Relations. See also article 4 (*agrément*).

What does "consent" mean in practice? It means, at a minimum, that the receiving State has agreed with the sending State that the sending State shall send the person to the receiving State as an official visitor entitled to immunity. It is not normally sufficient, to establish "consent", that the immigration authorities have permitted the person to enter, or that a visa has been issued. Even the issue of a diplomatic or official visa does not necessarily amount to consent to a special mission. Practice varies from State to State, and the visa-issuing authorities are not necessarily thinking in terms of immunities. Such visas may be issued simply as a courtesy. Consent must be consent to the special mission itself, not simply to a visit by the individual concerned. It is not, however, necessary that the sending and receiving States use the term "special mission": such niceties are not to be expected, and customary law addresses official visitors in general. The necessary consent may be implied from all the surrounding circumstances.[110] For example, if the visit is led by one of the so-called "troika" (Head of State, Head of Government, Minister for Foreign Affairs) or other holders of high office to whom similar considerations apply (such as the Minister of Defence or a Minister for Foreign Trade) then it may be presumed that any consent to the visit is consent to a visit or special mission entailing immunity.

Although it seems to be generally agreed to be a requirement that the sending and receiving States have agreed on the specific questions to be dealt with by a special mission or the specific task to be performed, such agreement does not need to be detailed. Indeed, *Tabatabai* is authority for the proposition that it can be quite general in nature. As for the nature of the questions or tasks, it seems unlikely that a mission purely to conclude commercial contracts on behalf of the Government would be accepted as a special mission.[111]

That, at least under customary international law, there is flexibility as regards the requirement that consent be given in advance is illustrated by the *Tabatabai* case.[112] There is no strict requirement that consent must be given prior to the arrival of the members of the special mission in the territory of the receiving State.

How is it to be ascertained that consent has been given? Domestic courts will usually accept the word of the Executive on this matter. That is the case, for example, in the United Kingdom when a Foreign

---

[110] See the letter from the FCO's Director for Protocol in the *Khurts Bat* case, see note 176 below.
[111] See, for example, Parker LJ's remarks in the *Teja* Case, see note 162 below.
[112] See note 137 below.

Office certificate is issued; the position seems to be essentially the same in the United States, and probably in other countries too. In any event, domestic practice in this regard is likely to be quite flexible.

c. Whether Consent is given is a Matter of Policy

Whether a receiving State is actually willing to consent to a particular official visit as a visit attracting immunity is essentially a matter of policy. It is not a matter regulated by international law, though at least in the case of a visit led by a Head of State, Head of Government or Minister for Foreign Affairs (and those holders of high office in the State equated with them) it may well be that consent to the mission automatically includes consent to the visit as one attracting immunity.

States may wish to develop policy criteria, as well as procedures, for the cases in which they are prepared to give their consent, or they may prefer to decide case-by-case. If policy guidelines are developed, they may include, for example, that the visit should be "high-level" (a term which may or may not be defined) and/or that its functions should be of the kind that would normally be conducted by a permanent diplomatic mission (nowadays a very broad category of functions). States may also wish to develop procedures which they would normally expect to be followed in certain cases.

d. The Status of Persons on High-Level Official Visits

The scale of immunities to which official visitors are entitled is governed by the principle of functional necessity. They enjoy such immunities as are necessary for the efficient conduct of their functions.[113] In particular, they enjoy, for the duration of the visit, the like inviolability of the person and immunity from criminal jurisdiction as persons of equivalent rank accredited to a permanent diplomatic mission.[114] This includes the receiving State's obligation to treat them with due respect and to take all appropriate steps to prevent any attack on their persons,

---

[113] Convention on Special Missions, preamble.
[114] *Khurts Bat*, see note 15, para. 26 (Moses LJ). However, there may be differences, e.g. as regards traffic cases, inviolability of the premises of the mission.

freedom or dignity.¹¹⁵ It also includes immunity from service of legal process.¹¹⁶

As regards other privileges and immunities, including immunity from civil jurisdiction, the position under customary international law is less clear. During the elaboration of the *Convention on Special Missions* there were two broad approaches: that the members of a special mission should in all respects enjoy the same immunities and privileges as the corresponding members of a permanent diplomatic mission; and that, as regards immunity from civil jurisdiction they should only enjoy "official act" immunity.¹¹⁷ One of the main reasons for the limited participation in the Convention is what is seen as an excessive immunity from civil jurisdiction, going beyond what is required by functional necessity.¹¹⁸ Given this, it seems difficult to argue that under customary law the immunity of members of special missions from civil or administrative jurisdiction extends beyond official acts and any measures that might involve an element of constraint (such as the serving of a subpoena to produce evidence or any other demand to appear as a witness). As regards other matters, such as the inviolability of archives and papers, and the right of free communication, these are to be granted so far as practical (though if the sending State has a permanent diplomatic mission in the State concerned such facilities and privileges may not in practice be needed).

VI. Conclusion

We have seen that at least three separate heads of immunity may come into play in the case of any particular official visit: (i) the immunity *ratione personae* of holders of high-ranking office; (ii) "official act" immunity; and (iii) the immunity of official visitors, including those on special missions. As regards the third head, the rules of customary international law are both wider and narrower than the provisions of the *Convention on Special Missions*. They are wider in that the class of official visitors who may be entitled to immunity is broader than that foreseen in the Convention. They are narrower in that the range of privi-

---

[115] Article 29, Vienna Convention on Diplomatic Relations; article 29, Convention on Special Missions.
[116] E. Denza, *Diplomatic Law*, 3rd edition, 2008, 268-269.
[117] Przetacznik, see note 2, 594, 599-600; Donnarumma (1972), see note 2, 46.
[118] See notes 76-78.

leges and immunities is more limited, being essentially confined to immunity from criminal jurisdiction and inviolability of the person.

There now seems to be a "settled answer"[119] to the question of the customary law on the immunity of official visitors. This is to be welcomed. The law in this field is an important part of what the ICJ has described as "the whole corpus of the international rules of which diplomatic and consular law is comprised", rules the "fundamental character" of which it strongly affirmed.[120] Emphasising the "extreme importance" of these rules, the International Court has referred to:

> "the edifice of law carefully constructed by mankind over a period of centuries, the maintenance of which is vital for the security and well-being of the complex international community of the present day, to which it is more essential than ever that the rules developed to ensure the ordered progress of relations between its members should be constantly and scrupulously respected."[121]

---

[119] See note 3.
[120] *United States Diplomatic and Consular Staff in Tehran,* ICJ Reports 1980, 3 et seq. (42, para. 91).
[121] Ibid., 43 (para. 92).

Annex

State Practice

The State practice set out in this Annex covers Austria, Belgium, Finland, France, Germany, the Netherlands, the United Kingdom, and the United States of America. It does not pretend to be exhaustive. Indeed, there is no doubt a good deal of practice in this as in other fields which does not receive much if any publicity.

Austria

Austria is a party to the *Convention on Special Missions*. Nevertheless, *vis-à-vis* most States it is the rules of customary international law that apply. The leading case is the *Syrian National Immunity* case.[122] This decision of the Austrian Supreme Court is important for its references to the customary international law on immunity. The case is an impressive statement of the central importance of consent, and applies the rules of the *Convention on Special Missions* by analogy in a wider context.

The lower Court (Oberlandesgericht) had held that Dr. S. was entitled to immunity both as a representative of a Member State on a visit to UNIDO, and because he was on an *ad hoc* mission to UNIDO. The Supreme Court overturned the decision on both grounds. As to the second ground, the Supreme Court considered *inter alia* the analogy with special missions within the meaning of the *Convention on Special Missions*, holding that an *ad hoc* mission to UNIDO could not come into existence without the consent of that organization. The Judgment of the Supreme Court contains the following passage,

> "An ad-hoc mission means a legation, limited in duration, which represents a State and is sent by that State to another State, with the latter's consent, for the purpose of dealing with specific issues with that State or to fulfil a specific task in relation to it ... the position of such ad hoc State representatives ... is determined primarily by the relevant agreement on the official headquarters of that organization, secondarily by customary international law."

---

[122] *Oberster Gerichtshof*, 120s3/98, Judgment of 12 February 1998, *ILR* 127 (2005), 88-93.

The Court concluded,

> "None of these legal sources can support the assumption that an ad hoc mission to UNIDO may come into being without the consent of that organisation. In the case in point, UNIDO would be comparable to the recipient State of an ad hoc legation; that State has the right to cooperate, through its consent, in the despatch to it of such a mission, so that unwanted missions cannot arise ... the prior agreement of UNIDO is required in order to cause a visit by a State representative to become an ad hoc legation. If that requirement is not satisfied, a special mission does not exist."

Belgium

In the *Arrest Warrant* case, Belgium stressed that it was not claiming to enforce arrest warrants against "representatives of foreign States who visit Belgium on the basis of an official invitation, making it clear that such persons would be immune from enforcement of an arrest warrant in Belgium."[123]

Belgium's Law of 1993 on crimes under international humanitarian law, amended in 1999, was highly controversial. It introduced wide universal jurisdiction and removed immunity in respect of many crimes.[124] When it was amended in 2003 a new provision was included as article 1 *bis* of the Preliminary Title of the Code of Criminal Procedure, as amended in 2003, paragraph 2 of which provides,

> "In accordance with international law, no act of constraint relating to the exercise of a prosecution may be imposed during their stay, against any person who has been officially invited to stay in the territory of the Kingdom by the Belgian authorities or by an international organization established in Belgium and with which Belgium has concluded a headquarters agreement."

This provision confers immunity from execution in criminal matters upon any person officially invited by a Belgian authority or certain in-

---

[123] *Arrest Warrant of 11 April 2000 (Democratic Republic of the Congo v. Belgium),* see note 25, 28, para. 65. See also Belgium's Counter-Memorial, para. 1.12.

[124] S. Ratner, "Belgium's War Crimes Statute: A Postmortem", *AJIL* 97 (2003), 888-897.

ternational organizations, whether or not that person is a representative of a State or an international organization.[125]

Finland

Finland signed the *Convention on Special Missions* in 1970, but has not ratified it. In 1973, it enacted legislation in part modelled on the Convention. The Act applies "to special missions of foreign States sent here with the consent of the Government of Finland and with functions mutually agreed upon by the respective States." It provides, *inter alia*, that "[t]he person of members of ... the special mission and their family shall be inviolable", and that "[t]he members of ... the special mission shall enjoy the same immunity from criminal, civil and administrative jurisdiction and executive power as the members of diplomatic missions in Finland ..."[126]

France

The *French Property Commission in Egypt* case (1961-1962)[127] concerned the arrest and trial in Egypt of three members of the French Property Commission in Cairo, a body established by agreement between Egypt and France to handle property rights of French nationals in Egypt which had been sequestered following Suez (1956). The three were accused, principally, of espionage, plotting against the State and planning to assassinate President Nasser. The trial took place in secret and it is not known what arguments were made in Court. After the

---

[125] Law of 17 April 1878 concerning the Preliminary Title of the Code of Criminal Procedure, Art. 1 *bis*, para. 2: "Conformément au droit international, un acte de contrainte relatif à l'exercice de l'action publique ne peut être posé pendant la durée de leur séjour, à l'encontre de toute personne ayant été officiellement invitée à sojourner sur le territoire du Royaume par les autorités belges ou par une organisation internationale établie en Belgique et avec laquelle la Belgique a conclu un accord."

[126] Act on the Privileges and Immunities of International Conferences and Special Missions, enacted on 15 June 1973 (572/73) and amended on 20 December 1991 (1649/91) (referred to as the Privilege Act), Sections 1, 9 and 10. The Act applies also to delegations to conferences and certain intergovernmental organizations.

[127] Watts (1963), see note 2; *The State v. Mattei and others*, in: *ILR* 34 (1967), 175-179, *A.F.D.I.* 8 (1962), 1064; Ch. Rousseau, "Egypte et France", *RGDIP* 66 (1962), 601-617; Louis, see note 2.

hearing but before the Court's decision, the trial was suspended "for high reasons of State" and the accused were immediately released. In the course of these events, the French Government issued a press release saying *inter alia* that,

> "[t]he French Foreign Ministry officials who were arrested were members of an official mission accredited by the French Government, in accord with the Egyptian Government, for the purpose of implementing an international agreement; they were entitled to certain privileges and immunities, in accordance with the general principles of international law, under which special missions enjoy a status similar to that of regular diplomatic missions ...
>
> As regards the argument that the persons involved enjoyed a special status, that of special missions (a term used to designate official missions of one State to another State, charged with diplomatic functions of a special and temporary nature) – this argument does not hold, for this status is no different from that of the permanent diplomatic missions, in particular as concerns judicial immunity."[128]

A more recent statement on the matter by the French Government is to be found in its Counter-Memorial in *Djibouti* v. *France*.[129]

On 1 April 2004, Jean-François H. (N'Dengue), Director-General of Police of the Republic of the Congo, was arrested in France in connection with allegations of crimes against humanity, torture and acts of barbary and kidnapping committed in 1999 at the river port of Brazzaville known as "le Beach". Later that day, the Director of the Cabinet of the French Minister for Foreign Affairs sent to the Procureur de la République of Meaux a note from the Protocol Service, reading:

---

[128] Watts (1963), see note 2, 1389-1390 (Press release of 6 December 1961, issued by the French Permanent Mission to the United Nations).

[129] *Certain Questions of Mutual Judicial Assistance in Criminal Matters (Djibouti* v. *France)*, see note 25, Counter-Memorial of France, para 4.34 "Lorsque des personnes ont, comme en l'espèce, des fonctions essentiellement internes, il n'est pas nécessaire qu'elles soient protégées par des immunités en tout temps et en toutes circonstances; il suffit qu'elles puissent bénéficier d'immunités lorsqu'elles se rendent à l'étranger, pour le compte de leur Etat, dans le cadre d'une mission officielle. Tel est l'objet des immunités reconnues aux membres des missions spéciales, qui constituent une garantie suffisante pour des personnes exerçant une fonction, telle que celle de procureur de la République ou de chef de la sécurité nationale, qui n'implique pas de fréquents déplacements à l'étranger."

"The Ministry of Foreign Affairs confirms that the Ambassador of the Congo in France has certified that Jean-François H., holder of a document signed by the President of the Republic of the Congo, is on official mission in France since 19 March 2004; that in this capacity, and by virtue of customary international law, he benefits from immunities from jurisdiction and execution."[130]

Based on this note, the Procureur de la République requested that the proceedings against Jean-François H. be stopped, and this was done.[131] Subsequently, in a Judgment dated 20 June 2007, the *Court of Appeal of Versailles* found that this note "was without any ambiguity as regards the immunity of Jean-François H. notwithstanding the non-ratification by France of the New York Convention on Special Missions of 8 December 1969", and held "that Jean-François H., at the time of his arrest, benefited from immunity from jurisdiction and execution, which applied whatever the nature of the crimes."[132]

In another French case, *Hubert X*, a dual French-Burkinabé national, claimed immunity on the ground that he was on a diplomatic mission on behalf of Burkina Faso. In its decision of 23 September 2009,[133] the Criminal Chamber of the *Cour de Cassation* noted that the French Foreign Ministry had indicated by a note dated 28 May 2009 that,

"– a diplomatic passport is simply a travel document which does not confer on its holder any diplomatic immunity; – Hubert X is not accredited in France; – that the presence of Hubert X in France is not within the framework of a special mission; – that in consequence

---

[130] "Le Ministère des affaires étrangères confirme que l'Ambassadeur du Congo en France a certifié que M. N'Dengue, porteur d'un document signé par le président de la République du Congo, est en mission officielle en France à compter du 19 mars 2004, qu'à ce titre, et en vertu du droit international coutumier, il bénéficie d'immunités de juridiction et d'exécution." (reproduced in the Judgment of 9 April 2008 of the Criminal Chamber of the *Cour de Cassation* – No. de pourvoi: 07-86412).

[131] For the facts, see the Judgment of 20 June 2007 of the *Cour d'Appel de Versailles*, Chambre de l'Instruction, 10ème chamber-section A.

[132] The relevant part of the *Cour d'Appel*'s Judgment is set out in the Judgment of 9 April 2008, see note 130. The *Cour de Cassation* turned down the appeal on other grounds, but seems to have concluded that the *Cour d'Appel* had not been competent to deal with immunity and was moreover wrong, since the Director-General of Police was only entitled to official act immunity.

[133] No. de pourvoi: 09-84759.

Hubert X is subject to common law and cannot claim any immunity."[134]

The *Cour de Cassation* upheld the lower Court, finding that *Hubert X* had no immunity since he was not accredited in France, and "his presence in France was not within the framework of a special mission." The Chamber stressed the need for the sending State to ensure that it had received *agrément* and that it was for the sending state to prove prior accreditation, not the receiving State.

Thus French practice, particularly as evidenced by statements of the Executive, tends to support the view that under customary international law official visitors to France enjoy immunity from criminal jurisdiction.

Germany

Section 20 of the German Law on the Constitution of the Courts (Gerichtsverfassungsgesetz – GVG) provides that,

> "German jurisdiction also shall not apply to representatives of other states and persons accompanying them who are staying in territory of application of this Act at the official invitation of the Federal Republic of Germany.
>
> Moreover, German jurisdiction also shall not apply to persons other than those designated in subsection (1) and in sections 18 [*diplomatic missions*] and 19 [*consular posts*] insofar as they are exempt therefrom pursuant to the general rules of international law or on the basis of international agreements or other legislation."

Section 20 (1), sometimes known as the *lex Honecker*, was enacted to protect the German Democratic Republic leader when he made an official visit to the Federal Republic of Germany. But it has wider application, covering all representatives of other States, and persons accompanying them, who are in Germany pursuant to an official invitation of the Federal Republic of Germany. It covers, for example, not only Heads of State and members of Governments but also other persons who are present at the invitation of the Government and who are there-

---

[134] "– un passeport diplomatique est un simple titre de voyage qui ne confère à son titulaire aucune immunité diplomatique; – Hubert X n'est pas accrédité en France: – que la présence d'Hubert X en France ne s'inscrit pas dans le cadre d'une mission spéciale; – qu'en conséquence Hubert X relève du droit commun et ne peut se prévaloir d'aucune immunité".

fore immune from jurisdiction according to the general rules of inter-State intercourse, such as military observers under OSCE-agreements.[135] An invitation may be extended by any federal constitutional organ (President, Government, the Bundestag, and the Bundesrat). As the Minister of State in the German Chancellery put it, the Government wanted to set out in a law an exception from criminal jurisdiction for "guests of the Federal Republic."[136]

The leading German case on official visitors, one of the leading cases worldwide, is *Tabatabai*.[137] This case, which eventually reached the Criminal Chamber of the Federal Supreme Court, concerned a member of the political leadership in Iran who was arrested at Düsseldorf airport when opium was found in his luggage. He claimed to be on a secret mission to Germany and other Western countries. The various German courts that considered the matter between 1983 and 1986 (Regional Court, Higher Regional Court, Federal Supreme Court), in some cases more than once, were essentially in agreement as to the customary international law status of the law on special missions and its main outlines. But they disagreed on the application of the law to the facts, particularly on whether the Foreign Ministries of the Federal Republic of Germany and Iran had agreed upon a sufficiently specific mission to be performed by *Tabatabai*, and on whether they had not in fact agreed on the special mission in order to shield *Tabatabai* personally from the jurisdiction of the German criminal courts rather than to protect the mission.[138]

---

[135] Deutscher Bundestag – 10. Wahlperiode – 74. Sitzung. Bonn, den 7. Juni 1984, 5386 (State Secretary in the Federal Ministry of Justice).

[136] In an interview in the *Spiegel* 1984, the Minister of State in the German Chancellery, Philipp Jenninger, denied that the law was especially passed for Honecker: "Wir haben nicht die Absicht, eine Lex Honecker zu machen. Aber es ist in der Tat dafür ein allgemeines Bedürfnis vorhanden. Und da kann man auch diese Situation miteinbeziehen. Wir wollen für Gäste der Bundesrepublik eine Ausnahme von der Strafverfolgung im Gesetz festlegen. Dies haben wir vor, aber – wie gesagt – nicht ausgerichtet auf den Besuch von Honecker", <http://www.spiegel.de>.

[137] BGHSt 32 (1984), 275; *NJW* 37 (1984), 2048; *ILR* 80 (1989) 388-424 (411); K. Bockslaff/ M. Koch, "The Tabatabai Case: The Immunity of Special Envoys and the Limits of Judicial Review", *GYIL* 25 (1982), 539-584; Wolf, see note 2; Herdegen, see note 2, 576; Franey, see note 2, 139-143.

[138] The Iranian Foreign Ministry's letter of 31 January 1983, and the German Foreign Office's reaction thereto, are reproduced in the Judgment of 27 February 1984: *ILR*, see note 137, 413.

In its Judgment of 27 February 1984, the Federal Supreme Court said,

> "It is contentious amongst scholars of international law whether its provisions [*the provisions of the Convention on Special Missions*] are already now the basis of State practice as customary international law. ... However, the question of the customary validity of the Convention is not the decisive issue ... It is in any case established that, irrespective of the draft Convention, there is a customary rule of international law, based on State practice and opinio juris which makes it possible for an ad hoc envoy, who has been charged with a special political mission by the sending State, to be granted immunity by individual agreement with the host State for that mission and its associated status, and therefore for such envoys to be on a par with members of the permanent missions of States protected by international treaty law ..."[139]

Since *Tabatabai*, the customary law status of provisions of the *Convention on Special Missions* has been confirmed in a further German case. The *Vietnamese National* case concerned the arrest of a Vietnamese national who had failed to comply with an order to attend an identity parade (to determine his nationality) before Vietnamese officials in the offices of a German authority in Germany. (The procedure took place under a bilateral Germany-Vietnam Re-admission Agreement.) The question before the Court was whether the identity parade was an action of the German authorities (and thus governed by German administrative law) or not. The Higher Administrative Court explained that its conclusion that the identity parade was not governed by German administrative law was,

> "confirmed by the status in international law of the Vietnamese officials who carried out this procedure in Germany. Their presence was considered by the Federal Government as a consented-to special mission (see art. 1 (a) of the UN Convention on Special Missions of 8 December 1969). This Convention, which Germany thus far had not signed, is in its greater part recognized and applied by the Federal Government as customary international law. As such it is part of federal law and has a higher rank than ordinary laws. The Vietnamese officials taking part in the special mission enjoy at least im-

---

[139] Ibid., 418-419.

munity for their official acts and personal inviolability (arts. 29, 31 and 41 of the Convention)."[140]

In 2006, a French Judge (Judge Bruguière) had indicted Mrs. Rose Kabuye, Chief of State Protocol in the Office of President Kagame of Rwanda, in connection with allegations of aiding and abetting the assassination of former President Habyarimana of Rwanda. France sought her extradition from Germany on a European arrest warrant. In April 2008, the German authorities declined to arrest her on the ground that she had immunity since she was accompanying the Rwandan President on an official visit to Germany. Some months later, on 9 November 2008, the German police arrested her at Frankfurt and extradited her to France, saying that on this occasion she was present in Germany on a private visit.[141]

In summary, the German authorities and courts clearly accept that there are customary international law rules concerning official visitors, and in particular that "there is a customary rule of international law, based on State practice and *opinio juris* which makes it possible for an ad hoc envoy, who has been charged with a special political mission by the sending State, to be granted immunity by individual agreement with the host State for that mission and its associated status."[142]

Netherlands

The Dutch International Crimes Act[143] provides, in section 16, that,

"Criminal prosecution for one of the crimes referred to in this Act is excluded with respect to:

foreign heads of state, heads of government and ministers of foreign affairs, as long as they are in office, and other persons insofar as their immunity is recognised under international law;

persons who have immunity under any convention applicable to the Netherlands within the Kingdom."

---

[140] *Oberverwaltungsgericht* of Berlin-Brandenburg, Judgment of 15 June 2006: OVG 8 S 39.06 (overturning a decision of the Administrative Court Berlin).

[141] V. Thalmann, "French Justice's Endeavours to Substitute for the ICTR", *Journal of International Criminal Justice* 6 (2008), 995-1002; Akande/ Shah, see note 2, 822.

[142] See note 139 above.

[143] *Wet internationale misdrijven* (WIM), Act of 19 June 2003, Bulletin of Acts and Decrees 2003, 270.

In a report published in May 2011, prepared at the request of the Foreign Minister, the Dutch Advisory Committee on Issues of Public International Law (CAVV) said,

> " ... the CAVV recognises that the smooth conduct of international relations requires that persons other than the threesome discussed above should, when the occasion arises, be able to rely on being able to perform their duties on behalf of the state without interference and, where necessary, claim full immunity. If a representative of a state pays an official visit to another state, this person should, in the opinion of the CAVV, be able to claim full immunity, even in cases concerning international crimes. In this context, the CAVV would prefer to employ the term 'full immunity' rather than 'personal immunity' since the immunity is not linked to the position of the person claiming immunity but to his duties at a given moment. The CAVV bases the granting of immunity in such cases on customary international law."[144]

In its response to this report,[145] the Dutch Government agreed with the main conclusions and recommendations. The Government stated its belief "that the rule on immunity set out in section 16 of the International Crimes Act can continue to function as a good guiding principle" and agreed "that section 16 of the International Crimes Act adequately reflects the current state of international law." The Government continued,

> "The rule set out in section 16 (a) is not limited to the three categories of representatives specified, but extends to 'other persons insofar as their immunity is recognised under international law'. In the CAVV's opinion, all members of official missions may be entitled to full immunity under customary international law. The government endorses this. Members of official missions can be seen as 'temporary diplomats'. They, like diplomats, require this immunity so they can carry out their mission for the sending state without interference. However, unlike diplomats, members of official missions only

---

[144] Advisory Committee on Issues of Public International Law (CAVV), Advisory Report on the Immunity of Foreign State Officials, see note 103, 31.

[145] Letter from the Minister of Foreign Affairs to the President of the House of Representatives of the States General, dated 19 October 2011, enclosure (TK 2011-2012, 33000 V, nr. 9).

require this immunity for a limited period, namely the duration of the mission to the receiving state."[146]

United Kingdom

In the law of England and Wales, the position as regards the customary international law on official visitors is the same as in the case of State and diplomatic immunity before they were placed on a statutory footing. In fact, the main area of customary law that has been consistently applied by English courts – that is, recognised as a part or a source of English law – is that of international immunities. The underlying position was explained by Moses LJ in *Khurts Bat* as follows,

> "whilst not all the rules of customary international law are what might loosely be described as part of the law of England, English courts should apply the rules of customary law relating to immunities and recognise that those rules are a part of or one of the sources of English law."[147]

On 26 April 2011 the Government responded to a Parliamentary Question as follows,

> "The Government signed the Special Missions Convention on 17 December 1970, but have not yet ratified it. The Government have kept the question of ratification under review, though ratification would entail the passage of primary legislation. However developments in customary international law regarding special missions and certain high-level official visitors that have been recognised by our

---

[146] The Government also explained that it was of the opinion "that it would be preferable to clarify that all members of official missions are entitled to full immunity in a letter to the States General. Developments within relevant areas of international law have not yet fully crystallised; accordingly, it would be better not to amend section 16 of the International Crimes Act for the time being. The government will therefore draft a letter to the States General in the near future, setting out in greater detail that members of official missions are entitled to full immunity and therefore belong in the category 'other persons insofar as their immunity is recognised under international law' as referred to in section 16 (a) of the International Crimes Act. The letter will also state the conditions that need to be met before official missions can claim immunity."

[147] *Khurts Bat*, see note 15, para. 22 (Moses LJ). The Administrative Court found that the rules of customary international law on the inviolability and immunity of persons on a "special mission" were part of the law of England, and were to be applied as such by the English courts.

courts require that appropriate privileges and immunities are extended to visitors on special missions and other high-level visitors."[148]

There was an intention to ratify the Convention at the time of signature in 1970, and steps were taken between 1970 and 1979 to enact the necessary legislation to enable effect to be given to the Convention, including the preparations of a draft Bill. But this did not happen; presumably other Bills were accorded higher priority.[149] Two things were of particular interest during this process. First, the Foreign and Commonwealth Office noted the uncertainty of the then rules of customary international law, and even more so the rules that the English courts would apply. The latest reiteration of this assessment dates from December 1974.[150] Second, the Foreign and Commonwealth Office, still no doubt concerned at the excessive scale of privileges and immunities under the Convention, repeatedly stated its understanding of the lim-

---

[148] Hansard Commons, 26 April 2011: Column 404W.

[149] According to papers available at The National Archives, signature was agreed by the Cabinet's Home Affairs Committee in November 1970 (Foreign and Commonwealth Office, Convention on Special Missions, Memorandum by the Parliamentary Under Secretary of State, HA(70)35 of 13 October 1970; HA(70) 7th Mtg, 20 November 1970). In May 1973, and again (after a change of Government) in December 1974, the Minister of State for Foreign and Commonwealth Affairs proposed to the Cabinet's Home (and Social) Affairs Committee that a Bill should be introduced to enable the United Kingdom to ratify and implement the Convention (Convention on Special Missions, Memorandum by the Minister of State for Foreign and Commonwealth Affairs, HS(73)73 of 2 May 1973; Convention on Special Missions, Memorandum by the Minister of State for Foreign and Commonwealth Affairs, H(74)88 of 17 December 1974). Policy approval was given both in 1973 and in 1975 (H(75) 3rd Mtg, 7 March 1975). A series of draft Bills was prepared by Parliamentary Counsel, the last of which was dated 28 April 1976. But it would seem that Parliamentary time was not found to take it forward. A further effort to revive the Bill was made in 1979, but to no avail (E. Wilmshurst, *Letter to the Office of the Parliamentary Counsel*, 9 March 1979).

[150] Convention on Special Missions, Memorandum by the Minister of State for Foreign and Commonwealth Affairs, Annex B (The Convention on Special Missions and existing law): H(74)88 of 17 December 1974. Earlier versions of this paper were similar: see HA(70)35 of 13 October 1970, Annex B; HS(73)73 of 2 May 1973, Annex B; letter from Sir Vincent Evans to Parliamentary Counsel of 10 August 1973, Annex I.

ited scope of the term "special mission" as used in the Convention. In 1970, the Foreign and Commonwealth Office said the following,

"[The Convention] governs the sending and reception and the status, privileges and immunities of special missions, that is to say temporary <u>ad hoc</u> missions sent by one State to another to carry out functions essentially similar to those of permanent diplomatic missions. Examples of missions that would be covered are: official ministerial visits to foreign countries; negotiating teams sent to conclude a commercial treaty or a frontier agreement; official representatives sent to a coronation or a state funeral [or ...]; members of bilateral intergovernmental economic commissions etc."[151]

The draft Bill's 1 (2) provided that, in the articles of the Convention that were to have the force of law in the United Kingdom,

"'special mission' shall be construed as including a mission falling within the definition in Article 1 if, and only if, Her Majesty's Government have consented to the mission's being treated as a special mission for the purposes of those Articles; ... "

This definition, with its requirement that a mission would only be a special mission for the purposes of the Act if it was accepted as such by the United Kingdom Government, was crucial and would have resolved in domestic law the difficulty of defining the term that had not been fully overcome during the negotiation of the Convention. It was evidently considered to be consistent with the Convention,[152] and the approach was accepted as valid under customary international law in *Khurts Bat*,[153] though the intention was, for the avoidance of doubt, to make an interpretative declaration to this effect upon ratification of the convention.[154]

---

[151] Convention on Special Missions, Memorandum by the Parliamentary Under Secretary of State, Foreign and Commonwealth Office, HA(70)35 of 13 October 1970, para. 2.

[152] For a contrary view, see Donnarumma (1972), see note 2, 38, n. 22.

[153] Para. 29 (Moses LJ), cited at note 108 above.

[154] The draft Bill contained a Clause 3, modelled on Section 4 of the Diplomatic Privileges Act 1964, providing for a conclusive certificate as to fact, reading: "If in any proceedings any question arises whether or not any person is entitled to any privilege or immunity under this Act a certificate issued by or under the authority of the Secretary of State stating any fact relating to that question shall be conclusive evidence of that fact." A positive certificate under this Clause would have followed the lines of those issued

As the British Government said in Parliament on 18 October 2011, "[i]n Foreign and Commonwealth Office (FCO) practice, there are no prescribed formalities for consenting to a special mission, but such consent may be inferred from the circumstances of any given visit",[155] and that "each visit is treated on its own merits."[156]

The United Kingdom Government has recently had occasion to state its view generally on the law of special missions in response to Parliamentary Questions. On 13 December 2010, the Minister of State at the FCO answered a question as follows,

"There are various forms of immunity that may operate in proceedings before UK courts, including, State immunity, diplomatic immunity and special missions immunity. State and diplomatic immunity are addressed in legislation; special missions immunity derives from customary international law. Each of these aspects of immunity have been addressed in UK court judgments, to which reference must be made when determining whether immunity applies in any given case.

Whether a visiting Minister of a foreign Government is entitled to immunity from arrest in the UK will depend on the status of the person concerned, whether they are travelling on official Government business, as well as on other considerations. By virtue of their office, immunities will attach to visiting Heads of State, Heads of Government and Ministers of Foreign Affairs, as well as, by extension, other Ministers who travel by virtue of their office. The extent to which such immunities may attach to other visiting senior officials will fall to be determined case-by-case depending on their status and the reasons for their visit to the UK."[157]

---

under the Diplomatic Privileges Act 1964, and would have no doubt been similar to that issued in respect of Ms Tzipi Livni (at note 178 below).

[155] Hansard, HC Deb, 18 October 2011, Column 896W.

[156] Hansard, HC Deb, 18 October 2011, Column 897W. See also the letter from the Director of Protocol cited at note 176 below.

[157] The first paragraph of the reply was omitted in error when the question was first answered on 11 November 2010: 11 November 2010, Vol. 518 Column 435W. The answer set out above is the answer that should have been given, as explained on 13 December 2010 in a Parliamentary Written Question (Correction): Hansard, HC Deb, 13 December 2010, Column 72WS.

There have been a number of cases in the English courts concerning official visitors. Some are relatively old. The more recent ones reflect an awareness of the current importance of *ad hoc* diplomacy.

In *Service* v. *Castaneda*,[158] Knight-Bruce VC accepted that Castaneda was in England as an envoy on a special mission for the Spanish Queen (to settle claims arising out of the services of the British Auxiliary Legion of Spain). The Vice-Chancellor considered it unnecessary to establish whether Castaneda brought himself strictly within the wording of the Statute of Anne (concerning Ambassadors) as "on the language of his affidavit (which as yet has received no contradiction) ... he brings himself within that common law which exists equally with the statute, to protect him from that particular process."[159] The action for an injunction was accordingly dissolved.

Several decades later, in *Fenton Textile Association* v. *Krassin*,[160] Scrutton LJ expressed the opinion that a representative attracted immunity even though not formally accredited to His Majesty as a diplomat if the Government was negotiating with that person "as representing a recognised foreign state, about matters of concern between nation and nation without further definition of his position."[161] However, Krassin's immunity was in fact governed by the Trade Agreement between the United Kingdom and the Russian Soviet Federative Socialist Republic, which did not extend to immunities from civil suit and so his claim for immunity failed.

In *R.* v. *Governor of Pentonville Prison, ex parte Teja*,[162] the Divisional Court seems to have accepted in principle that Teja might be on a special mission and thus entitled to immunity. But this was not established on the facts. Costa Rica had issued Teja with a letter of credence stating it had appointed him as an economic advisor to be established in Switzerland where he would soon be accredited to undertake a study on the possible development of an integral steel industry; accordingly, he ought to be accorded diplomatic immunity under the Diplomatic Privileges Act 1964. He was arrested while passing through England for two days. Lord Parker rejected Costa Rica's contention in forthright terms,

---

[158] (1845) 1 Holt Equity Reports 159.
[159] Ibid., 170.
[160] (1921) 38 TLR 259.
[161] Ibid., 170.
[162] (1971) 2 Q.B. 274.

"I confess that at the very outset this argument ... seemed to me to produce a frightening result in that any foreign country could claim immunity for representatives sent to this country unilaterally whether this country agreed or not. As I see it, it is fundamental to the claiming of immunity by reason of being a diplomatic agent that the diplomatic agent should have been in some form accepted or received by this country."[163]

Lord Parker did accept that Costa Rica intended Mr. Teja to go on a special mission covered by the *Convention on Special Missions*, not in force in the United Kingdom, not the 1961 Vienna Convention on Diplomatic Relations. Even then, he considered,

"it is almost impossible to say that a man who is employed by a government to go to foreign countries to conclude purely commercial agreements, and not to negotiate in any way or have contact with the other government, can be said to be engaged on a diplomatic mission at all. He was there merely as a commercial agent of the government for the purposes of concluding a commercial contract. He was not there representing his state to deal with other states. For all these reasons I am quite satisfied that this man could not claim under article 39 diplomatic privileges and immunities from the moment he landed in this country."[164]

The District Judge at Central London/City of Westminster Magistrates' Court has recognized the immunity of official visitors under cus-

---

[163] Ibid., 282B-C.

[164] Ibid., 283F-H. In *R v. Governor of Pentonville Prison, ex parte Osman (No. 2)*, *ILR* 88 (1992), 378, a Foreign Office official had submitted an affidavit in this case saying that "Her Majesty's Government has not ratified the New York Convention on Special Missions and does not regard it as being declaratory of international customary law" (385). The Divisional Court said, *obiter*: "What is the effect of these documents [letters of Full Powers etc.]? One possibility might have been to suggest that the applicant was head of a special mission. This suggestion has rightly been disclaimed. There was nothing 'special' about the tasks entrusted to the applicant by the letters of Full Powers. No notification of such a mission was ever given to HMG or any other government. If it had been, the applicant's status would not have been recognized in English law, since the United Kingdom has nor enacted legislation pursuant to the Convention on Special Missions of 1969. ... " (393). There does not seem to have been argument about the rules of customary law in this case, decided in 1988, and the *obiter dictum* is in any event overtaken by the decision in *Khurts Bat*, see note 15.

tomary international law/English law in a number of cases.[165] In *Re Bo Xilai*,[166] Judge Workman held that Mr. Bo was entitled to immunity under customary international law both *ratione personae* in light of his high office and because he was in the United Kingdom performing official duties as Minister for Commerce and International Trade of the People's Republic of China, as part of an official delegation for the State visit of the President of the People's Republic of China. He was "a member of a Special Mission and as such has immunity under customary international law."

In *Court of Appeal Paris, France* v. *Durbar*,[167] the Paris Court of Appeal sought Durbar's surrender following his conviction, *in absentia*, for embezzlement. In holding that the defendant did not enjoy immunity, Judge Evans accepted the existence in principle of special mission immunity under customary international law. But on the facts he rejected Durbar's assertion that at the time of his arrest in France he had been on a special mission sent by the Central African Republic; there was no evidence whatsoever to support it, and it would in any event not have subsisted in relation to the present proceedings.[168]

In *Re Ehud Barak*,[169] Judge Wickham was satisfied that, in addition to enjoying immunity *ratione personae* by virtue of his office, Mr. Barak, the Israeli Defence Minister, was entitled to special mission immunity under customary international law. Her decision was based on information from the Foreign and Commonwealth Office that he was,

"in the United Kingdom both for the purposes of attending the Labour Party Conference and to attend official meetings with the Foreign Secretary (arranged prior to Mr. Barak's arrival in the UK) and with the Prime Minister and the Defence Secretary (requested by the Israeli Embassy prior to Mr. Barak's arrival in the UK but confirmed subsequently). These bilateral meetings are to discuss official high-

---

[165] Franey, see note 2, 135-149.
[166] 8 November 2005, *ILR* 128 (2006), 713-715; *BYIL* 76 (2005), 601-603.
[167] City of Westminster Magistrates' Court, 16 June 2008 (unreported): Franey, see note 2, 147-149.
[168] In a subsequent decision, dated 7 November 2008, District Judge *Evans* rejected, on the facts, Mr. Durbar's claim that, having since been appointed Minister by the Central African Republic, he was entitled to immunity as the holder of high office in the State (under the *Arrest Warrant* principle).
[169] 29 September 2009 (unreported), Franey, see note 2, 146-147.

level engagement between the UK and Israel, including the Middle East Peace Process."[170]

In *Re Mikhael Gorbachev*,[171] Judge Wickham was told by the Foreign and Commonwealth Office, in response to her request for information, that the former Head of State of the USSR was "in the United Kingdom both for the purpose of attending a fundraising event this evening and to attend an official meeting with the Prime Minister." The Judge was "satisfied that Mr Gorbachev is entitled to immunity under customary international law as a member of a Special Mission. This immunity is in accordance with article 31 of the Convention on Special Missions ... " The Judge referred in addition to immunity *ratione materiae*, adding that she was not satisfied that the elements of the offence alleged (torture) had been made out.

In *Khurts Bat*,[172] the appellant had been arrested on the basis of a European arrest warrant alleging that he kidnapped and seriously mistreated a Mongolian national in Germany (and France). In the City of Westminster Magistrates' Court, Judge Purdy rejected the two immunity grounds then put forward by Khurts Bat to resist extradition to Germany: that he was entitled to immunity on the ground that he was visiting the United Kingdom on a special mission; and that he was entitled to immunity *ratione personae* as the holder of high-ranking office within the State. The Judge accepted the principle of special mission immunity, but found that in the case before him there could not be said to be a special mission, which "requires mutual consent in clear terms."[173] Khurts Bat appealed to the High Court, asserting *inter alia* that he was entitled to inviolability of the person and immunity from suit in respect of extradition proceedings because, at the time of his arrest at Heathrow on a European arrest warrant, he was a member of a special mission sent by the Republic of Mongolia to the United Kingdom with the consent of the latter.[174] The claim to immunity was re-

---

[170] Franey, see note 2, 146-147.
[171] City of Westminster Magistrates' Court, 30 March 2011 (unreported, text on file with the author). See the Westminster News, <http://www.sketchnews.co.uk>.
[172] *Khurts Bat*, see note 15.
[173] City of Westminster Magistrates' Court, 18 February 2011 (unreported, text on file with the author).
[174] The Appellant, and the Republic of Mongolia (which intervened as an interested party), also claimed in the Administrative Court that he was entitled to inviolability of the person and immunity from suit as a high-ranking

jected by the Administrative Court.¹⁷⁵ Neither of the requirements referred to at page 32 above was met, as was conclusively established by a letter to the District Court from the Director of Protocol and Vice-Marshal of the Diplomatic Corps.¹⁷⁶

On 6 October 2011, the Director of Public Prosecutions (DPP), acting under section 1(4A)(1) of the Magistrates' Courts Act 1980,¹⁷⁷ de-

---

official enjoying immunity *ratione personae*, as well as immunity *ratione materiae* in respect of the offences charged in the European arrest warrant. Each of these claims was rejected.

175   The Appellant did not appeal further to the Supreme Court, and was returned to Germany in August 2011 pursuant to the European Arrest Warrant. He was released in September 2011.

176   The letter from the Director of Protocol read as follows: "Ultimately the question of whether Mr Khurts Bat came to the UK on 18 September 2010 on a Special Mission is a question of law for the court to determine. However there are relevant facts within the knowledge of Her Majesty's Government, which may assist the court in reaching conclusions on the law. In the view of Her Majesty's Government a Special Mission is a means to conduct ad hoc diplomacy in relation to specific international business, beyond the framework of permanent diplomatic relations that is now set out in [the Vienna Convention on Diplomatic Relations]. As is the case for permanent diplomatic relations, the fundamental aspect of a Special Mission is the mutuality of consent of both the sending and the receiving States to the Special Mission. Whilst in FCO practice there are no prescribed formalities, such consent would normally be demonstrated by, for example, an invitation by the receiving State and an acceptance by the sending State, an agreed programme of meetings, an agreed agenda of business and so on. In the case of Mr Khurts Bat, the FCO did not consent to his visit as a Special Mission, no invitation was issued, no meeting was arranged, no subjects of business were agreed or prepared. The FCO therefore did not consider that Mr Khurts Bat came to the UK on 18 September on a Special Mission."

177   Section 1(4A)(1) of the Magistrates' Courts Act 1980 (c. 43), inserted by section 153 of the Police Reform and Social Responsibility Act 2011 (c. 13), provides that where a person who is not a public prosecutor lays an information before a justice of the peace in respect of certain offences (including grave breaches of the Geneva Conventions and torture) alleged to have been committed outside the United Kingdom, no warrant shall be issued under the section without the consent of the Director of Public Prosecutions. In response to a Parliamentary Question, a Home Office Minister explained that "Section 153 of the Police Reform and Social Responsibility Act 2011, which came into force on 15 September 2011, requires the consent of the Director of Public Prosecutions to be given before an arrest warrant can be issued in a private prosecution for offences of universal ju-

clined to give his consent to a private prosecutor for the issue of a warrant to arrest Ms. Tzipi Livni, the Israeli opposition leader, who was visiting London. The private prosecutor had sought a warrant to arrest Ms. Livni in relation to war crimes alleged to have been committed when she was Foreign Minister of Israel. At the request of the DPP, the Foreign and Commonwealth Office certified that "the Foreign and Commonwealth Office has consented to the visit to the United Kingdom of Ms Tzipi Livni on 05-06 October 2011 as a special mission, and she has been received as such."[178] On the same day, the Crown Prosecution Service issued a statement explaining the basis on which he had refused to give consent.[179]

---

risdiction. These are offences – including certain war crimes, torture, and hostage-taking – which can be prosecuted here even if committed outside the UK by someone who is not a British national. The Director of Public Prosecutions is well aware that speed is important in dealing with applications of this kind, and he has made clear that it is open to anyone who wants to pursue a crime of universal jurisdiction to engage with the Crown Prosecution Service as early as possible." (Hansard, HC Deb, 17 Oct 2011, Column 653W).

[178] The certificate read in full: "Under the authority of Her Majesty's Principal Secretary of State for Foreign and Commonwealth Affairs conferred on me, I, Simon Martin, Director of Protocol, hereby certify that the Foreign and Commonwealth Office has consented to the visit to the United Kingdom of Ms Tzipi Livni on 05-06 October 2011 as a special mission, and she has been received as such." See also the Parliamentary Answers at Hansard, HC Deb, 18 October 2011, Column 896W-Column 897W.

[179] *CPS Statement in relation to Ms Tzipi Livni's visit to the UK* (CPS News Brief, 6 October 2011). The statement included the following: "On a previous occasion the High Court of England and Wales has considered the legal effect of such a certificate. In Bat v German Federal Court and The Government of Mongolia and The Secretary of State for Foreign and Commonwealth Affairs [2011] EWCH 2029 (Admin), the High Court ruled that a 'special mission' performs temporarily those functions ordinarily taken care of by a permanent diplomatic mission and that accordingly a 'special mission' is afforded immunity from suit and legal process for the duration of the mission. The High Court also ruled that it is not open to a court to call into question the classification of a mission as a 'special mission' by the Foreign and Commonwealth Office. The immunity attracted by those on special missions has also been recognised in a number of decisions made by District Judges. The ruling of the High Court is binding on all magistrates' courts. Accordingly the Director of Public Prosecutions has concluded that a Magistrates' Court would be bound to refuse any application for the arrest of Ms Livni for the duration of this visit. In those cir-

In summary, in the United Kingdom there is extensive practice of the executive and of the courts, based on and supporting the existence of rules of customary international law on the immunity and inviolability of official visitors, including persons on special missions. These customary rules form part of the law of England, and are applied directly by the courts.

United States of America

The United States view of the customary international law on official visitors was explained in 2008, by the then State Department Legal Adviser, John B. Bellinger III, in the following terms:

"Another immunity that may be accorded to foreign officials is special mission immunity, which is also grounded in customary international law and federal common law (Like most countries, the United States has not joined the Special Missions Convention). The doctrine of special mission immunity, like diplomatic immunity, is necessary to facilitate high level contacts between governments through invitational visits. The Executive Branch has made suggestions of special mission immunity in cases such as one filed against Prince Charles in 1978 while he was here on an official visit. *Kilroy v. Charles Windsor, Prince of Wales*, Civ. No. C-78-291 (N.D. Ohio, 1978). This past summer, in response to a request for views by the federal district court for the D.C. Circuit, the Executive Branch submitted a suggestion of special mission immunity on behalf of a Chinese Minister of Commerce who was served while attending bilateral trade talks hosted by the United States, in *Li Weixum v. Bo Xilai*, D.C.C.Civ. No. 04-0649 (RJL)."[180]

The US Restatement of 1987 includes the following:

"*Immunity for high officials and special missions.*

High officials of a foreign state and their staffs on an official visit or in transit, including those attending international conferences as of-

---

cumstances, the Director of Public Prosecutions has refused to give his consent to the private prosecutor to make an application to the court for an arrest warrant."

[180] J.B. Bellinger III, *Immunities*, Opinio Juris blog (18 January 2007), see under <http://opiniojuris.org/2007/01/18/immunities>. See also id., "The Dog that Caught the Car: Observations on the Past, Present, and Future Approaches of the Office of the Legal Adviser to Official Acts Immunities", *Vand. J. Transnat'l L.* 44 (2011), 819 (831-832).

ficial representatives of their country, enjoy immunities like those of diplomatic agents when the effect of exercising jurisdiction against the official would be to violate the immunity of the foreign state. Many such officials would enjoy immunity equivalent in all instances to that enjoyed by diplomatic agents under the Convention on Special Missions, Reporters' Note 13, if that Convention were to come into effect."[181]

In a number of cases, United States courts have accepted the view of the US Government, conveyed to the Court, as to the status of persons on what are often referred to in the United States as "special diplomatic missions." The starting point for the law of international immunities in the United States is the early Supreme Court case of *The Schooner Exchange* v. *McFaddon*, in which Marshall CJ held that whenever a sovereign, a representative of a foreign State or a foreign army is present within the territory by consent, it is to be implied that the local sovereign confers immunity from local jurisdiction. The importance of consent is evident in this early decision.[182]

In *Chong Boon Kim* v. *Kim Yong Shik*, the US Attorney submitted a suggestion of immunity to the Circuit Court of the First Circuit, State of Hawaii, saying that,

"Under customary rules of international law, recognized and applied by the United States, the head of a foreign government, its foreign minister, and those designated by him as members of his official party are immune from the jurisdiction of United States federal and state courts."

---

[181] *Restatement (Third) of Foreign Relations Law of the United States*, 1987, Vol. 1, para. 464 cmt. *i*. Reporters' Note 13 includes the following: "Although the law as to 'itinerant envoys,' special representatives, representatives to international conferences, and other participants in diplomacy remains uncertain, the Convention on Special Missions reflects what is increasingly practiced and in many respects may emerge as customary international law."

[182] 11 US 116 (1812): "A sovereign committing the interests of his nation with a foreign power, to the care of a person whom he has selected for that purpose, cannot intend to subject his minister in any degree to that power; and, therefore, a consent to receive him, implies a consent that he shall possess those privileges which his principal intended he should retain – privileges which are essential to the dignity of his sovereign, and to the duties he is bound to perform." (139).

The Court dismissed the action as to *Kim Yong Shik*, Foreign Minister of the Republic of Korea, on the basis of lack of jurisdiction.[183]

Kilroy v. *Charles Windsor, Prince of Wales*[184] concerned a suit brought against the Heir to the British Throne for alleged deprivation of plaintiff's rights under the Constitution and laws of the United States. (The plaintiff had been removed from an event at Cleveland State University by US Department of State officials, after putting forward a question to the Prince, alleging that the British Government tortured prisoners in Northern Ireland.) The Department of Justice filed a Suggestion of Immunity before the Court, arguing that "[u]nder customary rules of international law ... other diplomatic representatives, including senior officials on special diplomatic missions, are immune from the jurisdiction of United States." A letter to the Department of Justice stated that "[t]he Department of State regards the visit of Prince Charles as a special diplomatic mission and considers the Prince to have been an official diplomatic envoy while present in the United States on that mission." The Court held that the Prince of Wales enjoyed immunity.

In *Philippines* v. *Marcos*, a subpoena was served on the Solicitor General of the Philippines, who was in the United States to give a speech. The State Department's Suggestion of Immunity stated that "Solicitor General Ordinez is present in San Francisco as the representative of the Government of the Philippines in the performance of official functions of that Government. Under these circumstances the Department believes that it would be appropriate to recognize and allow the immunity of Solicitor General Ordonez from service of process ..." The Court accepted that the Solicitor General was entitled to "diplomatic immunity" even though the Suggestion of Immunity had issued after he had arrived in the United States and been served with the subpoena.[185]

---

[183] Civ. No. C12565 (Cir. Ct 1st Dir. Haw. 1963), *AJIL* 68 (1964), 186-187; see also Whiteman, see note 2, 41-42.

[184] *Kilroy* v. *Windsor (Prince Charles, Prince of Wales)*, Civ. No. C-78-291 (N.D. Ohio, 1978); Washington, D.C. International Law Institute (ed.), *Digest of United States Practice in International Law*, 1978, 641; *ILR* 81 (1990), 605.

[185] United States District Court, N.D. California, *Republic of Philippines by the Central Bank of the Philippines* v. *Ferdinand E. Marcos, et al.*, 665 F.Supp.793 (N.D. Cal. 1987). The Statement of Interest and Suggestion of Immunity in *Bo Xilai* (*Li Weixum et al.* v. *Bo Xilai*, 568 F.Supp.2d 35) states (at 8) that "court granted Philippine Solicitor General diplomatic immu-

Li Weixum v. *Bo Xilai*,[186] concerned a suit brought against the Minister of Commerce of the People's Republic of China by Falun Gong members, for alleged human rights violations committed while he served as governor of Liaoning Province from 2001 to 2004. The Minister was in the United States pursuant to an invitation of the Executive Branch to participate in an annual meeting of the U.S.-China Joint Commission on Commerce and Trade. The Department of Justice filed a Statement of Interest and Suggestion of Immunity, asserting that "upon an Executive Branch determination, senior foreign officials on special diplomatic missions are immune from personal jurisdiction where jurisdiction is based solely on their presence in the United States during their mission."[187] The Court deferred to the views of the Executive that Minister Bo Xilai was on a "special diplomatic mission" and found it lacked jurisdiction to try him.[188]

In summary, it is clear from United States practice and case-law that the US Government considers that official visitors, accepted as such by the Executive, are entitled to immunity for the duration of their visit. US practice thus supports the existence of customary rules regarding the immunity of official visitors. It also demonstrates that the applicability of this immunity is dependent on the consent and recognition, accorded by the receiving State's Executive, of the official visit as such. As can be seen from the case-law, where the Executive expressed its con-

---

nity, misunderstanding U.S. position that he was entitled to special missions immunity."

[186] See *Bo Xilai*, above.

[187] *Li Weixum et al.* v. *Bo Xilai*, Department of Justice Statement of Interest and Suggestion of Immunity, 568 F.Supp.2d 35 (D.D.C 2006) (No. 1:04-cv-00649), 5.

[188] In *USA* v. *Sissoko* (995 F.Supp. 1469, 1997), *ILR* 121 (2002), 599, Counsel on behalf of The Gambia filed a motion to dismiss charges of paying a gratuity against Foutanga Sissoko, designated as a "Special Adviser to a Special Mission", a designation accepted by the United States (ibid., 1470). The court rejected the motion, finding that the UN Convention on Special Missions was not customary law. In doing so, it based itself on the fact that neither the United States, The Gambia nor any member of the UN Security Council had signed the Convention. (The United Kingdom had in fact signed the Convention). The court appears not to have considered the possible existence of rules of customary international law independent of the Convention on Special Missions. And it distinguished the case from others, as there was no Suggestion of Immunity and the only recognition of the United States of Sissoko was the visa he was issued, without the expression of any other form of consent.

sent via a statement of interest asserting immunity from jurisdiction, based on customary international law, the judiciary accepts the position of the Executive Branch.

Responsibility in International Law

Volker Roeben

I. Introduction
II. Responsibility as an Institution of International Law
   1. The Idea of International Responsibility
   2. Guaranteeing International Responsibility Law
III. Responsibility for Sustainable Development
   1. Responsibility in the Rio Declaration
   2. The Climate Change Regime
      a. The Common Responsibility of Each State Party: Reflective Responsibility
      b. Differentiated Responsibilities of States Parties: Standards for Outcomes
   3. The Rio Declaration and the Law of the Sea
   4. Conclusions
IV. Responsibility for the Global Economy
   1. Responsibility in the G20 Washington Declaration
   2. Designing an Oversight Regime for the Global Financial Markets
   3. The G20 and the Responsibility of Third States
   4. Conclusions
V. Responsibility for Peace and Stability within States
   1. Responsibility in the 2005 World Summit Outcome
   2. Post-conflict Peace-Building
      a. Primary Responsibility of Each State Emerging from Conflict
      b. The United Nations as Addressee of Accountability of States
   3. The "Responsibility to Protect"
      a. Primary Responsibility of Each State to Protect Civilians from Genocide, War Crimes, Ethnic Cleansing and Crimes against Humanity
      b. The Responsibility of the United Nations to Guarantee and to Act
      c. Responsibility of Each State Represented on the Governance of United Nations Organs
   4. Conclusions
VI. Responsibility as an Institution of International Law: Concluding Reflections

Abstract

International legal materials refer to "common but differentiated responsibility", the "responsibility to protect", or the "responsibility for the global economy". These terms are manifestations of a single institution of international responsibility, which undergirds much international law development since the 1990s. Institutions combine an idea and a legal reality. The idea of responsibility is that it establishes a relation between the vectors of moral agent, object, addressee to which the agent is accountable, and criteria of assessment.

In the context of international law, states are the primary agents of responsibility, with international organisations being assigned secondary responsibility. Accountability generally lies to the international community, acting through appropriate bodies which assess whether actors meet their assigned responsibility according to defined standards. This matrix of international responsibility is normatively guaranteed and concretised through an international law-making process that proceeds from the recognition in a non-binding document of responsibility as foundational principle for an area of law to the development of binding treaty law and alternative forms of international law-making. The thus conceptualised institution of international responsibility is then shown to manifest itself in three reference areas of international law: sustainable development, international financial markets, and state-internal peace and stability including the Responsibility to Protect civilians. The article concludes by drawing normative implications for the development and interpretation of international law that falls within the ambit of the institution of international responsibility.

Keywords

Law of the Global Economy; International Responsibility; Institutions of International Law; International Law-making; Responsibility to Protect; Sustainable Development

I. Introduction

Responsibility has a bewildering array of senses or meanings each of which occupies a distinctive role.[1] Historically, the term responsibility first appears in legal texts of the 15th century where responsibility refers to the justification or defence of an action in court,[2] and in the 19th century it denotes parliamentary ministerial responsibility to compensate for the theory that the king is not responsible and therefore legally can do no wrong.[3] For contemporary society responsibility is a key category of self-reflection which therein seeks reassurance after the loss of metaphysics and the end of utopian expectations of social progress.[4] Law shares the concept and terminology of responsibility with other disciplines such as philosophy and ethics,[5] and (international) political theory.[6] Responsibility plays, of course, an important role in legal philosophy, albeit its account refers mostly to the domestic context. In positive legal theory responsibility is an established concept denoting mainly the consequences of individual action in torts and criminal law.[7]

---

[1] J. Crawford/ J. Watkins, "International Responsibility", in: J. Tasioulas/ S. Besson (eds), *The Philosophy of International Law*, 2010, 293 et seq. (hereinafter Philosophy of International Law); D. Miller, *National Responsibility and Global Justice*, 2007, 82 et seq. (hereinafter National Responsibility).

[2] See W. Korff/ G. Wilhelms, "Verantwortung", in: W. Kasper (ed.), *Lexikon für Theologie und Kirche*, 3rd edition, 2001, 600 et seq.

[3] Sir W. Blackstone, *Commentaries*, Book III, Chapter XVII, available at <http://avalonlaw.yale.edu>; C. von Rotteck, "Lehrbuch der allgemeinen Staatslehre", in: id., *Lehrbuch des Vernunftrechts und der Staatswissenschaften*, Vol. 2, 2nd edition, 1804, reprinted 1964, 249-251.

[4] M. Vogt, "Grenzen und Methoden der Verantwortung in der Risikogesellschaft", in: J. Beaufort/ E. Gumpert/ M. Vogt (eds), *Fortschritt und Risiko. Zur Dialektik der Verantwortung in (post-)moderner Gesellschaft*, 2003, 85 et seq.

[5] See e.g. H. Jonas, *The Imperative of Responsibility*, 1985; F. Kaufmann, *Der Ruf nach Verantwortung. Risiko und Ethik in einer unüberschaubaren Welt*, 1992, 11 et seq.

[6] National Responsibility, see note 1.

[7] H.L.A. Hart, "Postscript: Responsibility and Retribution", in: *Punishment and Responsibility*, 1968, 210 et seq.; G.P. Fletcher, "Punishment and Responsibility", in: D. Patterson (ed.), *A Companion to Philosophy of Law and Legal Theory*, 1996, 514; J. Gardner, "The Mark of Responsibility", *Oxford Journal of Legal Studies* 23 (2003), 157 et seq.; C. Kutz, "Responsibility", in: J. Coleman/ S. Shapiro (eds), *The Oxford Handbook of Juris-*

Responsibility has also been used in a political theory underpinning the legal relation between individual rights and their limitations in the public interest which must be traceable to the objectives or public goods enshrined in a Constitution.[8] Recent accounts of "international responsibility" in the philosophy of international law put emphasis on moral responsibility as a yardstick for the law of state responsibility[9] or more generally the instrumental value of the state.[10]

Contemporary international law also makes a range of uses of the term responsibility. Here responsibility may denote a competence, as is the case for Article 24 UN Charter which provides that the UN Security Council has "primary responsibility for the maintenance of international peace and security."[11] Responsibility may denote primary obligations for states, for instance in the 1982 UN Convention on the Law of the Sea,[12] which is distinguishable from the use of the term responsibility within the customary law of state responsibility concerned with secondary legal consequences attaching to the violation of states' primary international law obligations.[13] Responsibility may also denote

---

prudence and the Philosophy of Law, 2002, 548 et seq.; J. Raz, "Responsibility and the Negligence Standard", *Oxford Journal of Legal Studies* 30 (2010), 1 et seq.

8   R. Dworkin, "Hard cases", in: *Taking Rights Seriously*, 1975, 88 et seq., see also T. Nagel, "Ruthlessness in Public Life", in: *Mortal Questions,* 1979, 75 et seq.

9   Crawford/ Watkins, see note 1.

10 L. Murphy, "International Responsibility", in: Philosophy of International Law, see note 1, 299 et seq.

11 See Security Council, Presidential Statement, SCOR 61st Sess., 6389th Mtg, Doc. S/PRST/2010/18 of 23 September 2010: "The Security Council reaffirms its primary responsibility under the Charter of the United Nations for the maintenance of international peace and security. The Council in this regard recalls its resolutions and statements of its President in relation to preventive diplomacy, peacemaking, peacekeeping and peacebuilding."

12 "Responsibilities and Obligations of States sponsoring Persons and Entities with respect to Activities in the Area", Sea-bed Disputes Chamber of the International Tribunal for the Law of the Sea, Case No. 17, Advisory Opinion of 1 February 2011 (hereinafter Responsibilities Opinion).

13 Article 28 ILC Articles on Responsibility of States for Internationally Wrongful Acts, annexed to A/RES/56/83 of 12 December 2001, in: Report of the ILC, 53rd Sess., Doc. A/56/10 (hereinafter Articles on State Responsibility).

individual criminal liability under international law.¹⁴ Concepts such as "the responsibility to protect" or "common but differentiated responsibility" are finding their way into international law instruments. Recent broader debates invoke responsibility in the sense of fundamental obligations of states, be it in respect of international terrorism¹⁵ or for the respect of fundamental human rights in other states.¹⁶ Finally, in the theory of organisation¹⁷ and of global administrative law¹⁸ responsibility is sometimes treated as a term for accountability.

There is thus copious evidence of the importance of responsibility for the theory and practice of international law. But this only leaves the more pressing question as to what responsibility in international law means: is there a concept of responsibility of international law that overarches the terminological senses and debates? The search for a single understanding of responsibility in international law requires one to realise that, seen from the perspective of law, responsibility – like justice – is not a quintessentially legal concept or term. It is rather a regulative principle that occupies a meta-level shared with other disciplines using identical terminology. From that meta-level law observes itself and makes strategic decisions about its relationship with other parts of society. Just as justice remains the ultimate objective of law, responsibility marks the essence of any system of law. It constitutes its largely invisi-

---

14   Statute of the International Tribunal for the Prosecution of Persons Responsible for Serious Violations of International Humanitarian Law committed in the Territory of the Former Yugoslavia since 1991, arts 1, 7 and S/RES/827 (1993) of 25 May 1993.

15   See T. Reinold, "State Weakness, Irregular Warfare, and the Right to Self-Defense Post-9/11", *AJIL* 105 (2011), 244 et seq. (responsibility in the sense of an obligation to prevent a state's territory to be used by terrorists for launching attacks on another state).

16   See M. Hakimi, "State Bystander Responsibility", *EJIL* 21 (2010), 341 et seq. (responsibility to denote the obligation of a state in respect of another state's human rights observation).

17   See R.W. Grant/ R.O. Keohane, "Accountability and Abuses of Power in World Politics", *American Political Science Review* 99 (2005), 35 et seq. (35-37); Y. Papadopoulos, "Problems of Democratic Accountability in Network and Multilevel Governance", *ELJ* 13 (2007), 477 et seq.

18   See R. Stewart, "Administrative Law for the 21st century", *N.Y.U.L. Rev.* 78 (2003), 437 et seq.; A.C. Aman, "The Limits of Globalization and the Future of Administrative Law: From Government to Governance", *Ind. J. Global Legal Stud.* 8 (2001), 379 et seq.

ble foundational structure which may be rendered visible by means of legal principles.

More precisely, responsibility is an institution. An institution is an idea or a set of ideas with the claim to constitute normative reality.[19] Institutions are not agents for the free production of legal norms. Rather law recognises institutions as necessary conditions for its normative contents. Institutions are law's contact points with social reality. An institution requires convincing power on the level of ideas, it needs social recognition, and it depends on normative guarantees at all levels from principles through rule-making to concrete decisions of cases.[20] International law presupposes or reconfirms such institutions, integrating them with the international political system and assigning them functions. The ICJ has recognised this for the institution of the self-determination of peoples.[21] The understanding of responsibility as an institution of international law will be substantiated subsequently in Part II. There then follow discussions of international responsibility in the reference contexts of sustainable development (Part III.), regulation of the global financial markets (Part IV.), and peace and stability within states (Part V.). Concluding that an institution of responsibility is embedded in contemporary international law, Part VI. will clarify certain normative implications of that finding.

II. Responsibility as an Institution of International Law

Institutions couple an idea with a claim to normative reality. What is the idea of international responsibility and what are the mechanisms of the normative concretisation of this idea?

---

[19] See U. Di Fabio, "Verantwortung als Verfassungsinstitut", in: W. Knies (ed.), *Staat, Amt, Verantwortung. Festschrift für Karl Fromme*, 2002, 15 et seq. (20).

[20] Ibid., 15-40.

[21] See Legal Consequences for States of the Continued Presence of South Africa in Namibia (South West Africa) notwithstanding Security Council Resolution 276 (1970), ICJ Reports 1971, 16 et seq., para. 52 (hereinafter Namibia Opinion); Western Sahara, ICJ Reports 1975, 12 et seq. (31-33); East Timor (Portugal v. Australia), ICJ Reports 1995, 90 et seq. (102, para. 29); Legal Consequences of the Construction of a Wall in the Occupied Palestinian Territory, ICJ Reports 2004, 136 et seq. (171, para. 88) (hereinafter Wall Opinion) (from political concept to objective legal principle to subjective right with *erga omnes*-effect).

1. The Idea of International Responsibility

The conceptual analysis of the idea of responsibility may start with the etymological insight that "responsibility" denotes linguistic interaction: answer-ability.[22] At the heart of responsibility is indeed the idea of attributing consequences and their control. Responsibility is thus relational. It marks the relation between subject (moral agent), object (action or thing, moral patient), and a designated body (addressee) who disposes of effective sanctioning powers.[23] Modern thinking presupposes that this addressee be legitimate and has criteria of assessment. All matters of responsibility play out within this matrix made up of the three vectors of who is responsible for what to whom.[24] Responsibility is in particular the normative core of all public organisation in society, so that the art of organisation in essence becomes the art of the clear delimitation and attribution of responsibilities.[25] That has long been accepted for the organisation of the constitutional state.[26] But it is true also for the organisation of the international space above the state. The matrix of international responsibility then would consist of the following three vectors: in respect of the question of who can be assigned with international responsibility, responsibility presupposes that there is space for own decision-making by the responsible actor. Only a competent actor can be said to be making decisions for which it and it alone is answerable. Responsibility and sovereignty thus imply each other.[27] Sovereignty under international law guarantees each state residual competences for internal matters. For matters not under its jurisdiction, each state is competent to enter into cooperation with other states and to implement the results of that cooperation domestically. The sovereign veil can be pierced and responsibility be attributed to state organs, namely regulators. It is also within the logic of the idea of responsibility that it reaches further down into the state. Thus, individuals running a

---

[22] J.R. Lucas, *Responsibility*, 1993, 5 et seq.
[23] Vogt, see note 4, 89.
[24] O. Höffe, *Moral als Preis der Moderne*, 1993, 23.
[25] K. Bayertz, *Verantwortung. Prinzip oder Problem?*, 1995, 43.
[26] Cf. Di Fabio, see note 19, 20-40; L. Fisler Damrosch, "War and Uncertainty. (On Democratic Ground: New Perspectives on John Hart Ely)", *Yale L. J.* 114 (2005), 1405 et seq.
[27] See F.M. Deng/ S. Kimaro/ T. Lyons/ D. Rothchild/ I.W. Zartman, *Sovereignty as Responsibility: Conflict Management in Africa*, 1996, 1 et seq.

state's government can bear international (criminal) responsibility.[28] States are, however, not the exclusive competent actors and therefore subjects of responsibility in the international sphere. That role can also be played by international organisations and their organs if and where competences have been conferred upon them,[29] or by other forms of institutionalised cooperation between states to the extent that they exercise formal or informal public authority.[30] But to the extent that private conduct is of consequence at the international level it becomes possible to attribute consequences of private action for an international public good. Assigning them with responsibility renders the private parties accountable at the international level to a designated body. At the level of the implementation of this individual or private responsibility, there is then the need to respect the applicable human or other individual rights.

What can international responsibility be assigned for? This denotes the remit of responsibility: the public good for which responsibility is assigned, and the questions of whether conduct or omission are relevant and whether responsibility is to be attributed for the past or the future. Primary and secondary responsibilities among relevant actors have to be clearly identified. The remit of an actor's responsibility is determined on the basis of norms. Such norms are shaped particularly by international law whose structure ensures that the duties of responsible actors can be determined in a practical manner.[31] This does not exclude that in

---

[28] Rome Statute of the ICC, arts 25, 27, UNTS Vol. 2187 No. 38544. On aggression within the meaning of article 5 (1)(d) Statute of the ICC as a leadership crime see C. Kreß/ L. von Holtzendorff, "The Kampala Compromise on the Crime of Aggression", *Journal of International Criminal Justice* 8 (2010), 1179 et seq. (1189). By contrast, the once hotly discussed criminal responsibility of states has been largely dropped, see D. Bodansky/ J.R. Crook, "Symposium: The ILC's State Responsibility Articles", *AJIL* 96 (2002), 772 et seq. (784).

[29] The UN Charter uses responsibility in this sense of competence in many of its stipulations on the principal organs, cf. Arts 13 (2), 60 for the General Assembly; Arts 24 (1), 26 for the Security Council; Article 60 for ECOSOC.

[30] See A. von Bogdandy et al. (eds), *The Exercise of Public Authority by International Institutions*, 2009.

[31] See generally P. Weil, "Towards Relative Normativity in International Law?", *AJIL* 77 (1983), 413 et seq. (functions and qualities of international law norms).

certain instances standards may reach into the political sphere.[32] International responsibility first presupposes that an international public good which lies in the interest of the international community as a whole can be identified. There is no fixed or predetermined list of such international goods, their identification is the province of the international political and legal systems as is the attribution of responsibility for them. Conceptually, there are two categories of international public goods: there are public goods that require international cooperation and those that are the subject of internal action. Sustainable development and regulation of the global economy are such international goods in need of cooperative action by all or most states, while lawful peace and security are state internal matters.

In respect of such goods, each state will be responsible for reflecting on the objectives as well as the design of the regulation and organisation to achieve these objectives. Since each state owns this responsibility none can cede control either over the process of reflection or over the implementation of the results of the reflections, including any international organisation that may be founded or resorted to in the furtherance of the common objective.[33] If the cooperation extends into the future, in other words if it is a programme rather than a one-off event, then the reflective responsibility extends over time. This will comprise all points of the process of negotiating, entering into and complying with internationally legally binding commitments. Reflective responsibility entails a strong element of discretion in the design of the cooperative mechanisms. But the design of cooperation is subject to certain substantive standards relating to effectiveness, equity, and transparency. The cooperative design would namely have to provide for a clear identi-

---

[32] This concentration on responsibility criteria distinguishes the institution of responsibility from broader accountability theories such as those put forward by M. Bovens, "Analysing and Assessing Public Accountability: A Conceptual Framework", *European Law Review* 13 (2007), 447 et seq. (450); see also M. Bovens/ D. Curtin/ P.T. Hart (eds), *Studying the Real World of EU Accountability: Framework and Design in the Real World of EU Accountability – What Deficit?*, 2010, 35 et seq.

[33] Cf. Joined cases 2 BvE 2/08, 2 BvE 5/08, 2 BvR 1010/08, 2 BvR 1022/08, 2 BvR 1259/08, 2 BvR 182/09, Federal Constitutional Court of Germany, BVerfGE 123, 267, translation under <www.bundesverfassungsgericht.de>, (on the constitutionality of the EU Treaty of Lisbon, discussing reflective "konzeptionelle" responsibility of the European Union Member States and the principle of conferred powers on the European Union) (hereinafter Lisbon judgment).

fication of primary and secondary responsibilities among relevant actors, shaping the demarcation of the obligations of states and the competences of international organisations. But there are also international public goods relating to matters under the jurisdiction of each state. Neither international or supranational organisations nor other states can displace the sovereign in its responsibility for regulating these matters in line with international standards.[34] Yet responsibility may come to be recognised to additionally lie with other international actors, as responsibility to guarantee or to act. As a consequence, again the need arises to define the concomitant obligations, rights and competences of all actors.

Responsibility always lies towards another body. Responsibility necessarily implies a hierarchical relationship of the responsible actor with the designated body to which accountability lies. Acting for the international community, an organisation such as the United Nations can fulfil the role of the designated body to which the responsible actor is accountable. A state's international responsibility implies accountability to a designated international body competent to set standards for the conduct of states, assess each state's performance against them and sanction its findings. Accountability in this sense includes that the institution to which accountability lies has effective sanctions at its disposal, in other words powers of compliance control. The consequences of responsibility must be defined. Mere factual results of own action or omission cannot be accounted for as sanction. International responsibility is attributed *in the interest* of the international community.[35] International responsibility is not a single issue topic confined to one area of law. Rather this institution sits at a medium level of generality, extending over a range of subject areas of that segment or "layer"[36] of interna-

---

[34] Retaining such competence may be demanded in constitutional law as a precondition for effective democratic responsibility, cf. Lisbon judgment. Accordingly Member States have not transferred certain critical competences to the European Union, not even through the Lisbon Treaty.

[35] According to arts 42 (b), 48 (1)(b) Articles on Responsibility of States for Internationally Wrongful Acts, see note 13, states have certain obligations to the "international community as a whole", giving legal form to the recognition and safeguarding of collective goods. For the term international community as a whole see Commentaries, article 25, para. 18; J.R. Crawford, "Responsibilities of the International Community as a Whole", *Ind. J. Global Legal Stud.* 8 (2000-01), 303 et seq. (314-315).

[36] See J.H.H. Weiler, "The Geology of International Law – Governance, Democracy and Legitimacy", *ZaöRV/ HJIL* 64 (2004), 556 et seq.

tional law that advances wider community objectives and harnesses the state.[37]

It is then clear how international responsibility can be distinguished from state responsibility and other forms of liability in international law.[38] Assigning actors with responsibility will often result in the establishment of primary obligations for them. Liability then expresses the idea that a legally defined consequence attaches to the violation of a primary obligation incumbent on the responsible agent. Liability may be institutionalised in different ways,[39] and in international law it is expressed as the customary law of state responsibility as well as the often treaty-based liability with or without fault in international law and it will often include the occurrence of damages. Liability may be established for public goods, the safeguard of which lies in the interest of the international community as a whole. States are liable for consequences resulting from their own action, and that may include a lack of supervision of private actors. Responsibility and liability as two different senses of the term responsibility are both in operation in the international legal system but at different stages.[40]

2. Guaranteeing International Responsibility Law

The institution of international responsibility depends on normative guarantees at all levels from principles through rule-making down to concrete decisions. In the decentralised international law context such guarantees cannot be derived from a single constitution – in the sense of a document at the apex of a normative hierarchy. In a world of sover-

---

[37] See E. Hey, "International Public Law", *International Law Forum* 6 (2004), 149 et seq.
[38] Conceptual clarity is particularly in demand in international law which may tend to use responsibility as synonymous for liability, Crawford/ Watkins, see note 1, 284.
[39] Such as censure in public law, punishment in criminal law, liability in private law.
[40] Cf. Crawford/ Watkins, see note 1, 284 (referring for responsibility to judicial process). In reality, the structure of primary substantive responsibility-related obligations and the corresponding legal interest to invoke them is also relevant at the level of enforcing liability, see Responsibilities Opinion, see note 12, para. 180 (*erga omnes* obligation for states to protect the marine environment of the Area means that all states may claim compensation for damage to that environment).

eigns, what rather matters is the ability of states dynamically to produce authoritative texts on international responsibility along the matrix outlined above. Guaranteeing international responsibility is thus intimately wedded to the contemporary process of international law-making. This process is grounded in foundational political documents, which serve as reference points for subsequent law-making encompassing instruments ranging from treaty law to alternative forms of law-making including administrative-style rule-making. The process has been powerfully elucidated by the Sea-bed Disputes Chamber of the International Tribunal for the Law of the Sea in the recent Advisory Opinion on *Responsibilities and Obligations of States sponsoring Persons and Entities with Respect to Activities in the Area.*[41] The Chamber there discusses the "precautionary principle", linking it to the Rio Declaration. The politically binding Rio Declaration, so the Chamber finds, is the starting point for a process of concretising this principle into binding law. There could be several forms of legal implementation in the law of the sea, ranging from the treaties to the secondary law of rules adopted by the International Sea-bed Authority.[42] The cumulative effect of concretising of the principle through treaty or sub-treaty norms could then cause the principle to crystallise in customary international law.[43] The Chamber thus identifies a cascading process that allows moving from the first recognition of a broad principle in a politically binding document to the legally binding concretisation of the rationale underlying the principle.

The same concretisation process is available for international responsibility.[44] The process takes as its starting point a foundational document which for a new area under consideration first adopts the terminology of responsibility and assigns relevant actors with responsibilities. This

---

[41] See note 12. On the position of the International Tribunal for the Law of the Sea within the Law of the Sea Convention's dispute settlement system and the broader international regime for the settlement of disputes see B.H. Oxman, "A Tribute to Louis Sohn – Is the Dispute Settlement System under the Law of the Sea Convention Working?, *Geo. Wash. L. Rev.* 39 (2007), 655 et seq. (656-659).

[42] Responsibilities Opinion, see note 12, paras 126-35, 161.

[43] In the event, the Chamber found that the environmental impact assessment requirement was customary international law, Responsibilities Opinion, see note 12, para. 145, while the precautionary principle was (only) launched on the way to becoming customary international law, para. 135.

[44] Regardless of the fact that the idea of responsibility is situated at a higher level of abstraction than the more specific environmental principles featuring in the Responsibilities Opinion.

foundational document will be of a non-binding political nature. The document of universal or near universal acceptability is then concretised through binding international law. Such binding law can be treaty law, secondary law adopted by international organisations, or alternative forms of international law-making. The collective self-attribution of responsibility by states is rooted in the consent principle that traditionally underpins the legitimacy of international law. But responsibility may also be attributed by a group of states to third states. The consent principle cannot legitimise responsibility attribution to a non-consenting state. Such external responsibility attribution can, however, derive legitimation from the group of states claiming to be acting in the interest of the international community. This presupposes that these states constitute a representative group of states which includes those most interested in the matter and that there is an objective justification for also attributing responsibility to the non-represented state. The creation of responsibility related norms of international law is thus in essence a deductive process. This differentiates it from the other well-established categories of public-interest norms in international law: *ius cogens* and *erga omnes* norms both develop essentially inductively through converging state practice.

III. Responsibility for Sustainable Development

The article will now turn to examining the law of sustainable development as reference area for the institution of responsibility. Sustainable development is by now an established branch of international law. The 1992 Rio Declaration is its foundational text, grounding it in the idea of responsibility. The Rio Declaration has then been concretised in the international legal regimes on the global commons, namely the climate and the oceans along the matrix of responsibility.

1. Responsibility in the Rio Declaration

The UN Conference on Environment and Development (UNCED) held in Rio de Janeiro in 1992 produced as a central outcome the Rio Declaration.[45] The non-binding Rio Declaration has become the foun-

---

[45] Report of the UN Conference on Environment and Development, Rio Declaration, Doc. A/CONF.151/26/Vol.1 of 12 August 1992.

dational document of sustainable development law by setting forth its principles.[46] In particular, the Rio Declaration bases international efforts at achieving sustainable development on the idea of responsibility in its Principles No. 1, 2 and 7. Rio Principle No. 1 sets out sustainable development as an objective or public good and identifies humanity as a chief beneficiary of international efforts undertaken in pursuit of this objective.[47] Taken together, Rio Principles No. 2 and 7 break down the objective of sustainable development into the matrix of responsibilities: Principle No. 2 establishes the responsibility of each state for matters under its jurisdiction. The Principle does so by pairing the sovereign right of each state to exploit its own resources pursuant to their own environmental and developmental policies with the "responsibility to ensure that activities within their jurisdiction or control do not cause damage to the environment of other States or of areas beyond the limits of national jurisdiction."[48] Principle No. 7 is then concerned with defining the concomitant responsibility of each state for global ecosystems. The Principle introduces "common but differentiated responsibilities" of states for sustainable development in the following terms:

"States shall co-operate in a spirit of global partnership to conserve, protect and restore the health and integrity of the Earth's ecosystem. *In view of the different contributions to global environmental degradation, states have common but differentiated responsibilities. The developed countries acknowledge the responsibility that they bear in the international pursuit of sustainable development in view of the pressures their societies place on the global environment and of the technologies and financial resources they command.*"(emphasis added)

---

[46] On the principles of international environmental law see J. Brunnée, "The Stockholm Declaration and the Structure and Processes of International Environmental Law", in: A. Chircop/ T. McDorman (eds), *Future of Ocean Regime Building: Essays in Tribute to D.M. Johnston*, 2008, 41 et seq.; P. Birnie/A. Boyle/ C. Redgwell, *International Law and the Environment*, 3rd edition, 2009, 181 et seq. (hereinafter International Law and the Environment); P. Sands, *Principles of International Environmental Law*, 1995, 181 et seq.

[47] Principle No. 1: "Human Beings are at the centre of concerns for sustainable development. They are entitled to a healthy and productive life in harmony with nature."

[48] Identical to Principle No. 21 of the Stockholm Declaration of the UN Conference on the Human Environment 1972, but for adding "developmental" policies.

While there is no shortage of voices in the literature discussing the theoretical[49] and practical[50] relevance of common but differentiated responsibilities for international sustainable development law, Rio Principle No. 7 is best understood as founding the international protection of the global environment on the idea of responsibility. Principle No. 7 establishes as a public good the protection of global ecosystems as an essential part of sustainable development. Recognition of the causal link between human-induced pressures and current trends in environmental degradation is the ground for assigning states with the responsibility for cooperative action to protect the global environment and achieve sustainable development. This responsibility is common to all states and thus it is attributed to each state. It comprises the responsibility to reflect on the design of a regime for the world's ecosystems and to assume duties under the thus designed regime. In a second step, both higher pressures and higher capacities and financial resources ground attributing special or greater responsibility to developed states within the cooperative design.

There are also standards that any such design has to meet so that it will be effective[51] and reflective of burden-sharing between developed and developing states in line with equity and capacity. Principle No. 7 is concerned with the past, present and future impact and the present and future capacity of states. That implies that the qualification of a state as developed or developing is only a proxy for the actual impact on the environment and the remedial capacity of each state at any given moment in time. The Rio Declaration itself contains further indications of the differentiated treatment accorded to developed and developing states. For instance, by stating that the precautionary approach shall be applied by states "according to their capabilities", the first sentence of Principle No. 15 introduces the possibility of differences in application of the precautionary approach in light of the different capabilities of each state.[52] The Rio Declaration thus puts the idea of responsibility at

---

[49] Cf. C.D. Stone, "Common but Differentiated Responsibilities in International Law", *AJIL* 98 (2004), 276 et seq. (276-81) with E.A. Posner/ C.R. Sunstein, "Climate Change Justice", *Geo. L. J.* 96 (2008), 1565 et seq. (1565-1607).

[50] International Law and the Environment, see note 46, 132-36.

[51] "conserve, protect and restore the health and integrity of the Earth's ecosystem."

[52] Principle No. 15: "In order to protect the environment, the precautionary approach shall be widely applied by States according to their capabilities. Where there are threats of serious or irreversible damage, lack of full scien-

the heart of sustainable development governance. The non-binding Declaration drives the process of developing binding international law. What follows is an analysis of the legal regimes concerned with global climate (see below under 2.) and the oceans (see below under 3.), each striving for universal membership, and of the way they concretise common but differentiated responsibilities.[53]

2. The Climate Change Regime

Spawned at UNCED, the 1992 UN Framework Convention on Climate Change (FCCC) recognises that climate change is indeed a "common concern of humankind" necessitating international cooperative action.[54] The FCCC, in its arts 3 and 4, incorporates Rio Principle No. 7 into the climate change regime, giving it legal force. Article 3 (1) FCCC essentially restates Principle No. 7 for the climate change context,[55] and article 4 FCCC further concretises article 3 by creating two categories of obligations, those common to all Parties and those incumbent on developed Parties as defined by Annex I only.[56] Arts 3, 4 of the FCCC concretise Rio Principle No. 7 along the matrix of responsibility identified above. There is recognition of the causal link between anthropogenic carbon dioxide emissions and current trends in global warming which grounds the need and responsibility for climate protection through binding international law. Humanity is the ultimate beneficiary

---

tific certainty shall not be used as a reason for postponing cost-effective measures to prevent environmental degradation."

[53] Elements of differentiated treatment of developed and developing countries can be found in a number of international environmental law treaties. For a comprehensive account see L. Rajamani, *Differential Treatment in International Environmental Law*, 2006.

[54] Framework Convention on Climate Change, UNTS Vol. 1771 No. 30822, Preamble (hereinafter FCCC).

[55] FCCC article 3 (1): "[t]he Parties should protect the climate system for the benefit of present and future generations of humankind, on the basis of equity and respective capabilities. Accordingly, the developed country Parties should take the lead in combating climate change and the adverse effects thereof." The formula of article 3 FCCC or elements thereof are also incorporated in supplemental climate-change instruments adopted subsequently. The Preamble of the Kyoto Protocol declares the Parties to the Protocol as being guided by article 3 FCCC.

[56] FCCC article 4 (2)(f) provides that the list of States Parties contained in Annex I is open to amendment by the COP.

of such protection efforts, but accountability of each State Party lies with the States Parties organised within the Conference of the Parties (COP). Each State Party is responsible for cooperative climate protection, both through collectively reflecting on its governance and through the readiness to undertake individual measures. Differentiated emissions, respective capabilities and equity mean that responsibility for protective measures should differentiate between developing and developed States Parties.[57]

Developed States Parties thus have heightened or leadership responsibility to bring about this framework through their continuous readiness to take the necessary measures on the basis of legally binding obligations. The practice of States Parties shows, through the FCCC itself and then through the subsequent supplementing agreements, largely comporting with this matrix, that they have collectively been reflecting on a regime of climate protection (a), which corresponds with the substantive standards inherent in the formula of common but differentiated responsibilities (b).

a. The Common Responsibility of Each State Party: Reflective Responsibility

The responsibility to be engaged in reflecting on climate protection as a cooperative enterprise is common to all Parties, regardless of their status as enshrined under the FCCC or any Protocol to it. Article 2 FCCC establishes how States Parties to the Convention intend to exercise their reflective responsibility. Article 2 provides that the Convention's ultimate objective of stabilising "greenhouse gas concentrations in the atmosphere at a level that would prevent dangerous anthropogenic interference with the climate system" will be achieved through the adoption of "this Convention and any related legal instruments that the Conference of the Parties may adopt." Climate protection, then, is conceived of as a matter of progressively developing instruments that are legally binding or that have at least an equivalent effect.

---

[57] See Proceedings of the 96th Annual Mtg of the American Society of International Law, "Common but Differentiated Responsibility", *ASIL Proceedings* 96 (2002), 358 et seq. (358) (remarks of C.C. Joyner) (industrialised countries are responsible for the majority of these emissions, and thus the FCCC excludes developing countries from binding emissions reductions requirements).

The FCCC itself is designed as framework convention. As such, it sets out broad principles for the protection of the global climate but not firm legal commitments. These are to be set out in subsequent Protocols to the Convention (article 17 FCCC). Since it is for the COP to adopt any such supplemental instruments, each state must be involved in the design of the instruments and each state is accountable for that design as well as its readiness to adopt the instrument.

States have adhered to and refined this concept through successive stages of designing instruments. The Parties to the FCCC supplemented it with the Kyoto Protocol.[58] This treaty sets forth firm, quantified and timetabled emissions reduction commitments for Annex I States Parties. The Kyoto Protocol also contains a conceptual innovation in providing for economically efficient climate change protection through the Protocol's flexibility mechanisms.[59] There is compliance control through administrative means elaborated by legislative-type decisions of the COP serving as the meeting of the Parties. The Kyoto Protocol's commitments will expire in 2012. States Parties to the FCCC have identified the need for agreeing on a successor regime in the Bali Plan of Action adopted in 2007.[60] The non-binding Bali Plan of Action sets forth substantive parameters for the future regime, namely in that it provides for mitigation and adaptation measures, the continuation of the flexibility mechanisms and a special fund for the support of climate protection projects in developing countries.[61] It also institutes two open-ended negotiating processes under the FCCC and under the Kyoto Protocol,[62] with the participation of all states.[63] These processes

---

[58] Kyoto Protocol to the United Nations Framework Convention on Climate Change, UNTS Vol. 2303 No. 30822 (hereinafter Kyoto Protocol).

[59] See I.H. Rowlands, "Atmosphere and Outer Space", in: D. Bodansky/ J. Brunnée/ E. Hey (eds), *Oxford Handbook of International Environmental Law*, 2006, 315 et seq. (330-331) (hereinafter Handbook).

[60] Conference of the Parties to the United Nations Framework Convention on Climate Change, 13th Sess., Bali, 3-15 December 2007, Decision 1/CP.13, Bali Action Plan, Doc. FCCC/CP/2007/6/Add.1 of 14 March 2008) (hereinafter Bali Action Plan).

[61] For industrialised states, the Bali Action Plan contemplates "[n]ationally appropriate mitigation commitments or actions, including quantified emission limitation and reduction objectives, ..." whereas for developing countries it envisages only "[n]ationally appropriate mitigation actions ....", Bali Action Plan, see note 60, para. 1(b)(i)-(ii).

[62] The AWG-LCA held its first session in March 2008, United Nations Framework Convention on Climate Change Ad Hoc Working Group on

led first to the political compromise of the so-called Copenhagen Accord that States Parties "took note of"[64] which was then the basis for the agreement reached at the meeting of the COP in Cancun.[65] The Cancun COP adopted a decision that sets forth the parameters of the post-Kyoto regime.[66] There will be mitigation and adaptation and there will be a green fund. Annex I Parties are expected to communicate their intended emissions reduction commitments for the period after 2012 on an individual basis to the COP through its Subsidiary Body on Scientific and Technological Advice (SBSTA). Non-Annex I Parties undertake to communicate their Nationally Appropriate Mitigation Action to the COP. Communications are formally recognised by the COP. These communications to the COP are not legally binding. But something equivalent is being achieved. Because communications are being made to the COP as the representative "supreme" body of the FCCC, each State Party is thereby recognising that the COP can hold it accountable for its targets. This is political accountability in the sense that the instance to which accountability lies can take political sanctions to express its sentiment as to whether negotiating standards of good faith have been fulfilled. The complementary decision adopted by the COP serving as the meeting of the Parties for the Kyoto-Protocol provides this. As a result of the Cancun Accord there is a subtle change in the structure of commitments that now resemble the individually negotiated and agreed schedules of commitments by means of which WTO

Long-Term Cooperative Action under the Convention, First Sess., Bangkok, 1 March - 8 April 2008. For documentation see <http://unfccc.int/meetings>.

[63] Views Regarding the Work Programme of the Ad Hoc Working Group on Long-Term Cooperative Action under the Convention, Doc. FCCC/AWGLCA/2008/MISC.1 of 3 March 2008, see under <http://unfccc.int>. See J. Brunnée, "From BALI to Copenhagen: Towards a Shared Vision for a Post-2012 Climate Regime?", *Maryland Journal of International Law* 25 (2010), 86 et seq.

[64] Conference of the Parties to the United Nations Framework Convention on Climate Change, 15th Sess., 7-18 December 2009, Copenhagen, Draft Decision/CP 15; Proposal by the President, Copenhagen Accord (hereinafter Copenhagen Accord), Doc. FCCC/CP/2009/L.7 of 18 December 2009, see under <http://unfccc.int>.

[65] See D. Bodansky, "The Copenhagen Climate Change Conference: A Post-mortem", *AJIL* 104 (2010), 230 et seq.; L. Rajamani, "The Making and Unmaking of the Copenhagen Accord", *ICLQ* 59 (2010), 824 et seq.

[66] L. Rajamani, "The Cancun Climate Agreements: Reading the Text, Subtext and Tea Leaves", *ICLQ* 60 (2011), 499 et seq.

Member States bind their tariffs and other obstacles to trade in goods or services.

Subsequent state practice has thus confirmed the three essential elements of article 2 FCCC: the establishment of a process of negotiating instruments that have legal or equivalent effect, the continuing involvement of each State Party in it, and the role of the COP as accountability addressee of each State Party. Through their practice States Parties have not only confirmed but further elaborated the original conception set out in article 2 FCCC. Evidence of that is the move from state group based greenhouse gas reduction commitments in the Kyoto-Protocol to the individual communications foreseen in the Cancun decisions. Reflective responsibility has thus resulted in states renouncing the hitherto established one-off approach of elaborating a treaty and then applying it. Instead law-making on the climate has become an iterative process passing through characteristic stages. This process has aptly been labelled a "convention-cum-protocol approach."[67] The first stage is a multilateral law-making treaty in the form of a framework convention, which sets out broad principles and objectives. Subsequently, States Parties are to be guided by these objectives and principles in defining more specific obligations. States' law-development responsibility then translates into a responsibility to respect the law agreed at relevant intervals. But the underlying law-development responsibilities remain active and come to the fore again at the end of the period of time covered by the treaty. Discharge of their continuous reflective responsibility then requires states to enter into negotiations with a view to drawing up a successor instrument. All States Parties are responsible for entering into and conducting negotiations through the multilateral process under the FCCC. That does not exclude the raising of climate change matters in other near-fora, but decision-making ought to be left to the inclusive UN process. Negotiations must be conducted in good faith, which, as a minimum, requires that constructive efforts must be undertaken to develop negotiating positions on the issues that each state considers critical.[68] Reflective responsibility implies that

---

[67] P. Sand, "The Evolution of International Environmental Law", in: Handbook, see note 59, 29, 35 et seq.; D. Bodansky, "The Framework Convention/Protocol Approach", in: *Framework Convention on Tobacco Control Technical Briefing Services*, 1999.

[68] The ICJ first devised an obligation to negotiate in good faith in the North Sea Continental Shelf cases, ICJ Reports 1969, 3 et seq. (para. 85). Case concerning Application of the International Convention on the Elimination of All Forms of Racial Discrimination (Georgia v. Russian Federa-

States Parties remain ready to adapt or modify regulatory techniques if need be.

b. Differentiated Responsibilities of States Parties: Standards for Outcomes

As shown above, already Rio Principle No. 7 makes clear that common but differentiated responsibilities also enunciate substantive standards as to effectiveness and burden-sharing that the climate protection regime has to comply with. Article 2 FCCC establishes a negotiating responsibility for all States Parties. The outcome of that negotiated process is only vaguely determined, i.e. the human induced temperature rise must remain manageable. In addition, it must reflect regard for the scientific consensus on the underlying threats to the global commons.[69] The critical standard is the differentiated responsibilities which must reflect the differentiated capacities for contribution to climate change and for the fight against it. Under article 3 (1) FCCC, differentiation of the burden to be shouldered by states for the protection of the climate needs to take place on the basis of responsibility understood as causation[70] and capacities or financial resources to take remedial action. To this has been added the explicit consideration of equity, which relates to the allocation of climate protection efforts between developed and developing states.[71] This results in a rough dividing line between develop-

---

tion), Judgment of 1 April 2011, paras 122-184, available at <http://www.icj-cij.org>, has clarified that good faith requires a state, as a minimum, transparently to raise the issues it considers important. The reasoning of the Court in the case applied to settling disputes under a convention peacefully through negotiations prior to its seisin, but may be taken to reflect the structure of any good faith obligation to negotiate in international law.

[69] The normative basis is article 1 (2) FCCC which establishes the causal link between anthropogenic emissions and the resulting climate change. This science based analysis of the problem leads to informed solutions based on or at least informed by science. See R.K. Pachauri et al. (eds), *Climate Change, 2007: Synthesis Report*, 66-67, Intergovernmental Panel on Climate Change, 2007, available at <http://www.ipcc.ch>

[70] See National Responsibility, see note 1, 83-90 (discussing the role of establishing causation for identifying responsibility for a given situation – outcome responsibility – as opposed to assigning responsibility for dealing with it – remedial responsibility).

[71] This is neither distributive nor corrective justice. But see Posner/ Sunstein, see note 49, 1583, 1591.

ing and developed countries. The attribution of primary ("leadership") responsibility to developed States Parties yields their accountability not just for internal mitigation and adaptation action as internationally agreed but also for support for emission reduction efforts in developing States Parties. The assumption underlying differential or secondary responsibility of developing countries is that they lack relevant capacity both in respect of emitting greenhouse gases and in respect of mitigating any such emissions. It is for this critical assumption that there are no quantitative emission reduction obligations imposed on them. This would point to a duty for each State Party to evaluate, in good faith, on which side of the dividing line between developing and developed states it falls at the precise moment of negotiations.

Practice of states conforms to this principle. Article 3 (1) FCCC enshrines the common but differentiated responsibilities for climate change, and article 4 FCCC introduces distinct categories of States Parties as Annex I and non-Annex I countries. Higher standards of conduct are explicitly set for Annex I (developed) states, both in the FCCC and the Kyoto Protocol supplementing it. The Kyoto Protocol implements the idea of differentiated responsibility by establishing timetabled and quantified emission reduction commitments for Annex I States Parties only. States Parties other than Annex I countries have a much diminished but still relevant complementary responsibility to play in the development and operation of viable climate change. That categorisation as an Annex I or non-Annex I State Party at the time of the adoption of the FCCC is a proxy as the underlying principle of capability only is reflected in that the Annexes are open to amendment by the COP.[72] More forcefully, the Bali Plan uses the more flexible categories of developed and developing states[73] and the Cancun decisions allow the underlying rationale to play out even more forcefully by pro-

---

[72] See Conference of the Parties to the United Nations Framework Convention on Climate Change, Request from a Group of Countries of Central Asia and the Caucasus, Albania and Moldova regarding their Status under the Convention, Decision 35/CP.7, Doc. FCCC/CP/2001/13/Add.4 of 21 January 2002, page 25.

[73] Bali Action Plan, see note 60, para. 1 (b)(i)-(ii); see Brunnée, see note 63, 101; C. Spence et al., "Great Expectations: Understanding Bali and the Climate Change Negotiation Process", *RECIEL* 17 (2008), 142 et seq. (150).

viding for individual communications from all developing states as well.[74]

3. The Rio Declaration and the Law of the Sea

Rio Principle No. 7 allows for context-specific implementation as long as the main conceptual planks of the principle are maintained. The implementation of the principle of common but differentiated responsibilities in the Rio-spawned regime on the global climate has been discussed above. This regime relies on multilateral law-making treaties. The global commons of the oceans are also subject to a multilateral law-making treaty in the form of the 1982 UN Convention on the Law of the Sea.[75] While the LOS Convention predates the Rio Declaration, the International Tribunal for the Law of the Sea has not hesitated to refer to the Rio Declaration as a conceptual starting point for understanding the Convention.[76] The Convention can therefore be considered as an instantiation of the Rio Declaration principles and common but differentiated responsibilities.[77] Referred to as a "constitution for the oceans"[78] in the sense that it comprehensively covers all ocean uses, the Convention instantiates its vision of common but differentiated responsibilities of States Parties in particular in the regulation of the exploration and exploitation of the mineral resources of the sea-bed per Part

---

[74] On the evidence of the communications received so far there is a differentiation within the group of Non-Annex I Parties between the more and the less developed states. China, in particular, has communicated a substantial policy commitment. See Subsidiary Body for Scientific and Technological Advice, Compilation of Economy-Wide Emission Reduction Targets to be Implemented by Parties included in Annex I to the Convention, Doc. FCCC/SB/2011/INF.1 of 10 March 2011.

[75] United Nations Convention on the Law of the Sea, UNTS Vol. 1834 No. 31363 (hereinafter UNCLOS or LOS Convention).

[76] Responsibilities Opinion, see note 12, para. 125.

[77] See C.D. Stone, "Common but Differentiated Responsibilities in International Law", *AJIL* 98 (2004), 276 et seq. (276) speaking of "close cognates" to common but differentiated responsibilities.

[78] T. Koh, *The Law of the Sea: Official Text of the UN Convention on the Law of the Sea*, 1983, xxxiii.

XI UNLCOS and the 1994 Implementation Agreement relating to Part XI UNCLOS.[79] [80]

Such mining activity of potentially high economic interest would by necessity implicate the sensitive marine environment of the deep sea. The LOS Convention contains a fundamental principle of the protection of the marine environment.[81] In order to protect the marine environment of the deep sea-bed the Convention establishes "responsibilities" for states when engaging in mining. Responsibility thus appears as a legal term in several provisions of Part XI UNCLOS. The structure of these provisions has been clarified by the Sea-bed Disputes Chamber of the International Tribunal for the Law of the Sea in its Responsibilities Advisory Opinion.[82] The Chamber found that these provisions must be seen as enshrining primary obligations for states in the interest of the protection of the marine environment, not secondary obligations within the meaning of the law of state responsibility.[83] States are under direct obligations for their own conduct. They also have indirect obligations for the conduct of private parties (undertakings) wishing to explore or exploit the area whereby states need not just to "sponsor" and thus control the private parties but also have the obligation to take appropriate legislative action in the national legal orders to control private action. The obligation involved is substantively a due diligence obligation in the sense that there is no prescribed or finite measure to be taken but that standards depend on the circumstances and are subject to evolution.[84] It includes everything that is comprised by the direct obligations a state is under, namely the implementation of the precautionary ap-

---

[79] Agreement Relating to the Implementation of Part XI of the United Nations Convention on the Law of the Sea of 10 December 1982, UNTS Vol. 1836 No. 31364.

[80] See E. Posner/ A.O. Sykes, "Economic Foundations of the Law of the Sea", *AJIL* 114 (2010), 569 et seq. (587-588) (summary of the state of the law resulting from Part XI UNCLOS and the 1994 Implementation Agreement).

[81] "… the duty to cooperate is a fundamental principle in the prevention of pollution of the marine environment", Case No. 10, The Mox Plant Case (Ireland v. United Kingdom), Provisional Measures, para. 82, ITLOS 3 December 2001; Case Concerning Land Reclamation by Singapore in and around the Straits of Johor (Malaysia v. Singapore), Provisional Measures, para. 92, ITLOS 8 October 2003.

[82] Responsibilities Opinion, see note 12.

[83] Responsibilities Opinion, ibid., paras 64-71, 107-116.

[84] Responsibilities Opinion, ibid., paras 117-120.

proach and best environmental practices.[85] These direct and indirect obligations are incumbent on *all* states – both developed and developing – that choose to engage in sponsoring exploration and exploitation of the mineral resources of the deep sea-bed to the same degree. They are imposed in the interest of mankind.[86] Differential treatment of developing countries for the protection of the marine environment is indeed only possible to a very limited extent as equality of treatment for all states sponsoring activities in the area is essential to prevent regulatory arbitrage ("sponsor states of convenience") being harmful to the protection of the environment of the deep sea. But developing states receive special access rights to the mining activities that the International Sea-bed Authority itself will be undertaking for the benefit of mankind.[87] Also, developed states should support developing states through provision of training.[88]

The regime for the Area enshrined in Part XI UNCLOS and the 1994 Implementation Agreement thus concretises common but differentiated responsibilities of States Parties for the protection of the marine environment of the deep sea-bed. Each state engaging in mining in the Area is assigned with the responsibility to protect the marine environment. In remarkable distinction from the climate change regime, primary environmental protection obligations of states are not differentiated in any significant measure. Rather developed and developing states are under more or less the same stringent obligations, and there is the same accountability of both groups of states to the International Sea-bed Authority. Non-differentiation in respect of the environmental protection objective of sustainable development can, however, be squared with the underlying rationale of common but differentiated responsibilities: Differentiated responsibilities are attributed on the basis of different contributions of developed and developing states to environmental degradation and different capacities of both groups of states to halt environmental degradation in the future. Neither rationale is applicable in the context of the deep sea-bed mining regime. There is no differentiation in the responsibilities of states for the protection of the

---

[85] Responsibilities Opinion, ibid., paras 123, 125-137.
[86] Responsibilities Opinion, ibid., para. 158. Para. 180 clarifies that the beneficiary of the protection of the marine environment is "mankind" as much as it is the beneficiary of the mining activities carried out in the Area (article 140 UNCLOS).
[87] Responsibilities Opinion, ibid., para. 157.
[88] Responsibilities Opinion, ibid., para. 163.

environment because deep sea-bed mineral exploitation is in fact an activity that has no differential impact depending on who is undertaking it.

The rationale of different capacities creating differentiated obligations plays out, however, in that developed states have to assist developing states through training and other means to meet their marine environmental protection requirements. Common but differentiated responsibilities also contain the seeds for a strong consideration of equity. In the context of the deep sea-bed mineral exploitation, equity translates into participation in its economic benefits. This is then realised through the international mechanism of the International Sea-bed Authority.

4. Conclusions

Critical parts of the law of sustainable development are built around the institution of responsibility. Principle No. 7 of the Rio Declaration is the foundational text. The foundational document is then implemented in the diverse issue-areas such as climate and the deep sea-bed. Across the variations, the core idea of Principle No. 7 is, however, borne out in both areas:[89] each state bears reflective responsibility for the best collective protective efforts, and is accountable for its own efforts. Substantive obligations can then vary depending on the status of each State Party as developed or developing, to the extent that this is compatible with the objective of protecting the global environmental good in the interest of humanity.

IV. Responsibility for the Global Economy

Despite the framework of international financial standards developed since the end of the Bretton Woods system, in 2008 and 2009 the world

---

[89] J. Brunnée/ S. Toope, *Legitimacy and Legality in International Law*, 2010, 151 et seq. offer an alternative account of how the principle of common but differentiated responsibilities acquires social reality in international law. It is a "norm" to the extent that it is supported by resilient shared understandings of relevant actors and meets specified criteria of legality, generality, promulgation, non-retroactivity, non-contradiction, constancy and predictability.

was engulfed in the worst economic and financial crisis since the 1930s, prompting a complete overhaul of the international financial architecture.[90] The new architecture has been grounded in responsibility with the Washington Declaration of the Group of Twenty as its foundational text.

1. Responsibility in the G20 Washington Declaration

The process of designing a new international financial architecture has been using the informal intergovernmental forum of the Group of Twenty (G20),[91] which was originally conceived as a loose grouping bringing together the finance ministers and central bank governors of a number of leading industrialised and critical emerging economies which met for the first time in 1999.[92] Yet in November 2008, the G20 met at the level of Heads of State or Government in Washington ("Leaders' Summit"), producing the Washington Declaration and Plan of Action.[93] While the Washington Declaration does not expressly employ the ter-

---

[90] See M. Giovanoli, "The International Financial Architecture", in: M. Giovanoli/ D. Devos (eds), *International Monetary and Financial Law*, 2010, 1.01.

[91] See A.S. Alexandroff/ J. Kirton, "The 'Great' Recession and the Emergence of the G-20 Leaders' Summit", in: A.S. Alexandroff/ A.F. Cooper (eds), *Rising States, Rising Institutions: Challenges For Global Governance*, 2010, 193 et seq.; A.F. Cooper, "The G20 as an Improvised Crisis Committee and/or a Contested 'Steering Committee' for the World", *Int'l Aff.* 86 (2010), 741 et seq. (G20 as a "steering committee" or a "crisis committee" for regulatory deliverables).

[92] Initially the G20 started out as the G22 and was formed for a one-time meeting. It briefly became the G33 and finally upon the recommendation of the G7 finance ministers became the G20. See P.I. Hajnal, "The G8 System and the G20: Evolution, Role and Documentation", 2007, 151 et seq. Members of the G20 are Argentina, Australia, Brazil, Canada, China, France, Germany, India, Indonesia, Italy, Japan, Mexico, Russia, Saudi Arabia, South Africa, Korea, Turkey, United Kingdom, United States, and the European Union. Spain and the Netherlands have attended as observers, as have ASEAN, the Financial Stability Board, IMF, the New Partnership for Africa's Development (NEPAD), the United Nations, the IBRD and the WTO.

[93] *Declaration of the Summit on Financial Markets and the World Economy*, of 15 November 2008, available at <www.g20.org/Documents> (hereinafter Washington Declaration).

minology of responsibility, it contains an implicit acknowledgement of responsibility by the G20 states. This implicit acknowledgement lies in the Declaration identifying past government actions and omissions as causative of the crisis of the financial markets and in identifying the need to take adequate action to prevent a recurrence of the crisis.[94] The Declaration thereby puts in place the critical elements for shaping its approach to financial market regulation as a matter of responsibility. The Declaration identifies the public good of a functioning global financial market and more widely of a return to growth for the international economy. Consequences for that public good are attributed to action taken by each participating state.[95] Accountability of each of the participating states is established. The G20 states claim not to act (only) in their own interest but rather as stewards of the global financial markets and more widely the global economy.[96] The Washington Declaration thereby expresses that the intended beneficiary of the thus assumed responsibility are not just the G20 states themselves but the international community as a whole. In 2010, the Pittsburgh Leaders' statement then made explicit what the Washington Declaration had implied: the G20 states self-assign themselves with responsibility for the global economy.[97] The non-binding Washington Declaration thus puts the idea of responsibility at the centre of the cooperative construction of a new global financial architecture. The non-binding Declaration has initiated a concretising law-making process on the regulation of financial markets that combines the production of standards at the international level with their implementation at the national level.

---

[94] See Washington Declaration, ibid., paras 3-7.
[95] See Washington Declaration, ibid., para. 2.
[96] See Washington Declaration, ibid., para. 1.
[97] *Leaders' Statement: The Pittsburgh Summit of 24-25 September 2009. The Framework for Strong, Sustainable and Balanced Growth*, Annex I, paras 1-4: "The Framework for Strong, Sustainable and Balanced Growth we launched in Pittsburgh is the means to achieving our shared objectives. *G-20 members have a responsibility to the community of nations to assure the overall health of the global economy*. We are committed to assess the collective consistency of our policy actions and to strengthen our policy frameworks in order to meet our common objectives. Through our collective policy action, we will ensure growth is sustained, more balanced, shared across all countries and regions of the world, and consistent with our development goals." (emphasis added), (hereinafter Pittsburgh Leaders' Statement) <http://www.g20.org/Documents>.

What follows is an analysis of the emerging oversight of a globally integrated financial regime and the way it concretises the idea of responsibility for the G20 states (2) and for other states (3).

2. Designing an Oversight Regime for the Global Financial Markets

The design by the G20 states of a regulatory regime for the global financial markets is based on attribution of specific responsibilities to all relevant actors: the states, national regulators, and private international financial institutions.

The states themselves represented by their leaders assume the responsibility to reflect on the design of the regime for the global financial markets. Through the Washington Declaration, the G20 states had started to sketch the future governance of the financial markets. In line with *continuous reflective* responsibility, states have kept the development of the G20 as the core governance body under close review since the initial meeting in Washington. Since the initial meeting there has been a rapid succession of follow-up meetings of the G20 at the level of Heads of State or Government.[98] The "summit declaration" or "leaders' statement" issued by the G20 at the issue of each meeting mark the progress of consensus on the organisation, the principles, the instruments, and the standards that should govern the cooperative enterprise, finally declaring the G20 the premier forum for their international economic cooperation.[99] Exercise of their reflective responsibility in this way by states has resulted in the design from scratch of a specific forum for cooperation that does not conform to existing templates. Theirs is a horizontal treaty-less mechanism that allows for political coordination

---

[98] A second meeting took place in London in the spring of 2009, a third meeting was held in September 2009 in Pittsburgh, a fourth in June 2010 in Toronto, a fifth in Seoul in November 2010, and a sixth in Cannes in November 2011. Annual meetings are envisaged thereafter. More regular meetings still are being held at the level of the G20 finance ministers to implement the agreements reached by the principals and to prepare their next meeting.

[99] Pittsburgh Leaders' Statement, see note 97, preambular para. 19. The *Toronto Summit Declaration of 26-27 June 2010*, para. 1, states accordingly: "In Toronto, we held our first Summit of the G-20 in its new capacity as the premier forum for our international economic cooperation", <http://www.g20.org/Documents> (hereinafter Toronto Summit Declaration).

and management but also rule-making.[100] Through it, states are effectively accountable for their domestic financial and economic action and record of compliance with agreed policies to the international community as organised in the G20.[101] Action by states through the G20 must conform to standards and can be assessed against it. The Washington Declaration and subsequent summit declarations specify that regulatory action of the G20 will have to accord to the standards of sound regulation, transparency, inclusiveness, and accountability in the sense of enforceability,[102] and similar standards will also govern the reform of the international financial institutions[103] and the organisation of the forum of the G20 itself. A standard of differentiated responsibilities does not feature. This reflects the assumption that effective regulation of the

---

[100] As opposed to a vertical approach involving an international organisation such as the IMF to head the process or a Meeting of Parties to an international treaty. See generally on government networks and their norm-generating effects A.M. Slaughter, *A New World Order*, 2004. For the use of Meetings of Parties for international lawmaking in a range of sectors see V. Röben, "Conference (Meetings) of States Parties", in: R. Wolfrum (ed.), *Max Planck Encyclopedia of Public International Law*, 2012, Vol. I, 605 et seq.

[101] Under the Mutual Assessment Process (MAP) the G20 states can collectively evaluate each member's record of compliance with previously agreed policies and regulatory standards, Toronto Summit Declaration, see note 99, para. 9; see IMF, *Factsheet: The G-20 Mutual Assessment Process*, 11 November 2010 <http://www.imf.org/external/np/exr/facts>. At the London Summit, the G20 asked the WTO along with UNCTAD and the OECD to "monitor and report publicly on G20 adherence to their undertakings on resisting protectionism and promoting global trade and investment", *The London Summit April 2009, The Global Plan for Recovery and Reform*, para. 20, <http://www.g20.org/Documents> (hereinafter London Leaders' Statement); Doc. WTO/OECD/UNCTAD, *Report on G20 Trade and Investment Measures September 2009 to February 2010 of 8 March 2010*, <http://www.unctad.org/en/docs>, and related Pittsburgh Leaders' Statement, see note 97, para. 48. International accountability of each state is complemented by its national responsibility, see R.M. Nelson, "The G-20 and International Economic Cooperation: Background and Implications for Congress", *Congress Research Service* 1 (2010), R40977, <fas.org/sgp/crs/row/R40977.pdf.>

[102] Washington Declaration, see note 93, para. 9; Pittsburgh Leaders' Statement, see note 97, para. 5.

[103] London Leaders' Statement, see note 101, para. 20.

global financial markets requires uniformity to avoid regulatory arbitrage.[104]

Through the G20, states have contrived to set up machinery to produce policy coordination as well as financial market regulation. Management capacity has been complemented by rule-making capacity.[105] The machinery links political levels of decision-makers with expert-staffed levels of decision-making, trusted with proposing and implementing political decisions. At their summit meetings, leaders task finance ministers to come up with concrete proposals at the follow-up meeting. These are followed up by meetings of senior civil servants/regulators to further implement the political decisions into technical arrangements through standard-setting bodies susceptible of being applied by national authorities. Critically, regulators are addressed as agents having responsibilities of their own for cooperatively reaching certain regulatory outcomes.[106] Their responsibility corresponds to their competence since financial regulation is still fully under the national competence of states with the exception of the European Union. Regulators are accountable to the G20 and receive guidance on that basis. The central forum for this cooperation is the Financial Stability Board (FSB) set up by the G20.[107] The FSB is made up of finance ministries and a regulator,[108] and its task is to implement the decisions taken

---

[104] However, equity considerations underlie the G20-Declaration on Delivering Resources through the International Financial Institutions, providing for a massive increase of financial resources for the IMF and various multilateral development banks, to meet the needs of emerging and developing countries, London 2 April 2009 <http://www.g20.org/Documents>.

[105] For an early account see D. Zaring, "International Law by Other Means: The Twilight Existence of International Financial Regulatory Organizations", *Tex. Int'l L. J.* 33 (1998), 281 et seq.

[106] Washington Declaration, see note 93, para. 8.

[107] Established at the London Leaders' Summit of the G20, see note 101, para. 15. The FSB was preceded by the Financial Stability Forum which was itself preceded by the Joint Forum on Financial Conglomerates, see Slaughter, see note 100, 135. The FSB has adopted a non-binding Charter to enhance its transparency. Cf. FSB Charter, article 1: "The Financial Stability Board (FSB) is established to coordinate at the international level the work of national financial authorities and international standard setting bodies (SSBs) in order to develop and promote the implementation of effective regulatory, supervisory and other financial sector policies ... "

[108] FSB Charter, article 4: "(1) The following bodies are eligible to be a Member: (a) National and regional authorities responsible for maintaining financial stability, namely ministries of finance, central banks, supervisory and

at the political level within its remit. This cyclical process will bring about, at the international level, internationally agreed and backed non-binding standards for regulation. These standards will actually be translated into binding national law. While the FSB is to set new standards, the organisationally powerful IMF would then monitor and enforce compliance with them,[109] even though the FSB seems to increasingly assume this compliance control function itself.[110] Standards may be agreed upon within the FSB itself or in various standard-setting bodies which informally report to the FSB. For instance, under the new FSB standards for compensation, supervisors will require that 40 to 60 per cent of all senior bankers' bonuses come in the form of deferred compensation over time.[111] At the London Summit the G20 decided to reduce reliance on credit rating agencies, and the FSB responded to this G20 goal with Principles for Reducing Reliance on CRA (Credit Rating Agency) Ratings,[112] which were endorsed at the Seoul Summit.[113] In addition to the FSB, the Basel Committee on Banking Supervision (BCBS) is an important standard-setting body and venue for regulators' cooperation.[114] The attribution of own responsibility through the G20 has fed into the process of national banking supervisors agreeing within

---

regulatory authorities; (b) International financial institutions; and (c) International standard setting, regulatory, supervisory and central bank bodies." For the membership of the FSB <http://www.financialstabilityboard.org>.

[109] Washington Declaration, see note 93.

[110] There is a toolbox including peer review under the FSB's Framework for Strengthening Adherence to International Standards of 9 January 2010, <http://www.financialstabilityboard.org>. The FSB has completed its first peer review on compensation, *Thematic Review on Compensation, Peer Review Report, March 2010* <http://www.financialstabilityboard.org>. The results feed into the regular progress reports on actions taken since the last summit prepared by the rotating G20 chair.

[111] The FSB Principles for Sound Compensation Practices and their Implementation Standards, 2 April 2009, were endorsed by the Pittsburgh Leaders' Statement, see note 97, para. 17. See L.A. Bebchuk/ J.M. Fried, "Paying For Long-Term Performance", *University of Pennsylvania Law Review* 158 (2010), 1915 et seq. (1919).

[112] FSB, Principles for Reducing Reliance on Credit Rating Agency (CRA) Ratings 27 October 2010, <http://www.financialstabilityboard.org>.

[113] Leaders' Declaration, *The G20 Seoul Summit*, 11-12 November 2010, para. 37 (hereinafter Seoul Leaders' Declaration).

[114] Supported by the BIS, the BCBS "generates global public goods of information and expertise" in the area of banking supervision. It drafts standards relating to capital adequacy requirements of banks.

the BCBS on the critical common standards for the equity reserves that banks need to hold.[115] Consensus was first reached by the finance ministers on capital requirements for banks (Basel III), which were then further implemented by the Basel Committee.[116] These "Basel standards" are not binding *per se*, but each regulator's state is in turn responsible for implementing them internally in binding law.[117] The G20 also makes use of the International Organization of Securities Commissions (IOSCO), a network of securities' regulators, which has come up with the May 2010 Principles Regarding Cross-border Supervisory Cooperation.[118]

While these processes use the channels of regulatory rule-making by public authorities, the Washington Declaration enters uncharted territory by assigning private actors with direct responsibility for the international financial markets.[119] The position of these private parties can be analysed through the responsibility prism. They are thus designated as international moral agents that have to account for their handling of financial risks. They are deemed internationally accountable against standards being set by the G20. In subsequent steps, the G20 states

---

[115] In September 2010, the BCBS announced the international regulatory framework for banks (Basel III), which established a 7 per cent minimum common equity requirement as well as an additional counter-cyclical buffer including up to 2.5 per cent of risk-weighted assets (Basel III: A Global Regulatory Framework for more resilient Banks and Banking Systems of 16 December 2010, <http://www.bis.orgl>). The Leaders Statement of the Seoul Summit, 11-12 November 2010, endorsed the Basel III framework.

[116] Progress Report on the Actions of the London and Washington G20 Summits, 48, 5 September 2009.

[117] Progress in the Implementation of the G20 Recommendations for Strengthening Financial Stability, FSB of 15 February 2011, <http://www.financialstabilityboard.org> "All members will now put in place the necessary regulations and/or legislation to implement the Basel III framework on 1 January 2013, such that it can be fully phased in by 1 January 2019." The Enhancements to the Basel II framework, BCBS of 14 July 2009, <www.bis.org>, were implemented by EU Directive 2009/111/EC, amending the "Basel II" or "CRD" Directive (2006/48/EC), 2009 OJ 17/9.

[118] IOSCO, *Principles Regarding Cross-border Supervisory Cooperation*, <http://www.iosco.org>.

[119] Washington Declaration, see note 93, para. 3. This entails "enhancing required disclosure on complex financial products and ensuring complete and accurate disclosure by firms of their financial conditions. Incentives should be aligned to avoid excessive risk-taking."

have specified the category of private actors that bear this responsibility. They have created the category of Systemically Important Financial Institutions (SIFIs). SIFIs will be made subject to regulation developed by the FSB,[120] and globally systemic firms (G-SIFIs) will be made the subject of an individualised process of supervision through international supervisory colleges.[121]

3. The G20 and the Responsibility of Third States

The Washington Declaration constitutes an instance of self-attributed responsibilities by the states represented in the G20. But the London Leaders' Statement also innovates by assigning responsibility for global financial markets to third states.[122] By acting through the G20 rather than a more formal international organisation or a treaty with a meeting of parties, states had established a principle of lightly institutionalised harmonisation of national legislation with adherence to certain substantive standards. Practice of the G20 states conforms and fleshes out this conceptualisation. That is also true for assigning non-traditional actors with international responsibility. While the G20 comprises a large enough portion of the world's economy for laying down rules that will affect much of the global economy and have a significant compliance pull, a significant number of issues require action on the part of non-represented, third states. Off-shore tax havens figure prominently here. Such havens are sometimes under the remit of the G20 states, but there are also third states. These third states are assigned responsibility externally by the G20 states. The legitimating basis for this is the G20 claim to overall responsibility for the global economy, the beneficiary of which, in the last instance, is humanity, backed by the G20 representing a large share of the international economy. Concretisation of such third-state responsibility in binding law will still have to correspond with the applicable rules of the law of treaties, namely the *pacta tertiis*

---

[120] The Seoul Leaders' Declaration, see note 113, paras 30-31, 11-12 November 2010, endorsed the FSB's policy framework for reducing the moral hazard of systemically important financial institutions (SIFIs). See FSB, "Effective Resolution of Systemically Important Financial Institutions", Consultative Document of 19 July 2011, available under <http://www.financialstabilityboard.org>

[121] Seoul Leaders' Declaration, see note 113, para. 31. See already *Declaration on Strengthening the Financial System*, 2 April 2009.

[122] London Leaders' Summit, see note 101, para. 15.

rule.[123] States not represented at the G20 therefore have the right to decide whether to enter into any bilateral or multilateral agreement proposed to them. But their responsibility would mean that they are politically accountable for the position taken at the G20. In the event, bilateral treaties on tax issues have been entered into by all of the said third states.[124]

4. Conclusions

Responsibility forms the normative core both of the established field of sustainable development law and of the emerging regulation of the global financial markets and the global economy more broadly. Both areas follow the matrix of responsibility for matters of concern to the international community. An international public good is identified, every state is assigned reflective responsibility, a body is identified to which accountability lies, which has the power of sanctioning, and standards of accountability are determined – effectiveness, transparency, equity, differentiated obligations. Private parties and third states may also be assigned responsibilities.

In both areas, the matrix of international responsibility is being concretised through processes of law-making grounded in a foundational political document which first adopts the terminology of responsibility. As is the case with the Rio Declaration for sustainable development, the Washington Declaration of the G20 is a foundational document adopted by a representative body of states for the regulation of the financial markets. Each document then serves as reference point for a

---

[123] Article 34 Vienna Convention on the Law of Treaties, UNTS Vol. 1155 No. 18232.

[124] See OECD, Tax-Co-operation 2009 of 31 August 2009 with press release: "OECD-Assessment shows bank secrecy as a shield for tax evaders coming to an end." Several treaties have been concluded by the G20 members Germany, the United Kingdom and the United States on the basis of the OECD-model Agreement on Exchange of Information on Tax Matters, <http://www.oecd.org>, drafted by OECD Member States and non-OECD states through the Global Forum on Transparency and Exchange of Information. See in particular: United Kingdom-Liechtenstein (Tax Information Exchange Agreement, 8 December 2008); United Kingdom-Switzerland (Swiss Federal Department of Finance Press Release, 24 August 2011); Germany-Switzerland (Press Release, 10 August 2011); United States-Switzerland (Press Release, 19 June 2009).

law-making process that encompasses a range of instruments of traditional treaty law – as in sustainable development – and alternative law-making forms such as the regulatory processes pioneered in the regulation of the global financial markets.[125]

V. Responsibility for Peace and Stability within States

Sustainable development and regulation of the global economy are international goods in need of cooperative action by all or most states. But international responsibility also structures the governance of areas fully under the jurisdiction of each state, in other words: state-internal matters.

1. Responsibility in the 2005 World Summit Outcome

The 2005 World Summit Outcome[126] marks the Outcome of the UN World Summit held in 2005, that brought together all Member States represented at the level of Heads of State or Government.[127] The Outcome is a resolution of the UN General Assembly and thus technically distinguishable from the Rio Declaration adopted by UNCED and the Washington Declaration adopted by the G20. But the Outcome is functionally comparable to both the Rio and the Washington Declarations. Like those, the Outcome represents the political commitment of the participating states undertaken at the level of Heads of State or Government, expressing the intention of the international community to ground its future course of action in critical state-internal matters on

---

[125] On choice of instruments see generally J.H. Jackson, "International Economic Law in Times that are interesting", *JIEL* 3 (2000), 3 et seq., (8) ("treaties are often an awkward albeit necessary method of designing institutions needed in today's interdependent world, but they do not solve many problems"); C. Lipson, "Why are some International Agreements informal", *International Organizations* 45 (1991), 495 et seq., (537-538) (benefits of informal agreements *vis-à-vis* treaties).

[126] The 2005 World Summit Outcome, A/RES/60/1 of 16 September 2005 (hereinafter 2005 World Summit Outcome). See generally A.M. Slaughter, "Security, Solidarity, and Sovereignty: The Grand Themes of UN Reform", *AJIL* 99 (2005), 619 et seq.

[127] A/RES/59/291 of 15 April 2005.

the idea of responsibility.[128] The critical state-internal matters addressed are post-conflict peace-building, basic human security – the Responsibility to Protect –, and development.[129] In respect of responsibilities for these state-internal matters, the Outcome adopts a uniform approach which distinguishes primary and secondary responsibilities. Primary responsibility for the public goods of development, peace and stability, and basic human security is attributed to each state.[130] That implies its accountability to the international community. The international community acting through the United Nations has secondary responsibility that comprises a responsibility to guarantee and a responsibility to act preventively and responsively. This responsibilities-matrix of the Outcome has then been concretised mainly by subsequent action of the principal organs of the United Nations. The following discussion of peace-building will in particular focus on the standards of accountability for states (see below under 2.), while the discussion of the Responsibility to Protect will demonstrate the United Nations own responsibility to act which must in turn not undermine the primary responsibility of each state for its internal affairs (see below under 3.).

---

[128] General Assembly resolutions may be evidence of or result in customary international law but do not have legal effect as such, Military and Paramilitary Activities in and against Nicaragua (Nicaragua v. United States), ICJ Reports 1986, 14 et seq. (paras 187-190); Wall Opinion, see note 21, para. 87.

[129] The 2005 World Summit Outcome, see note 126, also covers a broad range of economic and social areas, including for instance a demand that the governance structure of the Bretton Woods institutions include more representation from developing countries and economies in transition. This demand has been taken up by the G20 with respect to "emerging and developing economies, including the poorest countries." Pittsburgh Leaders' Statement, see note 97, para. 20, which then led to the Articles of Agreement of the IMF being amended in 2010, not yet in effect.

[130] 2005 World Summit Outcome, see note 126, para. 22, "We reaffirm that each country must take primary responsibility for its own development and that the role of national policies and development strategies cannot be overemphasized in the achievement of sustainable development. We also recognize that national efforts should be complemented by supportive global programmes, measures and policies aimed at expanding the development opportunities of developing countries, while taking into account national conditions and ensuring respect for national ownership, strategies and sovereignty." For reasons of space, only post-conflict peace-building and the Responsibility to Protect will be discussed, leaving development to one side.

2. Post-conflict Peace-Building

The Outcome only sketches the approach to peace-building in post-conflict situations. It explicitly deals with the set up of a Peacebuilding Commission at the UN level,[131] but subsequent pronouncements of the UN Security Council confirm that each state is primarily responsible for its post-conflict peace-building.

a. Primary Responsibility of Each State Emerging from Conflict

The UN Security Council has re-emphasised in general terms that "the primary responsibility for peace-building lies with governments and relevant national actors, including civil society, in countries emerging from conflict."[132] Primary responsibility ensures national ownership of any peace-building processes.[133] Beyond peace-building after conflict, the Security Council has extended the reach of the principle to all instances in which internal peace and stability of a state is in question. This is demonstrated by the case of Cyprus. In respect of the ongoing division of the country, the Security Council has emphasised that "the responsibility for finding a solution to the internal conflict" lies primarily with the state (of Cyprus).[134] By the same token, this state is accountable to the international community pursuant to certain stan-

---

[131] 2005 World Summit Outcome, see note 126, para. 97, "Emphasizing the need for a coordinated, coherent and integrated approach to post-conflict peacebuilding and reconciliation with a view to achieving sustainable peace, recognizing the need for a dedicated institutional mechanism to address the special needs of countries emerging from conflict towards recovery, reintegration and reconstruction and to assist them in laying the foundation for sustainable development, and recognizing the vital role of the United Nations in that regard, we decide to establish a Peacebuilding Commission as an intergovernmental advisory body." See also Explanatory note on the Peacebuilding Commision, Secretary-General, Doc. A/59/2005/Add. 2.

[132] SC Presidential Statement, para. 2, Doc. S/PRST/2011/2; SC Presidential Statement, para. 4, Doc. S/PRST/ 2011/4.

[133] 2005 World Summit Outcome, see note 126, para. 5, refers to self-determination, and the reference to self-determination must be understood as constituting both the ground of the primary responsibility of each state and the limit to the possible role of the international community in prescribing standards for the conduct of state internal affairs.

[134] S/RES/1986 (2011) of 13 June 2011 preambular para. 3 "Echoing the Secretary-General's firm belief that the responsibility for finding a solution lies first and foremost with the Cypriots themselves ..."

dards, concerning, for instance, the conduct of negotiations.[135] The United Nation's role is to support these negotiations.[136]

b. The United Nations as Addressee of Accountability of States

By virtue of being the primarily responsible actor, each state is accountable for the consequences of its action for internal peace and stability. That accountability lies towards the United Nations. Within the United Nations, competence for post-conflict peace-building is asserted to lie with the Security Council by virtue of Article 24 UN Charter, with the Security Council interpreting the controlling term "international peace and security" to extend to achieving sustainable peace after a country emerges from conflict.[137] The vantage point from which the United Nations approach the internal organisation of a state is the impact that this organisation has on the state's internal stability, and, by ramification, international stability.[138] Demands are formulated to ensure that a state is stable and internally peaceful rather than become a failed state or a pariah state.[139] There is also growing understanding that representative state organs are essential to the successful development of developing states, and as such form the legitimate objective of strategic efforts of the international community.[140] As expressed in a number of recent

---

[135] Ibid., paras 1-10.

[136] Ibid., preambular para. 3 "... reaffirming the primary role of the United Nations in assisting the parties to bring the Cyprus conflict and division of the island to a comprehensive and durable settlement."

[137] SC Presidential Statement, Doc. S/PRST/2011/4 para. 1 "The Security Council reaffirms its primary responsibility under the Charter of the United Nations for the maintenance of international peace and security and its readiness to strive for sustainable peace in all situations under its consideration."

[138] Identified threats to global stability will justify and require concerted efforts of a legislative and administrative nature by both states and the Security Council. Terrorism and proliferation of weapons of mass destruction have been identified as such global stability risks, for the former see S/RES/1373 (2001) of 28 September 2001, for the latter see S/RES/1540 (2004) of 28 April 2004.

[139] Joint Article on Libya: the pathway to peace, Prime Minister Cameron and President Obama, <http://www.number10.gov.uk>.

[140] See World Bank, *World Development Report 2011*. International efforts should be directed towards building government institutions in states which can mediate political and communal conflicts. The report acknowl-

general statements by the Security Council, achieving state-internal stability requires "representative institutions" that ensure that, as a minimum, rulers have the consent of the governed and that internal and communal conflicts can be successfully and peacefully mediated.[141] On that basis, the Security Council concretises the accountability of each state emerging from conflict through criteria for the internal organisation of these states. The said Presidential statements have been followed up by mandatory Security Council action based on UN Charter Chapter VII. A democratic state organisation based on elections marks one end of the organisational spectrum,[142] which starts, at the other end, with minimum standards for collective decision-making, "institution building" and representation of traditionally under-represented groups such as women and minorities.[143] Territorial international administration in post-conflict situations by the United Nations has consistently been directed toward establishing democratic

---

edges that there is not one single form or template for democracy, and that in each case, a culturally acceptable form must be found.

[141] SC Presidential Statement, Doc. S/PRST/2011/2, para. 1 "The Security Council restates the previous Statements of its President on post-conflict peacebuilding. The Council stresses the importance of institution building as a critical component of peacebuilding and emphasizes the importance of a more effective and coherent national and international response to it, so that countries emerging from conflict can deliver core government functions, including managing political disputes peacefully, providing security and maintaining stability, protecting their population, ensuring respect for the rule of law, revitalising the economy and providing basic services, which are essential to achieving durable peace. The Council emphasizes the importance of national ownership in this regard"; SC Presidential Statement, para. 3, Doc. S/PRST/2011/4 "The Security Council reiterates that, in order to support a country emerge sustainably from conflict, there is a need for a comprehensive and integrated approach that incorporates and strengthens coherence between political, security, development, human rights and rule of law activities."

[142] A state's opting for democracy will receive a positive assessment from the Council, an expression of support, and even the indication of positive measures that the Council and the UN Member States should take in support of national efforts, S/RES/1944 (2010) of 14 October 2010. For previous practice see N. Petersen, *Demokratie als teleologisches Prinzip*, 2009.

[143] Cf. S/RES/1820 (2008) of 19 June 2008, op. para. 11 (standards to ensure the representation of women as a matter of internal peace).

governance structures.¹⁴⁴ There is also rich practice of the Security Council operationalising the peaceful exercise of any self-determination claims in the colonial and in the non-colonial contexts through criteria for the domestic structures of the new states typically emerging from conflict.¹⁴⁵ In a non-colonial context, the proper representation of any group bearer of the right to self-determination within a state's governance institutions will realise that group's "internal" self-determination, foreclosing the group's rights to "external" self-determination through secession. If the case so warrants, the Security Council can move from establishing standards for internal peace-building processes to addressing any factors that might stand in the way or hinder their implementation by deploying a variety of instruments including targeted measures (individual sanctions) and forcible measures under Chapter VII of the UN Charter.

For that purpose, a situation internal to a state can be determined to constitute a "threat to the peace, breach of the peace, or act of aggression" within the meaning of Article 39 UN Charter, clearing the threshold for forcible and non-forcible measures under Chapter VII, Arts 41-42. This template is now being established by the Security Council through its recent action e.g. regarding the Ivory Coast. This state has been emerging from a civil conflict; there has been a third-party brokered peace process, which includes presidential and parliamentary elections. S/RES/1962 sets forth the critical considerations that will justify measures of the Council under Chapter VII on the situation in that state.¹⁴⁶ S/RES/1975 protects the outcome of the presidential

---

[144] See R. Wolfrum, "International Administration in Post-Conflict Situations by the United Nations and Other International Actors", in: A. v. Bogdandy/ R. Wolfrum (eds), *Max Planck UNYB* 9 (2005), 649 et seq.

[145] See U. Saxer, *Die internationale Steuerung der Selbstbestimmung und der Staatsentstehung*, 2010; M. Benzing, "Midwifing a New State: The United Nations in East Timor", *Max Planck UNYB*, see note 144, 295 et seq.

[146] S/RES/1962 (2010) of 20 December 2010, preambular paras 2-4 "Congratulating the Ivorian people for the holding of the two rounds of the Presidential election on 31 October 2010 and 28 November 2010 with a massive and peaceful participation. Condemning in the strongest possible terms the attempts to usurp the will of the people and undermine the integrity of the electoral process and any progress in the peace process in Côte d'Ivoire. Expressing grave concern at the risk of escalation of violence, recalling that the Ivorian leaders bear primary responsibility for ensuring peace and protecting the civilian population in Côte d'Ivoire and demanding that all stakeholders and parties to conflict act with maximum restraint to prevent

elections, through binding requests addressed to the main players.[147] It urges the defeated incumbent to immediately step aside and condemns him for not accepting the overall political solution proposed by the High-Level Panel put in place by the African Union.[148] Beforehand all Ivorian state institutions, including the armed forces, were urged to yield to the authority vested by the Ivorian people in the newly elected President.[149] S/RES/1980, preambular para. 5, then welcomes the fact that the elected President has taken office in accordance.

The Council also put so-called targeted sanctions in place to support implementation of the peace process and the elections.[150] This sanctions regime is specifically to serve stabilisation throughout the country, the holding of the parliamentary elections and the implementation of the key steps of the peace process.[151] The implementation of these measures is backed up by available military means.[152] The Council took forcible measures under UN Charter Chapter VII when the defeated incumbent resorted to force against the newly elected president.[153] Any measures

---

a recurrence of violence and ensure the protection of civilians." The motivation as well as the robustness of the measures taken by the Council here closely resemble those under Responsibility to Protect.

[147] S/RES/1975 (2011) of 30 March 2011.

[148] Ibid., op. para. 3.

[149] S/RES/1962 (2010) of 20 December 2010, op. para. 1.

[150] Ibid. op. para. 16: "Reaffirms its readiness to impose measures, including targeted sanctions, against persons who, among other things, threaten the peace process and national reconciliation, including by seeking to undermine the outcome of the electoral process, obstruct the work of UNOCI and other international actors and commit serious violations of human rights and international humanitarian law, as set out by Resolution 1946 (2010)." S/RES/1980 (2011) of 28 April 2011, op. para. 1 renews the targeted sanctions under Chapter VII directed against individuals.

[151] See in this respect S/RES/1962, see note 149, op. para. 8 "Stresses the importance of UNOCI's continued support to the Ivorian peace process in accordance with its mandate, especially the completion of the unfinished tasks including the legislative elections, ..., the strengthening of rule of law institutions, the reform of the security sector, and the promotion and protection of human rights with particular attention to the situation of children and women."

[152] Ibid., op. para. 14 "Recalls its authorization given to UNOCI to use all necessary means to carry out its mandate, within its capabilities and its areas of deployment."

[153] S/RES/1975, see note 147, op. para. 6, "Recalls its authorization and stresses its full support given to the UNOCI, while impartially implement-

taken by the Council on that basis remain, however, within the rationale of primary responsibility of the state concerned.[154] The United Nations also recognises that it has a critical own role to play in support of building countries' national institutions.[155] One important instrument is the Peacebuilding Commission established by concurrent General Assembly and Security Council resolutions, which also established a Peacebuilding Fund and a Peacebuilding Support Office.[156] That this involvement is again complementary to the primary responsibility of each state is implied, for instance through the composition of the Peace-Building Commission.[157]

3. The "Responsibility to Protect"

It would not seem to be a controversial statement that international law considers the security of civilian populations to be covered by the sovereignty of each state understood as objective competence and subjective right. Correspondingly, the UN's main concern had traditionally been with the security of states in their international relations. But the atrocities committed against civilian populations in Rwanda and on the Balkans in the 1990s caused basic human security in each state to arise

---

ing its mandate, to use all necessary means to carry out its mandate to protect civilians under imminent threat of physical violence, within its capabilities and its areas of deployment, including to prevent the use of heavy weapons against the civilian population and requests the Secretary-General to keep it urgently informed of measures taken and efforts made in this regard."

[154] S/RES/1980, see note 150, preambular para. 4 "Emphasizing the continued contribution to the stability in Côte d'Ivoire of the measures imposed by resolutions 1572 (2004), 1643 (2005) and 1975 (2011) and stressing that these measures aim at *supporting* the peace process in Côte d'Ivoire." (emphasis added).

[155] SC Presidential Statement, para. 4, Doc. S/PRST/2011/4 of 11 February 2011.

[156] S/RES/1645 (2005) of 20 December 2005; A/RES/60/180 of 20 December 2005.

[157] 2005 World Summit Outcome, see note 126, paras 97-105. The purpose of the Peacebuilding Commission is to bring together all relevant actors to marshal resources and to advise on and propose integrated strategies for post-conflict peacebuilding and recovery (para. 98).

as a concern for the international community.¹⁵⁸ By developing the "responsibility to protect" the 2005 World Summit Outcome established as an international public good the protection of civilian populations from four crimes and violations: genocide, war crimes, ethnic cleansing, and crimes against humanity.¹⁵⁹ In respect of this objective, the Outcome assigns states and the international community with responsibilities. It is the responsibility of "each individual state" to protect its populations from the four crimes,¹⁶⁰ including their prevention.¹⁶¹ Protection from the four crimes is a universal standard, applying to all UN Member States. But in respect of the objective of civilian protection, the Outcome also identifies an own responsibility of the international community to act preventively and responsively through the United Nations.¹⁶² The Outcome is a politically binding instrument adopted

---

[158] See reports in relation to the Rwandan genocide Doc. S/1999/1257 and the fall of Srebrenica Doc. A/54/549.

[159] 2005 World Summit Outcome, see note 126, at paras 138-139. For forerunners, cf. Report of the International Commission on Intervention and State Sovereignty, *The Responsibility to Protect*, 2001; High-level Panel on Threats, Challenges and Change, *A more secure World – Our shared Responsibility*, Doc. A/59/565 of 2 December 2004; Report of the UN Secretary-General, *In Larger Freedom: Towards Security, Development and Human Rights for All*, Doc. A/59/2005 of 21 March 2005. There is a burgeoning literature, to which is cited throughout this portion of the article.

[160] 2005 World Summit Outcome, see note 126, para. 138: "Each individual State has the responsibility to protect its populations from genocide, war crimes, ethnic cleansing and crimes against humanity. This responsibility entails the prevention of such crimes, including their incitement, through appropriate and necessary means. We accept that responsibility and will act in accordance with it. The international community should, as appropriate, encourage and help States to exercise this responsibility and support the United Nations in establishing an early warning capability."

[161] This language fits into the threefold standard of human rights and humanitarian obligations to "respect, protect and fulfil", cf. UN Human Rights Committee, *Nature of the General Legal Obligation Imposed on States Parties to the Covenant*, General Comment No. 31, Doc. CCPR/C/21/Rev.1/Add. 13 of 26 May 2004; cf. A. Peters, "The Responsibility to Protect: Spelling out the Hard Consequences for the UN Security Council and its Members", in: U. Fastenrath et al. (eds), *Essays in Honour of Bruno Simma*, 2011, 297 et seq. On the threefold human rights standard see generally W. Kälin/ J. Künzli, *The International Law of Human Rights Protection*, 2010, 96 et seq.

[162] 2005 World Summit Outcome, see note 126, para. 139: "The international community, through the United Nations, also has the responsibility to use

by the General Assembly at the level of Heads of State or Government. It has been followed up by normative activity of the UN principal organs under the UN Charter, ranging from the Secretary-General's report to the General Assembly on "Implementing the Responsibility to Protect"[163] and an extensive General Assembly debate[164] to UN Security Council measures binding under UN Charter Chapter VII.[165] This organisational secondary law-making concretises the Responsibility to Protect along the general matrix of international responsibility. Building on a multi-level governance model, primary responsibilities of each

---

appropriate diplomatic, humanitarian and other peaceful means, in accordance with Chapters VI and VIII of the Charter, to help to protect populations from genocide, war crimes, ethnic cleansing and crimes against humanity. In this context, we are prepared to take collective action, in a timely and decisive manner, through the Security Council, in accordance with the Charter, including Chapter VII, on a case-by-case basis and in cooperation with relevant regional organizations as appropriate, should peaceful means be inadequate and national authorities are manifestly failing to protect their populations from genocide, war crimes, ethnic cleansing and crimes against humanity. We stress the need for the General Assembly to continue consideration of the responsibility to protect populations from genocide, war crimes, ethnic cleansing and crimes against humanity and its implications, bearing in mind the principles of the Charter and international law. We also intend to commit ourselves, as necessary and appropriate, to helping States build capacity to protect their populations from genocide, war crimes, ethnic cleansing and crimes against humanity and to assisting those which are under stress before crises and conflicts break out."

[163] Report of the Secretary-General, *Implementing the Responsibility to Protect*, Doc. A/63/677 and related A/RES/63/308 of 14 September 2009, para. 1. "Takes note of the report of the Secretary-General and of the timely and productive debate organized by the President of the General Assembly on the responsibility to protect, held on 21, 23, 24 and 28 July 2009, with full participation by Member States; 2. Decides to continue its consideration of the responsibility to protect."

[164] Doc. A/63/PV.99.

[165] The 2005 World Summit Outcome, see note 126, was adopted by the UN General Assembly. As the United Nations is based on coordinated principal organs (Article 7 UN Charter) this resolution would not *per se* be binding on, in particular, the Security Council to the extent that this body bears "primary responsibility" for international security and world peace. The Council has, however, referred to the concept itself, absorbing it into its own practice, comprising general re-statements of the law and forcible and non-forcible measures pursuant to Chapter VII of the UN Charter. Pertinent Council resolutions will be discussed subsequently.

state and secondary responsibilities of the United Nations for the protection of civilians are demarcated, duties and possible sanctions for their non-fulfilment are determined, and lines of accountability are established.

a. Primary Responsibility of Each State to Protect Civilians from Genocide, War Crimes, Ethnic Cleansing and Crimes against Humanity

The Secretary General's report on implementation offers a conceptual clarification of the 2005 World Summit Outcome's Responsibility to Protect concept by distinguishing a three Pillar strategy: Pillar one comprises the protection responsibilities of the state, Pillar two the international assistance and capacity-building, and Pillar three timely and decisive response. The three Pillars mark functions that are assigned to states and the United Nations. Each state is assigned with the Responsibility to Protect its civilian populations from the four crimes, this overall responsibility of each state is primary over the secondary responsibility of the United Nations.[166] This backs up the assertion that Responsibility to Protect is no distraction from but rather presupposes sovereignty.[167] Guaranteeing each state the space for own protective action is indeed a necessary prerequisite for attributing the consequences of its decisions to it. Each state is accountable for its decisions to the international community which will assess them against internationally defined criteria. The 2005 World Summit Outcome already identifies the broad standard to prevent the commission of the four crimes. This universal standard, applying to all UN Member States, is in need of further concretisation.

In a first step, the standard is backed up and fleshed out by relevant international treaty law, which needs to be faithfully embodied in national legislation.[168] The Genocide Convention e.g. establishes the threefold obligation for States Parties to prevent genocide[169] and to

---

[166] Report, see note 163, para. 14.
[167] Ibid., para. 10 ("responsible sovereignty").
[168] Ibid., para. 17.
[169] Article I; cf. further Application of the Convention on the Prevention and Punishment of the Crime of Genocide (Bosnia and Herzegovina v. Serbia and Montenegro), ICJ Reports 2007, 43 et seq. (221, para. 430) (due diligence obligation to prevent the extraterritorial commission of genocide) (hereinafter Genocide Convention case).

punish individuals for its commission[170] (obligation to protect) as well not to actively commit genocide through its own organs or actors it controls (obligation to respect). In respect of war crimes, the Geneva Conventions also impose obligations of respect and protection including prevention.[171] Crimes against humanity are punishable individual offences under international criminal law, and respective obligations for states are laid down in the statutes of the International Criminal Tribunals and of the ICC.[172] Further concretisation of the protective standard is the province of the United Nations. The Secretary-General's report specifies the protection responsibilities of the state.[173] Significantly, UN Security Council resolutions under UN Charter Chapter VII have defined specific standards for states to meet their protective responsibility. The Security Council did so in S/RES/1674 on the protection of civilians in armed conflict[174] and in S/RES/1882 on the topic of children and armed conflict.[175] These resolutions set forth general restatements of the law, but add that states need to comply with them as an expression of their responsibility.

b. The Responsibility of the United Nations to Guarantee and to Act

The UN's own Responsibility to Protect civilians is secondary to each state's primary responsibility. The United Nations must therefore not substitute itself for the choices of each state. But it must also be able to take action to ensure that the state discharges this responsibility within the standards applicable. The United Nations responsibility comprises two elements, a responsibility to guarantee and a responsibility to act.

---

[170] Article I; and Genocide Convention case, see above, 226, para. 439.
[171] Wall Opinion case, see note 21, paras 158-159 (duty for states to ensure respect for common article I of the Geneva Conventions regardless of whether they are parties to a specific dispute including other states).
[172] Cf. A. Cassese/ G. Acquaviva/ M. Fan/ A. Whiting, *International Criminal Law*, 2011 (ethnic cleansing is not a defined crime under international criminal law).
[173] Report, see note 163, paras 14-22.
[174] S/RES/1674 (2006) of 28 April 2006, op. para. 4 reaffirmed paras 138 and 139 of the 2005 World Summit Outcome Document, see note 126. This reaffirmation was recalled in S/RES/1706 (2006) of 13 August 2006.
[175] S/RES/1882 (2009) of 4 August 2009, preambular para. 3 "Stressing the primary role of national Governments in providing protection and relief to all children affected by armed conflicts."

The 2005 World Summit Outcome establishes the United Nations as the body to which each state is accountable for discharge of its protective responsibility. Assuming this role of accountability body is the responsibility of the United Nations. It thus has the responsibility to guarantee that states fulfil their primary responsibility. For that purpose the United Nations may progressively develop standards, assess performance against these standards, and for that purpose it may take observational action through its own organs and other organs. The United Nations may, as a consequence of its assessment, take enforcement action. Sanctionability of assessments is inherent to the idea of accountability. In the case of accountability of a state to an international organisation, the sanctionability of assessments becomes a question of the competences of the organisation. The United Nations can assess the failure of a state to meet its protection responsibility and take action on the basis of Charter Chapter VII with the dual objective of directly protecting civilians and indirectly sanctioning the government for its failure. A government that has been found manifestly to fail the Responsibility to Protect-test may be presumed to have lost the consent of the governed and will eventually have to step aside.

It is a consequence of the forceful statement in the 2005 World Summit Outcome, para. 139, that the United Nations has not only the responsibility *to guarantee* but also has responsibility *to act*. The own responsibility of the United Nations to act extends to assistance and response action, that is Pillar 2 and 3 in the terminology of the Secretary-General's Implementation report. On the basis of UN Charter Chapters VI and VIII, the United Nations will take action through its own organs aimed at preventing crises from arising in the first place including establishing an early warning facility.[176] The international community, acting through the United Nations, must be ready to build capacity to prevent any of the four crimes being committed and to assist in situations of stress. Pillar 3 is timely and decisive response and it is again the responsibility of the United Nations.[177] Responsive action by means of Security Council measures pursuant to Chapter VII UN Charter may take place in the case of a "manifest failure" on the part of the state to fulfil its responsibility where a crisis could not be prevented.[178] The range of means includes military force.[179] The objective

---

[176] Report, see note 163, paras 28-39.
[177] Ibid., paras 49-67.
[178] The Council may intervene at an early point to prevent a crisis from escalating, cf. Report, see note 163, para. 11 lit. (c) (referring to Council in-

of such preventive and responsive action by the United Nations can, however, only be restitution of the state-internal political process, in other words the primary responsibility of the state.

In particular the Security Council has substantially added to the legal concretisation of the Responsibility to Protect, namely by referring to it in resolutions adopted under Chapter VII, authorising forcible measures concerning the situations in Libya and in the Ivory Coast. In the Libyan situation, the Security Council has invoked the Responsibility to Protect in its resolution S/RES/1973 adopted under Chapter VII, which authorises the deployment of "all necessary measures" by Member States to protect civilians in Libya from the large-scale use of force by the Libyan government.[180] Security Council action further concretises the individual criminal responsibility of the Libyan leadership by referring the situation in Libya to the Prosecutor of the ICC.[181] In the Ivorian situation, invocation of a Responsibility to Protect civilians and human rights has motivated the authorisation of a UN force and the French troops supporting it to use "all necessary means" to protect civilians from the use of force by the defeated incumbent president's forces.[182] The Ivorian intervention thus pushes the boundaries of possible UN Security Council action through the direct authorisation of peacekeepers as a result of a state's government failure to fulfil its protective responsibilities.[183] In these instances, the Security Council has invoked the state's Responsibility to Protect for motivating its measures

---

    volvement in Kenya after disputed elections pursuant to SC Presidential Statement, SCOR 60th Sess., 5831st Mtg, Doc. S/PRST/2008/4 of 6 February 2008).

[179] 2005 World Summit Outcome, see note 126, para. 139 "should peaceful means be inadequate and national authorities are manifestly failing to protect their populations ..."

[180] S/RES/1973 (2011) of 17 March 2011.

[181] S/RES/1970 (2011) of 26 February 2011, op. paras 4-8.

[182] See text at notes 146 et seq.

[183] S/RES/1962 (2010) of 20 December 2010 recalls that the Ivorian leaders bear primary responsibility for ensuring peace and protecting the civilian population in Côte d'Ivoire. S/RES/1975 of 30 March 2011 preambular para. 9 contains recognition of the responsibility to protect civilians: "... reaffirming the primary responsibility of each State to protect civilians and reiterating that parties to armed conflicts bear the primary responsibility to take all feasible steps to ensure the protection of civilians and facilitate the rapid and unimpeded passage of humanitarian assistance and the safety of humanitarian personnel ..."

under Chapter VII. This practice of the Security Council concretises the Responsibility to Protect into secondary (Council) but also primary (Charter) law.

Three functions of the Council's referral to the Responsibility to Protect have to be distinguished. First, there is the level of the Charter itself. Responsibility presupposes competence to act. Do the United Nations and in particular the UN Security Council have the competence to respond to a state failing to protect its populations by taking over the protection task? The UN Charter entrusts the Security Council with the primary responsibility for the maintenance of "international peace and security", and for that purpose the Security Council under Chapter VII UN Charter has powers to take decisions that are legally binding on all members of the organisation.[184] But does this denote the competence of the UN Security Council to take forcible measures in respect of what is essentially a state-internal situation? It first offers a general interpretation of the criterion "any threat to the peace" that Article 39 UN Charter establishes as a threshold for any Security Council action under Chapter VII.[185] In other words the Responsibility to Protect clarifies that the commission of any of the four crimes in a state *per se* can constitute a "threat to the peace". Responsibility to Protect here drives the legal development at the level of the treaty. Second, Responsibility to Protect is of relevance in determining the exercise of that power by the Security Council. In other words, Responsibility to Protect serves to guide the exercise of the discretion that the Security

---

[184] In addition to its power to repel threats to international peace and security, the Security Council has assumed (quasi-)legislative powers in areas as diverse as anti-terrorism and non-proliferation, see G. Abi-Saab, "The Security Council as Legislator and Executive in its Fight Against Terrorism and Against Proliferation of Weapons of Mass Destruction: The Question of Legitimacy", in: R. Wolfrum/ V. Röben (eds), *Legitimacy in International Law*, 2008, 109 et seq.

[185] The Council had acted essentially in internal situations before, Somalia being a case in point, S/RES/794 (1992) of 3 December 1992, op. para. 10, cf. further C.E. Philipp, "Somalia – A Very Special Case, Cross Cutting Issues", *Max Planck UNYB*, see note 144, 517 et seq. But the Responsibility to Protect provides a general rationale for acting in internal situations. The Council is thus interpreting the threshold criterion of "international peace and security" in a general fashion, akin to an exercise of legislative power. On such legislation on the level of the primary UN Charter see M. Wood, *The UN Security Council and International Law*, 2006; Namibia Opinion, see note 21, para. 22.

Council enjoys under Chapter VII, Arts 41 and 42 ("may"). The moment that the Council recognises that Responsibility to Protect is implicated in a given instance, however, accountability of the Council is established. The Security Council then assumes the burden of argumentation as to whether an intervention to protect civilians is required. Third, Responsibility to Protect is grounded and limited to what the Council can do in individual instances. Its responsive action in pursuit of Responsibility to Protect must not arrogate the primary responsibility of each state to protect its populations through means of its free choosing. Council action must not go further than restoring a state of affairs where the state concerned can again assume its primary responsibility. Interpretation of the Charter and each resolution adopted under Chapter VII must comply with this understanding. Fourth, intervention of the UN Security Council in Member States in pursuit of the Responsibility to Protect requires observance of an inclusive procedure by the Council involving the regional context of the state deemed to be violating its primary protective responsibilities.

The 2005 World Summit Outcome already refers to legitimacy of the Council as depending on procedural inclusiveness,[186] and the Security Council envisages that its procedure will have to involve any regional security system concerned.[187] Chapter VIII UN Charter indeed provides for regional systems of collective security to prevent regional crises, bring them to the Council's attention, and to carry out measures authorised by the Council.[188] The Security Council has explicitly mentioned the referral of the situation in Libya by the Arab League pursuant to its Charter as one of the grounds justifying Resolution 1973.[189]

---

[186] 2005 World Summit Outcome, see note 126, para. 154.
[187] See S/RES/1809 (2008) of 16 April 2008.
[188] UN Charter, Arts 52-53, provide that crises shall be dealt with at the regional level to the extent possible. According to Article 52 (2) UN Charter Member States of the UN shall make "every effort to achieve pacific settlement of local disputes through such regional arrangements or by such regional agencies before referring them to the Security Council." Correspondingly, Article 52 (3) UN Charter obliges the Security Council to "encourage the development of pacific settlement of local disputes through such regional arrangements or by such regional agencies either on the initiative of the states concerned or by reference from the Security Council". Article 53 UN Charter even envisages that the competent regional organisation may carry out enforcement action upon authorisation by the UN Security Council.
[189] S/RES/1973, see note 180, preambular para. 12.

And in the case of the Ivory Coast, the Council has referred to action of the African Union requesting that state's government to respect its fundamental norms. The Security Council then took these references into account, triggering action by it under Chapter VII.[190]

The UN Security Council is responsible for its preventive and responsive action. The 2005 World Summit Outcome recognises the responsibility not just of the international community but implicitly that of the Security Council as well, and this is made explicit in the Secretary-General's Implementation report and has been acknowledged in Security Council practice. Accountability of the Security Council lies with the UN General Assembly as the body representative of UN membership as a whole. This accountability is of a political nature. In other words, the Security Council can be held to account politically by the General Assembly, which may define political criteria. Responsibility to Protect itself would be the most important criterion for the exercise of the Council's powers under Chapter VII, even though further more detailed criteria for consistent action would be needed.[191]

In addition to this role as addressee the General Assembly is a responsible actor itself both under the second and the third Pillar.[192] The General Assembly has indeed become active through the Human Rights Council. Membership of this subsidiary organ of the General Assembly depends on a state's human rights record. And on that basis, the Council has been supporting and supplementing Security Council interventions in Libya[193] and in the Ivory Coast.[194]

---

[190] The controlling terms of these provisions make reference to international situations. However, in parallel to the threshold contained in Article 39 UN Charter, the relevant criteria in Arts 52 and 53 UN Charter are open to being interpreted as encompassing the state-internal situations involving the Responsibility to Protect. Such interpretation of Arts 52 and 53 may be inferred from the Security Council accepting referrals by regional security systems to it of instances of state-internal unrest and use of force against civilians.

[191] Report, see note 163, para. 62, and In Larger Freedom, see note 159, para. 126. See J. Brunnée, "International Law and Collective Concerns: Reflections on the Responsibility to Protect", in: T. Malick Ndiaye/ R. Wolfrum (eds), *Liber amicorum Judge Thomas Mensah,* 2007, 35 et seq. (43-48), (discussing negotiating history).

[192] The General Assembly's peace and security functions are addressed in UN Charter Arts 11, 12, 14, and 15.

[193] A/HRC/RES/S-15/1 of 25 February 2011, S/RES/1970 (2011) of 26 February 2011 preambular para. 5 "Welcoming the Human Rights Council reso-

c. Responsibility of Each State Represented on the Governance of United Nations Organs

The collective responsibility of the international community and of the UN principal organs does not preclude that it be further broken down to individual states represented on the governance of these organs. This first of all concerns the 15 UN Member States represented in the UN Security Council at any one time but particularly the 5 permanent members. Complementing the powers of UN Security Council membership with the duty to exercise these in a certain way would be in tune with the idea of responsibility.[195] But it would need further authoritative recognition. The 2005 World Summit Outcome document only established the responsibility of the international community for responding to a state's failure to meet its primary protective responsibility through the Security Council.[196] But the Secretary-General's report suggests that each state represented on the Security Council and in particular that each permanent member has an own responsibility and "should" consider the use of the veto in instances where the Responsibility to Protect is manifestly implicated.[197] While the General Assem-

---

lution A/HRC/RES/S-15/1 of 25 February 2011, including the decision to urgently dispatch an independent international commission of inquiry to investigate all alleged violations of international human rights law in the Libyan Arab Jamahiriya, to establish the facts and circumstances of such violations and of the crimes perpetrated, and where possible identify those responsible."

[194] A/HRC/16/25 in connection with S/RES/1975 (2011) of 30 March 2011.

[195] And more broadly solidarity, L. Boisson de Chazournes, "Responsibility to Protect: Reflecting Solidarity?", in: R. Wolfrum/ C. Kojima (eds), *Solidarity: A Structural Principle of International Law*, 2010, 93 et seq.

[196] 2005 World Summit Outcome, see note 126, para. 139: "timely and decisive manner ... on a case-by-case basis ...". This preparedness is conditioned on a manifest failure of the state to protect, the inadequacy of peaceful means, respect of the Charter law, and cooperation with relevant regional organisations as appropriate.

[197] Report, see note 163, para. 61: "Within the Security Council, the five permanent members bear particular responsibility because of the privileges of tenure and the veto power they have been granted under the Charter. I would urge them to refrain from employing or threatening to employ the veto in situations of manifest failure to meet obligations relating to the responsibility to protect, as defined in paragraph 139 of the 2005 World Summit Outcome document, and to reach a mutual understanding to that effect."

bly has not yet given authoritative recognition to individual responsibility qua Security Council membership,[198] as permanent members the United States and the United Kingdom have accepted this responsibility incumbent on them qua membership of the Council in a joint statement at the level of Heads of State and Government.[199] It is, furthermore, only consequent that their individual protective responsibility also attaches to membership in the UN General Assembly.[200]

4. Conclusions

The international responsibility for post-conflict peace-building and the Responsibility to Protect from the crimes of genocide, war crimes, ethnic cleansing and crimes against humanity is grounded in the 2005 World Summit Outcome. In respect of these state-internal matters, starting from a multi-level global governance model comprising states and international organisations, each state, the United Nations, and states represented on the governance structure of the United Nations are conceived of as actors to whom responsibilities ought to be attributed in such a way that the common objective be best achieved. The po-

---

[198] A/RES/63/308 of 14 September 2009 "takes note of the report of the Secretary-General."

[199] Joint Statement of Prime Minister Cameron and President Obama: "We are reluctant to use force but when our interests and values come together we know that we have a responsibility to act. This is why we mobilised the international community to protect the Libyan people from Colonel Gaddafi's regime", see note 141. These states assume a responsibility to act for the benefit of the population of the state concerned while a secondary beneficiary may be their own population. On the legal qualification of joint statements see Aegean Sea Continental Shelf case (Greece v. Turkey), ICJ Reports 1978, 3 et seq. (para. 98); Case Concerning Maritime Delimitation and Territorial Questions between Qatar and Bahrain (Qatar v. Bahrain), ICJ Reports 1994, 112 et seq. (para. 26); Case Concerning Pulp Mills on the River Uruguay (Argentina v. Uruguay), ICJ Judgment of 20 April 2010, paras 128, 149, <http://www.icj-cij.org>.

[200] Report, see note 163, para. 61: "… All Member States, not just the 15 members of the Security Council, should be acutely aware of both public expectations and shared responsibilities. If the General Assembly is to play a leading role in shaping a United Nations response, then all 192 Member States should share the responsibility to make it an effective instrument for advancing the principles relating to the responsibility to protect expressed so clearly in paragraphs 138 and 139 of the Summit Outcome."

litically binding 2005 World Summit Outcome has then been concretised through secondary law-making by the UN principal organs namely the UN Security Council. The Security Council has underlined the primary responsibility of each state for internal peace and stability. The United Nations have secondary responsibility only. But Security Council measures also establish that by virtue of its primary responsibility each state is accountable pursuant to criteria set by it. In terms of the criteria that states have to meet, there is a powerful trend requiring states to secure internal peace and stability through representative institutions. A state's responsibility will also involve assessment by the Council of whether the state has effectively complied with the criteria. The UN Security Council assesses the internal situation of states from an early point on when a crisis threatens to develop, formulating viewpoints and issuing decisions as appropriate. As a crisis evolves, there then arises a point when the UN Security Council may take responsive action under Chapter VII UN Charter. Post-conflict peace building and the Responsibility to Protect overlap here as the UN Security Council will invoke the state's Responsibility to Protect in either case to justify resort to forcible measures. But the United Nations is not free in its actions either. Rather it is responsible itself to the international community, in particular as to whether it will itself take collective protective action as consequence of the manifest failure of the primarily responsible territorial state. An own responsibility of states serving on the governance structure of the United Nations is also emerging. That is true particularly for the members of the UN Security Council in the exercise of their special powers.

Responsibility for post-conflict peace-building and the Responsibility to Protect converge. Both concepts involve the definition, imposition of standards for the institutional set-up of the state,[201] the assessment of whether standards have been met, and the sanctionability of the assessment.

The idea of responsibility powerfully structures the approach of the international community to state-internal matters relevant for international peace and stability and the protection of civilians but this objective is its ground and its limit. The reach of the institution of responsibility is thus not automatically congruent with community interests protected by *erga omnes* or *ius cogens* norms. United Nations practice

---

[201] The 2005 World Summit Outcome, see note 126, paras 119-145, discusses the Responsibility to Protect together with democracy and the rule of law in its section dealing with human rights.

on post-conflict peace-building and the Responsibility to Protect demonstrates that responsibility remains a concept that the United Nations has been careful to reserve for the internal matters considered to be most significant for global stability. While international law contains a host of legally binding human rights norms, the international institution of responsibility for them has not yet been extended to them.

Through the appropriate normative processes, there may, however, be constituted international responsibility for human rights protection along the lines of the matrix of responsibility for state-internal matters. That this may come to pass in the future is indicated by certain pronouncements of the United Nations that each state is responsible for the protection of human rights. Also, there is currently no international responsibility for individual states to ensure respect of human rights obligations in another state generally. International law at this juncture does not provide for the requisite comprehensive powers for states to enforce another state's human rights obligations. The 1948 Genocide Convention obligates States Parties to prevent the extraterritorial commission of genocide, but that would not confer a right to intervene in another state.[202]

There are also only limited powers for states to act under the customary international law of state responsibility. A state that is not materially injured by another state violating its multilateral treaty obligations can require cessation. Reparation must be tended to the entire group of states to which the obligations are owed.[203] In the human rights context, reparation can be made only once for the benefit of the individuals concerned. Even to the extent that international human rights norms constitute *ius cogens,* a state is limited to non-recognition and invoking other states' obligation to cooperate to remove the conse-

---

[202] Genocide Convention case, see note 169, para. 430 ("A State does not incur [state] responsibility simply because the desired result is not achieved; [state] responsibility is however incurred if the State manifestly failed to take all measures to prevent genocide which were within its power ... The State's capacity to influence must also be assessed by legal criteria, since it is clear that every State may only act within the limits permitted by international law.").

[203] Articles on Responsibility of States for Internationally Wrongful Acts, see note 13, article 48. The law of state responsibility attaches "legal consequences" to the breach by a state of any obligation under international law binding on that state provided there are no circumstances precluding wrongfulness. The resulting secondary obligations for that state comprise cessation of the violation and/or making reparation for it.

quences of the breach of the *ius cogens* norm.[204] A state may also resort to judicial enforcement, seeking a declaration that another state has violated its obligations under the applicable human rights treaty.[205] The powers that accrue to states in respect of the human rights obligations incumbent on other states remain limited,[206] there is currently no basis for an attribution of the consequences of ongoing human rights violations in other states. This particularly clearly demonstrates the function of the institution of responsibility to concretise norms into doctrine and to link this doctrine with enforcement machinery.

VI. Responsibility as an Institution of International Law: Concluding Reflections

The institution of international responsibility underlies much of the most dynamic law of the international community. The critical idea is to identify international public goods for which each state and any competent international organisation ought to be assigned responsibilities. Responsible actors would be accountable to designated bodies for controlling consequences of their action for these goods, and accountability would be assessed against standards and can be sanctioned. Safeguarding such international public goods must benefit the international community as a whole. They fall broadly into one of two groups. There are those of a transjurisdictional or global nature requiring cooperation between states. Others are under the jurisdiction of each state. Standards of accountability vary accordingly. This matrix of international responsibility acquires legal reality through a dynamic law-making process that concretises political commitments into binding law leading to enforceable doctrine. The process involves characteristic stages: a foundational document grounds the approach of the international community to a new field or area of responsibility. This foundational

---

[204] Articles on Responsibility of States for Internationally Wrongful Acts, see note 13, article 41.
[205] Many UN human rights treaties contain a clause conferring jurisdiction on the ICJ, see Case Concerning Application of the International Convention on the Elimination of All Forms of Racial Discrimination (Georgia v. Russian Federation), see note 68.
[206] On non-forcible intervention in other states' domestic affairs see L.F. Damrosch, "Politics Across Borders: Nonintervention and Nonforcible Influence over Domestic Affairs", *AJIL* 83 (1989), 1 et seq.

document is political in nature but it typically carries the legitimacy of having been adopted by the domestically responsible Heads of State or Government. The foundational reference text is then concretised through an iterative law-making process that involves, as sources of law, classic treaties as well as alternatives to treaty making including the secondary law of international organisations. The institution of international responsibility sits at the centre of some of the most dynamic areas of contemporary international law. Climate change regulation is based on common but differentiated responsibilities for sustainable development, the regulation of the international financial market is based on the G20 responsibility for the global economy, state-internal peace and security is based on the responsibility to secure lawful stability, and the protection of civilians is founded on the responsibility to protect. Seen together, these reference areas reflect the importance, the contours, and the functions of responsibility as an institution of the law of the international community. Critical among these functions is to help concretise broad norms into doctrine and to link this doctrine with an enforcement machinery. Understood as an institution, responsibility can indeed deliver a single concept encompassing the various senses in which the form is used in international law and international law doctrine. It encompasses the senses of competence, obligation and liability.

Identifying international responsibility as an institution of international law allows understanding in what ways international law has been evolving. The emergence of an institution of responsibility is a central marker for the underlying shift in the fundamental function of international law from serving sovereigns pursuing their national interests to serving the pursuit of common objectives and community interests.

The institution will identifiably remain distinct from its implementation. In other words, the implementation at any one time does not exhaust the meaning of the institution. There is a residual normative content of which several effects can be identified: first, the institution comprises only a segment of international law differentiating it from other parts, giving it identity and aiding in the interpretation of individual norms. Second, the institution allows us normatively to link disparate developments in the law, to see their interconnectedness, and thus allowing the systemic study of new functionalities in the existing law. Third, it may serve to evaluate legal developments, becoming a catalyst for the development of new law shaped by, reflecting the set of ideas behind the institution, and justifying the rolling out of a regulatory framework to improve on the present state of things. Finally, seen against the background of responsibilities states attribute to themselves or which are attributed to them, the classic consent rationale justifying international law commitment loses importance. The institution of responsibility itself includes a reference to a meta-basis of obligation. This is a basis of obligation not grounded in consent in the sense that there is no free disposition about the obligations to be incurred. This article points to the process of negotiating, entering into and complying with internationally legally binding commitments. Rather states have to become engaged in the process.

Assessing the Existence of the Right to Translation under the International Covenant on Civil and Political Rights

John H. Dingfelder Stone[*]

---

[*] Paper from the Seminar: *Modern Developments of Public International Law*, held at the Max Planck Institute, February 2012 by Prof. Dr. Dr. h.c. Rüdiger Wolfrum.

I. Introduction
II. The International Covenant on Civil and Political Rights
III. European Court of Human Rights
IV. The *Ad Hoc* Tribunals
   1. The Legal Framework
   2. Evaluation of the Case Law from the *Ad Hoc* Tribunals
   3. Assessment
V. The Rome Statute of the International Criminal Court
   1. The Legal Framework
   2. The Impact of the Rome Statute on the Interpretation of the International Covenant on Civil and Political Rights
VI. Conclusion

Abstract

The right to an interpreter for criminal defendants who do not speak the language of the court is guaranteed in article 14 (3)(f) International Covenant on Civil and Political Rights (ICCPR). However, the right to an interpreter is normally understood to only cover oral communications in the courtroom; it generally does not guarantee the translation of written documents or evidence. There is a growing awareness, though, that the translation of such documents may be required for a defendant to receive a truly fair trial. This paper seeks to determine whether a right to translation exists for criminal defendants within the framework of the ICCPR. In addition to examining the ICCPR treaty regime itself, the article also analyzes the jurisprudence surrounding identical treaty language arising from the European Court of Human Rights and both *ad hoc* international criminal Tribunals. Finally, the article reviews the explicit grant of a right to translation given in the Rome Statute for the ICC and discusses whether this specific language can be taken as both a codification of the international jurisprudence in this area, as well as a clarification of the evolving international legal standard on the right to translation.

Keywords

Translation; Interpretation; International Law; Customary Law; International Criminal Law; Criminal Procedure

I. Introduction

The right to a fair trial is a basic norm of international law.[1] However, the "right to a fair trial" is more than simply a singular right, rather it describes a collection of other individual rights and principles meant to ensure the eventual fulfillment of a "fair trial" for criminal defendants. Many of these individual rights that make up the overall right to a fair trial, such as the right to prepare and present a defense and the right to be presumed innocent, have become so familiar and accepted throughout the world that they are as familiar to non-lawyers as they are to lawyers. Indeed, the pervasiveness of these rights throughout national jurisdictions has led many scholars to conclude that the right to a fair trial, and specifically its codification in article 14 ICCPR,[2] represents customary international law.[3] Some scholars have even gone so far as to argue that the right to a fair trial, and presumably the individual rights contained therein, qualify as a peremptory norm.[4]

As is often said, the devil is in the details. It is easy enough to say that, for instance, the presumption of innocence is a norm of customary international law, but it is less easy to actually determine the detailed content of that particular norm. Within the folds of each of these article 14 rights exist manifest complexities and nuances. This paper will concern itself with one of these complexities, specifically with regard to one of article 14's lesser-known fair trial rights. The paper's purpose will be to discern whether the right to a fair trial, as embodied in article 14 ICCPR, entitles a criminal defendant to have access to translated documents during his criminal proceedings: a so-called "right to translation".

---

[1] See D. Weissbrodt/ R. Wolfrum, "Preface", in: D. Weissbrodt/ R. Wolfrum (eds), *The Right to a Fair Trial*, 1997.
[2] UNTS Vol. 999 No. 14668.
[3] See P. Robinson, "The Right to a Fair Trial in International Law, with Specific Reference to the Work of the ICTY", *Berkeley Journal of International Law Publicist* 3 (2009), 1 et seq. (6-7, 11); according to Doswald-Beck, the fair trial standard has materialized to such a degree that it can be claimed to have acquired the status of "one of the fundamental pillars of international law to protect individuals against arbitrary treatment", see L. Doswald-Beck, "Fair Trial, Right to, International Protection", in: R. Wolfrum (ed.), *Max Planck Encyclopedia of Public International Law*, 2012, Vol. IV, 1104 et seq., para. 1.
[4] Robinson, see note 3, 6-7, 11; G. Boas/ J.L. Bischoff/ N.L. Reid/ B.D. Taylor III, *International Criminal Procedure*, 2011, 12.

In this context it is necessary to distinguish between the concepts of "interpretation" and "translation". "Interpretation", from a linguistic standpoint, involves the transfer of *oral* content from one language to another, whereas "translation" concerns the same process in relation to *written* documents.[5] Article 14 (3)(f) ICCPR specifically guarantees a criminal defendant the right to "have the free assistance of an interpreter if he cannot understand or speak the language used in court." In other words, the right to an oral interpretation is explicitly enumerated. The right to the "translation" of written documents, however, is not expressly granted in the ICCPR.

Nowak has argued that it is doubtful that the ICCPR contains such a right, given that several proposals for its specific inclusion were rejected during the drafting of the Covenant.[6] However, Nowak also questions the logic of this omission, asserting that it is "highly doubtful" whether a criminal defendant can receive a fair trial absent the ability to read and understand the documentary evidence presented against him at trial.[7] This would appear to be even more troublesome in civil law jurisdictions where the case file and written evidence play such an obvious and substantial role in the process.[8] Thus, there is a legitimate question as to whether criminal defendants maintain a right to the translation of documentary evidence under the ICCPR.

II. The International Covenant on Civil and Political Rights

Given the acceptance of the ICCPR by an unheralded number of states,[9] as well as its generally-agreed-upon status as customary interna-

---

[5] See V. Benmaman, "Legal Interpreting: An Emerging Profession", *Modern Language Journal* 76 (1992), 445 et seq.
[6] See M. Nowak, *U.N. Covenant on Civil and Political Rights: CCPR Commentary*, 2005, 343.
[7] Ibid.
[8] See S. Trechsel, *Human Rights in Criminal Proceedings*, 2005, 338.
[9] As of April 2012, there were 167 State Parties to the ICCPR. Ratifying nations represent approximately 78 per cent of the world population (cf. CIA Factbook). It should also be noted that the vast majority of the uncovered population might arise from China, which as a non-ratifying signatory state, still has the obligation not to actively defeat the purpose of the treaty,

tional law, it represents the logical starting point for the discussion. As mentioned, the ICCPR does not explicitly mention a right to translation. Thus, if the right is to exist, it must be seen as part of one of the expressly enumerated rights. In this instance, the jurisprudence of the Human Rights Committee (HRC), as the main interpretive body with respect to the ICCPR, is of some use. The leading case in this respect is *Harward v. Norway*.[10]

In *Harward v. Norway*, the applicant asserted that he was not provided with adequate translations of four documents used against him at his criminal trial, and that he was therefore denied the right to have adequate time and facilities to prepare his defense.[11] The HRC held that the right to a fair trial required that the defense be given the "opportunity to familiarize itself with the documentary evidence against an accused", but that this did not necessarily require the translation of relevant documents specifically for the accused, so long as they were furnished to the accused's counsel, who presumably would be linguistically capable of reading and understanding their contents.[12] Although this case would seem to preclude the necessity to translate any relevant documents for the defendant as a fair trial requirement, the decision must be read with some element of caution.

In its opinion, the HRC placed some emphasis on the "particular circumstances of the case", one of which was the fact that the defendant in *Harward v. Norway* had been assigned a competent court interpreter who was capable of translating any necessary documents for the defendant at the request of his defense counsel.[13] Thus, while the decision may seem to categorically deny any right to the translation of relevant documents, this denial rests substantially upon the fact that the accused, in fact, was given the opportunity to have the documents translated by his interpreter, and chose not to avail himself of that opportunity. Furthermore, the HRC was careful to stress in its opinion that the defendant's right to have adequate facilities to prepare his defense, specifically, was not violated.[14] The possibility that a right to the translation of

---

      see article 18 Vienna Convention on the Law of Treaties, UNTS Vol. 1155 No. 18232.

[10]   *Harward v. Norway*, Communication No. 451/1991, Doc. CCPR/C/51/D/451/1991 of 16 August 1994.

[11]   See *Harward v. Norway*, see note 10, paras 3.3, 3.4.

[12]   Ibid., para. 9.5.

[13]   Ibid.

[14]   Ibid.

necessary documents might arise from some other provisions of the ICCPR, or from customary international law itself, is therefore not foreclosed by the decision.

In this respect, the right to an interpreter as enshrined in article 14 (3)(f) ICCPR is of some relevance, since it is meant, at its core, to guarantee that the defendant can both understand and participate in the court proceedings against him.[15] It is perhaps true, as the HRC determined in *Harward* v. *Norway*, that translations may not be necessary in order to adequately prepare a defense, especially where the defendant has access to a court interpreter and is represented by counsel who can read the original documents. However, this does not necessarily mean that the same defendant will be able to understand and participate in the proceedings absent these translations,[16] especially where the oral witness testimony that is being interpreted for the defendant continuously refers to non-translated written documents. In this manner, the lack of translated materials, where those materials are necessary to the oral proceeding, can not only render that proceeding incomprehensible to a linguistically incompetent defendant, but also impair that defendant's ability to participate effectively in his own defense.

As such, it is entirely logical to say that, even though the right to have adequate time and facilities to prepare a defense does not entitle a defendant to the translation of necessary documents, the right to a court interpreter does. Indeed, several other international actors, specifically the European Court of Human Rights (ECtHR) and the International Criminal Tribunal for Rwanda (ICTR), have reached this very conclusion: finding a right to the translation of written documents within the defendant's right to the interpretation of oral evidence.[17] Given that this is an area neither considered in, nor foreclosed by the HRC's *Harward* v. *Norway* decision, it is instructive to examine these other precedents, among others, in order to assess to what extent they may contribute to the determination of an ICCPR right in this context.

---

[15] See *Guesdon* v. *France*, Communication No. 219/1986, Doc. CCPR/C/39/D/219/1986 of 25 July 1990, para. 10.2.
[16] See Nowak, see note 6, 343.
[17] See Trechsel, see note 8, 338.

III. European Court of Human Rights

The right to an interpreter is guaranteed in article 6 (3)(e) European Convention for the Protection of Human Rights and Fundamental Freedoms (ECHR).[18] It uses identical language to article 14 (3)(f) ICCPR.[19] As such, although certainly not conclusive, interpretations by the ECtHR of the article 6 ECHR right are at worst persuasive authority as to the meaning of the ICCPR right to an interpreter.[20] The ECtHR has dealt with the right to translation most directly in *Kamasinski v. Austria*.[21] In *Kamasinski v. Austria*, the applicant alleged several violations of article 6 ECHR arising from his criminal proceedings, among which was the allegation that he had suffered from a "lack of written translation of official documents at the different stages of the procedure."[22] Upon considering the applicant's appeal, the ECtHR elaborated that the right to an interpreter applied "not only to oral statements made at trial hearings but also to documentary material."[23] The court further asserted that the right entitled the applicant to the "translation or interpretation of all those documents or statements in the proceedings instituted against him which it is necessary for him to understand ... in order to have the benefit of a fair trial."[24] The ECtHR noted, however, that the article 6 right did not extend so far as to entitle the defendant to translations of each and every written piece of evi-

---

[18] UNTS Vol. 213 No. 2889.
[19] Cf. article 6 (3)(e) ECHR ("to have the free assistance of an interpreter if he cannot understand or speak the language used in court") with article 14 (3)(f) ICCPR ("[t]o have the free assistance of an interpreter if he cannot understand or speak the language used in court"); see also Nowak, see note 6, 343.
[20] Both Nowak and Van Dijk support the proposition that ECtHR's interpretation of the right to a fair trial may be useful in interpreting the similar ICCPR provisions; Nowak, see note 6, 307.
[21] *Kamasinski v. Austria*, Series A, No. 168, Application No. 9783/82 of 19 December 1989.
[22] Ibid., para. 72.
[23] Ibid., para. 74; see also in accord *Luedicke, Belkacem and Koç v. Germany*, Series A, No. 29, Application Nos 6210/73; 6877/75; 7132/75 of 28 November 1978, para. 48; *Hermi v. Italy*, Application No. 18114/02 of 18 October 2006, para. 69.
[24] Ibid.

dence in the procedure, since not every prosecutorial document would be essential to the applicant's understanding of the proceedings.[25]

Thus, from *Kamasinski v. Austria*, one can see that the ECtHR, interpreting language that is identical to that contained in the ICCPR, moved in an entirely different direction than the HRC, by explicitly recognizing a right to the translation of "necessary" documents. This can be explained primarily by the context in which the applicant's claim was brought. While the HRC focused on the ability to prepare a defense, and thus placed emphasis on the capacity of the defendant's counsel to understand the evidence, the ECtHR stressed the defendant's ability himself to understand the evidence as a means to understanding the proceedings. Aside from the express recognition of a right to translated documents, the necessary result of the ECtHR's emphasis on the defendant's comprehension of the proceedings is that the right to translation is logically limited to only those documents that will alleviate any inability of the defendant to do so. In addition, it has been subsequently held that the oral interpretation of written documents in court by a courtroom interpreter (known as a "sight translation")[26] is sufficient to satisfy the defendant's right to understand the proceedings.[27]

Thus, in the estimation of the ECtHR, the right to translation is not an absolute right, but rather a limited entitlement meant only to fulfill the underlying purposes behind the explicit right to an interpreter. Whether this service is performed by a translator beforehand or an interpreter at the time is not relevant. As mentioned, this is not an issue or argument that was expressly considered by the HRC in *Harward v. Norway*, though it should be noted that the applicant in *Harward v. Norway* was afforded a court interpreter capable of fulfilling this purpose.[28]

---

[25] See *Kamasinski v. Austria*, see note 21, para. 74.
[26] See E.M. de Jongh, "Foreign Language Interpreters in the Courtroom: The Case for Linguistic and Cultural Proficiency", *Modern Language Journal* 75 (1991), 285 et seq. (288).
[27] See *Hermi v. Italy*, see note 23, para. 70.
[28] See *Harward v. Norway*, see note 10, para. 9.5

IV. The *Ad Hoc* Tribunals

1. The Legal Framework

The most extensive jurisprudence on the right to translation arises in the context of the International Criminal Tribunal for the former Yugoslavia (ICTY) and the ICTR. Each Tribunal was established by a resolution of the United Nations Security Council adopted under Chapter VII of the United Nations Charter.[29] Since the power of the Security Council to create the Tribunals through binding resolutions arises from a treaty (the United Nations Charter), it has been argued that the Statutes themselves should be treated as analogous to treaties.[30] Irrespective of whether or not the Statutes may be considered analogous to treaties, they were clearly meant to represent and stay within the norms of customary international law.[31] This was specifically emphasized by the UN Secretary-General with regard to the defendant's fair trial rights.[32] Thus, their content can be perceived as representing customary international law norms, and the jurisprudence of the two Tribunals in this area can therefore be considered interpretations of the contemporary status of customary international law.[33] While this viewpoint concerning the impact of judicial decisions on the content of customary international law is not without its critics,[34] it is enough to note here that the relevant language pertaining to the right to a fair trial in both the ICTY and ICTR Statutes is virtually identical to that contained in article 14 ICCPR on the same subject.[35] Therefore, even if the ICTY and ICTR

---

[29] For the ICTY, see S/RES/827 (1993) of 25 May 1993; for the ICTR, see S/RES/955 (1994) of 8 November 1994. ICTY Statute – reprinted at *ILM* 32 (1993), 1192 et seq. ICTR Statute – reprinted at *ILM* 33 (1994), 1598 et seq.

[30] See R. Cryer, "Of Custom, Treaties, Scholars and the Gavel: The Influence of the International Criminal Tribunals on the ICRC Customary Law Study", *Journal of Conflict & Security Law* 11 (2006), 239 et seq. (242).

[31] See G. Werle, *Principles of International Criminal Law*, 2005, 50.

[32] See Report of the Secretary-General pursuant to para. 2 of S/RES/808 (1993) of 22 February 1993, para. 106.

[33] See Cryer, see note 30, 6.

[34] Ibid.

[35] Cf. article 14 (1) ICCPR "All persons shall be equal before the courts and tribunals" with article 20 (1) ICTR Statute "All persons shall be equal before the International Tribunal for Rwanda" and article 21 (1) ICTY Statute "All persons shall be equal before the International Tribunal"; cf. article 14

are incapable of affirmatively determining the content of customary international law in the area of the right to a fair trial, their interpretation of language that is identical to that found in the ICCPR is relevant in attempting to determine the content of the ICCPR rights.

The working languages of each Tribunal are English and French.[36] However, they each regularly accommodate both witnesses and defendants who neither understand nor speak these working languages. As such, the standard working practice is to automatically provide interpretation at each oral proceeding, in order to fulfill the defendant's right to an interpreter.[37] Such interpretation practices, however, do not solve the linguistic issues concerning documents and evidence, all of which must be presented to the court in one of the working languages.[38] Considering that the Prosecutor's evidence alone in a case can easily exceed 10,000 pages of documents,[39] a sight translation for the defendant of each document (as allowed under ECtHR jurisprudence) is impractical given the amount of delay in the proceedings this would cause. As such, the Tribunals have been forced to deal with the issue straight on, and the result has been a very rich and detailed view of the right to translation in the context of an international criminal trial.

---

(3)(f) ICCPR's language "have the free assistance of an interpreter if he cannot understand or speak the language used in court" with the language of article 21 (4)(f) ICTY Statute "have the free assistance of an interpreter if he cannot understand or speak the language used in the International Tribunal" and article 20 (4)(f) ICTR Statute "have the free assistance of an interpreter if he or she cannot understand or speak the language used in the International Tribunal for Rwanda"; and finally note the identical nature of article 14 (3)(a) ICCPR, article 20 (4)(a) ICTR Statute and article 21 (4)(a) ICTY Statute.

[36] Arts 33 ICTY Statute; 31 ICTR Statute.

[37] For the ICTY, see *Prosecutor v. Delalić* (Case No. IT-96-21-T), Trial Chamber, Decision on Defence Application for Forwarding the Documents in the Language of the Accused, 25 September 1996, para. 12; for the ICTR, see *Prosecutor v. Muhimana*, Case No. ICTR-95-1B, Trial Chamber, Decision on the Defence Motion for the Translation of Prosecution and Procedural Documents into Kinyarwanda, the Language of the Accused, and into French, the Language of His Counsel, 6 November 2001, para. 34.

[38] See *Delalić*, see note 37, paras 6, 10.

[39] See ICTY, *Prosecutor v. Šešelj*, Case No. IT-03-67-T, Trial Chamber, Second Order concerning the Translation of Documents the Accused Intends to Tender as Defence Evidence, 19 February 2008.

2. Evaluation of the Case Law from the *Ad Hoc* Tribunals

The first major case arising concerning document translation was *Prosecutor* v. *Delalić* of the ICTY, in which the Defense requested that "all 'transcripts and other documents'" be provided to the accused in his native language of Bosnian during the pre-trial phase of the case.[40] The Tribunal held that the Defense was not entitled to the translation of every transcript or document, but rather was entitled only to translated versions of any and all evidence that would be submitted by the Prosecution at trial, any materials submitted in support of the indictment against the accused, and any orders or decisions issued by the Tribunal.[41] For all other evidence (such as prosecutorial discovery, correspondence, or transcripts), the working languages of the Tribunal were sufficient and no pre-trial translation for the accused into Bosnian was necessary.[42] In so holding, the ICTY based its decision *not* upon the accused's right to an interpreter (as the ECtHR had done), but rather upon the concepts of equality before the Tribunal and the accused's right to be informed of the charges against him in a language that he understood.[43] Thus, pre-trial translations of relevant documents were required to ensure that the Defense (including the accused) and the Prosecutor were able to interact on an equal footing before the Tribunal, and also to allow the accused to understand the evidence that would be presented at trial to prove his guilt. Although the ICTY buttressed its holding using the article 21 (4)(a) language of understanding "the nature and cause of the charge against" the accused, its reasoning is somewhat similar to that of the ECtHR in *Kamasinski* v. *Austria*, in that it is primarily concerned with the accused's ability to understand the evidence presented at trial.

In the 2001 case of *Prosecutor* v. *Muhimana*, the ICTR was faced with a similar request from an accused to have "all" documents translated into his native language of Kinyarwanda.[44] Following *Prosecutor* v. *Delalić*, the ICTR likewise ruled that the accused was not entitled to the translation of every document in the case, but instead was limited to those documents allowed under *Prosecutor* v. *Delalić*, as well as any and all prior statements from witnesses that the Prosecution anticipated

---

[40] See *Delalić*, see note 37, para. 1.
[41] Ibid., Disposition.
[42] Ibid.
[43] Ibid., para. 6, citing specifically article 21 (1) and (4)(a) ICTY Statute.
[44] See *Prosecutor* v. *Muhimana*, see note 37, para. 3.

calling at trial.⁴⁵ The ICTR, however, while placing great emphasis on *Prosecutor v. Delalić*, distanced itself from the ICTY's decision and reasoning in one important respect: it explicitly based its ruling in part upon the accused's right to an interpreter.⁴⁶ The Tribunal stated that, in its opinion, "the right of an accused to have the free assistance of an interpreter ... covers, not only oral proceedings, but also ... some documents relating to this case."⁴⁷ In doing so, the ICTR both cited with approval and discussed at length the jurisprudence of the ECtHR, specifically *Kamasinski v. Austria*.⁴⁸ In every other respect, the rules laid down in *Prosecutor v. Delalić* were followed.

For its part, the ICTY has continued to both follow and refine the rules that originated in the *Prosecutor v. Delalić* opinion. Concerning the pre-trial stage, the ICTY now requires the translation not only of the documents listed in *Prosecutor v. Delalić*, but also any prior "statements obtained by the Prosecutor from the Accused", any statements by witnesses that the Prosecution will likely call to testify, any statements by witnesses that will be entered into evidence in lieu of oral testimony (Rule 92*bis* statements), as well as any "[e]xculpatory material disclosed by the Prosecutor according to Article 68 of the [ICTY] Rules."⁴⁹ In addition, where the accused has chosen to represent himself, the Tribunal has extended the right to translation to include any motions filed by the Prosecutor and any Defense briefs filed by counsel for co-accused (if there are co-accused in the case).⁵⁰ During the trial phase of the case, the right to translation also has been held to require the possible translation of any exhibits tendered by the Prosecutor.⁵¹ In addition, the ICTY has clarified extra classes of documents of which the accused is not entitled to a translation, including any pre-trial briefs

---

45 Ibid., paras 22-26.
46 Ibid., para. 16.
47 Ibid.
48 Ibid., paras 16-21.
49 ICTY, *Prosecutor v. Ljubičić*, Case No. IT-00-41-PT, Trial Chamber, Decision on the Defence Counsel's Request for Translation of All Documents, 20 November 2002.
50 See ICTY, *Prosecutor v. Prlić*, Case No. IT-04-74-PT, Pre-Trial Judge, Order for the Translation of Documents, 17 January 2006, see also ICTY, *Prosecutor v. Šešelj*, Case No. IT-03-67-T, Trial Chamber, Order on the Translation of Documents, 6 March 2003.
51 See *Prosecutor v. Ljubičić*, see note 49.

filed by the Prosecutor⁵² and any unrelated materials such as "case-law of other jurisdictions, books, and other literature."⁵³

As an enforcement mechanism for its translation rulings, the Tribunal has further held that any untranslated document may not be submitted as evidence.⁵⁴ Needless to say, given that the documents in each case can easily number in the thousands of pages,⁵⁵ the work required to sort through, organize, classify and then submit the required documents to the Registry for translation in any given case is substantial (as are the financial costs involved). This has, on occasions, led to significant delays by parties, which might, in theory, jeopardize that party's ability to enter evidence into the record.⁵⁶ In practice, however, the ICTY has been highly accommodating of time delays caused by individual parties, thus alleviating any concern in this respect.⁵⁷ However, delays are not solely the provenance of the parties; the translation workload placed upon the Registry has also played its part.⁵⁸ These delays have caused unease at both Tribunals, raising the specter of possible violations of the accused's right to an expeditious trial.⁵⁹ In the end, however, the accused's ability to understand the evidence (through translation) has been placed ahead of any concerns regarding expediency, judicial efficiency and costs.⁶⁰

---

52   See ICTY, *Prosecutor v. Popović*, Case No. IT-05-88-PT, Trial Chamber, Decision on Joint Defence Motions Requesting the Translation of the Pre-trial Brief and Specific Motions, 24 May 2006.
53   ICTY *Prosecutor v. Šešelj*, Case No. IT-03-67-T, Trial Chamber, Decision on Request for Material Cited in Prosecution Pre-trial Brief, 12 July 2006.
54   See ICTY *Prosecutor v. Naletilić*, Case No. IT-98-34-T, Trial Chamber, Decision on Defence's Motion concerning Translation of All Documents, 18 October 2001.
55   See *Prosecutor v. Šešelj*, see note 39.
56   See ICTY, *Prosecutor v. Milutinović*, Case No. IT-05-87-T, Trial Chamber, Decision on *Lukić* Defence Motion for Reconsideration of Denial of Extension of Time and Leave to File Replies, 10 June 2008.
57   Ibid.
58   See C.P.R. Romano/ A. Nollkaemper/ J.K. Kleffner (eds), *Internationalized Criminal Courts and Tribunals: Sierra Leone, East Timor, Kosovo, and Cambodia*, 2004, 342.
59   See ICTY, *Prosecutor v. Milošević*, Case No. IT-02-54-T, Trial Chamber, Decision on Prosecution Motion for Permission to Disclose Witness Statements in English, 19 September 2001; see also *Prosecutor v. Ljubičić*, see note 49; *Prosecutor v. Naletilić*, see note 54.
60   Ibid.

3. Assessment

The considerable jurisprudence of the *ad hoc* Tribunals concerning the right to translation can be seen as both a clarification and an expansion of the ECtHR's doctrine in this area. While the ECtHR has focused mainly on the concept of "necessity", entitling the accused only to the translation of those documents that are "necessary" in order to ensure the comprehensibility of the oral proceedings, the *ad hoc* Tribunals have addressed different concerns. They have mainly set out to alleviate any inequalities before the Tribunals effecting either party, while simultaneously seeking to ensure that the accused will be able to understand the evidence that will be used against him at trial. It is logical to assume that the ECtHR doctrine would guarantee, in practical effect, the translation of many of the same documents covered by the *ad hoc* Tribunals' jurisprudence, especially the evidence presented at trial. Yet, it is also likely that the *ad hoc* Tribunals' rules in this area go some way past what the ECtHR jurisprudence would require in criminal proceedings.

This divergence in coverage between the ECtHR and *ad hoc* Tribunals can be largely attributed to the different levels of importance that each jurisdiction places on the reasons why translations are necessary. The ECtHR is focused on the right of the accused to understand the oral proceedings (and thus invoke the right to an interpreter as the justifying provision), while the *ad hoc* Tribunals are focused on the concept of equality before the Tribunals and the necessity of the accused to understand the evidence supporting the charges against him. Since each is focused on alleviating a different problem, they logically arrive at different solutions. The result is that the *ad hoc* Tribunals have set out a more expansive, and significantly more detailed, entitlement than the ECtHR has.

That the right to translation has been more fleshed out by the *ad hoc* Tribunals is both a positive and a negative development in regard to the interpretation of the identical ICCPR provisions. On the one hand, the extra attention lavished upon the question has necessarily resulted in increased analysis by well-respected and well-qualified independent judges.[61] That their opinions may be of some persuasive influence on the eventual interpretation of the analogous ICCPR provisions can only be seen as a positive development. On the other hand, it is worth asking whether the decisions and practices of the Tribunals can really be

---

[61] See Cryer, see note 30, 245-246 (regarding the general influence of judicial decisions, and their specific use as a source of international law).

that helpful. While it is true that the language difference between the ICCPR and the relevant Tribunal Statutes is minimal, the circumstances in which each provision must be applied could not be more distinct.

The ICCPR is meant to set the minimum guarantees pertaining to the right to a fair trial in domestic jurisdictions, as is the nearly identical provision of the ECHR. The Tribunal provisions, however, are meant to cover the necessities of a fair trial in specific international criminal Tribunals. These dissimilar contexts make a great deal of difference,[62] since few domestic jurisdictions have the necessary experience of dealing with a multiple language trial or the built-in translation and court interpretation services that the *ad hoc* Tribunals possess. The different realities in each jurisdiction call into question the relevance of the Tribunals' jurisprudence for national courts, since the Tribunal rulings can be seen as developing international criminal procedural thresholds for a fair trial, and not necessarily domestic thresholds.

In other words, when the ICTY rules that all exculpatory evidence must be translated for the accused, this may very well be seen as a necessity given the specific rules applied in the context of a multilingual international Tribunal with a well-functioning translation department where the disclosure of such evidence is required by that Tribunal's internal rules.[63] Whether the pre-trial translation of such evidence would be necessary in a domestic proceeding operating under different rules and with different budgetary realities is highly questionable. There is, in essence, a difference between national criminal procedures required by international law and those criminal procedures required at international criminal Tribunals (so-called international criminal procedure). As such, the expansive entitlement to translated documents as practiced by the *ad hoc* Tribunals, while certainly laudable, may not be the best guide as to the possible content of a right to translation under the ICCPR, regardless of the similarity in language between the *ad hoc* Tribunal Statutes and the Covenant.

Yet, though the more detailed regime expounded by the *ad hoc* Tribunals may not be completely applicable to national jurisdictions, the jurisprudence of the Tribunals is still rather instructive on certain issues. First, the unmistakable thrust of the Tribunals' opinions is in favor of a right to translation. As for the content of this right, leaving argument

---

[62] See Robinson, see note 3, 9 (arguing that "there is no gainsaying that context is significant in construing provisions of the ICTY's Statute and Rules").

[63] See Rule 68 ICTY Rules of Procedure and Evidence, Doc. IT/32/Rev. 46.

over the details aside, it would appear to set the minimum bar at least at the same level as the ECtHR in *Kamasinski* v. *Austria*. Second, the *ad hoc* Tribunals supported their "right to translation" using different provisions of the right to a fair trial than the ECtHR did (though the ICTR also acknowledged the importance of the right to an interpreter as a source provision). This is important for the simple reason that the HRC denied the existence of a right to translation without considering the specific fair trial provisions relied upon in the *ad hoc* jurisprudence. Thus, it cannot be discounted that the concept of equality (or the right to understand the charges, or both) might also eventually be seen as a source provision for a right to translation under the ICCPR. At the end of the day, the endorsement of the right to translation by the *ad hoc* Tribunals, and their implicit or explicit approval of the ECtHR case law on the issue, is significant as to the eventual outcome of the debate over whether or not such a right exists under the ICCPR. To what extent the detailed expansion of the right contributes to the overall debate, or eventually helps define or clarify the boundaries of an ICCPR right, is yet to be determined. One place where the *ad hoc* Tribunals' decisions have already had an impact, however, is with the founding of the ICC.

V. The Rome Statute of the International Criminal Court

1. The Legal Framework

The relative success of the *ad hoc* Tribunals at the international level helped lead to the founding of the ICC through the successful negotiation and entry into force of the Rome Statute of the ICC (Rome Statute).[64] Supplementing the Rome Statute are the ICC Rules of Procedure and Evidence,[65] which are "based in part on the experience and practice of the ICTY and ICTR."[66] As such, the entire development and structure of the ICC can be seen as heavily influenced by both the success of the *ad hoc* Tribunals, as well as their actual jurisprudence.

---

[64] UNTS Vol. 2187 No. 38544; see also W.A. Schabas, *An Introduction to the International Criminal Court*, 2001, 12.

[65] See ICC Rules of Procedure and Evidence, Official Records ICC-ASP/1/3.

[66] M.C. Bassiouni, "The Sources and Content of International Criminal Law: A Theoretical Framework", in: K. Koufa (ed.), *The New International Criminal Law: 2001 International Law Session*, 2003, 19 et seq. (184-185).

Unlike the *ad hoc* Tribunal Statutes, the Rome Statute specifically addresses the necessity of translations to the guarantee of a fair trial. Article 55 (1)(c) Rome Statute guarantees an individual under investigation the right to have a competent interpreter while being questioned, as well as "such translations as are necessary to meet the requirements of fairness." In addition, and more importantly in this context, article 67 (1)(f) Rome Statute states that the accused is entitled to "have, free of any cost, the assistance of a competent interpreter and such translations as are necessary to meet the requirements of fairness, if any of the proceedings of or documents presented to the court are not in a language which the accused fully understands and speaks." From these provisions, several things are immediately clear.

First, the right to translation is specifically guaranteed, which is a clear break from the previous treaties and Statutes that have been discussed. Second, the right to translation is located alongside the right to an interpreter in both provisions, thus adding credence to the ECtHR's interpretation that these two entitlements are necessarily connected when seeking to ensure that the accused is able to understand any oral proceedings (or interrogations, as the case may be). Third, the right, as formulated, substantially mirrors the ECtHR's language of "necessity". The Rome Statute speaks of those documents that are "necessary to meet the requirements of fairness" while the ECtHR protects those documents that are "necessary for [the accused] to understand ... in order to have the benefit of a fair trial."[67] In each instance, the fairness of the proceedings, and what is necessary to achieve that fairness, is of paramount concern.

Given the similarities between the Rome Statute and the ECtHR jurisprudence on this issue, the argument can be made that the Rome Statute effectively codified the ECtHR standards as to the right to translation. The fact that the drafters of the Statute specifically altered the "normal" fair trial provisions (as can be seen in the identical wording of the ECHR, ICCPR, and Statutes of the ICTY and ICTR) to include language expressly granting a right that was, to that point at least, a court-created entitlement, lends credence to the idea that the Rome Statute meant to codify and clarify that right. In effect, the drafters meant to explicitly acknowledge a right to translation that other jurisdictions had implicitly found necessary to the fairness of a trial. That the language used, and its placement within the right to interpreter pro-

---

[67] Cf. article 67 (1)(f) Rome Statute with *Kamasinski v. Austria*, see note 21, para. 74.

vision, reflect the jurisprudence of the ECtHR is likely no accident, but rather more probably a conscious choice meant to reflect what the drafters perceived as the majority rule in this area. If the idea was to make explicit what had previously only been implicit, then recognizing a baseline standard that had already found backing in the ECtHR and *ad hoc* Tribunals would seem a logical adoption.

The ICC's foremost decision in this area adds support to this theory. In *Prosecutor v. Lubanga*, the accused sought the translation of certain procedural and evidentiary documents into a language which he was capable of understanding (French, in this instance).[68] The ICC ruled that the Rome Statute did not entitle the accused to the translation of "all procedural documents and all evidentiary materials", but rather only a smaller subset of these documents.[69] In so holding, the ICC relied extensively on *Kamasinski v. Austria* and the ECtHR's jurisprudence as to the implicit right to translation under the ECHR.[70] The Court even went so far as to affirm that its interpretation of the explicit right to translation found in the Rome Statute was "fully consistent with the case law of the [ECtHR] on this matter."[71] That the ICC would seek to align the Rome Statute's right to translation provision with the ECtHR's jurisprudence in this area can be taken as evidence that the court acknowledged the ECtHR standard as the authoritative rule, even with regard to the interpretation of an independent treaty provision. Whether the drafters of the Rome Statute intended to codify this standard or not is less important than the outcome of their efforts: the ECtHR standard was explicitly recognized as determinative as to the right to translation embodied in article 67 (1)(f) Rome Statute.

2. The Impact of the Rome Statute on the Interpretation of the International Covenant on Civil and Political Rights

The question is whether this specific endorsement of the right has any effect on the interpretation of the ICCPR. As mentioned, the language of the Rome Statute is substantially different from the ICCPR. Thus, unlike the *ad hoc* Tribunals' analysis of identical language, any jurispru-

---

[68] See ICC *Prosecutor v. Lubanga Dyilo,* Case No. ICC-01/04-01/06-268, 4 August 2006, 2.
[69] Ibid., 6.
[70] Ibid., 5.
[71] Ibid., 6.

dence emanating from the ICC on this issue is likely unhelpful as to the content of the ICCPR's language. Rather, it is the Rome Statute itself that provides the most potential impact on the interpretation of the ICCPR. If one accepts that the ICCPR embodies the contemporary customary international law standards pertaining to the right to a fair trial (even to the point of being *jus cogens*), while simultaneously accepting that the Rome Statute is meant to confirm and clarify those very same standards,[72] then it becomes clear that the text of the Rome Statute itself can play a significant role in the interpretation of the ICCPR's provisions in that area. In other words, the very fact that the Rome Statute is more precise as to fair trial standards (and purports that these are a reflection of customary international law) than the ICCPR (which also represents the same standards) can be taken to mean that the language in the Rome Statute is a clarification of what the ICCPR is meant to embody. In this interpretation, the provisions of the Rome Statute in this area are nothing more than a more detailed explanation of the more general ICCPR provisions, or, at a minimum, the customary international law standards which the ICCPR's provisions are meant to represent.

Utilizing the Rome Statute as a source for the interpretation of the ICCPR is not without legal precedent. Article 31 (3)(c) Vienna Convention on the Law of Treaties, when addressing the general rules of treaty interpretation, dictates that "(3) [t]here shall be taken into account, together with the context: ... (c) any relevant rules of international law applicable in the relations between the parties."[73] Among the "relevant rules" that must be taken into consideration are customary international law norms.[74] Although in the past many courts have shown reluctance to overtly refer to customary norms when interpreting treaty provisions,[75] in recent times the practice has grown in both importance and acceptance.[76] Now, informing the interpretation of a treaty provi-

---

[72] See Cryer, see note 30, 10; Werle, see note 31, 49.
[73] Article 31 (3)(c) Vienna Convention on the Law of Treaties, see note 9.
[74] See C. McLachlan, "The Principle of Systematic Integration and Article 31(3)(c) of the Vienna Convention", *ICLQ* 54 (2005), 279 et seq. (290-291). Other treaties are also generally considered "relevant rules" that must be taken into consideration as interpretive help, but their actual usage is still relatively controversial and as such, less helpful.
[75] See P. Sands, "Treaty, Custom and the Cross-fertilization of International Law", *Yale Human Rights & Development Law Journal* 1 (1998), 85 et seq. (95).
[76] See McLachlan, see note 74, 280.

sion using the relevant customary international law norms in that area is seen simply as fitting the provision into its "proper place within the larger normative order."[77] Given that the ICCPR provision is less specific than the Rome Statute provision, and the latter can be interpreted as a clarification of the former, it is not only entirely appropriate to look to the Rome Statute as evidence of customary international law in this instance, but exceedingly useful as well.

There is, however, a minor logical flaw in this argument. If the Rome Statute was intended to codify a more detailed and precise version of an already existing general customary law norm (the ICCPR standard), then it is not altogether clear why this would be necessary. If it is taken for granted that the right to translation already exists as a necessary part of the right to a fair trial under customary law, then there would appear no need to explicitly sanction this right. This is especially true given the unproblematic recognition of the right by both the ECtHR and the *ad hoc* Tribunals. It can just as easily be argued that the codification of the right to translation was made explicit specifically because the right was up to that point not an accepted part of the right to a fair trial under international law. In other words, the States Parties made the right explicit because they feared that the right would not necessarily exist as part of the ICC's procedures if they had not. Seen in this light, the Rome Statute, rather than advancing the development of the right to translation, can be taken as evidence that the right did not exist absent specific expression.

Furthermore, there is some doubt as to whether the Rome Statute itself actually embodies customary international law in this area. Werle, while acknowledging that the Rome Statute is meant to conform to and clarify existing customary international law standards in criminal law, draws a distinction between substantive and procedural criminal law standards.[78] He argues that although the substantive criminal law provisions reflect customary law, the procedural standards enshrined in the Rome Statute likely do not.[79] Likewise, just as with the *ad hoc* Tribunals, it can be argued that the provisions of the Rome Statute, even if accepted as customary international law standards in this area, actually reflect norms of international criminal procedure, and not national procedural requirements that would be relevant to the interpretation of the ICCPR.

---

[77] Ibid., 312.
[78] See Werle, see note 31, 50.
[79] Ibid.

Cryer as well doubts whether the Rome Statute accurately reflects customary international law in every instance, asserting that in some instances it either falls short of contemporary standards or goes too far.[80] Even the minimum level assertion of the Rome Statute's embodiment of customary international law, that it at least reflects the *opinio juris* of a "great number of states",[81] does little to support the notion that the Rome Statute embodies customary international law standards, since several of the most powerful and populous nations have failed to ratify it.[82] While it is highly unlikely that these nations abstained from supporting the ICC due to the Rome Statute's provisions on the right to translation, their nonparticipation in this Treaty does nothing to support the assertion that the Rome Statute represents contemporary norms of customary international law in this area either.

And yet, despite the arguments given above, there is still a case to be made that the procedural rules of the Rome Statute do indeed reflect contemporary standards specifically as to the right to a fair trial. As Bassiouni has argued, the procedural rules of the ICC, as well as the *ad hoc* Tribunals are not only "based on general principles of procedural law which emerge from the laws and practices of the world's major criminal justice systems," they also mirror the rules and principles enshrined in numerous international and regional treaties.[83] As such, they represent a "convergence of international, regional, and national legal norms that represent contemporary standards of procedural due process."[84]

Moreover, even if the overall procedural standards reflected in the Rome Statute do not, as a whole, represent established norms of customary international law, it is still possible to argue that the treaty's specific right to translation standard itself does indeed merit such a distinction. One may reject the argument that the entirety of the procedural rules of the ICC represents customary international law norms, and yet still accept the assertion that specific provisions therein do reflect such standards, so long as they have sufficient international sup-

---

[80] See Cryer, see note 30, 10.
[81] ICTY, *Prosecutor v. Furundžija*, Case No. IT-95-17/1-T, Trial Chamber, Judgment, 10 December 1998, para. 227.
[82] For instance, China, India, the United States of America, and Russia (comprising nearly 43 per cent of the world's population, according to the CIA Factbook) have all failed to ratify the Rome Statute.
[83] Bassiouni, see note 66, 185.
[84] Ibid.

port. In this instance, it may plausibly be argued that the right to translation, given that it has been recognized by several different highly influential international jurisdictions with virtually no direct objections from the international community, has garnered such extensive support. That each of these courts (the ICTY, ICTR, and the ECtHR) have pointed to different parts of the right to a fair trial as the origin of the right to translation does little to undermine the existence of that right. Rather, it simply makes the determination of the eventual content of that right harder to assess. At an absolute minimum, the specific insertion of a right to translation into the Rome Statute serves as evidence of a larger movement towards acknowledgment of the right to translation at the international level.

VI. Conclusion

In the end, the question as to whether or not a right to translation exists under the ICCPR is far from settled. It would perhaps be easier to simply say that the right to translation exists as a norm of customary international law, and leave aside any enquiry into the ICCPR. However, it is not a foregone conclusion that a customary norm exists in this context either. As mentioned above, both the *ad hoc* Tribunal Statutes and the Rome Statute purport to represent customary international law, but the question must be asked whether they supposedly represent customary norms as to national or international criminal procedures. A fairly convincing argument can be made that the procedural fair trial guarantees embodied in the international Statutes represent customary international law applicable to any criminal proceedings before an international criminal Tribunal or court. Yet, it is less clear that these procedural guarantees would (or even could) apply equally to domestic criminal prosecutions in national courts; the contexts are different enough to make their applicability questionable. As such, while the international Statutes may represent customary international law standards on the right to a fair trial (and a right to translation), they probably only do so at the international level, which renders them largely unhelpful to the establishment of a truly universal standard. The practice of the ECtHR, on the other hand, does support the creation of such a standard, since it relates to domestic prosecutions. Standing alone, though, its jurisprudence would appear insufficient as evidence of such a universal norm.

Thus, considering the uncertainty surrounding the existence of a customary international law norm in this context, the ICCPR remains the best hope as to the universal existence of a right to translation. That the HRC expressly denied the existence of such a right in *Harward* v. *Norway* is problematic, but hardly conclusive to the issue. In its Decision, the HRC placed great emphasis on the particular circumstances of the case and limited its consideration to whether the right to have adequate time and facilities to prepare a defense required the translation of documents.[85] It implicitly left open the possibility that other facets of the right to a fair trial might entitle an accused to a right to translation. This is precisely what the ECtHR and *ad hoc* Tribunals have found. Within the context of the right to an interpreter, and thus the guarantee of understanding the oral proceedings, both the ECtHR and the ICTR have explicitly found that such a right to translation does exist.[86] The ICTY has implicitly endorsed this rationale as well, while simultaneously finding the right to translation in the notions of equality before the court and the right to understand the evidence supporting any determination of guilt.[87] For its part, the Rome Statute represents evidence that the development of the right has reached a point that it can be codified as an accepted part of the right to fair trial.[88]

Combined with the HRC's lack of an explicit statement on the issue, the practice of these other international actors leaves open the possibility that the right to translation does indeed exist within the framework of the ICCPR. Whether or not the HRC ultimately chooses to endorse this interpretation of the right to a fair trial is, of course, an open question. Yet the positive movement in this direction by several different international actors lends credence to the theory that, while not inevitable, this is more likely to occur than not.

---

[85] See *Harward* v. *Norway*, see note 10.
[86] See *Prosecutor* v. *Muhimana*, see note 37; *Kamasinski* v. *Austria*, see note 21.
[87] See *Prosecutor* v. *Delalić*, see note 37.
[88] See Rome Statute, see note 64.

Human Rights Within a Multilayered Constitution: The Example of Freedom of Expression and the WTO

Maya Hertig Randall

I. Introduction
II. Multilayered Governance
   1. Characteristics
   2. Relationship and Interaction between the Various Layers of Governance
   3. The Example of the EU and the ECHR
   4. Insights for the WTO
III. Free Speech Functions and Values
   1. Economic Perspective
      a. The Impact of Speech on the Functioning of Markets
      b. The Specificity of the Speech Market
      c. Implications for the Protection and Regulation of Speech
   2. Free Speech Theory
      a. The Argument from Autonomy
      b. The Argument from Democracy
      c. The Argument from Truth
   3. Synthesis
IV. Free Speech and Free Trade within the Multilayered Constitution
   1. The National Level
   2. The Regional Level
      a. Human Rights Regimes
      b. Free Trade Regimes (The European Union)
   3. The Global Level
      a. The ICCPR
      b. The ICESCR
      c. Customary International Law
   4. Synthesis
V. Integrating Freedom of Speech within the WTO
   1. GATT and GATS
      a. "Defensive" Use of Free Speech
      b. "Offensive" Use of Free Speech
   2. TRIPS
      a. "Defensive" Uses
      b. "Offensive" Uses
VI. Conclusion

Abstract

This article focuses on the interface of the WTO with a quintessential civil and political right, the right to freedom of expression. It analyses both potential synergies and conflicts between WTO law and free speech. Since the WTO operates within a multilayered governance structure, the article adopts a comparative approach, examining the protection and relationship of free speech and free trade on the domestic, regional and global layers. Building on these findings, the article argues that the WTO judiciary should interpret exception clauses broadly and grant members sufficient leeway to implement free speech-enhancing policies. Such "defensive uses" of freedom of expression should be admissible even if they are not underpinned by a universally shared conception of free speech. By contrast, "offensive" uses of freedom of expression require a more cautious approach. They should preclude the justification of a WTO inconsistent measure in two cases: firstly, when it was found in breach of free speech by an international human rights monitoring body, and secondly, when it consists in a policy of state censorship and repression targeting political speech, broadly defined, and thus contravenes customary international law. Both defensive and offensive uses of free speech are ultimately supportive of the WTO's legitimacy and mandate.

Keywords

Multilayered Governance; Freedom of Expression; WTO; Trade and Human Rights; Global Constitutionalism

I. Introduction

How do human rights and the law of the WTO relate to each other? This "trade-and" question[1] has attracted much attention and spawned

---

[1] This expression is inspired by J.P. Trachtman, "Trade and ... Problems, Cost-Benefit Analysis and Subsidiarity", *EJIL* 9 (1998), 32 et seq.

considerable controversy.² Trade specialists have argued that "human rights and trade are mutually supportive. Human rights are essential to the good functioning of the multilateral trading system, and trade and

---

2   For general studies on the relationship between human rights and the WTO, see S. Joseph, *Blame it on the WTO?*, 2011; S. Joseph/ D. Kinley/ J. Waincyme (eds), *The World Trade Organization and Human Rights: Interdisciplinary Perspectives*, 2009; J. Harrison, *The Human Rights Impact of the World Trade Organization*, 2007; C.J. Lopez Hurtado, *The WTO Legal System and International Human Rights*, 2006; D. Kinley, *Civilising Globalisation: Human Rights and the Global Economy*, 2009, in particular at 60 et seq.; T. Cottier/ J. Pauwelyn/ E. Bürgi Bonanomi (eds), *Human Rights and International Trade*, 2005; W. Benedek, "The World Trade Organization and Human Rights", in: W. Benedek/ K. De Feyter/ F. Marrella (eds), *Economic Globalisation and Human Rights*, 2007, 137-169; B. Konstantinov, "Human Rights and the WTO: Are They Really Oil and Water?", *JWT* 43 (2009), 317 et seq.; R. Wai, "Countering, Branding, Dealing: Using Economic and Social Rights in and Around the International Trade Regime", *EJIL* 14 (2003), 35 et seq.; C. Dommen, "Raising Human Rights Concerns in the World Trade Organization: Actors, Processes and Possible Strategies", *HRQ* 24 (2002), 24 et seq.; S. Leader, "Trade and Human Rights II", in: P.F.J. Macrory/ A.E. Appleton/ M.G. Plummer, *The World Trade Organization: Legal, Economic and Political Analysis*, Vol. 2, 2005, 664-695; A.E. Appleton, "The World Trade Organization: Implications for Human Rights and Democracy", *Thesaurus Acroasium* 29 (2000), 415 et seq.; R. Howse/ M. Mutua, "Protecting Human Rights in a Global Economy. Challenges for the World Trade Organization", in: *Rights and Democracy*, 2000; J. Bhagwati, "Trade Linkage and Human Rights", in: J. Bhagwati/ M. Hirs (eds), *The Uruguay Round and Beyond: Essays in Honor of Arthur Dunkel*, 1998, 241-250; S.H. Cleveland, "Human Rights Sanctions and the World Trade Organization", in: F. Francioni (ed.), *Environment, Human Rights and International Trade*, 2001, 199-261; T. Flory/ N. Ligneul, "Commerce international, droits de l'homme, mondialisation: les droits de l'homme et l'Organisation mondial du commerce", in: *Commerce mondiale et protection des droits de l'homme: les droits de l'homme à l'épreuve de la globalisation des échanges économiques*, 2001, 179-191; H. Lim, "Trade and Human Rights: What's At Issue?", *JWT* 35 (2001), 275 et seq.; A.H. Qureshi, "International Trade and Human Rights from the Perspective of the WTO", in: F. Weiss/ E. Denter/ P. de Waart (eds), *International Economic Law with a Human Face*, 1998, 159-173; P. Stirling, "The Use of Trade Sanctions as an Enforcement Mechanism for Basic Human Rights: A Proposal for Addition to the World Trade Organization", *Am. U. J. Int'l L. & Pol'y* 11 (1996), 1 et seq.

WTO rules contribute to the realization of human rights."³ Human rights lawyers, by contrast, tend to highlight the different normative foundations of international trade and human rights law and the potential for conflict between the two regimes, accusing the other camp of conflating economic interests with rights derived from human dignity and protecting the most fundamental interests of humanity.⁴ A report of the former Sub-Commission on the Promotion and Protection of Human Rights went as far as to describe the WTO as a "nightmare for human rights in developing countries."⁵ Reflecting these antagonistic

---

3   Speech by P. Lamy at the Colloquium on Human Rights and the Global Economy, Geneva, 13 January 2010, <http://www.wto.org>; the mutually reinforcing nature of trade and human rights has been mainly stressed in the writings of Petersmann. See e.g. E.U. Petersmann, "From 'Negative' to 'Positive' Integration in the WTO: Time for 'Mainstreaming Human Rights' into WTO Law", *CML Rev.* 37 (2000), 1363 et seq.; id., "Human Rights and the Law of the World Trade Organization", *JWT* 37 (2003), 241 et seq.; id. "Trade and Human Rights I", in: Macrory/ Appleton/ Plummer, see note 2, 623-662; id., "Time for a United Nations 'Global Compact' for Integrating Human Rights Law of Worldwide Organizations: Lessons from European Integration", *EJIL* 13 (2002), 621 et seq.; id., "Human Rights, International Economic Law and Constitutional Justice", *EJIL* 19 (2008), 769 et seq. The human rights dimension of the WTO is also emphasised by Qureshi, see note 2 and Lim, see note 2.
4   P. Alston, "Resisting the Merger and Acquisition of Human Rights by Trade Law: A Reply to Petersmann," *EJIL* 13 (2002), 815 et seq.; Lopez Hurtado, see note 2, 22 et seq. M. Cohn, "The World Trade Organization: Elevating Property Interests Above Human Rights", *Ga. J. Int'l & Comp. L.* 29 (2001), 247 et seq.; A.C. Habbard/ M. Guiraud, "The World Trade Organisation and Human Rights", FIDH Position Paper, November 1999, <http://www.fidh.org/rapports>; F. Garcia, "Global Market and Human Rights: Trading Away the Human Rights Principle", *Brook. J. Int'l L.* 25 (1999), 51 et seq. (63), holding that the normative foundations of international trade law and human rights are "if not incompatible, then at least in fundamental tension"; for a comment, see S. Charnovitz, "The Globalization of Economic Human Rights", *Brook. J. Int'l L.* 25 (1999), 113 et seq.; for a more general claim that classical economics and human rights are incompatible, see M. Couret Branco, *Economics versus Human Rights*, 2009, 3-4.
5   J. Oloko-Onyango/ D. Udagama, "The Realization of Economic, Cultural and Social Rights: Globalization and its Impact on the Full Enjoyment of Human Rights", Report of the Expert Group of the Sub-Commission on the Promotion and Protection of Human Rights, 15 June 2000, Doc. E/CN.4/Sub.2/2000/13, also known as the "Nightmare Report"; for a

views, the relationship between trade and human rights has been described as a "history of suspicion,"⁶ "governed by distrust."⁷ The communication between human rights and trade lawyers was referred to as a dialogue of the deaf.⁸

So far, most studies have focused either on the general relationship between human rights and trade regimes or on the impact of the WTO on second and third generation rights (e.g. economic and social rights and solidarity rights),⁹ in particular labour rights, the right to health, the right to food and the right to development. The link between the multilateral trading system and first generation rights (e.g. civil and po-

---

    critical analysis, see P. Ala'i, "A Human Rights Critique of the WTO: Some Preliminary Observations", *Geo. Wash. Int'l L. Rev.* 33 (2000-2002), 537 et seq. For a more nuanced analysis, see the more recent reports by the Office of the High Commissioner for Human Rights (OHCHR), "Liberalisation of Trade and Services and Human Rights", Doc. E/CN.4/Sub.2/2002/9, 25 June 2002 (Report on GATS); id., "Globalisation and its Impact on the Full Enjoyment of Human Rights", Doc. E/CN.4/2002/54, 15 January 2002 (Report on the Agreement on Agriculture); id., "The Impact of the Agreement on Trade-Related Aspects of Intellectual Property Rights on Human Rights", Doc. E/CN.4/Sub.2/2001/13, 27 June 2001 (Report on the TRIPS Agreement); for an analysis of these reports, see Harrison, see note 2, 127 et seq.

6 Lamy, see note 3.
7 Ibid.
8 T. Cottier/ J. Pauwelyn/ E. Bürgi Bonanomi, "Linking Trade Regulation and Human Rights in International Law: An Overview", in: Cottier/ Pauwelyn/ Bürgi Bonanomi, see note 2, 7, referring to the controversy between Alston and Petersmann in the *EJIL* 2002 (see the references under note 3 and note 4). Criticism of Petersmann's work has also been voiced by R. Howse, "Human Rights in the WTO: Whose Rights, What Humanity? Comment on Petersmann", *EJIL* 13 (2002), 651 et seq.; id., "Human Rights, International Economic Law and Constitutional Justice: A Reply", *EJIL* 19 (2008), 945 et seq., replying to Petersmann 2008, see note 3; for a reply by E.U. Petersmann, see id., "Taking Human Dignity, Poverty and Empowerment of Individuals more Seriously: Rejoinder to Alston", *EJIL* 13 (2002), 845 et seq. and "Human Rights, International Economic Law and 'Constitutional Justice': A Rejoinder by E.U. Petersmann", available under <http://www.ejiltalk.org>.
9 On the classic distinction between three generations of human rights and a critical assessment, see e.g. C. Tomuschat, *Human Rights: Between Idealism and Realism*, 2008, 25-68; T. Meron, "On a Hierarchy of International Human Rights", *AJIL* 80 (1986), 1 et seq.

litical rights) has received far less attention.[10] This study is aimed at filling this gap. It will explore the interface between the WTO and a quintessential first generation right, the right to free speech. Following Howse's criticism of the excessively abstract nature of the "trade and human rights debate",[11] the present contribution will reject the assumption that the relationship between free speech and free trade can be adequately described in terms of *either* synergies *or* conflicts.

Using the example of free speech, this article also purports to nuance another divide between trade and the human rights specialists: some of the former argue that the "WTO is more than a commercial agreement; it is a human rights agreement",[12] designed to protect economic and property rights which are not essentially different from human rights.[13] Human rights lawyers retort that human rights are deontological. They are, like persons, aims in themselves, whereas free trade has essentially an instrumentalist value that consists in enhancing social welfare.[14] As will be shown, the distinction between means and ends is far from simple.[15] This claim has particular weight as far as freedom of speech is concerned. Political philosophers have tended to highlight both the intrinsic and the instrumentalist value of free speech as a *moral* right. In-

---

[10] This may be because first generation rights (apart from the right to property) are considered irrelevant for international trade. For such a view, see Flory/ Ligneul, see note 2, 180; for an essay focusing on the relationship between freedom of expression and international trade, see T. Cottier/ S. Khorana, "Linkage between Freedom of Expression and Unfair Competition Rules in International Trade: The Hertel Case and Beyond", in: Cottier/ Pauwelyn/ Bürgi Bonanomi, see note 2, 245-272; the linkage between freedom of speech and free trade is also explored by E.U. Petersmann, "Theories of Justice, Human Rights and the Constitution of International Markets", *Loyola of Los Angeles Law Review* 37 (2003), 407 et seq. (443 et seq.)

[11] Howse, see note 8.

[12] S. Charnovitz, "The WTO and the Rights of the Individual", *Intereconomics* 36 (2001), 98 et seq. (108), available at <http://www.worldtradelaw.net>.

[13] Petersmann is the most prominent exponent of this view; see his writings under note 3.

[14] Alston, see note 4, 826: "Human rights are recognized for all on the basis of the inherent human dignity of all persons. Trade-related rights are granted to individuals for instrumentalist reasons. Individuals are seen as objects rather than as holders of rights"; see also Garcia, see note 4, 62 et seq.; for a more nuanced view, see Charnovitz, see note 4, 115.

[15] This is acknowledged by Alston, see note 4, 827 et seq.

terpreting free speech provisions as a *legal* right, constitutional courts and human rights monitoring bodies, in particular the European Court of Human Rights (ECtHR), have adopted the same approach.

The emphasis on an instrumentalist rationale is one reason which has led to an overlap – and sometimes to interference – between human rights and free trade regimes, mainly on the regional but also on the global level. Since the WTO forms part of a multilayered governance structure, the question of what role free speech plays, or ought to play within the global trading system cannot be analysed in isolation. The WTO's norms, functions and rulings need to be coordinated with those of other international regimes (situated on either the global or regional level) as well as with domestic legal orders. For this reason, the present contribution opens with a section analysing the characteristics of the multilayered governance structure within which the WTO operates, focusing on the interaction between the various layers and on the different strategies of mutual accommodation (II.). The following section will focus on the linkages between free trade and free speech from both an economic vantage point and from the perspective of free speech theorists. It will highlight the interaction between free speech and free trade, as well as both intrinsic and instrumentalist rationales for protecting freedom of expression (III.). Thereafter, the paper will adopt a comparative perspective and examine to what extent free speech and free trade are protected on the various layers of governance. This analysis will also help to identify the impact of the various theoretical rationales on positive law and to show the overlap between free trade and human rights regimes (IV.). Building on the findings of the first three parts, the paper will move on to examine how free speech concerns are relevant for and can be accommodated within the WTO (V.). Section VI. concludes by summarising the main findings.

II. Multilayered Governance

1. Characteristics

Theories of multilayered governance[16] are attempts to conceptualise the complex reality that traditional governmental functions (such as guaranteeing security and collective welfare, protecting fundamental rights

---

[16] For a helpful introduction and overview, see M. Zürn/ H. Enderlein/ S. Walti (eds), *Handbook on Multi-level Governance*, 2010.

of citizens and regulating the economy) are no longer exercised predominantly on the domestic level. With the increasing international cooperation of states, regulatory powers have been transferred from the national to the regional and global level. The function of governing ceases to be confined within a single constitutional order and an overarching unified political authority, a *government*. Instead, *governance* is a more diffuse "overall process of regulating and ordering issues of public interest."[17] It implies the interaction of various layers, which together form what has been described as a "multilayered constitution",[18] a "multilevel system",[19] an "overall constitutional structure"[20] or a "five storey house", composed of a global, regional, national, sub-national and a municipal floor.[21] With respect to the "lower" national and sub-national levels, the functions of the "higher" regional and global levels are two-fold: firstly, they compensate for the declining capacity of the nation state to address common concerns that defy territorial borders.[22] Secondly, the "higher" levels act as a check against "state failures".[23] The checking function has been an important rationale for the emer-

---

[17] A. Peters, "Compensatory Constitutionalism: The Function and Potential of Fundamental International Norms and Structures", *LJIL* 19 (2006), 579 et seq. (580).

[18] See N. Bamforth/ P. Leyland (eds), *Public Law in a Multi-Layered Constitution*, 2003; in a similar vein, see I. Pernice/ R. Kanitz, "Fundamental Rights and Multilevel Constitutionalism in Europe", in: Walter Hallstein-Institut (ed.), *WHI Paper 7/2004*.

[19] See e.g. H.J. Blanke, "Der Unionsvertrag von Maastricht", *Die öffentliche Verwaltung* 46 (1993), 412 et seq. (422) (translated by the author); in a similar vein, see C. O'Cinneide, "Human Rights and Within Multi-layered Systems of Constitutional Governance: Rights Cosmopolitanism and Domestic Particularism in Tension", UC Working Papers in Law, *Criminology & Socio-Legal Studies*, Research Paper No. 12/2009, available at <http://papers.ssrn.com>; see also A. van Hoek/ T. Hol/ O. Jansen et al. (eds), *Multilevel Governance in Enforcement and Adjudication*, 2006.

[20] T. Cottier/ M. Hertig, "The Prospects of 21st Century Constitutionalism", in: A. von Bogdandy/ R. Wolfrum (eds), *Max Planck UNYB 7* (2003), 261 et seq. (298).

[21] T. Cottier, "Reforming the Swiss Federal Constitution: An International Lawyer's Perspective", in: M. Butler/ M. Pender/ J. Chalrey (eds), *The Making of Modern Switzerland 1948-1998*, 2000, 75–96; Cottier/ Hertig, see note 20, 299 et seq.

[22] Peters, see note 17, has described this function in terms of "compensatory constitutionalism".

[23] See Cottier/ Hertig, see note 20, 267.

gence of both international human rights and trade regimes, including more ambitious regimes of (economic) integration like the European Union (EU). Reflecting the traumatic experience that even democratically elected national governments could turn into a formidable threat to their own citizens, the insight prevailed after World War II that state power needed to be constrained not only from within (through domestic constitutions and judicial review) but also from without, by the international legal order. International human rights were thus proclaimed as a reaction to the "barbarous acts which have outraged the conscience of mankind"[24] and as an essential element in securing peace among nations. Preventing war was also an important rationale for the creation of the General Agreement on Tariffs and Trade (GATT, the first building block of the multilateral trading system on the global level), and economic integration on the European level. The welfare enhancing and civilising effects of trade, leading to greater interdependence and cooperation among nations,[25] were seen as an antidote to the protectionist policies preceding World War II.[26]

---

[24] See the Preamble of the Universal Declaration of Human Rights (UDHR) of 10 December 1948.

[25] See C. de Montesquieu, "Book XX. of Laws in Relation to Commerce, Considered in its Nature and Distinctions of the Spirit of Laws", first published in French in 1758; "Commerce is a cure for the most destructive prejudices; for it is almost a general rule that wherever we find agreeable manners, there commerce flourishes; and that wherever there is commerce, there we meet with agreeable manners. (...) 2. Of the Spirit of Commerce. Peace is the natural effect of trade. Two nations who traffic with each other become reciprocally dependent; for if one has an interest in buying, the other has an interest in selling: and thus their union is founded on their mutual necessities.(...) The spirit of trade produces in the mind of a man a certain sense of exact justice, opposite, on the one hand, to robbery, and on the other to those moral virtues which forbid our always adhering rigidly to the rules of private interest, and suffer us to neglect this for the advantage of others." For a critical analysis of Montesquieu's arguments and a comparison with the writings of Kant, D. Lang, "Kant et Montesquieu: A propos des vertus pacificatrices du commerce et des relations entre les nations", in: R. Theis/ L.K. Sosoe (eds), *Les sources de la philosophie kantienne au XVIIe et XVIIIe siècles*, 2005, 252-262. The case that peace and trade are linked has also been made from a different philosophical vantage point by John Stuart Mill, who stressed that "[i]t is commerce which is rapidly rendering war obsolete, by strengthening and multiplying the personal interests which are in natural opposition to it. And it may be said without exaggeration that the great extent and rapid increase of international trade,

The image of superimposed layers of governance, and the emphasis on the checking function, evokes theories of federalism. The analogy between multilayered constitutional governance and a federal polity has limited explanatory power, however, as federalism is too simplistic a template to capture the complexity of the governance system in a globalised world.[27]

Firstly, federalism is fixed on a given territory, which implies that the "lower" levels of governance are subsumed within the "higher" level. By contrast, contemporary international regimes (such as the EU, the European Convention on Human Rights (ECHR) and the WTO) are functionally or sectorally defined and have different memberships.[28] This leads to "the possibility of overlap without subsumption".[29] For each state, different supra-national layers assert authority in a given area without calling into question the state's territorial jurisdiction in other fields.[30] Contemporary states are thus "embedded in multiple and overlapping layers of constitutional governance."[31] Secondly, federalism evokes the image of a relatively straightforward hierarchy among separate and uniform levels, whereas the relationship between the various layers of contemporary regimes is more complex. On the one hand, the global and regional levels are both heterogeneous, as they do not consist of a unified constitutional framework but of international regimes (or "sub-layers") with overlapping membership, operating under different institutional umbrellas, and pursuing different objectives. On the other hand, a hierarchy between the regional and the global level is generally absent, as they both form part of the international legal order. For instance, no clear vertical subordination exists between the ECHR and the WTO. This raises the question of the relationship and the interaction between the various layers of governance.

---

in being the principal guarantee of the peace of the world, is the great permanent security for the uninterrupted progress of the ideas, the institutions, and the character of the human race" (see J.S. Mill, "Chapter XVII: Of International Trade", in: id., *The Collected Works of John Stuart Mill, Volume III— Principles of Political Economy Part II*, 1848).

26   See e.g. Harrison, see note 2, 7 et seq.
27   See A. Peters, *Elemente einer Theorie der Verfassung Europas*, 2001, 189 et seq. with further references.
28   N. Walker, "The Idea of Constitutional Pluralism", *Modern Law Review* 65 (2002), 317 et seq. (346).
29   Walker, see note 28, 346.
30   Ibid.
31   Cinneide, see note 19, 3.

2. Relationship and Interaction between the Various Layers of Governance

Authors stressing the multilayered structure of contemporary governance have different visions of how the various layers and sub-layers relate. They fall, broadly speaking, into two camps: stressing the checking function of "higher" over "lower" levels of governance, one strand of thought conceives of their relationship in terms of hierarchy.[32] Some exponents of this view have argued, however, that the supremacy of "higher" layers is a principle and not a strict rule of conflict. Viewed as a system of *mutual* checks and balances, multilayered constitutionalism posits that "lower" levels retain the capacity to safeguard fundamental values of their respective legal order against encroachment by "higher" levels.[33] The possibility for "lower" levels to "revolt" against "higher" layers accounts for the reality that their interaction cannot be adequately described in terms of "top down" command but is based on dialogue and mutual consideration.[34]

Another strand of thought, adhering to network theories or theories of constitutional pluralism, conceives of the relationship between layers and sub-layers in terms of heterarchy instead of hierarchy.[35] As there is "no Archimedean point", no neutral or external perspective from which to determine the relationship between various layers,[36] the latter is assessed from the internal point of each layer or sub-layer, and is "inter-

---

[32] See e.g. Cottier/ Hertig, see note 20, 307 et seq.
[33] Id., see note 20, 310 et seq.
[34] Id., see note 20, 313 et seq.
[35] From a perspective of constitutional pluralism, see e.g. Walker, see note 28, 337 (who describes the post-Westphalian order as a "multi-level order" (334)); for other authors defending the theory of constitutional pluralism, see e.g. M.P. Maduro, "Contrapunctual Law: Europe's Constitutional Pluralism in Action", in: N. Walker (ed.), *Sovereignty in Transition*, 2003, 501-537; for an analysis of different visions of constitutional pluralism, see M. Avbelj/ J. Komárek (eds), *Four Visions of Constitutional Pluralism*, EUI Working Paper LAW No. 2008/21; for the vision of a "loosely knit global constitutional network", see Peters, see note 17, 601 et seq. For other authors favouring network theories, see e.g. F. Ost/ M. van de Kerchove, *De la pyramide au réseau. Pour une théorie dialectique du droit*, 2002; K.H. Ladeur, "Towards a Legal Theory of Supranationality – The Viability of the Network Concept", *ELJ* 3 (1997), 33 et seq.
[36] See Walker, see note 28, 338; id., "Sovereignty and Differentiated Integration in the European Union", *ELJ* 4 (1998) 356 et seq. (361 et seq.).

active rather than hierarchical."³⁷ Conflicting claims and visions are settled through dialogue "over time in a process of constant 'mutual accommodation'".³⁸

Although they start from different premises, both strands of thought share some common ground: they stress the communicative interaction between the various layers of constitutional governance. The explanatory force of each model, however, varies in this author's view depending on the layers the relationship of which is to be analysed.

Whilst the "hierarchical" model is adequate to describe the relation between national and subnational layers of governance, the "network" model captures well the interaction between different regimes pertaining to the national, regional or international (sub)layers which are not institutionally linked in terms of membership. The cross-fertilisation and mutual borrowing among international human rights bodies,³⁹ for instance, or among different constitutional courts, is entirely voluntary and can be described in terms of "horizontal dialogue".⁴⁰ The same holds true when supreme courts from jurisdictions outside Europe cite judgments of the ECtHR, or, conversely, when the ECtHR corrobo-

---

37   N. MacCormick, *Questioning Sovereignty. Law, State and Nation in the European Commonwealth*, 1999, 118.
38   A. Torres Pérez, *Conflict of Rights in the European Union*, 2009, 111.
39   See L. Hennebel, "Les références croisées entre les juridictions internationales des droits de l'homme", in: *Le dialogue des juges. Actes du colloque organisé le 28 avril 2006 à l'Université libre de Bruxelles*, 2007, 31–76.
40   For the distinction between different forms on judicial dialogue based on the presence or absence of subordination, see L. Burgorgue-Larsen, "De l'internationalisation du dialogue des juges. Missive doctrinale à l'attention de Bruno Genevois", in: *Le dialogue des juges: mélanges en l'honneur du Président Bruno Genevois*, 2009, 94-130 (98 et seq.); A. Rosas, "The European Court of Justice in Context: Forms and Patterns of Judicial Dialogue", *European Journal of Legal Studies* 1 (2007), 1 et seq.; on the importance of judicial dialogue more generally, see e.g. A.M. Slaughter, *A New World Order*, 2004, 65 et seq.; id., "A Global Community of Courts", *Harv. Int'l L. J.* 44 (2003), 191 et seq.; C. McCrudden, "A Common Law of Human Rights?: Transnational Judicial Conversations on Constitutional Rights", *Oxford Journal of Legal Studies* 20 (2000), 499 et seq.; V. Jackson, "Comparative Constitutional Federalism and Transnational Judicial Discourse", *International Journal of Constitutional Law* 2 (2004), 91 et seq.

rates its findings with references to constitutional courts such as the Canadian Supreme Court[41] or the Supreme Court of Israel.[42]

It is more challenging to capture the relationship between the supranational (regional and global) and the national (sub-)layers which are connected in terms of membership (as is for instance the case for the WTO and the EU, or for the 47 Member States of the Council of Europe with respect to the ECHR). Both "pluralist" and "hierarchical" accounts have some drawbacks. Whilst adherents of the first model rightly point out that dispute settlement bodies on "higher" layers lack the "final word on the question of legal validity" of acts adopted on "lower layers",[43] which makes the relationship between international and domestic layers different from the hierarchical subordination between national and subnational courts, they minimise the extent to which "transnational frameworks are in practice often invoked to trump or overrule" particular rules and practices prevalent at the national level.[44] Attempting to find some middle ground between both theories, Rosas described the inter-layer relationship as "semi-vertical",[45] which reflects quite accurately the practice of states with regard to supra-national polities such as the EU, the ECHR and the WTO.[46] From the "hierarchical" vantage point, semi-verticality entails an understanding of supremacy of supranational layers over domestic ones as the main ordering principle, and the pre-eminence of national standards as an exception. From a normative point of view, this approach can among others be justified on functionalist grounds.[47] Su-

---

[41] ECtHR, App. No. 2346/02, *Pretty v. the United Kingdom*, [2002] 35 EHRR 1, paras 17 et seq., paras 66, 74.

[42] ECtHR (GC), App. No. 6339/05 *Evans v. the United Kingdom*, ECHR 2007-I, paras 49 et seq., para. 80.

[43] A. Stone Sweet, "A Cosmopolitan Legal Order: Constitutional Pluralism and Rights Adjudication in Europe", <http://ssrn.com/abstract=1913657>, 7.

[44] Cinneide, see note 19, 12 (from which also the quote in the middle of the sentence is drawn).

[45] See Rosas, see note 40, 9.

[46] The profound impact of the ECHR on the Member States is highlighted in the study by H. Keller/ A. Stone Sweet, *A Europe of Rights. The Impact of the ECHR on National Legal Systems*, 2008.

[47] Cottier/ Hertig, see note 20, 307 et seq., stressing also the input legitimacy of "higher" levels of governance, based on various mechanisms of participation and consent of "lower" levels. For a Kantian perspective, which stresses that solutions adopted by domestic courts need to be generalisable,

premacy of "higher" levels is essential to achieve the common objectives pursued by cooperation on the regional and global level and enables "higher" levels to act as a check on "lower" levels.[48]

Thinking in terms of vertically ordered layers has prompted scholars to complement the principle of supremacy with another ordering principle well-known in federalist theories, the principle of subsidiarity. As a normative claim, subsidiarity is based on the premise that "lower" levels are closer to the citizens and posits that tasks should not be assigned to "higher" levels unless they cannot be adequately fulfilled on a lower level. Viewed descriptively, subsidiarity helps to explain the generally higher levels of integration achieved on "lower" than on "higher" levels of governance[49] and cautions against transposing solutions adopted within the more homogeneous domestic level to the regional level, or within the more consolidated regional to the global level. Apart form the allocation of powers, the principle of subsidiarity also plays an important role as regards the relationship between the judicial or quasi-judicial guardians of the various polities. In human rights law, the requirement to exhaust domestic remedies, and the ECtHR' s doctrine of judicial deference (known as the margin of appreciation doctrine)[50] are

---

see M. Andenas/ E. Bjorge, "National Implementation of ECHR Rights: Kant's Categorical Imperative and the Convention", *University of Oslo Faculty of Law Legal Studies Research Paper Series* No. 2011-15 (2011).

[48] See also P.L. Lindseth, "'Weak' Constitutionalism? Reflections on Comitology and Transnational Governance in the European Union", *Oxford Journal of Legal Studies* 21 (2001), 145 et seq., stressing the autonomous regulatory interest of transnational governance in general, and of the EU, in particular, which is "to constrain, and in some sense to overcome, the propensity of Nation States to parochialism and self-interest" (148).

[49] In the field of human rights, this point was made by Pedro Nikken, judge of the Inter-American Court of Human Rights. Holding "that it is easier to conclude more advanced treaties where fewer cultural and political differences exist among the States that negotiate them", he concludes that it is not surprising that the American Convention on Human Rights is more advanced "than the Covenant [i.e. the ICCPRs of 1966], which aspires to be an instrument that binds all of the governments of the planet." (concurring opinion in I.A. Court H.R., *Compulsory Membership in an Association Prescribed by Law for the Practice of Journalism*, Advisory Opinion OC-5/85 of 13 November 1985, Series A5).

[50] On the margin of appreciation doctrine, see e.g. H.C. Yourow, *The Margin of Appreciation Doctrine in the Dynamics of European Human Rights Jurisprudence*, 1996; J. Schokkenbrock, "The Basis, Nature and Application of the Margin-of-Appreciation Doctrine in the Case-Law of the European

aimed at reducing "inter-layer irritation"[51] and at finding an adequate balance between the universalist and unifying ethos underlying international human rights and the particularist nature of national polities.

The "semi-verticality", and the ordering principles of supremacy and subsidiarity can also be incorporated within the "pluralist" or "network" model. Such an approach would be based on the idea that communication with the various knots or sites of the constitutional network is based on certain mutually respected rules and expectations. On the one hand, polities which are territorially or functionally part of another polity are expected to comply with the norms or rulings of the latter, but can in turn assume that the institutions (in particular the judicial ones) will not unduly expand their jurisdiction and encroach on their autonomy.[52]

The relationship between the various sub-layers of the regional and the global level is more complex. Unless they are connected in terms of membership (as is the case for the EU and the WTO), the "hierarchical" model offers little guidance on how to deal with inter-layer irritation resulting from the functional or sectoral overlap between different international regimes. By contrast with domestic constitutional orders, which provide for a unified institutional framework to balance and arbitrate between competing values, the same issue can be dealt with on the regional and global levels within different polities pursuing different objectives. For the purpose of this study, the relationship between global and regional human rights regimes and economic regimes (such as the EU or the WTO) are cases in point. Although the experience of the EU cannot be simply transposed to the WTO, it offers some valuable insights on how trade and human rights relate to each other.

3. The Example of the EU and the ECHR

The example of the EU has shown that the legitimacy of the ECtHR has generally been superior to that of the European Court of Justice

---

Court of Human Rights", *HRLJ* 19 (1998), 30 et seq.; P. Mahoney, "Judicial Activism and Judicial Self-restraint in the European Court of Human Rights: Two Sides of the Same Coin", *HRLJ* 11 (1990), 57 et seq.

51 Cinneide, see note 19, 1.
52 See Walker, see note 28, 329.

(ECJ) when it comes to the protection of human rights.[53] Until the EU accedes to the ECHR, as stipulated in the Lisbon Treaty,[54] the coordination between the two European transnational courts will continue to be based on mutual dialogue, and mainly on the ECJ's endeavour to align its case law to the Strasbourg jurisprudence.[55] Aware that the ECtHR's case law is a benchmark against which the legitimacy of EU law is measured, the ECJ frequently cites ECtHR's judgments and treats them with deference. Nevertheless, there has been a tendency to

---

[53] See J. Fudge, "Constitutionalizing Labour Rights in Europe", in: T. Campbell/ K.D. Ewing/ A. Tomins (eds), *The Legal Protection of Human Rights. Sceptical Essays*, 2010, 244-267, (264).

[54] See article 6 para. 2 of the Treaty on European Union, as amended by the Lisbon Treaty, which holds that "[t]he Union shall accede to the European Convention for the Protection of Human Rights and Fundamental Freedoms." Although the EU is not yet a member of the ECHR, the Strasbourg Court has affirmed its jurisdiction to examine whether Member States violate the Convention when implementing EU law. Holding that the Member States cannot free themselves from their obligations under the Convention by transferring powers to an international organization, the ECtHR has, however, taken into account the interest in international cooperation by limiting its standard of review to sanctioning manifest deficiencies of EU acts (see the famous judgment ECtHR App. No. 45036/98 *Bosphorus Hava Yollari Turizm v. Ireland*, ECHR 2005-VI; the Court seems to be willing to adopt this deferential standard of review with regard to international organisations that provide for a system of human rights protection which, from a substantive and procedural point of view, is equivalent to that under the Convention, a condition the Court deemed fulfilled by the EU).

[55] The relationship between the EU and the ECHR is not a one way street; see e.g. ECtHR App. No. 28957/95 *Christine Goodwin v. the United Kingdom*, ECHR 2002-VI, in which the ECtHR referred to article 9 of the Charter of Fundamental Rights of the European Union ("Charter" or "EU Charter"), *Official Journal of the European Union* 2007/C 303/01, which guarantees the right to marry. The Court noted that the said provision deliberately departed from the wording of article 12 ECHR, as it omitted the reference to men and women. Thereafter, the ECtHR adopted a purposive interpretation of article 12 ECHR and found that the impossibility for a transsexual to marry due to the lack of legal recognition of his new sex following gender re-assignment breached the Convention. For an overview of further references to the EU Charter by the ECtHR, see F. Benoît-Rohmer, "Droits fondamentaux. L'Union européenne et les droits fondamentaux depuis l'entrée en vigueur du Traité de Lisbonne", *RTDE* 47 (2011), 145 et seq. (157 et seq.).

view the ECJ's rulings in the sphere of human rights with suspicion. The opinion is not uncommon that the judicial guardians of an initially economically inspired treaty lack the institutional competence and sensitivity to deal with human rights issues and will be prone to subordinating fundamental rights to economic interests. The Irish abortion saga is the most telling example in this respect. Ireland's virtually absolute protection of the life of the unborn child came under the scrutiny of both the ECtHR and the ECJ. Each Court approached the issue from a different perspective, reflecting the different functions of the ECHR and the EU. In *Open Door Well Woman*,[56] the ECtHR found that the absolute ban on informing Irish women about abortion and on British medical facilities carrying out terminations of pregnancies infringed freedom of expression, guaranteed in article 10 of the Convention. In *Grogan*,[57] by contrast, the ECJ approached the issue from the vantage point of freedom to provide services, one of the four fundamental economic freedoms enshrined in the EU Treaty.[58] Considering abortion as a medical service, the Court found that it also protected the potential recipients of the service (i.e. the pregnant women). By contrast with the Advocate General's opinion, it did not hold, however, that the freedom to receive a service implied a freestanding right to receive information. Instead, it side-stepped the issue in holding that the case at hand was beyond the reach of EU law because the information was disseminated by students, a source unconnected with the service provider (i.e. the British medical facilities). Both international rulings fuelled controversy within Ireland; however, the ECtHR's judgment, although finding a violation, was far less fiercely disputed than the ECJ's finding that it lacked competence to decide the issue.[59] Envisaging abortion through

---

[56] ECtHR App. No. 14234/88 *Open Door Counselling Ltd and Dublin Well Women Centre Ltd and others v. Ireland*, Series A 246 A 1992.

[57] ECJ Case C-159/90 *SPUC v. Grogan* (1991) ECR I-4685.

[58] Article 56 of the Treaty on the Functioning of the European Union (TFEU).

[59] For commentaries and criticism of the *Grogan* case, see D. Rossa Phelan, "The Right to Life of the Unborn v. the Promotion of Trade in Court of Justice and the Normative Shaping of the European Union", *Modern Law Review* 55 (1992), 670 et seq.; id., *Revolt or Revolution. The Constitutional Boundaries of the European Community*, 1997; J. Coppel/ A. O'Neill, "The European Court of Justice: Taking Rights Seriously?", *CML Rev.* 29 (1992), 669 et seq.; D. Curtin, "Case C-159/90, Society for the Protection of the Unborn Child (Ireland) Ltd v Grogan and others", *CML Rev.* 29 (1992), 585 et seq.

an economic prism prompted charges that the ECJ did not take fundamental rights seriously and used them as a means to further economic interests.⁶⁰ The conflict was finally settled with an additional protocol to the Maastricht Treaty exempting Irish abortion policy from EU law.⁶¹

Interestingly, it was the Luxembourg Court's reasoning and methodology in *Grogan* rather than the outcome that triggered resistance. By contrast with the ECtHR, the ECJ lacks general jurisdiction to decide whether Member States' actions are consistent with human rights. It can only assess whether this is the case in the sphere of EU law.⁶² Scrutinizing whether national law unduly inhibits the free movement of goods, persons, capital or services is, however, a core competence of the ECJ. The Court's mission as a guardian of the single market implies that the four freedoms form the starting point of the analysis, and that human rights (such as the right to life or freedom of expression) are considered as exceptions to the four market freedoms. This approach has been perceived as placing fundamental rights "on the defensive", relegating them to second place with respect to economic freedoms. It is, however, important to note that fundamental rights can be invoked at the level of the exceptions to the market freedoms as either a "shield" or as a "sword". In the first case, the Member State invokes the human right as a justification for the limitation of a market freedom, as Ireland did in relying on the right to life of the unborn child to prohibit information about abortion services outside Ireland. In the second case, the bearer of the fundamental market freedom argues that the state's action infringes both a free movement guarantee and a fundamental right. Accordingly, the students in *Grogan* based their argument not only on the free movement of services but also on freedom of expression.⁶³

---

⁶⁰ See the references under note 59.
⁶¹ The Protocol is reproduced *verbatim* in the Lisbon Treaty, see Protocol 35 to the Treaty on European Union. According to this Protocol, "[n]othing in the Treaties (...) shall affect the application in Ireland of Article 40.3.3 of the Constitution of Ireland."
⁶² See article 51 para. 1 of the EU Charter.
⁶³ For another well-known case, see ECJ Case C-60/00 *Mary Carpenter v. Secretary of State for the Home Department* (2002) ECR I-6279. In this case, the ECJ found that the removal from the United Kingdom of a Filipino woman, married to a British citizen, for the sole reason that she had breached national immigration rules was a disproportionate restriction of the right to family life (article 8 ECHR). The Court held that the case was within the ambit of EU law, as Mr. Carpenter, who ran an advertising

The possibility of both synergies and conflicts between fundamental rights and market freedoms has given rise to fears that the ECJ would readily rely on fundamental rights so as to strengthen economic integration, whilst being reluctant to let human rights concerns trump economic interests. Cases in which the ECJ struck the balance between competing rights in favour of fundamental rights have thus received greater approval than those in which economic freedoms prevailed. The judgments *Omega*[64] and *Schmidberger*,[65] on the one hand, and *Viking*[66] and *Laval*,[67] on the other hand, illustrate this claim.

In *Omega*, the Court accepted that Germany's prohibition of a "playing at killing" game (named Laserdrom) which entailed simulated shooting at human figures was a legitimate restriction of free movement of goods and services, as it was aimed at protecting human dignity. The Court reached this conclusion although few other national constitu-

---

agency, often travelled to other Member States for professional reasons, whilst his wife was caring for his children. Based on this reasoning, the ECJ found that Mrs Carpenter's removal would hinder Mr. Carpenter's freedom to provide services and that the restriction to this right had to be interpreted in the light of fundamental rights, including article 8 ECHR. The Court's ruling, which is based on a very tenuous link with an economic freedom, can in our view be read as the Court's genuine concern for the fundamental rights of a foreigner. Nevertheless, some commentators have referred to it as exemplifying that the Luxembourg Court does not protect fundamental rights for the sole sake of the individual but only to the extent that the latter is useful from an economic point of view (see e.g. J.P. Müller, "Koordination des Grundrechtschutzes in Europa – Einleitungsreferat", *RDS II* 9 (2005), 26 et seq.).

[64] ECJ Case C 36/02 *Omega Spielhallen- und Automatenaufstellungs-GmbH v. Oberbürgermeisterin der Bundesstadt Bonn* (2004) ECR I-9609. For an analysis, see e.g. J. Morijn, "Balancing Fundamental Rights and Common Market Freedoms in Union Law: Schmidberger and Omega in the Light of the European Constitution", *ELJ* 12 (2006), 15 et seq.

[65] ECJ Case C–112/00 *Schmidberger v. Austria* (2003) ECR I–5659. For a commentary, see e.g. A. Biondi, "Free Trade, a Mountain Road and the Right to Protest: European Economic Freedoms and Fundamental Individual Rights", *European Human Rights Law Review* 9 (2004), 51 et seq.; Morijn, see note 64; C. Brown, "Case-note: Schmidberger", *CML Rev.* 40 (2003), 1499 et seq.

[66] ECJ Case C-438/05 *Seaman's Union (FSU) v. Viking Line* (2007) ECR I-10779.

[67] ECJ C-341/05 *Laval un Partneri Ltd v. Svenska Byggnadsarbetareförbundet* (2007) ECR I-11767.

tions explicitly protected human dignity as a freestanding right and afforded it as stringent protection as the German Basic Law. The ECJ granted the Member States some leeway, since,

> "the specific circumstances which may justify recourse to the concept of public policy may vary from one country to another and from one era to another."[68]

Recalling that fundamental rights form part of EU law, the Court held that their protection was a legitimate interest which could justify restrictions of the fundamental freedoms. The protection of human dignity was thus compatible with the EU legal order. The fact that states other than Germany did not enshrine human dignity as a freestanding human right and granted it less stringent protection was immaterial: the ECJ held that,

> "[i]t is not indispensable in that respect for the restrictive measure issued by the authorities of a Member State to correspond to a conception shared by all Member States as regards the precise way in which the fundamental right or legitimate interest in question is to be protected."[69]

The ECJ confirmed this reasoning in a case handed down in 2010,[70] in which it mentioned moreover that the EU was to respect the national identity of the Member States.[71]

In *Schmidberger*, the ECJ borrowed from the famous margin of appreciation doctrine of the ECtHR and held explicitly that states were afforded discretion when relying on fundamental rights to justify restrictions to free movement guarantees. Although the Court was un-

---

[68] ECJ *Omega*, see note 64, para. 31.
[69] Ibid., para. 37.
[70] Case C-208/09, *Ilonka Sayn-Wittgenstein v. Landeshauptmann von Wien* of 22 December 2010 (nyr) in which the Court admitted that the Austrian law on the abolition of nobility was a sufficient public policy justification to limit the right to free movement by refusing to recognise the full name of a citizen from another Member State. The Court held that the Austrian law expressed the more general principle of equality before the law of all Austrian citizens, which was also a general principle recognised within the EU legal order (paras 88-89). Quoting *Omega,* the ECJ expressed its willingness to grant the national authorities a margin of discretion and confirmed that diverging conceptions among the Member States did not prevent a fundamental right from being successfully invoked as a public policy exception (paras 87 and 91).
[71] ECJ *Ilonka Sayn-Wittgnstein*, see note 70, para. 92.

willing to subscribe to the view that fundamental rights enjoyed a preferred position *vis-à-vis* economic freedoms, it found that freedom of expression and assembly, trumped free movement concerns in the case at hand. Austria had thus not infringed free movement of goods in allowing peaceful demonstrations against environmental pollution to obstruct the traffic on the Brenner Pass.

The Court's approach was far less deferential in *Viking* and *Laval*. This time, the scales of the balance tipped in favour of economic freedoms. In both cases, coercive actions taken by trade unions in old Member States with a strong tradition of social rights (Sweden and Finland) with the aim of protecting their members against competition from inexpensive labour from new Member States (Latvia and Estonia) were deemed disproportionate. By contrast with *Schmidberger* and *Omega*, *Viking* and *Laval* met with strong scepticism and have been contrasted with the ECtHR more protective stance towards labour rights.[72]

The analysis of human rights concerns at the level of exceptions to economic freedoms, and the perception of the ECJ as a Court mainly concerned with economic integration, makes it vulnerable to charges of a neoliberal bias or of an instrumentalist use of human rights.[73] The fact that within the framework of EU law, the economic freedoms are the main focus of analysis, and human rights can only be accommodated via the exception clauses, gives rise to the suspicion of axiological priority between both sets of norms: economic rights are viewed as coming first, whereas human rights are relegated to second place.[74] Moreover, as the *Grogan* case illustrates, the economic language employed by the Court

---

[72] See e.g. Fudge, see note 53, 260 et seq.

[73] See e.g. Coppel/ O'Neill, see note 59; in a similar vein, Alston, see note 4, 823, referring to L. Besselink, "Case Note", *CML Rev.* 38 (2001), 437 et seq. (454).

[74] For a criticism of construing fundamental rights as exceptions to market freedoms, see Morijn, see note 64, 39 et seq.; Brown, see note 65; Müller, see note 63, 15; for a more general claim according to which in case of conflicts between rights, the right which is considered at the level of derogations is placed at a disadvantage, see E. Brems, "Conflicting Human Rights: An Exploration in the Context of the Right to a Fair Trial in the European Convention for the Protection of Human Rights and Fundamental Freedoms", *HRQ* 27 (2005), 294 et seq. (305); O. De Schutter/ F. Tulkens, "Rights in Conflict: The European Court of Human Rights as a Pragmatic Institution", in: E. Brems (ed.), *Conflicts Between Fundamental Rights*, 2008, 169-216, 190.

fails to attract support in sensitive matters.⁷⁵ Viewing abortion mainly

---

75 The economic language is more evident in the Advocate General's opinion. He first affirmed that abortion was a "service" in the sense of the EU Treaty and that the free movement of services provision protected not only the service provider but also the recipient. He then raised the question whether the information at issue fell within the ambit of the fundamental freedom. He answered in the affirmative, holding that: "In the judgment in GB-Inno-BM the Court emphasized, in connection with offering goods for sale, the interest of consumer information. It stated (in para. 8) that consumers' freedom to shop in another Member State is compromised if they are deprived of access in their own country to advertising available in the country where purchases are made. I can see no reason why the position should be otherwise with regard to information provided about a service: individuals' freedom to go to another country in order to receive a service supplied there may also be compromised if they are denied access in their own country to information concerning, in particular, the identity and location of the provider of the services and/or the services which he provides." (para. 18, internal footnotes omitted). "19. In my view, the answer given also holds good where the information comes from a person who is not himself the provider of the services and does not act on his behalf. The freedom recognized by the Court of a recipient of services to go to another Member State and the right comprised therein to access to (lawfully provided) information relating to the services and the provider of those services ensue from fundamental rules of the Treaty to which the most extensive possible effectiveness must be given. As a fundamental principle of the Treaty, the freedom to supply services must – subject to limitations arising out of imperative requirements or other justifying grounds, which I shall discuss later – be respected by all, just as it may be promoted by all, inter alia by means of the provision of information, whether or not for consideration, concerning services which the provider of information supplies himself or which are supplied by another person." Thereafter, the Advocate General turned to the question whether free movement of services applied to non-discriminatory restrictions. In support of his affirmative answer, he held that: "To allow measures which are non-discriminatory but detrimental to intra-Community trade in services to fall a priori outside the scope of Article 59 of the EEC Treaty would detract substantially from the effectiveness of the principle of the free movement of services, which in an economy in which the tertiary sector is continuing to expand will increase in importance. It would also give rise to an undesirable divergence between the Court's case-law on trade in goods and that on trade in services in situations in which only the service or the recipient of the service crosses the internal frontiers of the Community and which do not genuinely differ from situations in which goods or purchasers cross frontiers, and in situations in which services, for instance in the financial sector, are frequently presented as 'products'. (para. 20). 21. My conclusion is, therefore, that na-

in terms of a service has been seen as trivialising basic human rights concerns. Issues which would be considered by a constitutional or a human rights court, including women's rights to privacy and the right to receive information on health, received no mention in the ECJ's ruling. The Luxembourg Court thus neglected the expressive function of the law in *Grogan*, as it failed to explain to what extent EU law encapsulated more than mere economic concerns.[76] The ECJ's consequent reasoning in the Irish abortion case contrasts with more recent case law in the field of free movement of persons and European citizenship. Stressing the importance of EU-citizenship as the "fundamental status of nationals of the Member State",[77] the Court has progressively decoupled free movement from the pursuit of an economic activity in another Member State, interpreting residence and free movement rights as basic entitlements inherent in the citizenship status.[78] The incorporation of the EU Charter of Fundamental Rights in the EU legal order through the Lisbon Treaty may accelerate the departure from a predominantly economic focus of the European integration project,[79] leading to further rapprochement and fusion between the four basic economic freedoms (some of which are enshrined in the Charter[80]) and fundamental rights.

---

tional rules which, albeit not discriminatory, may, overtly or covertly, actually or potentially, impede intra-Community trade in services fall in principle within the scope of Articles 59 and 60 of the EEC Treaty."

[76] On the claim that the fundamental freedoms enshrine values other than merely economic ones, see J.H.H. Weiler/ N.J.S. Lockhart, "'Taking Rights Seriously' Seriously: The European Court of Justice and its Fundamental Rights Jurisprudence", *CML Rev.* 32 (1995), 579 et seq. (597 et seq.) and G. de Burca, "Fundamental Human Rights and the Reach of EC Law", *Oxford Journal of Legal Studies* 13 (1993), 283 et seq. (298 et seq.).

[77] ECJ Case C–184/99 *Rudy Grzelczyk v. CPAS* (2001) ECR I–6193.

[78] For an analysis of this trend, see F. Wollenschläger, "A New Fundamental Freedom beyond Market Integration: Union Citizenship and its Dynamics for Shifting the Economic Paradigm of European Integration", *ELJ* 17 (2010), 1 et seq.; M. Hertig Randall, "Der Schutz von Grundrechten und individuellen Freiheiten in der Europäischen Union aus schweizerischer Sicht", *Revue de Droit Suisse* Vol. I, 126 (2007), 487 et seq. (499 et seq.).

[79] See in particular the recent Case C-34/09 *Gerardo Ruiz Zambrano v. Office national de l'emploi (ONEM)* of 8 March 2011 (nyr), including the opinion of Advocate General Sharpston of 30 September 2010.

[80] See article 15 para. 2 of the Charter, which enshrines the freedom of every EU citizen "to seek employment, to work, to exercise the right of establishment and to provide services in any Member State." This provision

4. Insights for the WTO

A development similar to that outlined for the EU is very unlikely to occur within the WTO, the purpose of which is far more modest than that of European integration. Nevertheless, the interplay between the EU and the ECHR offers some insight as to the relationship between the international human rights regime and the multilateral trading system.[81] Firstly, owing to its economic mandate, the legitimacy of the WTO in the field of human rights is very likely to be less than that of international human rights bodies. Trade experts adjudicating human rights issues will be viewed with scepticism.[82] There will be concerns that they are structurally biased and "see every policy [including human rights] as a potential trade restriction."[83] When human rights claims are raised within the dispute settlement system of the WTO, the legitimacy of the rulings will also depend on Panels deferring to rulings of human rights bodies. Secondly, as human rights concerns within the WTO

---

forms part of a broader guarantee of economic liberty, referred to below Section IV. 2. b.

[81] On the benefits and limits of a comparative analysis between the EU and the WTO, see S. Zleptig, *Non-economic objectives in WTO Law: Justification provisions of GATT, GATS, SPS and TBT Agreements*, 2010, 7 et seq., which includes a comparative section on human rights at 199 et seq. For other comparative studies between the EU and the WTO, see F. Ortino, *Basic Legal Instruments for the Liberalisation of Trade. A Comparative Analysis of EC and WTO Law*, 2004, 2 et seq.; J.H.H. Weiler, "Cain and Abel – Convergence and Divergence in International Trade Law", in: id. (ed.), *The EU, the WTO and the NAFTA. Towards a Common Law of International Trade*, 2000, 1 et seq.; G. Búrca/ J. Scott (eds), *The EU and the WTO. Legal and Constitutional Aspects*, 2000.

[82] See e.g. Kinley, see note 2, 75; Cleveland, see note 2, 258, holding that due to the WTO's institutional competence, "any balancing of trade and human rights concerns that is conducted by that body is likely to undervalue human rights norms"; G.B. Dinwoodie, "A New Copyright Order: Why National Courts Should Create Global Norms", *University of Pennsylvania Law Review* 149 (2000), 469 et seq. (508) (criticising the insufficiently inclusive perspectives of the WTO dispute settlement proceedings and the "trade-blinkered positions" which national governments also tend to adopt in the WTO).

[83] M. Koskenniemi, "International Law: Between Fragmentation and Constitutionalism", 2006, 5, <http://www.ejls.eu/1/3UK.htm>; on the structural bias of international bodies, see id., *From Apology to Utopia. The Structure of International Legal Argument*, 2005, 600 et seq.

framework, like in EU law, are most easily accommodated at the level of the exception clauses, the perception of an economic bias is hard to refute. Not surprisingly, treating human rights as mere defences in trade disputes has already given rise to concerns.[84] It has been argued that this approach entails the idea of a "presumption of guilt", as "human rights norms might too closely be associated with restrictions to trade."[85] Thirdly, rulings ignoring human rights defences advanced by Member States or subjecting them to exact scrutiny risk fuelling substantial controversy. Fourthly, if a human right is invoked "as a sword", e.g. in support of the complainant state, purely economic analysis may prompt the charge of an instrumentalist use of human rights, as it fails to take into account the expressive function of the law. The adjudicative branch of the WTO would thus need to approach freedom of speech issues not only from an economic vantage point. It would also need to take into account the point of view of free speech theory prevalent in the rulings of constitutional and human rights courts. As will be shown in the following section, there is some convergence between these approaches, explaining the jurisdictional overlap between trade and human rights regimes.

III. Free Speech Functions and Values

1. Economic Perspective

An economic perspective helps to explain why free speech issues are a relevant concern for free trade regimes and have led to jurisdictional overlap within the EU, as the *Grogan* case has shown. Economists have stressed the impact of speech on the functioning of markets (a.), providing utilitarian rationales for both the constitutional protection and the

---

[84] See e.g. Harrison, see note 2, 215 et seq.; the High Commissioner for Human Rights' Report on GATS, see note 5, also points out the difference between a human rights approach and the treatment of human rights at the level of exceptions in international trade law, holding that "a human rights approach would place the promotion of human rights at the centre of the objectives of GATS rather than as permitted exceptions." It concludes, however, that "these links nonetheless provide an entry point for a human rights approach to liberalization and a means of ensuring that the essentially commercial objectives of GATS can be implemented with respect for human rights" (para. 63).

[85] Harrison, see note 2, 215.

regulation of expression. As speech can be produced and sold, it is viewed from the economic vantage point as a service or a commodity. The "speech market", however, differs from the market of other commodities in important ways (b.). Its specificities need to be taken into account when assessing the need for constitutional protection and regulation (c.).

a. The Impact of Speech on the Functioning of Markets

Economists have highlighted the importance of speech in the functioning of markets since the 1960s.[86] If consumers lack adequate information, or have to spend excessive amounts of time or money searching for it, their purchasing decisions do not lead to the optimal allocation of resources. Insufficient information, both from the quantitative and qualitative point of view, has thus been recognised as giving rise to market failures. The school of information economics highlights the role of advertising (also termed "commercial speech") as an important source of consumer information. Advertising, however, owing to its one-sided nature, is an insufficient source of information and may, if false or misleading, exacerbate informational deficiencies. The theory of information asymmetry holds that producers and sellers are generally better informed about products or services than consumers, which adversely affects the functioning of markets. In extreme cases, it may fundamentally undermine the trust in the trading partners and cause the market to collapse.[87] The more difficult it is for consumers to check for themselves relevant product characteristics before purchase, the more pervasive informational asymmetries are. When it comes to production and process methods (including, for instance, the respect for environmental or labour standards), consumers are heavily dependent on the information provided by the seller or manufacturer, who may, however, have no economic incentive to make it available. Moreover, the geographical distance separating producers and consumers, and the differ-

---

[86] See the seminal article by G.J. Stigler, "The Economics of Information", *Journal of Political Economy* 69 (1961), 213 et seq.; the best known representatives of this school are Joseph E. Stiglitz, George Akerlof and Andrew Michael Spence. They were awarded the Nobel Prize in Economics in 2001. For an overview of the school of information economics, see e.g. J.P. Mackaay, *Economics of Information and Law*, 1980.

[87] See the famous article by G.A. Akerlof, "The Market for 'Lemons': Quality Uncertainty and the Market Mechanism", *Quarterly Journal of Economics* 84 (1970), 488 et seq.

ences between national product and production standards, make it even more difficult for consumers to assess the qualities of commodities, not to mention the growing complexity and diversity of products and services. Technological progress and economic globalisation thus further enhance the informational advantages of producers and sellers over consumers. For this reason, a well-functioning global economy depends not only on the free movement of goods and services across frontiers, but also on the free flow of information about their characteristics and production methods. As the American free speech specialist Lee C. Bollinger has argued, in a globalised economy, free speech violations occurring in one country also affect citizens in other states.[88] Political repression of the domestic media reporting health hazards of certain products, questioning the viability of the financial sector, or decrying corruption of the state apparatus impact on both the political and the economic sphere. Therefore, both the free marketplace of goods and services and the free marketplace of ideas ought to be of concern for the WTO.[89] Interestingly, highlighting the specificities of the speech market, some scholars have argued that economic approaches to regulation (e.g. public choice theory) provide a stronger reason for according constitutional protection to freedom of speech than to economic freedom (including the right to trade).[90]

b. The Specificity of the Speech Market

The starting point of economic approaches arguing for a higher level of protection of speech than economic activity[91] is that unlike most commodities, information is not a private but a public good. This property

---

[88] "Columbia President Says First Amendment Should be Global", 4 May 2010, The Epoch Times, <http://www.theepochtimes.com>.

[89] Ibid.

[90] The following section draws on M. Hertig Randall, "Commercial Speech under the European Convention on Human Rights: Subordinate or Equal?", *Human Rights Law Review* 6 (2006), 53 et seq. (82 et seq.) and id., "La société civile face à la société commerciale: quelques réflexions sur la liberté d'expression dans un contexte commercial polities", in: F. Bohnet/ P. Wessner (eds), *Droit des sociétés. Mélanges en l'honneur de Roland Ruedin*, 2006, 477 et seq. (482 et seq.).

[91] See mainly D. Farber, "Commentary: Free Speech Without Romance: Public Choices and the First Amendment", *Harv. L. Rev.* 105 (1991), 554 et seq.

entails that information is generally under-produced.[92] Since it can be shared and disseminated at a low cost, it tends to benefit not only the paying customer but also third parties. The beneficiaries of information thus have an incentive to "free-ride". From this perspective, intellectual property rights (IPRs) are a means to counter free-riding and to encourage the production of information. Nevertheless, producers cannot translate all the social benefits flowing from the distribution of information into personal gain and, therefore, lack the motivation to produce as much information as would be socially optimal. For the same reason, they have less incentive to oppose censorship of information than to challenge governmental regulations on goods other than information. With regard to lobbying efforts from recipients of the information, the free-riding problem exacerbates the general ineffectiveness of consumer pressure groups as compared with other special interest groups. Government will thus be inclined to yield to demands for restrictions on information. In summary, information tends to be both under-produced by the market and over-regulated by the state. Elevating freedom of expression to a fundamental right can thus be understood, under public-choice theory, as an attempt to counteract these problems.

These general considerations do not apply to the same extent to all speech, as the public good features can be more or less pronounced depending on the type of expression at issue. At one end of the spectrum lies information, which, like that contained in the medical file of a patient, is of little use to anyone other than the recipient. Whilst such information has predominantly private goods characteristics, political speech lies at the other end of the spectrum. It is, in Farber's words, a "double" public good. Firstly, the information conveyed through political speech has the characteristics of a public good for the reasons described above. Secondly, political participation can be considered as an-

---

[92] The characteristics of public goods are their non-rivalry and non-excludability. The first property entails that the consumption of the good by one person does not preclude consumption or simultaneous use by others, and the second refers to the impossibility (or excessive difficulty) of excluding others from using the public good. By contrast with most consumer goods, which are private goods, clean air, for instance, is a public good: it is non-rivalous, since it is available to everybody, in as much as one person's use of clean air does not preclude others from breathing clean air simultaneously; it is non-excludable, as it would be virtually impossible to limit the use of clean air to those willing to pay for it, and to exclude people unwilling to pay for clean air (by shouldering the costs of anti-pollution policies) from its benefit.

other public good; indeed, as the influence of a single vote is marginal, individuals will generally benefit from a certain policy independently of whether they supported it or not. Since citizens can "free-ride" on the political engagement of others, they are also less inclined to seek information on public affairs and to oppose governmental restrictions on information.

Commercial speech lies on the spectrum somewhere between purely private and political speech. It has the characteristics of a "weak" public good. Although, unlike the information contained in a medical file, it is generally directed at the public at large, it resembles a private good in as much as advertising increases the speaker's turnover. Most of the benefits of the information thus accrue to the producer. The direct profit motive means that the market for advertising is entirely dependent on the market for the commercialised product or service. In that sense, advertising has been described as a complementary product to the main commodity, entirely financed through sales revenues. It is the wholly ancillary nature of commercial speech,[93] and its direct profit motive, which distinguishes it from other types of information with more pronounced public good characteristics. Although filmmakers and authors may also pursue an economic interest, unlike commercial speech, their work does not have the advantage of being financed through the profits of a main commodity. This explains why they are much more dependent on state subsidies than advertising.

The commercial speaker's direct profit motive offers an incentive to producers and sellers to provide consumers with some, but not all, the relevant information. Although any advertisement contains some incompressible element of information, and therefore has some utility to consumers, it fails to provide information not directed to further sales, let alone unfavourable facts.[94] Owing to the inherent bias of advertising, the functioning of markets relies on other information sources, such as

---

[93] See N. Kaldor, "The Economic Aspects of Advertising", *Review of Economic Studies* 17 (1950), 1 et seq.

[94] Economists hold that the incentives to disseminate negative information about competitors' products via comparative advertising are limited, see e.g. R. Pitofsky, "Beyond Nader: Consumer Protection and the Regulation of Advertising", *Harv. L. Rev.* 90 (1977), 661 et seq.; R. Posner, "Free Speech in an Economic Perspective", *Suffolk University Law Review* 20 (1986), 2 et seq. (40).

the media,[95] scientific reports, consumer organisations and other NGOs. As it lacks the direct profit motive characteristic of commercial speech, such "non commercial information" will be under-produced as compared with advertising. Moreover, producers of non-commercial information will be less inclined to oppose speech-restrictive measures than commercial speakers. Producers and sellers, by contrast, will generally have a strong incentive to refute and seek suppression of statements detrimental to their commercial interests. Moreover, their speech is less likely to be chilled through governmental regulation than non-commercial expression. Put differently, on the speech market, commercial speech has a competitive advantage over non-commercial counterspeech. This imbalance needs to be taken into account when expression is constitutionally protected and regulated.

c. Implications for the Protection and Regulation of Speech

Several regulatory strategies are aimed at addressing deficiencies of the speech market caused by the public good characteristics of information and at combating "informational failures" of the marketplace of goods and services. Disclosure requirements and subsidies to consumer organisations are aimed at increasing the creation and dissemination of under-produced information. As already mentioned, entrenching freedom of speech in constitutions can be viewed from an economic perspective as a strategy to counter the danger of overregulation, resulting in the suppression of socially beneficial speech. Under the utilitarian framework typical of economic analysis, constitutional protection of freedom of speech does not entail free speech absolutism but is aimed at ensuring that free speech interests receive sufficient weight on the scales when balanced against competing interests.[96] Based on a cost-benefit-analysis characteristic of utilitarian approaches, the suppression of speech is justified if the harm the expression does is likely to outweigh

---

[95] The dependency of the media on commercial advertising entails the risk that the media are reluctant to publish speech critical of market players or their products, see e.g. E.C. Baker, *Advertising and a Democratic Press*, 1994, in particular Chapter 2; L. Soley, *Censorship, Inc,: The Corporate Threat to Free Speech in the United States*, 2002.

[96] According to this vision, rights are particularly important interests which can be outweighed but count for more than other interests in utilitarian calculations. See J. Waldron, "Introduction", in: id., *Theories of Rights*, 1984, 15 which contains an outline of competing theories of rights.

its potential benefits.[97] Considering the difficulties in assessing the harms and benefits of speech, error costs need to be included in the analysis. Owing to information asymmetries between producers and consumers, these costs are likely to be higher for non-commercial sources like consumer magazines. Unlike manufacturers and sellers, they generally have less information about product characteristics and manufacturing processes and will find it more difficult than producers to counter charges of making false or misleading statements. Due to the bigger error costs, the risk of the suppression of socially valuable speech is thus higher for non-commercial statements. The fact that non-commercial speech is more likely to be chilled than commercial speech reinforces this conclusion. Put differently, allowing some false or misleading statements is the price to be paid for avoiding self-censorship of truthful speech. The error costs and the chilling effect of speech regulation underscore the complexity of assessing whether the suppression of speech in a given case is justified. Both factors argue for caution. When faced with non-commercial statements, there are good reasons to tip the balance in favour of free speech.

2. Free Speech Theory

The previous section has shown that the functioning of markets depends on sufficient information, both from commercial and non-commercial sources. Whilst market transparency calls for regulation of expression, the specificities of the speech market justify according free speech constitutional protection, which tilts the scales in favour of free speech concerns. Protecting free speech based on welfarist considerations is an unusual way to approach freedom of expression. Human rights advocates are bound to retort that fundamental rights are valuable *per se* and not for the sake of economic efficiency. Free speech theory, however, shows a more complex picture, and illustrates the more general problem that little consensus exists about the foundations of human rights. Behind the simple statement that human rights are entitlements which every human being holds by virtue of the sole fact of being human lurks the problem of the indeterminate nature of these rights.[98] As regards free speech, political philosophers have advanced a

---

[97] See e.g. Posner, see note 94.
[98] On the indeterminate nature of human rights, see e.g. J. Griffin, *On Human Rights*, 2008, 9 et seq.; M.K. Addo, *The Legal Nature of International*

range of competing theories highlighting different rationales for the protection of the right to free expression.[99] Protecting dissent,[100] furthering tolerance,[101] facilitating the peaceful evolution of society,[102] and checking the abuse of power[103] have been considered important free speech functions.

The following section will not consider all of them. It will briefly sketch the three most prominent rationales for the protection of freedom of expression, which are arguments based on autonomy (a.), democracy (b.) and truth (c.). The purpose of this overview is twofold: firstly, it is aimed at showing that free speech theorists have defended freedom of expression both as a means and as an end.[104] The opposition between economic approaches and philosophical arguments is thus less pronounced than often assumed. Secondly, the analysis will show the extent to which existing justifications for free speech lead to results similar to those of the economic approach sketched above, and are relevant for the functioning of markets.

a. The Argument from Autonomy

From a human rights perspective, the argument from autonomy is the most obvious justification of freedom of expression. It is directly linked to the foundational value of human rights, to human dignity, i.e. the intrinsic worth of every member of the human family.[105] In the Western tradition, dignity is grounded on autonomy, meaning the ability of persons endowed with reason[106] to form their own conception of a

---

Human Rights, 2010, 19-81; for an overview of various foundations of human rights, see J.J. Shestack, "The Philosophic Foundations of Human Rights", *HRQ* 20 (1998), 201 et seq.

[99] For an analysis of free speech theory, see mainly F. Schauer, *Free Speech: A Philosophical Inquiry*, 1982; E. Barendt, *Freedom of Speech*, 2005.

[100] S. Shiffrin, *Dissent, Injustice and the Meaning of America*, 1999.

[101] L.C. Bollinger, *The Tolerant Society*, 1986.

[102] See T.I. Emerson, "Toward a General Theory of the First Amendment", *Yale L. J.* 72 (1962-1963), 877 et seq., who also relies on other free speech values.

[103] V. Blasi, "The Checking Value in First Amendment Theory", *American Bar Foundation Research Journal* 72 (1977), 521 et seq.

[104] This expression is inspired by the famous concurring opinion of Justice Brandeis in *Whitney v. California*, see below note 149.

[105] Cf. the Preamble of the UDHR.

[106] See article 1 of the UDHR.

worthwhile life and to pursue it.[107] Respecting people's dignity thus entails treating them as normative agents, i.e. as "self-deciders", or in Rousseauist and Kantian terms, as "self-legislators."[108] This vision of autonomy does not necessarily call for the protection of a general right to liberty, but for the freedom to define one's conception of a worthwhile life and to pursue it, within the limits of the same freedom granted to all. Accordingly, international human rights instruments do not protect a general right to liberty. They focus on specific rights considered particularly relevant for moral agency and, as history has shown, are at a high risk of being infringed.[109] Both conditions are fulfilled for free speech. Censorship of unpopular ideas has marked the history of humankind and given rise to vindications of freedom of expression as a right constitutive of normative agency. Forming and pursuing one's conception of a worthwhile life requires the capacity for critical reflection, which is inconceivable without language, deliberation and exchange with others. In that vein, Kant argued that the Enlightenment, defined as "man's emergence from his self-incurred immaturity",[110] required one to make public use of one's reason. Persons acting as "self-deciders", moreover, need sufficient information about available options. In that sense, freedom of expression has been described as a condition for the exercise or enjoyment of other human rights. Information about contraceptives or abortion facilities, for instance, enables women to exercise their right to privacy and is connected to their right to health. Taking another example, information about contents and production methods of food may be necessary for the exercise of freedom of religion, since many religious beliefs require respect for dietary practices. As these examples show, even if one takes a narrow view of autonomy and limits it to those choices most relevant to forming and pursuing a conception of a good life (which would not extend to all consumption choices), the free flow of information about products and services is in many instances a condition of normative agency.[111]

---

[107] Griffin, see note 98, 152 et seq.
[108] See Griffin, see note 98, 157.
[109] See e.g. A. Dershowitz, *Rights from Wrongs*, 2005.
[110] I. Kant, "An Answer to the Question: 'What is Enlightenment'", 1874.
[111] For a narrow view of autonomy, see Griffin, see note 98, 239 et seq., who defines the scope of freedom of expression as "freedom to state, discuss, and debate anything relevant to our functioning as normative agents." For broader views, see e.g. R. Dworkin, *Freedom's Law. The Moral Reading of the American Constitution*, 3rd edition, 1999, 200; M. Redish, "Self-

b. The Argument from Democracy

The argument from democracy is closely linked to the argument from autonomy, stressing people's status as "self-legislators" and "self-governors", e.g. their right to participate, directly or indirectly in public affairs and in the elaboration of rules they are subject to. Nevertheless, it is generally considered an instrumentalist defence of free speech, as it views freedom of expression as a means to guarantee democratic self-government, considered a public, and not just a private interest.

The argument from democracy places debates and the flow of information on matters of public concern at the heart of freedom of expression. It calls for strong protection of the media and other institutions of civil society (such as associations and NGOs) which inform the citizenry, check and criticise those in power and shape public opinion on matters relevant to collective self-determination. Moreover, under the argument of democracy, the protection of minority views is crucial for several reasons. Firstly, it gives minorities the sense of co-authorship and inclusion. When outvoted, the chance of having had the opportunity to voice one's concerns and to retain the ability to do so with a view to changing existing laws and policies is essential. Secondly, vigorous protection of non-conforming, dissident opinions is crucial for the fairness of the political process. It prevents current majorities from blocking the channels of communication and from insulating themselves against criticism. Highlighting the high risk of wrongly suppressing political speech because of the self-interest and partisan bias of power-holders, and the danger of chilling political speech, free speech theorists' concern with democracy also explains their willingness to protect not only non-conformist, but also some false speech, such as defamatory statements about politicians. Whilst the autonomy-based defence does not justify the pre-eminence of freedom of expression when it clashes with other human rights, such as reputational and privacy rights, under the argument from democracy, the public interest in securing uninhibited debate on public matters tilts the scales in favour of free speech.

At first sight, the argument from democracy may seem to have little relevance to speech related to the commercial marketplace. However, although distinct, the commercial and the political spheres increasingly overlap. Consumers regard many purchasing decisions not merely as

---

Realization, Democracy and Freedom of Expression: A Reply to Professor Baker", *University of Pennsylvania Law Review* 130 (1982), 678 et seq.

economic acts aimed at satisfying subjective preferences, but view consumption itself as an act of political or moral significance.[112] Various factors have contributed to the politicisation of consumption decisions. For instance, privatisation of formerly public functions has blurred the traditional line between the public and the private sphere[113] and has weakened citizens' ability to both influence and control the exercise of these powers through traditional democratic channels. Under these circumstances, indirect influence through consumption decisions fulfils a compensatory role. Similarly, technical progress and enhanced product complexity have acted as an incentive to "vote with one's dollars" when democratic participation and deliberation are marginalised:[114] increased product complexity and constant technological change have called for more flexible ways of regulation than traditional legislative procedures, fuelling a trend to confer regulatory powers upon private standard-setting bodies or governmental agencies composed to a large extent of experts. Whilst insulation from the ordinary political processes is advantageous in terms of efficiency,[115] it raises difficulties in terms of input legitimacy.[116]

Globalisation compounds these difficulties. As product regulation frequently has spill-over effects on other jurisdictions, diverging national norms act as a barrier to trade, which needs to be addressed on a global level, most prominently within the WTO. Similar to the experience within the EU, the judicial branch of the WTO has played an important role in disciplining national protectionism. At the same time, it favours deregulation, often referred to as "negative integration", giving rise to the need for flanking measures. Such measures of "positive inte-

---

[112] See e.g. D.A. Kysar, "Preferences for Processes: The Process/Product Distinction and the Regulation of Consumer Choice", *Harv. L. Rev.* 118 (2004), 525 et seq. For a more general analysis of the evolution of consumption, see R. Mason, *The Economics of Conspicuous Consumption: Theory and Thought Since 1700*, 1998.

[113] A.C. Aman, "Information, Privacy, and Technology: Citizens, Clients, or Consumers?", in: J. Beatson/ Y. Cripps (eds), *Freedom of Expression and Freedom of Information. Essays in Honour of Sir David Williams*, 2001, 325-348 (332).

[114] See Kysar, see note 112, 525 et seq.; A.C. Aman, *The Democracy Deficit: Taming Globalization Through Law Reform*, 2004, 134.

[115] See e.g. G. Majone, *Regulating Europe*, 1996.

[116] See J.H.H. Weiler, "Epilogue: 'Comitology' As Revolution – Infranationalism, Constitutionalism and Democracy", in: C. Joerges/ E. Vos (eds), *EU Committees: Social Regulation, Law and Politics*, 1999, 339–350.

gration" concern, for instance, the definition and enforcement of minimal labour and environmental standards and the regulation of genetically modified organisms.[117] However, these issues often turned out to be virtually intractable. In this context, citizens use their purchasing power as both a stick and a carrot for economic actors to satisfy certain minimal standards. Typically, many of these standards are not limited to consumer preferences regarding product quality and price but also extend to the way the product is made. These "preferences for processes"[118] frequently reflect visions of justice and fairness traditionally debated in democratic fora. The virulent criticism addressed to big corporations for failing to respect minimal labour and environmental standards is a prominent example of how the roles of citizens and consumers have increasingly been blurred.

Globalisation has also been a context favourable to the rise of big corporations, the financial assets of which may exceed those of small or developing countries and enables these corporations to exert greater influence on the political process.[119] In this context, corporate power needs to be checked no less than state power.[120] Unfair business practices, mismanagement, disregard for environmental and labour standards, the marketing of unsafe products, and the excessive risks taken by financial institutions are clear examples of conduct which ought to be prevented and checked through free speech. Oversight is particularly important for corporations deemed too big to fail, as their difficulties have a strong impact on the financial system, the labour market, social security systems and ultimately on the taxpayer. The social, economic and environmental impact of corporations often calls for political action, making speech on corporate issues clearly a matter of public con-

---

[117] It comes as no surprise that the question of how a fair balance can be achieved between the interest in international trade and competing interests, pertaining for instance to environmental issues, labour standards, and human rights, has given rise to much controversy. For an overview of these "trade and ... " issues or the "linkage debate", see e.g. the articles published under the heading "Symposium: The Boundaries of the WTO", *AJIL* 96 (2002), 1 et seq.

[118] See Kysar, see note 112, 525.

[119] See e.g. D. Jackson, "Note: The Corporate Defamation Plaintiff in the Era of Slapps: Revisiting New York Times v. Sullivan", *William & Mary Bill of Rights Journal* 9 (2001), 491 et seq. (492).

[120] In favour of greater corporate oversight and accountability, see F. Rigaux, "Introduction générale", *RUDH* No. 13 (special number) (1993), 3 et seq. (15).

cern. These developments are not to be understood as amounting to the claim that consumer decisions are equivalent to citizens' participation in democratic decision-making. As Aman highlights, consumer choice tends to be reactionary, whilst the role of the citizen is more creative, aimed at defining policies which, depending on the view of democracy adopted, implement the common good or accommodate citizens' conflicting interests. Nevertheless, the trends described above imply that consumer choice is frequently the only, albeit imperfect, substitute for citizens' participation. The political dimension of many consumption decisions and the indirect control exercised by corporate power through the consumers thus cannot be denied.

The Canadian Supreme Court eloquently highlighted the blurring of the commercial and the political sphere in a case involving "counter-advertising", e.g. the criticism of a product or a service by a dissatisfied customer (in the case at hand, of an insurance company). The Supreme Court held that "counter-advertising" was not merely a form of speech derived from commercial expression, but "assists in circulating information and protecting the interests of society just as much as does advertising or certain forms of political expression. This type of communication may be of considerable social importance, *even beyond the merely commercial sphere."*[121] In the same vein, the Court characterised "counter-advertising" as "a form of the expression of opinion that has an important effect on the social and economic life of a society. *It is a right not only of consumers, but of citizens."*[122]

In conclusion, due to the overlap and interdependence between the political and the commercial sphere, the argument from democracy justifies the protection of expression which from an economic vantage point is considered as contributing to market transparency and the efficient allocation of resources. The same holds true for the third classic defence in favour of freedom of expression, the argument from truth.

c. The Argument from Truth

It is not surprising that the truth-seeking function of freedom of thought and expression has been stressed by a utilitarian scholar. In his famous defence in favour of free speech, John Stuart Mill emphasised

---

[121] Emphasis added.
[122] Emphasis added.

the societal value of freedom of expression.[123] As human beings are partial and fallible, uninhibited debate, reflecting all sides of an argument, is the only means to gain knowledge and for society to progress. Silencing an opinion was thus for Mill not only a private injury to the speaker, but detrimental to the listeners, and to the whole "human race."[124]

As regards the scope of the argument from truth, Mill considered "freedom of opinion and sentiment on all subjects, practical or speculative, scientific, moral, or theological"[125] as covered by the free speech principle. Although the argument from truth is particularly relevant in the domains mentioned, no reason exists to exclude the commercial sphere. Highlighting the conformist pressures of society, Mill vindicated free speech in particular for unpopular and minority views. Due to the structural imbalance between commercial and non-commercial expression, his defence requires strong protection of non-commercial speakers voicing criticism of commercial practices.

3. Synthesis

This section has outlined the function and values underlying freedom of expression from an economic perspective and from the perspective of classic free speech theory. It has shown that there is common ground between both approaches. Firstly, instrumentalist reasoning, which is typical of economic analysis, is not wholly foreign to classic free speech theory. Under the argument from truth, speech is protected mainly as means; the argument from democracy is not only clearly connected to personal autonomy and dignity, but also considers democracy a collective interest furthered by free speech. Moreover, both rationales protect freedom of speech not only for the speaker's sake but take into account the interest of the listeners, or more broadly, the interests of the public at large in receiving ideas and information necessary to take part in public decision making or the collective quest for truth. Secondly, the economic analysis highlights the strong dependency of markets on adequate information, stemming both from commercial and non-

---

[123] J.S. Mill, *On Liberty*, 1859, mainly Chapter II: *Of the Liberty of Thought and Discussion*, available on the website of the Online Library of Liberty, <http://oll.libertyfund.org>.
[124] Ibid.
[125] Ibid., Chapter I.

commercial speakers, including for instance the media, NGOs and consumer organisations. The structural imbalance of the information market in favour of commercial speech justifies stronger protection of non-commercial than of commercial expression. The same conclusion can be reached under the argument from democracy and the argument from truth, which both insist on the need to protect dissenting and minority views. The scope of both arguments can be construed broadly enough so as to encompass speech relevant for the commercial marketplace. The same holds true for the autonomy-based defence, which covers, under a narrow reading, at least market-related information relevant for the exercise of other human rights or necessary to shape one's conception of a worthwhile life.

These insights reveal a more complex picture than views drawing clear lines between the instrumentalist approach relevant to trade and economic analysis and the dignitarian defence of human rights. They also show that courts operating either within a human rights or an economic framework may reach similar outcomes. These arguments will become more evident in the following section, which will analyse the role and function of freedom of speech and free trade on the various constitutional layers and sub-layers.

IV. Free Speech and Free Trade within the Multilayered Constitution

Whilst the previous section explored freedom of expression as a *moral* right, the present one focuses on both free speech and free trade as *legal* rights. Such analysis prepares the ground for the integration of freedom of speech concerns within the WTO. Seen as one part of a multilayered constitution, the multilateral trading system cannot be addressed in isolation. Concerns for the coherence of the constitutional structure as a whole make it necessary to explore the functions and values pursued within regimes situated on the same or on different levels of governance.

1. The National Level

In light of the number and diversity of national legal orders, only general observations can be made about the constitutional protection of freedom of speech and the "right to trade" (more frequently termed "economic freedom" or "economic liberty"), understood as a comprehensive right of both natural and legal persons to choose and pursue an economic activity. The main point is that as regards the recognition of the right, a broader consensus exists with respect to freedom of expression than concerning a right to trade. Whilst many, if not most, constitutions enshrine free speech,[126] economic freedom enjoys less support. Focusing on some prominent WTO members, the Constitution of China, for instance, guarantees freedom of expression[127] but only protects the right and duty to work.[128] Based on the title and wording of the constitutional provision, it is designed to protect a social and not a liberty right. In a similar vein, the Constitution of Japan refers to the "right and obligation to work."[129] It explicitly confers to every person only the right to "*choose* his occupation",[130] and solely "*to the extent that it does not interfere with the public welfare.*"[131] The Canadian Charter of Rights and Freedoms does not explicitly protect economic liberty beyond a guarantee similar to the interstate commerce clause enshrined in the US Constitution or the free movement rights within the EU legal order.[132] In Brazil,[133] India[134] and South Africa,[135] the constitutions provide for economic rights, which are worded mainly as rights of individuals to choose and engage in an economic activity. As regards the level of protection, the South African Constitution explicitly distinguishes between the right to *choose* a trade, occupation or profession freely and the right to *practice* the said activities, holding that "[t]he

---

[126] See the comparative study with further reference by A. Stone, "The Comparative Constitutional Law of Freedom of Expression", *University of Melbourne Legal Studies Research Paper* No. 476 (2010), available at <http://papers.ssrn.com>. The author holds that "Rights of freedom of expression can be found in constitutions drawn from all continents: throughout western Europe as well as in the constitutions of the new democracies of Eastern Europe, in constitutions in Asia, South America, Africa and Australasia" (at 1).
[127] Article 41 of the Constitution of China.
[128] Article 42, ibid.
[129] Article 27 of the Constitution of Japan. As regards freedom of expression, it is guaranteed in article 21 of this Constitution.
[130] Article 22, ibid., emphasis added.
[131] Ibid., emphasis added.
[132] Article 6 para. 2 of the Charter.
[133] Article 5 XIII of the Constitution of Brazil.
[134] Article 19 para. 1 lit. g of the Constitution of India.
[135] Article 22 of the Constitution of South Africa.

practice of a trade, occupation or profession may be regulated by law."[136] Turning to the Council of Europe, most, but not all[137] constitutions explicitly[138] protect more or less broadly construed economic liberty rights.[139] With regard to the scope of the right, some constitutional texts refer only to the right to work, which is interpreted (also) as a liberty right, and sometimes as a broader right of economic liberty.[140] Among the European legal orders, the Swiss Constitution stands out as being among the oldest constitutional texts to enshrine a very comprehensive right of economic freedom, protecting the choice, access and exercise of an economic activity by both individuals and corporations, which includes the right to trade within Switzerland and with third countries.[141] This right was enshrined in the Swiss Constitution of 1874

[136] Ibid.

[137] See the Human Rights Act 1998 in the United Kingdom, and the Constitution of Bosnia and Herzegovina, which only enshrines free movement guarantees, see article 1 para. 4 of the Constitution of 1 December 1995.

[138] In some constitutional orders, economic liberty has been recognised as an implied right; see e.g. the case law of the French Conseil Constitutionnel, Decision No. 81-132 of 16 January 1982, in which it was inferred from the general right to liberty, protected in article 4 of the Declaration of Rights of Men and Citizens of 1789, that entrepreneurial freedom ("liberté d'entreprendre") could not be subject to arbitrary of abusive restrictions.

[139] For a comparative analysis of the right to pursue an economic activity, see H. Schiwer, *Der Schutz der "Unternehmerischen Freiheit" nach Art. 16 der Charta der Grundrechte der Europäischen Union – Eine Darstellung der tatsächlichen Reichweite und Intensität der grundrechtlichen Gewährleistung aus rechtsvergleichender Perspektive*, 2008; for a succinct overview, see D. Schreiter, *Wirtschaftsgrundrechte von Unternehmen in der Europäischen Grundrechtecharta unter besonderer Berücksichtigung des sachlichen Anwendungsbereichs der verbürgten Garantien*, 2009, 102 et seq.

[140] Similar to the right to work, the right to occupational freedom has been broadly interpreted in some jurisdictions as protecting entrepreneurial freedom; this is for instance the case in Germany, see e.g. Schreiter, see note 139, 104.

[141] Article 27 of the Swiss Constitution. On economic liberty within the Swiss constitutional order, see e.g. J.P. Müller/ M. Schefer, *Grundrechte in der Schweiz*, 4th edition, 2008, 1042 et seq.; A. Auer/ G. Malinverni/ M. Hottelier, *Droit constitutionnel Suisse*, Vol. 2, 2nd edition, 2006, 415 et seq.; K.A. Vallender/ P. Hettich/ J. Lehne, *Wirtschaftsfreiheit und begrenzte Staatsverantwortung: Grundzüge des Wirtschaftsverfassungs- und Wirtschaftsverwaltungsrechts*, 4th edition, 2006; D. Hofmann, *La liberté économique suisse face au droit européen*, 2005.

essentially for instrumental reasons. Similar to the US interstate commerce clause, it was mainly designed to further the economic integration of the newly created federal state by overcoming barriers to trade among the constituent states. Apart from the creation of a single market, the constitutional protection of economic freedom is based on the assumption that a free market economy is more conducive to general welfare than state interventionism. In addition to the welfarist justification, economic freedom is also considered as an essential safeguard of individual liberty and self-development. Like other human rights, historical experience underpins this vision of economic liberty. The excessive influence of guilds was not only detrimental to general welfare but also to individual self-development and equality.[142] The diverse functions of economic freedom vary depending on the content and the bearer and the components of the right in question. The human rights dimension is clearly more relevant for individual actors and the right to choose and access an economic activity; with respect to corporate actors and the free pursuit of an economic activity, the instrumental justifications are paramount.[143]

As regards the level of protection, some constitutions explicitly contain broad limitation clauses or qualifications aimed at preventing a neoliberal interpretation of economic liberty rights.[144] Although the

---

[142] The historical legacy of communism also explains why most Central and Eastern European constitutions protect economic liberty; for an enumeration of the various constitutional provisions, see M. Ruffet, "Ad Art. 15 GRCh", in: C. Callies/ M. Ruffet (eds), *Das Verfassungsrecht der Europäischen Union mit Europäischer Grundrechtecharta, Kommentar*, 3rd edition, 2007, 2598, footnote 2.

[143] See e.g. J.P. Müller, "Allgemeine Bemerkungen zu den Grundrechten", in: D. Thürer/ J.F. Aubert and J.P. Müller (eds), *Verfassungsrecht der Schweiz*, 2001, 626 no. 9

[144] See for instance article 11 para. 6 of the Constitution of Luxembourg (subjecting the right "to any restrictions that may be imposed by the legislature"); article 41 of the Constitution of Italy, holding that freedom of enterprise "may not be carried out against the common good or in a way that may harm public security, liberty, or human dignity" (para. 2) and that "[t]he law determines appropriate planning and controls so that public and private economic activities may be directed and coordinated towards social ends." (para. 3); article 45 para. 3.2. of the Constitution of Ireland, according to which "[t]he State shall endeavour to secure that private enterprise shall be so conducted as to ensure reasonable efficiency in the production and distribution of goods and as to protect the public against unjust exploitation"; article 59 of the Constitution of Azerbaijan (protecting the right to

admissible restrictions and the conceptions of the relationship between the state and the economy vary across the European legal orders,[145] the necessity to limit economic freedoms and to reconcile them with other policy goals, including environmental and social policy, is common ground.[146]

As is well known, the heritage of the United States is different. The Supreme Court's neoliberal approach during the *Lochner* era[147] has discredited economic liberty as an individual right to an extent which European scholars find hard to understand.[148] The dialogue of the deaf as regards the status of free trade within the WTO is partly due to differing historical legacies.

Compared with economic freedom, free speech as a human right and the underlying free speech values enjoy broader support on both sides of the Atlantic. European courts and the United States Supreme Court, for instance, emphasise the importance of freedom of speech both as an end in itself and as a means for securing democracy and social progress (i.e. truth).[149]

---

carry out a business activity "according to existing legislation"), and article 48 para. 2 of the Constitution of Turkey, holding that "[t]he state shall take measures to ensure that private enterprises operate in accordance with national economic requirements and social objectives and in conditions of security and stability."

[145] See M.P. Maduro, "Reforming the Market or the State?: Article 30 and the European Constitution: Economic Freedom and Political Rights", *ELJ* 3 (1997), 55 et seq. (65 et seq.) (noting that ordo-liberal constitutional concepts are not embedded in the constitutional tradition of the Member States).

[146] See e.g. for a comparative analysis of economic freedom and its limitations in Spain, France and Switzerland, A. Capitani, *"Les libertés de l'entrepreneur". Recherches sur la protection constitutionnelle des droits et libertés à caractère économique. Aspects de droit comparé espagnol, français et suisse*, 2008, 155 et seq., concluding that although economic liberties "are from a formal point of view not hierarchically inferior, their level of protection is reduced" (at 191, no. 406, translated by the author).

[147] See the famous judgment *Lochner v. New York*, 98 U.S. 45 (1905).

[148] In Europe, the legacy of *Lochnerism* tends to be referred to as a general argument against judicial review. See e.g. for the Scandinavian countries, R. Helgadóttir, *The Influence of American Theories on Judicial Review in Nordic Constitutional Law*, 2006.

[149] See e.g. the famous concurring opinion of Justice Brandeis in *Whitney v. California*, 274 U.S. 357 (1927), holding that: "Those who won our inde-

However, substantial differences exist with respect to the level of protection afforded to freedom of expression and the method of adjudication.[150] Whilst European courts generally engage in balancing free speech against competing values and rights, adopting a methodology not foreign to economic analysis,[151] the United States Supreme Court favours a rules-oriented approach based on distinctions between various categories of speech and the purpose of the governmental measure. When the speech at issue is not considered as "low value" speech and enjoys full constitutional protection, there is virtually no room for restriction based on the content of the expression.[152] Hate speech regulations, for instance, which are widespread in Europe, are thus constitutionally proscribed in the United States.[153] To take another example:

---

pendence believed that the final end of the State was to make men free to develop their faculties, and that, in its government, the deliberative forces should prevail over the arbitrary. They valued liberty both as an end, and as a means. They believed liberty to be the secret of happiness, and courage to be the secret of liberty. They believed that freedom to think as you will and to speak as you think are means indispensable to the discovery and spread of political truth; (…)". For a famous European free speech case, see the seminal *Lüth* judgment of the German Constitutional Court, BVerfGE 7, 198 (for an English translation, see <http://www.utexas.edu>. The Court held that: "The basic right to freedom of expression, the most immediate aspect of the human personality in society, is one of the most precious rights of man (Declaration of the Rights of Man and Citizen (1789) Art. 11). It is absolutely essential to a free and democratic state, for it alone permits that constant spiritual interaction, the conflict of opinion, which is its vital element (…). In a certain sense it is the basis of freedom itself, 'the matrix, the indispensable condition of nearly every other form of freedom' (Cardozo)."

[150] For a study on the United States Supreme Court's free speech methodology from a European perspective, see I. Hare, "Method and Objectivity in Free Speech Adjudication: Lessons from America", *ICLQ* 54 (2005), 49 et seq. For comparative studies including jurisdictions other than Europe and the United States, see e.g. Stone, see note 126; M.H. Good, "Freedom of Expression in Comparative Perspective: Japan's Quiet Revolution", *HRQ* 7 (1985), 429 et seq.; R.J. Krotoszynski, *The First Amendment in Cross-cultural Perspective: A Comparative Legal Analysis of Freedom of Speech*, 2006.

[151] See above Section III. 1. c.

[152] See note 150.

[153] For a comparative study of hate speech and other forms of controversial speech, see the contributions in I. Hare/ J. Weinstein (eds), *Extreme Speech and Democracy*, 2009; M. Rosenfeld, "Hate Speech in Constitutional Juris-

whilst the German conception of human dignity justifies the prohibition of "playing at killing" games, as evidenced by the *Omega* case,[154] the American attachment to free speech leaves virtually no room to regulate the sale of violent video games to minors.[155]

Again, history accounts for some of these differences: in Europe, the experience of the Holocaust has led to vigorous protection of human dignity, whilst in the United States, the legacy of the McCarthy era has highlighted the proneness of government to stifle unorthodox views. Moreover, the mistrust of government is greater in the United States,[156] favouring a predominantly negative understanding of rights. In the field of free speech, this approach is encapsulated in the metaphor of the free marketplace of ideas[157] which government must not interfere with. In Europe, courts more frequently hold that the state has not only the duty to abstain but also to protect fundamental rights against infringement by private parties and to promote free speech values, such as media pluralism.[158] In the light of these differences between Europe and the United States, it is not surprising to find even more discrepancies, both as regards interpretation and effective implementation of freedom

---

prudence: A Comparative Analysis", *Cardozo Law Review* 24 (2003), 1523 et seq.

[154] See above Section II. 3.

[155] See *Brown et al. v. Entertainment Merchants Association et al.* U.S. No. 08-1448, decided on 27 June 2011.

[156] See D. Feldman, "Content Neutrality", in: I. Loveland (ed.), *Importing the First Amendment. Freedom of Expression in American, English and European Law*, 1998, 139-171; E. Barendt, "Importing United States Free Speech Jurisprudence?", in: T. Campbell/ W. Sadurski (eds), *Freedom of Communication*, 1994, 57-76 (64).

[157] The metaphor has its origins in the famous dissenting opinion of Justice Holmes in *Abrams v. United States*, 50 U.S. 616 (1919), which refers to the "free trade in ideas".

[158] See for instance the following Decisions of the French Conseil Constitutionnel, which recognized pluralism as a constitutional value derived from freedom of speech (Decision No. 84-181 DC of 10 October 1984, in which the Conseil Constitutionnel rejects the metaphor of uninhibited free trade in ideas, holding that pluralism needs to be protected against both public and private power and cannot be left to the market alone; see also Decision No. 86-217 DC of 18 September 1986 and Decision No. 89-271 DC of 11 January 1990).

Hertig Randall, Human Rights Within a Multilayered Constitution

of expression,[159] if further jurisdictions are taken into account. A well-known example is the controversy surrounding the thorny issue of defamation of religion, which has divided states in the Human Rights Council[160] and at the 2009 World Conference Against Racism, Racial Discrimination, Xenophobia and Related Intolerance (Durban II), held in Geneva.

Turning to the economic sphere, courts have also taken differing views on advertising. In some jurisdictions, including Japan,[161] the Netherlands,[162] Switzerland, Germany and France, commercial speech does not fall within the ambit of freedom of expression. By contrast, the United States Supreme Court,[163] and, following its example, the Cana-

---

[159] As regards effective implementation of freedom of expression, see e.g. the cases decided by the African Commission on Human Rights listed below, see note 174, which highlight the grave deficiencies in certain countries.

[160] The first resolution on this subject was adopted under the auspices of the United Nations Commission on Human Rights following the initiative of Pakistan in 1999. Ever since, a similar resolution has been adopted every year, within the Commission and its successor, the Human Rights Council. For the most recent ones, see Resolution 10/22, "Combating defamation of religions" of 26 March 2009, Doc. A/HRC/RES/10/22; and Resolution 13/16, "Combating defamation of religions" of 25 March 2010, Doc. A/HRC/RES/13/16; the vote on both resolutions shows that the Council is strongly divided on this issue. The first was adopted with 23 against 11 votes with 13 abstentions, the second with 20 against 17 votes with 8 abstentions. For an analysis of the various resolutions adopted on this subject, see S. Parmar, "The Challenge of 'Defamation of Religions' to Freedom of Expression and the International Human Rights System", *European Human Rights Law Review* 9 (2009), 353 et seq. There are, however, signs of a rapprochement between the two camps, as the concept of defamation of religions was abandoned in the latest resolution, see Resolution 16/13, "Freedom of religion or belief" of 24 March 2011, Doc. A/HRC/RES/16/13, adopted by consensus.

[161] See Krotoszynski, see note 150, 214 et seq.; but see S. Matsui, "Freedom of Expression in Japan", *Osaka University Law Review* 38 (1990), 13 et seq. (28 et seq.) (holding that the constitutional protection of commercial speech is controversial).

[162] Article 7 para. 4 of the Dutch Constitution explicitly exempts commercial advertising from the scope of freedom of the press and freedom of expression.

[163] See the seminal case *Virginia Citizens Consumer Council*, 425 U.S. 748 (1976).

dian Supreme Court,[164] have extended the scope of the free speech guarantee to commercial expression and accord it a considerable level of protection.[165] Nevertheless, both courts clearly admit broader limitations of commercial than of political speech, a trend confirmed in other jurisdictions.

2. The Regional Level

a. Human Rights Regimes

Regional human rights regimes do not guarantee a self-standing, comprehensive right of economic liberty. By contrast, all four general human rights treaties concluded on the regional level – the European Convention on Human Rights of 1950,[166] the American Convention on Human Rights of 1969,[167] the African (Banjul) Charter on Human and Peoples' Rights of 1981[168] and the Arab Charter on Human Rights of 2004[169] – protect freedom of speech. The case law within the European, the American and the African human rights regimes draws both on the

---

[164] See the seminal case *Rocket v. Royal College of Dental Surgeons of Ontario* [1990] 2 S.C.R. 232.

[165] Cf., for instance, the following cases on tobacco advertising handed down by the United States Supreme Court, the Canadian Supreme Court, and the ECJ: *Lorillard Tobacco v. Reilly*, 533 U.S. 525 (2001); *RJR – MacDonald Inc. v. Canada (Attorney General)*, [1995] 3 S.C.R. 199; ECJ, Case C-380/03 *Germany v. European Parliament and Council* ("Tobacco Advertising II") (2006) ECR I-11573. For comparative studies on commercial speech, see e.g. J. Krzeminska-Vamvaka, *Freedom of Commercial Speech in Europe*, 2008; V. Skouris, *Advertising and Constitutional Rights in Europe*, 1994; B.E.H. Johnson/ K.H. Youmsee, "Commercial Speech and Free Expression: The United States and Europe Compared", *Journal of International Media and Entertainment Law* 2 (2009), 159 et seq.; A. Hatje, "Werbung und Grundrechtsschutz in rechtsvergleichender Sicht", in: J. Schwarze (ed.), *Werbung und Werbeverbote im Lichte des europäischen Gemeinschaftsrechts*, 1999, 37 et seq.; see also R.A. Shiner, *Freedom of Commercial Expression*, 2003; K.K. Gower, "Looking Northward: Canada's Approach to Commercial Expression", *Communication Law and Policy* 10 (2005), 29 et seq.

[166] Article 10 ECHR.

[167] Article 13 American Convention.

[168] Article 9 African Charter.

[169] Article 32 Arab Charter.

arguments from autonomy and democracy. It highlights that freedom of expression is not only protected for the sake of the individual but also for the sake of the interest of the community as a whole. In the words of the ECtHR, "[f]reedom of expression constitutes one of the essential foundations of a democratic society and one of the basic conditions for its progress and for each individual's self-fulfilment",[170] or, as the Inter-American Court of Human Rights put it, free speech is "a cornerstone in the mere existence of a democratic society" and "a condition for the community to be fully informed when making their choices."[171] It is both "a right that belongs to each individual" and "a collective right to receive any information whatsoever."[172] According to the African Commission on Human Rights, freedom of expression is "vital to an individual's personal development, his political consciousness, and participation in the conduct of public affairs in his country."[173] As a consequence, the supervisory organs of all three regional human rights regimes accord political speech a high level of protection: restrictions targeting the media, NGOs, political parties and politicians are subject to strict scrutiny;[174] in the same vein, politicians' reputation

---

[170] See e.g. App. No. 25181/94 *Hertel v. Switzerland*, ECHR 1998-VI, para. 46, quoting the famous judgment App. No. 5493/72 *Handyside v. the United Kingdom*, Series A24 (1976), para. 49.

[171] I.A. Court H.R., *Compulsory Membership*, see note 49, para. 70.

[172] Ibid., para. 30.

[173] ACom.HPR, Comm. nos. 105/93, 128/94, 130/94 and 152/96 *Media Rights Agenda and Others v. Nigeria* (1998), para. 54.

[174] For a comparison of the ECtHR's and the Inter-American Court's case law on freedom of expression, see E.A. Bertoni, "The Inter-American Court of Human Rights and the European Court of Human Rights: A Dialogue on Freedom of Expression Standards", *European Human Rights Law Review* 3 (2009), 332 et seq.; all the decisions on freedom of expression rendered by the African Commission concern political expression, see ACom.HPR, Comm. nos. 105/93, 128/94, 130/94 and 152/96 *Media Rights Agenda and Others v. Nigeria* (1998) (seizure of 50,000 copies of a magazine critical of the government); ACom.HPR, Comm. no. 225/98 *Huri-Laws v. Nigeria* (Persecution of a human rights organization's employees and raids of its offices); ACom.HPR, Comm. no. 212/98 (1999), *Amnesty International v. Zambia* (politically motivated deportations of politicians and of a businessman); ACom.HPR, Comm. nos. 48/90, 50/91, 52/91, 89/93 *Amnesty International and Others v. Sudan* (1999) (detention of people belonging to opposition parties or trade unions); ACom.HPR, Comm. nos. 147/95 and 149/96, *Dawda Jawara v. The Gambia* (2000) (arrests, detentions, expulsions and intimidation of journalists); ACom.HPR, Comm. no. 250/2002

and privacy enjoy a lesser degree of protection than that of private figures.[175] The argument from truth holds a less prominent place than the argument from democracy but also finds expression in the case law of the European and the Inter-American Court of Human Rights. It is implicit in a broad vision of political speech and the reference to the *progress* of a democratic society.[176] The similarity between the rulings of the regional human rights bodies is not a coincidence. As the Inter-American Court's extensive references to the Strasbourg case law show, cross-fertilisation has favoured convergence.[177] It is not surprising that the oldest regional human rights regime – the European Convention – has been more important as a source of inspiration to its regional counterparts than the other way round. The consolidation of the American and African body of free speech cases may, however, lead to a two-way dialogue. The fact that the "younger" American Convention and its free speech guarantee were designed to provide more generous protection than article 10 of the older European human rights instrument, and may give rise to more progressive case law, could be conductive to such a development.[178]

Liesbeth Zegveld and Messie Ephrem v. Eritrea (2003) (detention of 15 senior officials belonging to the same political party who had been openly critical of Government policies).

[175] For the European human rights regime, see the famous judgments ECtHR, App. No. 9815/82, *Lingens v. Austria*, Series A03-B (1986), 8 EHRR 407; ECtHR, App. No. 11798/85 *Castells v. Spain*, Series A236 (1992), 14 EHRR 445; for the American system, see e.g. Inter-American Court, *Herrera Ulloa v. Costa Rica*, judgment of 31 August 2004, Series C107; *Ricardo Canese v. Paraguay*, judgment of 31 August 2004; *Jorge Fontevecchia and Hector D'Amico v. Argentina*, judgment of 29 November 2011 and for the African system, see ACom.HPR, Comm. nos. 105/93, 128/94, 130/94 and 152/96 *Media Rights Agenda and Others v. Nigeria* (1998) para. 74: "People who assume highly visible public roles must necessarily face a higher degree of criticism than private citizens; otherwise public debate may be stifled altogether."

[176] See the quote accompanying note 170 and ECtHR, App. No. 13470/87 *Otto-Preminger-Institut v. Austria*, Series A295-A, para. 49 (1994), holding that speech gratuitously offensive to religious feelings of others does "not contribute to any form of public debate capable of furthering *progress* in human affairs" (emphasis added).

[177] For a detailed analysis, see Bertoni, see note 174.

[178] See Bertoni, see note 174, 352; such development can already be observed on the European level, as the ECtHR sometimes refers to the more recent

So far, however, the Strasbourg Court has to our knowledge been the only one called upon to decide free speech cases directly related to the economic marketplace. Information about the remuneration of the chairman of a big corporation in an ongoing labour dispute,[179] speech criticising commercial seal hunting methods,[180] the limited opening times of veterinary practices,[181] the complications and lack of care after cosmetic surgery carried out by a renowned physician,[182] a TV spot exhorting the public to consume less meat for the sake of animal protection,[183] and claims made by a scientist alleging the health hazard of micro waved food,[184] were all considered as speech on matters of public concern and afforded a high level of protection. In the case mentioned last, *Hertel v. Switzerland*, the Court held that "what is at stake is not a given individual's purely 'commercial' statements, but his participation in a debate affecting the general interest, for example, over public health." It concluded that it had to "carefully examine whether the measures in issue were proportionate to the aim pursued"[185] and found that the fact that the scientist's opinion was a "minority one and may appear to be devoid of merit since, in a sphere in which it is unlikely that any certainty exists, it would be particularly unreasonable to restrict freedom of expression only to generally accepted ideas."[186] In the context of defamation proceedings instigated by a transnational corporation against Greenpeace activists, the Court referred to the "general interest in promoting the free circulation of information and ideas about the activities of commercial entities" and the risk of such expres-

---

EU Charter of Fundamental Rights so as to adopt a purposive interpretation of the Convention (see Benoît-Rohmer, see note 55).

[179] ECtHR (GC), App. No. 29183 *Fressoz and Roire v. France* (1999) 31 EHRR 28.
[180] ECtHR, App. No. 21980/93 *Bladet Tromso and Stensaas v. Norway* (1999) 29 EHRR 125.
[181] ECtHR, App. No. 8734/79 *Barthold v. Germany*, Series A90 (1985).
[182] ECtHR, App. No. 26132/95 *Bergens Tidende v. Norway* (2001) 31 EHRR 15.
[183] ECtHR, App. No. 24699/94 *Verein gegen Tierfabriken Schweiz (VgT) v. Switzerland*, ECHR 2001-VI; ECtHR (GC), App. No. 32772/02 *Verein gegen Tierfabriken Schweiz (VgT) v. Switzerland* (No. 2).
[184] *Hertel*, see note 170.
[185] *Hertel*, ibid., para. 47.
[186] *Hertel*, ibid., para. 50.

sion being chilled.[187] It also held "that large public companies inevitably and knowingly lay themselves open to close scrutiny of their acts, and, as in the case of the businessmen and women who manage them, the limits of acceptable criticism are wider in the case of such companies."[188]

The Court's willingness to accord speech on matters of public concern a high level of protection has caused it to venture into commercial territory, leading to an overlap with the WTO regime, specifically, with the Agreement on Trade-Related Aspects of Intellectual Property Rights (TRIPS Agreement). In a series of cases concerning domestic copyright legislation, the ECtHR analysed copyright legislation in the light of freedom of expression.[189] As mentioned above, from an economic point of view, IPRs seek to address market failures of the "information market" caused by the public goods feature of information. Their instrumental value, which consists in favouring the production of information and innovation, is thus related to both free speech functions and the economic marketplace. Whilst IPRs are designed to further free speech values, the exclusive rights they create can at the same time act as a barrier to the dissemination of information. Faced with a conflict between IPRs and freedom of expression, the ECtHR found that injunctions based on the Austrian Copyright Act prohibiting the media from disseminating photographs of politicians or individuals involved in matters of public concern infringed free speech.[190]

---

[187] ECtHR, App. No. 68416/01 *Steel and Morris v. the United Kingdom*, ECHR 2005-II, para. 95.

[188] *Steel and Morris*, para. 94, referring to ECtHR, App. No. 17101/90 *Fayed v. the United Kingdom*, Series A294-B, para. 75.

[189] L.R. Helfer, "The New Innovation Frontier? Intellectual Property and the European Court of Human Rights", *Harv. Int'l L. J.* 49 (2008), 1 et seq. (46).

[190] See ECtHR, App. No. 35841/02, *Oesterreichischer Rundfunk v. Austria* (2006), which concerned the dissemination of images showing the head of a neo-Nazi organisation during his release on parole. The Court stressed that the subject matter was of public concern and that the news "related to a sphere in which restrictions on freedom of expression are to be strictly construed." The Court thus had to "exercise caution when the measures taken by the national authorities are such as to dissuade the media from taking part in the discussion of matters of public interest" (para. 66); App. No. 34315/96, *Krone Verlags GmbH & Co KG v. Austria* (2003), 57 EHRR 1059, concerning a politician criticised for not having earned all his income lawfully, and App. No. 10520/02, *Verlagsgruppe News GmbH v.*

The ECtHR also moved into the economic sphere by extending the reach of freedom of expression to commercial speech, including commercial advertising and statements made by competitors sanctioned pursuant to unfair competition law.[191] The Court, however, distinguishes commercial expression from speech on matters of public concern and grants the Member States a wide margin of appreciation. In one of the first commercial speech cases, *Markt intern*, the Court held, for instance, that a "margin of appreciation is essential in commercial matters and, in particular, in an area as complex and fluctuating as that of unfair competition. Otherwise, the European Court of Human Rights would have to undertake a re-examination of the facts and all the circumstances of each case. The Court must confine its review to the question whether the measures taken on the national level are justifiable in principle and proportionate."[192]

Due to this deferential standard of review, the Court generally finds no violation in commercial speech cases.[193]

Stretching the reach of the Convention even wider, the Court found in *Autronic*[194] that a corporation specialised in home electronics which was refused permission to receive a Soviet television programme via a Soviet satellite so as to demonstrate the performance of private dish antennas at a trade fair was expression protected under article 10 ECHR. Neither the applicant's status as a legal corporation, nor the fact that the content of the speech was of no interest to the corporation itself or to the public, were relevant in the Court's view. In this case, article 10 ECHR was thus in substance given the scope and purpose of economic freedom, since the protected interests at stake were exclusively commercial.

Austria (No. 2) (2006), concerning pending investigations on the suspicion of tax evasion against a "business magnate" (para. 36), e.g. the owner and publisher of a widely-read weekly.

[191] For an overview and analysis of the ECtHR's commercial speech doctrine, see Hertig Randall, see note 90.

[192] ECtHR, App. No. 10572/83, *Markt intern Verlag GmbH and Klaus Beermann v. Germany*, Series A165 (1989) 12 EHRR 161, para. 33.

[193] See Hertig Randall, see note 90.

[194] ECtHR, App. No. 12726/87 *Autronic AG v. Switzerland*, Series A178 (1990) 12 ECHR 485.

Autronic illustrates the ECtHR's tendency to interpret the Convention generously.[195] In addition to freedom of expression, the Court admits that corporations are holders of other rights,[196] including, for instance, the right to privacy (article 8 ECHR) and fair trial guarantees (article 6 ECHR), and that they have standing to file an application.[197] Accordingly, the Court has held that not only individual premises (mainly a person's home) but also corporate premises are protected under article 8 ECHR.[198] As regards the right to property, the Court has taken economic interests into account in protecting also intellectual property, including trademarks of multinational corporations.[199] The ECtHR's approach is difficult to explain based on a vision of human rights protecting human dignity.[200] Instrumentalist considerations, in-

---

[195] For a recent contribution on the ECtHR's interpretive methodology, see G. Letsas, "Strasbourg's Interpretive Ethic: Lessons for the International Lawyer", *EJIL* 21 (2010), 507 et seq.

[196] For studies on the role of corporate actors under the ECHR, see e.g. M. Emberland, *Human Rights of Companies. Exploring the Structure of ECHR Protection*, 2006; V. Martenet, "Les sociétés commerciales devant la Cour européenne des droits de l'homme", in: Bohnet/ Wessner, see note 90, 503-521. For a critical stance, see A. Grear, "Challenging Corporate 'Humanity': Legal Disembodiment, Embodiment and Human Rights", *Human Rights Law Review* 7 (2007), 511 et seq.

[197] Article 34 para. 1 ECHR grants standing not only to "any person" but also to a "non-governmental organisation or group of individuals claiming to be the victim of a violation by one of the High Contracting Parties of the rights set forth in the Convention." The Court considers corporations as non-governmental organisations and admits that they have standing. See X.B. Ruedin/ P.E. Ruedin, "Les personnes morales dans la procédure de requête individuelle devant la Cour européenne des droits de l'Homme", in: Bohnet/ Wessner, see note 90, 27-48.

[198] ECtHR, App. No. 37971/97, *Société Colas Est and others v. France*, ECHR 2002-III. For a commentary, see M. Emberland, "Protection against Unwarranted Searches and Seizures of Corporate Premises under art. 8 of the European Convention on Human Rights: *the Colas Est SA v France Approach*", *Mich. J. Int'l L.* 25 (2003), 77 et seq.

[199] ECtHR (GC), App. No. 73049/01 *Anheuser-Busch Inc. v. Portugal* (2007) 45 EHRR 36, para. 72. For an analysis, see Helfer, see note 189, describing the case as "especially striking" (at 3) and that it sits "uneasily with a treaty whose principal objective is to protect the civil and political liberties of individuals" (at 4).

[200] See M. Hertig Randall, "Personnes morales et titularité des droits fondamentaux", in: R. Trigo Trindade/ H. Peter/ C. Bovet (eds), *Economie, En-*

cluding the objective to limit state power, to safeguard the rule of law,[201] to create minimal standards across Europe, or, from a sceptic's viewpoint, to entrench capitalism,[202] seem more relevant justification for the extensive reach of the Convention.[203] The Court's interpretation of fundamental rights takes into account that the drafters conceived them as both an aim and a means. As reflected in the Preamble of the ECHR and the Statute of the Council of Europe, fundamental rights are also protected as a means to safeguard democracy and to prevent totalitarianism, and to create common values conducive to European integration.[204] The Court's interpretation of the Convention as a "constitutional instrument of a European public order"[205] reflects this vision.

---

vironnement, Ethique, De la responsabilité sociale et sociétale, Liber Amicorum Anne Petitpierre-Sauvain, 2009, 181-191.

[201] See Emberland, see note 196, Chapter 4.

[202] D. Nicol, *The Constitutional Protection of Capitalism*, 2010; id., "Business Rights as Human Rights", in: Campbell/ Wing/ Tomkins, see note 53, 229-243.

[203] The Inter-American Court of Human Rights also favours a generous interpretation of Convention rights. Although standing is limited to natural persons, the Court's case law protects economic interests (for instance those of investors) via a broad interpretation of the right to property. See L. Lixinski, "Treaty Interpretation by the Inter-American Court of Human Rights: Expansionism at the Service of the Unity of International Law", *EJIL* 32 (2010), 585 et seq. (598 et seq.).

[204] See the Preamble of the ECHR, which states that: "Considering that the *aim* of the Council of Europe is the achievement of *greater unity* between its Members and that one of the *methods* by which the aim is to be pursued is the *maintenance and further realization of Human Rights and Fundamental Freedoms*" (emphasis added). See also the Preamble and article 1 lit. a. and b of the Statute of the Council of Europe, which holds that: "a. The aim of the Council of Europe is to achieve a greater unity between its members for the purpose of safeguarding and realising the ideals and principles which are their common heritage and facilitating their economic and social progress. This aim shall be pursued through the organs of the Council by discussion of questions of common concern and by agreements and common action in economic, social, cultural, scientific, legal and administrative matters and in the maintenance and further realisation of human rights and fundamental freedoms."

[205] ECtHR, App. No. 15318/89 *Loizidou v. Turkey*, Series A310, para. 75 (1995); on the ECHR as a European public order, see J.A. Frowein, "The European Convention on Human Rights as the Public Order of Europe", in: *Collected Courses of the Academy of European Law*, Vol. I.2, 1992, 267-358.

"The Convention thus seeks to advance human rights as instrumental to the cause of a Europe united by shared values. It is part of a regime on human rights, but at the same time is linked in a sense to the regime on European integration of the European Union (EU)."[206]

b. Free Trade Regimes (The European Union)

Whilst the Strasbourg court's case law has broadly construed Convention rights, including freedom of expression, and has ventured into the commercial sphere, the judicial guardian of the EU legal order, the ECJ, has moved, as discussed above,[207] from the economic into the human rights sphere. To sketch this evolution with a special focus on freedom of expression, it is useful to distinguish between judicial control of EU acts and measures of the Member States.

The genesis of human rights protection against EU acts is a particularly interesting example of interaction between various layers and sub-layers of governance.[208] Having posited the principle of supremacy of EU law over domestic law, the ECJ faced resistance from national courts, some of which were unwilling to abide by EU measures deemed incompatible with fundamental rights protected in domestic constitutions.[209] Partly in response to these challenges, the ECJ incorporated fundamental rights into the EU legal order as general principles of law. Whilst asserting the autonomy and supremacy of EU law, including that of EU fundamental rights,[210] the Court aimed at achieving inter-

---

[206] S. Ratner, "Regulatory Takings in Institutional Context: Beyond the Fear of Fragmented International Law", *AJIL* 102 (2008), 475 et seq. (496).

[207] Above Section II. 3.

[208] On fundamental rights in the EU legal order, see e.g. P. Alston/ M. Bustelo (eds), *The EU and Human Rights*, 1999; D. Ehlers (ed.), *European Fundamental Rights and Freedoms*, 2007.

[209] The best known cases are those handed down by the German Constitutional Court, see BVerfGE 37, 271 ("Solange I"); BVerfGE 73, 339 ("Solange II"); BVerfGE 89, 155 ("Maastricht Judgment"); BVerfGE 102, 147 ("Banana Judgment"); BVerfGE 123, 267 ("Lisbon Judgment").

[210] See mainly ECJ, Case 11/70 *Internationale Handelsgesellschaft mbH v. Einfuhr- und Vorratsstelle für Getreide und Futtermittel* (1970) ECR 1161, paras 3 and 4: The ECJ stressed that the "law stemming from the Treaty, an independent source of law cannot because of its very nature be overridden by rules of national law", including "fundamental rights as formulated by the constitution" of the Member States. Its validity had to be assessed in the light of EU law, of which fundamental rights formed an integral part.

layer coherence and had recourse to domestic constitutional law as well as the ECHR as sources of inspiration.[211]

The unwritten Bill of Rights fashioned through the ECJ's case law has meanwhile been codified. Adopted in 2000 as a political instrument, the EU Charter of Fundamental Rights, proclaimed on 7 December 2000, became legally binding in 2009.[212] It protects both freedom of expression and economic freedom in two separate provisions. Article 15 enshrines the freedom to choose an occupation and the right to engage in work, and article 16 sets out the freedom to conduct a business. Whilst there is an overlap between the two provisions, and little agreement on their respective scope,[213] the adoption of two distinct provisions takes into account the differing constitutional traditions of the Member States. Reflecting a more limited consensus, the freedom to conduct a business is, according to the wording of article 16, "recognised" "in accordance with Community law and *national laws and practices.*"[214] No such qualification exists in article 15, which enjoys broader support as a human right.

Before the Charter became part of the EU legal order, the ECJ had already reviewed EU measures in the light of fundamental rights. It examined, for instance, far-reaching bans on advertising and sponsoring for tobacco products in the light of freedom of expression.[215] Referring to the case law of the ECtHR's commercial speech cases, it adopted a

---

[211] Article 6 para. 3 of the Treaty on European Union codifies the ECJ's case law: "Fundamental rights, as guaranteed by the European Convention for the Protection of Human Rights and Fundamental Freedoms and as they result from the constitutional traditions common to the Member States, shall constitute general principles of the Union's law."

[212] This date corresponds to the entry into force of the Lisbon Treaty, which incorporates the Charter and confers it the same status as the EU-Treaties (see article 6 of the EU-Treaty). To this effect, the Charter was slightly amended and proclaimed again in December 2007.

[213] See J. von Bernsdorff, "Article 16", in: J. Meyer (ed.), *Charta der Grundrechte der Europäischen Union*, 3rd edition, 2011, 296 et seq., No. 10; H.D. Jarass, *Charta der Grundrechte der Europäischen Union. Kommentar*, 2010, 167, 4; Schreiter, see note 139, 111 et seq.

[214] Emphasis added.

[215] ECJ, "Tobacco Advertising II", see note 165; for a free speech case outside the commercial sphere, see Case C-274/99 *P. Connolly v. Commission* (2001) ECR I-1611, concerning the dismissal of an employee of the European Commission for having published a book highly critical of the EU policies he worked on.

deferential standard of review and upheld the directive in question. The tobacco directive case illustrates two more general trends in the ECJ's case law on fundamental rights: firstly, the tendency to construe EU fundamental rights in the light of the ECHR, and secondly the Court's willingness to grant the EU legislative branch a wide margin of discretion.[216]

Reflecting the Court's understanding of itself as the judicial guardian of the single market based on free movement of persons, goods, services and capital, the Luxembourg judges have engaged in closer scrutiny of national measures restricting trade between Member States. Having conferred upon the four freedoms the status of directly applicable individual rights, the Court reviewed a considerable number of cases which are relevant for freedom of expression. Placing the emphasis on market access,[217] which depends on the availability of information to consumers,[218] the ECJ has scrutinised advertising or marketing restrictions that have a detrimental impact on foreign goods or services in the light of

---

[216] See the well-known Case 160/88 *Fedesa v. Council* (1988) ECR 6399, in which the ECJ upheld the ban on hormones in beef, by contrast with the Appellate Body, see WTO, Appellate Body Report, *EC Measures concerning Meat and Meat Products (EC – Hormones)*, Doc. WT/DS26/AB/R, adopted 13 February 1998); the deferential standard of review is also underlined by commentators with respect to economic freedoms enshrined in arts 15 and 16 of the Charter, see e.g. Bernsdorff, see note 213, 290, No. 18.

[217] In the famous Case C-267 and 268/91 *Keck and Mithouard* (1993) ECR I-6097, the ECJ excluded selling arrangements, which include some forms of advertising, from the scope of free movement of goods. The Court has, however, interpreted this exception narrowly and does not apply it to advertising restrictions that affect foreign products more adversely than domestic products. This is generally the case, as foreign producers depend more on advertising for market access than domestic ones. For the evolution of the case law, see e.g. Case C-71/02 *Herbert Karner Industrie-Auktionen GmbH v. Roostwijk GmbH* (2004) ECR I-3025, para. 37 et seq.

[218] The ECJ stressed the importance of consumer information for the functioning of markets, for instance in Case C-362/88 *GB-INNO v. Confederation du Commerce Luxembourgeois* (1990) ECR I-667, holding that free movement of goods could not be interpreted as "meaning that national legislation which denies the consumer access to certain kinds of information may be justified by mandatory requirements concerning consumer protection" (para. 18). Based on this view, the Court found the prohibition on mentioning the initial price and the duration of the sales in advertising to be contrary to EU law.

the free movement guarantees.²¹⁹ Despite the focus on free movement, the Court has shown willingness to uphold domestic measures aimed at protecting human health, including bans on alcohol advertising.²²⁰ In more recent cases, it not only relied on free movement of goods but considered, in line with the *Grogan*, *Omega* and *Schmidberger* cases,²²¹ that restrictions of fundamental freedoms had to be interpreted in the light of fundamental rights, including article 10 ECHR. Due to the deferential standard of review applicable to commercial speech, however, the reference to the Convention did not result in a higher level of protection than that flowing from free movement guarantees alone.²²²

Outside the commercial speech cases, freedom of expression had more teeth. In *ERT*, for instance, the Court relied on article 10 ECHR, as well as on freedom to provide services, to find a domestic broadcasting monopoly in breach of EU law.²²³ The Court also assessed domestic

---

[219] For studies on restrictions of free speech in the EU legal order, see D. Buschle, *Kommunikationsfreiheit in den Grundrechten und Grundfreiheiten des EG-Vertrages*, 2004; on commercial speech, see Schwarze, see note 165; G. Perau, *Werbeverbote im Gemeinschaftsrecht*, 1997; for a study focusing on advertising restrictions and free movement of goods and services, see R. Greaves, "Advertising Restrictions and the Free Movement of Goods and Services", *European Law Review* 23 (1998), 305 et seq.

[220] See e.g. ECJ, Joined Cases C-1/190 and 176/90 *Aragonesa de Publicidad Exterior and Publivía* (1991) ECR I-4151 concerning the ban on advertising of beverages with a high alcohol content at specified places; the ECJ found the ban to be compatible with free movement of goods; Case C-405/98 *KO v. Gourmet International Products* (2001) ECR I-1795, concerning the prohibition of advertising of alcoholic beverages in magazines; ECJ, C-262/02 *Commission v. France* (GC) (2004) ECR I-6569 and ECJ, C-429/02, *Bacardi France S.A. v. Télévision française 1 SA (TF1) and Others* (GC) (2004) ECR I-6613, both finding a French ban on indirect television advertising for alcoholic beverages during the retransmission of bi-national sporting events taking place in other Member States compatible with free movement of services.

[221] See above Section II. 3.

[222] See e.g. Karner, see note 217, concerning the prohibition on mentioning in advertisements that the goods for sale originate from an insolvent estate if the goods in question have ceased to be part of it. Although the ECJ examined the advertising restriction in question in the light of freedom of expression, it referred to the ECtHR's case law on commercial speech and held that Member States enjoyed considerable discretion (see para. 51).

[223] ECJ, Case C-260/89 *Elliniki Radiophonia Tileorassi AE v. Dimotiki Etairia Pliroforissis and Sotirios Kouvelas* (1991) ECR I-2925; this case contrasted

measures in the light of freedom of expression in *Familiapress*.[224] The case concerned a ban on the distribution of a German magazine in Austria on the grounds that it contained prize competitions contrary to national unfair competition law provisions. In the proceedings, the Austrian Government argued that the domestic legislation was aimed at protecting press diversity, as the local press was unable to use equally costly marketing strategies. The Court agreed with the Austrian Government, and held, referring to the case law of the ECtHR, that,

> "[m]aintenance of press diversity may constitute an overriding requirement justifying a restriction on free movement of goods" since it "helps to safeguard freedom of expression, as protected by Article 10 of the European Convention on Human Rights and Fundamental Freedoms, which is one of the fundamental rights guaranteed by the Community legal order."[225]

At the same time, the Court referred to its *ERT* judgment and found that the overriding requirements invoked to derogate from free movement of goods had to be interpreted in the light of fundamental rights, including freedom of expression. As the domestic measure interfered with press freedom, the domestic court which had referred the matter to the ECJ was asked to balance the individual right to free speech and free movement of goods against press pluralism, a value also derived from freedom of expression. Interestingly, the Court thus left the issue to the Austrian court to decide but indicated a series of factors which needed to be taken into account, such as the competitive relationship of various press products, the impact of marketing strategy on consumers and the market shares of individual publishers and press groups on the Austrian market.

---

with the Court's earlier *Cinéthèque* ruling, in which it held that it lacked the competence to examine the domestic measure (resulting in a ban on the plaintiff's videocassettes) in the light of fundamental rights, see ECJ, Joined Cases 60 and 61/84 *Cinéthèque SA v. Fédération Nationale des Cinémas Français* (1985) ECR 2605.

[224] ECJ, Case C-368/95 *Vereinigte Familiapress Zeitungsverlag- und vertriebs GmbH v. Heinrich Bauer Verlag* (1997) ECR I-3689.

[225] *Familiapress*, see note 224, para. 18. The ECJ referred to the famous judgment of the ECtHR, App. No. 914/88; 15041/89; 15717/89 *Informationsverein Lentia and Others v. Austria*, Series A 276 (1993). On media pluralism within the Council of Europe, see e.g. E. Komorek, "Is Media Pluralism a Human Right? The European Court of Human Rights, the Council of Europe and the Issue of Media Pluralism", *European Human Rights Law Review* 3 (2009), 395 et seq.

3. The Global Level

On the global level, freedom of expression forms part of the International Bill of Rights, this is the Universal Declaration of Human Rights of 1948 (UDHR), and the two International Covenants of 1966. It is anchored in article 19 UDHR, as well as article 19 of the International Covenant on Civil and Political Rights (ICCPR) (a.). It is also inherent in certain rights contained in the International Covenant on Economic, Social and Cultural Rights (ICESCR) (b.). Similar to the regional human rights treaties, neither Covenant protects a free-standing right to trade. The question whether and to what extent the right in question forms part of customary international law thus only needs to be explored for the right to free speech, the consensus underpinning economic liberty being too slim (c.).

a. The ICCPR

The ICCPR has to date been ratified by 167 states. Its supervisory body, the Human Rights Committee, has stressed that "[t]he right to freedom of expression is of paramount importance in any democratic society."[226] Like its regional counterparts, it thus considers political expression as core speech. Interestingly, the Human Rights Committee also adopted a protective stance towards commercial speech. In its communication *John Ballantyne et al. v. Canada*,[227] it not only considered advertising as protected expression, but also rejected the view that different categories of speech "can be subject to varying degrees of limitation, with the result that some forms of expression may suffer broader restrictions than others."[228] This finding is nevertheless limited for two main reasons. Firstly, *John Ballantyne et al. v. Canada* did not concern a typical commercial speech case, involving, for instance, regulation of false or misleading advertising or bans motivated by health reasons. The communication was filed by an English-speaking shopkeeper who challenged the language law of Quebec prohibiting commercial shop signs in a language other than French. The right of an individual to express

---

[226] HRC, Communication No. 628/1995 *Tae-Hoon Park v. Republic of Korea* (1998), para. 10.3; Communication No. 1173/2003 *Benhadj v. Algeria* (2007), para. 8.10.
[227] HRC, Communications Nos. 359/1989 and 385/1989 *Ballantyne, Davidson and McIntyre v. Canada* (1991).
[228] Ibid., para. 11.3.

oneself in the language of his or her choice does not raise fundamentally different issues depending on the content and purpose of the speech at issue. Secondly, the Human Rights Committee's new general comment on freedom of expression[229] and its drafting history show that the status of commercial speech is controversial. Whilst listing political discourse, commentary on one's own and on public affairs, discussion of human rights, journalism, cultural and artistic expression, teaching and religious discourse among the forms of protected speech[230] did not stir up controversy, there was no consensus on commercial speech. For this reason, commercial speech was first put inside brackets which were removed in later drafts and replaced with the formula that commercial speech *may* also be included within the scope of article 19.[231] At the same time, the reference to *John Ballantyne et al. v. Canada* was deleted in order to show that commercial expression was not on the same footing as other categories of speech.[232]

As regards the functions and values of freedom of expression, the general comment refers, in addition to the argument from democracy, also to the argument from autonomy.[233] It also holds that free speech is a "necessary condition for the realisation of the principles of transparency and accountability that are, in turn, essential for the promotion and protection of human rights."[234] Whilst the essential role of the media is acknowledged, the precise obligations states have to secure pluralism have been controversial, as reflected in the relatively weak wording that states "*should* take particular care to encourage an independent and diverse media."[235]

International obligations not to inhibit the flow of information can also be derived from the ICESCR. This fact is of practical relevance for states that have not ratified the ICCPR, as is the case for China.

---

[229] HRC, "General Comment No. 34: Article 19: Freedoms of Opinion and Expression", 21 July 2011, Doc. CPR/C/GC/34, which replaces the very cursory General Comment No. 10 of 1983 on article 19.
[230] Ibid., para. 11.
[231] General Comment No. 34, see note 229, para. 11.
[232] See the information available at <http://www.ishr.ch/treaty-bodies> and <http://intlawgrrls.blogspot.com>.
[233] Para. 1.
[234] Para. 2 bis.
[235] Para. 13, see for a similarly cautious wording also para. 15.

b. The ICESCR

Illustrating the indivisibility and interdependence of human rights, and the overlap between various sub-layers of the international human rights regimes, the Committee on Economic, Social and Cultural Rights (CESCR) has adopted a broad vision of the rights enshrined in the Covenant. With regard to article 12 ICESCR, the Committee holds, for instance, that "the right to health is closely related to and dependent upon the realization of other human rights, as contained in the International Bill of Rights, including [...] access to information. These and other rights and freedoms address integral components of the right to health."[236] The right to health thus "contains both freedoms and entitlements",[237] including components of freedom of expression, e.g. the right to seek, receive and impart information and ideas concerning health issues.[238] Based on this view, states that censor or suppress "health-related education and information, including on sexual and reproductive health"[239] violate their duty to respect the right to health.[240] From the vantage point of free speech theory, the Committee's view can be read as emphasising the argument from autonomy, which calls for a strong level of protection of expression considered as a condition for the exercise of other human rights.[241]

c. Customary International Law

For states which have not ratified the Covenant or have made reservations to article 19 ICCPR, the question arises whether or to what extent freedom of expression has the status of customary international law. Scholars are divided on this issue. Some consider that all the rights enshrined in the UDHR (which includes freedom of expression) have gained the status of customary law.[242] Others adopt a narrower view,[243]

---

[236] General Comment No. 14: The Right to the Highest attainable Standard of Health, Art. 12 of the Covenant, 11 August 2000, Doc. E/C.12/2000/4, para. 3.
[237] Ibid., para. 8.
[238] Ibid., para. 12.
[239] Ibid., para. 11.
[240] Ibid., paras 34 et seq.
[241] See above Section III. 2. a.
[242] See e.g. H. Hannum, "The Status of the Universal Declaration of Human Rights in National and International Law", *Ga. J. Int'l & Comp. L.* 25 (1995-1996), 287 et seq.; L.B. Sohn, "The Human Rights Law of the Char-

proposing or referring to more or less extensive rights catalogues that generally do not encompass free speech.²⁴⁴ In support of the first view, one may stress that the UDHR forms the basis of Universal Periodic Review within the Human Rights Council. The practice of all the 193 State Parties to the United Nations is thus regularly examined in the light of the Universal Declaration. Against such an extensive vision of customary international law, it has been argued that it devalues this source of law.²⁴⁵ However, the claim that freedom of expression forms part of customary international law is supported by two further arguments: firstly, the existence of this right is underpinned by a broad consensus, as freedom of speech is protected within most domestic constitutions, all regional human rights instruments, and in the ICCPR with

---

ter", *Tex. Int'l L. J.* 12 (1977), 129 et seq. (133); M.S. McDougal/ H. Lasswell/ L.C. Chen, *Human Rights and World Public Order*, 1980, 272; Habbard/ Guiraud, see note 4; J.P. Humphrey, "The International Bill of Rights: Scope and Implementation", *William and Mary Law Review* 17 (1976), 527 et seq. (529).

243 See e.g. B. Simma/ P. Alston, "The Sources of Human Rights Law: Custom, Jus Cogens and General Principle", *Austr. Yb. Int'l L.* 12 (1992), 82 et seq. (91); W. Kälin/ J. Künzli, *Universeller Menschenrechtsschutz*, 2nd edition, 2008; among authors writing about the interface of human rights and international economic law, see Alston, see note 4, 829; Howse/ Mutua, see note 2, 10; A. McBeth, *International Economic Actors and Human Rights*, 2010, 30.

244 According to the Restatement (third) of Foreign Relations Law of the United States (1986), para. 702, "[a] state violates international law if, as a matter of state policy, it practices, encourages, or condones (a) genocide, (b) slavery or slave trade, (c) the murder or causing the disappearance of individuals, (d) torture or other cruel, inhuman, or degrading treatment or punishment, (e) prolonged arbitrary detention, (f) systematic racial discrimination, or (g) a consistent pattern of gross violations of internationally recognized human rights." The Human Rights Committee has suggested a more extensive catalogue, see HRC, General Comment No. 24: Issues relating to Reservations made upon Ratification or Accession to the Covenant or the Optional Protocols thereto, or in Relation to Declarations under Article 41 of the Covenant, 4 November 1994, Doc. CCPR/C/21/Rev.1/Add.6, para. 8. For an author holding that free speech is part of customary international law, see M. Panizzon, "GATS and the Regulation of International Trade in Services", in: M. Panizzon/ N. Pohl/ P. Sauvé (eds), *GATS and the Regulation of International Trade in Services*, 534-560, 554; C.B. Graber, *Handel und Kultur im Audiovisionsrecht der WTO. Völkerrechtliche, ökonomische und kulturpolitische Grundlagen einer globalen Medienordnung*, 2003, 119.

245 See Simma/ Alston, see note 243.

nearly universal membership. Secondly, within the Charter-based human rights mechanisms, a thematic mandate "on the Promotion and Protection of the Right to Freedom of Opinion and Expression" was instituted in 1993.[246] This indicates that the members of the UN consider freedom of expression to be protected within general international law.

Affirming that freedom of expression forms part of customary international law, however, carries the risk of glossing over the differences among various domestic and international regimes as regards the status of various categories of speech.[247] Based on the Human Rights Committee's view, which considers both reservations to and derogations from freedom of opinion to be non-permissible, the right to hold an opinion ought to be considered as forming part of customary public international law.[248] It is submitted that state measures engaging in repression or censorship of political speech also infringe freedom of speech *qua* customary international law.[249] Although freedom of political expression is far from being effectively realised on the domestic level, the case law of many constitutional courts, all three regional human rights courts and the Human Rights Committee reflects a consensus on the particular importance of political speech, broadly defined.[250] Such a line

---

[246] See Commission on Human Rights Resolution 1993/45 and Human Rights Council Resolutions 7/36 and 16/4. For the genesis of this resolution and the claim that it is based on the assumption that freedom of expression forms part of public international law independently of human rights treaties, see B. Rudolf, *Die thematischen Berichterstatter und Arbeitsgruppen der UN-Menschenrechtskommission*, 2000, 335 et seq.

[247] Some of the main issues on which state practices diverge are mentioned above Section IV. 1.

[248] See also HRC, General Comment No. 24, see note 244, para. 8, which considers freedom of thought, conscience and religion as forming part of customary international law.

[249] If repression and censorship are systematic and thus form part of state policy, such practices can be considered as a "consistent pattern of gross violations" of freedom of expression in the sense of the Restatement (third) of Foreign Relations Law of the United States, see note 244.

[250] With regard to human rights norms, it has been argued that the *opinio iuris* carries more weight than state practice (see e.g. T. Meron, "The Continuing Role of Custom in the Formation of International Humanitarian Law", *AJIL* 90 (1996), 238 et seq. (239-240)). Without this reasoning, the widely acknowledged claim that the prohibition of torture forms part of customary international law (or even *ius cogens*) would be impossible to maintain in the light of the widespread practice of torture.

of reasoning would also be compatible with views claiming that public international law has evolved towards admitting a "right to democracy".[251] Independently of the existence of such a right, it can be argued that transparency is essential to check any form of government. This argument is important for the purpose of this survey considering that WTO members are almost equally split between "free" and "not free" states.[252]

4. Synthesis

The previous sections examined the status and function of freedom of expression and economic freedom within the multilayered constitution. This cursory analysis offers several insights. Firstly, whilst freedom of expression is protected as a freestanding right on every layer of governance, the same does not hold true for economic freedom. Human rights regimes, similarly to some domestic constitutions, do not enshrine a comprehensive guarantee of economic liberty. Considerable diversity exists even among the Member States of the EU. Despite the entrenchment of the four market freedoms on the EU level, the domestic constitutional orders protect economic liberty to various degrees. Secondly, and not surprisingly, there are also differences with regard to the interpretation and application of free speech. However, there is wide consensus that political expression, understood in broad terms, is core speech and deserves a high level of protection. Pursuant to the case law

---

[251] See the seminal contribution by T. Franck, "The Emerging Right to Democratic Governance", *AJIL* 86 (1992), 46 et seq. For a cautionary note from an Asian perspective, see S. Varayudej, "A Right to Democracy in International Law: Its Implications for Asia", *Annual Survey of International & Comparative Law* 12 (2006), 1 et seq. The Human Rights Committee stresses the importance of freedom of expression for the right to political participation enshrined in article 25 ICCPR (see General Comment No. 25: The Right to Participate in Public Affairs, Voting Rights and the Right of Equal Access to Public Service (Art. 25), 12 July 1996, Doc. CCPR/C/21/Rev.1/Add.7, para. 12). Combined with the other components of this right, article 25 "will result in a functioning electoral democracy" (Varayudej, see note 251, 9).

[252] See the study by S.A. Aaronson/ J.M. Zimmermann, *Trade Imbalance: The Struggle to Weigh Human Rights Concerns in Trade Policymaking*, 2008. The authors base their study on the classification of states done by Freedomhouse. For a summary of their study, see Konstantinov, see note 2, 321 et seq.

of the ECtHR, political speech extends to "market relevant expression", such as speech critical of business practices or stressing the health hazard of certain products. By contrast to political expression, courts tend to adopt a deferential standard of review when examining restrictions on commercial expression (narrowly defined as advertising or speech targeting a competitor). Moreover, disagreement exists as to whether commercial speech falls within the ambit of freedom of expression. Thirdly, the practice of the courts on the various constitutional layers does not confirm visions of strict separation between various regimes and categories of rights. Human rights courts and constitutional courts tend to protect freedom of speech not exclusively on grounds of autonomy, e.g. as a right belonging to every human being by virtue of being human, but also take into account instrumentalist justifications. This trend is very pronounced in the case law of the ECtHR.

Similar to the broad interpretation of other Convention rights, the Strasbourg court has construed freedom of expression as protecting purely economically motivated corporate speech. Conversely, within the EU, the ECJ has been gradually moving from a utilitarian vision of the economic freedoms (in particular free movement of persons) to interpreting these rights as protecting human beings rather than economic actors. As a consequence of these trends, there are substantial overlap, rapprochement and interaction between the "ethical" and the "economic" Europe.[253] Both mutual influence and expansionism can also be observed in the relationships between various human rights courts. On the regional level, the case law of the ECtHR on freedom of expression has served as a source of inspiration to the other regional courts, without the relationship being a one-way street. On the global level, the CESCR has construed socioeconomic rights broadly. It has, for instance, interpreted the right to health also as a liberty right which comprises several components of freedom of expression. The trend towards cross-fertilisation, mutual borrowing and expansionism has so far been less pronounced within the WTO. Nevertheless, the view that the WTO is not a self-contained regime operating in clinical isolation from public international law,[254] and the Appellate Body's trend towards a

---

[253] The expression is borrowed from M. Delmas-Marty, "Commerce mondial et protection des droits de l'homme", in: *Commerce mondial et protection des droits de l'homme: les droits de l'homme à l'épreuve de la globalisation des échanges économiques*, 2001, 1-17 (9).

[254] See e.g. A. Lindroos/ M. Mehling, "Dispelling the Chimera of 'Self-Contained Regimes' International Law and the WTO", *EJIL* 16 (2005), 857 et seq.

less formalistic interpretation of the WTO treaties,[255] opens up space to integrate human rights concerns (including freedom of speech issues) within the multilateral trading system.

V. Integrating Freedom of Speech within the WTO

Before addressing the interface between freedom of expression and world trade law, it is useful to point out a few characteristics of the multilateral trading system which are relevant for the inter-linkage between human rights and free trade rules. The emphasis will be on the distinguishing features of the free trade regime as compared with human rights regimes. Firstly, although it has been argued that international trade law is aimed at protecting individual liberty of producers and consumers, the WTO remains an essentially member-driven organisation. By contrast with human rights regimes and the EU, individuals never have standing to enforce their rights or interests. The Dispute Settlement Understanding[256] (DSU) remains a mechanism to resolve inter-state disputes. Secondly, like the four market freedoms, WTO law has the function of securing market access for domestic economic actors against protectionist policies adopted by other states, whilst human rights law is primarily designed to protect citizens against their own state. Considered together, these facts make it hard to sustain the view that the WTO is conceived as protecting free trade as a human right, independently of whether free trade (mainly by corporate actors) is regarded as a human right. The WTO law remains anchored in the paradigm of reciprocity typical of inter-state relations,[257] which is ex-

---

[255] See I. Van Damme, "Treaty Interpretation by the WTO Appellate Body", *EJIL* 21 (2010), 605 et seq.

[256] Understanding on Rules and Procedures Governing the Settlement of Disputes.

[257] See J. Pauwelyn, "A Typology of Multilateral Treaty Obligations: Are WTO Obligations Bilateral or Collective in Nature?" *EJIL* 14 (2003), 907 et seq.; see also S. Charnovitz, "WTO Dispute Settlement as a Model for International Governance", in: A. Kiss/ D. Shelton/ K. Ishibashi (eds), *Economic Globalization and Compliance with International Environmental Agreements*, 2003, 245-253 (252); for a contrary view, see C. Carmody, "WTO Obligations as Collective", *EJIL* 17 (2006), 419 et seq.; see also Harrison, see note 2, 60 who mentions that "many trade lawyers would dispute this characterization of trade law and human rights law obligations" without taking sides himself.

plicitly rejected within human rights regimes. Although most human rights treaties provide not only for individual but also for inter-state complaints, the supervisory organs of the ECHR, and later of other human rights bodies, have stressed that a state complaining about human rights violations by another state before the competent treaty body does not defend its own interests but those of the community of states as a whole.[258] The so-called objective nature of human rights norms, and the absence of reciprocity, also means that a state cannot refuse to abide by its human rights obligations on the grounds that other states fail to honour their commitments. Within the WTO, by contrast, compensation and retaliation are available to a complainant state so as to induce the defendant state to comply with a Panel or Appellate Body ruling. Reciprocity is thus alive and well within the multilateral trading system. It is this very feature, combined with the compulsory nature of the DSU, which tends to confer pre-eminence to WTO law with respect to other international regimes. These characteristics of the WTO regime give rise to "sanctions envy"[259] and the resulting calls for linking trade law with norms from regimes whose enforcement mechanisms are much weaker. Whilst human rights enjoy perceived normative superior-

---

[258] See the famous admissibility decision of the European Commission of Human Rights in *Austria v. Italy* (known as the *Pfunders* case), App. No. 788/60, Yearbook of the European Convention on Human Rights, 1961, Vol. IV, 138-140, which described the specific nature and purpose of the Convention as follows: "The purpose of the High Contracting Parties in concluding the Convention was not to concede to each other reciprocal rights and obligations in pursuance of their individual national interests but to realise the aims and ideals of the Council of Europe, as expressed in its Statute, and to establish a common public order of the free democracies of Europe with the object of safeguarding their common heritage of political traditions, ideals, freedom and the rule of law. [...] it follows that the obligations undertaken [...] are essentially of an objective character, being designed to protect the fundamental rights of individual human beings from infringement by any of the High Contracting Parties than to create subjective and reciprocal rights for the High Contracting Parties themselves; [...] [I]t follows that a High Contracting Party, when it refers an alleged breach of the Convention to the Commission [...], is not to be regarded as exercising a right of action for the purpose of enforcing its own rights, but rather as bringing before the Commission an alleged violation of the public order of Europe." For a detailed analysis of the specific nature of human rights treaties, with references to other human rights regimes, see Addo, see note 98, 468 et seq.

[259] Charnovitz, see note 257, 252.

ity[260] over international trade law, the "hard enforced" WTO regime benefits from "de facto" pre-eminence over "soft-enforced" human rights regimes.[261] In other words, enforcement, which "has always been seen as the weak link in the international legal system, and it is surely the weak link of international human rights law",[262] is less of a problem for the WTO.

Compared with the judicial branch of the WTO, the legislative and the executive branch fares less well in terms of effectiveness. By contrast with the EU, the multilateral trading system lacks an independent institution representing the interests of the community of the Member States and law-making powers typical of supranationalism. This also limits the avenues along which to integrate human rights within the multilateral trading regime. Under the current institutional framework, the mechanisms available to accommodate human rights issues, including freedom of expression, are mainly treaty amendments, the adoption of waivers, accession discussions, the non-extension of privileges, Trade Policy Reviews (TPR) and dispute settlement.[263] As others have shown, the practical relevance of these avenues is quite limited. Human rights concerns, for instance, have so far not played an important role in accession negotiations or during TPR.[264] For this reason, most contributions on human rights and the WTO focus on dispute settlement, which is considered the most promising among the existing avenues. The advantage of this mechanism remains relative. So far, states have been reluctant to rely on human rights directly within the dispute settlement

---

[260] Of the regional human rights courts, both the Strasbourg Court and the Inter-American Court have made claims coming close to asserting the superiority of human rights law *vis-à-vis* other norms of international law. See the *Bosphorus* ruling of the ECtHR, see note 54 and E. De Wet, "The Emergence of International and Regional Value Systems as a Manifestation of the Emerging International Constitutional Order", *LJIL* 19 (2011), 611 et seq.; the Inter-American Court has supported this finding based on the objective nature of the ACHR, which it contrasted with the reciprocal nature of an investment treaty (see Lixinski, see note 203, 590 et seq. (598 et seq.)).

[261] See H. Hestermayer, *Human Rights and the WTO. The Case of Patents and Access to Medicine*, 2007, 206 et seq. (from which the terminology is borrowed); see also Konstantinov, see note 2, 330.

[262] L. Henkin, "Human Rights and 'State Sovereignty'", *Ga. J. Int'l & Comp. L.* 25 (1996), 31 et seq. (41).

[263] See Konstantinov, see note 2, 325.

[264] Id., see note 2, 325 et seq.

procedure.²⁶⁵ More generally, the fact that only governments have standing "acts as a key political filter", limiting both the number of cases and the arguments brought before the dispute settlement bodies.²⁶⁶ The preference for a negotiated settlement,²⁶⁷ and political reasons, may explain governments' reluctance to base their claims not only on WTO law but also on human rights law. Bargaining, and reaching a negotiated compromise over basic entitlements of human beings, appears much more problematic than a settlement over purely commercial interests.

Due to the paucity of precedents, the following sections are partly speculative, attempting to anticipate cases in which free speech concerns may be at issue. The analysis will first focus on the GATT and the General Agreement on Trade in Services (GATS) (1.) and then on the TRIPS Agreement (2.). It will be limited to cases where free speech is directly linked to the dispute at issue. Thus the compatibility of trade sanctions targeting human rights violations that are not directly trade-related will not be examined.²⁶⁸

1. GATT and GATS

To gain a clearer understanding of how freedom of expression may interact with the norms of trade liberalisation in the field of goods (GATT) and services (GATS), it is useful to adopt a comparative perspective. Drawing on the insights from the inter-linkage between freedom of expression and economic rights and freedoms on other layers of governance, in particular within the EU, the present analysis will distinguish between "defensive" and "offensive" uses of freedom of expression.²⁶⁹ The first group encompasses cases in which the complaining state invokes free speech as "a sword" to reinforce its claim that the defending state has breached GATT or GATS rules. The second con-

---

265 Id., see note 2, 331.
266 See Helfer, see note 189, 44; On the "political filters" with respect to WTO litigations, see A.O. Sykes, "Public versus Private Enforcement of International Economic Law: Standing and Remedy", *Journal of Legal Studies* 34 (2005), 631 et seq.
267 See Helfer, see note 189, 44, footnote 224.
268 On this issue, see e.g. Cleveland, see note 2 and Stirling, see note 2.
269 The terminology is borrowed from Coppel/ O'Neill, see note 59.

sists of cases in which the defending state relies on freedom of expression as "a shield", at the level of exceptions to free trade rules.

a. "Defensive" Use of Free Speech

What are the cases in which conflicts between freedom of expression and commitments are likely to occur under the GATT and the GATS? This question needs answering before possible avenues for reconciling free speech and WTO law are analysed. As discussed above, within the EU legal order, the ECJ was faced with a clear clash between market freedoms and free speech in the *Schmidberger* case. It has been argued that a similar scenario may also occur within the WTO legal order, as "politically motivated private demonstrations blocking freedom of transit"[270] may contravene Article V GATT. Although theoretically feasible, the state-centred nature of the dispute settlement mechanism makes it unlikely that a government would bring a claim against another state for allowing a peaceful demonstration to interrupt a specific transit route for a few hours. A state may have a bigger incentive to file a complaint in a scenario where private actors systematically and intentionally block the traffic of foreign goods in protest against "unfair" competition.

The ECJ was called to rule on similar facts in *Commission v. France*.[271] This case concerned the French Government's lack of action to secure free movement of Spanish agricultural products against blockages and acts of vandalism from French farmers over a period of more than ten years. Scrutinising this case in the light of free movement implied, however, that the ECJ admitted that the four economic freedoms imposed on the Member States not only the duty to refrain from taking protectionist measures but also the duty to protect free movement rights against interference from private parties. This activist ruling did not remain without comments on the European level. It is far from certain that a Panel or the Appellate Body, which operate in a more diverse setting than the ECJ, would, or should, confer an equally broad scope to the states' obligations under GATT.

---

[270] E.U. Petersmann, "The 'Human Rights Approach' Advocated by the UN High Commissioner for Human Rights and by the International Labour Organization: Is it Relevant for WTO Law and Policy?", *Journal of International Economic Law* 7 (2004), 605 et seq. (609).

[271] ECJ Case 265/95 *Commission v. France* (1997) ECR I-6959.

A more likely avenue for freedom of expression to enter the ambit of GATT and GATS would be with disputes involving "cultural products",[272] which were at issue, for instance, in the famous *Canada–Periodicals* case.[273] By contrast with *Familiapress* and similar cases decided by the ECJ, the Canadian Government did not rely on freedom of expression to justify the measures taken to protect the Canadian press against competition from U.S. products. More generally, measures taken by states to preserve the diversity of the local media, cinematography, literature and arts have so far rarely been analysed as free speech issues within the WTO.[274] Discussions[275] have mainly centred on linking WTO law with cultural rights protected under the ICESCR[276] and the UNESCO Convention on the Protection and Promotion of the Diversity of Cultural Expression.[277] The reluctance to frame the "trade and culture" debate as a free speech issue may partly be due to diverging interpretations of the scope and content of freedom of expression. As already mentioned,[278] the American vision of an unfettered free marketplace of ideas, coupled with a purely negative vision of fundamental rights contrasts, for instance, with the "European" vision considering media and press pluralism as a free speech value which the state needs to protect against the standardising forces of the market. As also discussed earlier,[279] the lack of consensus is reflected on the global level, too. As the drafting process of the new General Comment on article 19

---

[272] For a study on "cultural products" within the WTO, see e.g. J. Morijn, *Reframing human rights and trade: potential and limits of a human rights perspective of WTO law on cultural and educational goods and services*, 2010; T. Voon, *Cultural Products and the World Trade Organization*, 2007; Graber, see note 244.

[273] WTO Appellate Body Report, *Canada – Certain Measures Concerning Periodicals (Canada – Periodicals)*, Doc. WT/DS31/AB/R adopted 30 July 1997.

[274] For an exception, see Graber, see note 244, 102 et seq.

[275] For an overview of the discussion, see Voon, see note 272, 149 et seq.

[276] See article 27 para. 1 Universal Declaration: "Everyone has the right freely to participate in the cultural life of the community, to enjoy the arts and to share in scientific advancement and its benefits."

[277] UNESCO Convention on the Protection and Promotion of the Diversity of Cultural Expression, adopted 20 October 2005, entered into force 18 March 2007.

[278] See above Section IV. 1.

[279] See above Section IV. 3. a.

ICCPR has shown, the extent to which freedom of speech imposes on governments the duty to safeguard press pluralism is controversial.

Does the lack of a global consensus mean that states should be precluded from invoking freedom of expression as a defence against a complaint filed by another WTO member? An answer in the affirmative would in the author's view not take sufficiently into account the subsidiarity of "higher" with respect to "lower" layers of governance. The experience on the European level shows that the ECtHR's margin of appreciation doctrine is an important tool to accommodate national diversity. In the same vein, the ECJ's *Omega* jurisprudence allows states to justify restrictions of economic freedoms based on human rights defences, even absent a shared vision of the right in question.[280] Within the WTO, the public morals exception (Article XX (a) GATT and Article XIV (a) GATS)[281] is the most promising avenue to integrate human rights conceptions which are not shared by all members within the multilateral trading system.[282] This approach can build on WTO jurispru-

---

[280] See above Section II. 3.

[281] For studies of the public morals exception, see M. Wu, "Free Trade and the Protection of Public Morals: An analysis of the Newly Emerging Public Morals Clause Doctrine", *Yale J. Int'l L.* 33 (2008), 215 et seq.; N.F. Diebold, "The Morals and Order Exceptions in WTO: Balancing the Toothless Tiger and the Undermining Mole", *Journal of International Economic Law* 11 (2007), 43 et seq.; S. Charnovitz, "The Moral Exception in Trade Policy", *Va. J. Int'l L.* 38 (1998), 689 et seq.; C.T. Feddersen, "Focusing on Substantive Law in International Economic Relations: The Public Morals of GATT's Article XX(a) and 'Conventional' Rules of Interpretation'", *Minn. J. of Global Trade* 7 (1998), 75 et seq.

[282] This approach is supported amongst others by Harrison, see note 2, 200 et seq.; Voon, see note 272, 156 et seq.; see also the Report of the United Nations High Commissioner for Human Rights, "Human Rights and World Trade Agreements: Using General Exception Clauses to Protect Human Rights", Doc. HR/PUB05/05 (2005), 5; Howse/ Mutua, see note 2; M.J. Trebilcock/ R. Howse, "Trade Policy and Labor Standards", *Minn. J. Global Trade* 14 (2005), 261 et seq. (290); S. Zleptic, *Non-economic objectives in WTO law : justification provisions of GATT, GATS, SPS, and TBT Agreements*, 2010, 202 et seq.; S.J. Powell, "Place of Human Rights Law in World Trade Organization Rules", *Fla. J. Int'l L.* 16 (2004), 219 et seq. (223); Cleveland, see note 2, 157.

dence. In *U.S.–Gambling*,²⁸³ the Panel held with respect to the terms "public morals" and "public order" that,

"the content of these concepts for Members can vary in time and space, depending upon a range of factors, including prevailing social, cultural, ethical and religious values. Further, the Appellate Body has stated on several occasions that Members, in applying similar societal concepts, have the right to determine the level of protection that they consider appropriate. (…) More particularly, Members should be given some scope to define and apply for themselves the concepts of 'public morals' and 'public order' in their respective territories, according to their own systems and scales of values."²⁸⁴

The emphasis on the variability of public morals, and the willingness to grant members "some scope" to define and apply this concept, support the view that the Panel rejected a universalist vision of public morality. Varying in time, public morals are, as the Appellate Body held with respect to other exception clauses, "by definition, evolutionary."²⁸⁵ The fact that human rights law was in its infancy when GATT was drafted thus does not prevent contemporary human rights norms from informing the ordinary meaning of Article XX (a) according to the rules of interpretation of article 31 para. 1 Vienna Convention on the Law of Treaties (VCLT).²⁸⁶ Human rights moreover fit the Panel's defi-

---

283 WTO, Panel Report, *United States – Measures Affecting the Cross-Border Supply of Gambling and Betting Services (U.S.–Gambling)*, Doc. WT/DS285/R, Appellate Body Report adopted 20 April 2005.

284 Ibid., para. 6.461, internal footnotes omitted.

285 Appellate Body Report, *United States – Import Prohibition of Certain Shrimp and Shrimp Products (US – Shrimp)*, Doc. WT/DS58/AB/R, adopted 6 November 1998, para. 130, internal quotations omitted; on the evolutionary nature of the public moral exception, see Voon, see note 272, 156, and of the exception clauses more generally, Zleptic, see note 282, 203.

286 See also High Commissioner for Human Rights, see note 282, 5: "(…) But arguing for the exclusion of the norms and standards of international human rights on the basis of the ordinary meaning of the terms would be very difficult to sustain. For, '[i]n the modern world, the very idea of public morality has become inseparable from the concern for human personhood, dignity, and capacity reflected in fundamental rights. A conception of public morals or morality that excluded notions of fundamental rights would simply be contrary to the ordinary contemporary meaning of the concept.'" (quoting R. Howse, "Back to court after Shrimp/Turtle? Almost but not quite yet: India's short lived challenge to labor and environmental exceptions in the European Union's generalized system of preferences", *Am. U.*

nition of public morals in *U.S.–Gambling* as denoting "standards of right and wrong conduct maintained by or on behalf of a community or nation."[287] As Zleptic put it,

> "[i]f pornography, gambling, alcohol drinks or matters of religious concern are considered as core elements of the public morals exception, it is difficult to argue why human rights considerations should not fall within the same category. They can also be considered as constitutive of 'public order', defined as the 'preservation of the fundamental interests of a society, as reflected in public policy and law'",[288] and relating,

> "inter alia, to standards of law, security and morality."[289]

Whilst *U.S.–Gambling* does not support a universalist reading of "public morals", it does not seem to endorse an entirely particularist vision, either.[290] However, it offers no guidance as to the "thickness" of consensus necessary for the public morals exception to apply.[291] Defining the degree of convergence required is a difficult undertaking. At least if a certain conception of a human right finds support both within several jurisdictions of the national level and on the regional level, the consensus requirement ought to be considered as being met. This is the case with respect to the free speech value of pluralism, which is not only espoused by several European constitutional courts but also by the ECtHR and the ECJ. The UNESCO Convention, which refers in its title to "cultural expression",[292] points to even broader support.

Taking regional human rights instruments into account would, in the case of Europe, fit well with the ECtHR's description of the European Convention as a "constitutional instrument of a European public order."[293] This solution strikes a balance between the risks entailed by both universalism and particularism. It takes the principle of subsidiar-

---

Int'l L. Rev. 18 (2003), 1333 et seq. (1368); see also Trebilcock/ Howse, see note 282, stressing the "evolution of human rights as a core element in public morality in many postwar societies and at the international level."

[287] Panel Report, *U.S.–Gambling*, see note 283, para. 6.465.
[288] Panel Report, *U.S.–Gambling*, ibid., para. 6.467.
[289] Ibid.
[290] The Report refers to the practice of other jurisdictions before admitting the applicability of the public morals exception, see Panel Report, *U.S.-Gambling*, see note 283, paras 6.471- 6.474; see also Wu, see note 281, 233.
[291] See Wu, see note 281, 231 et seq.
[292] See above note 277.
[293] See above Section IV. 2. a. and *Loizidou v. Turkey*, see note 205.

ity seriously without compromising the checking function of "higher" over "lower" layers of governance[294] by preventing the "public morals exception" from being rendered ineffective in accommodating diverging domestic values, whilst taking seriously the concern that states may use unfettered discretion to adopt protectionist measures under the cover of "public morals". Robert Wai's assertion that "the multilateral nature of the international human rights regime partially protects against protectionist motives"[295] is pertinent also with respect to regional human rights instruments. Invoking free speech values as defences in disputes concerning "cultural products" would thus not be incompatible with the object and purpose of the WTO. More affirmatively, with respect to the media, pluralism enhances the diversity of information and public debate on matters of public concern, which include, as mentioned earlier,[296] both political and economic matters. Diverse media is also an important safeguard against abuses in the political and the commercial sphere. The importance of transparency for the functioning of markets makes it supportive of the objectives pursued by the WTO.

b. "Offensive" Use of Free Speech

As was shown above, synergies and overlaps between freedom of expression and free trade occur in the field of commercial speech, e.g. commercial advertising. This raises the question whether the WTO adjudicative branch ought to examine advertising restrictions not only in the light of GATT or GATS rules, but also in the light of freedom of expression. Referring to the *Hertel* case,[297] Petersmann, for instance, raises the question why human rights courts confer more extensive protection to commercial speech than trade courts.[298] This assertion, however, is based on a concept of commercial speech which is different from that used by constitutional and human rights courts.[299] The latter adopt a narrow vision of commercial expression and limit it to cases where the speaker has a direct profit motive, as is the case in commer-

---

[294] On the role of subsidiarity and the checking function within a multilayered constitution, see above Section II. 1. and 2.
[295] Wai, see note 2, 54.
[296] See above Section III. 2. b.
[297] See above Section IV. 2. a.
[298] Petersmann, see note 270, 610.
[299] See C.B. Graber, "The *Hertel* Case and the Distinction between Commercial and Non-Commercial Speech", in: Cottier/ Pauwelyn/ Bürgi Bonanomi, see note 2, 273-278.

cial advertising and speech by competitors falling within the ambit of unfair competition law. This was also the vision of the ECtHR in the *Hertel* case.[300] As mentioned above, the Strasbourg court distinguished the expression at issue in *Hertel* from standard commercial speech and treated it as political speech, understood in a broad sense. If commercial speech is understood in a narrow sense, there is little ground to argue that human rights courts treat this category of speech more favourably than trade courts. The analysis of freedom of expression on the different layers of governance has shown that both the ECtHR and the ECJ subject commercial speech to a lower level of scrutiny than political speech.[301] Although the Luxembourg court has interpreted derogations from free movement provisions in the light of freedom of expression, this has not resulted in a higher level of protection against advertising restrictions than that flowing from free movement of goods or free movement of services.[302] On the global level, the Human Rights Committee's work on drafting the new general comment on freedom of expression illustrates that there is little consensus on whether or not commercial speech is a form of protected expression under article 19 ICCPR.[303] In the light of this diversity, in the author's view it is inadvisable for Panels or the Appellate Body to frame advertising restrictions as free speech issues. Doing so is likely to trigger criticism, including the charge that human rights are used as a strategic tool to reinforce market access. This approach would be particularly controversial with respect to advertising restrictions based on health grounds. Bans on advertising alcoholic beverages or cigarettes apply in many jurisdictions. Viewing them as limitations of free speech entails the risk of according commercial speech an excessively high level of protection, generating conflicts with other human rights, in particular with the right to health.[304] Pursuant to the ICESCR, the duty to protect and fulfil the right to health requires states to take positive measures. In the light of the Framework Convention on Tobacco Control (FCTC), these include

---

[300] See above Section IV. 2. a.
[301] See above Section IV. 2. a. and b.
[302] See above Section IV. 2. b.
[303] See above Section IV. 3. a.
[304] Within the health community, concerns have been voiced that advertising restrictions may be sanctioned by WTO dispute settlement bodies, without them being framed as free speech issues. See e.g. E. Gould, "Trade Treaties and Alcohol Advertising Policy", *Journal of Public Health Policy* 26 (2005), 359 et seq.

restrictions on advertising.[305] Under these circumstances, the approach taken in the *Thailand Cigarettes* case[306] and in *U.S.–Gambling*[307] with respect to commercial speech is appropriate.

In the first case, Thailand's total ban on both direct and indirect advertising in all media, which applied indiscriminately to domestic and imported cigarettes, was found compatible with GATT.[308] The Panel considered the argument that the broad scope of the ban *de facto* disadvantaged imported products *vis-à-vis* domestic cigarettes and may thus amount to discrimination proscribed by Article III:4 GATT. It held, however, that even if this view were accepted, the national measure could be justified on public health grounds. Since advertising carries the risk of stimulating the demand for cigarettes, a total ban was deemed necessary in the sense of Article XX(b) GATT.[309]

In *U.S.-Gambling*, the Panel did not clearly distinguish between the supply of gambling services and the promotion thereof. Referring to the practice of other jurisdictions, including the case law of the ECJ,[310] it considered the public morals exception applicable.[311]

A human rights approach taking into account freedom of expression would have greater appeal with respect to information bans about a health-related service or product, as was the case in *Grogan*. Even if such measures were to come within the reach of WTO law, assessing them in the light of human rights would be a daunting task. The WTO judiciary would need to venture into highly sensitive areas, which may

---

[305] On the relationship between WTO law and the FCTC, see A.L. Taylor, "Trade, Human Rights, and the WHO Framework Convention on Tobacco Control: Just What the Doctor Ordered?", in: Cottier/ Pauwelyn/ Bürgi Bonanomi, see note 2, 322-333, and W. Meng, "Conflicting Rules in the WHO FCTC and their Impact. Commentary on Allyn L. Taylor", in: ibid., see note 2, 334-339; the fact that trade liberalisation has led to an increase in the number of smokers in developing countries is highlighted in the joint study of the WTO and the WHO on the WTO Agreements and public health, 2002, 71 et seq., available at <http://www.wto.org>.

[306] Panel Report, *Thailand – Restrictions on Importation of and Internal Taxes on Cigarettes (Thailand – Cigarettes)*, Doc. DS10/R - 37S/200, adopted 7 November 1990.

[307] Appellate Body Report, *U.S.–Gambling*, see note 283.

[308] The Panel found other measures which applied only to imported cigarettes to be GATT inconsistent.

[309] Panel Report, *Thailand – Cigarettes,* see note 306, 78.

[310] Panel Report, *U.S.–Gambling*, see note 283, para. 6.473, footnote 913.

[311] Panel Report, *U.S.–Gambling*, see note 283, paras 6.471-6.474.

undermine the legitimacy of a dispute settlement system conceived mainly for economic matters. Cases like *Grogan* moreover require weighing and balancing of competing fundamental rights. Apart from freedom of expression, the right to privacy and to health of the pregnant women, and the right to life of the foetus, are at issue. Finding an appropriate balance is a delicate task for which a dispute settlement body composed of trade experts is ill equipped. A finding of a violation risks prompting the charge of a "strategic" use of human rights. This problem would be compounded if a human rights body reached a different solution in a subsequent case. As *Grogan* shows, the opposite scenario is also conceivable. A Panel or the Appellate Body called upon to decide such matters is likely to be aware of its limitations and leave the defending state more discretion than a human rights body would. In *Grogan*, whilst the ECJ declined jurisdiction, the Advocate General engaged in the balancing process and considered the information ban compatible with the fundamental freedoms and fundamental rights protected in the EU legal order. As mentioned, the ECtHR reached the opposite result. Such diverging rulings are detrimental to the coherence of the international legal order and weaken both human rights and the legitimacy of the multilateral trading system. In cases similar to *Grogan*, it would be preferable for WTO dispute settlement bodies to analyse the issue from the vantage point of free trade rules. The reports could state the limited grounds of the ruling and mention that their findings do not imply compatibility with human rights law.

An offensive use of freedom of expression would, however, be justified in two constellations. Firstly, a state should not be able to successfully invoke an exception clause to justify a measure that was clearly found to be incompatible with freedom of expression by a regional or international human rights treaty body.[312] Under a reading of the public

---

[312] For a similar approach, see Wu, see note 281, 246, who requires, however, that the international treaty be ratified by the majority of WTO members. He posits this requirement, however, for "outward-looking measures", e.g. cases in which a WTO member invokes the public morals exception to enforce certain standards outside its own jurisdiction. He considers "inward-looking" measures (which are at issue when a WTO member invokes public morals as a defence) as being less problematic and subjects them to less stringent conditions. As the right to freedom of expression is enshrined both in the ICCPR (a treaty which binds the majority of WTO members) and in regional human rights instruments, preventing a WTO member from justifying a WTO-inconsistent measure which also violates freedom of expression does not hold that member to a standard foreign to other

morals exception which includes human rights, it makes sense to admit that the scope of the exception clause is at the same time limited by human rights, and cannot be invoked to justify a measure found in breach of freedom of expression by the competent human rights body. This approach also means that Panels or the Appellate Body would not accept domestic measures that infringe freedom of expression and are taken under the guise of preserving cultural diversity. The concern that such measures may be used to stifle freedom of expression is also reflected in the UNESCO Convention on the Protection and Promotion of the Diversity of Cultural Expression. Its article 2 para. 1 holds that,

> "Cultural diversity can be protected and promoted only if human rights and fundamental freedoms, such as freedom of expression, information and communication, as well as the ability of individuals to choose cultural expressions, are guaranteed. No one may invoke the provisions of this Convention in order to infringe human rights and fundamental freedoms as enshrined in the Universal Declaration of Human Rights or guaranteed by international law, or to limit the scope thereof."

Accepting that the public morals exception is itself limited by human rights law would have the merit of counteracting the fragmentation of international law. At the same time, it would also address fragmentation within states and create incentives for different governmental ministries to adopt a coherent approach. Trade ministries should not disregard human rights obligations freely entered into by their governments in the WTO forum. The fact that the scope of the public morals clause may vary depending on the international obligations entered into by each state, ought not be a decisive argument against the proposed approach, as variability is a characteristic feature of the public morals exception.

Secondly, the scope of the exception clauses ought also to be limited by *ius cogens* norms and rules of customary international law, which is of importance for states which are not bound to respect freedom of expression by virtue of a universal or a regional human rights convention. *Ius cogens* prevails over treaty law based on its hierarchical superior-

---

WTO members, although diverging interpretations of the same right are possible. Since the right of individual or state communications is optional under the ICCPR, taking into account regional human rights instruments makes it easier to satisfy the requirement that a domestic measure is in clear breach of freedom of expression.

ity.³¹³ Customary international law can be taken into account both via the "weak form of normative integration"³¹⁴ of article 31 (1) VCLT, and via the "more constricting and binding principle of integration found in Article 31 (3)(c) VCLT",³¹⁵ as "relevant rules of international law applicable in the relations between the parties." Whilst freedom of expression is generally not considered part of *ius cogens*, it may benefit from the protective ambit of imperative norms of international law. Practices like torture, forced disappearances and summary executions of journalists, which are widespread in certain states,³¹⁶ infringe both freedom of expression and *ius cogens* norms. As Panizzon has argued, they may impair the work of journalists and make broadcasters reluctant to send reporters to a country where their life and integrity is at risk. Grave human rights abuses may thus prevent foreign media from making use of the market access commitments made by the receiving country under GATS and are therefore trade-relevant.³¹⁷

As argued above,³¹⁸ free speech enjoys independent protection in the form of customary international law against state policies engaging in repression or censorship of political speech, broadly defined. With respect to the practice of some states (the most prominent example being China) of subjecting the media, including the Internet, to stringent content control, scholars have rightly argued that the WTO dispute settlement bodies should not accept a defence based on the public morals

---

313 Arts 53 and 64 VCLT.
314 T. Broude, "Principles of Normative Integration and the Allocation of International Authority: The WTO, the Vienna Convention on the Law of Treaties, and the Rio Declaration", *Loyola University Chicago International Law Review* 6 (2008), 173 et seq. (200). Whether treaties ratified by both parties to the dispute, or only those ratified by all WTO members, are to be considered as rules "applicable in the relations between the parties" in the sense of article 31 (3)(c) VCLT is controversial. As is well known, the Panel in *EC- Biotech* favoured the second interpretation (see WTO, Panel Report, *European Communities - Measures Affecting the Approval and Marketing of Biotech Products*, Doc. WT/DS291,292,293/R, adopted 21 November 2006; for a discussion of this ruling and other interpretations of article 31 (3)(c) VCLT, see e.g. Voon, see note 272, 137 et seq.; Harrison, see note 2, 200 et seq.
315 Broude, see note 314, 199.
316 See e.g. the free speech cases decided by the African Commission on Human Rights, see note 174.
317 Panizzon, see note 244, 541.
318 Above Section IV. 3. c.

exception. Doing so "would amount to granting a license to violate some core international human rights standards, the most important one of which being the right to freedom of expression."[319]

So far, both WTO members and its judiciary have shied away from raising free speech claims within the dispute settlement system, as the well-known *China–Publications*[320] case shows. The United States had initiated the complaint arguing that China violated obligations it had entered into in the Accession Protocol by limiting imports and distribution of cultural products to state-owned enterprises. As a consequence, foreign corporations were unable to import and distribute publications like books, magazines and newspapers in print and online, as well as sound recordings, films and DVDs. China argued that the restrictions on trading rights are necessary to safeguard public morals. This defence needs to be seen in the context of the pervasive system of

---

[319] H.S. Gao, "The Mighty Pen, the Almighty Dollar, and the Holy Hammer and Sickle", *Asian Journal of WTO & International Health Law and Policy* 2 (2007), 328 et seq.; for doubts that the public morals or the public order exception would cover blatant censorship, see also M. Panizzon, "How close will GATS get to Human Rights?", NCCR Working Paper No. 2006/14, 28, available at <http://papers.ssrn.com>; T. Wu, "The World Trade Law of Censorship and Internet Filtering", *Chi. J. Int'l L.* 7 (2006), 263 et seq. (284), holding that the applicability of the public order exception is "a hard question when the content blocked may be more of a threat either to the Party or to a favoured local company."

[320] WTO, Appellate Body Report, *China – Measures Affecting Trading Rights and Distribution Services for Certain Publications and Audiovisual Entertainment Products (China – Publications)*, Doc. WT/DS363/AB/R, adopted 19 January 2010. For commentaries, see J. Pauwelyn, "Squaring Free Trade in Culture with Chinese Censorship: The WTO Appellate Body Report in China-Audiovisuals", *Melbourne Journal of International Law* 11 (2008), 1 et seq.; X. Wu, "Case Note: China – Measures Affecting Trading Rights and Distribution Services for Certain Publications and Audiovisual Entertainment Products (Doc. WT/DS363/ABR)", *Chinese Journal of International Law* 9 (2010), 415 et seq.; J. Shi/ W. Chen, "The 'Specificity' of Cultural Products v. the 'Generality' of Trade Obligations: Reflecting on China – Publications and Audiovisual Products", *Journal of World Trade* 45 (2011), 159 et seq.; J. Ya Qin, "Pushing the Limits of Global Governance: Trading Rights, Censorship and WTO Jurisprudence – A Commentary on the China – Publications Case", *Chinese Journal of International Law* 10 (2011), 271 et seq.

content control applied in China.³²¹ Deemed politically sensitive, information and cultural products can only be imported and distributed by a limited number of selected state-owned entities which are also entrusted with content control. The statutory grounds for refusing dissemination of a cultural product are manifold and couched in broad and vague terms. They clearly go beyond the legitimate interests provided for in human rights agreements, such as public order, national security and public morals. China's rules and regulations also prohibit publications which "defy the basic principles of the Constitution, injure the national glory and interests, (…) infringe upon customs and habits of the nationalities, propagate evil cults or superstition, or disturb public order or destroys social stability."³²² These criteria are concretised through internal instructions from the Communist Party's Central Propaganda Department. These secret guidelines and directives ensure a maximum level of flexibility to adjust the censorship criteria to the political circumstances of the day. As a consequence, the criteria applied by the state-owned enterprises are opaque and the review process itself lacks transparency and respect for due process.³²³

Even though the systematic censorship applied to all imports and distribution of cultural products is anathema to the "freedom to seek, receive and impart information and ideas of all kinds, regardless of frontiers",³²⁴ the United States did not challenge the review process or the broad censorship criteria but accepted the claim made by China that content review pursued the aim of protecting public morals. Its argument was limited to questioning the necessity of the measure. The United States argued that excluding private enterprises from the import and distribution of cultural products was not necessary, since a less trade-disruptive measure was available: instead of entrusting the state-owned enterprises with content review, the Chinese Government could carry out censorship by a centralised agency. The Panel and the Appellate Body endorsed the United States' arguments, showing no inclination to engage with the politically sensitive nature of censorship. The Panel held that the protection of public morals is a crucial value. It considered that members are able to determine the appropriate level of pro-

---

[321] For a description of the censorship regime, see Qin, see note 320, 274 et seq.; see also B. Liebman, "Watchdog or Demagogue? The Media in the Chinese Legal System", *Colum. L. R.* 105 (2005), 1 et seq. (23-28).
[322] Qin, see note 320, 76, internal quotation marks omitted.
[323] Qin, ibid., 284.
[324] Article 19 para. 2 ICCPR.

tection, and that China had opted for a high level.³²⁵ As neither the United States, nor a third party, had challenged the content control as such, the Panel did not question *whether* but only *how* the review was to be carried out. It concluded that a centralised review system was a reasonable alternative available to China.

Although the party submissions, and both the Panel and the Appellate Body report, preferred to steer clear of human rights arguments, the question arises whether the ruling *de facto* favoured freedom of expression. Put differently, what are the human rights implications of *China–Publications*? Does the ruling point to synergies between the "right to trade" and the right to free speech, enabling WTO law to act as a handmaiden for human rights law? This is far from certain. Commentators have highlighted that China's duty to reform the content review process could have both positive and negative implications for freedom of expression.

On the one hand, it has been argued that the centralisation of content review in a newly created governmental agency may, in the long term, jeopardise the opacity of the whole procedure, as private importers would sooner or later challenge the lack of transparency and due process of content control and ask for the reasons why certain products did not pass the censors' scrutiny. The new review scheme may as a result be challenged in a new WTO complaint on the grounds that it is inconsistent with the transparency or due process obligations under the covered agreements (Article X GATT or Article III and VI GATS).³²⁶ Making the review process transparent would, however, run counter to the Communist Party's desire for maximum flexibility. Publicising the prohibited products may moreover fuel the public's interest and increase the risk of illegal circulation.³²⁷

On the other hand, centralised review may result in more stringent control of cultural products. Under the current system, the in-house reviewers of the state-owned enterprises are given considerable leeway in interpreting and applying the vague censorship criteria. The decentralised nature of the review enables censors to opt for a more liberal approach than that favoured by conservative members of the Party. Moreover, the state-owned enterprises' financial incentive in trading acts as a safeguard against an excessively rigid application of the censorship criteria. By contrast, employees of a centralised government

---

³²⁵ Panel Report, *China – Publications,* see note 320, paras 7.816-7.819.
³²⁶ See Qin, see note 320, 285-286.
³²⁷ Qin, ibid., 285.

agency responsible exclusively for content review would be insensitive to the economic impact of banning material from being imported and distributed. "Accountable to the central censorship agency only, the reviewers would be motivated to screen imports as rigorously and strictly as possible so as to justify their bureaucratic existence."[328] Lastly, the Chinese Government may choose to combine centralised review with the legal duty of all private importers to engage in self-censorship. This solution, already applied to Google, carries the risk of having a considerable chilling effect on freedom of expression, as private corporations may prefer to remain on the safe side and censor material which is not clearly caught by the censorship criteria[329].

In conclusion, the impact of *China–Publications*[330] on freedom of expression is difficult to assess. Although it is understandable that WTO members and the dispute settlement bodies preferred to avoid a politically charged issue like censorship, this is regrettable from a human rights perspective. Uncritically endorsing China's censorship scheme as conceived to protect the important interest of public morals may even have the detrimental effect of legitimising clear violations of freedom of expression. This would not be the case had the parties and the WTO judiciary been willing to construe the public morals exception in the light of human rights law. Had they gone down this road, it would have been necessary to engage clearly with policy arguments[331] and to show that freedom of expression was not only protected for the sake of "the right to trade" of foreign importers. As argued in the context of the EU, such narrow instrumentalist reasoning fails to take into account the expressive nature of human rights law. The claim could have been made that the WTO's objective of pursuing "sustainable development" entailed the respect for freedom,[332] including freedom of expression, as an essential right for both individual self-development

---

[328] Qin, ibid., 287, holding that this phenomenon has already been noticed with regard to Internet censorship, allegedly carried out by 30,000 employees.

[329] Qin, see note 320, 287.

[330] See note 320.

[331] For a criticism of the panel and the Appellate Body's reluctance to engage with policy arguments in *China – Publications,* see Qin, see note 320, 316, 321 (who does not however include freedom of expression among them).

[332] See Amartya Sen's famous understanding of development as freedom. See e.g. A. Sen, *Development as Freedom*, 1999; for an interpretation of sustainable development as including human rights, see also Howse/ Mutua, see note 2, 12.

and democracy. Moreover, the close connection between free speech and transparency, which is explicitly mentioned as an objective in GATS, could have been underscored. Lastly, the checking value of freedom of speech, both in the political and the economic sphere, could have been stressed. The free flow of information is, as argued above,[333] a necessary safeguard against abuses of political and economic power. Without robust and independent media willing to expose harmful commercial practices, the trust in trade liberalisation, and the functioning of the WTO, will be impaired in the long term.

2. TRIPS

a. "Defensive" Uses

Like for GATT and GATS, accommodating freedom of speech concerns within the TRIPS Agreement raises the question of possible conflicts between both sets of norms. Similarly to the two other covered agreements, the *Hertel* case was again invoked in the sphere of the TRIPS Agreement in order to highlight the need to apply WTO law consistently with the right to freedom of expression. Whilst it is true that rules of unfair competition law (in casu article 10 *bis* of the Paris Convention and thus the TRIPS Agreement) can have the effect of stifling freedom of expression, it seems unlikely that the judicial organs of the WTO would construe the relevant unfair competition rules so broadly as to extend to non commercial speech. Indeed, the Swiss Unfair Competition Act at issue in *Hertel* stands out for its singularly broad scope. Generally, unfair competition rules suppose some competitive relationship between the parties and the speaker's intention to further his or a third party's position on the market at the expense of a competitor.[334] Thus, they generally cover all statements (including those made by a scientist or the press) likely to impact on consumers' purchasing decisions.

The potential for conflict between freedom of expression and TRIPS is greater in the field of copyright and trademark law. As mentioned

---

[333] Section III. 2. b.
[334] See R. Baur, *UWG und Wirtschaftsberichterstattung – Vorschläge zur Reduktion des Haftungsrisikos*, 1995, 61 et seq., comparing Switzerland with Germany, France and Italy.

earlier,[335] the ECtHR has already shown willingness to subject copyright rules to scrutiny and to find a violation in cases where they inhibited speech on matters of public concern. Domestic courts have also rendered judgments on conflicts between IPRs and freedom of expression. As Helfer highlights, balancing one set of rights against the other is a "sensitive and policy-laden function",[336] including not only rights-based reasoning but also "utilitarian and social welfare arguments."[337] It is thus not surprising that national courts reach different outcomes on issues including, for instance, copyright limitations to permit quotation, news reporting, or the use of copyrighted work, such as songs, in satire and parody, for the purpose of social criticism or simple entertainment.[338] As famous brands are a common target of scorn and ridicule, there is also considerable scope for conflict between trademarks and freedom of expression.[339]

---

[335] See above Section IV. 2. a. and note 190.
[336] Helfer, see note 189, 49.
[337] Ibid.
[338] See P. Bernt Hugenholtz, "Copyright and Freedom of Expression in Europe", in: R.C. Dreyfuss/ D. Leenheer Zimmerman/ H. First (eds), *Expanding the Boundaries of Intellectual Property: Innovation Policy for the Knowledge Society*, 2001, 343 et seq. (362), showing the potential for conflict between intellectual property rights and article 10 ECHR. For other studies analysing the tension between freedom of expression and intellectual property rights, see e.g. C. Geiger, "'Constitutionalising' Intellectual Property Law? The Influence of Fundamental Rights on Intellectual Property in the European Union", *International Review of Intellectual Property & Competition Law* 37 (2006), 371 et seq.; id., "Fundamental Rights, a Safeguard for the Coherence of Intellectual Property Law?", *International Review of Intellectual Property & Competition Law* 35 (2004), 268 et seq.; S.J. Horowitz, "A Free Speech Theory of Copyright", *Stanford Technology Law Review* 2 (2009).
[339] For studies on trademark parodies and the conflict between freedom of expression and trademarks, see e.g. M. Hertig Randall, "Regard d'une constitutionnaliste sur la parodie des marques", in: P.V. Kunz/ D. Herren/ T. Cottier/ R. Matteotti (eds), *Wirtschaftsrecht in Theorie und Praxis. Festschrift für Roland von Büren*, 2009, 415-452, including references to American, German, French, Swiss and South African case law; for a comparative study in German and American law, see J. Grünberger, *Schutz geschäftlicher Kennzeichen gegen Parodie im deutschen und im amerikanischen Recht*, 1991; for an overview of French case law, see D. Voorhoof, "La liberté d'expression est-elle un argument légitime en faveur du non-respect du droit d'auteur?", in: A. Strowel/ F. Tulkens et al. (eds),

It is important to note that trademark and copyright law generally provide for exceptions so as to accommodate free speech concerns and other competing interests. However, the exception clauses and many other copyright and trademark provisions are highly indeterminate.[340] Conflicts may thus arise from differing interpretations. Assessing, for instance, whether limitations to copyright are confined to "certain special cases which do not conflict with a normal exploitation of the work and do not unreasonably prejudice the legitimate interests of the right holder" as required by article 13 of the TRIPS Agreement clearly entails the application of many open-textured terms. In the field of trademarks, article 17 of the TRIPS Agreement is also indeterminate.[341] Moreover, terms including the use of a trademark "in the course of trade" and "likelihood of confusion"[342] can be interpreted more or less broadly. The same holds true when the protection of well-known trademarks applies to uses "in relation to" goods or services which "would indicate a connection" with the owner of the registered trademark.[343] Based on an over-generous construction, any use of a mark which is not purely disinterested (such as a trademark parody disseminated in a magazine) may be considered as occurring "in the course of trade", including a category of expression much broader than commercial speech; "connection" with the rights owner or "likelihood of confusion" could be read as encompassing cases which involve the simple association evoked with a distinctive commercial sign. States would thus be required to adopt stringent protection against trademark dilution which would lead to a risk of stifling social criticism in the form of trademark parodies.[344]

Noting the potential for conflict between IPRs and the right to free speech, several authors have argued that dispute settlement bodies

---

Droit d'auteur et liberté d'expression, 2006, 39 et seq.; for a study of German law, see B. Schneider, *Die Markenparodie in Deutschland*, 2010.

[340] See N.W. Netanel, "Asserting Copyright's Democratic Principles in the Global Arena", *Vanderbilt Law Review* 51 (1998), 217 et seq. (309).

[341] "Members may provide limited exceptions to the rights conferred by a trademark, such as fair use of descriptive terms, provided that such exceptions take account of the legitimate interests of the owner of the trademark and of third parties."

[342] Article 16 para. 1 TRIPS Agreement.

[343] Article 16 para. 3 TRIPS Agreement.

[344] For potential conflicts with freedom of expression stemming from a maximalist reading of TRIPS, see L.P. Ramsey, "Free Speech and International Obligations to Protect Trademarks", *Yale J. Int'l L.* 25 (2010), 405 et seq. (427 et seq.).

ought to refrain from a "maximalist" interpretation of the TRIPS Agreement and construe its provisions in the light of freedom of expression.[345] Essentially two means are available to achieve consistency of IPRs with free speech values: firstly, the scope of copyright and trademark provisions can be construed narrowly so as to exclude, for instance, political or artistic speech from the ambit of the TRIPS Agreement; secondly, like in the field of the GATT and the GATS, states can be accorded sufficient leeway to create breathing space for robust exchange of ideas through a generous interpretation of the exception clauses.[346] This approach would offer the advantage of multi-level consistency,[347] enabling states to respect their international obligations under both TRIPS and human rights agreements, as well as the right of freedom of expression protected on the domestic level. It would be compatible with the purpose and object of the TRIPS Agreement, too. In its general provisions, the latter enables states to take measures necessary for the protection of other public policy goals.[348] It also recognises the instrumental value of IPRs and holds that their protection and enforcement "should contribute to the promotion of technological innovation and to the transfer and dissemination of technology, to the mutual advantage of producers and users of technological knowledge and in a manner conducive to social and economic welfare, and to a balance of rights and obligations."[349] Considering the importance of free speech for collective interests, including democracy and the functioning of the economic system, domestic measures aimed at protecting free speech values can be viewed as contributing to "social and economic welfare" and to striking a reasonable balance between the IPR holders rights and obligations. Moreover, TRIPS grants members some leeway as regards the implementation of their obligations and acknowledges the special need for flexibility for least developed countries.[350]

---

[345] See Ramsey, see note 344; Netanel, see note 340; a deferential approach is also recommended by the following authors, who do not, however, rely predominantly on freedom of speech in support of their view: L.R. Helfer, "Adjudicating Copyright Claims under the TRIPs Agreement: The Case for a European Human Rights Analogy", *Harv. Int'l L. J.* 39 (1998), 357 et seq.; Dinwoodie, see note 82, 512 et seq.

[346] See Ramsey, see note 344, 445 et seq.

[347] See C. Breining-Kaufmann, "The Matrix of Human Rights and Trade Law", in: Cottier/ Pauwelyn/ Bürgi Bonanomi, see note 2, 95-138 (118).

[348] Article 8 TRIPS Agreement.

[349] Article 7 TRIPS Agreement.

[350] Preamble and article 1 para. 1 TRIPS Agreement.

b. "Offensive" Uses

Whilst there are good reasons to interpret the TRIPS Agreement as leaving states sufficient discretion to adopt speech-protective laws, another question is whether TRIPS ought to be construed as *requiring* states to do so. If that were the case, the failure, for instance, of a state to exempt non-commercial uses from trademark law could constitute a breach of both TRIPS and human rights law. As Ramsay has argued, this approach would raise several difficulties.[351] Firstly, it would be hard to reconcile with the wording of TRIPS, which is termed as leaving states the *option* to pursue other policy goals.[352] Secondly, as IPRs are both an "engine of free expression"[353] and, if construed too broadly, an impediment to the free flow of information, the line between "speech enhancing" and "speech impeding" uses of IPRs is difficult to draw.[354] Moreover, the appropriate balance may vary depending on the social, political and economic context.[355] Granting states the ability to experiment and to "act as laboratories in the development of international rules"[356] would be in line with the idea of subsidiarity inherent in multilayered constitutionalism. It would also take seriously concerns that the WTO may not be the most appropriate forum to strike the subtle balance between IPRs and free speech concerns.[357] The fact that international human rights law so far offers little guidance on this issue exacerbates this difficulty.[358] Of the regional human rights regimes, only the ECtHR has to the author's knowledge so far addressed conflicts between IPRs and freedom of expression. Even those rulings are sparse and barely address the vast array of possible conflicts between both bodies of law. This raises the risk that subsequent rulings by human rights bodies will contradict activist rulings of the WTO adjudicative branch. Because of the perceived axiological superiority of human rights law over trade law, such contradictory rulings would be detrimental to the legitimacy of the multilateral trading system. The fact that

---

[351] Ramsey, see note 344, 456 et seq.
[352] See Netanel, see note 340, 281.
[353] This expression is borrowed from US SC, *Harper & Row Publishers Inc.*, 471 U.S. 539 (1985), 558.
[354] See Netanel, see note 340, 230.
[355] See id., see note 340, 277, 296; Dinwoodie, see note 82, 513 et seq.
[356] Dinwoodie, see note 82.
[357] See Ramsey, see note 344, 455; Dinwoodie, see note 82, 508.
[358] See Ramsey, see note 344, 451.

the WTO and its dispute settlement system are still in their early years magnifies this risk.[359]

Does it follow that "freedom imperialism"[360] via TRIPS is never justified? Put differently, is there some room for "offensive uses" of freedom of speech within the WTO in the field of intellectual property? The *China–IPR* case[361] would have offered an opportunity to address this question. Filed by the United States on the same day as *China–Publications*,[362] the complaint also concerned China's comprehensive censorship scheme, as works which had not successfully passed the review process were denied the protection of copyright. The broad and vague criteria, as exposed in the unappealed Panel report, extend to publications which "impair the prestige and interests of the State", "propagate cults and superstition", "undermine social stability", "jeopardize social ethics or fine national cultural traditions" and extend to "other contents banned by laws, administrative regulations and provisions of the State."[363] As observed in the context of the *China–Publications* case,[364] these criteria (not to mention the internal party guidelines)[365] give the reviewers almost unfettered discretion to refuse IPR protection to core political speech, which enjoys a high level of protection within all three regional human rights instruments as well as on the universal level. Moreover, good reasons exist to consider the denial of copyright protection as a measure limiting freedom of expression. On the one hand, the measure forms part of a broad scheme of content review. On the other hand, the refusal to grant copyright protection to non-conformist views denies authors revenues from their work. This makes them more dependent on the government and weak-

---

[359] See Helfer, see note 345, who argues that an initially deferential approach was an important factor for the legitimacy of the European human rights regime and favours the same approach within the WTO.

[360] Netanel, see note 340, 280, 282.

[361] WTO Appellate Body Report, *China – Measures Affecting the Protecting and Enforcement of Intellectual Property Rights (China – IPR)*, Doc. WT/DS362/R, adopted 20 March 2009. For an analysis from the vantage point of freedom of expression, see T. Broude, "It's Easily Done: The *China-Intellectual Property Rights Enforcement* Dispute and the Freedom of Expression", available at <http://ssrn.com>.

[362] See note 320.

[363] See Panel Report, *China – IPR*, see note 361, paras 7.77–7.79; for a comprehensive list, see Broude, see note 361, 13.

[364] See note 320.

[365] See above Section V. 1. b.

ens, as a result, the emergence of a civil society as a counterweight to the state.[366] In other words, the system of content review undermines the speech protective function of both IPRs and human rights law. Despite this, the United States failed to invoke freedom of expression or other human rights norms,[367] and the Panel chose the course of judicial minimalism. It "wishe[d] to emphasize that the United States claim did not challenge China's right to conduct content review" and that "[t]he Panel's findings do not affect China's right to conduct content review."[368] The Panel contented itself with finding that the denial of copyright was incompatible with the TRIPS Agreement. In response to China's defence based on article 17 of the Berne Convention for the Protection of Literary and Artistic Work of 1971 as incorporated by article 9 para. 1 TRIPS, the Panel opted for a narrow interpretation of the public order clause without, however, taking freedom of expression into account. Article 17 of the Berne Convention, entitled "Censorship", reads as follows,

> "The provisions of this Convention cannot in any way affect the right of the Government of each country of the Union to permit, to control, or to prohibit by legislation or regulation, the circulation, presentation, or exhibition of any work or production in regard to which the competent authority may find it necessary to exercise that right."

The Panel found that the reference to "circulation, presentation, or exhibition" does not cover all forms of exploitation of a work and thus does not justify the denial of all copyright.[369] It chose to look upon censorship and IPRs as two distinct issues, noting that,

> "copyright and government censorship address different rights and interests. Copyright protects private rights, as reflected in the fourth recital of the preamble of the TRIPS Agreement, whilst government censorship addresses public interests."[370]

---

[366] See Netanel, see note 340, 227.
[367] See article 15 para. 1 lit. (c) ICESCR, enshrining the right to "benefit from the protection of the moral and material interests resulting from any scientific, literary or artistic production of which he is the author."
[368] Panel Report, *China – IPR*, see note 361, para. 7.144.
[369] Ibid., para. 7.127.
[370] Ibid., para. 7.135.

Like for *China–Publications*,[371] the question arises whether the Panel ruling has a positive effect on freedom of expression, despite the strategy of "issue avoidance". Again, this is far from certain. Firstly, the infringed WTO provisions only require China to grant copyright protection to foreign authors. Denial of copyright thus remains possible with regard to Chinese works, enabling the state to exert control over domestic authors and to hinder the democratising effect of an emerging civil society. As regards foreign materials, this sanction will not be available any more pursuant to the Panel's ruling. As several commentators have noted, rigorous enforcement of copyright may in the Chinese context paradoxically be detrimental to the free flow of information.[372] Under a system of comprehensive censorship, enforcing copyright is in effect a powerful weapon in the hands of the censors with which to clamp down on the unofficial channels circulating unauthorised works. Thus, the consequence of *China–IPR* may well be not more speech, but more enforced silence.[373] Put differently, a ruling which is mindful of copyright's free speech enhancing and democratising function cannot be confined to the holding that article 17 of the Berne Convention precludes the denial of copyright to censored work, but needs to engage with the substantive criteria and the transparency of the review process. Under such an approach, article 17 of the Berne Convention would need to be construed in the light of customary human rights law and the object and purpose of TRIPS. Freedom of expression, and the welfare enhancing purpose of copyright, would limit the scope of the seemingly self-judging nature of the public order clause. In conclusion, whilst *China-IPR* at first sight seems to be a case in which freedom of expression and the multilateral trading system are mutually supportive,

---

[371] See note 320.

[372] Broude, see note 361, 15; the fact that deficient of enforcement favours the dissemination of information and ideas under conditions of censorship is also stressed by B.R. Byrne, "Regulating the Film Industry in China: A New Approach", in: *The IP and Entertainment Law Ledger*, 2010, <http://ledger.nyu-ipels.org>, section III; adopting a democratic vision of copyright, Netanel, see note 340, 252 et seq. also cautions against strong copyright protection and enforcement in non-democratic states.

[373] This sentence is inspired by the famous passage of Justice Brandeis in *Whitney v. California*, see note 149: "If there be time to expose through discussion the falsehood and fallacies, to avert the evil by the processes of education, the remedy to be applied is more speech, not enforced silence."

the disengagement from the human rights context makes it at best a "partial", maybe even a "pyrrhic victory for freedom of speech."[374]

VI. Conclusion

The present study has explored the interface between freedom of expression and free trade in the context of the multilateral trading system. Before analysing the potential for conflicts and synergies between free speech and WTO law, it examined the theoretical and institutional inter-linkages between freedom of expression and free trade. Both are intricate and manifold.

At the theoretical level, considerable overlap exists between economic approaches analysing the role and function of freedom of expression and free speech justifications advanced by political philosophers and constitutionalists. From an economic vantage point, freedom of expression is, like the individual right to trade, essential for the functioning of markets. Importantly, this approach not only focuses on commercial speech (e.g. mainly commercial advertising) but also requires protection of any market-relevant information, which includes speech from the media and civil society. Owing to the lack of direct profit motive and its pronounced public goods characteristics, speech from independent sources, like political speech, is more easily chilled than commercial speech. Economic approaches focusing on the regulation of speech account for this difference and support a higher level of protection for speech on matters of public concern than for commercial speech. Starting from different premises, free speech theorists generally arrive at the same conclusion. As was shown, under the three most common free speech justifications, freedom of expression is protected for the sake of autonomy, as a means to further democracy or the discovery of truth. All three rationales justify, in addition to a broad array of expression, also the protection of market-relevant information. Whilst the argument from autonomy corresponds to the deontological vision of human rights, the arguments from truth and democracy are, like economic free speech justifications, instrumental in nature. A pluralist account of freedom of expression thus provides for a richer understanding of the relationship between free speech and free trade than visions contrasting the deontological human right to free speech with the instrumental individual right to trade.

---

[374] Broude, see note 361, 12.

Considerable overlap exists also at the institutional level. A comparative analysis focusing on the role of freedom of expression and free trade on the domestic, regional and global layers of governance does not confirm strict separation between instrumentalist visions of free trade and deontological justifications of freedom of speech. Constitutional courts and human rights monitoring bodies stress both the intrinsic and the instrumentalist value of free speech. Whilst freedom of expression is protected as a free-standing right on every layer of governance, less consensus exists with regard to a comprehensive right of economic liberty. A more or less broadly defined right to pursue an economic activity is well established in Europe and within the EU, both for its intrinsic and its instrumental value. This vision is not shared by the United States and finds little support on the regional and the global level. As regards freedom of expression, the consensus among the various layers of governance varies depending on the type of speech at issue. The question whether freedom of expression extends, for instance, to commercial speech is controversial. By contrast, a broad consensus exists that political expression is core speech entitled to a high level of protection. Based on this finding, this article has argued that policies of state censorship and repression of political speech violate freedom of expression as a norm forming part of customary international law.

Apart from casting light on the status and level of protection of free speech and free trade within the multilayered constitution, the comparative analysis has stressed the lively interaction between the various layers of governance. It has also stressed the trend towards expansion of and overlap between international regimes. Based on a broad vision of political speech, the ECtHR, for instance, accords a high level of protection to market-relevant expression from independent sources, and thus effectively contributes to safeguarding transparency of the economic system. Conversely, the ECJ has extended its reach to human rights and systematically interprets them in the light of the ECtHR's case law. Whilst the protection of human rights against infringements from EU acts was seen as essential for the legitimacy of European governance, applying fundamental rights *vis-à-vis* the Member States has been less straightforward. More precisely, judgments in which the ECJ accepted states' reliance on a human right (including freedom of expression) as a justification for measures restricting market freedoms have stirred up little controversy. To the contrary, a deferential approach accommodating conceptions of human rights even if they are not shared by all Member States has been an important tool to implement the principle of subsidiarity inherent in multilayered governance. It also helps to counteract the common perception that an economically minded court is necessarily inclined to privilege economic interests and to relegate human rights to second place. By contrast with "defensive" recourse to human rights, "offensive" uses have tended to confirm fears of an economic bias. This has mainly been the case when a fundamental right limits the state's leeway to justify a domestic measure in sensitive areas, such as abortion, and when the court's reasoning is couched predominantly in economic terms.

The state-centred nature of the dispute settlement system, and the greater heterogeneity of WTO members, have not been very conducive to integrating human rights (including freedom of expression) within the multilateral trading system. Nevertheless, the European experience offers some insights for the WTO legal order. The perception of an economic bias poses no lesser threat to the legitimacy of Panels and the Appellate Body than it does to the ECJ.

As regards free speech, a potential for conflict exists in the field of TRIPS. An expansionist interpretation of TRIPS, coupled with a narrow construction of the exception clauses, risks encroaching on the regulatory autonomy of WTO members to accommodate speech enhancing policies (such as exceptions in favour of non-commercial speech, including satire and parody). An interpretation of the exception clauses in the light of free speech values, and a deferential standard of review, would avoid this danger. In the field of the GATT and the GATS, the public morals exception can be used to accommodate conceptions of freedom of expression even if they do not reflect a universalist standard. This is the case for example for cultural and press diversity, which tends to be viewed as a free speech value on both the domestic and regional level in Europe. As is widely known, this vision has not prevailed in the United States.

Limiting the reach of WTO law for the sake of freedom of expression should not be viewed as a "concession" granted to human rights concerns. Press diversity and sufficient breathing space for non commercial speech, are necessary to check both economic and political power. They are a prerequisite for market transparency, and, ultimately, for trust in free trade and a globalised economy.

The interdependence of the political and the economic sphere raises an important argument admitting also "offensive" uses of freedom of speech within the WTO. Drawing on the experience in the EU, and taking into account the greater diversity and more limited purpose of the global multilateral trading system than that of the European integration project, the present study has pointed out the risks of using freedom of speech as a sword. The WTO judiciary ought not to engage in the delicate interpretation and balancing inherent in fundamental rights jurisprudence. When a regional or international human rights body finds a state policy to be in breach of freedom of speech, the government should, however, not be able to justify the same policy based on the public morals defence within the forum of the WTO. Moreover, human rights protected by customary international law should also limit the scope of the exception clauses. An "offensive" use of freedom of speech would thus also apply to state policies of systematic repression and censorship of political speech (broadly defined).

The WTO judiciary has so far not been willing to go down this road. *China–Publications*[375] and *China–IPR*[376] show that complaining states, third parties, and the dispute settlement bodies have shied away from confronting China's comprehensive system of "content review" and have decided the disputes on narrower grounds. As a consequence, the free speech implications of the dispute were also ignored. Although both reports found against China, without challenging the legitimacy of content review in the first place, the narrow reforms necessary to comply with the WTO rulings may have a negative impact on the free flow of information. Although clearly connected, freedom of speech and international trade law passed each other like "ships in the night, without acknowledging each other's existence."[377] Within the multilateral trading system, free speech and free trade "pretend that they never have met: it's easily done."[378]

---

[375] See note 320.
[376] *China–IPR,* see note 361. For an analysis from the vantage point of freedom of expression, see Broude, see note 361.
[377] Broude, see note 361, 16.
[378] Id., see note 361, 17.

Responsibility of International Organizations – Introducing the ILC's DARIO

Mirka Möldner

I. Introduction
II. Some Background Information
    1. Development of the DARIO
    2. The Reasons behind the DARIO
    3. The Methodological Approach of the Commission
III. The Scope of the DARIO
IV. The Elements of Responsibility
    1. Attributable Conduct
        a. Conduct of Organs or Agents, Article 6 DARIO
        b. Conduct of Organs of a State or Organs or Agents of an International Organization, Article 7 DARIO
    2. Breach of an International Obligation
    3. Further Elements
V. Circumstances Precluding Wrongfulness
    1. Consent, Article 20 DARIO
    2. Self-Defense, Article 21 DARIO
    3. Countermeasures, Article 22 and Articles 51 to 57 DARIO
    4. *Force Majeure*, Article 23 DARIO
    5. Distress, Article 24 DARIO
    6. Necessity, Article 25 DARIO
VI. Consequences of an Internationally Wrongful Act and Invocation of Responsibility
    1. Consequences
    2. Invocation of Responsibility
VII. Responsibility in Cases of Connected Conduct of States and International Organizations
    1. Responsibility of an International Organization in Connection with the Act of a State or another International Organization, Articles 14 et seq. DARIO
        a. Aid or Assistance, Article 14 DARIO
        b. Direction and Control, Article 15 DARIO
        c. Coercion, Article 16 DARIO
        d. Circumvention, Article 17 DARIO
    2. Responsibility of a State in Connection with the Conduct of an International Organization
        a. Aid or Assistance, Article 58 DARIO
        b. Direction and Control, Article 59 DARIO
        c. Coercion, Article 60 DARIO
        d. Circumvention of International Obligations, Article 61 DARIO
        e. Acceptance or Causation of Reliance, Article 62 DARIO
VIII. Critique
    1. Comparing Apples and Oranges I: States vs. International Organizations
    2. Comparing Apples and Oranges II: The Variety of International Organizations

3. Putting the Cart before the Horse – The Lack of Primary Rules
  4. The DARIO as a Dry Run – The Lack of Practice
IX. Final Remarks

Abstract

The responsibility of international organizations is a field of international law which has gained importance in theory and practice especially within the last decades. As of 2002, also the International Law Commission started attending to the topic. It concluded its work in August 2011 by adopting on second reading a set of 67 *Draft Articles on Responsibility of International Organizations* (DARIO). The purpose of this contribution is to give an introduction and assessment of the content and potential of these articles and to evaluate the critique that has been raised so far. The DARIO are modelled after the Commission's previous and very successful work, the *Articles on State Responsibility* (ASR). Thus, the question can be posed whether the DARIO are likely to follow in the footsteps of its older sibling, the ASR, to become similarly successful.

Keywords

Responsibility of International Organizations; State Responsibility; Draft Articles on Responsibility of International Organizations; International Law Commission

I. Introduction

In August 2011, the ILC adopted the Draft Articles on Responsibility of International Organizations (DARIO).[1] At first sight, the DARIO seem to be the revised, extended version of the Commission's masterpiece, the Articles on State Responsibility (ASR).[2]

The purpose of this article is to present the keystones of the DARIO, to scratch the surface of some of the articles and their Commentary, and finally, to grapple with the main points of criticism that

---

[1] Report of the ILC, GAOR 66th Sess., Suppl. 10, Doc. A/66/10, 54 et seq.
[2] GAOR 56th Sess., Suppl. 10, Doc. A/56/10, 43 et seq.; because of the wide acceptance that the ASR have met and their wide reflection of customary international law, it seems appropriate to no longer speak of Draft Articles on State Responsibility but solely of Articles on State Responsibility.

have been raised so far. As the ASR have become a box office hit and the DARIO look the same, the question can be raised whether the DARIO thus have the same potential. The contribution will proceed as follows: it will start with some background information on the DARIO (II.) and will then describe the scope of the articles (III.), the conditions for responsibility to arise (IV.) and the circumstances precluding wrongfulness (V.). What the consequences of a wrongful act are and how responsibility of an international organization can be invoked will be dealt with in Section VI. In Section VII., the responsibility in cases of connected conduct is outlined. The article will conclude with an analysis of the critique raised so far (VIII.) and some final remarks (IX.).

II. Some Background Information

1. Development of the DARIO

The ILC included the topic "Responsibility of International Organizations" in its program of work only in 2002, although it had already detected the need for a law of responsibility of international organizations many years before.[3] The Special Rapporteur, Giorgio Gaja, drew up eight reports from 2002 to 2011. The Commission adopted the DARIO on first reading in 2009 and then on second reading in 2011. The Commission finished this work expeditiously – in comparison, it took the Commission 45 years (1956 – 2001), more than thirty reports, and the work of five Special Rapporteurs to conclude its work on the analogous topic of State Responsibility.

2. The Reasons behind the DARIO

When thinking about legal responsibility of international organizations one can first wonder why international organizations can be held responsible at all, namely by third, non-member states. The Commission states in article 3 DARIO:

---

[3] See A. El-Erian, Special Rapporteur on Relations between States and Intergovernmental Organizations, *First Report on Relations between States and Intergovernmental Organizations*, *ILCYB* 1963, Vol. II, 184, paras 172 et seq.

"Every internationally wrongful act of an international organization entails the international responsibility of that organization."

Some argue that this reflects a rule of international law, either by stating that it reflects a general principle of law[4] or by finding that this is a rule of international customary law.[5] Others base their reasoning on the international legal personality of international organizations.[6] Behind this legal argumentation one can find a political consideration which is based on the major role that international organizations nowadays play at the global level: because of their major role it would seem intolerable not to hold them responsible when violating international norms.[7]

The Commission bases article 3 DARIO on all of these legal considerations together: it seems to interpret the international responsibility of international organizations as being part of customary international law by relying on two references that can be interpreted as a proof for "practice" on the one hand and *opinio juris* on the other hand.[8] In addi-

---

[4] M.H. Arsanjani, "Claims Against International Organizations", *Yale Journal of World Public Order* 7 (1981), 131 et seq.

[5] E.g. M. Hirsch, *The Responsibility of International Organizations Toward Third Parties: Some Basic Principles*, 1995, 8; ILA, Final Report, *Accountability of International Organisations*, Berlin Conference 2004, 26, available at <http://www.ila-hq.org>.

[6] E.g. I. Brownlie, *Principles of Public International Law*, 2008, 683 et seq.; K. Ginther, "International Organizations, Responsibility", in: R. Bernhardt, *Encyclopedia of Public International Law II*, 1995, 1336; M. Hartwig, "International Organizations or Institutions, Responsibility and Liability", in: R. Wolfrum (ed.), *Max Planck Encyclopedia of Public International Law*, 2012, Vol. VI, 6 et seq., paras 11 et seq.

[7] E.g. Hirsch, see note 5, 8; E. Paasivirta and P.J. Kuijper speak of a public morals argument, id., "Does One Size Fit All?: The European Community and the Responsibility of International Organizations", *NYIL* 36 (2005), 169 et seq. (172 et seq.).

[8] The Commission draws upon two references: first, it cites the United Nations Secretary-General who stated, in a report on peacekeeping operations: "the principle of state responsibility-widely accepted to be applicable to international organizations-that damage caused in breach of an international obligation and which is attributable to the state (or to the Organization) entails the international responsibility of the state (or of the Organization) [...]." Second, the Commission refers to the Advisory Opinion of the ICJ on *Difference Relating to Immunity from Legal Process of a Special Rapporteur of the Commission on Human Rights*, ICJ Reports 1999, 88 et seq., para. 66, in which the Court said: "[...] the Court wishes to point out

tion, according to article 2 lit. (a) DARIO, the responsibility of an international organization is linked to its international legal personality.[9] Thereby the Commission clearly favors understanding the international legal personality of international organizations to be an "objective" personality, which does not need to be recognized by an injured state before considering whether the organization may be held internationally responsible according to the DARIO.[10] This last part of the sentence may at first sight seem to extend the rights of an injured state by according the possibility to refer directly to the injuring international organization. This possibility, however, has its downside as the injured party then has only limited possibility to refer to the Member States directly, because the DARIO do not establish a general concurrent or subsidiary responsibility of Member States.[11]

In the Commentary to article 3, the Commission states: "The general principle, as stated in article 3, applies to whichever entity commits an internationally wrongful act."[12] Thus, the Commission also relies on a general principle of law. It is especially noteworthy that the Commission here speaks of a general principle which applies for "whichever entity." It seems that the Commission here wants to pave the way for more international responsibility regimes.

Whereas the principle that international organizations may be held internationally responsible for their acts is widely accepted today, this may not be the case for all of the provisions contained in the DARIO.

---

that the question of immunity from legal process is distinct from the issue of compensation for any damages incurred as a result of acts performed by the United Nations or by its agents acting in their official capacity. The United Nations may be required to bear responsibility for the damage arising from such acts." See Commentary to article 3, see note 1, paras 1 et seq. with reference to Doc. A/51/389, 4, para. 6.

[9] This link has been pointed at by the Commission more strongly in its work on the ASR, see note 2, 4 and 34.

[10] Commentary to article 2, see note 1, para. 9; whether international organizations have such an objective international legal personality which does not depend on the recognition of a third party is still a matter of controversy, compare e.g. K. Schmalenbach, "International Organizations or Institutions, General Aspects", in: Max Planck Encyclopedia, see note 6, Vol. VI, 31 et seq.; C. Ryngaert/ H. Buchanan, "Member State Responsibility for the Acts of International Organizations", *Utrecht Law Review* 7 (2011), 131 et seq. (134 et seq.).

[11] See Section VII.

[12] Commentary to article 3, see note 1, para. 1.

The Commission makes clear in its General Commentary that, because of the absence of relevant practice with regard to some aspects, the DARIO to a certain extent constitute not a codification but rather a progressive development of the law.[13]

3. The Methodological Approach of the Commission

The DARIO will probably seem very familiar to all who have already been concerned with the ASR. This is because the Commission took the ASR as the basis for the DARIO. The DARIO follow the general outline of the ASR and many of the provisions are the same except that it says "international organization" instead of "state".[14] The Commission had already taken the same approach earlier, when it drafted the 1986 Vienna Convention on the Law of Treaties between States and International Organizations or between International Organizations on the basis of the 1969 Vienna Convention on the Law of Treaties.[15] The underlying assumption of the approach taken here is that, as states and international organizations are both subjects of international law, they should in principle be addressees of the same rules when breaching their international obligations.[16]

III. The Scope of the DARIO

According to article 1 the DARIO apply:

> "1. [...] to the international responsibility of an international organization for an internationally wrongful act.
>
> 2. [...] to the international responsibility of a State for an internationally wrongful act in connection with the conduct of an international organization."

---

[13] General Commentary to the DARIO, see note 1, para. 5; regarding the criticism raised thereto see Section VIII.

[14] When this contribution refers to the corresponding articles of the ASR, it may not always replicate this exception.

[15] Cf. thereto the analysis by C. Brölmann, "International Organizations and Treaties: Contractual Freedom and Institutional Constraint", in: J. Klabbers / Å. Wallendahl, *Research Handbook on the Law of International Organizations*, 2011, 285 et seq. (292 et seq.).

[16] To the critique thereon see Section VIII.

Ratione personae, the DARIO contain not only provisions on the responsibility of international organizations according to article 1 (1) DARIO, but to a certain extent also on the responsibility of states according to article 1 (2) DARIO. The latter was left out in the ASR, according to its article 57.

The understanding of "international organization" chosen here by the Commission is wider than, for example, that in the Vienna Conventions.[17]

Article 2 lit. (a) DARIO reads:

"For the purposes of the present draft articles,

(a) 'international organization' means an organization established by a treaty or other instrument governed by international law and possessing its own international legal personality. International organizations may include as members, in addition to States, other entities."

Thus, an international organization, as understood here, cannot only be established by an international treaty, but also by a resolution adopted by another international organization or by a conference of states.[18] Not only intergovernmental organizations are covered, but also international organizations that have been established with the participation of state organs other than governments or by other entities.[19] Also entities, such as the European Union, that have diverged from being a classical international organization, are included in that notion.[20] As the formulation "treaty or other instrument governed by interna-

---

[17] See article 1 (1) of the Vienna Convention on the Representation of States in their Relations with International Organizations of a Universal Character of 14 March 1975, Doc. A/CONF.67/16; article 2 (1) (n) of the Vienna Convention on Succession of States in Respect of Treaties of 23 August 1978; and article 2 (1) (i) of the Vienna Convention on the Law of Treaties between States and International Organizations or between International Organizations of 21 March 1986, Doc. A/CONF.129/15; this has been criticized by M. Mendelson, "The Definition of 'International Organization' in the International Law Commission's Current Project on the Responsibility of International Organizations", in: M. Ragazzi (ed.), *International Responsibility Today – Essays in Memory of Oscar Schachter*, 2005, 371 et seq.
[18] Commentary to article 2, see note 1, para. 5.
[19] Commentary to article 2, ibid., para. 3.
[20] On the criticism see Section VIII.

tional law" makes clear, organizations which are established through instruments governed by municipal law are not covered.[21]

The DARIO do not apply to the international responsibility of an individual.[22] This follows already from article 1 DARIO and is made clear again in article 66 DARIO.[23]

Ratione materiae, the DARIO are limited in their scope to the consequences of a breach of *international* law. The responsibility of an international organization because of a breach of *municipal* law does not fall within the scope of the DARIO.[24] This is indicated clearly throughout the articles by the requirement of an "internationally" wrongful act. According to article 5 "[t]he characterization of an act of an international organization as internationally wrongful is governed by international law."

IV. The Elements of Responsibility

Article 4 DARIO states that:

"There is an internationally wrongful act of an international organization when conduct consisting of an action or omission

(a) is attributable to that organization under international law; and

(b) constitutes a breach of an international obligation of that organization."

This is exactly the formulation as can be found in article 2 ASR. The Commission states in its Commentary that "article 4 expresses with regard to international organizations a general principle that applies to every internationally wrongful act, whoever its author."[25]

---

[21] Cf. Commentary to article 2, see note 1, para. 6.
[22] For this compare generally A. O'Shea, "Individual Criminal Responsibility", in: Max Planck Encyclopedia, see note 6, Vol. V, 141 et seq.
[23] Article 66 DARIO reads: "These draft articles are without prejudice to any question of the individual responsibility under international law of any person acting on behalf of an international organization or a State."
[24] Cf. Commentary to article 1, see note 1, para. 3.
[25] Commentary to article 4, ibid., para. 1.

1. Attributable Conduct

As article 4 DARIO explicitly states, there must be a conduct which either can be an action or an omission. An omission generally can only be relevant when there is an obligation for the international organization to act.[26] Whether the conduct can be attributed to the organization is addressed in articles 6 to 9 DARIO. This contribution will, in the following, mainly concentrate on article 6 and article 7 DARIO, as they are likely to cause the most difficulties.

a. Conduct of Organs or Agents, Article 6 DARIO

Attributable is, first of all, the conduct of an organ or agent of an international organization in the performance of its functions according to article 6 DARIO. What is meant by "organ" and "agent" can be found in article 2 DARIO. Pursuant to article 2 lit. (c) DARIO:

"'organ of an international organization' means any person or entity which has that status in accordance with the rules of the organization",

no matter if it is explicitly called "organ" or if it gains that status from its functions.[27]

Whereas the attribution of conduct of organs is well familiar from article 4 ASR, the attribution of conduct of agents as provided for in article 6 DARIO is different and thus deserves special attention.

Article 2 lit. (d) DARIO provides for a very wide understanding of the term "agent". According to this provision,

"'agent of an international organization' means an official or other person or entity, other than an organ, who is charged by the organization with carrying out, or helping to carry out, one of its functions, and thus through whom the organization acts."

This may be not only natural persons, but also other entities.[28]

The definition contained in article 2 lit. (d) DARIO is based on a passage of the Advisory Opinion of the ICJ on *Reparation for Injuries Suffered in the Service of the United Nations*, where the Court stated:

---

[26] Cf. Commentary to Chapter III DARIO, ibid., para. 2.
[27] Cf. Commentary to article 2, ibid., paras 20 et seq., and Commentary to article 6, ibid., para. 1.
[28] Commentary to article 2, ibid., para. 25.

"The Court understands the word 'agent' in the most liberal sense, that is to say, any person who, whether a paid official or not, and whether permanently employed or not, has been charged by an organ of the organization with carrying out, or helping to carry out, one of its functions – in short, any person through whom it acts."[29]

Because of the wide definition of "agent", article 6 DARIO is very comprehensive in its scope. This becomes particularly obvious when recalling article 8 ASR. The latter article deals with the attribution of the conduct of a person or group of persons to a state when acting on the instructions, or under the direction or control of that state.[30] For the question, whether the person or group of persons had acted "under the direction or control" of a state, different criteria have been developed by the ICJ in the *Nicaragua*[31] case on the one hand, and by the International Criminal Tribunal for the Former Yugoslavia (ICTY) in the *Tadić*[32] case on the other hand.[33] One cannot find an identically worded provision to article 8 ASR in the DARIO. Instead, the Commission subsumes this situation under article 6 DARIO. By this, the Commission wants the same criteria to be applied with regard to international organizations under article 6 DARIO as the ones developed with regard to states under article 8 ASR. This is made clear by the Commission in the Commentary to article 6 DARIO. Here, the Commission states: "[s]hould persons or groups of persons act under the instructions, or the direction or control, of an international organization, they would have to be regarded as agents according to the definition given in subparagraph (d) of article 2."[34]

---

[29] ICJ Reports 1949, 174 et seq. (177).

[30] Article 8 ASR provides: "The conduct of a person or group of persons shall be considered an act of a State under international law if the person or group of persons is in fact acting on the instructions of, or under the direction or control of, that State in carrying out the conduct."

[31] *Military and Paramilitary Activities in and against Nicaragua (Nicaragua v. United States of America)*, ICJ Reports 1986, 14 et seq.

[32] *Prosecutor v. Duško Tadić*, ICTY, Case IT-94-1-A (1999), *ILM* 38 (1999), 1518 et seq.

[33] See e.g. Commentary to article 8 ASR, see note 2, paras 4 et seq.; as to the criticism that has been expressed with regard to article 8 ASR and the attribution of conduct of private persons compare e.g. R. Wolfrum, "State Responsibility for Private Actors: An Old Problem of Renewed Relevance", in: Ragazzi, see note 17, 423 et seq.

[34] Commentary to article 6, see note 1, para. 11.

According to article 6 (1) DARIO, the conduct is only attributable if the organ or agent acted "in the performance of functions of that organ or agent ... ". For the determination of the functions, article 6 (2) DARIO refers to the "rules of the organization." The Commission finds though, that "in exceptional circumstances, functions may be considered as given to an organ or agent even if this could not be said to be based on the rules of the organization."[35] This clarification is especially relevant with regard to *de facto* organs or agents that can be subsumed under article 6 DARIO when acting under the instructions, the direction or control of an international organization (see above), as they may not be entrusted with functions pursuant to the rules of the organization.[36]

A conduct can also be attributed in case of an *ultra vires* act.[37] According to article 8 DARIO "[t]he conduct of an organ or agent of an international organization shall be considered an act of that organization under international law if the organ or agent acts in an official capacity and within the overall functions of that organization, even if the conduct exceeds the authority of that organ or agent or contravenes instructions."

b. Conduct of Organs of a State or Organs or Agents of an International Organization, Article 7 DARIO

The conduct of organs of a state as well as of organs or agents of an international organization that have been placed at the disposal of another international organization can be attributed according to article 7 DARIO, provided that the latter "exercises effective control over that conduct."[38] For this, the Commission states, "'operational' control would seem more significant than 'ultimate' control, since the latter

---

[35] Ibid., para. 9.
[36] Ibid., para. 11.
[37] To the wide acceptance of this and its bases see P. Klein, "The Attribution of Acts to International Organizations", in: J. Crawford/ A. Pellet/ S. Olleson, *The Law of International Responsibility*, 2010, 304 et seq.
[38] Article 7 reads: "The conduct of an organ of a State or an organ or agent of an international organization that is placed at the disposal of another international organization shall be considered under international law an act of the latter organization if the organization exercises effective control over that conduct."

hardly implies a role in the act in question."³⁹ To determine if an international organization has effective control, the "factual circumstances and particular context" are decisive.⁴⁰ The situation that the Commission refers to here explicitly is the one of military contingents that a state places at the disposal of the United Nations for a peacekeeping operation.⁴¹ In the Commentary,⁴² the Commission examines *inter alia* the jurisdiction of the European Court of Human Rights, which dealt with this situation in *Behrami and Saramati*,⁴³ and subsequently in *Kasumaj v. Greece*,⁴⁴ *Gajić v. Germany*⁴⁵ as well as *Berić and others v. Bosnia and Herzegovina*.⁴⁶. In those decisions, the Court had referred to the work of the Commission and also applied the criterion of "effective control". However, the Court there relied on "ultimate authority and control" rather than on "operational control". In *Al-Jedda v.*

---

39 Commentary to article 7, see note 1, para. 10; for more details on the discussion compare the various authors the Commission cites in its footnote 115, 89; compare also N. Tsagourias, "The Responsibility of International Organisations", in: M. Odello / R. Piotrowicz, *International Military Missions and International Law*, 2011, 245 et seq.; K.M. Larsen, "Attribution of Conduct in Peace Operations: The 'Ultimate Authority and Control' Test", *EJIL* 19 (2008), 509 et seq.

40 Commentary to article 7, see note 1, para. 4; an extensive evaluation of the responsibility practice of international organizations can be found at K. Schmalenbach, *Die Haftung Internationaler Organisationen im Rahmen von Militäreinsätzen und Territorialverwaltungen*, 2004.

41 Commentary to article 7, see note 1, para. 1.

42 Ibid., paras 10 et seq., compare also the references of the Commission to a long list of literature thereon in footnote 115.

43 ECtHR, *Behrami and Behrami v. France and Saramati v. France, Germany and Norway*, Decision (Grand Chamber) of 2 March 2007 on the admissibility of Applications No. 71412/01 and No. 78166/01. Compare thereto C.A. Bell, "Reassessing Multiple Attribution: The International Law Commission and the Behrami and Saramati Decision", *N.Y.U.J.Int'l L. & Pol.* 42 (2009-2010), 501 et seq.

44 Decision of 5 July 2007 on the Admissibility of Application No. 6974/05.

45 Decision of 28 August 2007 on the Admissibility of Application No. 31446/02.

46 Decision of 16 October 2007 on the Admissibility of Applications Nos 36357/04, 36360/04, 38346/04, 41705/04, 45190/04, 45578/04, 45579/04, 45580/04, 91/05, 97/05, 100/05, 1121/05, 1123/05, 1125/05, 1129/05, 1132/05, 1133/05, 1169/05, 1172/05, 1175/05, 1177/05, 1180/05, 1185/05, 20793/05 and 25496/05.

United Kingdom[47] on the other hand, the Court considered that "the United Nations Security Council had neither effective control nor ultimate authority and control over the acts and omissions of foreign troops within the Multi-National Force and that the applicant's detention was not, therefore, attributable to the United Nations."[48] In this formulation one may see an approximation of the Commission's and the Court's positions.

2. Breach of an International Obligation

As stated in article 4 lit. (b) DARIO, the action or omission must constitute a breach of an international obligation of the respective organization. According to article 10 (1) DARIO "[t]here is a breach of an international obligation by an international organization when an act of that international organization is not in conformity with what is required of it by that obligation, regardless of the origin or character of the obligation concerned."

The obligation that is breached cannot be found in the DARIO itself. The Commission even writes in the General Commentary that "[n]othing in the draft articles should be read as implying the existence or otherwise of any particular primary rule binding on international organizations."[49] Just like the ASR, the DARIO contain only secondary rules, as opposed to primary obligations.[50]

As the formulation "regardless of its origin" makes clear, the primary obligation can be found in any source of international law – e.g. in international treaties, customary international law or it can be established by a general principle.[51]

---

[47] Judgment (Grand Chamber), 7 July 2011, <http://cimskp.echr.coe.int>, para. 56.
[48] Ibid., para. 84.
[49] General Commentary to the DARIO, see note 1, para. 3.
[50] Criticism on this dichotomy and its inconsistent use has been raised by A. Nollkaemper/ D. Jacobs, "Shared Responsibility in International Law: A Conceptual Framework", *SHARES Research Paper* 03 (2011), ACIL 2011-07, 81 et seq., <www.sharesproject.nl>.
[51] These are the sources of international law the Commission names in the Commentary to article 10, see note 1, para. 2, as already in the Commentary to article 12 ASR, see note 2, para. 3; that sources of international law besides the ones contained in the catalogue of Article 38 (1) ICJ Statute

The Commission states in the Commentary to article 10 DARIO that "[a]n international obligation may be owed by an international organization to the international community as a whole, one or several states, whether members or nonmembers, another international organization or other international organizations and any other subject of international law."[52] As a consequence, this can also be an obligation owed to an individual as far as the individual is a subject of international law. In the General Commentary to the ASR, the Commission wrote this more explicitly when stating that "they apply to the whole field of the international obligations of States, whether the obligation is owed to one or several States, to an individual or group, or to the international community as a whole."

The Commission names some examples for international obligations owed to individuals by stating in the Commentary: "[w]ith regard to the international responsibility of international organizations, one significant area in which rights accrue to persons other than States or organizations is that of breaches by international organizations of their obligations under international law concerning employment. Another area is that of breaches committed by peacekeeping forces and affecting individuals."[53]

An international obligation may also arise for an international organization towards its members under the rules of the organization according to article 10 (2) DARIO. According to article 2 lit. (b) "'rules of the organization' means, in particular, the constituent instruments, decisions, resolutions and other acts of the international organization adopted in accordance with those instruments, and established practice of the organization." The formulation "towards its members" in article 10 (2) DARIO seems to suggest that only obligations owed to the members but not the ones owed to the personnel or other individuals are included. On the other hand, the Commission states in the Commentary that: "The wording in paragraph 2 is intended to include any international obligation that may arise from the rules of the organiza-

---

should be widely accepted, see R. Wolfrum, "Sources of International Law", in: Max Planck Encyclopedia, see note 6, Vol. IX, 299 et seq.; W. Graf Vitzthum, *Völkerrecht*, 2010, 66 et seq.

[52] Commentary to article 10, see note 1, para. 3.
[53] Commentary to article 33, ibid., para. 5; for the limited consequences arising for individuals and the impossibility for them to invoke responsibility themselves according to the DARIO see Section VI.

tion."⁵⁴ Moreover it states: "Paragraph 2 refers to the international obligations arising 'for an international organization towards its members', because these are the largest category of international obligations flowing from the rules of the organization. This reference is not intended to exclude the possibility that other rules of the organization may form part of international law."⁵⁵

The ILC has referred to the "rules of the organization" before.⁵⁶ The definition as contained in article 2 DARIO is mainly based on the definition of the 1986 Vienna Convention.⁵⁷ What constitutes an "established practice" of an organization has been discussed since then.⁵⁸ The "rules of international organizations", however, have a far greater importance in the DARIO than they had in the Vienna Convention, since, for example, they can be constitutive for the responsibility of an organization, as article 10 (2) DARIO makes clear.

The extent to which rules of international organizations are of an international law character is a matter of controversy.⁵⁹ As pointed out

---

54   Commentary to article 10, see note 1, para. 4.
55   Ibid., 98, para. 8.
56   See article 5 of the 1969 Vienna Convention on the Law of Treaties; article 3 of the 1975 Vienna Convention on the Representation of States in their Relations with International Organizations and article 2 of the 1986 Vienna Convention of the Law of Treaties between States and International Organizations or between International Organizations. However, only the latter contains a definition.
57   The Commission points this out in the Commentary to article 2, see note 1, para. 16.
58   See further on the issue C. Ahlborn, "The Rules of International Organizations and the Law of International Responsibility", ACIL Research Paper No. 2011-03 (*SHARES Series*), finalized 26 April 2011, <www.sharesproject.nt>, 19 et seq.; C. Peters, "Subsequent Practice and Established Practice of an International Organization: Two Sides of the Same Coin?", *Goettingen Journal of International Law* 3 (2011), 617 et seq.; that also the case law of the court of an organization should be seen as "established practice" of that organization has been argued e.g. by the European Commission, Doc. A/CN.4/545, 15; see also Paasivirta/ Kuijper, see note 7, 214 et seq.
59   This is also noted by the Commission in Commentary to article 10, see note 1, para. 5; compare ILA, *Committee on Accountability of International Organizations, First Report*, Taipei Conference 1998, 593 et seq.; see also M. Benzing, "International Organizations and Institutions, Secondary Law", in: Max Planck Encyclopedia, see note 6, Vol. VI, 74 et seq.; Ahlborn, see note 58 and id., "UNESCO Approves Palestinian Membership

above, only breaches of international law are covered by the scope of the DARIO. The Commission states that "to the extent that an obligation arising from the rules of the organization has to be regarded as an obligation under international law, the principles expressed in the present article apply. Breaches of obligations under the rules of the organization are not always breaches of obligations under international law."[60]

The Commission writes in the Commentary that "paragraph 2 does not attempt to express a clear-cut view on the issue." But by stating that a "breach of an international obligation [...] may arise for an international organization [...] under the rules of the organization" it clearly rejects the view that the secondary law of an international organization does not form part of international law but supports the opinion that secondary rules of international organizations form, at least to a certain extent, part of the sources of international law today.[61] The Commission, however, acknowledges that organizations that have obtained a high level of integration, such as the European Union, are a special case.[62] This acknowledgment is reflected again in the *lex specialis* rule as contained in article 64 DARIO.[63]

Bid - A Case for US Countermeasures Against the Organization?", who doubts that an international organization can incur international responsibility for a breach of its own rules, <http://www.ejiltalk.org> 2011.

[60] Commentary to article 10, see note 1, para. 7.

[61] Benzing, see note 59, states in para. 49 that: "It is safe to conclude that legal acts of international organizations and institutions, inasmuch as they are binding, have by now acquired the status of a source of international law."

[62] Commentary to article 10, see note 1, para. 5 with reference to the decision of the ECJ in *Costa v. E.N.E.L.*; compare on this issue e.g. A. von Bogdandy/ M. Smrkolj, "European Community and Union Law and International Law", in: Max Planck Encyclopedia, see note 6, Vol. III, 828 et seq., paras 2 et seq.

[63] Article 64 reads: "These draft articles do not apply where and to the extent that the conditions for the existence of an internationally wrongful act or the content or implementation of the international responsibility of an international organization, or of a State in connection with the conduct of an international organization, are governed by special rules of international law. Such special rules of international law may be contained in the rules of the organization applicable to the relations between an international organization and its members."; see also Section VIII.

3. Further Elements

Further elements to the ones described in article 4 DARIO are not required for international responsibility to arise according to the DARIO. However, further elements can be necessary according to the primary obligation. The primary obligation can require, for example, that there must be fault or that the injured party must have suffered a certain damage.[64]

V. Circumstances Precluding Wrongfulness

Even when the elements of responsibility are met, there may be circumstances that preclude the wrongfulness of the respective conduct.[65] These circumstances are set out in articles 20 to 27 DARIO, which correspond to articles 20 to 27 ASR.[66]

1. Consent, Article 20 DARIO

As one of these circumstances, article 20 DARIO sets out the valid consent of a state or an international organization to the commission of the act in question.[67] As in article 20 ASR, here the consent can also be given expressly or implicitly and it can be given in advance or even at the time the act is occurring. By contrast, a consent given after the conduct has occurred is a form of waiver or acquiescence and thus regulated in article 46 DARIO.[68] A consent given by an international or-

---

[64] Commentary to article 4, see note 1, para. 3; further elaborated in the Commentary to article 2 ASR, see note 2, paras 3, 9 et seq.
[65] One can argue that the conduct is actually "wrongful but excused", see V. Lowe, "Precluding Wrongfulness or Responsibility: A Plea for Excuses", *EJIL* 10 (1999), 405 et seq.; G. Dahm/ J. Delbrück/ R. Wolfrum, *Völkerrecht*, Band I/3, 2002, 919.
[66] On the criticism of these provisions see also Section VIII.
[67] Article 20 reads: "Valid consent by a State or an international organization to the commission of a given act by another international organization precludes the wrongfulness of that act in relation to that State or the former organization to the extent that the act remains within the limits of that consent."
[68] Article 46 reads: "The responsibility of an international organization may not be invoked if: (a) the injured State or international organization has val-

ganization "does not affect international obligations to the extent that they may also exist towards the members of the consenting organization, unless that organization has been empowered to express consent also on behalf of the members."[69]

2. Self-Defense, Article 21 DARIO

According to article 21 DARIO, "[t]he wrongfulness of an act of an international organization is precluded if and to the extent that the act constitutes a lawful measure of self-defence under international law."

The Commission had considered whether a distinction should be made between self-defense by states and self-defense by international organizations.[70] In the end, it decided that "[f]or reasons of coherency, the concept of self-defence which has [...] been elaborated with regard to States should be used also with regard to international organizations."[71] The conditions that must be met by an international organization in order to be acting in self-defense are a question of primary rules.[72] Only when an international organization complies with those rules, can the wrongfulness of the conduct be precluded. Self-defense is, as is well-known, an exception to the prohibition of the use of force.[73] The ILC also understands self-defense in the context of the DARIO this way.[74] Thus, the wrongfulness of the use of force by an international organization can be precluded when it acts in self-defense, which

---

idly waived the claim; (b) the injured State or international organization is to be considered as having, by reason of its conduct, validly acquiesced in the lapse of the claim."; compare also Commentary to article 20 ASR, see note 2, para. 3.

[69] Commentary to article 20, see note 1, para. 4.
[70] Cf. also M.H. Arsanjani, "Claims against International Organizations: Quis custodiet ipsos custodes?", *Yale Journal of World Public Order* 7 (1980-81), 131 et seq. (176); P. Klein, *La responsabilité des organisations internationales dans les ordres juridiques internes et en droit des gens*, 1998, 421; Schmalenbach, see note 40, 264 et seq.; M.C. Zwanenburg, *Accountability under International Humanitarian Law for United Nations and North Atlantic Treaty Organization Peace Support Operations*, 2004, 17.
[71] Commentary to article 21, see note 1, para. 2.
[72] Ibid., para. 4.
[73] See generally M. Bothe, "Friedenssicherung und Kriegsrecht", in: Vitzthum, see note 51, 655 et seq.
[74] Cf. Commentary to article 21, see note 1, para. 1.

may be seen a far-reaching conclusion.[75] In addition, it is noted by the Commission that the understanding of "self-defense" has been widened in practice with regard to UN peace-keeping and peace-enforcement missions to "defense of the mission".[76]

3. Countermeasures, Article 22 and Articles 51 to 57 DARIO

The Commission also decided to include provisions on countermeasures in the DARIO. The inclusion of provisions on countermeasures had already been a matter of controversy with regard to the ASR.[77] Thus one can imagine that the inclusion of countermeasures taken by international organizations, especially against states, would be no less a matter of discussion.[78] According to article 22 DARIO, the wrongfulness of an act of an international organization can be excluded also when this act constitutes a lawful countermeasure.[79] The countermea-

---

[75] This equalization of international organizations with states has been criticized see Section VIII.
[76] Commentary to article 21, see note 1, para. 3; see in greater detail the fourth report of the Special Rapporteur, 2006, Doc. A/CN.4/564, paras 16 et seq.; further examinations on the issue can be found at T. Findlay, *The Use of Force in UN Peace Operations*, 2002; compare also K.E. Cox, "Beyond Self-Defense: United Nations Peacekeeping Operations and the Use of Force", *Den. J. Int'l Law & Policy* 23 (1999), 239 et seq., and by M. Frulli, "Le operazioni di *peacekeeping* delle Nazioni Unite e l'uso della forza", *Riv. Dir. Int.* 84 (2001), 347 et seq.
[77] Cf. J. Crawford, *The International Law Commission's Articles on State Responsibility: Introduction, Text and Commentaries*, 2002, 47-49. For a definition of countermeasures with regard to states compare D. Alland, "The Definition of Countermeasures", in: Crawford/ Pellet/ Olleson, see note 37, 1135: "countermeasures are pacific unilateral reactions which are intrinsically unlawful, which are adopted by one or more states against another state, when the former consider that the latter has committed an internationally wrongful act which could justify such a reaction."
[78] Harsh criticism came e.g. from J. Alvarez, *Misadventures in Subjecthood*, 2010, <http://www.ejiltalk.org>.
[79] Article 22 reads: "1. Subject to paragraphs 2 and 3, the wrongfulness of an act of an international organization not in conformity with an international obligation towards a State or another international organization is precluded if and to the extent that the act constitutes a countermeasure taken in accordance with the substantive and procedural conditions required by international law, including those set forth in Chapter II of Part Four for

sure taken by the international organization is a reaction to the wrongful conduct of another international organization or a state and a remedy of the former against the wrongful act of the latter. Like the ASR, the DARIO or their Commentary also do not provide for a definition of countermeasures.[80] As an example of measures that have been called countermeasures in practice so far, the Commission names the "suspension of concessions or other obligations."[81]

Two situations need to be distinguished here: first, where a countermeasure is taken against another international organization. Second, where a countermeasure is taken against a state. The first situation, where an international organization takes countermeasures against another international organization, and its conditions, is dealt with in articles 51 to 57 DARIO. The situation that an international organization takes countermeasures against a state that has committed a wrongful act against the international organization, is not dealt with in articles 51 to 57 DARIO. Article 22 (1) DARIO refers to "the substantive and procedural conditions required by international law" instead. The Commission suggests applying the conditions set out for countermeasures taken by a state against another state in articles 49 to 54 ASR by analogy here.[82] When an international organization intends to take countermeasures against its members, it must additionally fulfill the requirements set out in article 22 (2) and (3) DARIO. The exercise of countermeasures by an international organization against its members may namely be prohibited by the rules of the organization.[83]

---

countermeasures taken against another international organization. 2. Subject to paragraph 3, an international organization may not take countermeasures against a responsible member State or international organization unless: (a) the conditions referred to in paragraph 1 are met; (b) the countermeasures are not inconsistent with the rules of the organization; and (c) no appropriate means are available for otherwise inducing compliance with the obligations of the responsible State or international organization concerning cessation of the breach and reparation. 3. Countermeasures may not be taken by an international organization against a member State or international organization in response to a breach of an international obligation under the rules of the organization unless such countermeasures are provided for by those rules."

[80] Cf. therefore e.g. Alland, see note 77.
[81] Commentary to article 51, see note 1, para. 4.
[82] Commentary to article 22, ibid., para. 2.
[83] Cf. also Ahlborn, see note 59.

4. *Force Majeure*, Article 23 DARIO

Significantly less controversial has been the case of *force majeure*. This is hardly surprising, given that the concept of *force majeure* is a widely accepted concept applicable not only to states but also to other subjects of law.[84] According to article 23 (1) DARIO the wrongfulness of an act of an international organization is precluded "if the act is due to *force majeure*, that is, the occurrence of an irresistible force or of an unforeseen event, beyond the control of the organization, making it materially impossible in the circumstances to perform the obligation."

Whereas the Special Rapporteur had still recommended in his fourth report[85] to include financial distress as a case of *force majeure*, the Commentary to the DARIO does not mention financial distress at all. The reason for this can be found in the statement of the Chairman of the Drafting Committee of 8 June 2006: "The Committee was of the view that there may be various reasons for financial distress of an international organization, such as poor management, non-payment of dues by member States, unanticipated expenses, etc., most of which could not be considered cases of force majeure. Financial distress of an international organization could amount to force majeure only in exceptional circumstances. [...] It was further agreed, that, while there may be circumstances that financial distress of an international organization may satisfy the requirement of force majeure, it was not prudent to use it as a prime example of a case of force majeure even in the commentary, since it might be misleading."[86]

5. Distress, Article 24 DARIO

When "the author of the act in question has no other reasonable way, in a situation of distress, of saving the author's life or the lives of other persons entrusted to the author's care" the wrongfulness of an act of an international organization not in conformity with an international obligation of that organization is precluded according to article 24 DARIO.

As an example of distress, the Commission refers to the Commentary on the corresponding article 24 ASR which names "aircraft and

---

[84] Cf. for the concept in general S. Hentrei/ X. Soley, "Force Majeure", in: Max Planck Encyclopedia, see note 6, Vol. IV, 151 et seq.
[85] Doc. A/CN.4/564, para. 31.
[86] Available at <http://www.un.org/law/ilc/>, see 5 et seq. of the statement.

ships entering State territory under stress of weather or following mechanical or navigational failure"[87] as the most common cases of distress and states also that "[a]lthough historically practice has focused on cases involving ships and aircraft, article 24 is not limited to such cases."[88] These examples show, despite this last cited sentence, that the field of application of cases of distress is very limited. In addition, the Commission decided to include a limitation *ratione personae*: the act must be committed for "saving the author's life or the lives of other persons entrusted to the author's care."

The Commission has discussed whether this requirement was too narrow as there may be situations where an international organization would intervene to prevent loss of life of individuals with whom it had no special relationship. The considerations of the Drafting Committee were very extensive here and even touched upon the issues of the Responsibility to Protect and humanitarian intervention. In the end it decided not to extent the scope of distress further as laid down in the ASR.[89]

6. Necessity, Article 25 DARIO

According to the Special Rapporteur, "[n]ecessity is probably the most controversial circumstance precluding wrongfulness. It has almost always been considered only in relation to States."[90] Nevertheless, "[t]he general view was that international organizations should be able to invoke necessity. But it was the general view that such a right should be circumscribed carefully."[91]

Article 25 DARIO, at first sight, looks basically the same as article 25 ASR, but there is one significant difference: whereas article 25 ASR refers to "an essential interest of the State or of the international com-

---

[87] Commentary to article 24 ASR, see note 2, para. 3.
[88] Ibid., para. 4.
[89] Statement of the Chairman of the Drafting Committee of 8 June 2006, see note 86, 6 et seq.
[90] Fourth Report of the Special Rapporteur, Doc. A/CN.4/564, para. 35; compare especially the discussion in the Sixth Committee of the UN General Assembly of 5 November 2004, Doc. A/CN.6/59/SR.22.
[91] This was the general view of the ILC, see Statement of the Chairman of the Drafting Committee of 8 June 2006, see note 86, 8.

munity as a whole"[92], an international organization can only invoke necessity "to safeguard [...] an essential interest of its member States or of the international community as a whole."[93] In addition, an international organization can only invoke necessity for an essential interest "when the organization has, in accordance with international law, the function to protect the interest in question" according to article 25 (1) lit. (a) DARIO.[94] Thus, an international organization cannot invoke necessity, according to article 25 DARIO, only for the protection of its own interests.[95]

The example for a case of necessity given in the Commentary reflects how remote the Commission has finally become from its initial considerations.[96] The Commission names access to the electronic ac-

---

[92] Commentary to article 25 ASR, see note 2, para. 2.
[93] Article 25 reads: "1. Necessity may not be invoked by an international organization as a ground for precluding the wrongfulness of an act not in conformity with an international obligation of that organization unless the act: (a) is the only means for the organization to safeguard against a grave and imminent peril an essential interest of its member States or of the international community as a whole when the organization has, in accordance with international law, the function to protect the interest in question; and (b) does not seriously impair an essential interest of the State or States towards which the international obligation exists, or of the international community as a whole. 2. In any case, necessity may not be invoked by an international organization as a ground for precluding wrongfulness if: (a) the international obligation in question excludes the possibility of invoking necessity; or (b) the organization has contributed to the situation of necessity."
[94] It is very interesting to see the development of this article. The Special Rapporteur had suggested in his fourth report (2006) only that there must be "an essential interest that the organization has the function to protect." In its report of 2006 (Doc. A/61/10), the Commission suggested that there must be "an essential interest of the international community as a whole" and "the organization [must have], in accordance with international law, the function to protect that interest."
[95] Cf. the criticism on the previous version of article 25, A. Reinisch, "Editorial: How Necessary is Necessity for International Organizations?", *International Organizations Law Review* 3 (2006), 177 et seq.
[96] Here the Committee also touched upon issues of humanitarian intervention e.g. as already in the context of distress, see above. Compare therefore also the literature on necessity in the context of state responsibility and human rights protection as a case of necessity: C. Ryngaert, "State Responsibility, Necessity and Human Rights", *NYIL* 41 (2010), 79 et seq.

count of an employee who was on leave as a case of urgency as the only example for necessity in the Commentary to article 25 DARIO.[97]

VI. Consequences of an Internationally Wrongful Act and Invocation of Responsibility

1. Consequences

Again when it comes to the legal consequences arising from an internationally wrongful act, articles 28 et seq. DARIO mirror articles 28 et seq. ASR. As in the case of state responsibility, an international organization may also have the continued duty to perform the obligation breached (article 29 DARIO), to cease the act if it is continuing (article 30 lit. (a) DARIO), and under certain circumstances to offer appropriate assurances and guarantees of non-repetition (article 30 lit. (b) DARIO).[98] Finally it has the duty to make reparation for the injury caused according to article 31, articles 34 et seq. DARIO. Reparation may be owed in the form of restitution, compensation and satisfaction, article 34 DARIO.[99] To a certain extent these consequences may also arise when circumstances precluding wrongfulness have been invoked according to article 27 DARIO.[100]

As articles 28 et seq. DARIO to the widest extent correspond to articles 28 et seq. ASR, in the following this contribution will concentrate

---

[97] Commentary to article 25, see note 1, para. 2.
[98] Article 29 reads: "The legal consequences of an internationally wrongful act under this Part do not affect the continued duty of the responsible international organization to perform the obligation breached."; article 30 DARIO reads: "The international organization responsible for the internationally wrongful act is under an obligation: (a) to cease that act, if it is continuing; (b) to offer appropriate assurances and guarantees of non-repetition, if circumstances so require."
[99] Article 34 reads: "Full reparation for the injury caused by the internationally wrongful act shall take the form of restitution, compensation and satisfaction, either singly or in combination, in accordance with the provisions of this Chapter."
[100] Article 27 reads: "The invocation of a circumstance precluding wrongfulness in accordance with this Chapter is without prejudice to: (a) compliance with the obligation in question, if and to the extent that the circumstance precluding wrongfulness no longer exists; (b) the question of compensation for any material loss caused by the act in question."

on the aspects that differ or may cause special problems with regard to international organizations.

According to article 31 (1) DARIO "[t]he responsible international organization is under an obligation to make full reparation for the injury caused by the internationally wrongful act." An international organization may, however, face difficulties in having the necessary means for making the required reparation, especially compensation.[101] When an international organization is financially not able to fulfill its obligation to pay compensation, the question can be raised whether an injured party can have recourse to the Member States. The existence of such a subsidiary obligation of Member States to pay for the debts of an international organization has been rejected by the Commission.[102] To ensure that the injured parties do not remain empty-handed, the Commission included article 40 (1) DARIO, according to which "the responsible international organization shall take all appropriate measures in accordance with its rules to ensure that its members provide it with the means for effectively fulfilling its obligations" arising as a consequence of an internationally wrongful act. In addition, according to article 40 (2) DARIO, "[t]he members of a responsible international organization shall take all the appropriate measures that may be required by the rules of the organization in order to enable the organization to fulfill its obligations" arising as a consequence of an internationally wrongful act.[103]

---

[101] Cf. also Summary of the International Law Discussion Group meeting held at Chatham House on Thursday, 10 February 2011, on Legal Responsibility of International Organizations in International Law, <http://www.chathamhouse.org>, 10.

[102] Commentary to article 40, see note 1, para. 2 with reference to comments of states and international organizations; in favor of such a subsidiary obligation on the other hand e.g. W. Meng, "Internationale Organisationen im völkerrechtlichen Deliktsrecht", *ZaöRV* 45 (1985), 325 et seq. (338); I. Seidl-Hohenveldern, "Responsibility of Member States of an International Organization for Acts of that Organization", in: id., *Collected Essays on International Investments and on International Organizations*, 1998, 63 et seq.

[103] This provision had been a matter of controversy. In an earlier draft it created a primary obligation for the Member States directly. It read: "The members of a responsible international organization are required to take, in accordance with the rules of the organization, all appropriate measures in order to provide the organization with the means for effectively fulfilling its obligations under the present chapter." See Titles and Texts of Draft Articles 31 to 45 [44] adopted by the Drafting Committee on 18, 19, 20 and 25

Despite its initial intention[104] not to do so, the Commission in article 40 (1) DARIO clearly lays down a primary obligation for international organizations. By its own definition, "primary rules of international law [are those rules], which establish obligations for international organizations, and secondary rules [are those rules], which consider the existence of a breach of an international obligation and its consequences for the responsible international organization."[105] The duty contained in article 40 (1) DARIO however, certainly does not describe the conditions for such a breach. In addition, article 40 (1) DARIO does not contain a rule on the consequences of the breach as it addresses another level than the obligations elsewhere contained in articles 28 et seq. DARIO. This already becomes apparent when looking at the relationship of the parties involved in the rest of the provisions on consequences according to articles 28 et seq. The parties concerned in article 40 (1) DARIO are the international organizations and its Member States, whereas apart from that the secondary rules address the relationship between the wrongfully acting international organization and the injured party.[106]

Finally, a crucial provision, when it comes to the consequences of the breach, is article 33 DARIO. According to article 33 (1) "[t]he obligations of the responsible international organization set out in this Part may be owed to one or more States, to one or more other organizations, or to the international community as a whole, depending in particular on the character and content of the international obligation and on the circumstances of the breach." The Commission thus decided in favor of a traditional approach as already taken analogously in article 33 ASR. It reflects a traditional view of the international legal system as a system focused on states, equating now to a certain extent international organizations, but not individuals or other entities.[107]

July 2007, Doc. A/CN.4/L720 as well as the statement of the Chairman of the Drafting Committee of 31 July 2007.

[104] Cf. General Commentary to the DARIO, see note 1, para. 3.

[105] Ibid.

[106] On the distinction between primary and secondary rules see above; on the difficulties to consequently abide by this dichotomy compare Nollkaemper/ Jacobs, see note 50, 81 et seq.

[107] Cf. for the analogous situation of State Responsibility also E. Brown Weiss, "Invoking State Responsibility in the Twenty-First Century", *AJIL* 96 (2002), 798 et seq.

The Commission concedes that international obligations exist towards individuals and can be breached by states and international organizations according to the ASR and the DARIO.[108] However, the consequences of these breaches with regard to individuals are not covered by the ASR or the DARIO.[109] According to article 33 (2) of the DARIO it "is without prejudice to any right, arising from the international responsibility of an international organization, which may accrue directly to any person or entity other than a State or an international organization." This provision refers to the consequences of breaches that may arise *vis-à-vis* individuals directly, e.g. according to human rights treaties.

2. Invocation of Responsibility

The DARIO also contain provisions regarding the invocation of responsibility in articles 43 et seq. According thereto, the responsibility of an international organization can be invoked by an injured state or an injured international organization (article 43)[110] and under certain circumstances also by a non-injured state or international organization (article 48).[111] There is no possibility for individuals or entities other

---

[108] See Section IV. 2.
[109] Commentary to article 33, see note 1, para. 5; this is criticized by A. von Bogdandy/ M. Steinbrück Platise, "DARIO and Human Rights Protection: Leaving the Individual in the Cold", *International Organizations Law Review* (forthcoming).
[110] Article 43 reads: "A State or an international organization is entitled as an injured State or an injured international organization to invoke the responsibility of another international organization if the obligation breached is owed to: (a) that State or the former international organization individually; (b) a group of States or international organizations including that State or the former international organization, or the international community as a whole, and the breach of the obligation: (i) specially affects that State or that international organization; or (ii) is of such a character as radically to change the position of all the other States and international organizations to which the obligation is owed with respect to the further performance of the obligation."
[111] Article 48 reads: "1. Where an international organization and one or more States or other international organizations are responsible for the same internationally wrongful act, the responsibility of each State or organization may be invoked in relation to that act. 2. Subsidiary responsibility may be invoked insofar as the invocation of the primary responsibility has not led

than states or international organizations to invoke responsibility directly according to the DARIO.[112] When there is no special rule entitling the individual to invoke responsibility itself (compare article 50 DARIO), the person will need to rely on diplomatic protection.[113] The rules on diplomatic protection have been elaborated by the Commission in the Draft Articles on Diplomatic Protection of 2006.[114] The Commission originally treated questions of diplomatic protection as part of the study on state responsibility.[115] Because of the limitation of the possibility to invoke responsibility, both topics remain closely connected. Article 45 (1) DARIO therefore refers to a rule that is central when exercising diplomatic protection, the rule of nationality of claims.[116]

Article 45 (2) DARIO makes clear that the local remedies rule can be applicable also with regard to claims against international organizations by states or other international organizations. According thereto, when an effective remedy within an international organization is avail-

---

to reparation. 3. Paragraphs 1 and 2: (a) do not permit any injured State or international organization to recover, by way of compensation, more than the damage it has suffered; (b) are without prejudice to any right of recourse that the State or international organization providing reparation may have against the other responsible States or international organizations."

[112] Cf. for the criticism von Bogdandy/ Steinbrück Platise, see note 109; this has also been criticized by Brown Weiss with regard to state responsibility, see note 107, 815; compare also the réplique of J. Crawford, "The ILC's Articles on Responsibility of States for Internationally Wrongful Acts: A Retrospect", *AJIL* 96 (2002), 874 et seq. (886 et seq.).

[113] Article 50 reads: "This Chapter is without prejudice to the entitlement that a person or entity other than a State or an international organization may have to invoke the international responsibility of an international organization."

[114] Draft Articles on Diplomatic Protection, ILC Report of the 58th Sess., 2006, Doc. A/61/10, 13 et seq.

[115] Cf. General Commentary to the Draft Articles on Diplomatic Protection, ibid., 22.

[116] Article 45 reads: "1. An injured State may not invoke the responsibility of an international organization if the claim is not brought in accordance with any applicable rule relating to the nationality of claims. 2. When the rule of exhaustion of local remedies applies to a claim, an injured State or international organization may not invoke the responsibility of another international organization if any available and effective remedy has not been exhausted."

able, an injured state or international organization may not invoke the responsibility before exhausting this remedy.[117]

VII. Responsibility in Cases of Connected Conduct of States and International Organizations

Articles 16 et seq. ASR contain rules on the responsibility of a state when it acts in connection with another state. Articles 14 et seq. DARIO as well as articles 58 et seq. DARIO complement these provisions. They are patterned after articles 16 et seq. ASR as the Commission tried to set up a coherent system of rules when a state acts in connection with the conduct of a state (articles 16 et seq. ASR) or an international organization (articles 58 et seq. DARIO) and *vice versa* when an international organization acts in connection with the act of a state or another international organization (articles 14 et seq. DARIO). Because of the corresponding content of articles 14 et seq. DARIO and articles 58 et seq. DARIO, they shall be dealt with here subsequently, despite their systematic position in the DARIO.

1. Responsibility of an International Organization in Connection with the Act of a State or another International Organization, Articles 14 et seq. DARIO

Under certain conditions, an international organization may be responsible for an act of a state or another international organization. Articles 14 et seq. DARIO set out these conditions.

a. Aid or Assistance, Article 14 DARIO

First, article 14 DARIO addresses the situation where an international organization "aids or assists a State or another international organiza-

---

[117] The Commission notes in the Commentary to article 45, see note 1, para. 7: "Although the term 'local remedies' may seem inappropriate in this context, because it seems to refer to remedies available in the territory of the responsible entity, it has generally been used in English texts as a term of art and as such has been included also in paragraph 2"; for an overview of the remedies available, which are still in an embryonic stage, compare e.g. Schmalenbach, see note 10.

tion in the commission of an internationally wrongful act."[118] Article 14 DARIO corresponds to article 16 ASR. The Commission writes in the Commentary: "The international responsibility that an entity may incur under international law for aiding or assisting another entity in the commission of an internationally wrongful act does not appear to depend on the nature and character of the entities concerned."[119] Thereby the Commission formulates another general rule applicable to all entities.

According to article 14 DARIO, the aiding or assisting international organization is responsible, given that it knew of the circumstances (lit. (a)) and that the act would be internationally wrongful when committed by the organization itself (lit. (b)). As the formulation "in the commission of an internationally wrongful act" suggests, the internationally wrongful conduct must actually be committed by the aided or assisted state. The wording of the precondition set out in article 14 lit. (a) DARIO is in fact misleading as according thereto, the mere "knowledge" would be sufficient. The Commission, however, states, with reference to the Commentary on article 16 ASR, that the international organization needs to "intend" to facilitate the occurrence of the wrongful conduct by the aid or assistance given. In addition, the Commission requires in the Commentary that the "aid or assistance should contribute 'significantly' to the commission of the act."[120]

b. Direction and Control, Article 15 DARIO

Second, corresponding to article 17 ASR, an international organization can be responsible when it directs and controls a state or another international organization in the commission of an internationally wrongful

---

[118] Article 14 reads: "An international organization which aids or assists a State or another international organization in the commission of an internationally wrongful act by the State or the latter organization is internationally responsible for doing so if: (a) the former organization does so with knowledge of the circumstances of the internationally wrongful act; and (b) the act would be internationally wrongful if committed by that organization."

[119] Commentary to article 14, see note 1, para. 1.

[120] A critical assessment of the article, especially when the aid or assistance exclusively consists of financial support can be found at A. Reinisch, "Aid or Assistance and Direction and Control between States and International Organizations in the Commission of Internationally Wrongful Acts", *International Organizations Law Review* 7 (2010), 63-77.

act, according to article 15 DARIO.[121] As in article 17 ASR, a narrow understanding of "direction" and "control" underlies article 15 DARIO: "[T]he term 'controls' refers to cases of domination over the commission of wrongful conduct and not simply the exercise of oversight, still less mere influence or concern", and "the word 'directs' does not encompass mere incitement or suggestion but rather connotes actual direction of an operative kind."[122] Again, the organization must be aware of the circumstances (lit. (a)) and the act would need to be internationally wrongful when committed by that organization itself (lit. (b)).[123] Also here, mere knowledge would not be enough, instead there must be an intention by the international organization and the internationally wrongful conduct must actually be committed.[124] To detect the intention of the international organization should, however, not be too difficult in such a case of direction and control.

c. Coercion, Article 16 DARIO

Third, article 16 DARIO deals with the situation when an international organization coerces a state or another international organization to commit an internationally wrongful act.[125] By referring to the Commentary of article 18 ASR, the Commission makes clear, that "coercion" here needs to be understood just as narrowly as in article 18 ASR: "Coercion for the purpose of article 18 has the same essential character as force majeure under article 23. Nothing less than conduct which forces the will of the coerced state will suffice, giving it no effective

---

[121] Article 15 reads: "An international organization which directs and controls a State or another international organization in the commission of an internationally wrongful act by the State or the latter organization is internationally responsible for that act if: (a) the former organization does so with knowledge of the circumstances of the internationally wrongful act; and (b) the act would be internationally wrongful if committed by that organization."
[122] Commentary to article 15, see note 1, para. 4, with reference to the Commentary on article 17 ASR, see note 2, 43, para. 7.
[123] For a further assessment compare Reinisch, see note 120.
[124] Cf. Commentary to article 15 DARIO, see note 1, para. 6.
[125] Article 16 reads: "An international organization which coerces a State or another international organization to commit an act is internationally responsible for that act if: (a) the act would, but for the coercion, be an internationally wrongful act of the coerced State or international organization; and (b) the coercing international organization does so with knowledge of the circumstances of the act."

choice but to comply with the wishes of the coercing State."[126] Unlike the previous articles, article 16 DARIO does not require the act to be wrongful if committed by the coercing organization. Instead the act needs to be wrongful for the coerced entity, (compare article 16 lit. (a) DARIO).

d. Circumvention, Article 17 DARIO

Finally, the most interesting provision here is the one that cannot be found correspondingly in the ASR, which is article 17 DARIO.[127] This provision takes into account that an international organization may circumvent its international obligations both through its decisions and authorizations. Article 17 DARIO describes two situations: first, when an international organization adopts a decision binding its Member States or international organizations to commit an act that would be internationally wrongful if committed by the former organization. The responsibility of the international organization is already triggered by the adoption of the binding decision – the bound Member State or international organization does not need to already have implemented the decision and thus have committed the act.

The second situation occurs when an international organization authorizes its Member States or international organizations to commit an act that would be internationally wrongful if committed by the former organization.[128] Unlike the case before, the act which is authorized

---

[126] Commentary to article 16, see note 1, para. 4, with reference to the Commentary to article 18 ASR, see note 2, para. 2.

[127] Article 17 reads: "1. An international organization incurs international responsibility if it circumvents one of its international obligations by adopting a decision binding member States or international organizations to commit an act that would be internationally wrongful if committed by the former organization. 2. An international organization incurs international responsibility if it circumvents one of its international obligations by authorizing member States or international organizations to commit an act that would be internationally wrongful if committed by the former organization and the act in question is committed because of that authorization. 3. Paragraphs 1 and 2 apply whether or not the act in question is internationally wrongful for the member States or international organizations to which the decision or authorization is addressed."

[128] For a critical examination of the inclusion of this situation in the DARIO, compare N. Blokker, "Abuse of the Members: Questions concerning the Draft Article 16 of the Draft Articles on Responsibility of International

needs to be actually committed. Moreover, it needs to be committed "because of that authorization", according to article 17 (2) DARIO.

In both cases the international organization circumvents one of its international obligations. "The term 'circumvention' implies an intention on the part of the international organization to take advantage of the separate legal personality of its members [...]."[129] The less discretion the international organization gives in its decision to the addressees, the more obvious may be the organization's intention to circumvent its obligation.

In its previous version of article 17 DARIO, the Commission had also referred to a third situation. It found, that "an international organization incurs international responsibility if it [...] recommends that a member State or international organization commit such an [internationally wrongful] act."[130] In his eighth report, the Special Rapporteur explained the reasons for the inclusion of "recommendations" by stating: "[t]he idea that an international organization may be responsible when it recommends a certain action to a member is based on the assumption that members are unlikely to ignore recommendations systematically. At least some of the members may be prompted to follow the recommendation."[131] In the present articles, this was dropped. Various international organizations as well as states had criticized the inclusion of responsibility because of non-binding recommendations in the DARIO, pointing to the considerable extension of responsibility that would result thereof.[132] An argument against the inclusion of recommendations in article 17 DARIO is that, as a Member State is not obliged to implement a recommendation, the implementation is based on its own decision (at least from a formal legal perspective), which

---

Organizations", *International Organizations Law Review* 7 (2010), 35 et seq. (46).

[129] Commentary to article 17, see note 1, para. 4.

[130] The current article 17 was article 16 back then, Report of the ILC, GAOR 64th Sess., Suppl. No. 10, Doc. A/64/10, 24.

[131] Eighth Report on Responsibility of International Organizations, Doc. A/CN.4/640, para. 56, 20.

[132] See the comments of inter alia the IMF (Doc. A/CN.4/637), of the European Commission or the International Labour Organization (both Doc. A/CN.4/637, Section II.B.12) or of the Nordic Countries (Doc. A/C.6/64/SR.15, para. 28).

outweighs the initial conduct (the recommendation) of the international organization.[133]

2. Responsibility of a State in Connection with the Conduct of an International Organization

Articles 58 et seq. DARIO contain rules on the responsibility of a state in connection with the conduct of an international organization. According to article 57 ASR, this had been left out in the ASR.[134] Articles 58 et seq. DARIO are patterned after articles 16 et seq. ASR, like articles 14 et seq. DARIO.

As can be inferred from the articles 58 et seq. DARIO, the mere membership in an international organization is not sufficient to trigger responsibility. In the Commentary, the Commission explicitly states that "[...] membership does not as such entail for member States international responsibility when the organization commits an internationally wrongful act."[135] Instead, there must be a certain conduct, be it aid or assistance (article 58 DARIO), direction and control (article 59 DARIO), coercion (article 60 DARIO), the circumvention of international obligations (article 61 DARIO), the acceptance of responsibility or a certain causation of reliance of the injured party (article 62 DARIO).

The question whether a state should be responsible for the wrongdoing of an international organization, solely because of its membership, has been a matter of controversy for a long time, especially since the collapse of the International Tin Council in 1985.[136] The ILC aligns with the Institute of International Law, which stated in its resolution of 1995 that: "[s]ave as specified in article 5, there is no general rule of international law whereby States members are, due solely to their mem-

---

[133] Cf. also the statement of the ILO, ibid., which speaks of a broken chain of causation; Blokker, see note 128, 43 et seq.

[134] Nevertheless, Member States may be responsible, next to the situations described in the DARIO, according to the ASR. Compare Commentary to article 62, see note 1, para. 1.

[135] Commentary to article 62, see note 1, para. 2.

[136] Cf. on this the analysis made by the Special Rapporteur in his Fourth Report, Doc. A/CN.4/564/Add.2, with references to a large list of literature in footnotes 160 et seq.

bership, liable, concurrently or subsidiarily, for the obligations of an international organization of which they are members."[137]

a. Aid or Assistance, Article 58 DARIO

Article 58 DARIO describes the reversed situation of article 14 DARIO.[138] Whereas in article 14 DARIO an international organization aids or assists a state (or another international organization) in the commission of a wrongful act, in article 58 DARIO a state aids or assists an international organization in the commission of a wrongful act. A state can thus not only be responsible when assisting or aiding another state (article 16 ASR), but also when assisting or aiding an international organization in the commission of a wrongful act (article 58 DARIO). Unfortunately, the Commission does not refer explicitly to the requirements, as stated above, that the relevant state organ intended, by the aid or assistance given, to facilitate the occurrence of the wrongful conduct, that the internationally wrongful conduct is actually committed by the aided or assisted international organization and also that the aid or assistance contributed "significantly" to the commission of the act.[139] However, as the Commission makes clear that article 58

---

[137] Article 6 (a) *Annuaire de l'Institut de Droit International*, Vol. 66-II (1996), 445; the ILA obviously was of the same view in its Berlin Report of 2004, see note 5, when it stated: "The question of concurrent or residual liability of Member states for non-fulfilment by IO-s of their obligations towards third parties has already been fully covered in the 1995 Resolution of the Institut de Droit International: 'The Legal Consequences for Member states of the Non-Fulfilment by International Organisations of their Obligations toward Third Parties'. The Committee did not therefore feel it necessary to go further into the matter.", compare on the other hand A. Stumer, "Liability of Member States for Acts of International Organizations: Reconsidering the Policy Objections", *Harv. Int'l L. J.*, 48 (2007), 553 et seq.

[138] Article 58 reads: "1. A State which aids or assists an international organization in the commission of an internationally wrongful act by the latter is internationally responsible for doing so if: (a) the State does so with knowledge of the circumstances of the internationally wrongful act; and (b) the act would be internationally wrongful if committed by that State. 2. An act by a State member of an international organization done in accordance with the rules of the organization does not as such engage the international responsibility of that State under the terms of this article."

[139] Commentary to article 16 ASR, see note 2, para. 5; the Special Rapporteur had pointed out that there should be some clarification in the Commentary,

DARIO is to be seen as the equivalent to article 14 DARIO and article 16 ASR, one can suppose that the Commission wanted these requirements to be applied here as well.[140]

On the other hand, article 58 (2) DARIO contains a provision that cannot be found in these two other articles. According to article 58 (2) DARIO, "[a]n act by a State member of an international organization done in accordance with the rules of the organization does not as such engage the international responsibility of that State under the terms of this draft article." Unfortunately, the Commission remains very unclear as to what exactly this means. To specify this provision, the Commission only states in the commentary abstractly that "[t]he factual context such as the size of membership and the nature of the involvement will probably be decisive."[141] The Special Rapporteur pointed out that "for the purpose of assessing whether aid or assistance occurs, much depends on the content of the obligation breached and on the circumstances."[142]

To understand article 58 (2) DARIO better, it is helpful to look into the eighth report of the Special Rapporteur.[143] Until then, no such provision had been included in article 58 DARIO, but only in the Commentary, which stated that "the influence that may amount to aid or assistance could not simply consist in participation in the decision-making process of the organization according to the pertinent rules of the organization."[144] This formulation, that was in fact a lot more narrow than the one now contained in article 58 (2) DARIO, has already been challenged.[145]

---

but apparently this was not effectuated by the Commission, see Seventh Report of the Special Rapporteur, 2009, Doc. A/CN./610, para. 75.

[140] Commentary to article 58, see note 1, para. 3: "The present article uses the same wording as article 16 on the Responsibility of States for internationally wrongful acts, because it would be hard to find reasons for applying a different rule when the aided or assisted entity is an international organization rather than a State."

[141] Commentary to article 58, see note 1, para. 4.

[142] Seventh Report of the Special Rapporteur, 2009, see note 139, para. 75.

[143] Eighth Report of the Special Rapporteur, 2011, Doc. A/CN.4/640, para. 103.

[144] Commentary to article 57, para. 2, Report of the ILC on the work of its 61st Sess., Doc. A/64/10.

[145] J. d'Aspremont, "Abuse of the Legal Personality of International Organizations and the Responsibility of Member States", *ILR* 129 (2007), 91 et seq. (97 et seq.); C. Ryngaert/ H. Buchanan, "Member State Responsibility

One main difficulty in a situation of aid and assistance by a state here is how to delineate when the conduct of the state needs to be seen as part of its function as a state on the one hand and when the conduct of the state needs to be seen as an action in its function as a member of an international organization on the other hand.

In most international organizations members of policy-making organs are representatives from governments. To see every action of that representative as the action of the state would of course completely undermine the separate legal personality of an international organization. On the other hand, one should not forget that the rules of an international organization cannot be applied to the detriment of a third party, as they are *res inter alios acta* to them. The extensiveness of the wording of this provision is especially problematic with regard to third parties. This needs to be kept in mind when interpreting article 58 (2) DARIO. The Commission states in the Commentary that "while the rules of the organization may affect international obligations for the relations between an organization and its members, they cannot have a similar effect in relation to non-members."[146]

b. Direction and Control, Article 59 DARIO

Also with regard to "direction and control", the Commission creates a coherent system for the situation where a state directs and controls another state or an international organization as well as the reversed situation, when an international organization directs and controls another international organization or a state, according to article 59, 15 DARIO and article 17 ASR.[147] For all three articles the same requirements apply. Article 59 (2) DARIO contains a provision parallel to the one in article

---

for the Acts of International Organizations", *Utrecht Law Review* 7 (2011), 131 et seq. (143); both refer to P. Klein, *La Responsabilité des Organizations Internationales Dans les Ordres Juridiques Internes et en Droit des Gens*, 1998, 469 et seq.

[146] Commentary to article 5, see note 1, para. 3.

[147] Article 59 reads: "1. A State which directs and controls an international organization in the commission of an internationally wrongful act by the latter is internationally responsible for that act if: (a) the State does so with knowledge of the circumstances of the internationally wrongful act; and (b) the act would be internationally wrongful if committed by that State. 2. An act by a State member of an international organization done in accordance with the rules of the organization does not as such engage the international responsibility of that State under the terms of this draft article."

58 (2) DARIO and thus, raises similar problems. The Commission states: "As in the case of aid or assistance, which is considered in article 58 and the related commentary, a distinction has to be made between participation by a member State in the decision making process of the organization according to its pertinent rules, and direction and control which would trigger the application of the present article. Since the latter conduct could take place within the framework of the organization, in borderline cases one would face the same problems that have been discussed in the commentary on the previous article."[148]

c. Coercion, Article 60 DARIO

A similar triplet can be found in the case of coercion, according to article 16, 60 DARIO and article 18 ASR.[149] The conditions applicable according to the three articles are essentially the same.[150] Article 60 DARIO contains no provisions like articles 58 (2) and 59 (2) DARIO "because it seems highly unlikely that an act of coercion could be taken by a State member of an international organization in accordance with the rules of the organization."[151]

d. Circumvention of International Obligations, Article 61 DARIO

Article 61 DARIO can be seen in connection with article 17 DARIO.[152] Whereas article 17 DARIO addresses the situation that an international organization circumvents its international obligation by, in a certain

---

[148] Commentary to article 58, see note 1, para. 2.
[149] Article 60 reads: "A State which coerces an international organization to commit an act is internationally responsible for that act if: (a) the act would, but for the coercion, be an internationally wrongful act of the coerced international organization; and (b) the coercing State does so with knowledge of the circumstances of the act."
[150] See above.
[151] Commentary to article 60, see note 1, para. 3.
[152] Article 61 reads: "1. A State member of an international organization incurs international responsibility if, by taking advantage of the fact that the organization has competence in relation to the subject-matter of one of the State's international obligations, it circumvents that obligation by causing the organization to commit an act that, if committed by the State, would have constituted a breach of the obligation. 2. Paragraph 1 applies whether or not the act in question is internationally wrongful for the international organization."

way, using a Member State or another international organization, article 61 DARIO addresses the reversed situation of a state taking advantage of an international organization of which it is a member.

As in article 17 DARIO, "circumvention" implies also in article 61 DARIO the existence of an intention to avoid compliance.[153] In addition, three conditions need to be met in order for responsibility to arise for a Member State under article 61: first, the international organization needs to have competence in relation to the subject matter of an international obligation of the state. Second, the Member State needs to have caused the organization to commit an act. The Commission speaks of the necessity of "a significant link between the conduct of the circumventing member State and that of the international organization."[154] Third, the act in question needs to constitute a breach of an international obligation if committed by the state.

e. Acceptance or Causation of Reliance, Article 62 DARIO

The last two cases of responsibility of states mentioned in the DARIO are those of acceptance of responsibility in article 62 (1) lit. (a), and of causation of reliance according to article 62 (1) lit. (b) DARIO.[155]

As provided for in article 62 (1) lit. (a) DARIO, a Member State is also responsible for an internationally wrongful act when it accepts responsibility for it towards the third party, expressly or implicitly, before or after the responsibility arises for the international organization.[156]

In addition, the Member State is responsible when its conduct has led the third party to rely on its responsibility, according to article 62 (1) lit. (b) DARIO. The Commission here lays down a provision which

---

[153] Commentary to article 61, see note 1, para. 2; Commentary to article 17, see note 1, para. 4. The Commission thus decided in favor of a subjective concept – other than in the preliminary version of article 61 DARIO where an objective approach had been pursued. Compare on this E. Paasivirta, "Responsibility of a Member State of an International Organization: Where Will It End?", *International Organizations Law Review* 7 (2010), 49 et seq. (58 et seq.).

[154] Commentary to article 61, see note 1, para. 7.

[155] Article 62 reads: "1. A State member of an international organization is responsible for an internationally wrongful act of that organization if: (a) it has accepted responsibility for that act towards the injured party; or (b) it has led the injured party to rely on its responsibility. 2. Any international responsibility of a State under paragraph 1 is presumed to be subsidiary."

[156] Cf. Commentary to article 62, see note 1, para. 6.

protects the good faith of third parties. Unfortunately, the Commission does not set up the further requirements to determine what constitutes sufficient causation of reliance. If understood widely, this provision could be applied in a way that would undermine the aforementioned decision against a general responsibility of Member States for the acts of an international organization. As stated above, "membership does not as such entail for member States international responsibility when the organization commits an internationally wrongful act."[157]

It will thus be necessary here to draw a line between conduct that solely reflects the exercise of membership on the one hand and the causation of reliance for third parties on the other hand. For this differentiation it will also be necessary to have in mind that Member States will intervene more in the decision-making process of an international organization when they know that they will probably be held responsible for the acts of the international organization.[158] When interpreting article 62 (1) lit. (b) DARIO one can also take into account the basic considerations that underlie article 58 (2) DARIO.[159]

VIII. Critique

The Commission has faced some critique for the DARIO. In the following, the main points of criticism shall be dealt with.

1. Comparing Apples and Oranges I: States vs. International Organizations

One of the main points of criticism raised has been that the ILC does not recognize sufficiently the differences between states and international organizations in the DARIO.[160] Some even found that the

---

[157] Id., see note 1, para. 2.
[158] See Fourth Report of the Special Rapporteur 2006, Doc. A/CN.4/564/Add.2, para. 94 with further references.
[159] The Special Rapporteur mentions in his Fourth Report (see above, para. 93) the relevance of voting behavior of a state for its responsibility. Similar considerations can be made in a situation according to article 58 DARIO.
[160] E.g. J. Wouters/ J. Odermatt, "Are All International Organizations Created Equal? Reflections on the ILC's Draft Articles of Responsibility of Inter-

DARIO have turned out to be only a "find and replace" exercise of the ILC - wherever the word "state" originally appeared it was replaced by the word "international organization."[161]

By equating international organizations to a large extent with states, the ILC has indeed been very progressive at least in some parts, e.g. when it comes to circumstances precluding wrongfulness.[162] However, probably no one would doubt that international organizations have become very powerful actors at the international level. Where functions have been conferred on them, they may act as independent subjects of international law in place of states. When they do so – carrying out tasks that have so far been fulfilled by states – it seems logical to hold them responsible equally for their conduct. It does not seem plausible that a completely different legal regime dealing with the legal consequences of breaches of international law by them should be established.[163]

On the contrary, this would lead to a large fragmentation of international law in that field. In addition, different legal regimes applicable for states on the one hand, and international organizations on the other, could create incentives for states to circumvent international responsibility by using the international legal personality of international organizations when their responsibility regime is shaped more leniently than that of states. *Vice versa*, the importance of international organizations could decrease, when their international responsibility is more encompassing than that of other subjects of international law, especially states.

2. Comparing Apples and Oranges II: The Variety of International Organizations

A second point that has been criticized is that the DARIO do not differentiate between the different kinds of international organizations,

---

national Organizations", *Global Governance Opinions* March 2012, <www.globalgovernancestudies.eu>.

[161] J.E. Alvarez, speech before the Canadian Council on International Law, 27 October 2006, <http://www.asil.org>.

[162] See Section V.

[163] See also Blokker, see note 128, 36.

namely with regard to regional economic integration organizations.[164] Often mentioned here are the problems of attribution that arise e.g. when acts of the EU are implemented by its Member States or in the case of mixed agreements of the EU and its Member States with third states.[165]

The implementation of the law of the EU is primarily carried out by the authorities of its Member States. When the EU is bound by an international obligation but the breach is actually committed through the conduct of Member States, the question is whether this conduct is attributable to the EU. As a reaction to the critique on the insufficient differentiation, the Commission has included a far-reaching *lex specialis* provision in article 64 DARIO. According thereto the DARIO "do not apply where and to the extent that the conditions for the existence of an internationally wrongful act or the content or implementation of the international responsibility of an international organization, or of a State in connection with the conduct of an international organization, are governed by special rules of international law. Such special rules of international law may be contained in the rules of the organization applicable to the relations between an international organization and its members." In the Commentary, the Commission explicitly refers to the problem of attribution in case of implementation as just described and sees this as a situation where special rules apply. With that provision, the Commission opens up the DARIO for a far-reaching differentiation between the various international organizations.

With regard to mixed agreements, whose characteristic is that the EU, its Member States and third states are parties to, it is a matter of controversy who is responsible for what obligation contained in the agreement.[166] The Commission addresses this problem in the Commen-

---

[164] See Paasivirta/ Kuijper, see note 7, 206; especially the European Commission pointed out that the special characteristics of the European Community (now European Union) need to be addressed, Doc. A/C.6/58/SR.14, paras 13 et seq.; Doc. A/CN.4/545, 5; confirmed again in 2011, Doc. A/C.6/66/SR.18, paras 38 et seq.

[165] Cf. S. Talmon, "Responsibility of International Organizations: Does the European Community Require Special Treatment", in: Ragazzi, see note 17, 405 et seq. (408 et seq.); Paasivirta/ Kuijper, see note 7, 184 et seq.

[166] For further details compare M. Möldner, "European Community and Union, Mixed Agreements", in: Max Planck Encyclopedia, see note 6, Vol. III, 854 et seq., paras 32 et seq.

tary to article 48 DARIO.¹⁶⁷ It decides in favor of a joint responsibility of the EU and its Member States when the agreement does not provide for the apportionment of the responsibility between the EU and its Member States,¹⁶⁸ which probably reflects the prevailing view on the issue.¹⁶⁹

3. Putting the Cart before the Horse – The Lack of Primary Rules

Third, it has been criticized that the secondary rules of the DARIO have been framed before even the primary rules have been clearly established.¹⁷⁰ It is certainly true that many primary rules are still controversial, e.g. when it comes to human rights obligations of international organizations. It would probably have been easier to establish the secondary obligations if the primary ones were already further developed. Examples of this again are circumstances precluding wrongfulness, e.g. self-defense, which are closely intertwined with questions of primary norms.¹⁷¹ Nevertheless, certain primary rules already undoubtedly exist, others are emerging.¹⁷² They would be toothless if they did not lead to any consequences. Considered from the perspective of the injured party, it is clearly favorable when generally applicable secondary rules exist.

---

[167] Article 48 reads: "1. Where an international organization and one or more States or other international organizations are responsible for the same internationally wrongful act, the responsibility of each State or organization may be invoked in relation to that act. 2. Subsidiary responsibility may be invoked insofar as the invocation of the primary responsibility has not led to reparation. 3. Paragraphs 1 and 2: (a) do not permit any injured State or international organization to recover, by way of compensation, more than the damage it has suffered; (b) are without prejudice to any right of recourse that the State or international organization providing reparation may have against the other responsible States or international organizations."
[168] Commentary to article 48, see note 1, para. 1.
[169] Cf. Möldner, see note 166, paras 32 et seq.
[170] Alvarez, see not 161, 12.
[171] See Section V.
[172] E.g. C.F. Amerasinghe, *Principles of the Institutional Law of International Organizations*, 2005, 400 et seq.

4. The DARIO as a Dry Run – The Lack of Practice

Fourth, it has been said that, whereas the ASR were based on the practice of states, the necessary practice is missing with regard to the DARIO.[173] The ILC confirms this by stating in the General Commentary to the DARIO that "[t]he fact that several of the present draft articles are based on limited practice moves the border between codification and progressive development in the direction of the latter."[174] However, this does not necessarily need to be seen as a negative aspect. The ILC has the mandate for both the codification and the progressive development of international law according to article 13 (1) lit. (a) UN Charter and article 1 (1) ILC Statute.[175] A predominance of progressive development by the Commission can also be seen positively as the mere codification may bear a risk of writing down only the past and thus impeding further developments of the rules.[176] Here, the progressive development of the rules seems to lead to an improvement of the position of injured parties, and to enhanced accountability of the injuring parties, which should be welcomed. Given the current, deficient situation of possibilities of legal redress, we probably could have waited for more than 45 years (which were needed for the work on the ASR to be concluded) if we had waited for an extensive practice to emerge. Such an extension of the working period of the ILC would then, without doubt, have led to further criticism.

IX. Final Remarks

Even though there may be some vagueness with regard to particular articles, the general approach of the Commission, to create a coherent system of responsibility for states and international organizations, should be supported. Responsibility as established here can serve as an

---

[173] J.E. Alvarez, "Memo to the State Department Advisory Committee: ILC's Draft Articles on the Responsibility of International Organizations", Meeting of June 21, 2010, <http://www.law.nyu.edu>.
[174] General Commentary to the DARIO, see note 1, para. 5.
[175] Article 1 (1) ILC Statute reads: "The International Law Commission shall have for its object the promotion of the progressive development of international law and its codification."
[176] Sir A. Watts, "Codification and Progressive Development of International Law", in: Max Planck Encyclopedia, see note 6, Vol. II, 282 et seq., para. 19.

important aspect of enhanced accountability of international organizations. Throughout the articles, the Commission repeatedly referred to general principles underlying the DARIO that would also be applicable to other subjects of international law committing an internationally wrongful act. This may open the door for the establishment of further, equally structured international responsibility regimes in the future. A drawback of the approach taken by the Commission is that it did not go further when it came to the rights of individuals. These were already limited in the ASR and are now equally limited in the DARIO, as the consequences of breaches with regard to individuals are not covered by the DARIO and individuals cannot invoke responsibility on their own.

The Commission has not only substantially but also procedurally pursued the same approach with the DARIO as with regard to the ASR, by recommending to the General Assembly to take note of the DARIO in a resolution, to annex them to the resolution, and to consider, at a later stage, the elaboration of a convention on the basis of the draft articles. This approach has proved very successful with regard to the ASR. They have become widely accepted in practice and in academia. The regime of state responsibility is of course older than that of responsibility of international organizations, and courts as well as the Commission have grappled with the former for a long period of time and thus have had time to develop it. The DARIO on the other hand are young, and still rather in their teenage stage of development. They can be given more time now to evolve in practice. As DARIO's older, adult sibling, the ASR has turned out so well, it can at least be hoped for the younger brother to turn out equally well - and thus become the Super-DARIO. What should, however, be developed now, out of its rather embryonic stage, are the remedies available to claim the responsibility of an international organization.

The Waters of Euphrates and Tigris: An International Law Perspective

A Study by Adele J. Kirschner and Katrin Tiroch[*]

---

[*] This Study was written as part of the MPIL Global Knowledge Transfer project on "Water Conflicts in International Law" financed by the German Ministry of Foreign Affairs, see <www.mpil.de/red/water>.
The authors would like to thank Prof. Dr. Dr. h.c. Rüdiger Wolfrum, Prof. Dr. Ulrich Beyerlin and Dr. Tilmann Röder for their invaluable comments on the article. Special thanks also go to Nicolas Bremer, Jie-Yoon Kim and David Reichwein for their kind assistance.

I.   Introduction
II.   Geography, Climate and Hydrological Setting
      1. Geography
         a. The Euphrates
         b. The Tigris
      2. Climate
      3. Hydrological Setting
III. Utilization of the Rivers and Development Plans
      1. Iraq
      2. Syria
      3. Turkey
      4. Conclusion
IV.   Historical Overview on Water Politics in the Euphrates and Tigris Region
      1. Developments before World War II
      2. Developments after World War II
V.   International Law in the Euphrates and Tigris Region
      1. International Water Law
         a. Introduction
         b. Equitable and Reasonable Utilization of an International Watercourse
         c. Obligation not to Cause Harm
         d. Procedural Obligations
         e. Environmental Protection
         f. Groundwater
         g. Vital Human Needs
         h. Water Principles in Islamic Law
      2. Bilateral Agreements
         a. Water Sharing Agreements before the 1990s
            aa. Turkey and Iraq
            bb. Syria and Turkey
            cc. Iraq and Syria
         b. Developments after 2000
VI.   Contentious Issues
      1. Euphrates and Tigris: Two Separate Rivers or One Integrated System?
      2. Terminology
      3. Different Ideas about Criteria to Determine Water Needs
      4. Turkish Position with Regard to the 1997 UN Watercourses Convention: Turkey as Persistent Objector to Customary International Law?
VII. Proposed Solutions
      1. Syria and Iraq
      2. Turkey
         a. Three Stages Plan for Optimum, Equitable and Reasonable Utilization of the Transboundary Watercourse of the Euphrates Basin (Three Stages Plan)
         b. The Peace Pipeline
VIII. Elements to be Considered for a Future Framework

1. Why do Iraq, Syria and Turkey Need a Trilateral Water Agreement?
   2. Elements to be Considered in a Trilateral Agreement
      a. General Remarks on Issues Essential for a Successful and Above All Sustainable Water Agreement
      b. Key Components
IX. Conclusion

Abstract

Competition over the scant resource water has been a recurring source of conflict between Iraq, Syria and Turkey, all three being riparian states of the Euphrates and Tigris Rivers. Despite several attempts at a common management of both watercourses, negotiations have not yet led to a final agreement. However, an equitable and sustainable allocation of this natural resource among the different countries would prove beneficial to all.

This article examines the relations between Iraq, Syria and Turkey with regard to their shared rivers, the Euphrates and the Tigris, from an international law perspective. It starts by giving an overview of the utilization and development of the rivers and a history of the water dispute. The authors then analyze the relevant law applicable in the region from a global and regional perspective and present the conflicting positions of the riparians by describing the underlying problems of the conflict. Then different solutions which have been proposed by the riparians are evaluated. Finally, the authors propose elements to be considered in a future sharing agreement, and give a short conclusion.

Keywords

International Water Law; Euphrates and Tigris Rivers; International Watercourses; Equitable Utilization of Shared Resources

I. Introduction

Water is a scant resource. Although water covers about two thirds of the earth's surface only about three per cent of this water is fresh water. In turn, the majority of this water is hardly accessible and distributed unequally. Whereas some regions have abundant water resources, others suffer from extreme scarcity. In light of growing water consumption and a steadily increasing world population, water is becoming ever more important and has an ever greater significance.

The question of water distribution and use is also of utmost importance for the Euphrates and Tigris region which has been struggling with water scarcity along with an increasing water demand for a long time. Competition over this scant resource has been a recurring source of conflict between the main riparian states Iraq, Syria and Turkey. Despite several attempts at a common management of both watercourses, negotiations have not yet led to a final agreement. However, an equitable and sustainable allocation of this natural resource among the different countries would prove beneficial to all.

This article examines the relations between Iraq, Syria and Turkey with regard to their shared rivers, the Euphrates and the Tigris, from an international law perspective. It commences with a short overview on the geography, climate and hydrological setting (II.), as well as on the utilization and development of the rivers (III.). The subsequent parts then focus on the history of the water dispute (IV.) and an analysis of the relevant law on a global and regional level (V.). Against this background the article then discusses the conflicting positions of the riparians by describing the underlying problems of the conflict (VI.). Finally different solutions which have been proposed by the riparians will be evaluated (VII.). The authors then conclude with a proposal for elements to be considered in a future sharing agreement (VIII.) and by giving a short conclusion (IX.).

II. Geography, Climate and Hydrological Setting

The following section will give a brief overview of the physical setting of the rivers Euphrates and Tigris. This includes the geography, climate and hydrology of the region. The consideration of the rivers' physical characteristics is a prerequisite for understanding the setting in which the riparian states operate.

1. Geography

The two rivers both originate in the mountainous region of southern Anatolia in eastern Turkey, with their sources lying barely 30 kilometers apart. The drainage basin[1] of the Euphrates is said to lie 28 per cent

---

[1] A drainage basin (also called catchment; catchment area; drainage area; river basin; watershed) is regarded as the entire drainage area of a stream, a

in Turkey, 17 per cent in Syria, 40 per cent in Iraq and 15 per cent in Saudi Arabia.[2] The Tigris drainage basin is described to stretch into Turkey (12 per cent), Syria (0.2 per cent), Iraq (54 per cent) and Iran (34 per cent). Although Saudi Arabia and Iran are frequently listed as drainage basin states,[3] they are usually not included in studies of the basin. This is due to the fact that the Saudi Arabian tributary is said to dry up in summer months and Iran has so far not made much use of the waters of the Tigris due to the difficult geographic and climatic conditions of the region.[4] Even though the Euphrates and the Tigris flow separately for the largest part, they are commonly considered together in studies.[5] Both rivers merge in their last 190 kilometers, forming the Shatt al-Arab[6] before flowing into the Persian Gulf. They are also connected by the man-made *Thartar* Canal in central Iraq.

a. The Euphrates

The Euphrates is noted to be between approximately 2,700 and 3,000 kilometers long, making it the longest river in southwest Asia west of

---

river or a lake; UNESCO/ WMO, *International Glossary of Hydrology*, see under <http://webworld.unesco.org> EN 0360, EN 0115.

[2] T. Naff/ R.C. Matson, *Water in the Middle East: Conflict or Cooperation?*, 1984, 83.

[3] See for example J.A. Allan, *The Middle East Water Question: Hydropolitics and the Global Economy*, 2008, 70 et seq.; Naff/ Matson, see note 2, 83.

[4] Reportedly Iran is, however, planning or has even already constructed several dams on tributaries of the Tigris and the Shatt al-Arab. Yet, current information regarding development plans in Iran is very hard to obtain; see I. Kaya, "The Euphrates-Tigris Basin: An Overview and Opportunities for Cooperation under International Law", *University of Arizona Arid Lands Newsletter* 44 (1998), see under <http://ag.arizona.edu>; S. Harms, *Branchenreport Wasser, Wirtschaftsplattform Irak 2010*, Chapter 3, see under <http://www.wp-irak.de>.

[5] Some authors even claim that both rivers form a single hydrological unit; see A. Kibaroglu, *Building a Regime for the Waters of the Euphrates-Tigris River Basin*, 2002, 160; N. Kliot, *Water Resources and Conflict in the Middle East*, 2005, 100; H. Elver, *Peaceful Uses of International Rivers: The Euphrates and Tigris Dispute*, 2002, 346. On this issue see under VI.1.

[6] On this issue, see R. Moschtaghi, "Shatt al Arab", in: R. Wolfrum (ed.), *Max Planck Encyclopedia of Public International Law*, 2012; D.A. Caponera, "The Legal Status of the Shatt-al-Arab (Tigris and Euphrates) River Basin", *Austrian J. Publ. Int'l Law* 45 (1993), 147 et seq.

the Indus.⁷ After the two rivers Kara-Su and Murat Su flow together in eastern Turkey to form the Euphrates, the river enters northwestern Syria before flowing down the length of Iraq on its way to the sea. While the drainage basin of the Euphrates is shared by five states, only two states significantly contribute to its water supply.⁸ The Euphrates receives most of its waters from Turkey supplying it with 88 per cent of the river's flow.⁹ While Syria contributes an additional 11 per cent, the remaining riparian Iraq hardly contributes to the water volume.¹⁰

b. The Tigris

The Tigris also flows southwards from Turkey, forming for a short distance the Turkish-Syrian border and later the Iraqi-Syrian border. It then flows down the length of Iraq, eventually joining the Euphrates near Qurna. The Tigris is measured to be approximately 1,840 km long.¹¹ Like the Euphrates it receives most of its water from Turkey (51 per cent), with Iraq and Iran respectively contributing 39 per cent and 10 per cent of the annual water volume.¹²

2. Climate

The Euphrates and the Tigris lie in a transition zone between humid continental and desert climates.¹³ The climate in south eastern Turkey, where the headwaters of both rivers flow, is generally characterized by wet winters and dry summers.¹⁴ The climate changes as the rivers flow south first through Syria and then through Iraq. Parts of Syria and the most of Iraq experience an arid climate with little precipitation.¹⁵

---

[7] See for example: J.F. Kolars/ W.A. Mitchell, *The Euphrates River and the Southeast Anatolia Development Project*, 1991, 3; Allan, see note 3, 70; Kibaroglu, see note 5, 162.
[8] Kaya, see note 4.
[9] Naff/ Matson, see note 2, 83 et seq.
[10] Ibid., 84.
[11] Kolars/ Mitchell, see note 7, 6; Kibaroglu, see note 5, 162.
[12] Allan, see note 3, 70.
[13] F.M. Lorenz/ E.J. Erickson, *The Euphrates Triangle: Security Implications of the Southeastern Anatolia Project*, 1999, 3.
[14] Kliot, see note 5, 104 et seq.
[15] Ibid.

Alongside the aridity the mean temperatures especially in summer are extremely high[16] resulting in a high water loss due to evaporation.[17]

3. Hydrological Setting

Both rivers receive most of their water from rainfall and melting snow in the mountains of southern Turkey.[18] Equally their flow varies greatly from season to season and from year to year.[19] This is not only due to climatic impacts such as for example water loss through evaporation, but also to years of rapid water use development disrupting the natural flow of the rivers. Scientists have, however, been able to identify three different flow seasons: the period of high discharge (March to June), the period of low discharge (July to October) and the period of average discharge (November to February).[20] The irregularity within the rivers' flow accompanied by an erratic documentation of stream flow data makes it difficult to determine the mean annual discharge of both rivers resulting in a great variation of available data.[21] Estimates roughly lie around 31,820 million cubic meters per year for the Euphrates and 42,230 million cubic meters per year for the Tigris.[22]

III. Utilization of the Rivers and Development Plans

Both rivers are characterized by a high level of competition over water by their co-riparians. This is especially reflected in the lack of coordination with regard to the development of water utilization projects which are outlined below.

---

[16] The mean average temperature in Iraq during the summer is said to lie at 30 degree Celsius; Kliot, see note 5, 108.

[17] Ibid.

[18] M.L. Kavvas et al., "A Study of Water Balances over the Euphrates-Tigris Watershed", *Physics and Chemistry of the Earth* 36 (2011), 197 et seq. (198).

[19] A. Kibaroglu et al., *Cooperation on Turkey's Transboundary Waters, Status Report commissioned by the German Federal Ministry for Environment, Nature Conservation and Nuclear Safety*, 2005, 57; FAO, "Irrigation of the Middle East Region in Figures", *Aquastat Water Reports* 34 (2009), 359.

[20] Kliot, see note 5, 109 et seq.; Naff/ Matson, see note 2, 86.

[21] Kliot, see note 5, 108 et seq.

[22] Naff/ Matson, see note 2, 86 et seq.

1. Iraq

Historically Iraq has been the principal user of the Euphrates and Tigris waters,[23] starting with the very beginnings of agricultural development in Mesopotamia in approximately 4000 B.C.[24] Consequently it is not surprising that Iraq was also the first state to begin utilizing the waters of the Euphrates and the Tigris in modern times by constructing new water works on the rivers.[25] In 1913 Iraq had finished the construction of the *al-Hindiya* Barrage which made it possible to divert water from the Euphrates into renewed irrigation canals, some of them dating from ancient times.[26]

With economic development, population growth and urbanization, the demand for water and water uses steadily increased. Iraq was especially keen to bring more land under irrigation. In the coming years it thus spent heavily on its hydrological infrastructure and built several other dams along both rivers.[27] Their main purposes were flood control, water diversion to irrigation canals and later also hydroelectric power production.[28] These investments were, however, also largely motivated by a fear of losing water, especially that of the Euphrates, through upstream development projects in Syria and Turkey, rather than by the country's actual needs.[29] It is against this background that Iraq constructed the *Tharthar* Canal north of Baghdad. As mentioned previously it links the Tigris to the Euphrates through the *Tharthar* Valley depression. This allows Iraq to transfer water in large quantities from the Tigris to the Euphrates, thereby controlling the flood flow of the Tigris, but also compensating possible shortfalls in the Euphrates

---

[23] Y. Lupu, "International Law and the Waters of the Euphrates and Tigris", *Geo. Int'l Envtl L. Rev.* 14 (2001-2002), 349 et seq. (350).
[24] Hilal, see note 5, 337.
[25] Naff/ Matson, see note 2, 89; Kliot, see note 5, 117.
[26] Kibaroglu, see note 5, 169.
[27] For an overview of barrages, regulators and lakes on the Euphrates and the Tigris in Iraq, cf. Kliot, see note 5, 118 et seq.
[28] Ibid., 143 et seq.; generation of hydroelectric power currently accounts for about 17 per cent of electric energy production in Iraq, cf. FAO, see note 19, 205.
[29] M. Biedler, "Hydropolitics of the Tigris – Euphrates River Basin with Implications for the European Union", *Centre Européen de Recherche Internationale et Stratégique: Research Paper* No. 1 (2004), 17 et seq.

basin.³⁰ As in most arid countries the agricultural sector is the biggest water consumer.³¹ Although it only adds 5 per cent in value to Iraq's GDP water withdrawal from this sector is estimated to lie at 79 per cent.³² Moreover, owing to outdated and ineffective water delivery systems much of this water is unfortunately not used efficiently.³³ According to most predictions water withdrawals in all sectors will increase and demands are soon expected to exceed Iraq's water supplies.³⁴

2. Syria

Syria's economy is largely dependent on agriculture and food security, this has always been among the highest priorities of government agenda,³⁵ thus the water in the Syrian part of the Euphrates basin is mainly used for irrigational purposes.³⁶ Although industrial and domestic uses take up only a small part of the total water resources consumption, pressure on water resources from these sectors is steadily increasing.³⁷

Syria did not really start developing the use of the Euphrates and the Tigris waters before the 1960s.³⁸ The first major project was the construction of the *Tabqa* Dam or *al-Thawtah* Dam on the Euphrates,

---

30   Kliot, see note 5, 120; Naff/ Matson, see note 2, 92.
31   FAO, see note 19, 205.
32   Ibid., 201.
33   N. Al-Mamouri, in: Harms, see note 4, Chapter 6; large parts of the water infrastructure were also severely damaged or even destroyed by the wars in 1991 and 2003; J.M. Trondalen, *Water and Peace for the People: Possible Solutions to Water Disputes in the Middle East*, 2008, 182.
34   See for example, Kliot, see note 5, 146; FAO, see note 19, 212 et seq.
35   M. Bazza/R. Najib, "Towards Improved Water Demand Management in Agriculture in the Syrian Arab Republic", paper presented on the First National Symposium on Management and Rationalization of Water Resources Use in Agriculture organized by the University of Damascus, Damascus, Arab Republic of Syria, 28-29 April 2003, 5, see under <ftp://ftp.fao.org/docrep/fao>.
36   Cf. FAO, see note 19, 344.
37   Cf. M. Salman, "Institutional Reform for Irrigation and Drainage in Syria: Diagnosis of Key Elements", in: FAO, *Syrian Expatriates Conference*, 2004, 1, see under <ftp://ftp.fao.org>.
38   Allan, see note 3, 72.

which is considered to be the largest dam in Syria.[39] The filling of the *Tabqa* Dam in 1974/1975 led to serious tensions with Syria's downstream neighbor Iraq since it caused a remarkable decrease in downstream flow.[40] With a special focus on expanding the country's irrigated area Syria has since been steadily increasing the development of its water uses.[41] As of 2008, 165 dams could be counted along its rivers. Yet the Euphrates is said to have currently 4 dams only.[42] Nevertheless it accounts for the major share of the country's water use.[43] Compared to the Euphrates the Tigris does not appear to play a big role in Syria's water development scheme. This may be because it only runs along a short stretch of the eastern Syrian border to Turkey.[44] However, according to Allan, Syria has recently conducted technical studies for an irrigation project using Tigris water.[45]

3. Turkey

Turkey began to develop plans to utilize the Euphrates at about the same time as Syria.[46] The main object of this development scheme was the exploitation of the rivers' energy potential.[47] Unlike Syria and Iraq, Turkey is not that heavily dependent on water for irrigation since it can also rely on natural precipitation.[48] In fact the development of hydroelectric energy has been given priority over other uses.[49] The first dam Turkey built on the Euphrates was the *Keban* Dam which was solely intended to generate hydroelectric power.[50] It was completed in 1973

---

[39] The *Tabqa* Dam forms the *Al Assad* Lake which has a storage capacity of 14.1 km³ and a total surface area of 674 km². It was constructed with financial and technical assistance of the Soviet Union and completed in 1973 (FAO, see note 19, 343).
[40] Naff/ Matson, see note 2, 90; see also under IV. 2.
[41] Trondalen, see note 33, 180.
[42] FAO, see note 19, 344.
[43] Salman, see note 37, 1.
[44] Biedler, see note 29, 15.
[45] Allan, see note 3, 72.
[46] Naff/ Matson, see note 2, 91.
[47] Biedler, see note 29, 10 et seq.
[48] Ibid., 10.
[49] Trondalen, see note 33, 180.
[50] Naff/ Matson, see note 2, 91.

and was by chance filled at about the same time as the *Tabqa* Dam in Syria. Unfortunately the filling of both dams also coincided with an extremely dry year leading to a severe water shortage downstream in Iraq.[51] The construction of the *Keban* Dam marked the beginning of a grand Turkish development scheme for the Euphrates and Tigris rivers.[52] In the 1980s it officially launched the *Güneydoğu Anadolu Projesi*[53] (GAP), a major multi-sector regional development project within the Turkish portions of the Euphrates and the Tigris basin, to develop the land and water resources in the region.[54] The project was originally scheduled to be completed in 2010,[55] however, in 2008 the Turkish government presented a new action plan postponing this target to 2012.[56]

4. Conclusion

When comparing the various uses of the Euphrates and the Tigris rivers by their riparian states it is striking that all three states have planned and implemented big development projects but little effort has been

---

[51] J.F. Kolars, "Problems of International River Management: The Case of the Euphrates", in: A.K. Biswas (ed.), *International Waters of the Middle East: From Euphrates-Tigris to Nile*, 1994, 44 et seq. (49); see also under IV. 2.

[52] Cf. Kibaroglu, see note 5, 223; according to Kibaroglu although the *Keban* Dam is not officially part of the South-East Anatolia Project it is an integral part of Turkey's overall development scheme.

[53] Turkish for Southeast Anatolia Project.

[54] It consists of major irrigation and hydropower schemes encompassing 22 dams, 19 hydroelectric power plants and irrigation systems that shall bring 1.7 million hectares of land under irrigation (GAP Program for the Development of Land and Water Resources, see under <http://www.gap.gov.tr>). The heart of the GAP and also the largest dam in Turkey is the *Atatürk* Dam on the Euphrates near Adiyaman (J.F. Kolars, "The Hydro-Imperative of Turkey's Search for Energy", *Middle East Journal* 40 (1986), 53 et seq. (63)). It has a storage capacity of 48.7 million cubic meters and is considered one of the largest dams in the world (Kolars/ Mitchell, see note 7, 38).

[55] Latest Point Reached in GAP, see under <http://www.gap.gov.tr>.

[56] Southeastern Anatolia Project Action Plan (2008-2012), May 2008, see under <http://includes.gap.gov.tr/files/ek-dosyalar_en/gap-action-plan/gap-action-plan.pdf>. According to a report on the latest situation of GAP activities at least the project in large shall be completed by 2012, Güneydoğu Anadolu Projesi son Durum (2010), 7.

made to coordinate these schemes.⁵⁷ All three states have, for example, developed immense water storage capacities over the years which have only fostered the individual accumulation of water rather than an attitude of sharing. Moreover, it also seems very questionable that the rivers' flow is large enough to actually fill these reservoirs.⁵⁸ It is thus no surprise that all this has led to ineffective and inefficient demand management practices and may be considered as one of the main factors influencing the water imbalance in the region.⁵⁹

IV. Historical Overview on Water Politics in the Euphrates and Tigris Region

1. Developments before World War II

Mesopotamia with its two great rivers the Euphrates and the Tigris is often described as the "cradle of civilization" as it gave rise to one of the earliest great cultures in history.⁶⁰ Yet, already in ancient times there was conflict over shared water resources. The two Mesopotamian city states of *Umma* and *Lagash* fought over water supplies more than 5000 years ago. However, these city states are also known for concluding the earliest recorded agreement to settle their disputes.⁶¹

From the 16th century to 1918 the entire Euphrates basin and most of the Tigris basin were part of the Ottoman Empire. Some treaties were concluded with Persia over the Tigris. These, however, mainly concerned boundaries or navigational issues and not water management or consumption.⁶² The origin of current state borders within the Eu-

---

57 Naff/ Matson, see note 2, 89.
58 Kliot, see note 5, 122.
59 Naff/ Matson, see note 2, 89.
60 G. Pring/ B. Salman Banaei, "Tigris and Euphrates Rivers", in: Wolfrum, see note 6, para. 11.
61 S.C. McCaffrey, *The Law of International Watercourses*, 2007, 59-60.
62 R.A. Lien, "Still Thirsting: Prospects for a Multilateral Treaty on the Euphrates and Tigris Rivers Following the Adoption of the United Nations Convention on International Watercourses", *B. U. Int'l L. J.* 16 (1998), 273 et seq. (278-279); J.W. Dellapenna, "The Two Rivers and the Lands Between: Mesopotamia and the International Law of Transboundary Waters", *Brigham Young University Journal of Public Law* 10 (1996), 213 et seq. (236).

phrates and the Tigris region lies in the redrawing of the political map after World War I. The pertinent area was divided between three states: France, the United Kingdom and Turkey. Iraq was attributed to the United Kingdom and Syria to France, both of which constituted so-called 'A' mandates according to article 22 Covenant of the League of Nations.[63] The remaining part was left to Turkey.[64] During this time some agreements including provisions, although mostly not very specific ones, on the use of both the Euphrates and the Tigris were concluded between the respective powers. These will shortly be described in the following.

1920: The Franco-British Convention

In 1920 France and the United Kingdom agreed on certain issues in connection with their mandates for Syria, the Lebanon, Palestine and Mesopotamia, such as boundary location and the joint use of a railway.[65] The treaty also referred to the utilization of the Euphrates and the Tigris rivers in its article 3 which provided for the formation of a commission. This commission was to review any Syrian irrigation plan that could affect the amount of water flowing into the area of the British mandate.[66]

---

[63] Covenant of the League of Nations 225 CTS 195; for further information on the topic, see: R. Gordon, "Mandates", in: Wolfrum, see note 6.

[64] For more detailed information on the breakup of the Ottoman Empire, please see e.g. H.N. Howard, *The Partition of Turkey: A Diplomatic History 1913-1923*, 1931.

[65] Franco-British Convention on Certain Points Connected with the Mandates for Syria, the Lebanon, Palestine and Mesopotamia (signed 23 December 1920), LNTS Vol. 22 No. 564.

[66] Article 3 Franco-British Convention on Certain Points Connected with the Mandates for Syria, the Lebanon, Palestine and Mesopotamia (see note 65) reads as follows: "The British and French Governments shall come to an agreement regarding the nomination of a commission, whose duty it will be to make a preliminary examination of any plan of irrigation formed by the Government of the French mandatory territory, the execution of which would be of a nature to diminish in any considerable degree the waters of the Tigris and Euphrates at the point where they enter the area of the British mandate in Mesopotamia."

1923: Lausanne Peace Treaty

The Lausanne Peace Treaty between Turkey and the Allies of 1923[67] only contained limited references to the management of shared water resources. Article 109 required that,

> "In default of any provisions to the contrary, when as the result of the fixing of a new frontier the hydraulic system (canalization, inundation, irrigation, drainage or similar matters) in a State is dependent on works executed within the territory of another State, or when use is made on the territory of a State, in virtue of pre-war usage, of water or hydraulic power, the source of which is on the territory of another State, an agreement shall be made between the States concerned to safeguard the interests and rights acquired by each of them. Failing an agreement, the matter shall be regulated by arbitration."[68]

1921 - 1930: Agreements between France and Turkey[69]

Between 1921 and 1930 France and Turkey entered into various agreements, some of which also contained provisions on the use of the Euphrates and the Tigris. The first pertinent provision can be found in a peace agreement concluded between the Former Minister of the French Republic and the Minister for Foreign Affairs of the Government of the Grand National Assembly of Angora of 1921[70] (hereinafter referred to as Angora Agreement),[71] which formally put an end to the state of war between the two states (article I).[72] Article XII of the Angora Agreement concerned the distribution and removal of water. It laid down the

---

[67] Treaty of Peace with Turkey, with related Documents (signed 24 July 1923), LNTS Vol. 28 No. 701.
[68] Article 109 Treaty of Peace with Turkey, ibid.
[69] Some authors also mention an agreement between Iraq and Turkey from 1930. Reportedly the two states pledged not to alter the course of the Euphrates river without each others' consent. Unfortunately the authors of this study were unable to obtain the mentioned document; Lupu, see note 23, 354-355, who, however, again refers to the article of Dellapenna, see note 62, 238.
[70] Agreement with a View to Promoting Peace, with Protocol relating thereto, Protocol concerning its coming into force, and Exchange of Notes (signed 20 October 1921, entered into force 28 October 1921), LNTS Vol. 54 No. 1284.
[71] Ankara was previously called Angora.
[72] Article I Agreement with a View to Promoting Peace, see note 70.

obligation to equitably utilize and share the Kuveik river between the Syrian city Aleppo and the Turkish district to the north.[73] It was assumed that the communities themselves were best suited to establish an equitable method of sharing the Kuveik waters.[74] The same article also addressed Aleppo's right to tap Euphrates waters for supply to satisfy the needs of the district. Thereby it even authorized Aleppo to organize, if necessary, its water supply from the Euphrates in Turkish territory. This, however, was to be done at the city's own expense. Further or more specific requirements for the utilization of this water were not laid down.

Another treaty was concluded in 1926 to strengthen cooperation and friendship between France and Turkey.[75] It again addressed the topic of water supply for Aleppo from the Kuveik and the Euphrates, yet again without further specifying this.[76] In addition to the two agreements, the Final Protocol of the Commission on the Delimitation of the Turkish-Syrian Frontier (1930)[77] mentions the Tigris river. This Commission had previously been established according to the Angora Agreement in order to delimit the border between the two neighboring states. Article II ascertains that the vicinity of the two states imposes particular obligations on the riparians requiring an agreement on their reciprocal rights. All issues concerning the Tigris – the treaty lists navigation, fishing, industrial and agricultural uses or river police – were to be determined on the basis of complete equality.[78]

In conclusion, one can observe that only sparse attention was paid to the utilization of the Euphrates and the Tigris rivers before World War II. This reflects the fact that the rivers were not much used by Tur-

---

[73] The Kuveik river flows from Turkey to northwestern Syria.
[74] Agreement with a View to Promoting Peace, see note 70, Exchange of Notes VIII.
[75] Convention of Friendship and Good-Neighbourly Relations between France and Turkey (signed 30 May 1926), LNTS Vol. 54 No. 1285.
[76] Article XIII Convention of Friendship and Good-Neighbourly Relations, see note 75.
[77] Protocole final d'abornement de la commission d'abornement de la frontière turco-syrienne agissant conformément au traité d'Angora du 20 octobre 1921, à la convention d'amitié et de bon voisinage du 30 Mai 1926 et au Protocole d'abornement du 22 Juin 1929 (signed 3 May 1930), Doc. ST/LEG/SER.B/12, 290.
[78] Article II Protocole final d'abornement, see note 77.

key and Syria at that time.⁷⁹ It is, however, interesting to note that some agreements indicate an acceptance of the principles of fair and equitable utilization of a shared water resource.⁸⁰ This is in particular the case with the Angora Agreement which contained (at the time) progressive stipulations with regard to equitable sharing of the Kuveik river.

2. Developments after World War II

After World War II Iraq and Syria had in the meantime both gained independence. In 1946 Iraq and Turkey concluded a comprehensive agreement which aimed at strengthening the neighborly cooperation between the two states.⁸¹ Protocol No.1 referred to the regulation and development of the waters of the Tigris and the Euphrates and of their tributaries. It included quite far-reaching rights and obligations in the interests of both parties, which will be discussed in detail below.⁸² However, Protocol No.1 was never implemented.

In the following decades water issues more and more came to the fore. Conflicts arose in particular when Turkey and Syria began to claim a larger share of their common water resources (mostly the Euphrates) and announced ambitious energy and irrigation projects. This coincided with Iraq expanding its development plans.⁸³ Since the 1960s the situation has been characterized by various crisis situations as a result of the three riparian states acting unilaterally. Yet, the period has also brought about bilateral and trilateral consultations and meetings. So far, these, however, were not very successful and produced few results.⁸⁴ Generally, one should note that there is scarce official information about these talks as the riparian states wanted to keep them off the

---

79 See Part III.; see also Dellapenna, see note 62, 237.
80 Lien, see note 62, 285; see article 12 Agreement with a View to Promoting Peace, see note 70; article II Protocole final d'abornement, see note 77; on the principle of equitable and reasonable utilization, see under V. 1. b.
81 Treaty of Friendship and Neighbourly Relations between Iraq and Turkey (signed 29 March 1946, it came into force 10 May 1948), UNTS Vol. 37 No. 580.
82 See under V. 2. a.
83 A. Kibaroglu, "Socioeconomic Development and Benefit Sharing in the Euphrates-Tigris River Basin", in: H. Shuval/ H. Dweik (eds), *Water Resources in the Middle East: Israeli-Palestinian Water Issues – From Conflict to Cooperation*, 2007, 185 et seq. (185).
84 Dellapenna, see note 62, 238.

records.⁸⁵ Moreover, the documentation found in literature, although in general consistent, varies in its details and sometimes is even contradictory. Nevertheless, one can distinguish certain developments and agreements which will be described in the following.

In the mid 1960s, the main topic of discussion concerned the building and impounding of the *Keban* (Turkey) and *Tabqa* (Syria) Dams, alongside with the *Haditha* Dam in Iraq, all situated on the Euphrates. The construction of the *Keban* Dam was supported by international donors, like the United States Aid for Development, reportedly pushing for conditions for the protection of downstream states. Accordingly Turkey agreed to ensure a minimal discharge of 350 m³/sec downstream of the dam. Prerequisite, however, was that the natural flow of the river made such a supply possible.⁸⁶

In 1965, a first round of tripartite negotiations commenced. The meetings were primarily of a technical nature and concerned updates on works, the exchange of data and other technical information on various dams.⁸⁷ It is noted that during these meetings, in order to have bargaining advantages, each country brought forward a maximum of demands on Euphrates waters: Iraq 14 billion cubic meters, Syria 13 billion cubic meters, Turkey 18 billion cubic meters. However, all demands taken together would have by far exceeded the annual yield of the river.⁸⁸ At the time the formation of a Joint Technical Committee (hereinafter referred to as JTC) was also discussed or possibly even implemented.⁸⁹ This does not become entirely clear from literature, at least apparently the parties held some kind of technical meetings in this period. Iraq even pushed for a permanent JTC to supervise a future water sharing agreement but this was rejected by Turkey. There was also disagreement over the functions the JTC should exercise,⁹⁰ as well as the scope of its jurisdiction (whether it should be limited to the Euphrates or also include the Tigris).⁹¹

---

85 R.M. Slim, "Turkey, Syria, Iraq: The Euphrates", in: G.O. Faure/ J.Z. Rubin (eds), *Culture and Negotiation*, 1993, 135 et seq. (139).
86 Kibaroglu, see note 5, 223.
87 Ibid., 224.
88 J. Waterbury, "Transboundary Water and the Challenge of Cooperation in the Middle East", in: P. Roger/ P. Lydon (eds), *Water in the Arab World: Perspectives and Prognoses*, 1994, 39 et seq. (56).
89 Cf. Kibaroglu, see note 5, 223-225; Elver, see note 5, 405.
90 Kibaroglu et al., see note 19, 61.
91 Kibaroglu, see note 5, 224; Elver, see note 5, 406.

Subsequently, Syria and Iraq held several bilateral meetings on technical matters concerning the distribution of Euphrates waters. Syria strongly opposed Iraq's position of having "established uses" or "acquired rights" during the negotiations and continued with the construction of the *Tabqa* Dam.[92] However, reportedly Syria informally accepted that Iraq was entitled to 59 per cent of the Euphrates water flow in normal years.[93]

In the 1970s delegations of the riparian states started meeting again trilaterally. The JTC was (re-)activated, yet only on an *ad hoc* basis. The main issue discussed still concerned the impounding of the *Keban* and *Tabqa* Dams. However, a water rights agreement as well as an agreement over a joint procedure for filling the two upstream dams without causing harm downstream once again was not reached. Eventually both the *Keban* and the *Tabqa* Dams were filled unilaterally within a year between 1974 and 1975.[94]

The almost simultaneous filling of the two dams in combination with the fact that 1974 constituted a particularly dry year, led to a serious crisis between Iraq and Syria,[95] since Iraq was already suffering from a severe water shortage. In addition, all this happened in the context of an already tense political environment with disagreements between the Ba'th parties of both states.[96] In 1974 the conflict still could be averted. Syria consented to slow down the impounding of the *Tabqa* Dam and to provide for additional amounts of Euphrates waters (200 million m³/year) to be released.[97] Yet, in 1975, the second season of filling the *Keban* and *Tabqa* Dams, the crisis broke out again. The relationship between the two states severed and resulted in mutual accusations. Iraq claimed that the water flow from the Euphrates had dropped tremendously, the normal flow of 920m³/sec having gone down to 197m³/sec. Syria, on the other hand, put the blame on Turkey. It maintained that only half of the previously normal flow had reached Syria. The Arab League was asked to intervene but was not able to successfully mediate between the two parties. In mid 1975, the conflict was on

---

[92] See under V. 2.
[93] Waterbury, see note 88, 56-57.
[94] Kibaroglu, see note 5, 225.
[95] Kliot, see note 5, 161.
[96] Elver, see note 5, 374; since 1968 there have been two distinct Ba'th parties in Syria and Iraq, see: E. Kienle, *Ba'th v. Ba'th: The Conflict between Syria and Iraq 1968-1989*, 1993, 3.
[97] Naff/ Matson, see note 2, 93; Kliot, see note 5, 161-162.

the verge of armed hostility. Both Syria and Iraq deployed their armies near the mutual border. Iraq even threatened to attack the *Tabqa* Dam. Eventually, last minute mediation on the parts of Saudi Arabia and the Soviet Union was able to avert a violent conflict. The parties reportedly also came to an understanding, which was not made public. It was, however, noted that Syria agreed as a gesture of goodwill to let 60 per cent of the Euphrates waters through to Iraq.[98]

Another JTC was formed again in 1980 between Turkey and Iraq,[99] with Syria joining in 1983 but it only met sporadically and cooperation was mainly on a technical level. Topics of discussion were centered on the GAP works being planned and built in southern Turkey. Of particular concern was the building of the *Ataturk* Dam. The JTC was to identify a reasonable and appropriate method for water allocation.[100] After 16 meetings it concluded its last meeting in 1993. It had split over the question of a formulation of a proposal to share the rivers and could not agree on a regime to determine the equitable utilization of their shared rivers.[101]

In the face of the completion of the Turkish *Ataturk* Dam, Syria and Turkey signed a protocol in 1987 in which Turkey pledged to let a yearly average of more than 500 m^3/sec of the Euphrates waters through to Syria.[102] In 1989, also Iraq and Syria agreed upon joint minutes fixing the water share between them: Iraq was to get 58 per cent and Syria the remainder of 42 per cent of the Euphrates waters.[103] The (partial) filling of the *Ataturk* Dam in 1990 then led to another tension

---

[98] Cf. Naff/ Matson, see note 2, 93-94, who cites private statements by Iraqi officials; see also Elver, see note 5, 375, who, however, does not cite a source.

[99] Some authors mention a Protocol of the Joint Economic Committee between Turkey and Iraq from 1980, which the authors of this study were, however, unable to obtain; see e.g. A.T. Wolf/ J.T. Newton, *Case Study Transboundary Dispute Resolution: the Tigris-Euphrates Basin*, 3; Elver, see note 5, 421, referring to a "Protocol for Techno-Economic Cooperation".

[100] Kibaroglu et al., see note 19, 61.

[101] Elver, see note 5, 407-408.

[102] Para. 6 Protocol on Matters Pertaining to Economic Cooperation between Turkey and the Syrian Arab Republic (signed and entered into force 17 July 1987) UNTS Vol. 1724 No. 30069; for a detailed discussion of the protocol see under V. 2. a. bb.

[103] Para. 1 Joint Minutes Concerning the Provisional Division of the Waters of the Euphrates River (Iraq-Syria) (signed 17 April 1989), see under <http://faolex.fao.org>.

between the three riparian states when Turkey (at least partly) cut off the water flow for about 30 days. Both Iraq and Syria protested against this measure and claimed that they had suffered severe damage (loss of crops, environmental damage etc.) because of the low level of water reaching their territories. Turkey, again, argued that the filling of the dam was a technical necessity and that it had duly warned its co-riparians in advance. Additionally, in an effort to reduce the damage and prove its good intentions, Turkey had increased the quantity of water in the months before the filling of the dam, i.e. it released more than the committed 500 m³/sec. Hence, the other riparian states had been given the possibility to store more water.[104]

Throughout the 1990s a variety of bilateral and trilateral talks were held but they repeatedly failed.[105] Iraq reportedly requested Turkey to increase the water flow to Syria to 700 m³/sec on various occasions, but this was rejected by Turkey.[106] Yet, Syria and Turkey concluded a joint communiqué on cooperation in January 1993.[107] In its para. 6 it refers to the protocol signed by the two states in 1987. The parties ambitiously agreed to seek a final solution settling the allocation of the Euphrates waters by the end of the year. However, again no such agreement was reached.

In 1996 the construction of the so called *Birecik* Dam in Turkey was accompanied by strong protests on the side of Iraq and Syria and led to another crisis.[108] Probably as a consequence, Iraq and Syria allied and apparently organized a joint water coordination committee. The parties conferred on possibilities of an equitable and reasonable sharing and

---

[104] Allan, see note 3, 73; Elver, see note 5, 376; see also Turkish Ministry of Foreign Affairs, "Water Issues between Turkey, Syria and Iraq", *Perceptions: Journal of International Affairs* 1 (1996), Chapter I.C.4.A.
[105] It should be noted that the information and literature on the events occurring after 1990 is even scarcer and harder to obtain than before.
[106] Turkish Ministry of Foreign Affairs, see note 104, Chapter I.C.5.
[107] Joint Communiqué on Cooperation between the Syrian Arab Republic and Turkey (signed and came into force 20 January 1993), UNTS Vol. 1724 No. 30070.
[108] Kibaroglu, see note 5, 229-230; A. Kibaroglu/ W. Scheumann, "Euphrates-Tigris River System: Political Rapprochement and Transboundary Water Cooperation", in: A. Kibaroglu/ W. Scheumann/ A. Kramer (eds), *Turkey's Water Policy: National Framework and International Cooperation*, 2011, 277 et seq. (282).

utilization of the Euphrates and Tigris waters and also decided to coordinate their positions on the issue against Turkey.[109]

Another Joint Communiqué was signed between Syria and Turkey in 2001.[110] It aims at (further) improving the relations, fostering dialogue and creating a coordination mechanism between the two countries. The agreement stipulates technical cooperation between both parties, including training programs, the identification, planning and implementation of joint projects, exchange programs and partnerships. An implementation protocol for the activities between the two parties, which identifies and specifies the activities to be carried out, was signed two years later.[111]

According to recent reports, there have lately been some activities in the field of cooperation on water issues. In 2007, Turkey and Syria decided to re-activate the JTC and held a series of meetings. They agreed to share information on meteorological patterns and water quality. This was followed in 2009 by a great variety of Memoranda of Understandings (MoUs) signed between the riparians. Turkey and Iraq agreed to cooperate in various fields, such as politics, economy, energy, culture, security as well as water and signed 48 MoUs.[112] The agreement on water issues *inter alia* concerned the exchange of data, information and expert knowledge, the efficient use of water resources and the strengthening of the JTC.[113] Similarly, Turkey and Syria enhanced their cooperation by signing 50 agreements and MoUs, four of which are noted to

---

[109] Wolf/ Newton, see note 99, 4.

[110] Joint Communiqué between the Republic of Turkey/ Prime Ministry/ Southeastern Anatolia Project Regional Development Administration (GAP) and the Arab Republic of Syria/ Ministry of Irrigation/ General Organization for Land Development (GOLD) (signed 23 August 2001), see under <http://ocid.nacse.org>.

[111] Implementation Document of Joint Communiqué (Programme for 2003) (25 July 2003), on file with the authors (unofficial transaltion); see also Kibaroglu, see note 83, 189.

[112] Strategic Foresight Group, *The Blue Peace: Rethinking Middle East Water*, 2011, 30-31, see under <http://www.strategicforesight.com>; see also: Kibaroglu/ Scheumann, see note 108, 293.

[113] The MoU between the Ministry of Environment and Forestry of the Republic of Turkey and the Ministry of Water Resources of the Republic of Iraq on Water (15 October 2009), on file with the authors (unofficial translation).

concern water issues.[114] Finally, sources also refer to a tripartite MoU from 2009 on strengthening cooperation, initiating water education programs, establishing joint measurement stations, monitoring and evaluating the impact of climate change and exchange of information on these issues.[115] However, there is little or no information to be found on the tripartite MoU of 2009 as well as the re-launched JTC.

To sum up, several formal and informal agreements were concluded after World War II. However, none addresses the question of water utilization and management of either the Euphrates or the Tigris comprehensively.[116] The precise content of the relevant agreements will be analyzed below.

V. International Law in the Euphrates and Tigris Region

1. International Water Law

The question of the respective riparian state's rights and obligations concerning the Euphrates and the Tigris waters is highly contested. The following part will give an overview of international law relevant for the Euphrates and the Tigris region. Its purpose is to give a general introduction to the core norms of international water law, which provide a legal framework leaving room for states to develop more specific norms.

---

[114] Strategic Foresight Group, see note 112, 30-31; see also: Kibaroglu/ Scheumann, see note 108, 293-294; out of the four MoUs mentioned the following three MoUs concern the Euphrates and Tigris rivers and are on file with the authors: MoU between the Government of the Republic of Turkey and the Government of the Syrian Arab Republic on Establishment of a Pumping Station in the Territories of the Syrian Arab Republic for Water Withdrawal from the Tigris River (23 September 2009); MoU in the Field of Remediation of Water Quality between the Government of the Republic of Turkey and the Government of the Syrian Arab Republic (23 September 2009); MoU between the Government of the Republic of Turkey and the Government of the Syrian Arab Republic in the Field of Efficient Utilization of Water Resources and Combating Drought (23 September 2009) (unofficial translations).

[115] Strategic Foresight Group, see note 112, 31; see also: Eviewweek, *Turkey, Syria, Iraq Sign MoU for Use of Water Resource (9 May 2009)*, 2009.

[116] In fact, after 1946 agreements mainly focused on the Euphrates river.

a. Introduction

As the demand for water increased at the beginning of the 19th century, the legal framework relating to the non-navigational utilization of international watercourses also started to develop more and more. Essential work was done in this field by the Institut de Droit International[117] as early as 1911. Later on also the work of the ILA[118] as well as the ILC[119] contributed fundamentally to the development of international water law. Important codifications of this area of international law *inter alia* are the 1966 ILA Helsinki Rules, further updated in 2004 by the Berlin Rules,[120] the 1997 Convention on the Law of the Non-Navigational Uses of International Watercourses (UN Watercourses Convention)[121] as well as on a regional level the 1992 UNECE Conven-

---

[117] The Institut de Droit International (IDI) was founded in 1873 in Belgium as an "exclusively learned society" composed of the world's leading international public lawyers. It is devoted to promoting the progress of international law [arts 1 and 3 Statute of the Institut de Droit International (10 September 1873, as amended), see under <http://www.idi-iil.org>].

[118] The ILA was founded in Brussels in 1873 as an international non-governmental organization with the objective to promote the study, clarification and development of international law and to further international understanding and respect for international law [article 3 (1) Constitution of the International Law Association (adopted August 2004), in: ILA, *Report of the Seventy-First Conference, Berlin 2004*, 2004, 42.]; see also T. Stein, "International Law Association (ILA)", in: Wolfrum, see note 6; for further information on the development of the legal rules and principles of international water law, see e.g., A. Teclaff, "Fiat or Custom: The Checkered Development of International Water Law", *Natural Resources Journal* 31 (1991), 45 et seq.

[119] The ILC was established by the General Assembly in 1947 for the promotion of the progressive development of international law and its codification [article 1 Statute of the International Law Commission, A/RES/174 (II) of 21 November 1947], see also P.S. Rao, "International Law Commission (ILC)", in: Wolfrum, see note 6.

[120] Committee on Water Resources, "Helsinki Rules on the Uses of the Waters of International Rivers", in: ILA, *Report of the Fifty-Second Conference (Helsinki 1966)*, 1967, 484 (ILA Helsinki Rules); Committee on Water Resources, "Water Resources Law – Fourth Report", in: ILA, *Report of the Seventy-First Conference*, see note 118, 334 (ILA Berlin Rules). It should be noted that these instruments do not constitute binding legal instruments.

[121] Convention on the Law of the Non-navigational Uses of International Watercourses (adopted and opened for signature 21 May 1997, not yet entered

tion on the Protection and Use of Transboundary Watercourses and International Lakes (UNECE Helsinki Convention).[122] Additionally, a multitude of sub-regional conventions and bilateral treaties concerning specific watercourses were signed.[123]

The UN Watercourses Convention is the only universally applicable Convention that establishes basic principles and rules for interstate cooperation on the management, use, apportionment as well as for the protection of international watercourses. Both Iraq and Syria have signed and ratified it.[124] In contrast, Turkey has not signed the Convention and was, moreover, among the three states that voted against its adoption in the UN General Assembly. Apart from that the Convention is still not in force since it has not yet received the necessary 35 ratifications. Therefore, the UN Watercourses Convention, as well as other regional and sub-regional conventions, is not directly applicable in the Euphrates and the Tigris region. Consequently, the question of a customary application of the fundamental norms of international water law arises. Unfortunately, there is still disagreement about the exact status, scope and interrelationship of these norms.[125] Albeit this fact the

---

into force) *ILM* 36 (1997), 700 et seq.; the UN Watercourses Convention was based on a draft prepared by the ILC, see Draft Articles on the Law of Non-navigational Uses of International Watercourses and Commentaries Thereto, 1994, GAOR 49th Sess., Suppl. 10, 195.

[122] Article 2 (1) Convention on the Protection and Use of Transboundary Watercourses and International Lakes (with Annexes), UNTS Vol. 1936 No. 33207.

[123] See for example Agreement on the Cooperation for the Sustainable Development of the Mekong River Basin, *ILM* 34 (1995), 864 et seq.; Convention on Cooperation for the Protection and Sustainable Use of the Danube River, OJ L 342 (12 December 1997), 19 et seq.; Convention on the Protection of the Rhine, OJ L 289/31; Indus Waters Treaty 1960, UNTS Vol. 419 No. 6032; Revised Protocol on Shared Watercourses in the Southern African Development Community (SADC), *ILM* 40 (2001), 321 et seq.

[124] Iraq accepted on 9 July 2001 and Syria ratified on 2 April 1998; according to article 18 of the Vienna Convention on the Law of Treaties, UNTS Vol. 1155 No. 18232, the two states are to refrain from acts that might defeat the purpose of the UN Watercourses Convention, see note 121, before it enters into force.

[125] Cf. O. McIntyre, "The Role of Customary Rules and Principles of International Environmental Law in the Protection of Shared International Freshwater Resources", *Natural Resources Journal* 46 (2006), 157 et seq.; P.M. Dupuy, "Formation of Customary Law and General Principles", in:

authors of this study generally contend that the norms described below are legally binding norms, i.e. norms of customary international law.[126] Even though one might not follow this approach, it cannot be denied that these fundamental norms will most likely influence the setting of terms in the debate and provide guidelines for voluntary compliance as well as for the negotiations of a future agreement.[127]

b. Equitable and Reasonable Utilization of an International Watercourse

Probably the pre-eminent norm in international water law regarding the management of an international watercourse is the principle of equitable and reasonable utilization.[128] As a matter of principle states have the sovereign right to use a shared freshwater resource within their territory. The norm, however, requires a state to use a water resource in a manner that is equitable and reasonable *vis-à-vis* other states.[129] The objective is to attain optimal utilization of and benefits from a water-

---

D. Bodansky/ J. Brunnée/ E. Hey (eds), *The Oxford Handbook of International Environmental Law*, 2007, 449 et seq. (450 et seq.).

[126] Although this view cannot be supported by an in-depth analysis, since this would go far beyond the scope of the study, separate references for each norm which underscore their customary legal status are provided.

[127] Cf. D. Bodansky, "Customary (and Not So Customary) International Environmental Law", *Ind. J. Global Legal Stud.* 3 (1995-1996), 105 et seq. (119), who also correctly states that "the international community should spend less time debating a norm's legal status and more time translating general norms into enforceable treaties", (105).

[128] For a discussion of the distinction between policies, legal rules and legal principles, see U. Beyerlin, "'Prinzipien' im Umweltvölkerrecht – ein pathologisches Phänomen?", in: H.J. Cremer et al. (eds), *Tradition und Weltoffenheit des Rechts: Festschrift für Helmut Steinberger*, 2002, 31 et seq.; id., "Different Types of Norms in International Environmental Law: Policies, Principles and Rules", in: Bodansky/ Brunnée/ Hey, see note 125, 425 et seq.; for the purposes of this study, the substantive norms of international water law (equitable and reasonable utilization and the obligation not to cause harm) will be referred by the terms *"principle"* of equitable and reasonable utilization and no harm *"rule"* since this is what they are generally called. This terminology, however, is used without prejudice whether either norm is considered a *"principle"* or *"rule"* of international law.

[129] S.C. McCaffrey, "International Watercourses", in: Wolfrum, see note 6, para. 11.

course, but in a sustainable manner consistent with its adequate protection. The principle of equitable and reasonable utilization is widely supported by state practice[130] and has been applied and confirmed by various international[131] and national court decisions.[132]

At the core of the principle lies the sovereign equality of all states. Hence, all watercourse states have a right to an equal share of the uses and benefits of an international watercourse and no state has *a priori* a superior claim on the shared resource.[133] Yet, states also have the correlative obligation not to exceed their rights and unduly interfere with the rights of other states.[134] It should also be clarified that equity does not mean equality of the share. Equal rights do not imply the equal apportionment of a watercourse. At the same time, the objective of an optimal utilization does not entail that a state capable of making the most

---

[130] For a survey of state practice, see ILC, Special Rapporteur McCaffrey, Second Report on the Law of the Non-navigational Uses of International Watercourses, Doc. A/CN.4/399 of 21 May 1986; this is supported by the consistent inclusions of the norm in treaties and other documents, cf. article 5 UN Watercourses Convention, see note 121; article IV ILA Helsinki Rules, see note 120; article 12 ILA Berlin Rules, see note 120; article 5 Agreement on the Cooperation for the Sustainable Development of the Mekong River Basin, see note 123; article 5 ILC Draft Articles on the Law of Non-navigational Uses of International Watercourses, see note 121; see also L. del Castillo-Laborde, "Equitable Utilization of Shared Resources", in: Wolfrum, see note 6, para. 16; McCaffrey, see note 61, 376 and references cited at 384 et seq.; see also references cited by C. Behrmann, *Das Prinzip der angemessenen und vernünftigen Nutzung und Teilhabe nach der VN-Wasserlaufkonvention*, 2008, 63-64 (fn 5).

[131] Cf. *Gabčikovo-Nagymaros Project (Hungary v. Slovakia)*, ICJ Reports 1997, 7 et seq. (paras 78, 85, 147); *Affaire du Lac Lanoux* (1957), 12 RIAA 281 (315); *Territorial Jurisdiction of the International Commission of the River Oder (United Kingdom v. Poland)* (10 September 1929), PCIJ Series A No. 23, 27.

[132] See e.g. *Kansas v. Colorado*, US Supreme Court [1907] 206 US 46; *New Jersey v. New York*, US Supreme Court [1931] 283 US 336; *Colorado v. New Mexico*, US Supreme Court [1984] 467 US 310; cf. also *Land Württemberg und Land Preußen gegen das Land Baden betreffend die Donauversinkung* before the German Staatsgerichtshof (Constitutional Court of the German Reich) (18 June 1927) (1927), 116 Entscheidungen des Reichsgerichts in Zivilsachen Anhang 18.

[133] Therefore, it is also irrelevant where the source of an international watercourse lies; see, Behrmann, see note 130, 65.

[134] Ibid., 64-65.

efficient – economically or technologically – or monetarily valuable use should have a prior claim against other states.[135]

The principle of equitable utilization is inherently of a rather flexible and general nature. It has to be adapted to a wide variety of situations and accommodate the different, often opposing interests of states. Thus, the norm implies a balancing of uses between the watercourse states concerned.[136] This, in turn, requires the examination of all relevant conditions pertaining to a particular situation. In order to assess their utilization correctly states then need to consider certain factors and criteria on which they can base their assessment and consult with other states. Such factors include *inter alia* geographical, social and economic circumstances, as well as existing and potential uses, conservation and protection measures and available alternatives.[137] Further it has to be taken into account that the factors are not static, but prone to change and alteration, either due to natural developments or man-made influences. Therefore, a determination of equitable and reasonable utilization must be continuously reviewed and reassessed, since changing circumstances require adjustments.[138]

c. Obligation not to Cause Harm

The second fundamental pillar of international water law is the obligation not to cause significant harm to other riparian states, also called no harm rule.[139] It means to prevent the causing of harm to other riparian

---

[135] Draft Articles on the Law of Non-navigational Uses of International Watercourses, see note 121, commentaries to article 5, paras (3), (8).
[136] McCaffrey, see note 129, para. 11.
[137] Cf. article 6 UN Watercourses Convention, see note 121; article IV ILA Helsinki Rules, see note 120; article 13 ILA Berlin Rules, see note 120.
[138] M.S. Helal, "Sharing Blue Gold: The 1997 UN Convention on the Law of the Non-navigational Uses of International Watercourses Ten Years On", *Colo. J. Int'l Envtl L. & Pol'y* 18 (2007), 337 et seq. (345).
[139] The customary status of this norm enjoys widespread support, see e.g.: article 7 UN Watercourses Convention, see note 121; article 2 (1) UNECE Helsinki Convention, see note 122; article X ILA Helsinki Rules, see note 120; article 16 ILA Berlin Rules, see note 120; Principle 21 UN Conference on the Human Environment, Stockholm Declaration of the UN Conference on the Human Environment (16 June 1972), Doc. A/CONF.48/14/Rev. 1, 3; Principle 2 UN Conference on Environment and Development, Rio Declaration on Environment and Development (14 June 1992), Doc. A/CONF. 151/26/Rev. 1 Vol. I, 3; *Affaire du Lac Lanoux*,

states through activities related to an international watercourse. Thereby harm may result from pollution or a decrease of water quantity due to other activities not necessarily related to a state's direct utilization of a watercourse, such as e.g. deforestation.[140]

The no harm rule is often linked to the doctrines of *sic utere tuo ut alienum non laedas* (so use your own as not to harm that of another), good neighborliness and/or of abuse of rights.[141] All three doctrines try to reconcile conflicting rights of different states.[142] The underlying rationale is that a state may not use or permit such use of its territory that causes injury to the rights or interests of other states.[143]

It should be pointed out that the no harm rule does not embody an absolute standard.[144] Several mitigating factors have to be taken into account. Firstly, state and conventional practice as well as case law require the harm to exceed a certain threshold, i.e. to be sufficiently serious or significant.[145] The determination of what is significant may, however, be different in each case. Secondly, the required standard of conduct is one

---

see note 131, 308; in support of the no harm rule but not on international water law itself: *Trail Smelter (United States of America v. Canada)* (1938/41), 3 RIAA 1905, 1965; *Corfu Channel (United Kingdom of Great Britain and Northern Ireland v. Albania) (Merits)*, ICJ Reports 1949, 4 et seq. (22); see also: McCaffrey, see note 61, 406 et seq.; O. McIntyre, *Environmental Protection of International Watercourses under International Law*, 2007, 87 et seq.; G. Handl, "Transboundary Impacts", in: Bodansky/ Brunnée/ Hey, see note 125, 531 et seq. (534).

140 McCaffrey, see note 61, 409.
141 Handl, see note 139, 533; McIntyre, see note 139, 89-90; McCaffrey, see note 61, 415-419.
142 McCaffrey, see note 61, 417.
143 This principle was most famously expressed in the *Trail Smelter* Case of 1949, see note 139, 1965: "[U]nder the principles of international law, as well as of the law of the United States, no State has the right to use or to permit the use of its territory in such a manner as to cause injury by fumes in or to the territory of another or the properties of persons therein, when the case is of serious consequence and the injury established by clear and convincing evidence".
144 Helal, see note 138, 361, 364; McCaffrey, see note 61, 408.
145 McIntyre, see note 139, 93; see also: T. Bruha/ C.A. Maaß, "Schutz der Süßwasserressourcen im Völkerrecht – Prinzipien, Instrumente und neuere Entwicklungen", in: T. Bruha/ H.J. Koch (eds), *Integrierte Gewässerpolitik: Gewässerschutz, Wassernutzung, Lebensraumschutz*, 2001, 69 et seq. (79-83); the term "significant" is used by the ILC and in article 7 UN Watercourses Convention, see note 121.

of due diligence. That means it does not entail responsibility for the mere occurrence of a result (obligation of result). Rather states shall take all reasonable measures not to cause significant harm (obligation of conduct). The concrete measures required are to be established taking into account the facts and circumstances of each particular situation as well as the capabilities of the state concerned. The standard of due diligence is mostly to be fulfilled on a national level and generally involves the adoption of adequate legislation and administrative measures as well as their enforcement.[146]

Finally, it is important to note that the rule does not only constrain activities of upstream states. It is clear that the environment of a downstream state may be factually harmed by an upstream use. However, there is also potential of harm the other way round. Heavy downstream use may have the legal effect of imposing limitations on an upstream state's utilization of a watercourse as its use may alter the equitable balance of uses between watercourse states. Thus, harm can also be of a legal nature. The upstream state may in effect be deprived of its right to use a watercourse or engage in a planned activity by downstream uses. Consequently, the obligation to prevent harm does not permit a downstream state to completely restrict the economic development of an upstream state.[147]

d. Procedural Obligations

Procedural norms play a vital role in international water law since they provide the normative framework which is necessary for the implementation of substantial obligations. In addition, procedural obligations can help to avoid disputes.

The most important of these obligations *inter alia* are: the obligation of prior notification, the obligation to exchange data and information, the obligation to consult with potentially affected states, the obligation to conduct an environmental impact assessment (EIA) and the central and embracing obligation to cooperate.[148] It is again maintained that all procedural obligations mentioned reflect customary international law.

---

[146] McIntyre, see note 139, 102.
[147] McCaffrey, see note 61, 410-415.
[148] B. Baker Röben, "International Freshwaters", in: F.L. Morrison/ R. Wolfrum (eds), *International, Regional and National Environmental Law*, 2000, 285 et seq. (303-304).

The following part aims to give an introduction to the procedural obligations in international water law.

The <u>obligation to notify</u>[149] requires a state to provide prior and timely notification to other watercourse states about planned activities within its territory or under its control that may have a significant adverse effect. A logic consequence of this is also that a state needs to be informed adequately in order to enable it to assess potential environmental implications of planned measures correctly. Therefore, it is necessary that a notification includes sufficient information, including the results of any EIA.[150] It should also be mentioned that the obligation is reciprocal in nature, i.e. it applies to upstream as well as downstream states.[151]

In addition to the requirement of prior notification, it is of crucial importance that states <u>regularly exchange data and information</u> concerning the condition of a watercourse.[152] The obligation is closely linked with the principle of equitable and reasonable utilization as without such data and information, the ongoing evaluation of uses

---

[149] Conventions and other instruments that contain similar obligations: see e.g. Principle 19 UN Conference on Environment and Development, Rio Declaration on Environment and Development, see note 139; article 14 Convention on Biological Diversity, UNTS Vol. 1760 No. 30619; arts 3 and 10 Convention on the Transboundary Effects of Industrial Accidents, *ILM* 31 (1992), 1333 et seq.; see Part III UN Watercourses Convention, see note 121; article 6 UNECE Helsinki Convention, see note 122; article 4 Revised Protocol on Shared Watercourses in the Southern African Development Community, see note 123; for further references see ILC, Special Rapporteur McCaffrey, *Third Report on the Law of the Non-navigational Uses of International Watercourses*, Doc. A/CN.4/406 of 11 December 1981, paras 63 et seq.; McCaffrey, see note 61, 473.

[150] Article 12 UN Watercourses Convention, see note 121; for further information see McIntyre, see note 139, 324-333.

[151] Helal, see note 138, 346; A. Grzybowski/ S.C. McCaffrey/ R.K. Paisley, "Beyond International Water Law: Successfully Negotiating Mutual Gains Agreements for International Watercourses", *Pacific McGeorge Global Business and Development Law Journal* 22 (2010), 139 et seq. (142).

[152] This obligation has been recognized in a variety of instruments, such as article 8 Convention on Long-Range Transboundary Air Pollution, UNTS Vol. 1302 No. 21623; article 5 Vienna Convention for the Protection of the Ozone Layer, UNTS Vol. 1513 No. 26164; arts 6 and 13 UNECE Helsinki Convention, see note 122; article 9 UN Watercourses Convention, see note 121; article 6 Indus Waters Treaty 1960, see note 123; for further references see McIntyre, see note 139, 333-337.

along with the weighing of all relevant factors as well as the adequate protection of a watercourse are rendered difficult, if not impossible.[153]

The duty to enter into consultations[154] with co-basin states is also closely connected to the two obligations mentioned previously. It arises in a variety of circumstances[155] and generally requires states to communicate in order to find strategies on how to accommodate different (often opposing) interests. It is, however, important to note that the duty to consult does not go as far as, for example, requiring the consent of an objecting state to a planned measure.[156] Consultations are a step in the process that precedes formal negotiation, i.e. they are not necessarily aimed at finding a compromise, but are rather discussions based *inter alia* on information exchange.[157] In this sense consultations provide a first opportunity for states to exchange their views and can thus support conflict prevention.

The practice to conduct an EIA has recently gained much acceptance among states; it is a binding norm of international law, as lately ruled by the ICJ in the so called *Pulp Mills Case*.[158] The obligation

---

[153] McCaffrey, see note 61, 478-479.

[154] A great variety of treaty instruments require states to enter into consultations; cf. e.g., article 5 Convention on Environmental Impact Assessment in a Transboundary Context (done 25 February 1991, entered into force 10 September 1997), *ILM* 30 (1991), 802 (Espoo Convention); article 4 Convention on the Transboundary Effects of Industrial Accidents, see note 149; article 5 Convention on Long-Range Transboundary Air Pollution, see note 152; for further references see McIntyre, see note 139, 337-344.

[155] See also arts 3 (5), 4, 7 (2), 11, 17, 18 (2) and (3), 19 (3), 21 (3), 24 (1), 26 (2), 30 UN Watercourses Convention, see note 121.

[156] McIntyre, see note 139, 337.

[157] Cf. McCaffrey, see note 61, 477.

[158] *Pulp Mills on the River Uruguay (Argentina v. Uruguay) (Judgment)* (20 April 2010), ICJ Doc. 2010 General List No. 135, para. 204; see also Principle 17 Rio Declaration on Environment and Development, see note 139; article 206 UN Convention on the Law of the Sea, UNTS Vol. 1833 No. 31363; article 4 (1) (f) UN Framework Convention on Climate Change (with Annexes), UNTS Vol. 1771 No. 30822; article 8 and Annex I Protocol on Environmental Protection to the Antarctic Treaty, *ILM* 30 (1991), 1455 et seq.; in general Espoo Convention, see note 154; article 11 (3) UNECE Helsinki Convention, see note 122; Chapter IV ILA Berlin Rules 2004, see note 120; see also P. Birnie/ A. Boyle, *International Law and the Environment*, 2009, 164; McIntyre, see note 139, 229-239; A. Epiney, "Environmental Impact Assessment", in: Wolfrum, see note 6, para. 63; U. Beyerlin, *International Environmental Law*, 2011, 233 et seq.

stipulates that states have to undertake an environmental impact assessment, "where there is a risk that the proposed industrial activity may have a significant adverse impact in a transboundary context, in particular, on a shared resource."[159] The idea is that a state first needs to have sufficient information and understand the environmental impact of an activity to be then able to take a decision and consequently prevent environmental harm.[160] Unfortunately, international law remains mostly silent on the specific scope and minimum core content of an EIA.[161] Hence, it is left to each state's domestic legal order to specify its elements. Even though the exact requirements are not specified, it is clear that the EIA has to be conducted prior to the implementation of the project and requires ongoing monitoring.[162]

Finally, the duty to cooperate[163] is considered as an overarching principle embracing all procedural obligations mentioned previously. The term cooperation generally describes "the voluntary coordinated action of two or more States which takes place under a legal regime and serves a specific objective. To this extent it marks the effort of States to accomplish an objective by joint action [...], where the activity of a single State cannot achieve the same result."[164] Hence, continuous cooperation is not only a necessary and indispensable requirement for the effective functioning of other procedural rules but also the driving force

---

[159] *Pulp Mills on the River Uruguay*, see note 158, para. 204.
[160] Epiney, see note 158, para. 1.
[161] Non-binding principles may be taken as guidelines; see e.g. UNEP, *Goals and Principles of Environmental Impact Assessment*, or see also, Espoo Convention, see note 154.
[162] *Pulp Mills on the River Uruguay*, see note 158, para. 205; for more information on EIA, see also UNEP, *Environmental Impact Assessment and Strategic Environmental Assessment: Towards an Integrated Approach*, 2004.
[163] The importance of cooperation concerning the utilization of international watercourses has been emphasized repeatedly; cf. Principle 7 Rio Declaration on Environment and Development, see note 139; article 8 ILC, Draft Articles on the Law of Non-navigational Uses of International Watercourses, see note 121; article 8 UN Watercourses Convention, see note 121; *Affaire du Lac Lanoux*, see note 131, 308; *Gabčikovo-Nagymaros Project*, see note 131, para. 17; for further references, see, ILC, Special Rapporteur McCaffrey, see note 149, paras 43 et seq.
[164] R. Wolfrum, "Cooperation, International Law of", in: id., see note 6, para. 2.

for the attainment as well as the maintenance of an equitable allocation of the uses and benefits of an international watercourse.

e. Environmental Protection

Traditionally the interests of riparian states mainly concerned the allocation of uses of shared freshwater resources. However, states have increasingly recognized the significance of the protection of the environment against pollution and other forms of harm. Alongside a better scientific understanding of the interdependence between different ecosystems, this has led to a trend towards more holistic and eco-system oriented approaches. Modern treaties and conventions no longer only consider the interests of states in utilizing a watercourse but are especially designed to ensure the ecological balance of a watercourse by prescribing environmental measures and standards.[165] Such measures, for example, relate to the prevention and reduction of pollution, the introduction of alien species, minimum flow guarantees and the general protection of the river's environment as well as the achievement of a good water quality.[166] This trend is reflected by the emergence and development of (customary) rules and principles in international environmental law including *inter alia* the obligation to prevent or minimize environmental harm, the precautionary principle, the polluter pays principle, sustainable development or the obligation to protect the eco-system.[167]

Environmental considerations do not (yet) play a big role in the Euphrates and the Tigris region even though both rivers are unfortunately highly polluted and suffer from environmental harm. In particular, rapid salinity increase and severe deterioration of the marshlands con-

---

[165] U. Beyerlin, *Umweltvölkerrecht*, 2000, 85; for treaties specifically concerning the protection of an international watercourse, see e.g. Convention on Cooperation for the Protection and Sustainable Use of the Danube River, see note 123; Convention on the Protection of the Rhine, see note 123.

[166] U. Beyerlin/ J. Grote Stoutenburg, "Environment, International Protection", in: Wolfrum, see note 6, para. 59.

[167] McIntyre, see note 139, 191 et seq.; see also, A. Nollkaemper, *The Legal Regime for Transboundary Water Pollution: Between Discretion and Constraint*, 1993; generally on principles of environmental law see R. Wolfrum, "International Environmental Law: Purposes, Principles and Means of Ensuring Compliance", in: F.L. Morrison/ R. Wolfrum (eds), *International, Regional and National Environmental Law*, 2000, 3; P. Sands, *Principles of International Environmental Law*, 2003.

stitute major problems.[168] It is, therefore, essential that any future agreement includes the issue of the environmental protection of the Euphrates and the Tigris river.

f. Groundwater

In the context of transboundary waters, attention needs also to be paid to groundwater. Within the Euphrates and the Tigris region, the three riparian states share groundwater resources, such the *Ceylanpinar* aquifer and the *Ras El Ain* karstic springs.[169]

Groundwater holds a special status in international water law. Although it is an important resource for freshwater, particularly in arid regions,[170] until recently it has received only little coverage in international law.[171] While the rules stipulated in the 1997 UN Watercourses Convention also apply to groundwater, they do so only in a limited way.[172] According to its definition of an international watercourse the Convention applies to groundwater when it is related to surface water, normally flowing into a common terminus.[173] This definition does not only exclude confined groundwater unrelated to surface water but also makes it difficult to determine to what extent aquifers with multiple termini (such as, for example, the groundwater associated with the Danube) fall under the scope of the convention.[174] Next to causing uncertainty this leaves out important transboundary aquifer systems, containing great amounts of freshwater resources. Moreover, the provisions

---

[168] Cf. D. Grey/ D. Blackmore, *Iraq – A Strategy to Negotiate with Co-Riparian States Responding to a "Note Verbale" to RBAS-UNDP* (April 2011), on file with the authors, 8.

[169] Kibaroglu et al., see note 19, 74.

[170] Aquifer systems constitute a strategic and also reliable freshwater reserve that can be drawn upon in cases of drought; see K. Mechlem, "Groundwater Protection", in: Wolfrum, see note 6, para. 5.

[171] According to Mechlem the reasons for this neglect lie *inter alia* in the complex nature of aquifers and longtime lack of available data on their behavior; see K. Mechlem, "International Groundwater Law: Towards Closing the Gaps?", *Yearbook of International Environmental Law* 14 (2003), 47 et seq. (53).

[172] Cf. ibid., 47 et seq.

[173] See article 2 UN Watercourses Convention, see note 121.

[174] Mechlem, see note 171, 54 et seq.

are tailored to surface water and do not cover the specific hydrological behavior of groundwater.[175]

In 2008 the UN General Assembly adopted Resolution 63/124,[176] containing a set of Draft Articles on the Law of Transboundary Aquifers which had been developed by the ILC between 2002 and 2008.[177] In spite of their non-binding nature,[178] these Draft Articles mark an important step in the development of international water law regarding the treatment of groundwater, more specifically transboundary aquifers.[179] They basically adapt the fundamental principles of international water law to the specific characteristics of groundwater.[180] Also, like the UN Watercourses Convention, the Draft Articles offer a framework for states to make appropriate arrangements for the proper management of

---

[175] It should be noted that not all international water law instruments suffer from this limitation. For example, the ILA Berlin Rules (2004), see note 120, stipulate rules for both surface and groundwater and on a regional level the UNECE Helsinki Convention, see note 122, also applies to surface as well as groundwater. The same goes for the Directive 2000/60/EC of the European Parliament and of the Council of 23 October 2000 Establishing a Framework for Community Action in the Field of Water Policy [2000] OJ L327/1; cf. Mechlem, see note 171, 57 et seq.

[176] The Law of Transboundary Aquifers, A/RES/63/124 of 11 December 2008.

[177] The ILC is tasked with the progressive development of international law and its codification [article 1 (1) Statute of the International Law Commission, see note 119]. Its members prepare draft conventions on subjects which have not yet been regulated, sufficiently developed or require more precise formulation and systematization in international law (article 15).

[178] Works of the ILC have the nature of recommendations and are thus, with the exception of codified rules of customary international law, not binding on states; Rao, see note 119, para. 5. The General Assembly has decided to examine the final form that may be given to the ILC, "Draft Articles on the Law of Transboundary Aquifers adopted by the Commission on First Reading", in: ILC, *Report of the International Law Commission Covering the Work of its 58th Sess. (1 May–9 June and 3 July–11 August 2006)*, GAOR 61 Sess., Suppl. 10, 192; A/RES/63/124, see note 176, para. 6.

[179] For the history of the development cf. Mechlem, see note 170. In this context the following non-governmental instruments of the ILA are also noteworthy: ILA Seoul Rules on International Groundwaters (Committee on Water Resources, "Rules on International Groundwaters", in: ILA, *Report of the Sixty-Second Conference (Seoul 1986)*, 1987, 251); ILA Berlin Rules, see note 120.

[180] Mechlem, see note 170, para. 20.

their transboundary aquifers, by taking into account the provisions of these draft articles.

g. Vital Human Needs

Water is essential for life. Without access to a sufficient supply of water humans have no chance of survival. Hence, when weighing different uses and negotiating a water-sharing agreement states should pay due respect to basic human needs. This is particularly the case for states suffering from water scarcity since they already face a great challenge of supplying their populations with sufficient amounts of water. The importance of securing fresh water access for basic human needs is also reflected in international water law. Although international water law generally does not recognize a hierarchy between uses,[181] it provides for a certain safeguard against neglecting the vital importance of water for humans.[182] Article 10 (2) of the UN Watercourses Convention, dealing with the relationship between different kinds of uses, for example calls upon states, when settling a conflict between different uses, to give "special regard [...] to the requirements of vital human needs."[183]

This requires sufficient water for sustaining human life, including drinking water and water for food production.[184] With regard to groundwater the ILC Draft Articles on the Law of Transboundary Aquifers even go a step further, requiring states to consider basic needs before a conflict of uses occurs,[185] namely within the process of determining an equitable and reasonable utilization.[186] Both provisions echo a growing trend in international water law highlighting the necessity to

---

[181] Cf. article 10 (1) UN Watercourses Convention, see note 121.
[182] S.C. McCaffrey, "The Human Right to Water", in: E. Brown-Weiss/ L. Boisson de Chazournes/ N. Bernasconi-Ostewalder (eds), *Fresh Water and International Economic Law*, 2005, 94 et seq. (100).
[183] Article 10 (2) UN Watercourses Convention, see note 121.
[184] Convention on the Law of the Non-navigational Uses of International Watercourses: Report of the Sixth Committee convening as the Working Group of the Whole, Doc. A/51/869 of 11 April 1997, 5.
[185] C. Leb, "Dig Deep: Conflict Prevention through Protection of Basic Water Rights: The Role of International Water Law in Conflict Prevention", Paper presented at the *International Conference "Transboundary Aquifers: Challenges and New Directions" (ISARM)*, UNESCO Paris, 6-8 December 2010, 4.
[186] Article 5 (2) ILC Draft Articles on the Law of Transboundary Aquifers, see note 178.

respect basic human needs in the management of transboundary water resources.[187] This trend is undoubtedly influenced by current developments in the field of human rights law, more specifically the human right to water.[188] While the rules governing international water law have not been devised as individual rights they do express the basic idea behind the right to water, that is, in making allocation decisions states should pay attention to vital human needs.[189] In sum, one can say that if vital human needs are at threat they should be prioritized over any other use to the extent necessary.[190]

h. Water Principles in Islamic Law

When examining the international law applicable in the Euphrates and the Tigris region special regard should be paid to Islamic law since Turkey, Syria and Iraq are all countries with largely Muslim populations. Even though Islamic law might not necessarily provide for a modern day solution of the Euphrates and Tigris conflict[191] and Turkey and

---

[187] Leb, see note 185, 5; several water sharing agreements refer to the human right to water or vital human needs, see e.g., Charte des Eaux du Fleuve Sénégal (Senegal River Charter) of 18 May 2002; see under <http://www.ecolex.org>; La Charte de L'eau du Basin Niger (Niger River Charter) signed 30 April 2008, see under <http://www.abn.ne>.

[188] On the human right to water see, e.g., E. Riedel/ P. Rothen (eds), *The Human Right to Water*, 2006; A. Kirschner, "The Human Right to Water and Sanitation", in: A. von Bogdandy/ R. Wolfrum (eds), *Max Planck UNYB* 15 (2011), 445 et seq. With particular focus on the Middle East see A.K. Biswas/ E. Rached/ C. Tortajada, *Water as a Human Right for the Middle East and North Africa*, 2008.

[189] McCaffrey, see note 182, 100 et seq.

[190] K. Bourquain, *Freshwater Access from a Human Rights Perspective: A Challenge to International Water and Human Rights Law*, 2008, 43; who criticizes that law does not make clear what the necessary minimum standard is which, in practice, makes the fulfillment of this aim doubtful.

[191] See for instance J.E. Cohen, "International Law and the Water Politics of the Euphrates", *N.Y.U.J.Int'L.&Pol.* 24 (1992), 503 et seq. (538). McCaffrey also points out that at the time Islamic water law was developed, people were not thinking about manipulating big rivers such as the Euphrates but rather concentrated on point sources and very small streams. Remarks of S.C. McCaffrey, "Water Resources in the Middle East", *ASIL Proceedings of the 80th Annual Meeting*, 1986, 249 et seq. (269).

Syria have secular laws,[192] it can perhaps provide for some valuable insight into the region's mindset towards water. Moreover it should not be disregarded that Islamic law, or the *sharia*,[193] has governed water issues in the Middle East for several centuries and its spirit has surely been in parts incorporated into modern secular water laws.[194]

The status of water in Islamic law perhaps becomes best apparent in the double meaning of the word *sharia*. Not only does it stand for the true moral path that Muslims must follow, but it also refers to access to the pure source of drinking water that must be preserved for humans.[195] In general, Islamic law governing the sharing and use of water is built upon common principles and guidelines rather than specific rules.[196] Islamic water law is based on the principle that water, in its natural state, is a common good and entitlement of all Muslims.[197] This is derived from a *hadith*[198] stating that "man holds three things in common, water,

---

[192] The new Iraqi Constitution is not secular. Although Islamic law is named as a source of legislation (article 2 Constitution of Iraq adopted 15 October 2005), in practice it is, however, not applied directly. On this issue see e.g. S. Hanish, "The Role of Islam in the Making of the New Iraqi Constitution", *Domes* 16 (2007), 30 et seq.; I. Coleman, "Women, Islam and the New Iraq", *Foreign Aff.* 85 (2006), 24 et seq. For an overview on the relationship between *sharia* and the Iraqi Constitution see T.J. Roeder/ T. Azizy, *Max Planck Materials on the Relation between Islamic Law and Constitutional Law in Selected Countries*, 2010, 12.

[193] *Sharia* is the name given by Muslims to the rules and regulations that govern the life of Muslims. *Sharia* is derived from several sources including the *koran*, the *hadith* (the practice of the Prophet Muhammed), the *ijma* (consensus of Islamic legal scholars) and *qiyas* (legal analogy); F. Griffel, "Introduction", in: A. Amanat/ F. Griffel (eds), *Sharia: Islamic Law in the Contemporary Context*, 2007, 3.

[194] T. Naff, "Conflict and Water Use in the Middle East", in: P. Rogers/ P. Lydon (eds), *Water in the Arab World*, 1994, 253 et seq. (268).

[195] Ibid.; Mallat even goes as far as calling it the "law of water", C. Mallat, "The Quest for Water Use Principles: Reflections on Sharia and Custom in the Middle East", in: J.A. Allan/ C. Mallat (eds), *Water in the Middle East: Legal, Political and Commercial Implication*, 1995, 127 et seq. (128).

[196] Naff, see note 194, 269.

[197] Ibid., 270; J.C. Wilkinson, "Muslim Land and Water Law", *Journal of Islamic Studies* 1 (1990), 54 et seq. (60).

[198] Next to the *koran* the *hadith* or "traditions" of the Prophet are considered as a source of Islamic law. They are said to be a record of Prophet Mohammed's behavior and words; A. Hourani, *History of the Arab People*, 2005, 66 and 69.

pasture, and fire."[199] No legal person or ruler may hence appropriate a river, or try to sell, rent or tax its water.[200] This prohibition though apparently does not pertain to artificial wells and irrigation canals. Under Islamic law, for example, one who digs a well is granted an ownership interest and exclusive rights in the water.[201] Regardless of how far these ownership rights may go,[202] under Islamic law no one has the right to deny any living being the right to quench its thirst.[203] Sharing water is considered a holy duty.[204]

Moreover, Islamic law establishes a clear priority of uses. Hereby water for drinking and domestic purposes is accorded top priority with humans taking precedents in use before animals.[205] Domestic uses again take priority over agricultural needs, such as water for irrigation. Once all these needs are satisfied, those living upstream have antecedent rights. This is largely based on the assumption that settlement proceeds from upper stretches of a watercourse onward downstream.[206] In principle this approach reflects a first in use, first in right position which is contrasted by modern international water law.

More in line with international water law is, however, the limitation which the *sharia* imposes on irrigation rights. Although hesitant with regard to according full property rights to water, the *sharia* accords several servitude rights such as the right to irrigate (right of *shirb*). The exercise of *shirb* is limited by a no harm provision: a person who irrigates

---

[199] Naff, see note 194, 270.

[200] Ibid. Wilkinson, see note 197, 60; both noting that products resulting from the use of water may, however, be levied.

[201] Elver, see note 5, 42.

[202] On this issue see for example C. Mallat, "Law and the Nile River: Emerging International Rules and the Sharia", in: P.P. Howell/ J.A. Allan (eds), *The Nile: Sharing a Scarce Resource*, 1994, 365 et seq. (372 et seq.).

[203] M.A. Civic, "A Comparative Analysis of the Israeli and Arab Water Law Traditions and Insights for Modern Water Sharing Agreements", *Den. J. Int'l L. & Pol'y* 26 (1998), 437 et seq.(443).

[204] Ibid., 442.

[205] Ibid.

[206] Naff, see note 194, 270 et seq., who also remarks that conversely this is not reflected in history since great civilizations like the Egyptians or Babylonians have proceeded upward in their settlement, i.e. starting at the lower end of the basin.

his/her land may not in doing so provoke harm to downhill or downstream neighbors.[207]

In sum, albeit its somewhat supple nature, Islamic water law clearly advocates a common responsibility of all Muslims to share their water resources as well as to avoid harming others when using them.[208]

2. Bilateral Agreements

The following section will discuss the main agreements so far reached within the region. The first part will focus on bilateral water sharing agreements between the three riparian states concluded before the 1990s: the 1946 Treaty of Friendship and Good Neighbourly Relations between Turkey and Iraq, the Protocol between Syria and Turkey of 1987 and the Joint Minutes between Iraq and Syria of 1989. The second part will consider the more recent developments referred to above.[209]

a. Water Sharing Agreements before the 1990s

aa. Turkey and Iraq

In 1946 Iraq and Turkey signed the Treaty of Friendship and Good Neighbourly Relations.[210] The treaty covers various issues, which are mainly dealt with in six Protocols annexed to the treaty.[211] Protocol No. 1 concerns the regulation of the waters of the Tigris and the Euphrates, including their tributaries. According to the preamble both parties recognized the importance of the construction of conservation works on the rivers for Iraq to regulate the water flow and prevent disastrous floods. Additionally, the need for permanent observation sta-

---

[207] Mallat, see note 202, 376.
[208] Cf. Lien, see note 62, 306.
[209] See under IV. 2.
[210] Treaty of Friendship and Neighbourly Relations between Iraq and Turkey, see note 81.
[211] Protocol No. 1 – Relative to the Regulation of the Waters of the Tigris and Euphrates and of their Tributaries; Protocol No. 2 – Relative to Mutual Assistance in Security Questions; Protocol No. 3 – Relative to Co-operation in Educational, Instructional and Cultural Matters; Protocol No. 4 – Relative to Postal, Telegraphic and Telephonic Communications; Protocol No. 5 – Relative to Economic Questions; Protocol No. 6 – Relative to the Frontier.

tions was laid down. It is noteworthy that the parties considered that the most suitable location for the construction works was likely to be within Turkish territory while the entire costs should be borne by Iraq. Moreover, parties should construct these works with a view to achieving greatest possible benefits for both states with regard to irrigation and power generation.[212]

To achieve these ends, the Protocol provides for quite extensive joint assessment, monitoring and information exchange mechanisms. It allows Iraq to send technical experts to Turkey so as to conduct investigations, collect information, as well as prepare plans for possible construction works on the various rivers. The Protocol further contains a set of obligations for Turkey. Firstly, Turkey shall provide the Iraqi experts with all necessary information, access, assistance and facilities as well as ensure the collaboration with Turkish experts.[213] It also was obliged to set up permanent observation stations to ensure their operation and maintenance as well as to regularly communicate measuring results to the competent Iraqi authorities. The Turkish government, moreover, generally accepted any other construction works on Turkish territory, on the condition that they were perceived necessary as a result of studies carried out by the experts of both countries. Yet, these works should be subject to a separate agreement.[214] Finally, Turkey was obliged to consult Iraq about any Turkish plans for construction works on the river. As far as possible, they should then be adapted to the interests of both parties.[215]

It is striking that the Protocol entails quite far reaching obligations, as well as restrictions on Turkish sovereignty. Presumably Turkey would nowadays hardly allow the construction of Iraqi conservation works on its territory. And *vice versa*, Iraq probably would not be interested in major water (control) infrastructure outside its borders. Another significant aspect of the Protocol is that it acknowledges the importance of cooperation, sharing of information and the need for consultation for the mutual benefit of both states. Yet, it includes no clear standards for such cooperation.[216]

This agreement stems from a time when Turkey was not (yet) making extensive use of the two rivers' waters. Subsequently, the relation-

---

[212] Preamble Protocol No. 1, see note 211.
[213] Article 2 Protocol No. 1, ibid.
[214] Article 4 Protocol No. 1, ibid.
[215] Article 5 Protocol No. 1, ibid.
[216] Lien, see note 62, 286.

ship between the two states, however, changed[217] and the planned measures were actually never implemented. Hence, the agreement lost its practical importance and supposedly fell into disuse.

bb. Syria and Turkey

Syria and Turkey signed the Protocol on Matters Pertaining to Economic Cooperation in 1987.[218] The Protocol is quite comprehensive. It endeavors to enhance cooperation for the mutual benefit of both states in various areas, such as *inter alia* petroleum and gas, electricity, banking, transport, telecommunication and trade. Paras 6-10 of the Protocol relate to water issues. The provision on the sharing of the resources of the Euphrates was included with a view to the upcoming impounding of the *Ataturk* Dam reservoir. Turkey agreed to let a yearly average flow of more than 500 m³/sec through to Syria. In case the monthly flow fell under the agreed level, Turkey had to make up the difference during subsequent months. However, the wording of the Protocol ("the Turkish side undertakes to …") does not suggest a very strong obligation. The agreement was considered provisional until a final allocation agreement on the Euphrates waters among the three riparians would be reached.[219] The two parties further agreed to allocate the Euphrates and the Tigris waters in the shortest time possible as well as to include Iraq.[220] A final agreement on the allocation of the Euphrates water has to date not come into existence.

Syria and Turkey also recognized the benefits of joint cooperation in the Protocol and it was agreed to expedite the work of the JTC. Moreover, the two states agreed in principle to construct and jointly operate projects for irrigation and hydro-power generation purposes.[221] Finally the Protocol touches upon the so-called "Peace Pipe Line" project proposed by Turkey.[222] It sets forth that Turkey informed Syria about the details of the project. Syria, then again, stated its interest in and principal endorsement of the project under the premise that Turkey commis-

---

[217] See under IV. 2.
[218] Protocol on Matters Pertaining to Economic Cooperation between Turkey and the Syrian Arab Republic, see note 102.
[219] Para. 6, ibid.
[220] Paras 6 and 7, ibid.
[221] Paras 8 and 9, ibid.
[222] For more details on the Peace Pipeline Project proposed by Turkey, see under VII. 2. b.

sions an international consultancy firm with a technical and economic feasibility study. Syria, furthermore, agreed to facilitate feasibility studies on the Syrian portion of the project and eventually to enter into negotiations if the results of the studies were positive.[223]

cc. Iraq and Syria

Finally, also Syria and Iraq agreed to share the Euphrates waters. In 1989 the Joint Minutes concerning the provisional division of the waters of the Euphrates river were signed by both parties.[224] In contrast to the preceding Syrian-Turkish agreement, which established a fixed minimum flow, Syria pledged to release 58 per cent of the Euphrates waters to Iraq. Syria was to keep the remaining quantity of 42 per cent.[225] This roughly corresponds to previous unofficial or unpublished records.[226] Once again, the wish to reach a trilateral agreement between the three riparian states was expressed. Moreover, the establishment of a JTC to deal with technical and administrative details of the implementation of the agreement was regarded as the best way to realize common interests.[227]

The difference between both agreements (1987 and 1989) is noteworthy, as both agreements favor Syria. In the earlier agreement Turkey bears the risk of not being able to provide enough water as it is obliged to ensure a yearly average flow based on a fixed quota. In the later agreement, on the other hand, Syria has negotiated a more flexible mechanism passing the risk on to Iraq by agreeing to provide a certain percentage of the water available. Hence, if there is less water available in Syria, Iraq receives less. Apart from that, one can notice that the pertinent parts of both agreements deal with one single issue: the allocation of water between riparian states. Water quality issues or other environmental concerns are not addressed. This mirrors the predominant preoccupation of the riparian states on quantity related water issues.

---

[223] Para. 10 Protocol on Matters Pertaining to Economic Cooperation between Turkey and the Syrian Arab Republic, see note 102.
[224] Joint Minutes Concerning the Provisional Division of the Waters of the Euphrates River (Iraq-Syria), see note 103.
[225] Para. 1, ibid.
[226] See also under IV. 2.
[227] Para. 2 Joint Minutes Concerning the Provisional Division of the Waters of the Euphrates River (Iraq-Syria), see note 103.

b. Developments after 2000

With the exception of the Joint Communiqué on Cooperation concluded between Syria and Turkey in January 1993 which hardly touched on the question of water,[228] the 1990s did not produce any agreements on water issues between the riparian states. In the new millennium the cooperation experienced a new impetus resulting in a variety of MoUs, joint communiqués and other agreements dealing with water issues.

The Joint Communiqué between the Republic of Turkey/ Prime Ministry/ Southeastern Anatolia Project Regional Development Administration (GAP) and the Arab Republic of Syria/ Ministry of Irrigation/ General Organization for Land Development (GOLD) of the Ministry of Irrigation of the Republic of Syria in 2001 after several meetings can be considered as a first breakthrough.[229] As already pointed out above, the agreement envisages technical cooperation between the parties including training programs, joint development projects as well as exchange programs and partnerships between all levels of staffs. An Implementation Protocol of 25 July 2003[230] complements and further specifies the projects, programs and activities to be carried out. In particular, four training programs were planned on (1) Participatory Irrigation Management in GAP, (2) Integrated Water Based Development: Examples from the GAP, (3) Women and Youth in Development: The GAP Experience, and (4) Project Cycle: Planning, Design and Implementation of Rural and Agricultural Development Projects. Furthermore, details were provided on a Twin Villages Project and a Joint Irrigated Agricultural Research Project (Twin Research Station). Additionally, an exchange program envisaged visits from Syrian engineers in Turkey to participate in the implementation of projects on the "Management, Operation and Maintenance of Irrigation Systems in the Southeastern Anatolia Region", "Participatory Rural Development" and "Improvement of Soil in the Leveled Lands Through the Use of Agricultural Residuals and Bio Fertilizers". Finally the protocol also

---

[228] Joint Communiqué on Cooperation between the Syrian Arab Republic and Turkey (signed and came into force 20 January 1993), see note 107.
[229] Joint Communiqué between the Republic of Turkey/ Prime Ministry/ Southeastern Anatolia Project Regional Development Administration (GAP) and the Arab Republic of Syria/ Ministry of Irrigation/ General Organization for Land Development (GOLD), see note 110.
[230] Implementation Document of Joint Communiqué (Programme for 2003), see note 111.

provides for some instructions on the execution of the activities stipulated.

Syria adopted agreements to set up pumping stations for water withdrawal from the Tigris river in 2002 with Iraq[231] and 2009 with Turkey respectively.[232] Both agreements lay down specific rules regarding the amount of water Syria may withdraw from the river. In return, Syria is required to report on all phases of implementation of the projects as well as on the quantity of water withdrawn. In the 2002 agreement the parties agreed to jointly monitor the river's discharges by setting up respective monitoring stations. It also foresees a joint technical committee to regularly determine the quantities of water drawn from the pumping station. Moreover, Iraq and Syria underscore their commitments to the UN Watercourses Convention by including a reference to it in article 7 which provides that all issues not provided for in the agreement shall be dealt with under the Convention. The 2009 agreement does not contain such far-reaching stipulations with regard to joint monitoring. However, it lays a strong emphasis on regular exchange of data and information. Apart from that, a final allocation agreement of the Euphrates and the Tigris waters between all three riparian states is once again envisaged.

In 2009 Turkey signed another three MoUs with its neighboring countries. Turkey and Syria signed two MoUs, one "in the Field of Efficient Utilization of Water Resources and Combating Drought"[233] and another one "in the Field of Remediation of Water Quality".[234] Both MoUs acknowledge the importance of sustainable development and stress that the protection of natural resources necessitates close cooperation between the parties. The third MoU was concluded between

---

[231] Agreement on Setting up a Syrian Pumping Station on the River Tigris between Syria and Iraq (done 9 April 2002), on file with authors (unofficial translation).

[232] MoU between the Government of the Republic of Turkey and the Government of the Syrian Arab Republic on Establishment of a Pumping Station in the Territories of the Syrian Arab Republic for Water Withdrawal from the Tigris River, see note 114.

[233] MoU between the Government of the Republic of Turkey and the Government of the Syrian Arab Republic in the Field of Efficient Utilization of Water Resources and Combating of Drought, see note 114.

[234] MoU in the Field of Remediation of Water Quality between the Government of the Republic of Turkey and the Government of the Syrian Arab Republic, see note 114.

Turkey and Iraq.[235] It also calls for cooperation as well as transfer of knowledge, experience and technology for the protection and utilization of water resources.

The new millennium marked a turning point in the relations between the three riparian states: the relations were overall improving and after about a decade of little interaction regarding water issues riparian states were fostering technical cooperation as well renewing their commitment towards cooperation regarding water issues. Whereas the agreements from early 2000 still lay the main focus on technical collaboration, it is interesting to note that by 2009 (in particular the 2009 MoUs) the focus of cooperation was moving towards the more efficient utilization of water resources alongside their protection. All riparians explicitly recognized the importance of a sustainable development approach in one of the MoUs. Moreover, this recent incorporation of sustainability considerations (drought mitigation, protection of the resource, preservation of water resources in quality and quantity etc.) might suggest that approaches are slowly shifting towards finding a more sustainable solution for the use of the Euphrates and the Tigris river.

All in all, despite of this positive development there is yet a long way to go. The riparian states are still following a piecemeal approach, settling single-issue subjects rather than adopting a more integrated view on river basin management. Allocation aspects and increasing water claims are still at the center of discussion whereas water quality concerns have been disregarded until very recently and still do not rank very high on the political agenda.[236]

VI. Contentious Issues

Having established the legal framework, this will now be contrasted to the different positions of the riparian states with regard to international

---

[235] MoU between the Ministry of Environment and Forestry of the Republic of Turkey and the Ministry of Water Resources of the Republic of Iraq on Water, see note 114.

[236] This conclusion is made on the basis of observations made by the authors at the International Conference "Advancing Cooperation in the Euphrates and Tigris Region: Institutional Development and Multidisciplinary Perspectives", 2-4 May 2012 Istanbul, see <www.mpil.de/red/water>.

law, including an analysis of the main contentious issues. The following four main points of dispute can be discerned:

1. Euphrates and Tigris: Two Separate Rivers or One Integrated System?

A major issue between the riparians is the question of whether the Euphrates and the Tigris can be considered as an integrated system, or whether they are to be discussed and treated separately. Syria and Iraq view the Euphrates and the Tigris as two separate rivers.[237] Turkey does not share this view, arguing that the two rivers come together at the *Shatt-al-Arab* and that with Lake *Tharthar* Iraq has even intentionally connected the two rivers.[238] These conflicting positions are explained by the fact that all three riparians hope to attain the most benefits from their respective claims. Syria and especially Iraq fear that if they were to consider the rivers as part of one system, then their claims to a larger share of the Euphrates river would be weakened.[239] Turkey, in turn, is trying to retain its development schemes for the Euphrates since, due to favorable geographic conditions, it is more suited for water development projects than the Tigris.[240]

According to international water law two rivers generally are considered as forming a single unit (watercourse system or drainage basin),[241] if they share a common terminus and their waters are to a cer-

---

[237] They claim that both rivers flow separately for most of their way and are clearly separated by hydrological boundaries. The confluence of both rivers to form the Shatt-al-Arab is considered negligible; Iraqi Ministry of Water Resources, *Facts on the Joint Waters with Turkey*, 1999, 29, 35 (on file with the authors).

[238] Biedler, see note 29, 21.

[239] Ibid.; this is due to the possibility of feeding irrigation areas not only with water from the Euphrates but also from the Tigris.

[240] Iraqi Ministry of Water Resources, see note 237, 35.

[241] Art. 2 (a) UN Watercourses Convention, see note 121, speaks of a "watercourse system", as opposed to a "drainage basin". The latter term is followed by other legal instruments such as the ILA Helsinki Rules (1966), (see note 120) and the ILA Berlin Rules (article 3 ILA Berlin Rules (2004), (see note 120). It is based on a geographical concept and is broader than the term "watercourse system". The term comprises an entire system of interconnected waters, including principal and secondary tributaries as well as groundwaters which are not connected to surface water. It is often criti-

tain extent interconnected,[242] or constitute by virtue of their relationship a unitary whole.[243] Undoubtedly, the Euphrates and the Tigris both flow into a common terminus at the *Shatt-al-Arab*. It is also through the *Shatt-al-Arab* that both rivers are also sufficiently interconnected, so that they can also be regarded as a unitary whole. Even though international water law might seem prone to a single basin approach, ultimately it does not impose an obligation to follow it. Rather it is a management decision over which the riparians need to find an understanding. Whether to conclude two separate agreements for both rivers, or, to have one agreement treating the Euphrates and the Tigris as a single or two separate watercourse systems is a matter which needs to be negotiated. Nonetheless, from an environmental perspective it can only be recommended to treat the rivers as a single unit since activities on both rivers can result in harm for the *Shatt-al-Arab* as well as the Persian Gulf.

2. Terminology

Another problem is posed by the lack of consensus regarding the use of terminology. Syria and Iraq consider the rivers, to be *international* rivers which should be treated as integrated entities by all riparian users.[244] They accordingly argue for an equal share of the waters between all three riparians.[245] Turkey on the contrary considers *international* rivers

---

cized for over-restricting the sovereignty of states, since it can extend the scope of application of international law also to small tributaries lying entirely within a national territory; cf. ILC, Special Rapporteur Kearny, First Report of the Law on Non-navigational Uses of International Watercourses (7 May 1976), Doc. A/CN.4/295 of 7 May 1976, 184 et seq.; see also, Commentary to article 3 Berlin Rules (2004), see note 120.

[242] Article 3 No. 5 ILA Berlin Rules, see note 120.
[243] Article 2 (a) UN Watercourses Convention, see note 121.
[244] Iraqi Ministry of Water Resources, see note 237, 29, 35; M. Jouejati, "Water Politics as High Politics: The Case of Turkey and Syria", in: H.J. Barkey (ed.), *Reluctant Neighbor: Turkey's Role in the Middle East*, 1996, 131 (136 et seq.). For a detailed analysis of this issue see N. Bremer, *Non-Navigational Use of the Euphrates and Tigris River System. The Regulation of the Distribution and Utilisation of the Water of Euphrates and Tigris through International Law illustrated at the example of the Ataturk Dam and the Ilisu Dam*, forthcoming, Part 1, E.II.2.
[245] Iraqi Ministry of Water Resources, see note 237, 29.

only to be those that constitute a boundary between two or more states.[246] It thus does not recognize the "international" character of the Euphrates and the Tigris, but claims that they are "transboundary" or "trans-border" rivers, falling under Turkey's exclusive sovereignty until they flow across the borders.[247] Accordingly the Euphrates becomes an "international" river only after it joins the Tigris to form the *Shatt-Al Arab*. Before this point each state shall enjoy full sovereign rights to use the water flowing through its territory.[248] Turkey's distinction between "international" and "transboundary" rivers is based on an understanding that associates different rights and obligations to these terms. While "international" rivers are to be *shared* through the median line or Talweg,[249] "transboundary" rivers should be used in an equitable and reasonable way.[250]

The use of different terminology when describing the Euphrates and the Tigris is not only a barrier to cooperation, but also makes it difficult to relate to international law. International law, as expressed by the 1997 UN Watercourses Convention,[251] defines a watercourse[252] as "international" when parts of it are situated in different states.[253] Parts of both the Euphrates and the Tigris are situated in different states. According to the UN Watercourses Convention they are therefore "international". This corresponds with the view of the lower riparians Syria and Iraq. Turkey's distinction between "transboundary" and "international" is closer to a historic differentiation drawn between watercourses that form or traverse boundaries, respectively called "contiguous" and "successive" international watercourses.[254] The legal rules governing both

---

[246] Kibaroglu et al., see note 19, 20.
[247] Republic of Turkey, "Turkey Water Report 2009", *Report of the General Directorate of State Hydraulic Works*, 2009, 48 et seq.
[248] Ibid.
[249] H. Chalabi/ T. Majzoub, "Turkey, the Waters of the Euphrates and Public International Law", in: J.A. Allan/ C. Mallat (eds), *Water in the Middle East: Legal, Political and Commercial Implications*, 1995, 211.
[250] Republic of Turkey Report, see note 247, 48; Kibaroglu et al., see note 19, 20.
[251] UN Watercourses Convention, see note 121.
[252] As stated above the use of the term "watercourse" does not affect the application of international law to a river, but rather extends the scope of this body of law to an entire watercourse system, see note 241.
[253] See article 20 UN Watercourses Convention, see note 121.
[254] This distinction was primarily made in the law of navigational uses of watercourses. On this issue see McCaffrey, see note 61, 41 et seq.

types of watercourses are, however, the same and do not differentiate.²⁵⁵ This is likewise underscored by the terminology used in other water law instruments, for example the UNECE Helsinki Convention uses the term "transboundary" for border as well as for cross-border rivers (article 1 (1)) without treating them differently. Equally the ILC has used both terms interchangeably, connecting the same meaning to both "transboundary" and "international".²⁵⁶ Turkey's distinction alongside its association of different obligations and rights regarding the use of "transboundary" and "international" rivers,²⁵⁷ is thus not reflected by international water law. Strictly speaking, since international law does not abide by a certain terminology, the underlying problem here is not really one of use of terms, but of the scope of rights a state possesses *vis-à-vis* its co-riparians.²⁵⁸

3. Different Ideas about Criteria to Determine Water Needs

It is a prerequisite for reaching a sharing-agreement between the riparians that the three states agree on criteria to determine reasonable utilization. As mentioned above the norm of equitable and reasonable utilization is flexible, but also ambiguous and requires definition as well as quantification.²⁵⁹ Whereas Iraq, Syria and Turkey basically all acknowledge this norm,²⁶⁰ controversy exists over the definition and determination of an equitable and reasonable share.²⁶¹ More precisely the riparians disagree on how to weight the different criteria when determining

---

²⁵⁵ Ibid., 45.
²⁵⁶ Cf. article 2 (a) ILC Draft Articles on the Law of Non-navigational Uses of International Watercourses, see note 121, defining international as "situated in different states" and article 2 (c) ILC Draft Articles on the Law of Transboundary Aquifers adopted by the Commission on First Reading, see note 178, also defining transboundary as "situated in different states."
²⁵⁷ E.g. equitably "sharing" or "allocating" waters.
²⁵⁸ Chalabi/ Majzoub, see note 249, 220.
²⁵⁹ W. Scheumann, "Conflicts on the Euphrates: an Analysis of Water and Non-water Issues", in: W. Scheumann/ M. Schiffler (eds), *Water in the Middle East: Potential for Conflicts and Prospects for* Cooperation, 1998, 113 et seq. (128).
²⁶⁰ Kibaroglu, see note 5, 244; Iraqi Ministry of Water Resources, see note 237, 29.
²⁶¹ Scheumann, see note 259, 128.

an equitable utilization.[262] While Syria and especially Iraq claim that they have acquired rights pertaining to prior or historical uses dating back from ancestral times and favor a mathematical approach by equally portioning the rivers, Turkey with its so-called Three Stages Plan[263] follows a rather needs-based approach claiming that waters should be allocated according to the needs of each riparian.[264] In doing so, Turkey has, however, made clear that an equitable use also encompasses and focuses on an optimal use, more precisely the efficient and effective utilization, of water.[265] With Syria and Iraq wanting to guard their already existing and partly historic water installations and Turkey promoting the development of new installations, no doubt having in mind the successful completion of the GAP Project, the two positions are clearly marked by the development plans of the respective countries.[266] Not surprisingly all three states pursue an approach out of which they expect the most advantages for their situation.[267]

In this respect international water law provides only little guidance and there is basically no norm to follow in determining a priority of uses.[268] Accordingly, for the most part, international water law leaves it up to states to agree on criteria for sharing. The main problem is not one of law but that all three states insist on their respective positions and are not willing to depart from them.

---

[262] For criteria, see under V. 1. b.
[263] Three Stages Plan for Optimum, Equitable and Reasonable Utilization of the Transboundary Watercourse of the Euphrates Basin (Three Stages Plan), see Turkish Ministry of Foreign Affairs, see note 104, Chapter IV; for full particulars see under VII. 2. a.
[264] Kibaroglu, see note 5, 244; Scheumann, see note 259, 128.
[265] Republic of Turkey Report, see note 247, 48.
[266] Scheumann, see note 259, 128.
[267] As explained above (see under V.1.b.), the principle of equitable and reasonable utilization does neither mean an equal apportionment in a mathematical sense nor does it favor the most efficient utilization of a water resource.
[268] Cohen, see note 191, 526; for example article 6 (3) of the UN Watercourses Convention, (see note 121), stipulates that "the weight [...] given to each factor [shall] [...] be determined by its importance in comparison with other relevant factors", thus clearly leaving this decision to the State Parties. Only in article 10 (2) there is a reference stipulating a certain priority of uses or certain criteria, where it reads that "in the event of a conflict between uses [...] special regard shall be given to the requirements of vital human needs."

4. Turkish Position with regard to the 1997 UN Watercourses Convention: Turkey as Persistent Objector to Customary International Law?

Finally, the Turkish position towards the UN Watercourses Convention is perceived as an impediment to reaching consensus on the rules applicable in the Euphrates and the Tigris region. As mentioned earlier, Turkey is not a party to the UN Watercourses Convention whereas Syria and Iraq are. Although this issue is brought up quite frequently it actually does not pose a problem.[269] Indeed the UN Convention is an important resource of international water law, albeit not being in force. Yet, as elaborated above, there is a body of customary international water law,[270] which stipulates rights and obligations with regard to transboundary water cooperation, so that recourse to the UN Convention is not necessary. These rules of customary international law are binding upon states and in principle once a rule of customary international law has been established a state cannot exempt itself unilaterally. An exception to this rule is made only when a state has persistently objected to a rule during its formative stage.[271] Turkey has more than once raised objections towards certain provisions of the UN Convention, such as for example the specific implementation of the obligation to prevent harm enshrined in article 7.[272] Against this background one could possibly argue that Turkey's reluctance voices a persistent objection to these rules. Yet, even though it has rejected certain provisions of the UN

---

[269] See for example Kibaroglu, see note 5, 257 et seq.
[270] Which is in part also reflected by the UN Watercourses Convention, see note 121, see under V. 1.
[271] O. Elias, "Persistent Objector", in: Wolfrum, see note 6, para. 1.
[272] Turkey has *inter alia* raised the following points during the negotiations of the UN Watercourses Convention: (1) in general it criticized that the Convention went far beyond the scope of a framework document, which should be limited to enacting basic principles; (2) it proposed to omit article 7 completely since according to its view the obligation to prevent harm is subsidiary to that of equitable and reasonable utilization; (3) the dispute settlement clause in article 33 should be omitted and it should be up to the states concerned to determine the rules of procedure since compulsory rules do not fit into a framework convention. See Convention on the Law of the Non-navigational Uses of International Watercourses: Draft Articles on the Law of the Non-navigational Uses of International Watercourses and Resolution on Confined Transboundary Groundwater, Report of the Secretary-General, Doc. A/51/275 of 6 August 1996, 12, 35, 53.

Convention, it has also frequently expressed its adherence to the core norms of international water law, such as the obligation to prevent harm and equitable and reasonable utilization.²⁷³ On the basis of such an express commitment it would be far-reaching to regard Turkey as a persistent objector in this case. All three riparians must hence adhere to the rules of customary international law.

VII. Proposed Solutions

Over the years all riparians have brought forward different proposals to reach a solution on the water-related problems in the region. They shall be discussed in the following.

1. Syria and Iraq

Syria and Iraq put forward somewhat similar plans to reach a sharing agreement between the riparian states. Both proposed that the allocation of the Euphrates and the Tigris waters be achieved through mathematical formulae. According to the Syrian proposal, in a first step, the riparian states declare their water demand from the Euphrates and the Tigris. The two rivers are treated separately. Then the total water supply capacity of both rivers is determined in each state. Depending on the results, there are two possibilities: if the total water demand does not surpass the total water supply capacity, the water is allocated according to the declared quantities. If the water demand is higher than the potential water discharge, the deficit will be deducted proportionally from the demand stipulated by each riparian state.²⁷⁴ Pursuant to

---

[273] See for example, Turkey's written comment on the Draft Articles on the Law of Non-navigational Uses of International Watercourses, see note 121, in Convention on the Law of the Non-navigational Uses of International Watercourses: Draft Articles, see note 272, 28 and Turkish Ministry of Foreign Affairs, see note 104, Chapter III.

[274] Ibid., Chapter II.A; or Kibaroglu, see note 5, 252, who cites the final Communiqués of the 16 Joint Technical Committee meetings (1980-1992) as source. It should, however, be mentioned that other authors describe the Syrian position somewhat differently; cf. Jouejati, see note 244, 144; Elver, see note 5, 415. The Syrian proposal is described as follows: 1. The JTC calculates the flow of the Euphrates and Tigris; 2. The JTC roughly estimates the quantity of water needed by each riparian for its projects (current and

the Iraqi proposal the water demand for realized, planned and future projects is to be put forward by each state. The next step envisages the exchange of data on the Euphrates and the Tigris. Finally, the JTC shall calculate the quotas for water allocation. Thereby projects under operation shall be prioritized over planned projects.[275]

Even though mathematical approaches may have certain advantages – an apportionment based on percentages allows, for example, for a flexible reaction in case of drought – the proposed approaches can be criticized on various grounds. One point of criticism is that the mathematical apportionment of a water resource neither contributes to improve the problem of water scarcity nor takes into account water quality issues which are among the most pressing concerns for both downstream riparians. Measures that ease the water shortage or tackle water quality issues are not provided for in the Iraqi and Syrian proposals. Additionally, a strict mathematical approach does not consider the great seasonal as well as annual variability of the rivers' water flow.[276] It is, furthermore, pointed out that water demand claims are open to arbitrariness as it allows states to declare their needs unilaterally.[277]

2. Turkey

a. Three Stages Plan for Optimum, Equitable and Reasonable Utilization of the Transboundary Watercourse of the Euphrates Basin (Three Stages Plan)[278]

The Three Stages Plan was introduced by Turkey in 1984 and has been continuously reiterated since.[279] It is Turkey's official plan of action for the optimal use and allocation of the Euphrates (and Tigris) river. The central idea is that it would neither be efficient nor equitable to utilize

---

future); 3. Finally, the JTC establishes the share each riparian state is entitled to. The states have the right to utilize their share according to their own needs.

[275] Kibaroglu et al., see note 19, 63; Turkish Ministry of Foreign Affairs, see note 104, Chapter II.A.
[276] Jouejati, see note 244, 144.
[277] Elver, see note 5, 415.
[278] Turkish Ministry of Foreign Affairs, see note 104, Chapter IV.
[279] Kibaroglu/ Scheumann, see note 108, 277 et seq. (284) ; Kibaroglu, see note 5, 254.

considerable quantities of a scant resource to irrigate infertile or less productive soil. Hence, a variety of factors, such as geographic and climatic conditions or economic expediency, should also be taken into account when allocating water.[280]

To this end water allocation should firstly be based on the assessment of the available water resources (Stage 1 – Inventory Studies of Water Resources). This *inter alia* includes the exchange and examination of available data, joint measurements, the estimation of water uses and losses and the calculation of natural flows. In a second step the land resources (soil conditions and quality, crop patterns, irrigation requirements etc.) would be studied, assessed and classified (Stage 2 – Inventory Studies of Land Resources). Finally, based on the previous assessments water and land resources should be evaluated jointly. The needs for the competing sectors would then be established and the water allocated accordingly (Stage 3 – Evaluation of Water and Land Resources). This stage covers *inter alia* the modernization and rehabilitation of ongoing projects, the improvement of irrigation, the determination of the total water consumption and demand as well as the determination of the economic viability of planned projects.[281] The plan of action is based on two principal premises. Firstly, the Euphrates and the Tigris are considered as one single transboundary watercourse system. Secondly, an equitable, rational and optimal utilization of a watercourse can only be realized through a joint scientific study determining the actual water needs of each riparian state. In this context the collection and sharing of joint data is of crucial importance since it is on this basis that the necessary means and measures to achieve the aim of an optimum water allocation are established.[282]

The Three Stages Plan was rejected by Iraq and Syria. The two states criticized the fact that the concept reflected the position of Turkey: i.e. that the Euphrates and the Tigris are transboundary rivers (as opposed to international rivers) and constitute a single system.[283] Furthermore, it was argued that the Turkish plan of action heavily infringed upon the sovereignty of the riparian states.[284] It was also noted that Syria and

---

[280] Chalabi/ Majzoub, see note 249, 213-214.
[281] Turkish Ministry of Foreign Affairs, see note 106, Chapter IV.
[282] Ibid.
[283] See under VI.
[284] Jouejati, see note 244, 143.

Iraq feared that Turkey would use the inventory studies on land resources to expose their supposedly inefficient agricultural practices.[285]

The Three Stages Plan is the most comprehensive water management plan brought forward by one of the riparian states. Unlike the other proposals, it does not exclusively concentrate on the quantitative aspect of water allocation but rather envisages a broad analysis of water and land resources encompassing both strategies on resource as well as on demand management. Moreover, the Plan recognizes the importance of data sharing, joint data gathering, data comparability and the application of advanced technology, which are undoubtedly reasonable approaches. Yet, the reluctance of Iraq and Syria to embrace the plan is also comprehensible. The Three Stages Plan in fact puts Turkey in a favorable position. Iraq for example suffers from very low water use efficiency and irrigation yields,[286] due to which it will probably not receive a very favorable classification in the assessment of water and land resources. Theoretically the plan is to be embraced, however, in practice it is probably extremely difficult if not impossible to implement. A minimum prerequisite would be a good and stable political environment and mutual trust between the riparian states. This is not the case at the moment. In addition, it can be stated that even though the implementation of the Plan probably would have a positive effect on the environment, environmental concerns still are not at the center of attention.

b. The Peace Pipeline

The proposal of a Peace Pipeline was introduced by Turkey at the end of the 1980s. Two pipelines were to supply water from Turkey (the *Ceyhan* and *Keyhan* rivers were named as possible sources) to Gulf and Middle East countries. One pipeline would supply water to Jordanian and Syrian cities. The other massive pipeline – the grander version – was supposed to go further south and export water to Saudi Arabia, Bahrain, Kuwait, Oman, Qatar and the United Arab Emirates.[287] However, the Peace Pipeline projects were never realized. Saudi Arabia and

---

[285] Kibaroglu, see note 5, 256-257.
[286] Grey/ Blackmore, see note 168, 7 (Report on file with the authors).
[287] It is interesting to note that the pipeline(s) could have had a positive side-effect for Syria. From the fall of the pipeline when entering Syrian territory, Syria could generate electric power; see B. Wachtel, "The Peace Canal Project: A Multiple Conflict Resolution Perspective for the Middle East", in: J. Isaac/ H. Shuval (eds), *Water and Peace in the Middle East*, 1994, 363 et seq. (368).

the Gulf States did not want to depend on the good will of both Turkey and Syria (the pipeline was to go through Syria).[288] Additionally, they feared sabotage or blackmail. Besides, it was maintained that the projects were not cost effective. Protests also came from Syria and Iraq. Whereas Syria did not want Israel to benefit from the project,[289] Iraq feared to receive less water since, even if the Peace Pipeline was not to be supplied with the Euphrates and Tigris waters, it was argued that Turkey would compensate its water loss from these waters. The Iraqis further claimed that such exports demonstrated that Turkey was storing more water than needed and as a consequence, the equitable shares of both downstream states should be larger.[290]

VIII. Elements to be Considered for a Future Framework

1. Why do Iraq, Syria and Turkey Need a Trilateral Water Agreement?

Already the nature of a "shared" resource implies cooperation. Actions or uses within one state almost always have effects on the environment in other states. Experience has shown that without cooperation the danger of overuse through unilateral development accompanied by environmental degradation or even depletion of the fresh water resource is very high. Eventually this may not only irreversibly harm the resource, but also confront states with the danger that they will not be able to provide their populations with enough water.

Coordinated development or even joint management brings about benefits for all riparian states (e.g. *inter alia* reduced costs for infrastructure, predictable water supply, flood control, effective pollution control).[291] Moreover, it is a necessary prerequisite for achieving and maintaining overall good water quality, alongside a healthy ecosystem. In order to maximize these reciprocal benefits and to ensure a sustainable utilization of their water resources, states need to overcome their

---

[288] Dellapenna, see note 62, 233-235.
[289] Jouejati, see note 244, 143.
[290] Dellapenna, see note 62, 233-235; 253-255.
[291] C.W. Sadoff/ D. Grey, "Beyond the River: the Benefits of Cooperation on International Rivers", *Water Policy* 4 (2002), 389 et seq. (393 et seq.); who distinguish between benefits "to", "from", "because" and "beyond" the river.

political differences and move away from competition and challenging each others' rights towards seeking joint action.[292] Recent efforts at cooperation show that the three riparians of the Euphrates and the Tigris river are becoming aware of the need to tackle common concerns.

In this context a treaty laying down specific obligations is more likely to be respected than general norms of international law alone.[293] At the same time if states manage to balance conflicting interests and find a satisfactory solution for all it would bring stability.[294] Where inequalities remain and a solution does not deliver equal benefits an agreement can provide for procedures such as a compensation mechanism to ensure an equal distribution of benefits and costs.[295] Finally a treaty can give all co-riparians better assurance that their partners are abiding by the rules.[296] In particular, treaty commitment is generally fostered by including an additional compliance control mechanism through which states can also assist each other in fulfilling treaty obligations.[297] This does in turn not only strengthen implementation but it also promotes mutual trust which is crucial for the successful and sustainable sharing of a resource.

2. Elements to be Considered in a Trilateral Agreement

It should have become quite obvious that the riparians of the Euphrates and the Tigris need to agree on a method how to share their waters in

---

[292] Grzybowski/ McCaffrey/ Paisley, see note 151, 143.
[293] K. Mechlem, "Water as Vehicle for Inter-state Cooperation: A Legal Perspective", *FAO Legal Paper Online* 32 (2003), 6.
[294] It should be noted that an agreement can also pave the way for greater cooperation resulting in benefits *beyond* the river such as regional security, see Sadoff/ Grey, see note 291, 393.
[295] A. Houdret/ A. Kramer/ A. Carius, "The Water Security Nexus: Challenges and Opportunities for Development Cooperation", *GTZ Concept Paper International Water Policy and Infrastructure Programme*, 2010, 18. Such a mechanism could for example require a lower riparian to contribute or even co-finance an upstream investment that shall reduce negative pollution effects downstream.
[296] Mechlem, see note 293, 7.
[297] S. Vinogradov/ P. Wouters/ P. Jones, *Transforming Potential Conflict into Cooperation Potential: The Role of International Law*, 2003, 66 et seq., who name typical elements of compliance control mechanisms to consist of *inter alia* reporting, review and evaluation procedures.

an equitable and sustainable way. All three states must urgently improve their cooperative management of the Euphrates and the Tigris basin to prevent further damage to the ecosystems of the rivers and to secure water supply for future generations. The following section shall give an overview of the elements which should be considered when negotiating a future framework.[298]

a. General Remarks on Issues Essential for a Successful and Above All Sustainable Water Agreement

In general it is pivotal for an agreement to be drafted in clear, precise and unambiguous language. This not only helps to prevent disputes over interpretation but also greatly facilitates the implementation of an agreement.[299] Furthermore, a treaty should be flexible enough to provide for its provisions to be adjusted, in particular with regard to natural impacts such as climate change. States should, however, be careful not to make it too flexible since this can also become a barrier to successful implementation.[300] Finally, state practice demonstrates that a broad and comprehensive approach towards overall basin management has proven to be more successful than a narrow one, focusing only on particular water issues. A sustainable and successful cooperative management concept is premised on a broad approach taking into account all aspects involved with the sharing of a common water resource, such as *inter alia* needs, uses, climate change, the hydrological cycle and the ecosystem.[301]

---

[298] The overview is largely based on a checklist developed by Vinogradov, Wouters and Jones who have identified the most important elements of the majority of watercourse agreements; Vinogradov/ Wouters/ Jones, see note 297.

[299] Vinogradov/ Wouters/ Jones, see note 297, 45.

[300] Agreements with a wording that is too flexible run the risk of being contested easily. Nevertheless agreements should provide for a certain degree of flexibility so that they can be adapted when new issues emerge or situations change.

[301] Houdret/ Kramer/ Carius, see note 295, 19.

b. Key Components

In particular, to provide for a sustainable agreement, experts have identified the most important elements to be considered in negotiations:[302]

– Scope

It is important to determine the exact scope of an agreement by providing for a clear definition of the waters covered by treaty provisions.[303] With regard to the Euphrates and the Tigris the riparians thus need to decide whether or not the rivers should be regarded as one or two separate watercourse systems. Although the question needs to be decided, it should be noted that a successful cooperative management concept is not dependent on its outcome. Iraq, Syria and Turkey are free to decide whether they would rather negotiate two (associated) agreements for the rivers or one unified one.[304]

– Substantive Rules

Every agreement centers on substantive rules (and principles) laying down the rights and obligations of its signatories. As noted earlier, international water law stipulates certain obligations for states sharing a watercourse (above all equitable and reasonable utilization; obligation to prevent harm). Riparians should draw from this framework of rights and obligations and incorporate it into their agreements by applying it to the specific situation. Of particular importance for a successful and sustainable agreement is finding a ratio of how to equitably and reasonably utilize a shared river, since any party who perceives a treaty to be inequitable will most likely attempt to obstruct its implementation.[305] An agreement which does not integrate these established rules of law will thus, in all likeliness, not be very successful.

An equitable and reasonable utilization is based on finding a framework for the allocation of existing and future uses. This framework

---

[302] Based on the checklist developed by Vinogradov, Wouters and Jones who have identified the most important elements of the majority of watercourse agreements, Vinogradov/ Wouters/ Jones, see note 297. The checklist has partially been adapted to the specificities of the Euphrates and Tigris region.
[303] Ibid., 46.
[304] Trondalen, see note 33, 196.
[305] Vinogradov/ Wouters/ Jones, see note 297, 53.

shall then govern the lawfulness of uses (existing and future).[306] It should, as far as possible, enable all riparians to attain the maximum possible benefits with the greatest satisfaction of all their needs. In order to actually achieve this, riparians need to take into account certain key issues, some of which are specified in the following:[307]

- *Vital Human Needs*

    When weighing different uses prior attention should be paid to vital human needs.[308] This requires the identification of a minimum amount of clean water needed to satisfy needs for drinking, domestic and sanitary purposes of the populations living along the banks of the Euphrates and the Tigris.

- *Existing and Proposed Uses*

    Moreover the riparians need to identify all existing uses and project their future requirements, such as for example the development of Turkey's agricultural uses in Southern Anatolia upon completion of the GAP. As much as the riparians need to identify existing uses they should also envisage proposed uses. As *Vinogradov* and his colleagues rightfully stress this does not imply the formulation of "a wish list but uses that are economically and environmentally feasible."[309] This would, for example, include calculations with regard to demands of Syria or Iraq for expansion of irrigation.

- *Alternative Resources*

    Additionally it is also important to indentify practicable alternative resources to meet the regions' water needs. Possible surface water shortfalls could for example be compensated through recourse to groundwater. This should, however, not be done with out considering safeguards to its adequate protection and the aspect of its hydrological interdependence with surface water.

- *Environmental Requirements*

    Last but not least riparians should look towards the integration of environmental concerns by identifying the environmental needs of both rivers and their related ecosystems (e.g. indentify the mini-

---

[306] Ibid., 74.
[307] The following issues were identified as key components when determining an equitable and reasonable utilization, see ibid., 74.
[308] See under V. 1. g.
[309] Vinogradov/ Wouters/ Jones, see note 297, 74.

mum in-stream flow necessary to protect the watercourse; introduce minimum standards for pollution control).

Finally, it is imperative to ensure that substantive rules are not only proclaimed but are actually also operationalized.[310] In that regard the importance of national water laws and policies must be highlighted. The most advanced international agreement is rendered useless if implementation on the national level is lacking.

– Procedural Rules

Long term successful cooperation cannot be achieved without finding an agreement on procedures to manage the watercourse and implement the substantive obligations. Without clear procedural rules a cooperation agreement can quickly turn into nothing but empty promises.

– Institutional Mechanisms

Many agreements on international watercourses include provisions providing for the establishment of institutional mechanisms in the form of joint bodies or commissions.[311] In fact it is hard to find any legal regime governing a transboundary watercourse which does not provide for some kind of institutional mechanism.[312] They not only promote the peaceful settlement of disputes but are also very helpful when it comes to coordinating management and development efforts between riparian states.

Iraq, Syria and Turkey have already gained some experiences in this regard from the JTC. Even though the JTC was not particularly successful, the example shows that the riparians were at least convinced of the advantages of an institutional mechanism. Today many different types of institutional arrangements and joint bodies with a great variety of forms and functions exist.[313] Albeit the fact that they are always established in relation to specific waters and address very par-

---

[310] Ibid., 53.
[311] Ibid., 57.
[312] Ibid., 62.
[313] The UNECE has distinguished three major types of institutional arrangements in international watercourse agreements: "(a) without designation of an institution to implement the agreement; (b) the appointment of plenipotentiaries (governmental representatives); and (c) the establishment of a joint commission"; see UNECE, "River Basin Commissions and other Institutions for Transboundary Water Cooperation: Capacity for Water Cooperation in Eastern Europe", *Caucasus and Central Asia* 1 (2009), 10.

ticular issues, experts have identified some principles of organization that are said to increase the efficiency of joint bodies, such as *inter alia* the importance of a broad competence and clearly defined powers.[314] The three riparians of the Euphrates and the Tigris should try to resume the discussions over the JTC and try to find an agreement on form and function of sustainable joint management mechanism(s).[315]

– Dispute Avoidance and Settlement Mechanisms

International water law is extremely sensitive to disputes. This is in part due to the general sensitivity of water issues as well as the use of broad rather flexible terminology. It is clear that the mere conclusion of an agreement will not make controversies disappear. Potential signatories need to envisage the possibility of disputes. Riparian states are thus well advised to design a conflict prevention, management and settlement mechanism to be included in their water sharing agreements.[316] International (water) law offers a wide range of different mechanisms which states can draw from, ranging from direct negotiations to third party involvement, comprising optional or mandatory arbitration and adjudication.[317]

---

[314] For more details see ibid., 39 et seq.

[315] Trondalen proposes the establishment of a new overarching international initiative he dubs the Euphrates and Tigris Basin Initiative (ETI), which is basically modeled on the Nile Basin Initiative launched by the riparians of the Nile River in 1999. According to his proposal this initiative shall be "a partnership initiated and led by the riparian States of the two rivers through a Council of Ministers with the full support of the international community, through an international organization such as [for example] the Arab development banks and institutions." He suggests that for the first phase the ETI shall start with a participatory process of dialogue and trust building which shall then ideally result in the formulation of a shared vision for the Euphrates and Tigris rivers. In a second phase this vision could then be translated into a more concrete program of action; for details see Trondalen, see note 33, 203 et seq.

[316] Vinogradov/ Wouters/ Jones, see note 297, 62.

[317] Ibid., 65 et seq.; for an overview of dispute settlement and prevention mechanisms in international water law, see McCaffrey, see note 61, 506 et seq.

IX. Conclusion

This is not the first study on the Euphrates and the Tigris rivers expressing the need for urgent action and underscoring the importance of finding a comprehensive trilateral solution (e.g. in form of a binding international agreement). Both rivers are still severely suffering from increasing water demands and deterioration of water quality. However times are changing, after many years of collaboration and frictions one has recently been able to witness a new dynamic of cooperation in the region, expressing itself for example in the relaunch of the JTC as well as the signing of the various MoUs. Unlike previous collaboration efforts the new initiatives seem to be following a more comprehensive approach focusing on multiple issues regarding the social and economic development of the region rather than focusing on water issues alone. Although the broadening of the negotiation agenda has proven beneficial to overcome the water negotiation deadlock and enhance dialogue, it still is a piecemeal approach, which does not necessarily solve the question of finding a sustainable trilateral or possible even multilateral (including other basin states) solution. Yet in the long term perspective improved relations and close socio- and economic ties between the riparian states may indeed pave the way for a comprehensive and sustainable resolution for the sharing of the rivers and a secure water future for the region.

Moreover, EU accession talks with Turkey present another driving factor for the latter to multiply its cooperation efforts.[318] Turkey has started harmonizing its domestic legislation with that of the EU in the field of environment and water resources making EU regulations a determining factor in Turkish water policies.[319] Nevertheless, with the recent turmoil in the Arab world and the fate of Syria being still uncertain, the political relations in the Euphrates and the Tigris region will most likely be influenced which could lead to a setback in cooperation on water issues. This should, however, not narrow the room for opti-

---

[318] For an overview of the EU Water Aquis and Turkey's progress up to date see A. Kibaroglu, "Legislative framework for Water Management in Turkey", see under <http://mpil.de/red/water>.

[319] A. Kibaroglu/ A. Kramer, "Turkey's Position toward International Water Law", in: Kibaroglu/ Scheumann/ Kramer, see note 108, 215 et seq. (227); A. Kibaroglu/ V. Sumer, "Diverging Water Management Paradigms between Turkey and the European Union", *Water International* 32 (2007), 739 et seq. (746).

mism. All three states in principle accept the core norms of international water law and have, at least individually, repeatedly stressed the importance of cooperation.

The LL.M. thesis being published below is the seventh in a series written in connection with a project introduced in 2004, by the Faculty of Law of the University of Heidelberg and the Universidad de Chile with scientific support from the Max Planck Institute for Comparative Public Law and International Law and the Institute for International Studies at the Universidad de Chile.

The project offers a one year Ph.D. course (International Law – Trade, Investments and Arbitration).

Chairs of the project are Prof. Rüdiger Wolfrum and Prof. María Teresa Infante Caffi.

Improving Compliance Mechanisms of the International Waste Trade Regime by Introducing Economic Compliance Incentives

University of Heidelberg, Max Planck Institute for Comparative Public Law and International Law and the University of Chile, March 2011

Daniela Wehlend

Table of Contents
I.   Introduction
II. Concept of Investigation
III. The Basel Convention: History, Scope, Mechanisms
    1. History and Background
    2. Scope
    3. Trade Restrictions and Exceptions
    4. Organs
    5. Regional Centers
    6. Finances
    7. Duties of the Member States
    8. Compliance Mechanism
    9. Criticized Deficiencies of the Basel Convention
    10. Financial Problems
IV. Compliance Theory and Means of Compliance in International Environmental Law
    1. Definitions of Compliance in International Environmental Law
    2. Basic Introduction to Compliance Theory
    3. Compliance and Treaty Design of MEAs
    4. Means to Ensure Compliance
        a. Confrontational Means
        b. Non-confrontational Means
            aa. Procedural Means: Reporting, Monitoring, Verification
            bb. Non-compliance Procedures
            cc. Facilitative Means
        c. Economic Incentives
        d. The Example of the Convention on Biological Diversity
        e. Compliance Assistance and Capacity-Building
    5. Financing Compliance with MEAs
    6. Possible Strategies to Enhance Compliance with and Funding of the Basel Convention
V.   Incentives to Grant Compliance Assistance for Developed State Parties in other selected MEAs
    1. Introduction
    2. Compliance and Funding Mechanisms of the Montreal Protocol on Substances that Deplete the Ozone Layer
        a. The Financial Mechanism of the Montreal Protocol: The Multilateral Fund
        b. Possible Conclusions from the MPMF
    3. Compliance and Funding Mechanisms of the Kyoto Protocol to the United Nations Framework Convention on Climate Change (UNFCCC)
        a. Flexible Mechanisms and Funding under the Kyoto Protocol
        b. Possible Conclusions from the Kyoto Protocol Flexible Mechanisms
VI. Conclusions

I. Introduction

Between February and May 2009 more than 1,400 tons of toxic waste were shipped into the Brazilian port of Santos, São Paulo and two other southern ports of the country.[1] This toxic waste, misleadingly marked as "recyclable plastics," came from the United Kingdom. It mostly consisted of used diapers, condoms, syringes, household waste and hospital waste, e.g. used blood bags. The containers were finally detected and held by Brazilian port and environmental authorities. Their United Kingdom counterparts had to take the waste back and start investigations in order to find out who was responsible for the illegal transport and the attempt to illegally dispose of these wastes.[2]

Not all cases of illegal traffic and disposal of hazardous wastes end up by being detected and returned. In 2006, hundreds of tons of toxic oil sludge that emitted the poisonous gas hydrogen sulfide were dumped in various sites around the city of Abidjan in Côte d'Ivoire. These dumping grounds, mostly landfills, were not adequately equipped for the safe disposal of these wastes. The Deputy Director of the Côte d'Ivoire Office of the Prime Minister reported – on 28 November 2006 to the Conference of the Parties of the Basel Convention on the Control of Transboundary Movement of Hazardous Wastes and their Disposal (hereinafter, Basel Convention)[3] – that the illegal dumping had caused more than 100,000 citizens to suffer from symptoms like nausea, vomiting, skin reactions, severe headaches and nose bleeds.[4] Indeed, sixty-nine people were hospitalized and at least ten people died of poisoning. Moreover, environmental consequences included air pollution, contamination of water sources, closure of the city's household waste treatment center for two months and contamination of the food chain. The incident further caused a halt for many economic activities. Fishermen, bakers and farmers had to discontinue their work and industries had to lay off workers.

---

[1] "Brazil demands return of UK waste", BBC Online 18 July 2009, available at <http://news.bbc.co.uk>.
[2] See note 1.
[3] Basel Convention on the Control of Transboundary Movements of Hazardous Wastes and their Disposal of 22 March 1989, available at <http://www.basel.int>.
[4] UNEP *Conference of the Parties to the Basel Convention on the Control of Transboundary Movements of Hazardous Wastes and their Disposal*, Report on the 8th Mtg, Doc. UNEP/CHW8/16, para. 25.

This waste had been transported on behalf of *Trafigura*, a multinational commodities trade company based in the Netherlands, but coordinating its shipping activities from London.[5] *Trafigura* ordered the toxic sludge to be sent to Côte d'Ivoire, where it was handed over to *Tommy* – an unqualified and ill-equipped local company. *Tommy* had accepted the disposal of the sludge for a much cheaper price than any European company. Nonetheless, *Tommy* then had its workers dump the waste in mostly open-air spaces in Abidjan. In July 2010, a Dutch court found *Trafigura* guilty of the illegal export of hazardous wastes.[6]

Illicit movement and dumping of toxic and dangerous products and wastes are serious problems. These types of acts are severe enough to be called a "serious threat to human rights, including the right to life, the enjoyment of the highest attainable standard of physical and mental health and …[to] other human rights affected by the illicit movement and dumping of toxic and dangerous products, including the rights to clean water, food, adequate housing and work, particularly of individual developing countries that do not have the technologies to process them."[7] In addition, even the enjoyment of "civil, political, economic, social and cultural rights and the right to development"[8] is feared to be in danger.

All the states that were directly or indirectly involved in the cases described above are State Parties to an international convention that was negotiated within the framework and under the auspices of UNEP. UNEP regulates toxic waste movements to foreign countries within the framework of the Basel Convention. The Basel Convention limits transboundary waste movements to the greatest extent possible by requiring that the generation of hazardous wastes should be avoided in the first place. Moreover, the Convention mandates that the treatment of the wastes should take place as close as possible to the site of the wastes' origin. Indeed, transboundary movements of hazardous wastes

---

[5] P. Murphy, "British Court to hear Ivorian waste class action", Reuters Online 2 February 2007, available at <http://www.reuters.com>.

[6] "Trafigura found guilty of exporting toxic waste", BBC Online 23 July 2010, available at <http://www.bbc.co.uk>.

[7] UN High Commissioner for Human Rights, *Adverse Effects of the Illicit Movement and Dumping of Toxic and Dangerous Products and Wastes on the Enjoyment of Human Rights*, Doc. E/CN.4/RES/2005/15.

[8] Human Rights Council Resolution, *The adverse Effects of the Movement and Dumping of toxic and dangerous Products and Wastes on the Enjoyment of Human Rights*, Doc. A/HRC/RES/12/18.

are only allowed when the technology necessary to treat the wastes in a safe way is not available in the country of the wastes' origin and when it is guaranteed that the country of destination possesses adequate disposal facilities. If a transboundary movement of hazardous wastes cannot be avoided by any means, the core obligation of the Basel Convention is to manage this movement and disposal in an environmentally sound manner.[9] This core obligation is expressed in procedures (based on the principle of prior informed consent) that keep each movement under permanent monitoring. Moreover, State Parties to the Basel Convention are required to criminalize the illegal traffic of hazardous wastes.

The Basel Convention was negotiated in the late 1980s, a decade in which several major incidents related to the illegal transport and disposal of hazardous wastes[10] led to public protests and a growth of awareness regarding the danger and harm of these activities. The large subscription to the Basel Convention – 178 Member States as of 2011 – shows that the subject matter does not lack general approval. Nonetheless, this thesis is based upon the determination that mere compliance with the Basel Convention is not adequate. In particular, it points out, that the illegal traffic of hazardous wastes to developing countries is barely under control.

---

[9] P. Birnie/ A. Boyle, *International Law and the Environment*, 2002, 433 et seq.
[10] The odysseys of the cargo ships *Karin B.* and *Khian Sea* were crucial for the ascending public call for making waste trade safer and fairer. The *Karin B.* carried toxic waste from Italy to Nigeria, resulting in the dumping of reported 6.000 drums of chlorinated solvents, waste resins, and some highly toxic polychlorinated biphenyls (PBCs) in Nigeria. The Italian government ordered the wastes back, when the case was made public, but Italian authorities objected the return, forcing the *Karin B.* to wander the Mediterranean and North Sea, before Italy finally accepted the wastes back. S. Greenhouse, "Toxic Waste Boomerang: Ciao Italy!", New York Times Online 3 September 1988, available at <http://query.nytimes.com>. The *Khian Sea* was carrying 28 million pounds of municipal and industrial incinerator ash from the city of Philadelphia (United States). The ash contained dangerous and toxic compounds, including aluminum, arsenic, chromium, copper, lead, mercury, nickel, zinc and dioxins. 2000 tons of ashes were dumped in Haiti, but when the nature of the ashes came out, further dumping was consequently denied by other states. Finally, the ashes disappeared and the ship showed up at an Asian port with an empty hold and a new name, *Pelicano*; "After two years, Ship dumps toxic Ash", New York Times Online 28 November 1988, available at, see above.

Moreover, the thesis deals with the separate and unclear future of the Basel Ban Amendment. The Basel Ban Amendment was adopted by the 2nd Conference of the Parties to the Basel Convention in 1994 and implemented as an amendment to the Convention by the third Conference of the Parties in 1995. It contained an immediate ban on the export of hazardous wastes from OECD to non OECD-countries. The Ban Amendment has not yet entered into force, as it has to be ratified by three-fourths of the Parties which accepted it. This is mainly due to a conflict regarding the interpretation of article 17.5 of the Ban Agreement.[11] So far, only the EU and EFTA have implemented a regulation prohibiting hazardous wastes transports for disposal to any state which is not a member of one of these two organizations.[12]

However, inspections in major European ports designated to detect illegal transport of hazardous wastes conducted by IMPEL-TSF,[13] reveal the ongoing regularity of violations. Between e.g. 2006 and 2008, 300 hazardous wastes shipments (each of them carrying waste freights of up to hundreds of tons of waste) were found to be in non-compliance with specific regulations. 40 per cent of these wastes shipments turned out to be illegal waste transports, while a further 60 per cent violated administrative rules.[14]

---

[11] See in detail below and article 17 para. 5 Basel Convention, "Instruments of ratification, approval, formal confirmation or acceptance of amendments shall be deposited with the Depositary. *Amendments adopted in accordance with paragraphs 3 or 4 above shall enter into force between Parties having accepted them on the ninetieth day after the receipt by the Depositary of their instrument of ratification, approval, formal confirmation or acceptance by at least three-fourths of the Parties who accepted them or by at least two thirds of the Parties to the protocol concerned who accepted them*, except as may otherwise be provided in such protocol. The amendments shall enter into force for any other Party on the ninetieth day after that Party deposits its instrument of ratification, approval, formal confirmation or acceptance of the amendments." (Emphasis added).

[12] EC Regulation on Shipments of Wastes, Doc. 1013/2006, arts 34 and 36.
Article 34 prohibits the exports of all wastes for disposal purposes to third countries (states which are not members of the EU or EFTA). According to article 36 of the Regulation, waste movements for recovery purposes are possible within the OECD.

[13] Transfrontier Shipment Branch of the European Union Network for the Implementation and Enforcement of Environmental Law, available at <http://impeltfs.eu>.

[14] The International Hazardous Waste Trade through Seaports, INECE-SESN Working Paper of 24 November 2009, 8, available at

From October 2008 to March 2011, further 3,897 transfrontier shipments of waste, which left European exit points, underwent physical inspections regarding compliance with the EC Waste Shipment Regulation. 833 of the inspected wastes shipments, which amount to slightly over 21 per cent, turned out to be in violation of the EC Waste Shipment Regulation requirements or related national requirements.[15]

These and other inspections indicate that the African continent is a favorite destination for many categories of European hazardous waste,[16] notwithstanding the fact that 51 African states are members of the Bamako Convention on the Ban of the Import into Africa and the Control of Transboundary Movement and Management of Hazardous Wastes within Africa[17] (hereinafter, Bamako Convention). It was negotiated and adopted in order to compensate the perceived flaws of the Basel Convention, and strictly bans imports of all kinds of hazardous wastes for both disposal and recycling purposes into its Member States.

It is therefore possible to conclude that an export prohibition in the region of the generation and an import prohibition in the region of destination taken together do not successfully prevent illegal transboundary waste movements and its disposal. This thesis argues that this unsatisfying situation is due to the fact that the Basel Convention and its offspring treaties do not address the source of the problem.

The attractiveness of disposing of wastes in developing countries and those with economies in transition is, *inter alia*, due to "the disappearance of landfill sites in industrialized countries, escalating disposal costs, and the difficulty of obtaining approval for incineration facilities."[18] The increased costs of hazardous wastes disposal – coupled with a permanent urgent need for space to dispose the immense quantities of hazardous wastes produced in industrialized societies and "an increasing demand [of many developing states] for secondary base materials from waste recycling – provides an incentive for some actors to make

---

<http://www.inece.org>. The Seaport Environmental Security Network of the International Network for Environmental Compliance and Enforcement is a partnership organization of government and non-government enforcement and compliance practitioners from more than 150 countries, more information available at <http://www.inece.org/seaport>.

[15] IMPEL-TFS Enforcement Actions, Actions II, Final Report of 28 April 2011, 21, available at <http://impeltfs.eu>.
[16] Id., see note 15, 43.
[17] African Union Treaties, Bamako Convention.
[18] Birnie/ Boyle, see note 9, 406 et seq.

profits through illegal operations."[19] Illegal waste movement is a profit-driven business which in most cases is conducted by private enterprises rather than state agencies, and is fueled by a constant demand for cheap waste solutions.

II. Concept of Investigation

This thesis aims to find new approaches to improve compliance with the Basel Convention. Chapter III. consists of an overview of the Basel Convention, its scope and mechanisms and the criticisms it faces. Parts IV. and V. are dedicated to the development of two different but very closely linked ideas about the development of a new compliance mechanism.

The first idea gives an initial basic overview of existing methods to ensure compliance with Multilateral Environmental Agreements (hereinafter, MEAs). It emphasizes the methods which probably respond most effectively to situations of non-compliance which derive from the predominance of economic needs and advantages over environmental considerations or from the incapability to comply. Specifically, the idea of (economic) incentives and compliance assistance, as the most feasible methods to enhance compliance, will be presented.

According to Wolfrum, compliance with MEAs, especially through State Parties with limited financial and technical resources, is best achieved by two mechanisms. "[E]ither by balancing environmental commitments by potential economic benefits which make adherence to the respective treaty and compliance therewith in general more acceptable or by assisting individual States in particular cases in the compliance with obligations entered into."[20] Regarding economic incentives used to enhance compliance with MEAs, hopes are high. For example, Montini identifies a "trend towards a progressive partial shift from the traditional command and control approach to an increased use of economic instruments for environmental regulation."[21] He further states,

---

[19] The International Hazardous Waste Trade through Seaports, see note 14, 4.
[20] R. Wolfrum, *Means of Ensuring Compliance with and Enforcement of International Environmental Law*, 1999, 110 et seq.
[21] M. Montini, "Improving Compliance with Multilateral Environmental Agreements through Positive Measures: The Case of the Kyoto Protocol on Climate Change", in: A. Kiss/ D. Shelton/ K. Ishibashi (eds), *Economic*

that "economic instruments are particularly helpful in the environmental sector insofar as they may help achieving the goal of sustainable development."[22]

Given that the developed compliance system should be, *inter alia*, based on economic or market-based approaches, a ban on transboundary movement of hazardous wastes to developing countries might be a misguided approach to the goal of a safer system of transboundary movements of hazardous wastes. Many developing countries lack the administrative structure to properly supervise compliance with the Basel Ban or with a regional Convention that bans the import of hazardous wastes and other wastes. Indeed, illegal waste traffic is promoted rather than abolished.

Further, a ban does not take into account that many developing countries resent being generally deemed incompetent to deal with hazardous wastes. Instead, a controlled permission to transport hazardous wastes to developing countries for disposal and recycling purposes could constitute an economically valuable option for these countries to develop a highly-productive and environmentally sound industry – if the right conditions are met. This thesis will highlight how controlled global movement of hazardous wastes could even improve compliance with the Basel Convention. Additional to an economically driven compliance system, the thesis will suggest "back-up" mechanisms that are not yet integrated in the Basel Convention. Examples of such mechanisms could be either random on-site inspections on waste treatment facilities in any country or movement permits based on the eligibility of waste treatment facilities.

The second idea departs from the fact that economic incentives and compliance assistance methods are both closely related to the finance mechanisms of MEAs. This is due to the fact that their application generally depends on the monetary resources available to a convention to use for this purpose. The Basel Convention indeed provides for a compliance assistance mechanism and a fund to finance compliance projects for State Parties in need. It suffers, though, from a chronic lack of resources. For example, voluntary State Party donations, which constitute the main source to finance compliance projects, are insufficient and generally not in time. Simultaneously to the review of compliance enhancement measures, this paper will scrutinize the finance systems ap-

---

Globalization and Compliance with International Environmental Agreements, 2003, 168 et seq.
22 Montini, see note 21, 168 et seq.

plied in other MEAs and the successful interplay that finance systems and economic incentives are able to develop if adequate market-based schemes are applied. It will present examples of MEAs whose performance regarding this interplay between incentives, assistance and funding is – put bluntly – much more successful than through the application of the Basel Convention. Specifically, two MEAs will be analyzed in Part V. in order to examine whether their strategies and mechanisms could be useful for the compliance system of the Basel Convention. The MEAs chosen to be examined for these purposes are the Montreal Protocol on Substances that Deplete the Ozone Layer[23] and the Kyoto Protocol to the United Nations Framework Convention on Climate Change.[24] Both MEAs are universal and rather old and, according to the treaty design distinction of Wolfrum, "result-orientated",[25] since they provide for rigorous reduction goals of the use and production of the respective substances they address, and for strict time-frames for countries to reach certain reduction levels. Nonetheless, these MEAs are chosen because they use economic incentives and compliance assistance measures, but they use different approaches: for example, the Montreal Protocol, similarly to the Basel Convention, bases its incentives and compliance support on the classical system of developed State Parties contributing to a fund that is used to finance compliance in developing State Parties. However, contrary to the Basel Convention Technical Trust Fund, contributions to the Multilateral Fund for the Implementation of the Montreal Protocol (MPMF) are obligatory. This fund applies a traditional incentives approach which does not address projects in developed State Parties. For its part, the Kyoto Protocol, apart from applying the classical approach of "developed States financing compliance in developing States", provides for some economic features which are amongst the most innovative of their kind: a market-based Emission Trading system, that can be joined by developed State Parties and a secondary funding system which, apart from receiving traditional state donations, is co-financed by the Clean Development Mechanism: the monetary equivalent of two per cent of those Emission

---

[23] Available at <http://unfccc.int>.
[24] Ibid.
[25] U. Beyerlin/ P. Stoll/ R. Wolfrum, "Conclusions drawn from the Conference on Ensuring Compliance with MEAs", in: U. Beyerlin/ P. Stoll/ R. Wolfrum (eds), *Ensuring Compliance with Multilateral Environmental Agreements: Academic Analysis and Views from Practice*, 2006, 260 et seq., see Chapter IV.

Trading Units, developed states generate through carrying out global-warming-projects in developing countries, go into the fund.

The stimuli and ideas extracted from literature and other MEAs will be recapitulated at the end of Part VI. The idea of a Basel Convention that facilitates legal waste trade and is supported by Member States motivated to improve the current situation by the incentives elaborated in this paper will be revisited.

III. The Basel Convention: History, Scope, Mechanisms

1. History and Background

The Basel Convention was negotiated following various high profile cases of major pollution and fraud regarding shipments of hazardous wastes for disposal purposes abroad. Acknowledging that the Convention's non-binding, recommendatory antecedent document, the "Cairo Guidelines and Principles for the Environmentally Sound Management of Hazardous Wastes" needed to be supplemented by a binding treaty, the Governing Council of the UNEP[26] mandated its Executive Director to form a working group designated to develop a global convention regarding transboundary movements of hazardous wastes. The working group's draft convention was adopted by the UNEP Governing Council in June 1987.[27] In the framework of an international conference held in Basel, Switzerland, from 20-22 March 1989, the draft convention was adopted by the participating parties. The Basel Convention entered into force on 5 May 1992, when the requirement of 20 ratifications was finally met. At present, the Basel Convention is one of the most extensive global MEAs. With currently 178 State Parties[28] it has almost universal membership. The United States, Haiti and Afghanistan are signatory states to the Basel Convention, but have not ratified it yet.[29]

---

[26] More information available at <http://www.unep.org>.
[27] UNEP *Report of the Governing Council on the Work of its 14th Sess.*, 8-19 June 1987, GAOR 42nd Sess. Suppl. No. 25; *Adoption of Draft Decision 14/30 on Environmentally Sound Management of Hazardous Wastes*, Doc. UNEP/GC.14/L.37–M, paras 125-127.
[28] Available at <http://www.basel.int/ratif/convention.htm>.
[29] Information available at, see above.

2. Scope

"Wastes" being defined in article 2, are defined as hazardous by the Basel Convention, when either listed in Annex I of the Convention or when considered to be hazardous by the domestic legislation of a Member State.[30] Wastes that belong to any category contained in Annex II that are subject to transboundary movement shall be "other wastes" for the purposes of the Convention.[31] Annex I includes, *inter alia*, clinical wastes from medical care in hospitals, waste substances and articles containing or being contaminated with polychlorinated biphenyls (PCBs) or waste containing arsenic, selenium or cadmium compounds.[32] Additionally, these wastes have to demonstrate at least one of the hazardous characteristics listed in Annex III, like flammability, toxicity or explosiveness.[33] "Other Wastes" include household wastes and residues arising from the incineration of household wastes.[34] Every State Party has the obligation to report to the Basel Secretariat within six months from the beginning of its membership, which wastes other than in Annex I of the Convention are considered to be hazardous under national legislation.[35] "Disposal", according to the Basel Convention, encompasses both disposal and recycling.[36]

Trade in hazardous substances not intended for disposal, such as chemicals, is not subject to regulation by the Basel Convention.[37] This issue is primarily addressed by the Rotterdam Convention on the Prior Informed Consent Procedure for Certain Hazardous Chemicals and Pesticides in International Trade (Rotterdam Convention),[38] developed by FAO and UNEP and adopted in 1998. Further excluded from the scope of the Basel Convention is radioactive waste,[39] given that it is

---

[30] Basel Convention, article 1 para. 1 lit. a and b.
[31] Ibid., article 1 para. 2.
[32] Ibid., Annex I Categories of Wastes to be Controlled, Y 1, 10, 23, 24, 25.
[33] Ibid., Annex III List of Hazardous Characteristics.
[34] Ibid., Annex II, Categories of Wastes requiring Special Consideration, Y 46, 47.
[35] Ibid., article 3 para.1.
[36] Ibid., article 2 para. 4 and Annex IV Disposal Operations.
[37] Birnie/ Boyle, see note 9, 430 et seq.
[38] More information available at <http://www.pic.int/home>.
[39] Basel Convention, article 1 para. 3.

subject to other regulatory regimes and wastes arising from the "normal operations of a ship.[40]"

3. Trade Restrictions and Exceptions

Though it constitutes its prime topic of regulation, the Basel Convention does not address the transboundary movement of hazardous wastes as the first issue. Rather, it calls upon the Member States to reduce the "generation [of hazardous wastes and other wastes] to a minimum in terms of quantity and/or hazardous potential"[41] and to dispose of their wastes in their own territories, "as far as it is compatible with environmentally sound and efficient management."[42] Kiss and Shelton would go as far as to say that "one of its [the Basel Convention's] objectives is to make the movement of hazardous wastes so costly and difficult that industry will find it more profitable to cut down on waste production."[43] In certain specified cases, the transboundary movement of hazardous wastes is prohibited. This is the case when a State Party decides to prohibit the import of any hazardous wastes covered by the Basel Convention into its national territory.[44] Further, export of hazardous wastes to non-parties[45] and to the world regions which are located in the area south of 60° South latitude[46] is prohibited. The Non-Party prohibition is subject to an exception when the wastes in question are covered by agreements or arrangements which are compatible with the environmentally sound management of hazardous wastes and other wastes as required by the Basel Convention.[47]

This is reflected e.g. in the OECD Guidance Manual for the Control of Transboundary Movements of Recoverable Wastes, Council Decision C (2001) 107/FINAL, 8, where it says: "The Decision recognized

---

[40] Ibid., article 1 para. 4.
[41] Ibid., Preamble, para. 3.
[42] Basel Convention, Preamble, para. 8.
[43] A. Kiss/ D. Shelton, *Guide to International Environmental Law*, 2007, 212 et seq.
[44] Basel Convention, article 4 para. 1 lit. a.
[45] Ibid., article 4 para. 5.
[46] Ibid., article 4 para. 6.
[47] Ibid., article 11. See also A. Daniel, "Hazardous Wastes, Transboundary Impacts", in: R. Wolfrum (ed.), *Max Planck Encyclopedia of Public International Law*, 2012.

the desirability of appropriately controlled international trade in waste materials destined for recovery, and that efficient and environmentally sound management of waste may justify some transfrontier movements in order to make use of adequate recovery or disposal facilities in other countries."[48] Many developing countries, though, considered transboundary waste trade an "unacceptable practice"[49] which they sought to abolish completely. This opinion prevailed especially amongst the Member States of the OAU.

Article 11 of the Basel Convention was designated to mitigate this divergence. Based on article 11, State Parties can enter into agreements on waste movements to and from non-parties or implement a stricter regime regarding transboundary waste movement than the Basel Convention. Article 11 grants the possibility for State Parties to enter into bilateral, multilateral and regional agreements, both with other State Parties and non-parties.

Current examples of regional conventions that regulate transboundary movements of hazardous wastes are, *inter alia*, the already mentioned Bamako Convention,[50] the Protocol on the Prevention of Pollution of the Mediterranean Sea by Transboundary Movements of Hazardous Wastes and their Disposal[51] from 1996, the Protocol to the UNEP Convention for the Protection of the Mediterranean Sea against Pollution and the Waigani Convention to Ban the Importation into Forum Island Countries of Hazardous and Radioactive Wastes and to Control the Transboundary Movement and Management of Hazardous Wastes within the South Pacific Region[52] from 1995. All of them prohibit the import of hazardous wastes into the territory of their State Parties.

As already mentioned, the second Conference of the State Parties to the Basel Convention in 1994 agreed on a complete ban on the movement of hazardous wastes from OECD to non-OECD countries intended for final disposal. Transboundary movements for recycling purposes should be phased out by 31 December 1997. The third Conference of the State Parties decided in 1995 to implement the ban as an

---

[48] See, for example: OECD, Guidance Manual for the Control of Transboundary Movements of Recoverable Wastes, Council Decision C (2001) 107/Final, 8 et seq.
[49] Birnie/ Boyle, see note 9, 428 et seq.
[50] See under "Introduction" in this paper.
[51] Available at <http://www.basel.int>.
[52] Available at <http://www.sprep.org>.

amendment to the Basel Convention.[53] The ban has not entered into force, as mentioned above, basically, because it is not clear to what date the ratification requirement of three-fourth of the State Parties refers. Supporters of the Basel Ban Amendment claim that the requirement of three-fourth historically refers to three-fourth of the total number of State Parties at the time of the amendment. This would equal 62 ratifications from the then 82 State Parties. To date 69 Parties have ratified the ban; accordingly, it could already have entered into force.[54] On 5 May 2004, though, the United Nations Office of Legal Affairs issued an interpretation of article 17 para. 5 Basel Convention, recommending a "current time approach" to interpret the ratification requirement. "In such circumstances, the Secretary-General [as depositary] is to calculate the number of acceptances on the basis of the number of parties to the treaty at the time of deposit of each instrument of acceptance of an amendment (the current time approach)."[55] A newer attempt to solve this deadlock was conducted by 118 Basel Member States at the 10th Conference of the Parties in Cartagena, Columbia, in October 2011, by agreeing on a possible bar for the entry into force of the Basel Ban Amendment. As decided in the so-called CLI ("Country Led Initiative") the Amendment will enter into force for those State Parties which want to adhere to it once additional 17 parties ratify it.[56]

4. Organs

The Organs of the Basel Convention are designated to achieve and monitor compliance with this MEA, to promote cooperation and to review and further develop the Convention's mechanisms and strategies. The head organ of the Basel Convention is the Conference of the Par-

---

[53] Basel Convention, article 4A para. 1 states that "[e]ach Party listed in Annex VII shall prohibit all transboundary movements of hazardous wastes which are destined for operations according to Annex IV A, to States not listed in Annex VII"; see also UNEP *Report of the 3rd Mtg of the Conference of the Parties to the Basel Convention on the Control of Transboundary Movements of Hazardous Wastes and their Disposal*, Doc. UNEP/CHW.3/34.
[54] Information available at <http://www.basel.int>.
[55] Recommendation of 5 May 2004 from the United Nations Office of Legal Affairs, available at <http://www.basel.int/legalmatters>.
[56] Indonesian-Swiss Country led Initiative to improve the effectiveness of the Basel Convention, Doc. UNEP/CH.10/5.

ties (hereinafter: COP), which consists of representatives of the governments of all State Parties. It is the governing body of the Basel Convention and meets at intervals of approximately one to three years. During these meetings, the COP is supposed to carry out a revision of the implementation processes in and the cooperation amongst the Basel Convention State Parties and on the results of compliance strategies developed in prior meetings. The COP decides on the *modus operandi* in order to maintain and improve compliance with the Basel Convention. In order to constantly improve the Basel Convention's performance, the COP has the faculty to not only amend the Convention and its Annexes,[57] but also to adopt protocols to the Convention[58] and to establish subsidiary bodies endowed with specified tasks and duties, when considered necessary.[59] The COP has made use of all of these possibilities. In order to be sufficiently prepared in these meetings, the COP has a permanently established assistant body, the Open Ended Working Group (OEWG), which is supposed to review the implementation of the COP's decisions and of the Convention in general.

The Secretariat is a permanent institution and serves as the administrative and executive body of the Basel Convention. Its office is located in Geneva, Switzerland. It is the center where all the information of the Member States regarding the Basel Convention is handed in, collected, interpreted and distributed to the COP and to the Member States. State Parties are supposed to report to the Secretariat, which then prepares and transmits reports based on the information received.[60] Further, the Secretariat prepares the COP and other meetings,[61] reports its own activities before the COP[62] and serves as a contact point for any technical party enquiry. The Secretariat also has an assistant body, the Extended Bureau. State Parties which are, *inter alia*, in search of technical know-how, assistance regarding the handling of the notification system of the Convention or a consulting firm in order to conduct examinations on wastes or treatment facilities[63] can approach the Secretariat in order to receive search assistance, data, or addresses, if available. The Secretariat's faculties are strictly limited to these competences of execution

---

[57] Basel Convention, article 15 para. 5 lit. b.
[58] Ibid., article 15 para. 5 lit. d.
[59] Ibid., article 15 para. 5 lit. e.
[60] Ibid., article 16 para. 1 lit. b.
[61] Ibid.
[62] Ibid., article 16 para. 1 lit. c.
[63] Ibid., article 16 para. 1 lit. g.

and assistance; it is not designated to do its own verification or control work on the reports that are submitted to it.

5. Regional Centers

The Basel Convention tries to respond to the gap regarding the availability of technology and funds that exists between developed State Parties and developing State Parties or Parties with economies in transition. Its preamble deals with the existing concern about "the limited capabilities of the developing countries to manage hazardous wastes and other wastes"[64] by immediately pronouncing an answer to the problem of technology transfer, especially to developing countries.[65] The idea of technology transfer stems from the overall concept of international cooperation to address the problem of transboundary waste movements and disposal.[66] While drafting the Basel Convention, the idea of creating regional centers which should assist with compliance and implementation and distribute technology and training to regions in need, was foreseen and implemented in article 14.[67] From 1994 on, the wish to establish Basel Convention Regional Centers – (hereinafter: BCRCs) was reiterated in several COP Decisions[68] and an election of headquar-

---

[64] Basel Convention, Preamble para. 20.
[65] Ibid., Preamble para. 21.
[66] Ibid., article 10 para. 2 lit. d.: "[t]o this end, the Parties shall: (…) cooperate actively, subject to their national laws, regulations and policies, in the transfer of technology and management systems related to the environmentally sound management of hazardous wastes and other wastes. They shall also co-operate in developing the technical capacity among Parties, especially those which may need and request technical assistance in this field."
[67] Ibid., article 14 para. 1: "[t]he Parties agree that, according to the specific needs of different regions and subregions, regional or sub-regional centres for training and technology transfers regarding the management of hazardous wastes and other wastes and the minimization of their generation should be established. The Parties shall decide on the establishment of appropriate funding mechanisms of a voluntary nature."
[68] UNEP *Report of the 1st Mtg Meeting of the Conference of the Parties to the Basel Convention*, Decision I/13, *Establishment of Regional Centers for Training and Technology Transfer*, Doc. UNEP/CHW.1/24; UNEP *Report of the 3rd Mtg of the Conference of the Parties to the Basel Convention*, Decision III/19, *Establishment of Regional or Sub-Regional Centres for Training and Technology Transfer Regarding the Management of Hazard-*

ters began. Today there exist 14 BCRCs (four in Africa, four in Asia, three in Central and Eastern Europe, three in Latin America). According to COP Decision VI/3, their core functions are to identify, develop and strengthen mechanisms for the transfer of technology, conduct training programs and workshops on environmentally sound management of wastes and on minimization of waste-generation.[69] They also should serve as focal points for the collection and provision of information regarding technology and know-how, implementation assistance, and conduct networking between State Parties.[70] Furthermore, they are supposed to coordinate regional cooperation between the Rotterdam, Stockholm and Basel Conventions. Most of the centers are founded as national legal entities of the host state. Each center is supposed to create its own funding strategy, which should involve the host states, the private sector, environmental NGOs and international organizations. The sources of the Basel Convention's own Technical Trust Fund are partly dedicated to the BCRCs.

6. Finances

The finance system of the Basel Convention is best described as a ragbag, since at first no coherent and encompassing strategy existed. Provisions regarding finances are found in separate articles in the Convention itself, but they refer more to the creation of financial back-up mechanisms for specific situations than to a general compliance funding system. According to article 6 para. 11, transboundary waste movements shall be covered by insurance, bond or other guarantee as may be required by a state of import or any state of transit which is a party.[71] Further, article 14 para. 2 states that "the establishment of a revolving fund to assist on an interim basis in case of emergency situations to minimize damage from accidents arising from transboundary move-

---

ous Wastes and other Wastes and the Minimization of their Generation, Doc. UNEP/CHW.3/35; UNEP *Report of the 7th Mtg of the Conference of the Parties to the Basel Convention*, Decision VII/9, *Basel Convention Regional Centres: Report on Progress*, Doc. UNEP/CHW.7/INF/7.

[69] UNEP *Report of the 6th Mtg of the Conference of the Parties to the Basel Convention*, Doc. UNEP/CHW.6/4.
[70] Ibid.
[71] Article 6 para. 11 Basel Convention.

ments of hazardous wastes and other wastes or during the disposal of those wastes" shall be considered by the Parties.[72]

A comprehensive attempt to concretize article 14 para. 2 Basel Convention was established through the foundation of two funds: a Trust Fund for the Basel Convention and a Trust Fund to Assist Developing Countries and Other Countries in Need of Technical Assistance in the implementation of the Basel Convention (Technical Trust Fund). Both were established during the first COP in 1992. The Trust Fund basically serves to cover "the ordinary expenditure of the Secretariat (…)"[73] and is financed by non-obligatory contributions of the State Parties. State Party contributions are based on the United Nations' scale of assessments.[74] Voluntary donations of Non-members or NGOs are also possible. The Technical Trust Fund was founded with the objective to "assist Developing Countries and other Countries in Need of Technical Assistance in the Implementation (…)"[75] and provides support for: (a) technical assistance, training, and capacity building; (b) the Basel Convention Regional Centers; (c) participation of the representatives of developing country parties and parties with economies in transition in Convention Meetings.[76] It is managed by the Secretariat, which is fully accountable to the COP. It is supposed to serve as the Basel Convention's main source to address the needs its State Parties might have in order to fulfill their obligations. It should especially be designated to grant financial support to compliance activities taking place in the world's economically weaker regions. Accordingly, it constitutes one of the Basel Convention's major compliance assistance instruments. According to the Study of Possible Options for Lasting and Sustainable Financial Mechanisms, conducted by UNEP and FAO, the Technical Trust Fund "has successfully provided assistance to numerous developing country party representatives so that they might attend convention meetings."[77]

The 5th COP in 1999 decided furthermore that parties suffering from an accident that occurred during a transnational movement of

---

[72] Ibid., article 14 para. 2.
[73] See note 68.
[74] Ibid.
[75] Available at <http://www.basel.int>.
[76] UNEP/FAO *Study of Possible Options for Lasting and Sustainable Financial Mechanisms*, Doc. UNEP/FAO/RC/COP.3/13.9 and E. Brown Weiss/ S. McCaffrey, *International Law and Policy*, 2nd edition 2006, 1070 et seq.
[77] UNEP/FAO, see note 76, 11 et seq.

hazardous wastes should be eligible to receive financial support from the Technical Trust Fund as emergency assistance and compensation for damage.[78] The Fund might also be used to cover costs that arise from a situation covered by the Basel Liability Protocol, if the liable perpetrator cannot be found or is not in a position to make the payment himself.[79] Until the waste is handed over to the disposer, the exporter or generator of the waste who has the obligation to notify the transnational movement according to article 6 Basel Convention is liable for damages. Later on the disposer is liable. The Technical Trust Fund is financed by voluntary donations of undefined amounts by State Parties and Non-Parties and, occasionally, by international organizations or NGOs. In the biennium 2008/2009, the Basel Convention Trust Fund had a total income (consisting of voluntary donations, interest income and miscellaneous income) of 7.2 Million US$.[80] In the same period, the Technical Trust Fund received 2.6 Million US$.[81] As of 30 September 2011, the Trust Fund had received only 4.1 Million US$,[82] while the Technical Trust Fund had received 1.1 Million US$ regarding the same period.[83]

7. Duties of the Member States

It is the Member States' first duty to take appropriate legal, administrative and other measures to implement and enforce the provisions of the Convention including measures to prevent and punish conduct in contravention of the Convention. Furthermore, State Parties have to comply with extensive and detailed information and publication requirements. First and foremost, these duties include the implementation of the Prior Informed Consent Procedure and the waste tracking system inherent to the Basel Convention. State Parties have to designate one or

---

[78] UNEP *Report of the 5th Mtg of the Conference of the Parties to the Basel Convention*, Doc. UNEP/CHW.5/29, 58 et seq.
[79] Ibid.
[80] Trust Fund for the Basel Convention: Status of Contributions as at 31 December 2008 and 30 September 2009.
[81] Technical Trust Fund For the Basel Convention: Status of Contributions as at 31 December 2008 and 30 September 2009.
[82] Trust Fund for the Basel Convention: Status of Contributions as at 30 September 2011.
[83] Technical Trust Fund for the Basel Convention. Status of Contributions as at 30 September 2011.

more competent authorities and one focal point,[84] which are in charge of the supervising and informational duties and have to respond to enquiries of national actors. These bodies have to be announced to the Secretariat within the first three months of the date the Convention enters into force for each State Party.

Through these bodies, which hand information over to the Secretariat, the Parties have to inform each other about any relevant decisions (e.g. a change of policies regarding the acceptance of imports of hazardous wastes into their territory) or occurrences (e.g. accidents).[85] Furthermore, before the end of each calendar year they have to hand over detailed information regarding the conduct of transboundary movements of hazardous wastes and other wastes, and their disposal in the previous year.[86] This information is compiled in a public annual report by the Secretary. The principle of the crucial Prior Informed Consent Procedure is that receiver and transit states have to give their "prior, informed and written consent"[87] before hazardous waste is moved into or through their territory. Transit states that are Parties to the Convention can waive this requirement.[88] However, if they wish to do so, they have to inform the other State Parties beforehand through the Secretariat.[89]

Crucial actors in a successful Prior Informed Consent Procedure are the competent authorities of the states of export, transit and import of the wastes. The authority of the exporting state (or the waste generator or exporter through the authority) notifies the purpose of a waste export/transit to the states of import or transit. This notification has to contain sufficient information in order to ensure that these states can make their decisions on an "informed" basis. A prospective state of import or transfer has to receive enough information to be able to "assess the possible environmental impacts of the proposed transfer, as a basis

---

[84] Basel Convention, article 5 paras 1 and 2.
[85] Ibid., article 13 para. 2 lit. e.
[86] The requested information has to contain data about, *inter alia*, the amount, categories, characteristics, origin and destination, transit states and disposal method of the wastes imported or exported, descriptions about the measures taken to reduce or eliminate waste generation, or information about measures taken in order to implement the Convention, Basel Convention, article 13 para. 3.
[87] Birnie/ Boyle, see note 9, 431 et seq.
[88] Basel Convention, article 6 para. 4.
[89] Ibid., article 13 para. 2.

for its decision whether or not to accept the proposed transfer."[90] The Basel Convention regulates what kind of information should be provided.[91] States of import and transit have to answer in writing through their respective competent authorities whether they consent to the movement, deny it, or whether they need further information.

The key of the system is that the competent authority of the State Party of export "shall not allow the generator or exporter to commence the transboundary movement until it has received written confirmation that: (a) The notifier has received the written consent of the State of import; and (b) The notifier has received from the State of import confirmation of the existence of a contract between the exporter and the disposer specifying environmentally sound management of the wastes in question."[92] It is due to the Prior Informed Consent Procedure that Birnie calls the Basel Convention a unique mechanism that is "thus based on a system of environmental responsibility shared among all states involved in each transaction."[93]

The tracking system is based on the use of a movement document that has to be signed by every person who is in charge during the ongoing transboundary movement. The movement document consists of a standardized set of information requirements that facilitate tracking.[94] As soon as the wastes arrive at their disposal site of destination, the disposer has to inform both the exporter and the competent authority of the exporting state of the arrival and of the completion of the due disposal. If these notifications do not arrive, the state of the exporter is supposed to alert the state of the importer.[95] As a general obligation, State Parties are supposed to promote the reduction of the generation of wastes to a minimum,[96] in order to ensure the availability of adequate disposal sites within their territory[97] and that the personnel involved is sufficiently trained.[98] Further, states are held to cooperate[99] and to en-

---

[90] K. Kummer-Peiry, "Prior informed consent", in: Wolfrum, see note 47, 1 et seq.
[91] Basel Convention, Annex V A.
[92] Ibid., article 6 para. 3 lit. a and b.
[93] Birnie/ Boyle, see note 9, 430 et seq.
[94] Daniel, see note 47, 4 et seq.
[95] Basel Convention, article 6 para. 9.
[96] Ibid., article 4 para. 2 lit. a.
[97] Ibid., article 4 para. 2 lit. b.
[98] Ibid., article 4 para. 2 lit. c.
[99] Ibid., article 10.

sure the environmentally sound management of wastes, both in their own territory and, as far as possible, in other states. A State Party to the Basel Convention that has reason to believe that hazardous wastes will not be treated in an environmentally sound manner in its own territory shall prohibit the import of the wastes in question.[100] When doubts arise about the ability of another State Party to treat wastes in an environmentally sound manner, states are supposed to prevent exports of wastes to these states.[101]

The Basel Convention does not provide a detailed description of "environmentally sound management"[102] of wastes, but the COP regularly establishes legally non-binding "technical guidelines."[103] They define what is meant by "environmentally sound management" of different types of wastes.[104] Parties have progressively been developing these guidelines since 1994, including the following criteria to assess the soundness of certain waste movements: whether the regulatory and enforcement infrastructure can ensure compliance; whether waste sites are authorized and are of adequate standard to deal with the waste in question; whether operators of wastes sites are adequately trained; whether sites are monitored; whether waste generation is minimized through best practice and clean production methods.[105] Birnie concludes that these guidelines are not obligatory. However, their adoption by the Parties gives them persuasive force as a basic standard for states in order to fulfill their obligations under the Basel Convention.[106]

---

[100] Ibid., article 4 para. 2 lit. g.
[101] Ibid., article 4 para. 2 lit. e.
[102] Basel Convention, article 2 para. 8 "'Environmentally sound management of hazardous wastes or other wastes' means taking all practicable steps to ensure that hazardous wastes or other wastes are managed in a manner which will protect human health and the environment against the adverse effects which may result from such wastes."
[103] Available at <http://www.basel.int>.
[104] Up to January 2011, 15 technical guidelines were existent, as draft documents or already adopted by the Conference of the Parties. They refer, *inter alia*, to environmentally sound management of Persistent Organic Polluters (POPs), dismantled ships, used car tires or substances containing polychlorinated biphenyls or DDT.
[105] Basel Convention Technical Working Group: *Guidance Document on the Preparation of Technical Guidelines for the Environmentally Sound Management of Wastes Subject to the Basel Convention*.
[106] Birnie/ Boyle, see note 9, 433 et seq.

Transboundary waste movements that take place without notification, without positive response from the state of import, with consent obtained fraudulently, are not in conformity with the documents accompanying the procedure or that will result in deliberate illegal disposal are deemed to be "illegal traffic" by the Basel Convention.[107] State Parties are supposed to consider illegal traffic in hazardous wastes and other wastes as criminal[108] and shall take appropriate legal measures in order to guarantee juridical prosecution.[109] The state of origin of the waste generally faces a duty to re-import the waste in question.[110]

In order to address the need to clarify responsibilities and indemnification duties in case of incidents related to transboundary movements of wastes, the COP adopted the Basel Protocol on Liability and Compensation for Damage Resulting from Transboundary Movements of Hazardous Wastes and their Disposal[111] (hereinafter: Liability Protocol) in 1999. This Protocol defines exactly the responsibilities of all actors involved in a transaction and is also effective regarding illegal traffic. The person that notified the shipment pursuant to article 6.1 Basel Convention is liable for damage resulting from a transboundary movement or disposal of hazardous wastes.[112] Liability shifts to the disposer once he has taken possession of the waste.[113] The Liability Protocol is not yet in force, demanding twenty ratifications to enter into force. By November 2011, it had only received ten ratifications.

8. Compliance Mechanism

In order to strengthen the assertiveness of the Basel Convention the Parties decided to implement a Mechanism for Promoting Implementation and Compliance. This mechanism was established by Decision VI/12 during the 6th COP in 2002 as a subsidiary body to the COP

---

[107] Basel Convention, article 9.
[108] Ibid., article 4 para. 3.
[109] Ibid., article 9 para. 5.
[110] Ibid., arts 8 and 9 para. 2 lit. a.
[111] Decision V/9 of the Conference of the Parties and the Open ended Working-Group, *Basel Protocol on Liability and Compensation for Damage Resulting from Transboundary Movements of Hazardous Wastes and Their Disposal*, available at <http://www.basel.int>.
[112] L. Bergkamp, *Liability and Environment*, 2001, 36 et seq.
[113] Bergkamp, see note 112, 36 et seq.

under article 15 para. 5 lit. e of the Convention.[114] The objective of the mechanism is to assist Parties to comply with their obligations under the Convention and to facilitate, promote, and monitor the implementation of and compliance with the obligations under the Basel Convention.[115] These faculties are conducted by the 15 member Basel Convention Implementation and Compliance Committee (hereinafter: Compliance Committee) and have to be exercised in a manner that is "non-confrontational, transparent, cost-effective and preventive in nature, simple, flexible, non-binding and oriented in the direction of helping parties to implement the provisions of the Basel Convention."[116]

There are two ways in which the Compliance Committee may act: Specific Submissions (article 9) and General Reviews (article 21). The specific submission procedure may be triggered by Parties which announce their own struggle complying with the Basel Convention[117] to the Committee (Self-Trigger) or by a Party that is concerned about incompliance of another Party with which it is directly involved under the Basel Convention.[118] This Party-to-Party Trigger is therefore narrowed to the possibility of announcing incompliance of other State Parties only in situations related to a specific transaction under the Basel Convention. Finally, the Secretariat may trigger compliance difficulties of a Party which are related to the reporting and information obligations under article 13 para. 3 of the Convention[119] (Secretariat Trigger). According to Shibata, the purpose of this restriction is to limit the authority of the Secretariat so that it will not actively investigate and search for possible compliance difficulties faced by the Parties.[120]

The Party-to-Party Trigger and the Secretariat Trigger require prior consultations with the Party in question before the Compliance Committee starts investigating. If these consultations do not render satisfactory results, the Committee may start a "facilitative procedure": it tries to determine the prime roots and causes of the compliance problem and

---

[114] UNEP Brochure, *The Basel Convention Mechanism for Promoting Implementation and Compliance*, 3 et seq.
[115] UNEP Basel Convention Compliance Committee, *Terms of Reference*, Doc. UNEP/P/CHW.6/40, Decision VI/12.
[116] Terms of Reference, article 3, see note 115.
[117] Ibid., article 9 lit. a.
[118] Ibid., article 9 lit. b.
[119] Ibid., article 9 lit. c.
[120] A. Shibata, "The Basel Compliance Mechanism", *RECIEL* 12 (2003), 183 et seq. (191).

offers assistance in solving it. It can provide the Party with advice, non-binding recommendations or information regarding the strengthening of the Party's domestic regulatory regime or the elaboration of voluntary compliance plans and follow-up agreements. The Committee does not provide financial and technical assistance, but it provides advice regarding access to this assistance.[121] As a secondary measure, the Committee may ask the COP to give further advice and make statements. In the worst case, the COP can issue a "Cautionary Statement."[122] It is the only measure under the mechanism which has a negative connotation.[123] As an auxiliary activity, the Compliance Committee may conduct general reviews on issues of compliance and implementation under the Convention. It can do so, if asked by the COP, or on its (own) decision regarding any general issue that may have arisen while undertaking its prime function of dealing with specific submissions.[124]

The success of the Compliance Committee is questionable. In its report to the 9th COP in June 2008, the Compliance Committee stated that by the date of its 6th Committee Meeting in February 2008 no specific submission according to article 9 of the Terms of Reference had been made.[125] At the same conference, the Committee itself presented a list of flaws that might cause this negligence,[126] *inter alia*, the inability of the Committee to initiate consideration of a particular case of implementation and compliance difficulties of which it becomes aware or the lack of resources to assist Parties that are determined to face difficulties in implementation and compliance.

9. Criticized Deficiencies of the Basel Convention

When the Basel Convention entered into force it was celebrated as a milestone that would make international waste trade fairer, safer and more transparent and would effectively fight illegal waste traffic. It was called "one of the international agreements at the forefront of integrat-

---

[121] Shibata, see note 120, 193.
[122] Terms of Reference, article 20 lit. b, see note 115.
[123] Shibata, see note 120, 194.
[124] Terms of Reference, arts 21 and 24, see note 115.
[125] *Report of the Compliance Committee and Work Program for the Committee for the Period 2009-2010*, Docs UNEP/CHW/CC/7/10 and UNEP/CHW/CC/7/5, article 26.
[126] See note 125, article 26 lit. a – e.

ing environmental justice principles into global international trade."[127] Transboundary movements of hazardous wastes would no longer be solely governed by international soft-law instruments, like the Cairo Guidelines, and national legislations regarding liability and conflict of laws, but would receive appropriate, treaty-based regulation. Today, criticisms of the Basel Convention range from calling it a "relative success"[128] to a "woeful shortfall in achieving environmental justice."[129] Severe incidents of waste pollution like the *Trafigura* Case in Côte d'Ivoire or the repeated detections of attempts to illegally move hazardous wastes from European ports to Africa or Asia indeed show that the Basel Convention is lacking teeth, especially when it comes to the prevention of illegal traffic of wastes and accidents related to it. Daniel describes four essential weaknesses of the Basel Convention regarding the performance of the State Parties: "Failure to report, failure to appoint competent authorities, failure to adopt implementing legislation and non-compliance related to illegal traffic."[130]

The following section will give a short overview about the most common criticisms of the Basel Convention. According to article 13 para. 3 State Parties are supposed to hand in an annual report of their activities regarding the transboundary movement of hazardous wastes to the COP through the Secretariat. This reporting system does not work effectively, which is, in the first place, due to the fact that some State Parties to the Basel Convention still fail to do adequate reporting or indeed any reporting at all. This is a crucial flaw, since reporting systems, together with inspection or external monitoring "constitute the foundation of any effective scheme of compliance control, for they provide the factual state of compliance by Parties with treaty obligations."[131] Even more drastic, Chayes, Handler Chayes and Mitchell

---

[127] V. Blayre Campbell, "Ghost Ships and Recycling Pollution: Sending America's Trash to Europe", *Tulsa Journal of Comparative and International Law* 12 (2004-2005), 189 et seq. (212).

[128] Birnie/ Boyle, see note 9, 438.

[129] L. Widawsky, "In my Backyard: How enabling Hazardous Waste Trade to Developing Nations can improve the Basel Convention's Ability to achieve Environmental Justice", *Lewis & Clark Law Schools Environmental Law* 38 (2008), 577 et seq. (581).

[130] Daniel, see note 47, 3.

[131] A. Shibata, "Ensuring Compliance with the Basel Convention – its unique features", in: Beyerlin/ Stoll/ Wolfrum, see note 25, 69.

state that "non-reporting is often small in itself but may prove to be indicative of more significant forms on noncompliance."[132]

No or insufficient reporting leads to a condition of non-transparency which frustrates any attempt to compare or assess a nation's compliance rates and might even serve as a disincentive to report properly for the other State Parties. Moreover, the Secretariat announced during the 7th Report Session of the Compliance Committee in June 2009 that by 2006 twelve Parties had not yet handed in any annual reports since the Basel Convention came into force for them, 112 Parties had handed in incomplete reports. Another 77 Parties had not yet submitted their 2006 report by the date of the Report Session.[133] By 20 July 2009, 92 Parties had not transmitted a report for 2007.[134] However, the malfunctioning of the reporting system cannot be attributed to the State Parties alone. The Secretariat has the obligation to "prepare and transmit reports based upon information received in accordance with Articles 3, 4, 6, 11 and 13 (...)."[135] Read together with article 13, the Secretariat may prepare its independent reports on the status of implementation by the Parties.[136] This includes that the Secretariat might even give its own statement about the annual compliance situation, including an opinion about each country's performance. But the Secretariat has restrained itself from making use of the possibility of making commentaries right to the Parties. In fact, "it has demonstrated some restraint, having prepared only a 'compilation' of the annual reports submitted by the Parties as well as more concise 'Country Fact Sheets'."[137] The latest comparable data regarding imports and exports of hazardous wastes and other wastes which are directly accessible to the State Parties and are not hidden in one of the numerous protocols provided on the home-

---

[132] A. Chayes/ A. Handler Chayes/ R.B. Mitchell, "Managing Compliance. A Comparative Perspective", in: E. Brown Weiss/ H. Jacobson (eds), *Engaging Countries: Strengthening Compliance with International Environmental Accords*, 2000, 39 et seq. (39).

[133] UNEP *Report of the 7th Sess. of the Basel Convention Implementation and Compliance Committee 25-26 June 2009*, Doc. UNEP/CHW/CC/7/10, item 4 of 3 August 2009.

[134] UNEP *Report Status of National Reporting 2007 by Parties to the Basel Convention pursuant to Article 13 para. 3 of the Convention, as of 20 July 2009*. This report does not differentiate between Parties which actually never have handed in a report or handed in an incomplete or invalid report.

[135] Basel Convention, article 16 para. 1 lit. b.

[136] Shibata, see note 131, 71.

[137] Ibid.

page of the Basel Convention date back to 2004. And last but not least, Shibata states, that the COP, which according to article 15 para. 5 Basel Convention "shall keep under continuous review and evaluation the effective implementation of this Convention", does not fulfill its task: "In practice, however, the COP and its subsidiary body, the Open-Ended Working Group (OEWG), undertakes neither a review of each individual report nor a substantive evaluation of the Secretariat's compilation reports."[138] He finally analyses: "Thus, while the reporting system has been formally established under the Basel Convention, in practice, this system has not been fully utilized as a compliance control mechanism."[139]

Another common point of criticism of the Basel Convention is the fact that there is no effective system of control. As far as compliance control is concerned, the Compliance Committee is permitted to act only in response to one of the triggers listed in article 9. It does not have any monitoring function regarding any given current waste transactions and does not review the annual reports.[140] The Secretariat's power to investigate and to review compliance with the Basel Convention in the Member States is similarly limited. Its facility to trigger the Compliance Committee is limited to situations of non-compliance with the Parties reporting obligations under article 13 para. 3.[141] The Verification provision in article 19 of the Basel Convention grants the possibility to Parties to inform the Secretariat of a possible breach of obligations by any other Party, if it has reason to suspect so.[142] In contrast to the Party-to-Party Trigger of the Compliance Mechanism, direct involvement under the Basel Convention with the Party in question is not required. Any Party can make allegations against any other Party, only with the condition to inform this Party at the same time as the Secretariat. However, article 19 does not reveal in any way, how the Secretariat is supposed to act when confronted with such an allegation. Ac-

---

[138] Ibid.
[139] Ibid., 72.
[140] Shibata is of the opinion that Parties did deny this function to the Compliance Committee. They argued that reviewing and analyzing all the annual reports would overburden the Committee and "drastically change the nature of the [compliance] mechanism", Shibata, see note 131, 72.
[141] Again, it was proposed to give the Secretariat the full competence to announce any act of non-compliance it became aware of through the annual reports. This was denied as well by most of the States Parties. See Shibata, see note 120.
[142] Basel Convention, article 19.

cording to Shibata, the power of the Secretariat would encompass neither investigations nor fact-finding missions[143] at the sites in questions.

An external compliance control mechanism is missing in the Basel Convention. External monitoring could be provided by e.g. the United Nations, by state authorities or by NGOs. In particular, NGOs seem to play a sometimes quasi-symbiotic role together with MEAs: they check the validity of Party reports and try to ensure that the State Parties' compliance performance and, especially, breaches of Convention obligations are made public. They also conduct their own research and generate compliance reports that are independent of the reports submitted by the Parties.[144] The Basel Convention refers to information submitted by "intergovernmental and non-governmental entities" as valid sources on which the Secretariat might prepare its reports.[145]

The Prior Informed Consent Procedure has also received criticism. Insufficiencies of this procedure are closely related to the fact that the Parties' performances under the Basel Convention are not assessed and controlled by any assigned authority. Like the annual reports, documents of this procedures do not undergo external reviews. Reliable information on whether a certain waste transaction in the scope of the Basel Convention will take place in an environmentally sound manner depends entirely on the persons, agencies and enterprises involved in the transaction in question. Besides, the process of Prior Informed Consent does not require prior inspection of waste facilities. It just requires that the state of import confirms the existence of a contract between the exporter and the disposer of the waste that specifies the environmentally sound treatment of the wastes in question.[146] For Widawsky, this level of ensuring environmentally sound management is low.[147] If the requirements of a proper procedure of Prior Informed

---

[143] Shibata, see note 131, 73.
[144] Kiss/ Shelton, see note 43, 304.
[145] Basel Convention, article 16 para. 1 lit. b: "The functions of the Secretariat shall be to prepare and transmit reports based upon information received in accordance with Articles 3, 4, 6, 11 and 13 as well as upon information derived from meetings of subsidiary bodies (...) as well as upon, as appropriate, information provided by relevant intergovernmental and non-governmental entities."
[146] Basel Convention, article 6 para. 3 lit. b.
[147] "Although the PIC procedure encourages pre-trade dialogue and consent among exporters and importers, its reliance on exporters and importers to verify that their facilities comply with ESM, without inspections of the facilities to substantiate this claim, is inadequate protection against untrained,

Consent are not fulfilled by the State Parties, illegal traffic, the "probably biggest problem facing the Basel Convention"[148] flourishes. Illegal traffic of hazardous wastes is a profit-driven crime and is almost always linked to environmentally unsound transport and disposal. In particular, those developing countries which lack adequate technologies, disposal facilities and personnel capacities to deal safely and in an environmentally sound way with hazardous materials suffer the impacts of hazardous wastes disposed in their territories. Fraud, corruption, the use of "shell companies", all undermine efforts to control the trade,[149] and in many cases it is not only the companies involved which conduct illegal waste trade – states, developing and developed ones, also participate in the transaction.

The Basel Convention is trying to regulate rather than to combat waste transactions. Exporters and generators of hazardous wastes, because they want to circumvent costly treatments and strict regulation in their own country seek options abroad that involve less stringent regulation and lower costs. Importers and recipient states often cooperate simply because of the possibility to earn high profit. Birnie criticizes: "A regime of shared responsibility may be desirable, but it is not clear that importing states will necessarily have the strongest interest in protecting themselves nor that exporting states will in practice do this for them."[150] Widawsky alleges that misrepresentation (which is only one of the elements that can constitute illegal traffic) is profitable, not only for the exporting companies, but also for the importers.[151] The jurisdiction, however, remains within the exclusive power of the individual states.

It adds to the problem that the Basel Ban Amendment, which was supposed to raise the level of protection for developing countries against streams of hazardous wastes they cannot deal with, has still not entered into force. However, due to the disadvantages and flaws that are inherent to ban concepts (like higher prevention and detection costs and a higher rate of illegal activity), it is questionable whether the Ban Amendment offers a step towards a sustainable global waste solution or if it might rather act as an obstacle. The Basel Ban Amendment had al-

---

conniving, careless, or poor nations or companies looking for profits from waste trading." Widawsky, see note 129, 605.

[148] Birnie/ Boyle, see note 9, 436.
[149] Ibid., 437.
[150] Ibid.
[151] Widawsky, see note 129, 605.

ready received heavy criticism while it was negotiated; in particular, the inclusion of recyclable waste in the ban was controversial and viewed as too restrictive in the eyes of many industrialized nations.[152]

The Basel Ban raises a two-fold problem. Apart from the question, whether a ban would jeopardize rather than strengthen the attempt to extinguish illegal movements of hazardous wastes, many experts perceive that the Basel Ban might collide with the rules of the WTO and the GATT.[153] As is known, the GATT establishes a system of non-discrimination, which is based on the principles of the Most Favorite Nation Clause (MFN; Article I), National Treatment (NT; Article III) and the Elimination of Quantitative Restrictions (Article XI).

Ishibashi expresses the concern that, while the provisions regarding trade restrictions and regulations of the Basel Convention itself might be covered by the General Exceptions Clause of Article XX[154] of the GATT, a ban which prohibits any trade between the parties themselves and between parties and non-parties, however, may constitute an infringement of the GATT/WTO provisions, if it is regarded as creating

---

[152] N. Bombier, "The Basel Convention's Complete Ban on Hazardous Waste Exports: Negotiating the Compatibility of Trade and Environment", *Journal of Environmental Law Practices 7* (1997), 325 et seq. (325).

[153] The GATT's central aims are the gradual elimination of barriers to international trade and the abolishment of protectionist state policies.

[154] The provisions which could affect the Basel Ban are Article XX, lit. b and g of the GATT. Article XX constitutes: "Subject to the requirement that such measures are not applied in a manner which would constitute a means of arbitrary or unjustifiable discrimination between countries where the same conditions prevail, or a disguised restriction on international trade, nothing in this Agreement shall be construed to prevent the adoption or enforcement by any contracting party of measures: (...) b) necessary to protect human, animal or plant life or health; (...) g) relating to the conservation of exhaustible natural resources if such measures are made effective in conjunction with restrictions on domestic production or consumption". Article XX requires the application of the least trade-restrictive measures necessary in order to achieve its protective aims. A ban probably never can be considered as the least trade-restrictive measure. Furthermore, the distinction drawn by the Basel Ban between developed countries and developing countries is based on the belonging of States to political organizations such as the OECD and the EU. According to K. Ishibashi, "it is not clear how to justify such discrimination."

arbitrary or unjustifiable discrimination.[155] However, no state has so far brought up an international dispute regarding a clash between the international waste trade regime and WTO rules.

10. Financial Problems

The financial problems of the Basel Convention probably constitute the root causes for, or at least a major contribution to, its unsatisfactory performance. The Basel Convention suffers from a general lack of funding. Both the Trust Fund and the Technical Trust Fund are too poorly provided with financial resources to facilitate all the activities the Basel Convention should realize in order to fulfill its own aims. In 2008 the Basel Convention Trust Fund had 3.6 Million US$ available;[156] by 30 September 2011 it had a sum of 4.1 US$ to hand.[157] The Basel Convention Technical Trust Fund, which is entirely based on voluntary financing, generally receives even fewer financial donations. In 2005 it was funded with 1,471,507 US$.[158] Remarkably, the United States, which have not ratified the Basel Convention yet, contributed 135,000 US$. In 2011 the Technical Trust Fund had only received 1,1 Million US$ by the end of September.[159] The most generous donators were EUROPAID (353,866 US$), Norway (200,378 US$) and, again, the United States (175,000 US$). Sadly, these funds are "insufficient to meet the Convention's needs"[160] and generally deprive the Convention's organs from fulfilling many of their tasks. The Basel Convention is only able to realize a few projects, not exclusively because of "severe funding con-

---

[155] K. Ishibashi, "Environmental Measures Restricting Waste Trade", in: K. Ishibashi/ A. Kiss/ D. Shelton (eds), *Economic Globalization and Compliance with International Environmental Agreements*, 2003, 69 et seq. (69).
[156] Trust Fund for the Basel Convention on the Control of Transboundary Movements of Hazardous Wastes and their Disposal. Status of contributions as at 31 December 2008, Annex I.
[157] Trust Fund for the Basel Convention on the Control of Transboundary Movements of Hazardous Wastes and their Disposal. Status of contributions as at 30 September 2011, Annex I.
[158] Basel Convention Trust Fund to Assist Developing Countries and other Countries in Need of Technical Assistance. Status of contributions 2005.
[159] See note 83, Annex II.
[160] Widawsky, see note 129, 602.

straints"[161] but also because nearly all the contributions are earmarked for specific uses.[162] The fact that there are almost no discretionary funds available makes it difficult for the Technical Trust Fund to develop a coherent strategy for project development and support. Just to compare: in order to clean up the pollution caused by the hazardous sludge dumped in the city of Abidjan in the *Trafigura* Case, the government of Côte d'Ivoire had to spend 22 Million Euros by December 2006.[163] The cleaning of the soil alone was then estimated to cost around 30 million Euros. The outcome of an immediate fundraising was low, except in the case of Japan, which donated 2 million US$ for the technical clean-up operation.[164] The Basel Convention Regional Centers, which are supposed to run their own finance mechanisms, but whose funds in reality depend directly on the contributions made to the Technical Trust Fund, face difficulties in doing effective work due to their sometimes "extremely precarious financial situation."[165] Experience has shown that the performance of the Centers is directly related to the amount of financial resources for activities administered by each centre.[166]

The Liability Protocol, which was described as "a significant step towards recourse action",[167] is not in force. Long explains, that many developing nations might have been reluctant to ratify the Protocol because, "contrary to their original need for assistance to cope with hazardous incidents, the Protocol as negotiated actually created significant loopholes in liability that would undermine developing nations' abili-

---

[161] Study of Possible Options for Lasting and Sustainable Financial Mechanisms, see note 76, 12.
[162] Ibid., 13.
[163] Just to compare: in order to clean up the pollution caused by the hazardous sludge dumped in the city of Abidjan in the *Trafigura* Case, the government of Côte d'Ivoire had to spend 22 Million Euros by December 2006, cf. UNEP *Report of the Conference of the Parties to the Basel Convention on the Control of Transboundary Movements of Hazardous Wastes and other Wastes in its 8th Mtg*, Doc. UNEP/CHW.8/16, 7.
[164] Ibid.
[165] *Report of the Review of the Operation of the Basel Convention Regional and Coordinating Centers as of 30 November 2009*, 11.
[166] Ibid.
[167] UNEP *Report of the 6th Mtg of the Conference of the Parties to the Basel Convention on the Control of Transboundary Movements of Hazardous Wastes and their Disposal*, Doc. UNEP/CHW.6/40, 59.

ties to deal with wastes."¹⁶⁸ This refers especially to article 4 of the Liability Protocol, which states that the concept of strict liability encompasses generators and exporters of hazardous wastes to be liable until the disposer has taken possession of the wastes. Developing State Parties often receive waste imports and host the disposers. And although the Basel Convention requires generators and exporters of hazardous wastes to ensure environmentally sound treatment of these wastes abroad, developing State Parties were afraid to be left alone with eventual clean-up and reparation costs. This loophole was said to give industrialized nations little incentive to ensure that environmentally sound facilities exist in the importing nation.¹⁶⁹ Furthermore, Parties tend to pay late. Delays in payment of the fund contributions and pledges that are never paid at all are a regular issue in each COP.¹⁷⁰ During the 9th COP, Parties decided to introduce penalties for contribution delays. Parties, whose contributions are in arrear for two or more years shall not be eligible to become a member of any bureau of the COP or its subsidiary bodies. Parties whose contributions are in arrear for four or more years shall not be entitled to vote at any meeting of the COP unless the Conference otherwise decides.¹⁷¹

---

¹⁶⁸ J.A. Long "Protocol on Liability and Compensation for Damage resulting from the Transboundary Movements of Hazardous Wastes and their Disposal", *Colo. J. Int'l Envtl. L. & Pol'y* 11 (2000), 253 et seq.

¹⁶⁹ Long, see note 168, 257-258.

¹⁷⁰ See the following statements: "The Conference expresses its concern over the delays in payment of the agreed contributions by Parties as well as voluntary contributions by Parties and non-Parties according to the agreement reached at the first meeting of the COP in accordance with which: 'all contributions are due to be paid in the year immediately preceding the year to which the contributions relate'", UNEP *Report of the Conference of the Parties to the Basel Convention on the Control of Transboundary Movements of Hazardous Wastes and other Wastes in its 4th Mtg*, Doc. UNEP/CHW.4/35, Decision IV/22; "The COP (...) expresses its concern over delays in payment of agreed contributions by Parties (...) and urges all Parties to pay their contributions promptly and full (...)", UNEP *Report of the Conference of the Parties to the Basel Convention on the Control of Transboundary Movements of Hazardous Wastes and other Wastes in its 9th Mtg*, Doc. UNEP/CHW.9/39, Decision IX/31.

¹⁷¹ UNEP *Report of the Conference of the Parties to the Basel Convention*, see note 170.

IV. Compliance Theory and Means of Compliance in International Environmental Law

1. Definitions of Compliance in International Environmental Law

Successful compliance with international agreements is defined in many ways. The UNEP Guidelines on Compliance with and Enforcement of Multilateral Environmental Agreements, a non-binding reference document designated to provide compliance advice for State Parties to MEAs of all kinds,[172] provide two different definitions: the section on Guidelines for Enhancing Compliance with Multilateral Environmental Agreements (Chapter I) refers to compliance as the "fulfillment by the contracting parties of their obligations under a multilateral environmental agreement and any amendments to the multilateral environmental agreement";[173] while the section on National Enforcement, and International Cooperation in combating Violations of Laws implementing Multilateral Environmental Agreements (Chapter II) describes compliance as the "state of conformity with obligations, imposed by a State, its competent authorities and agencies on the regulated community, whether directly or through conditions and requirements in permits, licenses and authorizations, in implementing multilateral environmental agreements."[174] The difference between these two aspects of compliance is clearly marked by the international approach of the former and the internal, national approach of the latter definition. The first definition refers to the compliance of State Parties with their respective international obligations. The second one refers to treaty-conforming national legislation that regulates the behavior of private actors within a State Party.

---

[172] In the light of many MEA Secretariats trying to develop successful compliance strategies, the UNEP incorporated the topic of compliance with, enforcement of, and implementation of, MEAs into its Work Program 2000 - 2001. The Guidelines were adopted by the 7th Special Sess. of the Governing Council of UNEP in 2002 and are now broadly available for use by governments, Convention Secretariats and all those interested. E. Maruma Mrema, "Cross-cutting Issues Related to Ensuring Compliance with MEAs", in: Beyerlin/ Stoll/ Wolfrum, see note 25, 201 et seq. (212).

[173] UNEP *Guidelines on Compliance with and Enforcement of Multilateral Environmental Agreements (2), UNEP Governing Council*, Decision SS.VII, 2004.

[174] Ibid., 8.

The Guidelines further distinguish between the terms of "Implementation" and "Enforcement", based on the different moments of regulation in which these acts come into effect. Implementation, therefore, "refers to, inter alia, all relevant laws, regulations, policies, and other measures and initiatives, that contracting parties adopt and/or take to meet their obligations under a multilateral environmental agreement and its amendments, if any."[175] Enforcement, on the other hand, encompasses the protection of these implemented regulations and the actions taken in a situation of breach: "Enforcement means the range of procedures and actions employed by a State, its competent authorities and agencies in order to ensure that organizations or persons, potentially failing to comply with environmental laws or regulations implementing multilateral environmental agreements, can be brought or returned into compliance and/or punished through civil, administrative or criminal action."[176] Enforcement includes a set of actions, i.e., the adoption of laws and regulations, reviews, etc., including various enabling activities and steps, which a state may take within its national territory to ensure compliance with an MEA (Guidelines 9 and 38).[177]

There exist other definitions which do not recognize the terms compliance, implementation and enforcement as different processes created by the adherence to a treaty, but as different stages of the compliance situation as a whole, on the national and the international level. According to Shelton, "Compliance includes implementation, but is broader, concerned with the factual matching of State behavior and international norms (...)."[178] Compliance (here used as an umbrella term encompassing compliance, implementation and enforcement) has different levels: first, there is compliance with the international treaty obligations the State Parties enter into. Since Parties to an MEA generally are states, compliance with MEAs therefore means "State Compliance" and might encompass, *inter alia*, reporting obligations or the establishment of na-

---

[175] Ibid., 2.
[176] Ibid., 9.
[177] Maruma Mrema, see note 172, 212, and *UNEP Guidelines on Compliance* see note 173, Guidelines 9 and 38.
[178] M. Fitzmaurice, "Compliance with Multilateral Environmental Agreements", *Hague Yearbook of International Law* 20 (2007-2008), 19 et seq., (23), citing D. Shelton, "Introduction: Law, Non-Law and the Problem of 'Soft-Law'", in: D. Shelton (ed.), *Commitment and Compliance. The Role of Non-Binding Norms in the International Legal System*, 2000, 5.

tional treaty authorities. As a "second step",[179] this level is complemented by the national legislation of a State Party that addresses persons or enterprises which are operating within the realm of the MEA in question and therefore affect the State Party's international performance. Their conduct needs to be regulated in conformity with the MEA in order to enable the state to comply. Within their national legislations, State Parties have to implement both the MEA in question and further regulations which secure and enforce compliance, and address non-compliance situations. The latter regulations apply different approaches and strategies. In a nutshell, they can be distinguished as confrontational, or adversarial measures that apply classical "control and command" structures; and non-confrontational or non-adversarial measures, which aim at facilitating compliance.[180]

2. Basic Introduction to Compliance Theory

A lot of research has already been done on possible reasons why states comply or do not comply with their obligations stemming from international treaties. This topic becomes even more sensitive in the realm of international environmental treaties, since they often do not provide for (immediate) advantages for the State Parties. They rather address the protection of global commons (like water, air, or the environment as a whole) and call for restrictions in certain (profitable) economic activities or for major financial contributions. Sometimes they address environmental issues which do not directly damage, nor even directly affect every state – like desertification, or the protection of certain plant or animal species. MEAs are "drafted and accepted in the interest of the whole humankind"[181] and "include obligations for all contracting parties without reciprocity."[182] As a rule, non-compliance with an obligation aimed at preserving and protecting certain global environmental goods does not have any direct detrimental impacts on an individual

---

[179] N. Matz, "Financial and other Incentives for Complying with MEA Obligations", in: Beyerlin/ Stoll/ Wolfrum, see note 25, 301 et seq. (303).
[180] Wolfrum, see note 20, 110 et seq.
[181] A. Kiss, "Reporting Obligations and Assessment of Reports", in: Beyerlin/ Stoll/ Wolfrum, see note 25, 229 et seq. (229).
[182] Kiss, see note 181, 229.

State Party.[183] It rather affects the treaty community of states as a whole.[184] Do State Parties not comply with their obligations stemming from an international treaty, because they do not achieve any (immediate) advantage from it? According to Chayes, Handler Chayes and Mitchell this is not the case. They refer to deliberate treaty violations as "dramatic, but rare exceptions rather than the rule"[185] and focus on incapability of states as the main cause of non-compliance: "As several country studies demonstrate, governments often fail to comply because they lack financial, administrative, informational, or regulatory capacities."[186] This problem can be especially pressing when the treaty targets private and individual behavior not directly under a government's control.[187]

Based on this assertion, the Managerial School on Compliance Theory was elaborated, an approach, according to which the "reasons for non-compliance are most likely to be found in the terms of an obligation, lack of capacity to carry out an obligation and a change of circumstances."[188] Accordingly, the strengthening of regulatory regimes requires "a strategy of integrated, active management of compliance that addresses the real sources of noncompliance, without necessarily expecting to achieve perfect implementation and compliance"[189] and they suggest management tools such as transparency, reporting, verification and monitoring, dispute resolution and capacity building as "the key to designing a regime to encourage compliance."[190] A central idea of their approach is that "a managerial model of compliance suggests that regimes usually keep noncompliance at acceptable levels by an interactive process of discourse among the parties, the treaty organization, and the

---

[183] U. Beyerlin/ P. Stoll/ R. Wolfrum, "Conclusions drawn from the Conference on Ensuring Compliance with MEAs", in: Beyerlin/ Stoll/ Wolfrum, see note 25, 359 et seq. (360).

[184] Beyerlin/ Stoll/ Wolfrum, see note 183, 360.

[185] Chayes/ Handler Chayes/ Mitchell, "Managing Compliance: A Comparative Perspective", in: Brown Weiss/ Jacobson, see note 132, 40 et seq. (40).

[186] Chayes et al., see note 132, 40.

[187] Ibid., 41.

[188] T.E. Crossen, "Multilateral Agreements and the Compliance Continuum", Geo. Int'l Envt'l L. Rev. 16 (2004), 473 et seq., (483), see also A. Chayes/ A. Handler Chayes, *The new Sovereignty: Compliance with International Regulatory Agreements*, 1995.

[189] Chayes et al., see note 132, 40.

[190] Crossen, see note 188, 12.

wider public."¹⁹¹ Maintaining the same logic of argumentation, a very strong constraint is pronounced against confrontational compliance means. Not only would their research "indicate that in the face of non-compliance, coercive [confrontational] sanctions¹⁹² are not only ineffective but inherently unsuitable,"¹⁹³ they would go as far as to state that "efforts to negotiate sanction clauses into treaties and to invoke unilateral sanctions for violations are largely a waste of time."¹⁹⁴

On the other end of the range of compliance theories, there are scholars who favor coercive means to achieve countries' compliance. Guzman presumes that countries' attitudes towards compliance are not driven by their economic and administrative capability to comply, but by a simple calculation whether a breach of or compliance with the MEA is more cost-efficient; and by the consideration, how badly the country's reputation on the international stage might be affected by a breach. According to Guzman, a country's decision to follow international law reflects a judgment that the costs of violation outweigh the benefits.¹⁹⁵ He calls for adversarial measures, especially sanctions as reasonable means to ensure and enforce compliance, although he admits that it is "difficult to achieve effective multilateral sanctions."¹⁹⁶ He argues that sanctions will work best in bilateral relationships and complex, ongoing relationships:¹⁹⁷ "By punishing offenders today, states increase the likelihood of compliance tomorrow because the threat of future punishment is credible."¹⁹⁸

The most prominent theory on treaty compliance that is in favor of sanctions is advanced by Downs and his colleagues.¹⁹⁹ Within their ap-

---

[191] Chayes et al., see note 132, 41.
[192] Introductory information on sanctions and other confrontational means, see Chapter 4. a.
[193] Chayes et al., see note 132, 41.
[194] Ibid.
[195] A.T. Guzman, "A Compliance-Based Theory of International Law", *Cal. L. Rev.* 90 (2002), 1823 et seq. (1853).
[196] Guzman, see note 195, 1868.
[197] Crossen, see note 188, 28 and Guzman, see note 195, 1868.
[198] Guzman, see note 195, 1868.
[199] G.W. Downs/ D.M. Rocke/ P.N. Barsoom, "Is the good news about compliance good news about cooperation?", *International Organizations* 50 (1996), 379 et seq. (379) and J. Brunnée, "Enforcement Mechanisms in International Law and International Environmental Law", in: Beyerlin/ Stoll/ Wolfrum, see note 25, 2 et seq., 11.

proach, sanctions are understood as a "broad range of measures that create costs or remove benefits",[200] which serve especially when non-compliance with an international treaty is an attractive option. This is the case where treaties require states to depart significantly from what they would have done in the absence of a treaty ("depth of cooperation").[201] Other authors argue that compliance with international treaties is not only due to the respective enforcement mechanisms, but to the treaty's structure as a whole. In the words of Mitchell: Regime design matters.[202] Brown Weiss and Jacobson established four groups of crucial variables which have to be taken into account while elaborating an effective international agreement: (1) the characteristics of the activity involved; (2) the characteristics of the accord; (3) the international environment; and (4) factors involving the country.[203] According to Brown Weiss and Jacobson, in the rarest of cases states willfully do not comply with their treaty obligations; compliance rather depends on conditions such as the number of actors involved, the acceptance and support of the treaty objectives by the international community (major international conferences, public opinion, media, international non-governmental organizations, and international financial organizations), precision and perceived equity of the obligations, the administrative capacity of a state or the effective application of enforcement measures like reporting requirements, incentives and sanctions.[204]

3. Compliance and Treaty Design of MEAs

Despite the research done in the field of compliance with international law obligations and especially with MEAs, and all the valid compliance

---

[200] G.W. Downs, "Enforcement and the Evolution of Cooperation", *Mich. J. Int'l L.* 19 (1998), 319 et seq. (320), found in Brunnée, see note 199, footnote 46 (11).
[201] Downs et al., see note 199, 383.
[202] R.B. Mitchell, "Regime design matters: intentional oil pollution and treaty compliance", in: B.J. Cohen/ Ch. Lipson (eds), *Theory and structure in international political economy: an international organization reader*, 1999, 207 et seq., 207.
[203] E. Brown Weiss/ H. Jacobson, "Assessing the record", in: E. Brown Weiss/ H. Jacobson (eds), *Engaging Countries: Strengthening Compliance with Environmental Accords*, 1998, 6 et seq.
[204] Brown Weiss/ Jacobson, see note 203, 528.

theories available,²⁰⁵ scholars nowadays agree upon the idea that no singular compliance strategy exists, which is applicable overall to MEAs. This is due to the heterogeneity of environmental issues and to the multiple structures that MEAs apply today. Compliance Mechanisms are as diverse as the treaties they are featured by. However, scholars seem to agree that sanctions are a "'last resort', after other methods have failed"²⁰⁶ and generally do not constitute the preferred compliance method in international environmental law. Classical dispute settlement solutions of international law have hardly been made use of, either.²⁰⁷ Brown Weiss and Jacobson further state that MEAs should not exclusively address states as Parties to the respective treaties, but should be able to modify, through them, the behavior of enterprises and individuals.²⁰⁸ Beyerlin, Wolfrum and Stoll point out, that opting for a certain method and procedure of compliance control "depends on the very type of the respective agreement, particularly the design and content of obligations that it imposes on its parties."²⁰⁹

Bringing the discussion back to the Basel Convention, Beyerlin, Stoll and Wolfrum make two important observations regarding its treaty design: first, the Basel Convention is an MEA that "clearly shows elements of bilateralism."²¹⁰ This implicates, that it might be most effi-

---

[205] A not exhaustive list of further theoreticians would encompass, e.g. Harold Koh or Thomas Franck. Koh seeks to explain compliance as arising from a three-part process of interaction, interpretation and internalization. Through a combination of, *inter alia*, lobbying, transnational public litigation, and norm sponsorship by prominent government and private sector figures – to which Koh refers to as "vertical" process - international norms are invoked, argued over and interpreted. See N. Craik, "The International Law of Environmental Impact Assessment", 2008, 188 et seq., citing H. Koh, "Why do Nations obey International Law", *Yale J. Int'l. L* 106 (1997), 106 et seq. According to his Fairness Theory, Franck argues that a perception that the law is substantively and procedurally fair encourages compliance. See Crossen, see note 188, 15 and T. Franck, "Fairness in International Law and Institutions", 1998.

[206] Brown Weiss/ McCaffrey, see note 76, 236 et seq.

[207] The Basel Convention requires its States Parties to settle their disputes regarding interpretation and application of, or compliance with the Convention through negotiations and other peaceful means. If these measures fail, the parties can agree to submit their case to the ICJ or to an arbitration tribunal. See Basel Convention, article 20 and Annex VI.

[208] Brown Weiss/ Jacobson, see note 203, 511.

[209] Beyerlin/ Stoll/ Wolfrum, see note 25, 359.

[210] Ibid., 260.

cient if the "directly affected State(s) unilaterally responded to the non-compliant State",[211] which affects the compliance enforcement methods that would serve such a treaty. Second, the Basel Convention mainly provides for "action-orientated" obligations, which generally have an "only abstractly defined objective."[212] They further lack a precise time limit for achieving this objective and a clear-cut definition of the action to be taken.[213] The opposite would be treaties with result-orientated obligations, which constitute clear aims (e.g. a certain amount of emission reduction within a defined period of time, as in the Kyoto Protocol).[214] As far as "action-orientated" treaties are concerned, Beyerlin, Stoll and Wolfrum resume that "the lack of efficiency of the control mechanisms identified in respect of this type of MEA is the direct result of the latter's design."[215] They further conclude, that "particular mechanisms still have to be developed which would provide for an efficient compliance control of action-orientated MEAs taking into consideration the objective they pursue."[216]

4. Means to Ensure Compliance

a. Confrontational Means

As stated above, mechanisms to ensure compliance are differentiated as confrontational and non-confrontational means. Confrontational means generally have a somewhat negative connotation and encompass sanctions or retaliatory actions, negative incentives and penalties.[217] Sanctions are of a coercive and punitive character and have to be "credible and potent"[218] in order to be effective. Furthermore, sanction provisions have to be backed up by a strong and credible enforcement structure. They lose effect if states are free to believe that incompliance will never lead to an actual launch of sanctions because of a lack of funding

---

[211] Ibid., 261.
[212] Ibid.
[213] Ibid.
[214] Ibid., 362.
[215] Ibid., 361.
[216] Ibid.
[217] E. Brown Weiss, "Strengthening National Compliance with International Environmental Agreements", *Env. Policy & Law* 27 (1997), 297 et seq.
[218] Mitchell, see note 202, 210.

or of political will. Sanctions may be economic, like trade embargos and import prohibitions for goods produced in the sanctioned country, or political, like the withdrawal of diplomatic missions from the territory of the sanctioned state. Moreover, there are negative incentives which are rather aimed at abolishing certain privileges.[219] Matz points out the example of a loan tied to certain conditionalities that might be called in if the state did not comply with those conditions.[220] Sanctions, on the contrary, "penalize non-compliant behavior by limiting the exercise of rights or reduce the position of a state below the ordinary."[221] The Basel Convention uses a prohibition of trade with Non-Parties[222] as a general objective; it does not, however, apply sanctions or other adversarial mechanisms to ensure compliance.

b. Non-confrontational Means

Non-confrontational means to enhance compliance with MEAs consist of procedural means, like reporting, monitoring and verification, site inspections and procedures to address situations of non-compliance. Furthermore, there are facilitative measures like financial and other economic incentives, compliance assistance, capacity building or technology transfer.

aa. Procedural Means: Reporting, Monitoring, Verification

Procedural means are core methods to enhance compliance with MEAs, because they allow that a State Party's performance regarding the obligations it assumed can be reviewed and evaluated. The UNEP Guidelines refer to reporting, monitoring and verification as "provisions that can help promote compliance, by, inter alia, potentially increasing public awareness."[223] Reporting, according to the UNEP Guidelines, requires Parties to make "regular, timely reports on compliance, using an appropriate common format."[224] Monitoring refers to the collection of these data, and "in accordance with provisions of a multilateral envi-

---

[219] Matz, see note 179, 312.
[220] Ibid.
[221] Ibid.
[222] Basel Convention, article 4 para. 5, "A Party shall not permit hazardous wastes or other wastes to be exported to a non-Party or to be imported from a non-Party."
[223] UNEP *Guidelines on Compliance*, see note 173, 3.
[224] See note 173.

ronmental agreement can be used to assess compliance with an agreement, identify compliance problems and indicate solutions."[225] Fitzmaurice further states that monitoring may encompass activities such as on-site field visits or regular conferences at which the states report.[226] The bodies assigned to collect and monitor the acquired data might be Secretariats to the MEAs, or special bodies, sometimes assisted by NGOs.[227] Finally, verification is the process of determination whether a party is compliant or not. The principal source of verification might be national reports.[228]

bb. Non-compliance Procedures

The UNEP Guidelines further recommend the inclusion of non-compliance mechanisms and bodies into MEAs, such as Compliance Committees. They should be used as "a vehicle to identify possible situations of non-compliance at an early stage and the causes of non-compliance and to formulate appropriate responses […]."[229] They should be non-adversarial and include procedural safeguards for the non-compliant State Party;[230] the power to emit final determinations of non-compliance, however, is supposed to remain with the Conference or Meeting of the Parties of the respective MEA, or to a body named by them.[231]

The Basel Convention generally and genuinely applies procedural means and a non-compliance procedure, providing for a reporting system managed by the Basel Convention Secretariat and a Compliance Committee, designated to address cases of non-compliance, when triggered to do so. It does not make use, however, of verification procedures in order to secure validity and correctness of the reports handed to the Secretariat. "Monitoring" within the Basel Convention is basically reduced to the generation of data compilations; on-site visits are not scheduled (the Compliance Committee, though, may hold "with the agreement of a Party(ies), information gatherings in its or their ter-

---

[225] Ibid.
[226] Fitzmaurice, see note 178, 3.
[227] Ibid.
[228] UNEP *Guidelines on Compliance*, see note 173.
[229] Ibid.
[230] Ibid.
[231] Ibid.

ritory for the purpose of fulfilling its functions)."[232] Shibata concludes, that the Basel Convention, "if the terms 'inspection' and 'external monitoring' were understood in the usual sense as used in international law […], does not provide such obligatory, pre-established systems of inspection or monitoring of the Parties' implementation of, and compliance with, the convention's obligations."[233]

cc. Facilitative Means

Facilitative means aim at enhancing compliance with MEAs by providing material help, like technology or funding, and immaterial support, like know-how. Many MEAs offer compliance assistance to their State Parties in order to make compliance possible in the first place. Matz distinguishes between incentives and compliance assistance as "the latter consist of transfers or of actions that enable a state to be compliant. Incentives are granted to induce compliance, they are granted when the development of a compliance project has been concluded successfully."[234]

c. Economic Incentives

In the UNEP Guidelines, economic compliance incentives are considered feasible mechanisms for both the implementation of an MEA into the national legal system and for the institutional framework to enforce compliance with the MEA on the national level. As far as national implementation is concerned, economic instruments are named as tools that parties can consider to make use of, as long as this is in conformity with their obligations under applicable international agreements.[235] Furthermore, states are held to make "use of economic instruments, including user fees, pollution fees and other measures promoting economically efficient compliance"[236] in order to enforce compliance and combat violations. According to Matz, incentives of a financial or other kind are most commonly known from national legal orders.[237] They might consist of tax advantages, e.g. for companies which successfully

---

[232] Terms of Reference, article 22 lit. d, see note 115.
[233] Shibata, see note 131, 72-73.
[234] Matz, see note 179, 306.
[235] UNEP *Guidelines on Compliance*, see note 173.
[236] Ibid.
[237] Matz, see note 179, 303.

comply with a certain emission regime or apply environmentally sound production technology, or of public financial awards granted to those who do so. The Rio Declaration of the United Nations Conference on Environment and Development[238] (UNCED) emphasizes the utility of economic instruments to enhance sustainable development, when being applied at the national level, in its Principle 16: National authorities should endeavor to promote the internalization of environmental costs and the use of economic instruments, taking into account the approach that the polluter should, in principle, bear the cost of pollution, with due regard to the public interest and without distorting international trade and investment.[239] International Environmental Declarations like the Rio Declaration and its successor documents refer to the overall goal of sustainable development rather than to the special field of compliance with MEAs. Since these aims are so closely linked, these documents provide feasible strategies for both aims. The Agenda 21 provides for more concrete economic mechanisms to implement national environmental policies and consequently calls for the "effective use of economic instruments and market and other incentives."[240] The Agenda 21 effectively links funding mechanisms which facilitate treaty regimes to globally finance and conduct environmentally sound and sustainable projects with economic incentives to comply with MEAs. It thereby emphasizes trade mechanisms and bilateral cooperation. Article 33.17 of Agenda 21 calls for the "mobilization of higher levels of foreign direct investment and technology transfers through national policies that promote investment and through joint ventures and other modalities"[241] and for "innovative financing", which includes, *inter alia*, "the use of economic and fiscal incentives and mechanisms" and "feasible tradable permits."[242] In the successor UNCED meeting to Rio, the World Summit on Sustainable Development in Johannesburg 2002, emphasized the importance the international community should give to economic mechanisms. The Johannesburg Plan of Implementation recognizes "the importance of foreign direct investment flows in support

---

[238] *Rio Declaration on Environment and Development*, Doc. A/CONF.151/26 (Vol. I).
[239] Rio Declaration, Principle 16, see note 238.
[240] Agenda 21, Doc. A/CONF.151/26/Rev.1 (Vol. I.), Chapter 8.
[241] Ibid., Chapter 33.17.
[242] Ibid., Chapter 33.18 lit. b and c.

of sustainable development"²⁴³ and "continues to enhance the mutual supportiveness of trade, environment and development with a view to achieving sustainable development [...]."²⁴⁴

As is shown above in the UNEP Guidelines and the Rio Declaration, international declarations regarding environmental law and sustainable development, often address economic incentives as a subject to be realized at national levels. The Basel Convention does not provide any incentive mechanism in its compliance system, but leaves their creation and implementation to the State Parties. The direct inclusion of economic incentives into MEAs might be more effective, though. Economic incentives that directly stem from MEAs need to be implemented in national law in order to be applied, like any other provision of international law. The advantage would be, though, that in this way MEAs directly provide an incentive framework as part of their treaty design, which could then be adapted as a whole and fully developed in the national legislations of State Parties. Incentive regulations, ready to be implemented by State Parties, benefit a treaty characteristic that is deemed essential to facilitate compliance with the UNEP Guidelines.²⁴⁵

A further positive aspect of specific compliance incentives which directly stem from an MEA is that these provisions probably receive a high level of acceptance from the State Parties. They might have participated in the treaty negotiations and therefore have accepted the incentive provisions beforehand or were able to inform themselves about these provisions before they adhered to the MEA in question and could make preparations. The strategy of preparing states for compliance before they ratify is especially considered in the Montreal Protocol, where prospective State Parties can apply for preparation support from the MPMF.

---

[243] UN Department for Economic and Social Affairs, Division for Sustainable Development, Johannesburg Plan of Implementation, Chapter X, article 84.

[244] Johannesburg Plan of Implementation, Chapter X, article 97, see note 243.

[245] UNEP *Guidelines on Compliance with and Enforcement of Multilateral Environmental Agreements*, see note 173, article 14 lit. a (3), "To assist in the assessment and ascertainment of compliance, the obligations of parties to multilateral environmental agreements should be stated clearly."

d. The Example of the Convention on Biological Diversity

There indeed exist MEAs which provide a compliance system based on economic incentives. The Convention on Biological Diversity[246] (CBD) provides – on a framework basis – the incentive of access to resources or resource markets[247] in order to achieve technical and scientific cooperation[248] between host states and states wishing to operate in their territory. This means, states which want to participate in the exploitation of genetic resources in the territory of another state, have to grant technical and scientific cooperation and technology transfer to the host state, especially, when the latter is not in the economic position to exploit its resources by itself. The concept of the CBD is that the benefits of the exploitation should be shared and the host states should be compensated for granting access to their resources. Article 16 para. 3 of the CBD generally obliges State Parties to take legislative, administrative or policy measures to transfer technology to those State Parties, in particu-

---

[246] Convention on Biological Diversity.
[247] Matz, see note 179, 315.
[248] Convention on Biological Diversity, article 18, "1. The Contracting Parties shall promote international technical and scientific cooperation in the field of conservation and sustainable use of biological diversity, where necessary, through the appropriate international and national institutions. 2. Each Contracting Party shall promote technical and scientific cooperation with other Contracting Parties, in particular developing countries, in implementing this Convention, inter alia, through the development and implementation of national policies. In promoting such cooperation, special attention should be given to the development and strengthening of national capabilities, by means of human resources development and institution building. 3. The Conference of the Parties, at its first meeting, shall determine how to establish a clearing-house mechanism to promote and facilitate technical and scientific cooperation. 4. The Contracting Parties shall, in accordance with national legislation and policies, encourage and develop methods of cooperation for the development and use of technologies, including indigenous and traditional technologies, in pursuance of the objectives of this Convention. For this purpose, the Contracting Parties shall also promote cooperation in the training of personnel and exchange of experts. 5. The Contracting Parties shall, subject to mutual agreement, promote the establishment of joint research programmes and joint ventures for the development of technologies relevant to the objectives of this Convention."

lar developing countries, which provide access to genetic resources.[249] The possibility to participate in the use of genetic resources and to have access to technologies and investigation equipment "attaches an economic value to biodiversity"[250] which shall serve as incentive for both host states and involved states to protect the resources and treat them sustainably. This principle is also called "benefit-sharing". Probably the most prominent MEA using economic and market-based incentives as a compliance enforcement mechanism is the Kyoto Protocol.

e. Compliance Assistance and Capacity-Building

Compliance assistance does not reward compliance as incentives do, but provides for funds and other means to facilitate compliance in the first place. Therefore, measures like capacity-building, technology transfer, awareness raising and financial transfers can serve as compliance assistance measures or as incentives, depending, when they are applied. The prospective of achieving compliance assistance may as well be seen as an incentive to adhere to or to comply with an MEA. However, compliance assistance consisting of transfers of financial resources in order to enable developing State Parties to comply with their obligations, e.g. by covering the incremental costs resulting from the implementation of an agreement, are a common feature of most modern international environmental agreements.[251]

Environmental treaties often implicate the capacity of the State (Parties) to govern,[252] and to translate and implement international MEA obligations feasibly into their domestic legislation. Where State Parties lack an efficient administration or the means to build such an administrative system themselves, capacity-building may be the most useful assistance method to facilitate compliance. The UNEP Guidelines recognize compliance assistance as a necessary measure in order to ensure the capability of particularly developing countries to comply with their MEA obligations: "The building and strengthening of capacities may be needed for developing countries that are parties to multilateral environmental agreements, particularly the least developed countries, as well as parties with economies in transition to assist such countries in

---

[249] Convention on Biological Diversity, article 16 para. 1; Wolfrum, see note 20, 114.
[250] Wolfrum, see note 20, 110 et seq.
[251] Matz, see note 179, 307.
[252] Chayes et al., see note 185, 52.

meeting their obligations under multilateral environmental agreements."²⁵³ This includes, *inter alia*, the provision of technology and funds, but refers particularly to the realization of adequate training for the locally competent authorities, in order to enable them to implement and overlook national compliance.

Gündling develops a three-step approach to the "fairly complex process"²⁵⁴ of capacity building. He states that first, "'Capacity' in the context of compliance with international law obligations may mean the availability of governmental institutions to implement international organizations at the national level and to ensure that the measures taken are enforced."²⁵⁵ This includes "environmental administrative structures, environmental rules and regulations, based on sound environmental policies, providing command and control measures where necessary and economic incentives where possible [...]."²⁵⁶ Second, he analyzes that compliance capacity needs resources: "This refers to the economic, technical and financial capabilities and means required for environmental management by both governmental and private actors."²⁵⁷ He points out an essential conclusion valid for the entire compliance debate in international environmental law: "A normative system providing for rules, regulations, standards and other requirements is useless if the addressees are not in a position to comply with them."²⁵⁸ As the third essential measure in order to build capacity, Gündling calls for the establishment and functioning of a non-governmental sector as "watchdog" for the governments and the private sectors alike.²⁵⁹

The Rio Declaration, Agenda 21 and the Johannesburg Plan call for capacity building.²⁶⁰ Concerning this matter, the Basel Convention only

---

253 UNEP *Guidelines on Compliance with and Enforcement of Multilateral Environmental Agreements*, see note 173, 6.
254 L. Gündling, "Compliance Assistance in International Environmental Law: Capacity-Building through Financial and Technology Transfer", *ZaöRV/HJIL* 56 (1996), 796 et seq. (800).
255 Gündling, see note 254, 800.
256 Ibid., 800.
257 Ibid.
258 Ibid.
259 Ibid., 801.
260 See, *inter alia*, Rio Declaration on Environment and Development, Principle 9: "States should cooperate to strengthen endogenous capacity-building for sustainable development by improving scientific understanding through exchanges of scientific and technological knowledge, and by enhancing the

contains a shallow provision regarding international cooperation,[261] which calls upon State Parties to work together in the fields of development and implementation of new environmentally low-waste technologies and to provide technology and capacity to manage it for countries in need, especially developing countries. The BCRCs constitute an attempt to facilitate technologies and adequate capacity training in developing countries, but – like the Technical Trust Fund, whose funds are supposed to finance capacity-building and technology transfer – they fall too short of financial supplies to permanently provide support. The Compliance Committee is – in a similarly imprecise way – held to review general issues of "accessing technical and financial support, particularly for developing countries, including technology transfer and capacity-building"[262] under the direction of the COP.

5. Financing Compliance with MEAs

Compliance with MEAs is costly. Costs stem, in principle, from internal measures State Parties have to take in order to create an administrative structure (focal points, responsible national authorities), and from the external duties State Parties assume, like periodic contributions to the MEA in question, or penalty payments for non-compliance. Departing from the viewpoint that developed countries carry the major responsibility for today's global environmental deterioration because they produce and consume most of the damaging substances, and further have more resources (like technology and funds) available, MEAs and international environmental declarations additionally tend to provide for developed State Parties to bear the biggest part of the costs which sustainable development parameters put on developing countries.[263]

---

development, adaptation, diffusion and transfer of technologies, including new and innovative technologies". Agenda 21, para. 34 para. 4: "There is a need for favourable access to and transfer of environmentally sound technologies, in particular to developing countries, through supportive measures that promote technology cooperation and that should enable transfer of necessary technological know-how as well as building up of economic, technical, and managerial capabilities for the efficient use and further development of transferred technology."

[261] Basel Convention, article 10 para. 2 lit. c and d and para. 10 lit. e.
[262] Terms of Reference, article 21 lit. c, see note 115.
[263] The Principle of Common, but Differentiated Responsibilities is, *inter alia*, manifested in Principle 7 of the Rio Declaration: "States shall cooperate in

Financial mechanisms of MEAS can be categorized according to their function, how they are administered, and how they are funded.[264] Brown Weiss and McCaffrey explain that with respect to function, a financial mechanism may serve either a funding or a coordinating function. A funding mechanism provides financial resources to help a country address its technical and capacity needs. In contrast, a coordinating mechanism primarily assists in resource mobilization by identifying possible outside sources of funding and other assistance and helping countries apply for them.[265] Furthermore, MEAs can be administered in a singular, stand-alone way or within the framework of an entity that operates multiple conventions. According to Brown Weiss, a stand-alone mechanism is treaty-specific, i.e., it administers a mechanism for a single MEA. In contrast a multipurpose operational entity administers the financial mechanisms of more than one MEA.[266] Finally, with respect to how a mechanism is funded, four types exist. A mechanism can be funded by voluntary contributors, by mandatory contributions, by sources other than contribution, or by a combination of these.[267] According to these definitions, the Basel Convention Technical Trust Fund can be described as a stand-alone, voluntary funding mechanism. It serves the Basel Convention alone and it receives direct funding on a voluntary basis. The MPMF has a similar structure as a single funding mechanism, but requires obligatory contributions from the State Parties.

---

    a spirit of global partnership to conserve, protect and restore the health and integrity of the Earth's ecosystem. In view of the different contributions to global environmental degradation, States have common but differentiated responsibilities. The developed countries acknowledge the responsibility that they bear in the international pursuit of sustainable development in view of the pressures their societies place on the global environment and of the technologies and financial resources they command." The Principle includes two elements: the first concerns the common responsibility of states for the protection of the environment, or parts of it, at the national, regional and global levels. The second concerns the need to take account of differing circumstances, particularly in relation to each state's contribution to the creation of a particular environmental problem and its ability to prevent, reduce and control the threat. See P. Sands, *Principles of International Environmental Law*, 2003, 286 et seq.

[264] Brown Weiss/ McCaffrey, see note 76, 1068.
[265] Ibid., 1068-1070.
[266] Ibid., 1069.
[267] Ibid.

Many international organizations, provide funds to finance environmentally sound developing projects. Typical forms of funding are requirement-bound loans or grants stemming from selective, purposeful funds these organizations administer. In 1991, the Global Environment Facility (GEF) was established by the World Bank, in cooperation with the UN and its relevant specialized agencies (UNEP, UNDP).[268] The GEF provides grants to developing countries and countries with economies in transition for projects related to biodiversity, climate change, international waters, land degradation, the ozone layer, and persistent organic pollutants.[269] It further constitutes the financial mechanism for four major environmental conventions: the Convention on Biological Diversity; the United Nations Framework Convention on Climate Change; the United Nations Convention to Combat Desertification; and the Stockholm Convention on Persistent Organic Pollutants. The GEF itself is funded by its Member States. The contributions it receives in periodic replenishment rounds are used to fund projects of different scales in countries eligible to apply for funding. In order to get grants from the GEF, countries either have to be a State Party to the respective treaty (for biodiversity and climate change projects) or fulfill the requirements needed to borrow from the World Bank or to receive UNDP technical assistance.[270] From 1991 until 1 December 2011, the GEF has allocated 10 billion US$ and (co-)financed about 2,800 projects. Four replenishment cycles have already been realized, the fifth started in November 2008. UNEP and FAO called the GEF an "effective and credible facility for funding activities that delivers significant global environmental benefits."[271] Montini describes the GEF as the "most important example of a financial mechanism devised for funding environmental protection at the global level."[272] Although being celebrated as a successful funding mechanism, the GEF faces the same difficulties as any contribution-based financial vehicle of an MEA. Brown Weiss writes that the main shortcoming of the GEF's financial resources is that they are relatively modest, given the critical and complex environmental challenges they are being asked to address.[273]

---

[268] Montini, see note 21, 163.
[269] Information available at <http://www.thegef.org>.
[270] Brown Weiss/ McCaffrey, see note 76, 1050.
[271] UNEP/ FAO Study, see note 76.
[272] Montini, see note 21, 163.
[273] Brown Weiss/ McCaffrey, see note 76, 1053.

6. Possible Strategies to Enhance Compliance with and Funding of the Basel Convention

Concluding the review of economic incentives and compliance assistance strategies which are used in MEAs or recommended in international environmental declarations and of the ways they are financed – what strategies could possibly be useful to enhance compliance with the Basel Convention?

A feasible basic approach might be to stop deeming movements of hazardous wastes from developed to developing countries as an evil and therefore undesirable trend which jeopardizes efforts to protect developing countries from environmental harms. On the contrary, it could be considered as trade in goods which brings economic benefits to the receiving countries, given that they are enabled to deal with the waste streams in an environmentally sound way. Global trade in hazardous wastes is an enormous and profitable business, and though environmentally sound technologies to deal with or to avoid hazardous wastes are on the rise in developing countries the world is still far away from generating significantly fewer quantities of hazardous wastes. As long as the disposal of hazardous wastes is cheaper and bureaucratically easier in developing countries, waste streams entering these countries, legally and illegally, probably will not run dry. The control of global waste flows will remain a "ubiquitous problem that affects both developing and developed nations",[274] which is "beautifully" demonstrated by the quantities of hazardous wastes still illegally leaving the EU to Africa and Asia.

The Basel Ban Amendment does not take up this idea. On the contrary, it sweepingly deems all developing countries as ineligible to deal with hazardous wastes. This approach might have been supported by many developing countries, especially among the African State Parties to the Basel Convention, but simultaneously faces rejection by those countries, which consider (some) hazardous wastes, e.g. electronic waste, as valuable sources for the extraction of prime materials. Widawsky states that although the Basel Ban was proposed as a mechanism to impose a strict rule in order to protect the health and safety of developing countries, it may be cutting of a source of income.[275] Instead of creating a ban, which is not yet in force, but hovering in space and defining the direction the Convention is taking, the Basel Convention

---

[274] Bombier, see note 152, 347.
[275] Widawsky, see note 129, 615.

should take up an approach according to which waste movements to developing countries are considered as preferable and where emphasis is put on regulations in order to enhance safety and profitability of these movements. Restrictive regional conventions like the Bamako Convention ought to be re-thought as well.

Developing countries need economic progress if they are to solve their environmental problems just as developed countries do.[276] But in order to be enabled to handle hazardous wastes in an environmentally sound way, developing states will need help and support from developed ones. Put bluntly, an import ban for hazardous wastes creates little incentives to State Parties which are in a position to help in building up waste treatment facilities to do so, because later they would not be able to use these facilities. The numerous regional conventions that prohibit the import of hazardous wastes to their State Parties also hinder developed countries, which aim for environmental protection in a framework that enables safe waste trading,[277] to actively build up waste infrastructure in developing countries.

How can legal waste trade with developing countries be made safe, environmentally sound and beneficial in a way that outweighs the economic "advantages" of illegal trading? The answer might be found in a system of feasible economic incentives and compliance assistance that addresses both developing and developed State Parties. A compliance system of the Basel Convention should directly respond to the economic activity that is behind the environmental issue in question (in this case: trade in hazardous wastes) and address the private actors in this field. The GEF also considers "enhanced private sector involvement"[278] as a crucial aspect for sustainable environmental projects to be successful.

Economic incentives in MEAs are traditionally focused on raising the attractiveness of compliance in developing State Parties. As far as global waste movements – a business attractive to actors on both the "winner" and "victim" country's side – are concerned, it might be a more useful approach to include developed countries, which produce and export the highest quantities of hazardous wastes into an incentive system. States and enterprises which invest in the development of safe

---

[276] Gündling, see note 254, 799.
[277] Widawsky, see note 129, 615.
[278] GEF Evaluation Office, GEF Annual Performance Report 2005, Doc. GEF/C.28/ME/2/Rev.1 (26) and Brown Weiss/ McCaffrey, see note 76, 1051.

waste treatment facilities or in capacity building in developing countries should be granted advantages for doing so. On the national level, State Parties to the Basel Convention could grant tax advantages or funding for entrepreneurs who carry out such projects in developing counties. However, special tax-related environmental measures are complex topics which alone raise a multitude of legal questions and would go far beyond the scope of this article.

On the MEA level, the Basel Convention could widen the access to funds of the Technical Trust Fund to developed State Parties and their national enterprises given that they finance or carry out environmentally sound waste projects or compliance assistance projects in developing State Parties. Gündling makes an important statement about the quality that assistance activities of developed states in developing ones should have in order to be effective and sustainable: "Projects need to be country-driven; counterparts in developing countries must feel that projects are their own. This implies that projects are coordinated and carried out basically by developing country institutions and that expatriate expertise is limited to what is absolutely necessary."[279] If developed countries genuinely acted up to this legitimate "ownership"[280] approach towards waste treatment projects in developing countries, they would lose predominance over the foreign projects they finance or carry out, possibly including over the intellectual property involved – a further disincentive to assist developing countries to comply with the Basel Convention.

Access to funds from the Technical Trust Fund not only for states which are in need of assistance, but also for those states and enterprises which actively assist, coupled with the possibility to legally move hazardous wastes to developing countries might contribute to the solution of two major dilemmas of the Basel Convention: illegal waste trade and poor financial conditions of the Convention's funding vehicles. These two approaches could – simply put – make compliance with the Basel Convention easier and more attractive. Developed State Parties accordingly would have a powerful incentive, not only to comply with their obligations under the Basel Convention, but also to assume their global responsibility as the leading generators of hazardous wastes and – more generally – under the global environmental principle of common, but differentiated responsibilities. The possibility to achieve funding for their own national investors willing to invest in or carry out waste

---

[279] Gündling, see note 254, 808-809.
[280] Ibid., 808.

treatment activities in developing countries perhaps would even enhance the willingness of State Parties to the Basel Convention to make adequate donations to the Technical Trust Fund and to genuinely pay their pledges.

In order to stabilize the two Funds of the Basel Convention and to avoid the permanent financial issues to which so many stand-alone conventions that are financed by State Party donations are prone, the funding system could be integrated into the GEF. This could happen in form of a reduced system that grants access to GEF funding to Basel-related projects like investments in waste treatment facilities or compliance assistance and capacity building projects in developing State Parties; or by making the GEF generally accountable to the Basel Convention by letting it operate its financial mechanisms. In order to prevent the scarcity of funds, authorities of the GEF pronounce an approach that also serves as a strategy for the Basel Convention: "Yet the private sector has historically been slow to invest in projects that produce global environmental benefits. In most cases, significantly expanding such investments may depend on the extent to which the conventions incorporate market mechanisms that provide incentives to attract private investment flows."[281]

Putting a feasible, investment-friendly system of economic incentives and rewards for compliance assistance in place might be an innovative adaptation for the compliance system of the Basel Convention. However, these measures cannot stand alone, but need to be backed up by functional treaty control and classical compliance enhancement mechanisms. Incentives to comply with the Basel Convention, whether granted in form of compliance assistance or in form of rewards for successfully completed compliance processes, still have to focus mainly on developing State Parties. And while trade in hazardous wastes may be carried out legally, illegal waste movement activities have to be tracked down tightly and be punished strictly by State Parties. As far as compliance control is regarded, the Basel Convention already contains reporting obligations for the State Parties and an encompassing PIC-requirement for transboundary movements of hazardous wastes. What is missing are internal or external bodies to verify the outcome of these systems of auto-control. Currently, neither PIC-documentation nor national reports are being reviewed in-depth before being published or compared by the Secretariat. Taking into consideration that bilateral re-

---

[281] GEF Annual Performance Report 2005, 28, see note 278 and Brown Weiss/ McCaffrey, see note 76, 1053.

sponse to non-compliance might be an effective tool within the realm of the Basel Convention, valid PIC-information is of utmost importance. It guarantees that State Parties are aware of breaches which affect them or are carried out by their nationals and can react appropriately.

Widawsky goes one step further and recommends the creation of a body that "inspects facilities to ensure their compliance with ESM standards set forth by the Parties."[282] Currently, the Compliance Committee of the Basel Convention may carry out on-site inspections if they are deemed necessary to conduct a proper non-compliance procedure. Widawsky, on the contrary, talks about on-site inspections as a more open, trade-friendly alternative to the Basel Ban which is less punitive towards those developing countries which actually seek participation in the global hazardous waste trade. These inspections might take place as a regular part of a PIC-procedure or even on request of countries regarding their own facilities. This body could therefore grant or deny authorization permits for facilities on the basis of these inspections.[283] A great advantage of these prior-to-trade inspections then would be that they ground their movement permits or denials on the eligibility of single facilities, and not sweepingly on the estimation of conditions of entire countries.

V. Incentives to Grant Compliance Assistance for Developed State Parties in other selected MEAs

1. Introduction

The last Chapter was dedicated to the attempt of developing ideas on how compliance with the Basel Convention could be improved. These considerations were based on the general discussion and current developments regarding compliance with international environmental law. The present Chapter is dedicated to review two different MEAs, the Kyoto Protocol to the United Nations Framework Convention on Climate Change and the Montreal Protocol on Substances that Deplete the Ozone Layer. The emphasis of the investigation is put on the economic incentives these treaties use in order to enhance compliance, and on the linkage of these incentives to compliance activities that developed State Parties carry out in developing Member States. This Chapter

---

[282] Widawsky, see note 129, 617.
[283] Ibid.

does not pretend to give an exhaustive analysis of these MEAs. *Inter alia*, the topic of compliance control mechanisms will be omitted. As stated above, the focus will be exclusively on incentive systems, on funding mechanisms, and on eventual linkages between treaty funding and compliance incentives used in these MEAs. The compliance mechanisms of both MEAs are – as a whole – clearly not eligible to be included into the Basel Convention. This examination aims at finding single aspects or principle patterns of the reviewed mechanisms which could, in an adapted form, improve the Basel Convention's approach to compliance.

2. Compliance and Funding Mechanisms of the Montreal Protocol on Substances that Deplete the Ozone Layer

The Montreal Protocol on Substances that Deplete the Ozone Layer was negotiated within the framework of the Vienna Convention for the Protection of the Ozone Layer (hereinafter: VCPOL) and came into force on 1 January 1989.[284] The VCPOL initiates research and information exchange, and the adoption of national policies to protect the ozone layer, but it does not require specific reduction levels of the consumption of Ozone Depleting Substances (ODS), mostly halo carbons, chlorofluorocarbons (CFCs), hydroclorofluorocarbons (HCFCs) and methyl-bromide.[285] The Montreal Protocol, concretizing the ideas of the VCPOL, provides for a reduction and final phase-out of the production and consumption of ODS. 96 chemicals are currently controlled. Developing State Parties are granted longer phase-out periods than developed State Parties, with an aspired phase-out of 99.5 per cent of almost all controlled substances by 2030.

a. The Financial Mechanism of the Montreal Protocol: The Multilateral Fund

The MPMF, the financial vehicle of the Montreal Protocol, is financed by mandatory contributions of the developed State Parties to the Montreal Protocol and is well respected by UNEP. As usual within the United Nations' treaty system, payments are based on the United Na-

---

[284] Information available at <http://ozone.unep.org>.
[285] K. Madhava Sarma/ S. Andersen/ D. Zaelke/ K. Taddonio, "Ozone Layer, International Protection", in: Wolfrum, see note 47.

tions assessment scale, but are agreed upon every three years by the States Parties. Accordingly, the Fund is replenished every three years. The main objective of the MPMF is to give compliance assistance to developing State Parties through the provision of funds and technology.[286] As of November 2011, 45 State Parties are considered contributors while 147 are eligible to receive funds.[287] Contributions can be paid in form of bilateral direct investments in ozone-sound projects, but only to an amount that equals up to twenty percent of the total contribution of a country. Such bilateral programs require the approval of the Executive Committee,[288] the managing body of the Fund, which consists of seven members from developed, and seven members from developing State Parties. The Fund accomplishes its aims by financing activities such as the closing of ODS production facilities, converting of existing manufacturing facilities, training personnel, paying royalties and patent rights on new technologies, and establishing national Ozone Offices.[289] Project development is conducted by the Executive Committee together with the four different Implementation Agencies of the MPMF: UNEP, UNDP, UNIDO and the IBRD.

The only countries eligible to receive support from the MPMF are developing countries. They can apply for funding designated to develop a compliance program before they become a State Party to the Montreal Protocol, in order to have a functioning compliance system in place by the time of accession. As a next step, they are eligible to receive support for the implementation of the required national Montreal Protocol institutions (National Ozone Units) and for personnel capacity building.[290] More complex projects, like performance based, multi-year agreements, encompass investment project activities (focusing on the conversion or shutting down of enterprises that use or produce ODS), regional management plans, and multi-year agreements between governments and the Executive Committee.[291] Frequently, projects are not entirely financed by the MPMF but need co-funding. All countries with economies in transition (not eligible to apply for funding from the MPMF) that are seeking assistance for a project designated to comply

---

[286] Brown Weiss/ McCaffrey, see note 76, 1074.
[287] Information available at <http://www.multilateralfund.org>.
[288] Madhava Sarma et al., see note 285, 4.
[289] Brown Weiss/ McCaffrey, see note 76, 1074.
[290] Ibid.
[291] Ibid., 1076.

with the Montreal Protocol, are eligible to apply for financial aid from the GEF.

The MPMF is frequently described as the most successful global multilateral environmental agreement.[292] Nevertheless, it faces the same difficulties as every global environmental fund, such as late payments or no payments at all. By 3 June 2011, 21 contributor Parties had paid their 2011 contributions either fully or partially, together having paid a sum of 38,45 million US$. This amounts to about a third of the overall agreed contribution sum for 2011, which is 133,34 million US$.[293] The situation was different in 2010, when contributions were almost completely fulfilled. Of the complete contribution sum of 133,34 million US$, 126,88 million US$ were actually paid.[294] A similarly satisfying outcome in pledges was reached in 2009. From its inception in 1991 to 2010, the fund had a total income of over 2,89 billion US$.[295]

b. Possible Conclusions from the MPMF

It seems possible to state, that the level of the Parties' funding commitment to the MPMF is traditionally high and that the MPMF has successfully managed to enforce compliance with its obligations in both developing and developed State Parties and therefore diminished the harmful effects of the use of ODS. Sarma calls the overall reduction of the use and consumption of ODS "impressive and beyond the mandate of the Montreal Protocol."[296] Indeed, reduction levels of the different ODS range between 85 and 99 per cent. Regarding both funding and project realization, the MPMF is substantially more effective than the Basel Convention Technical Trust Fund. The question is, if a simple status change of the Technical Trust Fund from "voluntary" to "mandatory" would raise the payment moral of State Parties. The more probable scenario might be that State Parties to the Basel Convention would not even agree to this change. Besides, the MPMF grants funding to de-

---

[292] Ibid., 1074.
[293] Report of the 63rd Mtg of the Executive Committee, Doc. UNEP/OzL.Pro/ExCom/64/3, Annex 1, Trust Fund for the Implementation of the Montreal Protocol, Report from the Treasurer: Status of Contributions and Disbursements as at 3 June 2011, 4.
[294] Report from the Treasurer, see note 293, 5.
[295] Ibid., 3.
[296] Madhava Sarma et al., see note 285, 7.

veloping State Parties only, an approach that the Basel Convention should overcome.

The MPMF, though, constitutes a successful example of developed countries accepting the costs of implementing the obligations of the Montreal Protocol in their territories and the greater part of the costs that occur in developing Member States for the same purpose. Would this be due to the "prominence" of the problem of ozone depletion or to a greater awareness of the fact that the use of ODS in any place in the world has negative global environmental effects? A reason for this behavior could be the intensive pre-examination and exact development of the projects prior to realization and the use of a country's eagerness towards compliance as an eligibility criterion, even before it becomes a Party to the Montreal Protocol. Furthermore, the strong involvement of many intergovernmental organizations which enjoy a reputation of being trustworthy and effective in the project development process.

What the Basel Convention possibly could copy from the MPMF is the way bilateral investments are being fostered and integrated into the funding system. In order to perform better, the Basel Convention has to develop a system that attracts foreign investment in waste treatment projects in developing countries. Insofar, the system of direct investments, which serve as discounts for the State Parties's contributions, could be adopted from the MPMF. Due to the importance of foreign investments in waste treatment facilities or capacity-building projects in developing countries, these direct investments could even cover more than the MPMF's 20 per cent of the total contribution of each State Party.

3. Compliance and Funding Mechanisms of the Kyoto Protocol to the United Nations Framework Convention on Climate Change (UNFCCC)

The Kyoto Protocol to the UNFCCC was adopted on 11 December 1997 and entered into force on 16 February 2005. Similar to the Montreal Protocol, the UNFCCC makes the aims of the Convention obligatory. It sets binding targets.[297] Annex I countries according to the UNFCCC are bound to reduce their greenhouse gas (GHG) emissions. This reduction amounts to an average of five per cent against 1990 levels

---

[297] The Kyoto Protocol has 192 Parties; information available at <http://unfccc.int>.

over the five-year period 2008 – 2012. Parties not listed in Annex I of the UNFCCC and Annex B of the Kyoto Protocol (which are mostly developing State Parties) are not bound by emission reduction targets, nor do they actively participate in the market mechanisms the Kyoto Protocol provides to reach its aims.

a. Flexible Mechanisms and Funding under the Kyoto Protocol

The Kyoto Protocol now might be the most market-based and incentive-driven existing MEA, applying a highly complex and innovative trade scheme that intensively connects compliance incentives with a funding mechanism. Put simply, the annual amount of allowed GHG emissions (measured in metric tons) is calculated and distributed to the countries participating in the reduction efforts. Further, the Kyoto Protocol creates four types of emission certificates: Assigned Amount Units (AAUs; the quantity of emissions permitted to each State Party), Removal Units (RMUs, they can be obtained by e.g. domestic reforestation programs), Emission Reduction Units (ERUs) and Certified Emission Reductions (CERs).

In order to fulfill their reduction obligations, State Parties have to carry out sufficient, autonomously funded "domestic action". On a complementary level, they can make use of the Flexibility Mechanisms in order to reduce costs and alleviate the burden of domestic reduction.[298] These mechanisms consist of Emission Trading (ET; article 17 Kyoto Protocol), Joint Implementation (JI; article 6 Kyoto Protocol) and the Clean Development Mechanism (CDM; article 12 Kyoto Pro-

---

[298] In order to be eligible to participate in the Mechanisms, Annex I Parties further need to meet the following criteria: they must have ratified the Kyoto Protocol, they must have calculated their assigned amount in terms of tones of CO2-equivalent emissions; they must have in place a national system for estimating emissions and removals of greenhouse gases within their territory; they must have in place a national registry to record and track the creation and movements of ERUs, CERs, AAUs, and RMUs [the mostly tradable reduction units created by the Kyoto Protocol], and must annually report such information to the Secretariat; and they must annually report information on emissions and removals to the Secretariat. Information available at <http://unfccc.int> and article 6 Kyoto Protocol. There exist further detailed eligibility criteria for each mechanism.

tocol). Their implementation is specified in the Marrakesh Accords of 2001.[299]

Joint Implementation allows commitment-bound Annex I State Parties to invest in emission-reduction projects in other Annex I countries,[300] thereby generating ERUs. Thus, the investing State Party can then obtain and "use" these ERUs "to partially satisfy its [own] limitation or reduction commitment."[301] The Clean Development Mechanism is similarly project-orientated, but refers to projects that Annex I State Parties carry out in the territory of developing State Parties which are not (yet) bound by emission reduction obligations. Montini explains that the peculiarity of the CDM is the fact that it is designed to accomplish a twofold objective.[302] On the one hand, it aims at assisting Annex I Parties to fulfill in part their limitation or reduction commitments; on the other, it aims at helping non-Annex I countries to achieve sustainable development.[303] A further difference to the JI is that CDM creates CERs, which are new tradable units, while JI leads to the transfer of existing Kyoto Units[304] from one participating state to the other.

The principle of Emission Trading is, that states which use fewer Kyoto Units than they are granted because they produce less GHG emissions, may sell part of their unit stock. States that emit more than they are eligible for may buy emission certificates. All four Kyoto Units can be used for ET. In order to prevent states from selling out their emission certificates instead of fulfilling their reduction objectives, they have to keep a commitment period in reserve.[305] States may not drop under a level equal to 90 per cent of its assigned amount.[306]

Public and private "Legal Entities" of the eligible State Parties are clearly given the possibility to participate in the Flexibility Mechanisms.[307] States are free to decide whether to allow such participation,[308]

---

[299] Report of the Conference of the Parties on its 7th Sess., held at Marrakesh from 29 October to 10 November 2001, Doc. FCCC/CP/2001/13/Add.4.
[300] Montini, see note 21, 157.
[301] Ibid., 174.
[302] Ibid.
[303] Montini, see note 21, 174.
[304] M. Schröder, "Joint Implementation", in: Wolfrum, see note 47.
[305] Schröder, see above.
[306] Ibid.
[307] Article 6 para. 3 and article 12 para. 9 Kyoto Protocol provide for the participation of legal entities in the JI and CDM programs. The Marrakesh

and they remain responsible under the Protocol for the activities of their nationals. Only international ET is feasible for the Kyoto Protocol's trading system, the sale of Kyoto Units from one national company to the other would not be recognized as a feasible transaction.

Schröder refers to Joint Implementation when he writes, that "being able to get involved both in the investing and the hosting side of a project, legal entities are likely to become the main drivers of the mechanism."[309] This assertion, however, might be appropriate for all the flexible mechanisms. Complementary to the flexible mechanisms with their restricted access, the UNFCCC and the Kyoto Protocol provide funding for projects that enhance the protection of the ozone layer. These funds are designated to serve the countries that are not eligible to participate in the Flexibility Mechanisms. At the 7th COP of the Kyoto Protocol 2001 (the same COP that decided on the Marrakesh Accords), State Parties decided to create an Adaptation Fund[310] in order to finance concrete adaptation projects and programs in developing countries that are parties to the Kyoto Protocol.[311] The Adaptation Fund has worked since 2009 and is financed by voluntary pledges of governments and by a share of proceeds from CDM projects. The monetary value of two per cent of the CERs that are issued for a CDM project has to be transferred to the Adaptation Fund.[312] As of 31 October 2010, about 202 million US$ were deposited in the Adaptation Fund; over 130 million US$ coming from the 2 per cent scale of created CERs, and the rest coming from governmental donations. By September 2010 two projects, one in Senegal and one in Honduras, were approved for financing by the Adaptation Fund.

The 7th COP also agreed on the creation of two more funds which should further serve the implementation and realization of GHG reduction projects worldwide. They should not be directly related with the Kyoto Protocol Mechanisms and only have a voluntary donation finance system: the Least Developed Country Fund[313] (LDC) has the

---

Accords (Annex to the Marrakesh Accords, article 5, see note 299) introduce legal entities to the Emission Trading system.

[308] Schröder, see note 304.
[309] Ibid.
[310] Report of the Conference of the Parties on its 7th Sess., see note 299, 52.
[311] Information available at <http://www.adaptation-fund.org>.
[312] Information available at <http://www.climatefundsupdate.org>; CDM projects in the World's Least Developed Countries are exempted.
[313] Report of the Conference of the Parties, see note 299, 43.

objective to address the special needs of 48 least developed countries regarding climate change adaptation and GHG reduction projects.[314] According to Climate Funds Update, the fund had e.g. received over 219 million US$ by 8 October 2010 from 22 developed donor states.

The second fund, the Special Climate Change Fund (SCCF) focuses on long-term projects that support country adaptation to climate change. It is accessible for all countries which are not listed in Annex I of the UNFCCC. It had received e.g. about 133 million US$ from 14 donor countries by 8 October 2010. In addition to its general role as the financial mechanism to the UNFCCC, the GEF administers both the LDC and the SCCF separately from the Climate Change Focal Area. The Adaptation Fund is administered by the Adaptation Fund Board, to which the GEF provides secretariat services on an interim basis.

b. Possible Conclusions from the Kyoto Protocol Flexible Mechanisms

What conclusions could possibly be drawn and what ideas that are feasible for the Basel Convention could be extracted from the mechanisms of the Kyoto Protocol? The Flexibility Mechanisms cannot be entirely transferred into another MEA that regulates a different subject (variations of Emission Trading, though, have successfully entered into various MEAs). The Kyoto Protocol has its own system of tradable permits. Wastes, on the contrary, are perhaps not eligible to be subject of a virtual trade, because they are traded and moved themselves.

What indeed might serve as a functioning compliance system of the Basel Convention are the general principles and ideas on which the Kyoto Protocol is built. Although things are not perfect, and by the end of the first GHG-reduction period 2008-2012 some developed nations will not have fulfilled their reduction obligations to the full extent, the Flexibility Mechanisms of the Kyoto Protocol still are an outstanding example of successful and innovative integration of economic incentives into the compliance system of an MEA. In particular, the Clean Development Mechanism typifies an approach, which rewards compliance assistance with economic benefits for the (developed) State Party that grants it. Kyoto Units obtained in a CDM-project abroad serve the assisting State Party to comply with its own reduction obligations. The CDM is therefore creating a "symbiotic" approach to compliance assistance, economic incentives and treaty funding. Financial

---

[314] Ibid. and <http://www.climatefundsupdate.org>.

outcomes of the CDM, though, are not directed into one of the Funds that belong to the Kyoto Protocol area, but are directly put into projects that serve to achieve the actual Kyoto goals.

Helping developing nations and protecting them from the harms of hazardous wastes is a major goal of the Basel Convention. Nevertheless, no waste reduction levels are defined in the Basel Convention; goals and approaches regarding this matter are left to the national legislations of the State Parties. What could be incorporated into the Basel Convention is the idea of the Clean Development Mechanism: State Parties which facilitate compliance assistance in developing countries in form of direct investment, training, capacity-building or bilateral trade possibilities, should be rewarded.

VI. Conclusions

It is not new that solutions to the flaws of the Basel Convention and methods to halt illegal waste trade have to be found within the realm of global economy. Principle 12 of the Rio Declaration states, *inter alia*, that "States should cooperate to promote a supportive and open international economic system that would lead to economic growth and sustainable development in all countries, to better address the problems of environmental degradation."[315] Abdul Haseeb Ansari puts it like this: "It is now said that trade is not an end in itself; rather, it is a means to achieving the end. The end is environmentally sustainable development."[316]

The Basel Convention, though, will not be able to reach a safe, sound, and economically beneficial waste trade system in a stand-alone way. In order to reach the optimal "Issue Linkage"[317] between trade and the protection of the environment from waste-related damages, measures have to be taken on all levels of law: within the global and regional waste trade regimes, the global trade regime of the WTO, within bilateral investment agreements and last but not least within national legislations. The Basel Convention, however, being the international

---

[315] Rio Declaration, see note 238.
[316] A.H. Ansari, "Free Trade Law and Environmental Law: Congruity or Conflict?", *IJIL* 41 (2001), 1 et seq. (1).
[317] D. Shelton, "The Impact of Economic Globalization on Compliance", in: K. Ishibashi/ A.Kiss/ D. Shelton (eds), *Economic Globalization and Compliance with International Environmental Agreements*, 2003, 40 et seq.

treaty at the forefront of the establishment of a safe global waste movement mechanism, urgently has to give up on cumbersome mechanisms that are hard to administer, like a complete trade ban, and needs to be adapted to the needs of a safe global waste trade.

As Beyerlin, Stoll and Wolfrum express, action-orientated MEAs like the Basel Convention need to provide their own control structure in order to be effective.[318] The establishment of an internal or external body which reviews the State Parties' annual reports and carries out on-site inspection procedures on waste treatment facilities, might constitute a promising measure to end the inefficiency of the current mechanisms. If not externalized, both tasks could be carried out by, or under the auspices of the Basel Convention Secretariat. As far as bilateral responses to breaches are concerned, verification of PIC-documentation might be a tool to enable State Parties to detect and respond to illegal waste movements into and from their territory. The Basel Convention, however, cannot provide a functioning national response system. A "review organ" of the Basel Convention, though, could, as a basic step, provide states with information regarding non-compliance in their territory or by their national private actors.

The Convention's main challenge, however, is to confront the flourishing illegal trade activities in hazardous wastes from developed to developing countries by increasing the attractiveness of compliance with its obligations. This means in the first place, that the Basel Ban Amendment should never enter into force, and that the concept of regional waste regimes prohibiting imports of hazardous wastes into their State Parties' territories should be rethought. So far, import bans, even coupled with export bans in states which are huge generators of hazardous wastes, have not led to overall satisfactory results. This is shown by the illegal hazardous waste flows that enter Africa from the European Union.

Still State Parties are perfectly able to prohibit the import of hazardous wastes into their territory, according to the regular provisions of the Basel Convention. But those developing State Parties which want to participate in the global waste trade should be enabled to do so. The implementation of economic compliance incentives for developing and developed State Parties alike and the improvement of the Basel Convention's financial mechanisms could constitute feasible steps to achieve this aim. As long as most developing countries do not possess sufficient means of their own to develop a modern waste industry infrastructure,

---

[318] Beyerlin/ Stoll/ Wolfrum, see note 25, 261.

developed states have to provide assistance, from capacity-building to entire investment projects in waste facilities. An improved Basel Convention compliance mechanism should be based on such considerations and, hence, reward assistance activities of developed State Parties and their national entities and make such projects subject to funding.

The idea of the Clean Development Mechanism applied by the Kyoto Protocol is an excellent example of rewarding developed State Parties for the compliance assistance or project investment they carry out in developing State Parties. Granting financial support to developed State Parties and their national enterprises which carry out environmentally sound and sustainable waste-related projects in developing State Parties, coupled with the actual possibility to then dispose hazardous wastes in these countries, might bring developed State Parties into compliance. The availability of adequate waste treatment facilities and the possibility to play a role in the global waste trade business might decrease the "attractiveness" for developing State Parties to accept illegal and harmful waste loads. In both developed and developing State Parties, these measures could "persuade" non-state actors into compliance, which is, according to Shelton, "a key factor in the environmental field, where most activities that cause harm to the environment are conducted by the private sector."[319] This system has to be backed up by strong and credible control mechanisms and strict national legislations regarding illegal waste traffic.

Due to its unique scope and topic, the Basel Convention will have to find an appropriate, tailor-made, and "attractive" compliance mechanism. In order to be applicable, this approach needs to be based on a functioning funding mechanism. The Technical Trust Fund, the designated project funding vehicle of the Basel Convention, should remain voluntary, but could increase its attractiveness by offering the possibility to finance projects which are carried out and financed by developed State Parties. A discount possibility which equals costs that stem from direct assistance in developing State Parties, as offered by the MPMF, could serve as a further incentive for Member States to pay their pledges and simultaneously dedicate themselves to waste treatment infrastructure in developing countries.

---

[319] Shelton, see note 317, 35.

Book Reviews

Antonios Tzanakopoulos: Disobeying the Security Council –
Countermeasures against Wrongful Sanctions
Oxford University Press, 2011, XXXII+243 pages, ISBN 978-0-19-960076-2

Extent and limits of the powers of the UN Security Council have been a topic of scholarly debate since the newly founded United Nations took up work after World War II. There was much discussion about the Security Council's power to impose general (S/RES/1373) and smart sanctions (S/RES/1267) and to establish judicial bodies like the ICTY and the ICTR under Chapter VII of the UN Charter. To this continuing debate, Tzanakopoulos adds a new and interesting twist by going beyond the usual stumbling blocks of the interpretation of delicate passages of the UN Charter and the classical shield of Chapter VII which in the eyes of many exempts the Security Council from too rigorous scrutiny.

A short introductory Chapter speaks about responsibility as a form of accountability. The carefully edited book is divided into three Parts of similar length: Part 1 deals with the engagement of responsibility; Part 2 discusses the determination of responsibility and Part 3 has the consequences of responsibility as its topic. This outline follows a logical order as the questions of engagement and determination of responsibility should be answered as preliminary questions before the consequences and especially the question of countermeasures can be addressed. The most import part of the book is contained in Chapter 7 on "implementation through self-enforcement" with a critical and thorough examination of whether states can resort to countermeasures against the United Nations in response to a wrongful act by the Security Council.

Tzanakopoulos argues in Chapter 1 that the control of the exercise of the power by international organizations and especially by the Security Council as the major organ of the United Nations, becomes more and more important. Such control could be best exercised through legal accountability using the concept of responsibility. The two following Chapters on the engagement of responsibility, consisting of attribution and the element of breach can be seen as representing a preliminary question and precondition for the treatment of the topic of countermeasures later in the book.

Attribution of actions is a specifically complex issue if international organizations are involved. Chapter 2 provides an illustrative list of recent and of conceivable Council action as a good complement to the more technical aspects of attribution. Since this Part often speaks of violations of the UN Charter, it could, as the author recognizes (pages 24/25), have been located in Chapter 3 of the book on the element of breach. It offers nonetheless a useful range of cases, such as the one to be found under the Section on attribution of Member State conduct to the United Nations. There are interesting thoughts in this Part on omissions, especially on the differences to state responsibility. Mention could have been made in this context of the Responsibility to Protect and the current state of debate on it.

Chapter 3 deals with the breach of an international obligation as the second element of the engagement of responsibility. The reader would expect this to be just an inevitable transit point of preliminary nature on the author's way to the treatment of the topic of countermeasures, reproducing the well-known discussion of the legal limits of the Security Council. Tzanakopoulos, however, not only addresses various obligations of the Security Council under the UN Charter, such as the compliance with the principle of proportionality and with procedural rules, and under general international law, along the differentiation between *ius cogens* and *ius dispositivum*. He also draws a functional analogy between countermeasures and sanctions, arguing that both these measures aim at inducing the recalcitrant state to comply with its international obligations. This analogy should allow for the application of general international law regulating countermeasures to sanctions imposed by the Security Council. Thus, the contents of article 50 (1)(b) and (d) of the Articles on the Responsibility of States for Internationally Wrongful Acts were applicable to the imposition of sanctions by the Security Council. This approach could add a new explanation to the old discussion of the Security Council's human rights obligations. Yet, the brief treatment of this interesting aspect does not elaborate on the different perspectives of countermeasures (bilateral between states, as far as article 50 of the Articles on the Responsibility of States for Internationally

Wrongful Acts is concerned) and sanctions (multilateral context of the UN as an organization) nor on the arguable reference in article 50 (1)(b) of the Articles on the Responsibility of States for Internationally Wrongful Acts to already existing human rights obligations (rather than itself constituting such) and the resulting implications for the question of the Security Council being bound by human rights. Still, the idea of this functional analogy remains an approach worth thinking about.

Chapter 4, as one of the two Chapters discussing the tricky topic of determination of responsibility covers first the question of judicial determination. The author defines "judicial review" as comprising the elements of internal, hierarchical, binding review of an inherent and systematic nature. He argues that there is no such judicial review since what could be performed by existing courts would be neither systematic, i.e. ensuring some regularity of control, nor binding in the sense of the definition. He concludes that in international law the determination of UN responsibility is done extra-judicially in a decentralized manner and therefore turns to such determination by states in Chapter 5 of the book.

The author concedes states the right of auto-interpretation of acts of international organizations and auto-determination of their violations of international law which he deems justified since the states were the addressees and "agents of execution" of such acts. Such right of determination was the necessary corollary of the lack of compulsory, centralized law-determination on the international level and would in principle subsist as long as there was no binding third party dispute settlement process. This picks up the *"Solange"* idea of the German Constitutional Court's decisions of the same name and the ECtHR's *Bosphorus* decision and is a convincing argument as it takes into consideration the legitimacy aspect of UN action and provides for a flexible and appropriate tool to support the proper mutual functioning of the domestic and international levels. The self-determination by states and the fact that a state is *iudex in causa sua* in such cases is justified by Tzanakopoulos with the argument that the impact of such auto-determination was eased by the presumption of legality existing with regard to Security Council action and by the fact that a state in a multilateral context had to seek support and a collective decision for such a determination. It must, however, be kept in mind that the ideal state of international law would show states following the acts of their own organization. This gets rather out of sight here. Again, the exemplifying case law (pages 119, 126-130, 131-136) gives a good illustration of state practice on the various conceivable case constellations.

In the third Part of his book, Tzanakopoulos unfolds his central thesis that states may, under certain circumstances, react to responsibility of the United Nations by applying the countermeasure of disobedience. Chapter 6 deals with the content of responsibility. The secondary obligations incumbent upon the United Nations as a consequence of its responsibility are cessation and reparation. The relatively short Chapter (the shortest of the book) gives a brief sketch of the named secondary obligations, their different limitations and their consequences if applied in cases of acts of the Security Council, with reparation typically consisting of "juridical" restitution, i.e. the reversal of respective resolutions of the Security Council. What Chapter VII of the UN Charter is for the work of the United Nations Chapter 7 of this book is for the thesis of the author, the most important part of the piece: the examination of whether states can resort to countermeasures against the United Nations in response to a wrongful act by the Security Council. While other countermeasures, such as withholding contributions or action in domestic courts are shortly discussed at the end of the Chapter, the emphasis is put on disobedience as a countermeasure.

The specific attraction of this approach lies in its potential to point to a clever way out of an old and increasingly pressing dilemma: measures taken by the UN Security Council are among the most powerful tools in international law but at the same time escape an effective control. There is no central, compulsory determination of engagement of responsibility of the United Nations. No international nor national court has the jurisdiction to examine them. And even if national courts or authorities did step in to review Security Council measures to find eventual violations of international law and subsequently to order non-compliance with such measures, the respective state would risk violating its obligation under Article 25 UN Charter to accept and carry out the decisions of the Security Council. Tzanakopoulos argues that as long as there is no central authority which could determine the engagement of responsibility, states retain their power to resort to countermeasures which were not explicitly excluded by the UN Charter. The author thoroughly examines how states' disobedience, i.e. their non-compliance with Security Council measures, can be legally qualified.

After discussing the concept of civil disobedience which is, however, not a legal argument, the author examines whether Article 25 UN Charter allows for non-compliance with Security Council measures in certain cases. He first arrives at the honest and open answer that interpretation cannot solve the question of the legal effects of UN resolutions that are not in conformity with the UN Charter. He then turns to the question of the legal consequences of such non-conforming resolutions, and more precisely to the discussion of the notion of "invalidity" and its relationship to that of "illegality".

Starting from the ICJ's approach to presume validity/legality of Security Council resolutions, Tzanakopoulos argues for two distinct presumptions: on the one hand, there was the presumption of validity according to which it is presumed that all acts of a UN organ are valid, if declared by its President or Chairperson to have been validly adopted. On the other hand, there was the presumption of legality according to which any action within the organization's purposes is considered to be *intra vires* and thus legal. While such legality could be rebutted by the proof that the action was *ultra vires*, the respective Security Council resolution would then be illegal but not invalid as it would still produce legal effects.

This is a decisive point of the book. The author needs this construction for his countermeasure argument: if an illegal resolution was invalid, states might be allowed to just disregard it since they were not bound by it. If, on the other hand, the presumption of legality was not rebuttable, states would never be allowed to take countermeasures which they are only allowed to take against an internationally wrongful act of an international organization (article 51 (1) Draft Articles on the Responsibility of International Organizations). The author's argument is valid: he tries to sort out the sometimes confusing discussion around the legal effects and consequences of Security Council resolutions which are not in conformity with the UN Charter by establishing two distinct categories of presumptions. Earlier in the book, the idea to use such presumptions was convincingly justified as a means to ensure that the self-determination of the UN's responsibility and subsequent disobedience is not rendered too easy an option for states (cf. page 121). And that illegal Security Council resolutions remain valid in view of the lack of judicial review (page 176) is acceptable as an argument considering the aspect of desirable legal certainty concerning the applicability of such resolutions.

The conclusion that the legal consequence of an *ultra vires* act of the Security Council is not its invalidity, but rather its illegality allows the author then to proceed to a detailed examination of disobedience (i.e. non-compliance) of states as a countermeasure according to articles 51 et seq. of the Draft Articles on the Responsibility of International Organizations against such illegal acts. He arrives at the conclusion that all

UN Member States have the right to take countermeasures against the United Nations and especially the countermeasure of disobedience.

Tzanakopoulos' approach entails several interesting aspects. It is not only new and innovative, but it also provides the legal framework that allows discussion of the political reactions of states to Security Council measures as legal matters, so that rules and standards of international law are applicable and enable a legal assessment of such disobedience. The countermeasure approach fits nicely in the given framework of international law, using the well-established concept of responsibility and countermeasures to argue that a state's own violation of Article 25 UN Charter is justified as the countermeasure response to a wrongful act by the United Nations. This appears to be an elegant way to avoid the difficult and contentious problems of interpretation of the UN Charter, especially with regard to what the limits of the Security Council under Chapter VII are and the question whether Article 25 UN Charter allows for disobedience in case of wrongful Security Council action. At the same time, Tzanakopoulos' proposal does not solve all the problems: there is still no answer to the question where Chapter VII powers end, there is still no central international control of Security Council action and many detailed questions of responsibility (e.g. concerning attribution) remain. The author's approach lends UN Member States a strong legal argument for taking countermeasures when they exercise their kind of indirect control of the Security Council. It should not be forgotten, though, that the ideal solution for the states would be to solve such problems in the governing bodies of the United Nations rather than to take the secondary avenue of countermeasures.

In sum, Tzanakopoulos presents a very detailed book where the treatment of one important legal question flows easily into the next without any distracting redundancy. He makes a convincing argument for the idea of employing disobedience as a countermeasure against Security Council resolutions and thus adds one beautiful stone on the way to complete the mosaic of the debate on the exercise of its powers by the Security Council and states' options of reaction to it. It might not be the last one in the whole picture but Tzanakopoulos with this diligent and thorough work makes it a particularly shiny one – provided that one reads the book as a skillful dogmatic classification of realities rather than as an instruction to states to be destructive *vis-à-vis* the UN Security Council.

Dr. Clemens A. Feinäugle, Geneva